Public Finance
and Expenditure
in a Federal System

Public Finance and Expenditure in a Federal System

Werner Z. Hirsch
University of California, Los Angeles

Anthony M. Rufolo
Portland State University

Harcourt Brace Jovanovich, Publishers
San Diego   New York   Chicago   Austin   Washington, D.C.
London   Sydney   Tokyo   Toronto

Preface //////

The United States, as a federal system, has three levels of government—national (also referred to as federal), state, and local. Because each level plays a vital role in our lives as citizens, it is important that we understand those roles and their interaction. To this end, we face the demanding task of constructing economic theories that can explain and possibly guide these governments in their manifold activities. This task is complicated by the wide variation in size, character, administrative structure, and capacity that characterize these different government bodies.

Changes in our national priorities over time have clearly demonstrated some of the strengths of a federal system of government. On the one hand, wars and major economic disruptions cannot be addressed by a fragmented group of decentralized governments. On the other hand, the unique ability of local or regional governments to respond to the day-to-day demands of their citizens cannot be duplicated by a strongly centralized organization.

The division of activities within a federal system has profound implications both for government and for the rest of the economy. And any analysis of government from an economic perspective should take this division into account. Most other textbooks on public finance, however, treat the state and local sectors as an add-on analysis. There is usually some discussion of the ability of the federal government to influence other levels of government through the use of grants, and perhaps there is a brief discussion of the property tax as primarily a local tax. However, most of these books ignore the major differences between state, local, and national governments and the complexity of their interactions. Moreover, they seldom if ever address the question of which level of government should provide what services, and how control over these services should be shared. This textbook attempts something new—to provide an integrated treatment of all levels of government.

A second important feature of the book is a balanced and comprehensive

91-969

treatment of both revenue and expenditure. Many public finance texts focus on taxation since this is the most direct application of microeconomic analysis to the public sector. And even when analysis of expenditure is included, it is largely limited to expenditures by the national government. Looking at all levels of government shows a broad array of both revenue sources and expenditure items. We discuss all major revenue sources and separate chapters are devoted to several important expenditure items.

Another feature that sets this text apart from its competitors is the two application chapters at the end of the book. These chapters provide a focused discussion of two topics—tax and expenditure limitations and fiscal crises—that can show how the methods of analysis developed in earlier sections can be used to address complex policy issues.

/// PLAN OF THE BOOK

Part One sets out to provide the basic framework needed to understand the economist's perspective on government and the basic methods needed for analysis. In addition to a summary of the basic economics of markets and the classic perspective on the role of government in the market system, there is an introduction to the economic analysis of public decision making (public choice and related topics) as well as a detailed discussion of the history and theory of federalism.

Part Two deals with the revenue sources available to government. It contains the standard analysis of the major taxes found in the United States, but it also includes a comprehensive discussion of other revenue sources. Interaction among taxes, sharing of tax bases by different levels of government, and tax base mobility receive more attention than in more typical treatments.

Part Three provides an analysis of expenditure by the public sector. It starts with an extensive discussion of the issues that arise in evaluating both the equity and efficiency of government expenditure. This is followed by a review of budget concepts for government and separate chapters dealing with four major areas of expenditure: transfer programs, national defense, education, and the control of crime. Again, attention is focused on how the responsibility for addressing various expenditure issues is distributed among the three levels of government.

The last section of the book is an attempt to bring much of the analysis into focus by applying it to two issues of primary importance to the funding of government: revenue and expenditure limitations and fiscal crises. The analysis of these issues helps highlight both the similarities and the differences of the various levels of government as well as their complex interactions.

In preparing this text, we have incurred obligations so numerous that it is not possible to individually identify and thank all those who deserve credit.

We benefited greatly from discussions with and advice from friends and colleagues, particularly at the University of California at Los Angeles and at Portland State University. And a number of colleagues from Meiji University and the University of Geneva who spent extended periods of time with us, also offered helpful advice. We are also indebted to a number of colleagues who were kind enough to review the manuscript—Steven G. Craig, University of Houston; Kathy Hayes, Southern Methodist University; Charles R. Knoeber, North Carolina State University; Sharon Megdal, MegEcon Consulting Group, Tucson; Michael Pritchett, Brigham Young University; Seymour Sacks, Syracuse University; Robert M. Schwab, University of Maryland; and Elbert Segelhorst, California State University—Long Beach. Finally, our numerous students, during the five years or so this volume was in preparation, helped us to continually refine and reformulate ideas, concepts, expositions, and policy implications.

Our thanks also go to Lorraine Grams who ably typed much of the manuscript and whose outstanding efficiency and timely assistance were invaluable. Special gratitude must go to our wives who showed understanding and patience when we were preoccupied with the preparation of this text.

Werner Z. Hirsch

Anthony M. Rufolo

Contents ///////

Public Finance
and Expenditure
in a Federal System

Introduction
and Background

Each specialized field of economic analysis has its own focus and draws upon different types of knowledge. Public finance and expenditure can be examined using the tools of economic analysis; however, a complete analysis of the public sector in the United States must take account of the distinct powers and obligations of the various levels of government as well as the interaction between these government units. The system of governments in the United States is known as a federalist system. Federalism is the permanent union of independent states. Each of the states retains some of the powers of government while others are ceded to the central government. It is important to understand this division of powers in analyzing the public sector in the United States.

In addition to the issues created by federalism, there are differences in the incentives that people face when acting in the political arena as compared to the market. These differences in incentives and rewards are important to understanding the actions likely to be taken and the effect of those actions on the ultimate allocation of resources in the economy.

This section starts by reviewing the key parts of

microeconomic analysis needed for studying the public sector. This includes an analysis of market failures, because market failures are most often used to justify the government's intervention in the market system. We then turn to the interaction of the fields of economics and political science, known as public choice. Public choice can be considered the application of the tools of economics to the choices made in the public sector. It is an important introduction to the differences in collective versus individual actions. This section ends with a more extensive discussion of the nature of federalism. In particular, we emphasize how autonomous units of government coordinate activities and interact with each other. ///

Chapter 1 //////

Government in the United States: Its Scope and Activities

The public sector in the United States is large by any definition of the term. It is a trillion-dollar business. Yet it is a mistake to refer to the public sector as if it were a single entity. It is, in fact, composed of over 80,000 separate jurisdictions with overlapping spatial boundaries, overlapping policy concerns, and overlapping revenue sources. While the federal government is certainly the largest of these units (it collects about two-thirds of all the revenue of government units in the United States), the importance of the state and local government sector should not be underrated. Governments at this level spend hundreds of billions each year, provide a wide range of services, and, if measured by direct civilian employment, employ over 80% of all government employees.[1] For example, in 1986, local government employment amounted to 9.8 million, state employment to 4.1 million, and federal civilian employment to 3.0 million.

Although government can be expressed by various measures the easiest is to simply state the dollar amount of taxes or expenditure. For example, we could say that the total public sector expenditure for 1987 was estimated to be $1,571 billion, an increase from the $1,487 billion in 1986.[2] However, this set of numbers has two disadvantages. First, few people have any comprehension of what such large numbers mean. Second, the dollar amounts are somewhat distorted by inflation and by growth in the economy.

One way around the problem is to adjust the numbers for the effects of inflation. This is usually called the "real" level of expenditure or taxation. Using inflation-adjusted numbers is a better way to make comparisons over time regarding government size, but this still does not put the numbers into a context that most people understand. To bring the numbers into the realm of

---

[1] Advisory Commission on Intergovernmental Relations (ACIR), *Significant Features of Fiscal Federalism, 1988 Edition*, volume 2, M-155II (Washington, D.C.: July 1988), p. 93.

[2] Ibid., p. 22.

everyday experience we can express them in per capita terms (in constant 1982 dollars) or as a percentage of gross national product (GNP), a measure often used to express the value of all goods and services produced in the U.S. Measured in 1982 dollars, total government expenditure in 1987 was estimated to be $5,481 for each man, woman, and child in the United States. Alternatively, it was 35.0% of GNP. Of this amount, the federal government spent 23.8% of GNP or $3,723 per person; and the state and local governments spent 11.2% of GNP or $1,758 per person.

Table 1-1 shows the growth of government spending in the U.S. since 1929 as a percentage of GNP. The total increased from about 10% of GNP in 1929 to about 20% of GNP after World War II, and then gradually increased to its current level of 35%. Most of the growth since 1969 is in the federal expenditure percentage. This is largely associated with the Social Security system, which increased in expenditures from 3.5% of GNP in 1969 to 6.5% in 1987.[3]

Despite the size of public expenditure in the United States and its growth as a percentage of GNP, by some measures the United States ranks as having one of the smallest public sectors of all the major industrialized nations. The public sector in the United States is large partly because the U.S. economy is large, but Figure 1-1 shows that taxes per capita are also high relative to many other countries. However, it also shows that the U.S. ranks much lower on taxes as a percentage of the domestic economy, because income per capita is also high. The international comparison of taxes is a little misleading as a measure of government size because of substantial differences in the deficits that are run in each country. For example, the figure shows Italy with taxes at 34.7% of Gross Domestic Product (a measure closely related to GNP) in 1985, yet another source reports expenditure by the Italian public sector at 59.2% of GNP in the same year.[4]

Another measure of the size of government is the level of employment in the public sector. Excluding the military, the public sector in the U.S. directly employed about 16.9 million people in 1986.[5] Of these, about 9.8 million were employed by local governments. Thus, the local public sector accounted for 58.1% of total public employment. This is because the local sector is most directly involved in providing services to people. Higher levels of government are more likely to be involved in transfer programs, which require less direct employment. Of course, the public sector also indirectly employed a large number of people involved in making things for government. For example, many employees in the private firms under contract to provide weapons to the government would be classified as government employees if the government chose to produce these items directly rather than contract for them. So the employment numbers are likely to understate the impact of government on the economy.

[3] Ibid., p. 32.
[4] *The Economist* (November 29, 1986), p. 101.
[5] ACIR, op. cit., p. 93.

Table 1-1 / **Government Expenditure as a Percentage of GNP**
Selected Years, 1929–1987

Calendar Year	Total Public Sector	Federal Government	Total State-Local Government	State Government	Local Government
1929	10.0%	2.5%	7.5%	2.1%	5.4%
1939	19.3	8.8	10.5	3.3	7.2
1949	23.0	15.3	7.8	3.0	4.8
1954	26.2	18.1	8.1	2.9	5.2
1959	26.6	17.1	9.5	3.4	6.1
1964	27.4	16.8	10.6	3.7	6.9
1969	30.1	17.7	12.4	4.5	7.9
1974	31.7	17.8	14.0	5.2	8.8
1979	30.6	17.6	13.1	5.0	8.1
1981	33.0	20.2	12.8	5.0	7.8
1982	35.1	22.0	13.1	5.2	7.9
1983	34.9	22.0	12.9	5.1	7.8
1984	33.9	21.3	12.6	5.1	7.5
1985	34.9	22.1	12.8	5.2	7.7
1986	35.1	21.9	13.2	5.4	7.9
1987	35.0	21.5	13.5	5.5	8.0

(Source: Advisory Commission on Intergovernmental Relations, *Significant Features of Fiscal Federalism, 1988 Edition*, vol. 2, M-155II (Washington, D.C.: July 1988), p. 24.)

Finally, the debt of all three levels of government has rapidly increased ever since 1939, but the pace of increase accelerated during the 1970s and 1980s. Thus, federal debt first exceeded $1 trillion in 1981; but it had grown to $2.4 trillion by 1987.[6] This amounts to $8,251 (in constant 1982 dollars) per person in debt for the federal government alone. The total of state and local debt has been about one-third the amount of the federal debt during the 1980s. Another important fact about the debt is that the federal debt declined from 97% of GNP in 1949 to 33% in 1981 before starting its current climb, which left it at 53% of GNP in 1987 and still climbing.[7]

We could give many different statistics to place government in various perspectives, but the main point should be clear. By whatever measure is used, government in the United States is large and important. Its size, however,

[6] Ibid., p. 28.
[7] Ibid., p. 29.

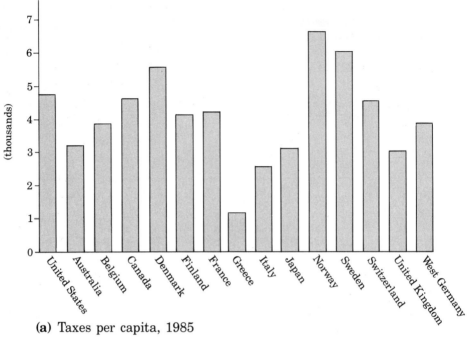

(a) Taxes per capita, 1985

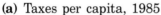

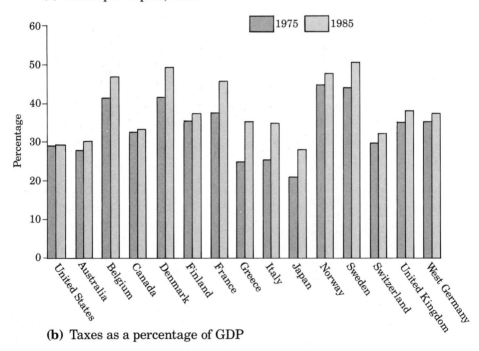

(b) Taxes as a percentage of GDP

***Figure 1-1* / General Government Expenditure as % of GNP**

(Source: *Statistical Abstract of the United States 1988*, U.S. Department of Commerce, Bureau of the Census, p. 810.)

should not hide its diversity. We turn next to a brief discussion of government in the United States.

/// CHALLENGES FACING GOVERNMENTS IN A CHANGING ENVIRONMENT

In all societies there is an ongoing debate about the role of government and its appropriate scope. The United States is no exception, and the recent reform movements in the Soviet Union and in China show that this debate is not limited to the largely market-oriented economies of the West. There can be little doubt that the private sector has impressive strengths in creating and distributing goods and services; but there often is unhappiness with the income distribution that the market's allocation of resources and goods and services generates. There are also complaints that the private sector produces the wrong mix of output and ignores some important costs that are not captured in market transactions. Tight government control of the economy may generate a more equal distribution of income or correct other problems; but experience shows that there is a high cost in terms of the quantity and quality of output produced by the economy.

All but the most ardent advocates of the market solution recognize that the private sector could not accomplish what it does without the aid of government. From the enforcement of contracts to the provision of roads for transportation, the reliance on government by the private sector is pervasive. Alternatively, a healthy private sector provides the resources for government to carry out these activities. Unfortunately, there is no clear-cut, ideal allocation of responsibility between the private and public sectors.

Perhaps it is inevitable that feelings about government are ambivalent. Aside from the wide array of services that government provides, it is the forum through which we address many of our most pressing problems. For example, when it became apparent that air was becoming increasingly toxic and rivers were becoming so polluted that one actually caught fire, the problem was addressed through the public sector. Yet the very powers that allow government to address serious problems allow it to tax private income and to take other actions that impinge on personal freedoms. When all of these powers are working for a common purpose the benefits are immense; but when these powers are misdirected or poorly handled, the waste and damage can also be immense.

Both the tax and the expenditure decisions of government have important effects on the allocation of resources in the economy. Governments collect taxes through a variety of levies placed directly on individuals or indirectly through businesses. These taxes raise revenue for the government but they also cause people to alter their behavior. The alterations in behavior vary significantly from one tax to another. Similarly, government expenditures can greatly influence people. Some are direct recipients of government transfers or salaries while others may respond to the services provided. Careful analysis of both the taxes and expenditures of government are needed to understand how the public sector affects the economy.

People and economic activity also affect the public sector, for example, when they move to new locations. Retirees move to warm climates for health and recreation. Working-age people move to parts of the country where the economy is most active. This movement may help both the economy as a whole and the people who move, yet it may create significant problems for the public sector. The jurisdictions that receive the influx of activity may be hard pressed to cope with the rapid increase in demand for services and infrastructure that development creates. There will be serious questions about how to finance the higher level of government activity and what the effects of both the financing choice and the infrastructure development will be for the future of the community. Will the boom suddenly level off and die, leaving the community with high bills to pay? Will there be continued growth, which will create even more problems if it is not planned for?

The communities that are losing population are likely to have even more problems than those receiving the population. There are likely to be certain fixed costs of government, which now must be spread over a smaller population. Further, those left behind in any migration tend to be people with low income and economic productivity. Hence, the central cities find themselves with higher concentrations of low-income residents as the higher-income ones move to the suburbs or other parts of the country. How should government respond? To what extent are the observed patterns caused by government behavior?

/// FEDERALISM AND THE DISTRIBUTION OF POWER AND OBLIGATIONS

In devising a system of governance for any country, a key question is whether to rely on a single centralized government or a fragmented one, and, if the latter, how decentralized it should be. Debate about this fundamental issue started while the U.S. Constitution was being drafted and has continued through most of U.S. history. Thus, the seminal debate between the supporters of Alexander Hamilton and those of Thomas Jefferson is surprisingly similar to the debates we have today. Hamilton called for centralization of power in the interests of efficiency and order; Jefferson demanded diffusion of power and the right of the citizen to be close to government and to participate in decisions. Jefferson warned, "When all government . . . shall be drawn to Washington as the center of all power, it . . . will become as venal and oppressive as the government from which we separated."[8] Further, he saw serious efficiency problems with a centralized government, warning, "Were we directed from Washington when to sow, and when to reap, we should soon want for bread,"[9] and, "If ever this vast country is brought under a single government, it will be one of the most extensive corruption, indifferent and incapable of a wholesome care."[10]

The principle of federalism is still sound: Have the smallest unit of government that is appropriate for the scale of a problem assume responsibility for that problem. To determine the size and level of government at which a particular good or service should be produced, we need to weigh and trade off the gains and losses of centralized authority. In this endeavor we should recognize that the financing can be separated from the rendering of public services. Although the rendering of services can be decentralized and accomplished by thousands of units of local government, federal or state revenues can be used to finance them. This has happened in the past, for example, in relation to highways and urban renewal, and we may see more of it in the future.

Thus, up to a point, dispersion of power and responsibility to subsidiary governments produces more gains than losses to society. In recent years much centralization, perhaps too much, has taken place. Modern technology has stripped us of the protection provided by distance and time, which once mitigated the effects of the actions of others, and has made us more vulnerable to imposed external costs. These interactions have in most cases led to further centralization of political and economic power. Some concentration of power has been a (perhaps unforeseen) byproduct of actions by groups strongly opposed to big government. An example is passage of Proposition 13 in California. It was designed to reduce property taxes levied by local governments, but this has resulted in the state making up much of the revenue lost by local governments. As a result of the state's enlarged role in funding cities, counties, and school districts, more power has been shifted to the state.

In the United States the multiplicity of government is common, but it is a relatively rare form of public organization. Most countries have a central government that directs all public activity in the country. (For example, in the United Kingdom, this power is seen to be lodged in Westminster.) In the U.S. the Constitution guarantees certain powers for the state governments and thus limits how much the central government can interfere with the lower levels of government. In turn, certain local governments have explicit charters that limit the ability of the state government to interfere. Moreover, states can and do delegate select powers to local governments.

---

[8] H. A. Washington, ed., *The Writings of Thomas Jefferson*, vol. 7 (Washington, D.C.: U.S. Congress, 1853–1854), p. 216.
[9] Ibid., vol. 1, p. 82.
[10] Ibid., vol. 7, p. 256.

In his classic study of the economic approach to federalism, Wallace Oates rejected a narrow definition of federalism in favor of one recognizing the importance of decentralization even when such power is delegated. He defines a federal government as one with:

> A public sector with both centralized and decentralized levels of decision-making in which choices made at each level concerning the provision of public services are determined largely by the demands for these services of the residents of (and perhaps by others who carry on activities in) the respective jurisdiction.[11]

The level of government at which action is taken may be at least as important as the action taken in terms of the ultimate effect it will have. This is because people have more choice about which jurisdiction to be part of if the activity is carried out by a lower level of government than they do if the activity is carried out by a higher level of government. This ability to move across jurisdictional boundaries constitutes a disciplining device and can place constraints on the activities of lower levels of government that do not exist at the higher levels. This fact, as well as the greater proximity of local governments to their constituents, makes them more responsive to their service demands.

Recognizing that some of these advantages are inherent in local governments, federal and state governments often mandate the former to carry out a variety of functions. Not always, however, are local governments provided with subventions to finance these activities. In either case, higher levels of government impose their power over their junior partners. We discuss these concerns below under the heading of intergovernmental relations, some being fiscal and others merely regulatory in nature.

Whatever the merits of the current system, it is clear that we will continue to have a separation of power and obligations for the foreseeable future. Thus, it is necessary to consider all three levels of government in an analysis of the public sector. This analysis is complicated by the fact that the world is replete with a host of interactions, not only between citizens and governmental units but also among different governments. Those interactions are related to externalities and spillovers, concepts which we define below. They have gained increasing prevalence as America has become more industrialized, urbanized, and mobile. For example, within the last two decades alone we have seen a significant movement of activity from the Northeast and North Central parts of the United States to the South and West. Within each region we also see the movement of the middle class and the upper class from central cities to suburban areas. Despite the talk of "gentrification" of the cities, i.e., the return of young, middle-class families to core cities, there is little evidence that the relative concentration of the poor in the downtown areas has been declining.

---

[11] Wallace Oates, *Fiscal Federalism* (New York: Harcourt Brace Jovanovich, 1972), p. 17.

There can be little doubt that, under these circumstances, federalism faces great challenges. The challenges, however, are more likely to be met if we better understand the underlying forces and complex relationships in a world of great mobility, rapid information flow, and widespread interdependence.

/// THE ECONOMICS OF A FEDERATED PUBLIC SECTOR

Many introductory economics texts have long defined economic problems as being the determination of "what, how, and for whom?"[12] Another perspective on the economic system, however, is to consider it as serving to allocate resources, coordinate activities, and provide incentives for individuals and firms to do what is efficient. The market system, if it is reasonably competitive, is noted for its ability to generate an efficient allocation of resources and to provide strong incentives for appropriate behavior with respect to production.

Many would argue that the political method of allocating final output has significant advantages over the market method. Whether this is true or not, there is a significant gap between the public sector and the market in the ability to coordinate activities and provide appropriate incentives for efficiency. Government functioning without the price system has great difficulty in solving the coordination problems of a complex economy. Making sure that the right resources are available in the economy is no easy task. Governments seem to have even greater problems in creating the incentives for efficiency in production and in use of resources. For many years, attention has been focused on the allocative failures of the market system, both in terms of what should be produced and how it should be distributed. While government can often overcome these allocative failures, it appears to have great difficulty in maintaining the coordination and incentive standards of the market. Thus, we study the public sector not only to make judgments about what it should do but also to see if there are ways of improving performance with respect to what is done.

Thus, while economists in general are concerned with the allocation of resources, those who pay special attention to the public sector of America focus on concepts, theories, tools of analysis and mechanisms to determine and implement an appropriate resource allocation of that sector. Within this context, choices must be made between governmental and private mechanisms, i.e., it must be decided which activities should be in the public and which in the private domain. As the U.S. economy has become increasingly interdependent, with just about everyone affecting everyone else, the role and scope of government has, of necessity, grown also. If government is preferred, then under federalism a choice must be made among levels of government. It must also be determined what specific responsibilities should be assigned to a

---

12 Armen Alchian and William Allen, *University Economics*, 2nd ed. (Belmont, CA: Wadsworth, 1967), p. 3.

particular government, i.e., production, financing, or both. In addition to this decision area, public sector economics is concerned with the question of what, how, when and for whom to produce and how to finance the activity. Solving these problems in the public sector is more demanding than in a market economy with its invisible hand.

This volume seeks to provide tools for solving these problems and for choosing between government or market activity, and among different governments, i.e., federal, state or specific local units. Unlike most public finance texts, this one takes explicit cognizance of the fact that our government is a federated one. Therefore, in addition to addressing the conventional public finance questions of raising and spending by government, we are concerned also with the allocation of public responsibilities to units of the three levels of government and with their implementation efforts.

There is a further concern to which we have already alluded. It relates to ways of analyzing specific governments and is aided by an analogy with the private sector. The federal government is very much like a monopolist. It has significant power, which people can do very little to avoid. At lower levels of government, the market analogy gets closer to that of competitive firms (although it would be a serious mistake to carry the analogy too far, since there are still major differences between the public and private sectors). People who do not like what one local government is doing have the option of getting out of the jurisdiction, i.e., voting with their feet. Thus, analyses of local governments, and to some extent states, must allow for the possibility that constituents may move away from jurisdictions that fail to meet their demands or to do so at acceptable tax levels, while taking into consideration relocation costs. This threat causes the local government to worry more about the consequences of its actions than does the federal government.

A further unique situation faces local and to some extent, state governments. Since their jurisdiction is over relatively limited territory, local governments face highly mobile tax bases. (As we will see below, a person is a tax base in relation to personal income and sales taxes. A physician, for example, may live in one jurisdiction and practice in a second while shopping in a third.) This fact makes revenue raising for local governments particularly difficult.

Among the questions with which we are concerned are the following: What is the role of government in the United States today? How do we determine the appropriate allocation of activities between the private sector and the public sector? How do we evaluate the assignment of responsibilities and how do we determine what services to provide and of what quantity and quality? Exactly what are the goals of government, how are they to be financed, and who, as a result, will bear what burden? Do the activities of government actually tend to achieve the objectives of government? How has government contributed to the increasing mobility of the population? Exactly what kinds of problems does mobility create for different governments?

This book seeks to show the basics of how to analyze some of these questions and other issues raised in this introductory chapter. There are still significant disagreements about the answer to many questions even among economists. The disagreements focus on different value judgments, estimates for key parameters, and opinions about what can safely be ignored in analyzing a particular issue. However, despite the disagreements there is a surprising amount of material on which there is agreement. This material relates to the methods used to analyze the public sector. We consider this to be most important, and our intention is to introduce you to these methods of analysis. Where there is widespread agreement about an analysis we will try to explain its nature. Where there is disagreement, we will try to show the basis of the disagreement. Sometimes these disagreements hinge on suppositions about the relationships between important variables or the estimates of certain key parameters. Where the disagreement is based on value judgments, it should at least be possible to see where those judgments enter the argument and how they affect the selection of policies.

No textbook can hope to cover such a broad and diverse field completely. This is especially true when the field is changing almost constantly. Hence, the book focuses on the basic analysis of each area addressed. With an understanding of the basics, the reader should be able to apply the analysis to a constantly changing situation. There are also a number of important areas, such as regulation and stabilization of the economy, which are not covered at all. Instead we focus on the raising and spending of money, on the provision of services, on allocating responsibilities to government on three levels, and analyzing how this activity affects the economy under federalism.

Chapter 2 //////

Economic Framework and Concepts

One of the first things new students of economics learn is that the competitive market system is an efficient way to allocate resources, but only if a variety of conditions are met. Shortly thereafter they learn of the many problems that can lead to inefficient resource allocation. They may also learn that the market system is dependent on a set of rules imposed from outside of the system and that the distribution of income resulting from the market system is not necessarily a desirable one. Thus, the stage is set for the analysis of the public sector.

Both the overall view of the economic system and the specific tools of economic analysis are needed to understand the economist's view of the public sector. It is important to know why the market system leads to efficiency in resource allocation if you want to know when it might be desirable to intervene in a market that is not operating properly. In addition, you need to know the basic methods of economic analysis to be able to analyze the effects of different policies. Hence, we start with an overview of the economic system and the basic methods of microeconomic analysis.[1]

/// DEMAND

In economics, demand refers to the relationship between quantity and price, which shows the maximum amount a person would purchase at any given price or alternatively the maximum amount a person would pay for one more unit of the good or service. Each interpretation is useful in certain circumstances. The relationship between price and quantity is a negative one

[1] For a complete treatment see an intermediate microeconomics text such as Jack Hirshleifer, *Price Theory and Applications*, 3rd ed. (New York: Prentice-Hall, 1986).

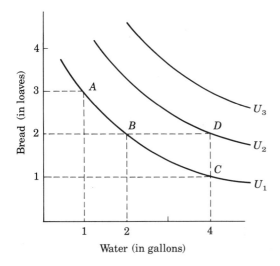

Figure 2-1 / **Indifference Curves**

for demand curves. As price increases, people buy fewer units of the good or service. We start by showing how an analysis of consumer behavior can help derive the demand relationship, and how this relationship can be interpreted as a measure of a person's willingness to pay for one more unit of the good or service.

Indifference Analysis and Demand Curves

Most analyses of consumer behavior start from indifference curves. An indifference curve is simply a representation of the various combinations of two goods that give a person equal levels of satisfaction. It is assumed that more of a good is always better, but that people are willing to accept less of one good if they are compensated with more of another. We can illustrate this in the case of two goods. In Figure 2-1, point A represents consumption of 3 loaves of bread and 1 gallon of water per day. The indifference curve U_1 goes through this point and connects it with all other combinations of bread and water that this consumer would judge to yield equal levels of utility. This person is indifferent among the various combinations of bread and water. For example, this consumer would trade one loaf of bread for one gallon of water to get to position B. The person feels neither better nor worse off because of this trade. If we wanted to induce the consumer to give up one more loaf of bread, we find that it will take more than one more gallon of water to compensate for the loss of the additional loaf of bread. In the figure, it takes two additional gallons of water to induce the person to give up the additional loaf of bread. Hence, at point C consumption consists of only one loaf of bread but four gallons of water. There is indifference between this and points A or B. We always expect that as the amount of one good declines relative to the other, the person will require more and more of the abundant good to compensate for giving up unit amounts of the less abundant good. Hence, we normally draw indifference curves so that they are convex to the origin as in Figure 2-1.

Higher indifference curves represent higher levels of satisfaction. Thus, point D is on a higher indifference curve than point B because it has the same amount of bread but more water. It is also higher than C because it has the same water but more bread. The slope of the indifference curve at any point shows the rate at which the individual is willing to trade one good for another at that point; this is the marginal rate of substitution (MRS) at that point.

The consumer's objective is to reach the highest possible indifference curve, since that would represent the highest level of satisfaction. However, the behavior of the consumer is constrained. We normally assume that the constraint takes the form of a budget constraint. This shows us the possible combinations that can be purchased with a fixed amount of money for specific prices. For example, if the price of bread is P_b, the price of water is P_w, and the person has income of I, then the equation $I \geq P_b B + P_w W$ says that expenditures must be less than or equal to income. This can be seen in Figure 2-2. The intercept on each axis is found simply by spending all of one's income on that good. Hence, I/P_b is the maximum amount of bread that can be purchased if all income is spent on bread. Solving the equation for a relationship between bread and water, we have $B \leq (I/P_b) - (P_w/P_b)(W)$. This set is shown as the shaded area in the figure. Since more is preferred to less, we usually ignore the inequality and focus on the budget line itself.

A brief numerical example helps to clarify this. Suppose that income is $100 per time period, the price of bread is $1 per unit, and water is $4 per unit.

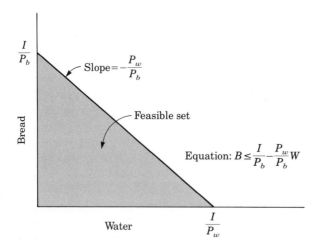

Figure 2-2 / Budget Lines

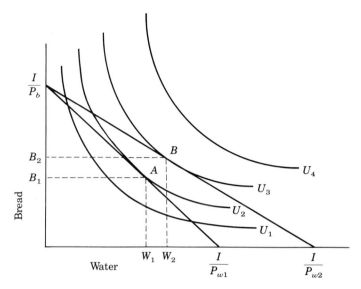

Figure 2-3 / Price Change

The person could buy a maximum of 100 units of bread per time period if all money is spent on bread. Alternatively, if all money is spent on water, the person could buy up to 25 units of water per time period. The equation for bread in terms of water consumption is $B = 100 - (4/1)(W)$. This shows that the consumer must give up four units of bread for each additional unit of water consumed.

As income goes up, the budget line shifts outward, reflecting a larger set of opportunities. As income declines, the budget line shifts inward, reflecting reduced opportunities. The slope of the budget line shows the ratio of prices. In our example the price of water is four times the price of bread and the individual must give up four loaves of bread to get one gallon of water. Increases in the price of water make the budget line steeper while decreases flatten it out. For example, if the price of water increased to $5 per unit, then the maximum amount of water the person could purchase would be 20 units and the budget line would show that it is necessary to give up five units of bread for each unit of water. Alternatively, increases in the price of bread flatten the line by bringing down the vertical intercept while decreases steepen it by raising the intercept.

In Figure 2-3 we superimpose a budget line on a set of indifference curves. Since the consumer wants to reach the highest level of satisfaction possible given the budget constraint, consumption will be at the point where an indifference curve is tangent to the budget line. Any indifference curve that cuts the budget line, such as U_1, cannot represent the highest level of satisfaction since higher indifference curves must also be available. Curves like U_4 represent levels of consumption that are not attainable with the given income level and prices. As the price changes, the slope of the budget line also changes and there is a new tangency. Thus, as the price of water falls to P_{w2}, the budget line flattens and the tangency at point B determines the new consumption pattern. The amount of water consumed goes up from W_1 to W_2. Note that the person is now on a higher indifference curve and hence better off. This occurs even though income is unchanged.

This change in consumption of water as the price of water changes is the basis for a demand curve. The demand curve for the individual assumes that income and all other prices are held constant. We vary the price of the good in question and pair the resulting quantity of the good with the new price to make a point on the demand curve. Figure 2-4 shows the quantity W_1 paired with the price P_{w1} and the quantity W_2 paired with the price P_{w2}. Further variations in the price would result in further variations in quantity and eventually we would be able to draw the full demand curve, which always has a downward slope.

It is important to remember that income and the price of other goods have been held constant. As they change, the whole demand curve is likely to shift. Thus, as income increases, the demand curves for most goods will move rightward, indicating that a larger quantity will be purchased at each possible price. However, it is possible for the demand curve for some items to shift to the left as income increases. Usually this occurs because a higher quality substitute is used; these items, therefore, are referred to as inferior goods. For example, as income increases steak may be substituted for hamburger; the demand for hamburger would then decline as income increased.

The market quantity demanded is generated by summing up the quantities that each person in the market would purchase at a given price. The sum of these quantities is paired with the price to become a point on the market

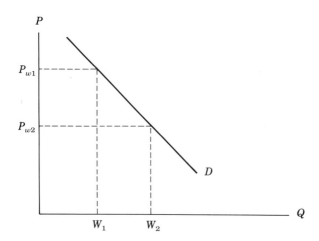

Figure 2-4 / Demand Curve

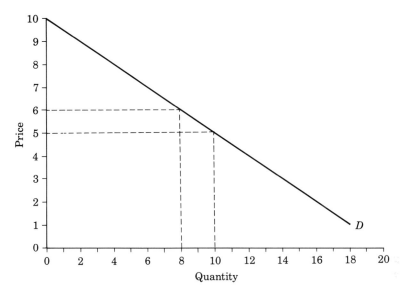

Figure 2-5 / **Demand Curve and Benefits**

demand curve. Thus, the curve is generated by horizontally summing up all the individual demand curves.

Willingness to Pay

The demand curve is sometimes referred to as a willingness-to-pay curve because it measures how much people are willing to pay for each additional unit of the good or service without being made any better or worse off. People buy additional units of a good or service until the last unit is worth exactly what it costs. All units before the last unit are worth more to the consumer than they cost. This must be true because the consumers would have purchased them even if the price were higher. We can see this in Figure 2-5. At a price of $5 the consumer will purchase 10 units. However, the other units must be worth more to the consumer than $5 apiece because this person still would have purchased them if the price were higher than $5. In fact, the diagram tells us that 8 of the units would have been purchased even if the price were as high as $6 per unit. Thus, the consumer is willing to pay more for the earlier units than for the later units. Even though the person does not pay more for the earlier units in a competitive market, the willingness to pay for them is higher.

Using this concept we can see that the area under the demand curve is an approximation of the total benefit a person gets from being able to consume a given quantity of the good or service. The willingness to pay is reduced for each additional unit; but the curve itself shows the maximum amount a person would have paid for each unit. In a certain sense, the sum of these maximum amounts represents the total value of the good or service to the consumer.[2]

The willingness-to-pay interpretation of the demand curve allows us to generate a way of measuring how much better off a person is when the market price of a good declines. This measure is called consumer surplus. Consider the demand curve illustrated in Figure 2-6. At price P_1 the person will purchase one unit. To induce the purchase of a second unit, price must be lowered to P_2. Recall that as price went down, the person moved to higher indifference curves. One indication of why that happens can be seen from the fact that at price P_2 the person buys both units for P_2 dollars apiece even though he or she would have paid the higher price P_1 for the first unit. The area under the demand curve and above the price represents the surplus the consumer gets from having this lower price. We hasten to add that this particular measurement is only an approximation; but it will do well for our purposes.[3]

If we then aggregate all the individual demand curves to get the aggregate or market demand curve, we still have a measure of willingness to pay for each unit of output. The output would only go to a person who valued it at least as much as the price. Hence, the price will tell us the willingness to pay for the last unit sold at that price. As price goes up, fewer units will be sold. If we consider price going up just enough to reduce sales by one unit, then the new price is the willingness to pay for the preceding unit. At no point would anyone value an additional unit at more than its market price. If they did, they would

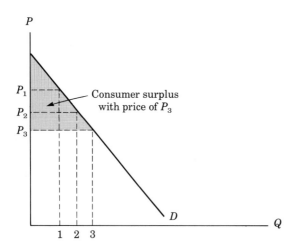

Figure 2-6 / Consumer Surplus

[2] There is an excellent treatment of these issues in E. J. Mishan, *Introduction to Normative Economics* (Oxford: Oxford University Press, 1981).
[3] See Mishan, op cit.

Box 2-1

////// Income and Willingness To Pay

One problem with using willingness to pay as the means of measuring the value of something is that those with little income are not counted very heavily. If you have no income and no wealth, then you are not "willing" to pay anything for any good or service. This does not mean that the person with no income does not want anything. We generally assume that each person's wants exceed the income available, so "wants" is a very imprecise measure of the benefit that a good or service will provide. Rather, each person's income is a constraint on the extent to which his or her wants can be satisfied. This constraint operates for all individuals. Willingness to pay is a measure of the relative value people place on different goods and services.

Those with little or no income therefore show little willingness to pay for things. This does not mean that the concept is not relevant for such groups. If a low-income person is unwilling to pay the cost of a particular good or service, this means that other goods or services that could be purchased with the money are valued more highly. If government determines that the willingness to pay for something is less than the cost of providing it, this means that the potential recipients would consider themselves to be better off with the money than they would be with the specific good or service. It may seem unfortunate that lack of income sometimes prevents some people from registering their desires for even basic commodities, such as health care; but this is a matter to be decided in the context of society's total willingness to redistribute income. Sometimes the redistributional benefits of certain programs may be deemed to outweigh any negative efficiency effects; but it is still important to know the efficiency cost of such a program. Overvaluing certain types of services so as to justify providing them to the poor is a very inefficient way to redistribute income.

simply purchase that unit. Similarly, by buying the good the consumer reveals that the unit is worth at least as much as the price, or he or she would not buy it. Of course, a person's income or wealth will influence what that person is willing to pay for a good or service. Economists make a distinction between wanting something and being ready and able to make a purchase. It is the latter concept that we use in the analysis (see Box 2-1).

The area under this aggregate demand curve is then a measure of the total benefit that a particular quantity of output will generate; the area under the demand curve but above the price is a measure of total consumer surplus for all consumers of this good at the given price.

We can think of consumer surplus as being the difference between the amount that a person would have been willing to pay for a given amount of a good or service rather than do without it altogether and the market expenditure. This difference is a measure of the benefit the person receives from having the good available in the market at the given price. At lower prices, consumer surplus would be higher, both because there is more consumer surplus on any one unit and because some additional units would be purchased and they are likely to add to the consumer surplus.

In this context we can also see why the demand curve can be treated as a marginal benefit curve. It shows the maximum price a person would have been willing to pay to purchase any particular unit of the good, given that he or she had already purchased all the prior units. This is so for each person who is purchasing the good. Thus the price associated with each unit of the good shows the maximum benefit that would be generated by that unit of output. Therefore, for each unit of output we can determine from the demand curve the consumers' willingness to pay for that additional unit; this will be a measure of the additional benefit that another unit of the good or service will generate.

Demand Elasticity

Elasticity of demand is a measure of the responsiveness of the quantity bought to changes in price. Thus, when we speak of an item with an elastic demand, it means that the quantity of that item that consumers offer to purchase is sensitive to changes in the price. Alternatively, when we speak of an inelastic demand, it means that consumers do not alter their purchases much as the price changes. This is illustrated in Figure 2-7. In part a of the figure, the demand curve shows that the amount of output consumers offer to purchase is not very sensitive to changes in price. This demand curve is said to be inelastic. In part b, the demand curve shows that the amount of output that consumers offer to purchase is very sensitive to the price. This is an example of an elastic demand curve. Price elasticity of demand, i.e., the demand elasticity with respect to price changes, can be defined as the negative of the percentage change in quantity over the percentage change in price. Since the demand curve is downward sloping, the price and quantity changes are in opposite directions and price elasticity is greater than or equal to zero.[4] Goods are often classified by their price elasticity of demand evaluated at equilibrium prices.

If the percentage change in quantity is less than the percentage change in price, the demand is inelastic; if the percentage change in quantity is greater than the percentage change in price, the good has an elastic demand; and if the percentage change in quantity is equal to the percentage change in price, the demand is unit elastic.

---

[4] In principle, elasticity changes at each point on a demand curve. Thus, attempts to calculate from the definition could give somewhat inconsistent results when the elasticity estimate is calculated for a price rise or fall and then for a movement back to the original level. It is possible to avoid this problem by using an estimate known as arc elasticity, which measures the elasticity between two discrete points. The formula and discussion can be found in most intermediate texts on microeconomic theory.

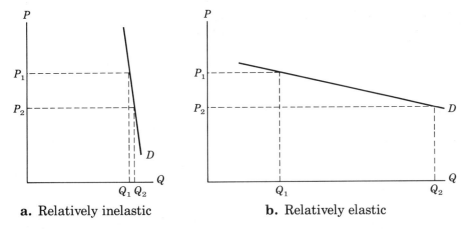

a. Relatively inelastic   **b.** Relatively elastic

Figure 2-7 / Elasticity of Demand

It is important to recognize that the demand curve and its associated elasticity are likely to be different if evaluated as long-term adjustments to price changes than if evaluated as short-term adjustments. Generally, people can make more significant changes in their consumption patterns over long time periods than they can over short time periods. Hence, the elasticity measure will tend to be lower in shorter time periods. For example, if the price of mass transit goes up some people will stop using it. This might be easy for those who have other alternatives, and their adjustment might be made quickly. However, some of the lost riders may have to purchase automobiles before they can alter their travel patterns. Hence, it is likely to take longer for them to actually stop using the mass transit system. Similarly, after the introduction of personal computers, prices fell substantially over a number of years, yet it took people time to determine how the computers could be used before actually purchasing them. As a general rule, price elasticities are higher in the long run. This holds for both the price elasticity of demand and the price elasticity of supply, which is a measure of how quantity supplied changes in response to market price changes.

We also consider the income elasticity of demand, i.e., demand elasticity with respect to income, which is defined as the percentage change in quantity over the percentage change in income. If the income elasticity of demand is positive, the good is defined as a normal good. However, if the income elasticity of demand is less than zero, the good is defined as an inferior good. Thus, the consumption of inferior goods declines as income increases while that of normal goods increases with rising income.

/// SUPPLY

Supply refers to the maximum amount offered for sale at a given price or, alternatively, the minimum price for which a particular amount is offered for sale. This minimum price can be interpreted as representing the value of the resources used up in producing the last unit of output.

Opportunity Cost

While we use price as a measure of the cost of a good or service, this is not its usual economic definition. The definition of cost is that which must be foregone to use the resources in a given way. Or, opportunity cost is the value of the highest valued alternative use of the resources, which for most goods purchased in a competitive market is the price. However, this assertion is a result of the analysis of how such markets work rather than an assumption about the market system. Hence, extensions of the analysis can show us situations where the price is not equal to the opportunity cost. We will return to some of these situations shortly. For now, consider why the price of output is likely to be a measure of the true opportunity cost of producing that good or service.

A firm decides to produce output in the short run if the price that the output will fetch on the market is at least equal to the marginal cost of production. If the price is above marginal cost, the firm will expand its output since each additional unit of output returns more in revenue than it costs to produce. Similarly, the firm will contract the level of output if marginal cost is above the price, for then the cost of producing the last unit of output is above the revenue received from its sale, and the firm would lose money on it. Thus, the profit-maximizing behavior of the firm leads it to produce up to the point where the price received for selling the good is just equal to the marginal cost of producing the last unit of output, and this is the opportunity cost of production.

Supply Curves

A supply curve for a firm shows the amount of output that the firm will offer for sale at any given price. Profit-maximizing firms operate where marginal cost equals marginal revenue ($MC = MR$); marginal revenue equals price for a competitive firm. Hence, the competitive firm operates where marginal cost equals price ($MC = P$). Thus, the supply curve for the competitive firm, which is traced out by varying price, is also the firm's marginal cost curve. Further, this marginal cost shows the opportunity cost to the economy of providing the last unit of output, where opportunity cost is used in its economic context as the value of the next best alternative use of resources. Again there are complications if we want to be exact; but this is good enough for our purposes.

Figure 2-8 shows that the output choice of the firm will respond to market price. If the price is $5, the firm will produce 9 units. At any production beyond this level the firm incurs costs greater than the price received for the new output. However, if the price rises to $6, the firm finds that the higher price

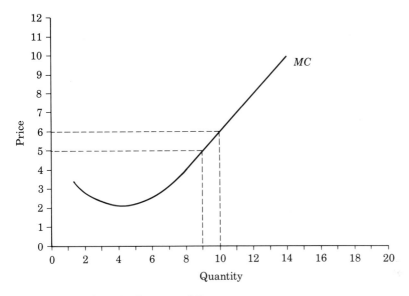

Figure 2-8 / **Supply Curve and Costs**

covers the higher costs of producing additional units and chooses to produce 10 units. Thus, the supply curve of the firm shows the opportunity cost of producing each additional unit of output, and the area under the marginal cost curve shows the total opportunity cost of producing a given level of output.

To get the market supply curve we simply add up the output that each individual firm offers to sell at each possible price. (Again a simplification that is acceptable for our purposes.) We pair the sum of these quantities with the price as a point on the market supply curve. This horizontal summation of the individual supply curves generates the market curve. The market supply curve then represents the marginal cost of producing one more unit of output.

Supply Elasticity

The price elasticity of supply is defined as the percentage change in quantity supplied over the percentage change in price. Since the supply curve is usually upward sloping, the elasticity of supply will be positive. The classifications are similar to those for elasticity of demand. If the percentage change in quantity is greater than the percentage change in price, the supply is elastic; and if the percentage change in quantity is less than the percentage change in price, the supply is inelastic.

The supply curves also will be more elastic in the long run than in the short run. Short-run marginal costs ignore all fixed costs since they are incurred whether or not the output is created in the short run. However, the long-run decision as to whether or not to keep the firm in business looks at the long-run cost curve; this is the appropriate measure of cost for the long-run decision. Fixed costs are not opportunity costs in the short run since the resources are used whether or not the firm operates; but they are costs in the long run since the firm could end such uses over an appropriate time horizon.

/// ECONOMIC EFFICIENCY

It is important to have criteria to evaluate the allocation of resources in the economy. So we briefly discuss the criteria used by economists before we finish our discussion of the allocation that results from market operation. First, goods and services should be produced in a technically efficient manner. The least amount of resources needed to produce a good or service should be used. Second, the combination of goods and services should be the one society values most highly given the possibilities available. Third, the output should be distributed correctly. The second and third criteria require some form of social value judgments. For the second, we assume that each individual is the best judge of what is valuable to him or her and that the system should make each person as well off as possible given that person's budget constraint. We assume that the third criterion involves some form of collective choice; but it is the criterion that economists are least able to address.

We can address some of these issues by considering the production possibility frontier. This construct shows the maximum amount of any one good that can be produced when a given amount of other goods are produced with the resources available. Figure 2-9 presents a production possibility curve that shows the tradeoff between bread and cheese production in a hypothetical economy. Point A represents an allocation such that the given levels of output could be produced using fewer resources than are in fact available within the economy. Thus, this economy can move to point B on the production possibility frontier and increase the level of output of both goods.

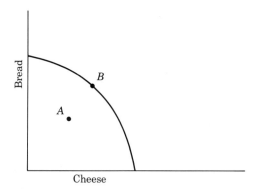

Figure 2-9 / **Production Possibility Curve and Efficiency**

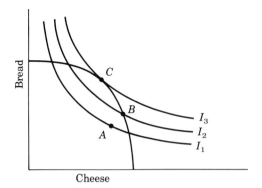

Figure 2-10 / **Allocative Efficiency**

A similar problem arises if the economy is producing the given level of output using the wrong combination of inputs. Each input has an opportunity cost in terms of the other goods or services that could have been produced using that input. This opportunity cost differs depending on the demand for various outputs relative to the resources available. Thus, resources will be relatively more or less scarce at various times and in various situations. Efficient production requires that the least valuable combination of resources be used to produce a given output. It is possible to produce extremely good electric wiring from gold; however, the other high-value uses of gold and its relative scarcity make this an inefficient use of gold. If, however, gold were to become much more plentiful than it now is or if the demand for it for other purposes were to fall, it might be very efficient to make more electric conductors of gold.

Technical efficiency is only part of the efficiency issue. We also want to be sure that the economy is producing the correct combination of goods. Thus, point B in Figure 2-9 represents a situation in which there is no waste of resources in the narrow sense; but it is possible to produce a set of outputs more desired by the economy than that represented by point B. In Figure 2-10 we have drawn in an indifference curve to show that combination C is preferred to combination B in this situation. Hence, B is not an efficient allocation of resources even if the output is produced in a technically efficient manner. Thus, the cheese producers in this economy may be very efficient at producing cheese, but point B simply represents too much cheese relative to bread given the preferences of the people in the economy.

Next, the economy must distribute the output according to the preferences of the consumers in the society. Thus, we would not want each person assigned only bread or only cheese for consumption. Some combination of the goods is most likely to maximize satisfaction of the individual, and it is important to allocate the goods in response to these preferences.

Finally, the distribution of output among the members of the economic system is important, but we can say relatively little about this. There must be some method by which society determines how output should be distributed. In the absence of any intervention, the output will be allocated in a market system according to the value of the inputs that a person owns. Thus, those with productive skills and other resources will get a relatively large share of any output while those with poor skills and no nonlabor resources will get little.

/// MARKET EQUILIBRIUM

A competitive market equilibrium allocates resources in an efficient manner. To achieve this allocation the market must meet certain criteria regarding its participants. The basic requirements are that there are many buyers and sellers, each of whom is so small relative to the total market transactions that the amount they buy and sell does not noticeably affect the market price. Each good is assumed to provide benefits only to the person who consumes it and each seller is assumed to pay all the costs of producing the output. Finally, each of the participants can freely enter or leave the market and has complete information on the prices in the market.

The intersection of supply and demand curves represents the market equilibrium position. When price is above equilibrium, there is an excess supply of the good, or the quantity that producers want to sell exceeds the quantity that consumers want to purchase. As suppliers attempt to sell the surplus output, they lower the price. When price is below the equilibrium level, the quantity demanded exceeds the quantity supplied and there is a shortage. As consumers compete for the existing units, they bid up the price. Only at the equilibrium is there no tendency for price to change.

Also, at the equilibrium, social welfare is maximized with respect to this good. Since the price faced by the producer and the consumer is the same in a competitive market, the opportunity cost of production is exactly equal to the consumer's willingness to pay for additional output. If we put the demand and supply curves into market form as in Figure 2-11, we see that the maximum difference between benefits and costs occurs at output Q^*. The total benefits are shown in the area under the demand curve and the opportunity costs are shown in the area under the supply curve. The greatest difference between the two is the shaded area. Any increase in quantity beyond Q^* reduces the net benefits because the opportunity cost is greater than the benefits. Of course, the quantity Q^* is the market equilibrium quantity, so the market equilibrium maximizes the net benefits of producing this good or service.

At any quantity below the equilibrium quantity, the benefits of an additional unit exceed the cost of producing it. Hence, this could not be a social optimum because more output would raise benefits by more than it would raise costs. At any quantity above equilibrium, the cost of the last unit was greater

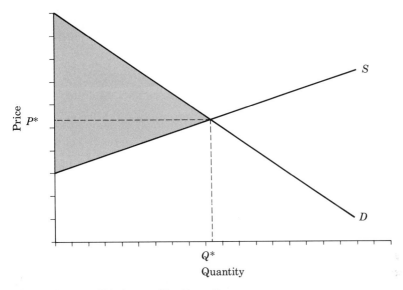

Figure 2-11 / **Maximum Net Benefit**

than the benefits it generated. Thus, it would be possible to raise total benefits by reducing output. The reduction in costs would more than offset the reduction in benefits. These concepts are illustrated in Figure 2-12. Part a shows the state of underproduction. This underproduction makes consumers worse off than they could be because the benefits from each additional unit up to the equilibrium quantity would be great enough to allow them to pay the equilibrium price and still be better off than they are without the additional units. It also makes producers worse off than they could be because they could produce the units for a cost less than the revenue they would receive from selling them at the equilibrium price. The sum of these lost opportunities is called a deadweight loss or efficiency loss to the economy. Part b shows the state of overproduction. Neither buyers nor sellers would voluntarily get to this quantity in a market. The buyers do not value the additional output enough even to pay the equilibrium price, while it would cost the producers more to provide the additional units of the good than the equilibrium price would cover. If this quantity were to be produced and distributed, there would be a lost opportunity to make better use of the resources used in the extra production. This lost opportunity is also called a deadweight loss or efficiency loss to the economy.

More generally a deadweight loss or efficiency loss is the reduction in the total value of output to society caused by producing the wrong amount of output, by producing the output without the least costly combination of resources, or by not distributing the output to those who value it most. In other words, it is a measure of the opportunities lost by deviating from the most efficient allocation of resources.

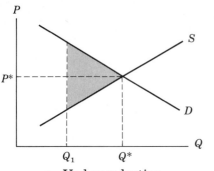

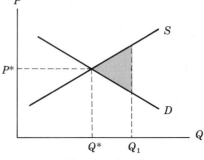

a. Underproduction   **b.** Overproduction

Figure 2-12 / Deadweight Loss

Note that deadweight losses are associated with deviations in output rather than price. As we see later, inefficiency can occur when prices are too low as well as when they are too high; but prices only direct the economy. The actual measure of welfare is associated with the use of resources in the economy.

While a competitive market system can lead to an allocation of resources that meets our criteria for efficiency, it cannot be relied on to generate these results in all circumstances.

/// MARKET FAILURE

Situations that prevent the market-determined allocation of resources from being efficient are referred to as market failures.[5] When this happens it is possible for the government to take action to improve the allocation of resources. This does not mean that government action necessarily improves the efficiency of the economy, only that there is potential for an improved allocation of resources.[6] There are three major reasons why markets may fail: market power, externalities, and public goods.

Market Power

Market power arises when either a buyer or seller in a market is large enough to be able to affect prices. In a competitive market each firm is so small that its output decisions have no significant effect on market price. However, a

---

[5] The classic article is Francis M. Bator, "The Anatomy of Market Failure," *Quarterly Journal of Economics* (1958); reprinted in Edwin Mansfield, ed., *Microeconomics: Selected Readings*, 3rd ed. (New York: W. W. Norton, 1979), pp. 425–450.

[6] For some reasons why government intervention may not improve the allocation of resources see Charles Wolf, Jr., "A Theory of Non-Market Failures," *The Public Interest* (Spring 1979), pp. 114–133.

monopolist is aware of even small effects on market price and underproduces. For example, if there are 1,000 firms and each sells 1,000 units at a price of $10.00 per unit, then no one firm is going to be concerned about changing the price by $0.01, for this amounts to only $10 per firm. Yet when this change is aggregated over all the firms, it amounts to $10,000. By definition, the monopolist owns all the other firms, so it would be concerned about the $10,000. In particular, one way to push price up a little is to cut production, and the monopolist would be expected to do this. This underproduction leads to an inefficient allocation of resources. Market price no longer reflects the marginal cost of production to the consumer, and the producer is not producing up to the point where the cost of the next unit produced is equal to price.

It is not necessary to have a monopolist for market power to exist. Whenever any buyer or seller is large enough to worry about the effect of its quantity decisions on market price, distortions will occur. Some economists think that this happens frequently while others think it is almost nonexistent in the United States except where government acts to create market power. Where market power does exist, there is the potential for government to improve the allocation of resources by either regulating the industry or providing the output itself. For example, the monopoly argument offers one explanation of the widespread regulation or ownership of utilities by state and local governments.

Externalities

Externalities are defined as benefits or costs generated outside of any market transaction. Specifically, an externality exists whenever the decision of such economic actors as households or firms directly affects, through non-market transactions, the benefits or costs of other economic actors. Positive externalities make someone better off without that person being required to reimburse the party responsible for the positive effect. However, since the person receiving the positive externality does not pay the person generating it, the person generating the externality does not have the incentive to produce or consume the efficient amount of the activity that generates these results. The originator of the externality only takes into account his or her own benefits when deciding how much to consume. Thus, the marginal benefit of the last unit consumed is likely to be above the marginal cost of producing it when all benefits are taken into account. An example of a positive externality is a vaccination against a communicable disease. The person who is vaccinated is better off because he or she will not get the disease. However, other people who are not vaccinated also benefit because there is one fewer person who might get the disease and pass it on to them. Few people consider this when deciding whether or not to be vaccinated, so the voluntary amount of vaccination purchased is likely to be too low.

More common examples of externalities are those associated with negative effects on others which are not controlled through a market exchange.

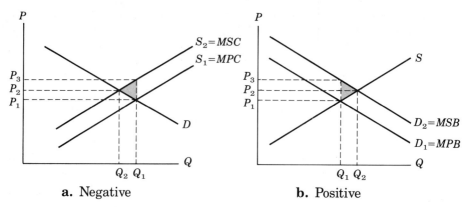

Figure 2-13 / Externalities

Most use of resources has a negative effect on others, but this negative is offset by the monetary payment for the resource. When there are externalities, the use of resources is not offset by a commensurate monetary payment and the producers (either individuals or companies) act as if their costs are lower than the true opportunity cost. Figure 2-13a shows two supply curves. S_1 represents the market supply curve generated by firms taking account of all the private costs of production. However, in this case social costs exceed private costs. Each firm generates a negative externality, a cost that it is not forced to pay. For example, the firm may be polluting the air or water. The market equilibrium is then at quantity Q_1, selling at price P_1; but the true social cost of the last unit of production is the price P_3. Because of the externality, too much of this good is produced.

It is possible that if the firm had to compensate those damaged by the pollution, it would find a method of production that creates less pollution per unit of output. However, if we ignore this possibility for the moment and treat the amount of pollution per unit of output as fixed, then the social optimum occurs where the demand curve intersects the marginal social cost curve. This is at price P_2 and quantity Q_2. At this intersection, the market price is higher but the total social cost is lower and people consume less of the output. At the market equilibrium, there is overproduction; this is associated with the dead-weight loss of the shaded triangle. Government action toward the internalization of this external cost could lead to an improvement in the allocation of resources.

Figure 2-13b shows the situation when there is a positive externality. D_1 shows the private demand for a good or service; but someone else gets benefits when the individual consumes this good or service, so the social demand curve is D_2. In this case, the private market leads to underconsumption as compared to the social optimum; and, again, there is the potential for some government action to lead to an improvement in the allocation of resources.

Public Goods

Public goods are defined as those goods for which consumption by any one person does not interfere with or reduce consumption by any other person. In contrast, whenever a person consumes a private good, the amount consumed is no longer available for anyone else to consume. It therefore does not matter to any one person how much others are consuming of private goods; but the choice of consumption for a public good is inherently a collective decision. In many cases, it is not possible to exclude anyone from consumption; but even where exclusion is possible, it would not be efficient. The marginal cost of allowing one more person to consume the existing amount of a public good is zero. Whatever price is set will exclude some people who value the good at less than this price but more than zero.

We can model a market for public goods even though this market would not exist in a decentralized system. Figure 2-14a shows the aggregation over individuals used to get a market demand curve for a private good. The aggregation is over the quantity that will be demanded by each person at each price. Thus at price P_1 person 1 consumes Q_1, person 2 consumes Q_2, and person 3 consumes Q_3. The market quantity is then $Q_1 + Q_2 + Q_3$ at price P_1. We generate the rest of the market demand curve by similarly aggregating quantities for each price. With a public good, however, the quantity is the same for everyone rather than the price. Nevertheless, we could still derive a demand curve for an individual that would show the quantity he or she would offer to purchase at any given price. In this case, we can interpret the price as the marginal value to the consumer of the last unit provided. When we know this marginal value, we can determine in principle the total value of the last unit by summing over price for each individual. This is shown in Figure 2-14b where the prices are aggregated over the quantity Q_1 to determine the value to the economy of one more unit of public good.

Unfortunately, the market demand curve generated in Figure 2-14b is not relevant for decentralized behavior. In the private good case, individuals only get the good if they pay for it. They increase their purchases up to the point where the value of the additional unit exactly offsets the cost. In the public good case, the quantity is determined by the purchases that everyone makes. In the figure, the marginal cost of the good is given by price P^* and the optimal quantity is then Q^*. However, persons 1 and 3 purchase none of the good at that price and person 2 purchases quantity Q_2. Thus, Q_2 becomes the decentralized quantity for this group, and this is clearly less than the efficient level. Further, persons 1 and 3 become "free riders" on the consumption of person 2, since they also get the benefits of the amount Q_2.

The classic example of a pure public good is national defense. Whatever defense is provided protects everyone in the country. Further, the contribution by each individual has a negligible effect on the total amount of defense produced. Hence, each individual would find it in his or her best interest not to

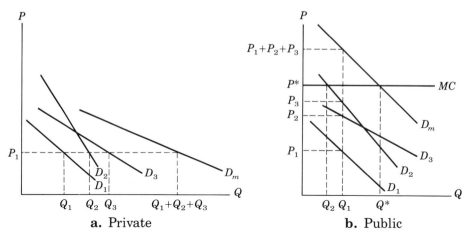

Figure 2-14 / **Public and Private Goods**

contribute toward national defense. If everyone makes such a decision no defense is provided. Therefore, government is usually called upon to provide public goods.

Few of the goods or services provided by government fall into the pure public good category. However, a large number fall into the category of crowdable public goods. A crowdable public good is one where consumption by one more person does not directly reduce consumption by others, but where it can interfere. For example, two people may be able to use a road without in any way interfering with each other; but as the number of users increases, each user finds interference with his or her use of the road. When such crowding takes place, it is often possible to generate prices that act very much like market prices. Further, geographic limits on benefits make it feasible for small units of government to provide many such services more efficiently than a larger government could.

/// OTHER GOVERNMENT ACTIVITIES

It would be a mistake to view efficient resource allocation as the only function of government from the economic perspective. Among the other functions of government are the stabilization of the economy and the distribution of resources within the economy. Some would add economic growth as another government function, but this should ideally come about as part of the efficient allocation of resources. Hence, we discuss the effects of government policies on economic growth at various places throughout the book, but we do not treat it as a separate type of issue.

Economic Stabilization

Even when individual markets are functioning efficiently, the economy may face the ups and downs of business cycles. While it is clear that individuals are unable to have any impact on a business cycle, there is great disagreement about the ability of government to act to stabilize the economy.

Virtually all economists accept that the government can affect the overall level of activity in the short run. However, there are disagreements about how this is done and about how long lasting the results are likely to be. There is disagreement about whether government affects the economy primarily by altering the amount of money in circulation or by making large changes in the level of taxation or spending. Further, there are serious disagreements about whether any such effects are permanent or are offset by other adjustments within the economy.

The ability to control the level of activity in the economy is treated in courses on macroeconomics; however, several aspects of tax and expenditure policy should be discussed briefly in the context of this volume. One is that stabilization policy is exclusively the domain of the federal government. Another is that the structure of certain tax and expenditure programs can work to offset some of the effects of the business cycle.

The need to assign the stabilization policy to the federal government is fairly obvious. The major tools of stabilization policy are the control of the money supply and tax and expenditure policy. State and local governments cannot affect the money supply, and they are frequently constrained to offer a balanced budget. Moreover, a unified nationwide policy is required. Hence, state and local governments could not conduct a countercyclical policy since the difficulty of coordination would make it unlikely that enough government units would act together to significantly affect the national economy.

The structure of tax and expenditure policies may help to stabilize the economy through what are known as automatic stabilizers. Specifically, receipts from certain taxes increase more rapidly than the economy during expansions and decrease more rapidly during contractions while expenditure programs work in the opposite direction. Thus, income tax collections automatically adjust as the economy goes up and down; and since the tax structure is what we later define as progressive, the adjustment is more than proportional. However, expenditures for food stamps and Aid to Families with Dependent Children (AFDC) go in the opposite direction of the economy. This is considered by some to be beneficial not because the federal government could not take such steps when necessary but because the lag between realization of changes in the economic situation and the implementation of offsetting policies can be quite long.

While there is disagreement about how effective these policies are, it does seem likely that the automatic stabilizers create more of an offset to economic fluctuations than would a set of taxes and expenditures that are invariant to the business cycle or that are procyclical in their patterns. Despite these advantages, the uncertainty of the magnitude of the effects, especially in the long run, makes this aspect of the decisions about how to tax and how to spend money relatively unimportant in the discussion of particular tax and expenditure programs. In fact, at the state and local level, countercyclical tax and expenditure programs are often considered to be a problem because they make for greater uncertainty in balancing the budget.

Redistribution

A final major function of government from the economic perspective is income redistribution. While a decentralized market economy can be expected to efficiently allocate society's scarce resources, there is no guarantee that the resulting distribution of final product will meet anyone's definition of a desirable distribution of income. In fact, advanced economics texts show that under purely competitive market conditions virtually any final distribution of income can be supported as an efficient allocation. Unfortunately, most distributions can be achieved only if assets can be freely redistributed before allowing the market system to take over. Aside from the inherent contradiction of redistributing assets at some time without anyone believing that they will again be redistributed at some point in the future, many of the productive assets in our economy are associated with human abilities and skills. These cannot be readily redistributed. Hence, any attempt to change the final distribution must occur by government intervening in the economy. In fact, virtually all government activity carries with it some element of redistribution, and other activities have redistribution as their major goal.

The structure of a federal system makes most redistribution ineffective at lower levels of government. The reason is that the tax base is relatively more mobile at the lower levels. Suppose that a small community were to enact a law taxing all income above the average at 100 percent and using the funds to provide grants to all receiving income below the community's average. There would be a strong incentive for those with above average income to move out of the jurisdiction and those with income below the community's average to move in. Of course, no such program exists in real life; but every government program has some redistributive elements. The bigger the redistributive elements are, the greater the incentive to move in response to them. Larger governments tend to offset this effect because of the greater cost associated with moving out of the jurisdiction. At the national level, the costs of moving are extremely high, although a very small number of people do change countries to avoid redistributive tax burdens. For example, some high-income British citizens once sought to change countries in response to Britain's very high tax rates. Thus, it is argued that strictly redistributive functions should be handled largely by the highest level of government possible and that higher levels of government can act to offset the redistributive elements of programs run at lower levels of government.

//// SUMMARY

We have presented a number of important economic concepts, many of which we use again and again in the rest of the book. They include demand, supply, market equilibrium, and market failures.

In addition to presenting concepts, we have sought to demonstrate that the market can yield efficient outcomes. Economists place significant emphasis on the efficiency of the market system in allocating resources. When the market is working according to the theory, it solves a large number of resource allocation problems and coordinates activity in an impressive manner.

Yet the system has a variety of potential problems. A number of factors can lead to market failure, in particular, situations where there is market power, where there are externalities, or where there are goods or services with the characteristics of a public good. In each of these circumstances, there is the possibility for government intervention to improve the allocation of resources. The major problem with market failure is that there are incentives to produce an inefficient level of output for the good or service with the market failure. However, the breakdown of the market incentive system also creates the possibility that production will itself be inefficient or that the allocation of output will be inefficient. These issues must be taken into account when evaluating the market under particular circumstances and when evaluating government alternatives to the market allocation.

In addition to the possibility of market failure, there is no general agreement that the allocation of income resulting from the market system will be acceptable to society. In theory it is possible to change the distribution of income without circumventing the market system, but there are no practical ways in which this can be done. Thus, when society decides to work toward a specific distribution, the government is called on to intervene in the allocation of resources, at least indirectly, as it tries to change the final distribution of output.

Chapter 3 //////

Framework for the Analysis of Government

The analysis of the allocation of resources in a market economy assumes that the market exists and that many of the institutional arrangements needed to have a market work correctly are already in place. For example, a market system would not work if there were no general agreement that each person has certain rights to have and exchange various goods and services, i.e., if there were no contract law and a government to enforce it. Thus, if there were no laws or enforcement mechanism to prevent someone from simply taking all the output you produce, you would have much less incentive to produce such output. Further, other people would be less inclined to purchase this output if they were uncertain of being able to keep what they obtain. In response to these considerations various types of institutions arise. It is not necessary that they be what we call government, but they often take that form.

The decision to form a government and the particular rules that government adopts can be analyzed in a variety of ways. The application of the tools of economic analysis to government and to political decision making is called public choice analysis. This branch of analysis seeks to find the reason for the form of organization we encounter and the effect of alternative decision rules on the outcome of political decision making. This is in contrast to the view that the decisions made in the political sphere should be taken as given when analyzing the effect of government actions on the economy. Thus, while most of the analysis in this book relates to the effect of government on the economy, it is also important to consider how choices are made about what government does and what constraints are placed on government activity. Hence this chapter presents some of the basic analysis of government from the economic perspective with emphasis on topics normally considered part of the public choice field.

Analysis of the effects of democratic voting as it relates to economic efficiency in the allocation of resources is central to the public choice field. In addition to the analysis of voting, public choice is concerned with the behavior of those who carry out the decisions made with respect to the public sector. This could be the formulation of the position held by a politician or political party or it could relate to the behavior of the bureaucrats in charge of implementing a particular program.

A further area of public choice is the analysis of what the outcome of public allocation of resources should be. In particular the issues of redistribution are addressed in some detail. The normative part of public choice has much less general agreement than does the positive or predictive analysis. Thus, this chapter focuses on the application of public choice analysis to the issue of the outcome of various types of voting mechanisms and to the analysis of the behavior of those within the public sector who are charged with implementing the policies determined by the political process. Many other topics, such as pressure groups and lobbying, could be covered in this context; but we have tried to focus on a few of the more central issues.

Before we turn to the analysis of the political process, we look at information and transaction costs in more detail. Such costs often seem to play an important role in the choice of institutional arrangement used to provide certain goods or services.

/// INFORMATION AND TRANSACTION COSTS

We have discussed the standard analysis of why government might intervene in a market economy, but some economists question the generality of the distinctions that were made. Often it is useful to look at the issue from a slightly different perspective. The public choice approach to the division of activities between the public and private sectors is based on treating people as if they act in the public arena to further their own best interests. Thus, the public sector is just a different way of allocating resources; but this method of allocating resources follows different rules from those found in the private sector. Further, it is usually assumed that the providers of services respond rationally to the incentives they receive, and these incentives may not promote efficient production or the appropriate level of output. According to this view, the choice of institutional arrangement is made in response to trade-offs of various types of costs which occur in different institutional configurations.

It may seem unusual to argue that people pursue self-interest through public sector organization. People are frequently upset about what government does, and many individuals will find themselves worse off because of specific government actions. Hence, choosing to have government make decisions for you may not seem to be a way to promote individual self-interest.

One response to this objection is that people are not necessarily concerned only with their own consumption. An individual may suffer when he or she sees another person going hungry or without adequate housing or medical care. Thus, support of government programs that take resources away from a person to achieve such goals may be quite rational.[1] However, another response is really at the heart of the public choice approach. This response is that government is a way of minimizing certain types of cost. If the benefits that government provides are greater than the costs it imposes on average, each of us is willing to accept higher costs in particular circumstances.

An example may help to clarify the general principle. People often buy subscriptions to magazines or newspapers even if they know that they will not read every issue. They do this because the net benefit of the subscription is higher than the net benefit of purchasing only those issues of specific interest. Because of economies in production and inventory control, producers are able to offer the subscription at a lower cost per issue than for individual purchases. The consumer gets the entire set of issues for a lower price but gives up the option of not buying some issues. Hence, for any one issue, the consumer may feel that the item was not worth its cost, but he or she has given up the option to act on that perception in order to gain the lower cost per unit with the subscription. Further, the consumer is not faced with the cost of evaluating each issue to decide if it is worth purchasing. The choice to participate in certain public sector activities may be similarly constrained so that a person could be unhappy with many specific actions of government and still feel that the result is better than taking all the activity away from government.[2]

Another way of looking at this is that the person chooses to give up options in a certain set of decisions in order to get a lower cost of making decisions or obtaining certain goods or services. The trade-off between the lower cost and the reduced options must be made on a higher level than that of the individual transactions.

This cost of decision making and conducting transactions is one key to determining the division of activities between the private sector and the various levels of government. Higher levels of government can make decisions for many people and reduce the cost of reaching decisions. In addition, they may be able to take advantage of economies of scale in production or distribution. Therefore, individuals may find that it is better to accept certain instances when they might have been better off acting on their own in order to reap the benefits of general collective action. The most important item is then to determine when action outside of the market is desirable and which type of organization should undertake the action.

Transaction Costs and Government

We have presented the standard approach to the theory of market failure. Under the assumptions we used, the market fails to allocate resources effi-

---

[1] Harold M. Hochman and James D. Rodgers, "Pareto-Optimal Redistribution," *American Economic Review* (September 1969), pp. 542–557; reprinted in William Breit et al., eds., *Readings in Microeconomics* (Times Mirror/Mosby College Publishing: 1986), pp. 468–481.

[2] James Buchanan and Gordon Tullock, *The Calculus of Consent* (University of Michigan Press: 1962) and Mancur Olsen, *The Logic of Collective Action* (Harvard University Press: 1965 and 1971) are two important and still widely read introductions to many of these issues.

ciently in certain well-defined cases. Then the government may step in and improve the allocation of resources. At this point it is tempting to ask why it would not be more efficient still to have the government allocate all resources. If it can step in to offset any of the market failures we have identified, why should we presume that it cannot do just as good a job when there are no market failures?[3] The answer to this question brings us to an analysis of transaction costs.

We can begin by considering the general nature of the economic problem. We assume that there are a large number of people and that each person has a set of goods and abilities. The problem is to organize the production and distribution of goods and services so as to best satisfy people's wants given the limited resources available. One possible solution is for people to use their own resources to produce goods for their own consumption; but this does not allow for all the gains that can be generated by trade and by specialization in production. Another possibility is for people to form groups. Each group could take inventory of all the resources it has, determine what could be produced, and reach some agreement on how the final output would be distributed. Those who are not satisfied with what their group proposes to give them could go and join another group.

This method of organizing the economy would be very costly in terms of negotiating the contracts that would bind group members. Yet in principle there is no reason why very complex agreements could not be worked out. The surprise is that such a system would generate exactly the same allocation decisions as the competitive market system. (See Box 3-1 for more detail on this conclusion.)

The problem with this system is that it does not fit the mechanism people think of when they consider a political system. People in the United States almost instantaneously think of voting when a political system is mentioned. Yet the democratic voting process is only one of many possible types of political forms. Why do we have representatives rather than subjecting all aspects of the public sector to individual votes? Further, for at least some public sector decisions it is possible to show disagreement by leaving that public sector. One can move out of a school district or municipality if one feels sufficient disagreement with local policies. The study of public choice looks at the reasons for certain types of institutional arrangements to provide particular goods or services within the context of the economic paradigm.

If the choices made in the public sector are no different in goals than those made in the private sector, then the major difference is the form of institution by which these allocations are made. This focus brings up many interesting aspects of public decision making. In particular it makes us look at the results

---

[3] There is a very good discussion of the issues in Kenneth Arrow, "The Organization of Economic Activity: Issues Pertinent to the Choice of Market versus Nonmarket Allocation" (Washington, DC: Joint Economic Committee of Congress, 1969); reprinted in Edwin Mansfield, ed., *Microeconomics: Selected Readings*, 3rd ed. (New York: W. W. Norton, 1979), pp. 490–508.

Box 3-1

////// Bargaining as a Choice Mechanism

The conclusion that a pure bargaining approach to the allocation of resources would lead to the same allocation as the competitive market system does not make sense to a lot of people, so let us look at it in more detail. We can define a coalition as a group of people and an assignment of goods and services within that group which does not use more than the resources available to the group. A set of coalitions would then determine the allocation of resources in the economy. We say that a coalition is blocked if there is some other coalition for which some people in the new coalition are better off and no one in the new coalition is worse off. The members of the old coalitions may be worse off because of this change as long as the members of the new group are not worse off. The new group is said to block the original allocation. A core is defined as the set of allocations that is not blocked. We can show that under certain conditions the core is the same as the competitive equilibrium.

This has very interesting implications for the use of the political system. For example, one argument about the political system as compared to the economic system is that it would be associated with more income redistribution. However, the core allocation can be thought of as the extreme political system. In this case, the income distribution is the same as it is in the perfectly competitive economic system. Hence, there is no redistribution from the competitive system. Thus, the expectation of more income redistribution is associated with the particular form of political system rather than with the use of the political system to determine the allocation of output.

---

of various institutions and it requires us to look more closely at the notion of market failure. We can try to determine whether different institutional arrangements would actually improve the allocation of resources.

Market Failure Reconsidered

Private markets exhibit a wide range of organization characteristics. One of the most important is the degree of competition within the market. A monopolist is concerned only with his or her own decisions and the actions of customers. By definition there are no competitors. At the other extreme, the large number of suppliers in a competitive market make the actions of any one rival virtually meaningless. Customers shift among producers in response to any small difference in price or quality among their output. The major reason for a monopolist in the traditional sense is the existence of economies of scale in the production of a good that are large relative to the size of the market. When such large economies of scale exist, it becomes necessary to look beyond the standard competitive model to analyze the behavior of the producer.

While it is relatively straightforward to analyze the actions of the monopolist, it is clearly the case that when a monopoly exists it would be possible for the customers and the monopolist to come to some terms whereby the amount of output is increased and everyone is made better off. The value of the additional output exceeds the cost to the monopolist of producing it.

In the standard analysis, the monopolist must charge each consumer the same price and must charge that price for each unit of output. However, there are certain exceptions to this general rule, and they often lead to more efficient behavior for the monopolist. One exception occurs when the monopolist can make each person an all-or-nothing offer and knows the person's demand function. In this case, the monopolist would get the greatest revenue by producing for each person the amount of output that maximizes net benefit. In other words, the monopolist charges those who place a very high value on the good a very high price and charges a low price to those with low demand. If the monopolist has enough information about the preferences of various consumers, it is possible to get the output back to the competitive level, although the monopolist will be able to keep a much larger amount of money than would a set of competitive firms.

Another theoretical possibility is for the consumers to get together and bargain with the monopolist for a better deal. The major impediment to such activities is the cost of reaching agreement among the consumers and of coordinating the activity of the group. Government regulation of the monopolist might be viewed as an alternative form of group action against the monopolist, but one that has a lower cost of bargaining and group formation.[4]

Given the profits that a monopolist can generate as compared to the competitive firms, it might also seem that producers in competitive markets would have an incentive to get together and form a cartel to act as a monopolist. This does not tend to happen because of the cost of forming and enforcing such an agreement. The agreement would have to cover not only the existing

---

[4] Another way to look at the issue of market failure and transaction costs is the theory of contestable markets. According to this theory, if the cost of entry and exit is low in each market, then the existence of possible entrants will force any existing monopolist to act as if it were a competitive producer. Any attempt to raise the price above the level of cost recovery would result in a large inflow of competitor firms and this threat would keep the existing firm striving to produce in the most efficient way possible. Again, note the importance of bargaining and transaction costs. In the absence of these costs, the market or some near market mechanism would lead to efficient resource allocation decisions. However, in the presence of these bargaining and transaction costs, the market is itself inefficient. For more detail see William J. Baumol, "Contestable Markets: An Uprising in the Theory of Industry Structure," *American Economic Review* (March 1982), pp. 1–15; reprinted in Breit, op. cit., pp. 363–376. Also see Harold Demsetz, "Why Regulate Utilities?" *Journal of Law and Economics* (April 1968), pp. 55–65; reprinted in Breit, op. cit., pp. 344–350.

producers but also any potential producers who might enter the market if the price were increased. However, there is no reason to believe that it would not happen if the bargaining and transaction costs could be reduced.

The second area of market imperfection that we addressed was the existence of externalities. We argued that in the presence of externalities the market would lead to either too little or too much production. Yet externalities are simply a case in which no market exists. The nonexistence of such markets is likely to be the result of the cost of bargaining and transacting rather than the nature of the good or service itself. For example, if a factory creates smoke that bothers people living in the area, the residents could offer to pay the factory to reduce its smoke output or they could take the factory to court to force it to stop. The action they take would be determined by the rights of each party. If the factory has the right to emit smoke, the residents would have to offer to pay for it to stop. However, if the residents have the right to clean air, the factory would have to offer to pay if it wanted to emit smoke. If the cost of reaching agreement is low, the result will depend on whether or not the residents value the clean air more or the factory values the right to make smoke more. Thus, if the factory has the right to create smoke but the residents value the clean air by more than the factory values the right to create smoke, then the residents can offer the factory enough money to get it to stop emitting smoke; and they are still better off than if the factory were emitting smoke and they had not made the payment.

Ronald Coase argues that the particular assignment of rights and responsibilities is unlikely to make any difference in the absence of transaction costs; he further argues that the lack of markets is not in itself any reason why an efficient allocation of resources could not occur if the cost of bargaining is low.[5] In such cases, there is some reallocation of actions that could make both parties better off. If this is the case, they have an incentive to find out what they could do to improve their interaction. He argues that bargaining and transaction costs interfere with such arrangements and that the assignment of rights and responsibilities should take such costs into account since certain types of actions are more likely, given a disparity in the costs of transacting between parties.

The other major type of market failure we considered was the existence of public goods. In the standard analysis, there is no incentive for the private market to provide such goods. However, the analysis also focuses on practical considerations such as the ability to exclude the noncontributor from consuming such goods. In most cases, the goods under discussion are not pure public goods. To serve someone else, either the service to other customers must be reduced or the capacity of the project must be increased. In either of these cases, the good is not a pure public good.

When the public good has some characteristics of a private good, the case

---

[5] Ronald Coase, "The Problem of Social Cost," *Journal of Law and Economics* (October 1960), pp. 1–44; reprinted in Mansfield, op. cit., pp. 359–382 and Breit, op. cit., pp. 414–440, as well as many other places.

for charges and exclusion can be made. However, the cost of determining the appropriate charge and imposing it can be quite high. If this is the case, again we have a problem of transaction and bargaining costs.

It is conceivable that with zero bargaining and transaction costs, even pure public goods could be provided efficiently through private agreements. It is in each person's best interest to reach such an agreement, but there is also a substantial incentive for each person to hold out and be a free rider. Even if everyone's preferences are known, unless a person can be excluded from consuming the public good, each person can share in the net benefit to a greater extent than others if they do not participate in paying for the good. Thus, each person has some incentive to hold out; but if everyone does this the system will not work. In this case, the use of coercion is necessary to get each person to contribute even if the efficient allocation is known and bargaining costs are low. However, there is the possibility of a decentralized solution if the cost of exclusion is low.

Information and transaction costs are a key determinant of the institutional arrangement that allows for the most efficient allocation of resources. Where such costs are low, the allocation will tend to be efficient. Where such costs are high, the choice of institutional arrangement becomes important, especially when the cost structure of information and bargaining differs according to the institutional arrangement.

Thus, the concept of market failure is not as clear-cut as it might appear at first glance. Instead, the cost of reaching an efficient allocation of resources differs depending on the characteristics of the good or service being considered. For some goods, the characteristics of the good and the market allow the unimpeded market mechanism to generate an efficient allocation of resources. However, for others the market mechanism breaks down and it is necessary to look at the cost of allocating resources through other mechanisms. Where bargaining and transaction costs are low, there may still be a possibility for an efficient allocation through private negotiations; however, the costs of such agreements may be quite large. In such cases, there is room to look at other types of arrangement for their provision. Democratic voting with majority rule is only one of many ways in which these issues may be addressed. Other types of institutional arrangements or changes in the legal structure may turn out to be more efficient than direct government intervention. Nevertheless, for the remainder of the book we focus on the evaluation of government activity.

/// COLLECTIVE CHOICE

When there is a market failure, a net gain is available by changing the allocation of resources. Thus, there should be some allocation of the cost and benefits to the individuals involved so that each can be made no worse off than he or she would be in the absence of the collective action. There must be some proposal that each would vote for relative to the nonprovision of the good or service. This allocation criterion is known as the unanimity rule, and it is traced back to K. Wicksell.[6] The unanimity rule necessarily means that everyone is made better off by collective action since no one would vote for such a change if it in fact made them worse off. However, it is also easy to see that the rule can lead to problems. Aside from the difficulty of communicating and voting, it creates the incentive for individuals to adopt strategic behavior, i.e., to vote against a proposal that would make them better off in the hopes of getting an even better deal.

Suppose that there is a society consisting of ten identical individuals, and that the group requires unanimity before it will take collective action. Further, each person is known to value the provision of the optimal level of common defense at $20, and this level of defense would cost $90 to provide. Obviously, if each were to contribute $9 to the provision of the collective good, then each would receive a net gain of $11 in terms of the value they place on the good. However, one person may decide to vote against this proposal and substitute one whereby he or she pays nothing toward the common defense and everyone else pays $10. From the perspective of the remaining nine, there is still a net gain of $10 from the provision of the collective good, so they are still better off than if there were no provision. However, additional members may now decide to engage in strategic behavior and the system may not achieve the provision of the collective good.

Even in the absence of strategic behavior, the problems with unanimity rules are severe. The time and information costs associated with trying to achieve an efficient allocation are likely to be immense. It is unlikely that the optimal allocation will be known before voting starts. Hence, there must be some discussion or preliminary proposals. The procedure would then have to continue in increments until a proposal was accepted that could not be improved. Not only does such a procedure imply vast patience on the part of the voters, but it also suffers from not having a well-defined outcome. There may be many possible decisions regarding the final amount provided and the tax shares of each contributor. The outcome is likely to be somewhat arbitrary.

Dictatorship is at the opposite extreme from unanimous consent to public actions. The cost of reaching a decision is obviously much smaller in this case. The major problem is that the dictator is not likely to take careful account of the preferences of everyone in the society. Thus, the public decision may be made quickly and easily, but the various members of society may be very unhappy about that decision. The more people who agree to a decision, the more we expect that any dissatisfaction associated with it will be reduced. Thus, there is some tradeoff between the cost of reaching a decision and the number of people likely to be unhappy with that decision.

---

[6] Cited in James M. Buchanan, *The Demand and Supply of Public Goods* (Chicago: Rand McNally, 1968), p. 27.

In practice, many voting rules simply call for a majority decision. However, majority rule may not make everyone better off and the total benefits may not exceed the total costs. All such a rule provides is that at least half of the people are better off under the change. It might be argued that if more than half of the population gains while less than half are net losers, the total benefits are likely to be greater than the total costs. Further, if an individual loses on any particular item, that person may gain on other votes. Thus, we may expect that decisions made under this procedure will average out to a net gain. However, there is likely to be some disagreement about whether this is going to be true or not, and that leads to much of the analysis of majority rule voting models.

Majority Rule Voting

It is generally accepted in the United States that most decisions in the public sector are made through some sort of voting mechanism. The existence of a voting mechanism is itself part of the choice made about how the public sector will operate. In particular, it is an acceptance that unanimity as a basis for decision making is not likely to be feasible. This is not true for small groups. Nor is majority rule the only form of voting mechanism. Many decisions require more than a majority rule; and in practice many decisions are made with less than a majority voting in favor of them because not everyone votes in every election. Further, the vast majority of allocation decisions in the public sector are made by elected representatives rather than by direct vote of the people.

The standard type of democratic voting is taken as a means of effectively articulating the demands of the society. Yet it is not at all clear that such a sanguine view is warranted. Perhaps the clearest possibility that voting might lead to some problems is associated with Condorcet's paradox, which was known at least as early as 1785.[7] It seems reasonable to expect any choice mechanism to meet certain rationality considerations. One of these is transitivity of preferences, which means that if A is preferred to B and B is preferred to C, then A is preferred to C. Any person who does not follow such ranking rules is likely to be judged a little eccentric, if nothing else. Yet Condorcet showed that a set of rational individuals will not necessarily end up with a set of rational group preferences under majority voting. Suppose that one-third of our voters prefer A to B and B to C, one-third prefer B to C but C to A, and one-third prefer C to A and A to B. Each person will have a consistent set of preferences but majority voting will not be consistent. If A is compared to B, A will receive two-thirds of the votes. If B is compared to C, B will receive two-thirds of the votes. it would thus appear that the group would also prefer A to C on the basis of transitivity of preferences; but in a vote C would receive two-thirds of the vote as compared to A.

---

[7] Cited in Arrow, op. cit.

This result is now commonly known as the cyclical majority phenomenon. It may seem to be of little direct importance; however, Kenneth Arrow has demonstrated that similar problems can exist in virtually all simple democratic voting.[8] Thus, there is reason to doubt that the political process can readily lead to an expression of society's goals and objectives; and there is even more concern that this process could lead to a consistent set of policies to achieve such goals once they were set.

A form of the cyclical majority problem might arise when policies are essentially redistributional. For example, it would seem that a majority of voters could tax the rest of society at 100% and redistribute the resources among themselves. Once such a policy were decided, however, it would be unstable. All of the minority could promise substantial gains to a few members of the majority to switch into their voting group so as to take control of all of the resources. The analysis discussed in Box 3-1 indicates that this will not happen if the costs of bargaining and information are zero. However, the costliness of forming groups and negotiating agreements means that some tendency toward this type of behavior could exist. Certainly the fear that a majority might not respect the rights of a minority led to many of the constitutional restrictions that the United States has on government power.

Because this is such an important issue in a demoracy, there has been considerable effort to determine the conditions under which the voting system breaks down and the likelihood of such conditions existing. To determine more carefully the situations in which the system has problems, we turn to an analysis of specific voting models.

Median Voter Model

The median voter model is the most complete economic model of voter behavior. It starts with the assumption that each person simply votes his or her self-interest on each issue. Further, the issues are generally simplified into "more" or "less" decisions on the output of some specific good or service, which is then financed by a prespecified tax on each person. Each person is assumed to know exactly what level of the good or service is to be provided and exactly how much that will cost in taxes. In this case each person has a demand curve for the good or service and there is a separate price for each peson. Thus, voters are expected to vote to increase or decrease the quantity of good or service depending on whether the quantity currently provided is above or below their desired quantity. The median voter is that voter whose most preferred choice is median among the choices of all voters.

Figure 3-1 illustrates the median voter model when each person pays an equal share of the cost of additional units. Assume that the good is a pure public good with cost of production constant at MC. The individual demand

---

[8] Kenneth Arrow, "A Difficulty in the Concept of Social Welfare," *Journal of Political Economy* (1950); reprinted in Mansfield, op. cit., pp. 453–469.

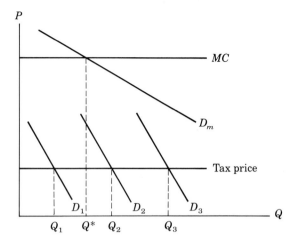

Figure 3-1 / Median Voter Model—Pure Public Good

curves are summed vertically to get the social demand curve. The intersection of this demand curve with the MC curve yields the optimal quantity of output Q^*. However, each individual is concerned only with his or her own benefits and costs. Thus, person 1 would vote to increase output up to Q_1 and vote against any output above this amount. Person 2 would similarly vote for increases up to Q_2 and against amounts above this. The voting equilibrium is thus at quantity Q_2. If the existing quantity is below that, a majority would vote for an increase in output while a majority would vote against any quantity above Q_2. Unfortunately, there is no guarantee that Q_2 is the social optimum. In the figure Q_2 is above the optimum; but it could just as easily have been below. For example, if person 3 were to have a change in taste that led to an increase in demand for this good, the D_3 curve would shift to the right and this would cause the social demand curve to shift to the right as well; but the median voter amount would remain unchanged.

Figure 3-2 illustrates the median voter model when the good is essentially a private good for which everyone is constrained to consume the same quantity. For example, this might refer to frequency of trash collection. Again, the voting scheme will lead to quantity Q_2 being provided. From the perspective of person 1, this quantity represents a deadweight loss of the shaded triangle above the D_1 demand curve and below the MC cost curve. This person does not value the additional output above Q_1 by the full cost of producing it. Similarly, there is a deadweight loss associated with the shaded triangle under the demand curve for person 3 but above the MC curve. This occurs because person 3 values additional output at above the cost of producing it. In this context, the efficient level of output would be one that minimizes the sum of deadweight losses for the various consumers; but there is no reason to expect the median voter quantity to achieve this objective. As we see when we turn to federalism,

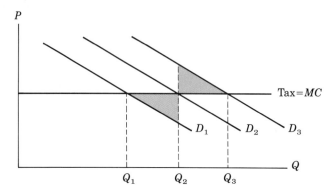

Figure 3-2 / **Median Voter Model—Private Good or Crowded Public Good**

a better solution might be to separate the consumers into different communities; but for now we retain the assumption of a fixed group and equal consumption.

Single-Peaked Preferences

A key reason for the determinateness of the median voter model is the assumption that each person has a well-defined downward sloping demand curve for the good or service under consideration. When this is coupled with a constant price per unit, the net quantity preference has a characteristic known as a single peak. Consider the demand curve in Figure 3-3. The individual would prefer to consume the quantity Q_2 if there were no constraint. However, the person can only vote whether to increase or decrease consumption. If we look at the net benefit the person receives, we see that this net benefit, which is the difference between the area under the demand curve and the cost to the individual, will start out fairly small and will grow until the quantity reaches Q_2. At this quantity, the level of net benefit is maximized. Any production beyond this point leads to a net loss for the individual as compared to the optimum. In other words, for additional output the benefit as shown by the area under the demand curve is less than the cost as shown by the area under the cost curve. This net loss on the additional units is subtracted from the net gain up to Q_2 in determining the net gain associated with these quantities of the output. Thus, the net gain peaks at Q_2 and then declines after that point, as shown in Figure 3-4. This occurs for each individual in similar circumstances. The particular point at which net benefits peak differs for different people, but each person has a curve that looks like the one in Figure 3-4. This peaking phenomenon is important if we are to have determinate outcomes from the median voter model. If all individuals have preference curves that behave in this way, the cyclical majority phenomenon will not occur.

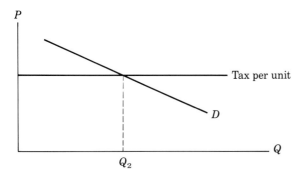

***Figure 3-3* / Voter's Demand for Public Output**

This particular formulation makes much sense when considering the case of a single good or service and a well-defined price for its provision. However, this is not necessarily the case that prevails in the provision of all goods and services. First, the finance mechanism is not such that each person faces an obvious price for the good or service. The tax may be such that the individual will pay different prices for different levels of output. For example, there may be matching funding from some other governmental unit which pays part of the cost for output up to some point, and the residents of the jurisdiction may then find the tax price jumping to the full cost for production above the subsidized level.

Another possibility is that the person may not have a well-defined demand curve for the public output. This could occur because the individual has the option of choosing some other method of providing the good or service. For example, in response to very low levels of public school quality, some families may choose to send their children to private schools. Thus, the net benefit of additional quality for public schools may be negative up to some point. At that point, the family will switch its children to public schools, and further im-

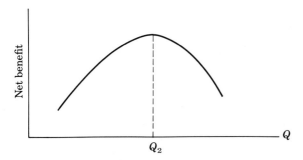

***Figure 3-4* / Net Benefit**

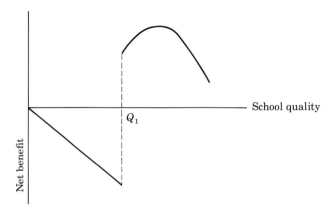

Figure 3-5 / **Multipeaked Preferences**

provements in quality may generate net benefits. Figure 3-5 illustrates this with a negative net benefit up to quality level Q_1. For lower quality than this, the family chooses to send the children to private school but must still pay the additional taxes associated with improving the public schools. At this point, the children are switched to public schools and additional quality generates positive net benefits. In this case it is entirely possible to get the cyclic majority phenomenon.

Finally, if we consider that most decisions are made on packages of public provision rather than on each item separately, the net benefits associated with a package might depend specifically on which items in the package receive additional funding as the level of funding is increased.

Logrolling

The major problems with the median voter model are that it does not allow for intensity of preferences and that voters are assumed to address one issue at a time. In fact, there are a variety of ways for people to make the intensity of their preferences count, and voters seldom vote on a single issue funded from a well-defined tax source. Rather, they vote on candidates who offer a specific (or not so specific) set of services and taxes. The package nature of the decision allows intensity of preferences to be felt. In choosing a candidate, a voter seldom finds one who would choose exactly what the voter would choose in all cases, so the voter must make compromises. It is in the process of making such compromises that the intensity of preferences can be important. Thus, for some voters, one issue may take precedence over all others. A candidate who offers these voters the best position on this item will receive their votes no matter what position he or she takes on other items. The candidate is in a position to trade off among various voters so as to get a majority who believe that his or her choices will leave them better off than the choices of any other candidate. This is called logrolling.

The problem with the logrolling model is that it is difficult to argue that the resulting decisions are any more efficient than those arising from the median voter model. This is particularly true when there are many decisions to be made. In this case, it is seldom in the best interest of each voter to become fully informed on each issue. Rather, voters only become informed about issues that are of interest to them. In this situation, it is argued, there is a strong tendency for government to provide too much in the way of benefits to small groups strongly interested in one program. For example, it is widely believed that in the short run the majority of Americans are hurt by farm subsidies. The subsidies require that the taxpayer provide money through taxes to purchase and store farm output; then the taxpayer is also likely to be hurt by the resulting higher food prices. However, the effect is small for any one family while it is very important for farmers. Hence, farmers strongly support such policies while the majority of the population is rather indifferent. Thus, the policies tend to continue. The same type of argument can be made for a large variety of government programs.

"Voting with Your Feet"

We tend to think of voting by marking a ballot as the only means to control the public sector environment in which we live; but there is another way to affect the amount of many publicly provided goods and services. This is to physically move from one jurisdiction to another. Charles Tiebout felt that the characterization of public goods often did not describe what government did.[9] In particular, he did not believe that adding population simply allowed more people to consume the public good without influencing what other people consume. Rather, he argued that most of the services provided by government are subject to crowding. If more people are to be served, then either the quality of the services declines or more resources must be used. Further, he argued, most goods and services are provided by local governments, and dissatisfied consumers can affect the level of output in two ways. They have the option of trying to change things through their voting behavior; but they can also move out of a jurisdiction if they are dissatisfied with the local public sector. This "voting with your feet" is deemed to have important implications for the decisions made at the local level. If one government is providing too much or too little of some service relative to what one family wants, then they can move to some other jurisdiction that has a mix closer to what they prefer.

Tiebout argued that this mobility leads to increased efficiency in that people come closer to satisfying their preferences than would be the case if

---

[9] Charles M. Tiebout, "A Pure Theory of Local Expenditures," *Journal of Political Economy* 64 (October 1956), pp. 416–424.

everyone had to consume the same amount of each good and service. Thus, if we look back at Figure 3-2 we see that there is inefficiency associated with each person being forced to consume the same amount of the good. Some feel that they are being forced to consume too much because they would be willing to take a lower level of service in exchange for lower taxes. Others feel that they are getting too little since they would be willing to pay the higher taxes needed to get the higher level of service. If they were to separate into communities where others had preferences similar to their own, each would be better off.

While there are important aspects in which Tiebout was correct, there are also some problems in applying his model too freely. First, the incentives for production efficiency that exist in the market do not exist in the local government area. If a private firm is producing inefficiently, sooner or later it will either go out of business or be bought by some other producer. Neither of these options really exist for local governments. Further, the price paid in a community is not tied to the package of services received. Hence, distortions are introduced into these location decisions. People are only concerned with the cost to them of living in a community rather than with the cost of providing them with services. Since many costs are linked to the number of people the community serves while local revenues are linked to the amount of property they consume, communities have an incentive to keep out families that consume little property and attract those who consume much property. Similarly, each family has some incentive to move into communities with a high tax base. Thus, we do not expect local governments to be as socially efficient as the "voting with your feet" model implies. Nevertheless, there are likely to be benefits associated with decentralization of government functions.

Offsetting the desirable aspects of a system of decentralized governments are some clear limits on what such governments can accomplish. First, they are not good at redistribution since those who provide above-average taxes have a tendency to move away. Second, they are not well suited for goods with extensive externalities or coordination problems, such as transit systems. Third, they are not large enough to take advantage of certain economies of scale. Fourth, the proliferation of governments is likely to raise administrative costs.

Nonmarket Failures

While we have a well-defined set of conditions under which the market mechanism may fail to provide the best allocation of goods and services, it is not always clear that the government intervention would improve things. Rather than assume that government always acts in the interest of efficiency, it is useful to consider what might prevent the government from being an efficient provider of goods and services. One set of issues is articulated by

Charles Wolf as a theory of nonmarket failures.[10] He sets out a series of conditions that are likely to lead to inefficiency in the government production or provision of a good or service. These are largely related to the incentives that exist in the public sector.

On the supply side, he identifies several major factors. To begin, there is the difficulty in measuring the output of many government activities, making it hard to evaluate production and efficiency. Instead of trying to evaluate output, we often look only at the inputs into the process, e.g., dollars per pupil spent rather than quality of education. Related to this is the difficulty of determining whether the output could be provided more efficiently by some other form of organization or production. Because there is no profit motive and no competition, the providers have the possibility of great inefficiency without losing their customers. Very inefficient private firms would either go out of business or be taken over by some other firm; but this is much less likely to happen if government is the funding source. On the demand side, he sees politicians as having a short time horizon extending primarily to the next election and leading to actions that appear to address current concerns rather than to actions that are beneficial in the long run.

Out of these characteristics, Wolf provides a set of likely problems associated with government provision. One is that the lack of profit incentive will translate into an inability to keep costs under control. This is manifested as a desire to grow, as a tendency to increase employment, and as an inappropriate response to innovation. In the latter case, there are instances of government attempting to gain the most technologically sophisticated inputs even if they are not cost effective, as well as resistance to the introduction of useful technology that would upset accepted routines. For example, the military is often accused of the former problem while many local governments appear to be very slow in adopting new technology.

The basic point is that in deciding whether to try to offset some market failure, we should consider an agency's internal incentives to determine how it will measure up against a competitive system. It is only by comparing the realistic behavior of the public sector with the realistic behavior of the private sector that we can determine appropriate actions.

/// IS GOVERNMENT TOO BIG?

While recent debates all seem to focus on whether government at all levels has grown too big, it is important to understand as well the arguments that government might be too small a portion of the economy. For many years, these arguments occupied much of the attention of both economists and the public at large. Such periods tend to occur when there are significant problems associ-

---

[10] Charles Wolf, Jr., "A Theory of Non-Market Failures," *The Public Interest* (Spring 1979), pp. 114–133.

ated with the ability of government to cope with growth. However, it may also be that the discussion just goes in cycles. There is already some evidence that the cities and states that have been most successful at curbing the growth of government are facing some problems associated with government's ability to handle the growing demands of the population.[11]

The arguments that government is too small usually relate to either externalities or to the absence of certain markets. For example, if the benefits from a particular local government's provision of a park spill over into adjacent communities, then that government will not take account of all benefits when deciding how many parks to have. Rather, it will only take account of the benefits to its own residents and, hence, underproduce parks. Similarly, it is argued that benefits to future generations are often ignored. Thus, a national park would provide benefits both to current generations and to future ones. Since the current government would be expected to worry only about current residents, it might underproduce national parks.

If the local parks decision is made at a very high level of government, the externality problem is not an important one. The higher level of government essentially internalizes the externalities because it encompasses all the recipients of benefits within its jurisdiction. However, this approach makes it difficult to vary the amount provided in response to community preferences.

There are other ways of offsetting any local tendency to ignore external benefits. One would be for the higher level of government to give the lower level incentives to produce more by offering to pay part of the cost. In principle this could offset the effects of the underproduction due to the externality; however, it suffers from the difficulty of setting one policy which is appropriate in all circumstances. Another possibility is for the local governments that receive benefits to offer to pay for part of the cost of providing the parks. This would effectively internalize the externality into the local decision-making process. The problem is one of bargaining and transaction costs. If they are low, the local governments can be expected to reach some type of agreement. However, if they are high there is little chance that the local governments will reach agreement.

The question of how we value the future benefits of a project is more difficult to analyze. We simply do not know how future generations will value national parks. They cannot contribute to our production of such items. To the extent that current citizens appropriately account for such future values, the process will take them into account. Since people do provide for their children, there is reason to believe that the political decision-making process does not ignore future benefits. However, if individuals do not account for these future benefits, there is no obvious way to get around such a market failure because much of the needed information simply does not exist.

On the opposite side are the arguments that government tends to be too

---

[11] For example, see Robert Reinhold, "Strict Limitations on Government Choke California," *Oregonian* (December 29, 1987), p. A2.

large. These positions relate both to government decision making and to the way government is organized. We have already seen the basic part of the decision-making analysis. It is argued that the benefits of many government programs are targeted on a small group of people. These people have a strong interest in getting the programs started or expanded. The costs, however, are spread out over a large group of people. These people individually bear little cost and frequently are not even aware of the cost they do bear. Hence, there is little incentive for them to oppose the program. Thus, it is argued that special interest groups create a distinct bias toward overexpansion of government.

Another possibility for the excessive expansion of government is related to the earlier argument about politicians ignoring the benefits that will occur in the future. It is asserted that they also tend to ignore future costs, because it can be politically attractive to provide current benefits and push the costs into the future. For example, an increase in promised public pensions may be partially substituted for current salary increases, with no additional money set aside to pay those pensions. This creates future problems since the funds to pay the pensions will have to be raised at some point; but that point usually comes after most of the politicians who originally supported such increases have left office. The same thing can happen by deferring needed maintenance to save current costs. The savings from such deferral are likely to be more than offset by future costs. There are many other less obvious programs where the opportunity to push costs off into the future may make a program look very attractive. If the costs were readily visible to current voters or if future voters had some say, there might be a different outcome; but there is no obvious way to generate such information.

Finally, there is the view that government tends to be too large because of the bureaucracy and its incentives. First, there is a tendency for those involved in a program at upper management levels to have some commitment to the program. Either they have worked in the bureau for a long time or they have special training in its area of coverage. Further, they are not responsible for raising the revenue they spend. Hence, they are likely to look only at the good that each program generates and to fight to keep and expand the scope of the bureau. In addition, the salary and rank of middle managers are often based on the number of employees they have. Hence, there is further incentive to expand and grow.

These incentives affect government decision making because bureaucrats tend to have some discretion as to how to spend funds allocated to their agency. Thus, they can apply any cuts in funds to programs that will provoke the most reaction.[12] For example, when faced with a cutback in funds, a school administrator may simply prepare to eliminate all sports programs. This is likely to generate support to replace the funds, whereas proposals to cut less visible

---

[12] An example of this is a reported attempt by the various armed forces to avoid their share of Defense Department cuts by proposing to cut weapons which they knew would be rescued by various members of Congress. Reported in *Los Angeles Times* (January 17, 1988), p. 1.

programs might have gone virtually unopposed. Further, government bureaucrats may have little incentive to improve efficiency. An improvement in efficiency would allow the same output to be produced with fewer resources; at least in the short run, this is not in the manager's best interest.

If it were less costly to determine the efficiency of government actions, there might be more possibility of changing the way decisions are made. However, the lack of competition makes it difficult to determine how cost effectively output is being produced. When there is private sector production of the same output, the private sector is almost always found to be the less costly producer. This is one reason why more governments are considering contracting with private producers to provide certain services. We cover this topic in more detail when we discuss government production in later chapters.

Size of Government

If all government growth were caused by increasing inefficiency, we would have real reason to be concerned about the economy. As noted earlier, growth at all levels of government has been significant both in absolute terms and as a percentage of GNP. However, a variety of arguments have been made as to why government should be expected to grow faster than the economy as a whole.[13]

One important reason is that the growth in the economy and the tendency for greater urban concentrations lead to an increase in the importance of externalities. As urbanization proceeds, externalities become more all-pervasive and burdensome because of the increasing number of generators and recipients. If people burn trash because their nearest neighbors are a mile away, the externality is not likely to be important; and, if it is important, it is likely that the neighbors could reach some agreement about how to control any problems. However, when you put a million people together and they all start to burn their trash, the externalities are very important. First, the environment cannot as readily absorb the concentration of pollutants. Second, each person's polluting will affect many other people.

One response to the trash problem is for government to start collecting trash so as to reduce the amount burned. Other responses include regulation of trash burning or establishing liability for damages done by smoke. The choice of mechanism depends on the relative costs of achieving the desired results, but the result is a larger government.

Another issue related to the size of government is associated with the differences in productivity growth in the production of goods and the production of services. The argument is basically that the production of goods is possible with fewer and fewer people per unit of output over time because capital can be substituted for labor in the production process. Hence, a larger percentage of the labor force will be associated with the production of services.

---

[13] William Baumol, "Macroeconomics of Unbalanced Growth," *American Economic Review* 57 (June 1967), pp. 415–426.

Certainly the relative importance of services in our economy has increased dramatically. To the extent that government is primarily a service provider, it would not be surprising to see it growing in line with other services.

/// SUMMARY

The market system ranks high on the count of efficiency when markets are competitively organized, all goods are private, there are no externalities, and information is freely available. When these conditions are not met, the government may be able to take actions that improve the allocation of resources. Further, government has the functions of stabilizing the economy and of redistributing income. However, it is necessary to look at how government is organized to see if it can actually achieve these objectives.

When there is a market failure, there is some possibility to reallocate resources so as to make some people better off without making anyone else worse off. However, the only way to guarantee that this efficiency objective is met is to have unanimous agreement about what should be done. There are many difficulties in trying to get such agreement. Realistically, we rely on voting models with some form of majority rule to decide on what government should do, or we rely on elected representatives to make such decisions.

Models of voting and government behavior point to potential problems with public sector allocations of resources. There is no obvious reason to expect that the decisions made through the political process represent a clear statement of voters' preferences. For example, the cyclical majority phenomenon might result in almost random determination of public policies with respect to a particular issue. Even when there is a determinate outcome, it may not be efficient. Output decisions may end up being too high or too low, and government is less likely than the private sector to be efficient in production. Some of these shortcomings can be overcome by a set of small decentralized governments, but this solution can create problems of its own.

There are many arguments that government may be too big, and other arguments that government is too small. While a variety of factors indicate that government should probably grow over time, it is not at all clear if it should be growing as a percentage of the economy or if it is too big at any one point in time. Further, there is reasonable consensus that there is room for much improvement in the efficiency with which government provides goods and services.

Our task then is threefold. We must look to see what governments actually do. We must analyze these activities with respect to the goals of government. Finally, we must look to see how efficient and effective the government is in conducting these activities. We propose to pay special attention to the choice of level of government and interactions between levels of government in our analysis.

Chapter 4   //////

Intergovernmental Relations under Federalism

Since its inception, the government of the United States has been based on the principle that provision and financing of governmental activities are best accomplished by a multilayered structure. The Tenth Amendment to the Constitution guides U.S. federalism by expressly protecting the rights of states to pursue their own agenda, provided the agenda does not conflict with clearly legislated federal objectives or constitutionally protected individual rights. State constitutions, through charters for the creation of local governments, offer protections for the activities of cities, counties, and special districts and delegate specific powers to them. It would be a mistake, however, to assume that American federalism is chiseled in granite. Instead of being static it is highly dynamic, changing in response to shifting demand and supply conditions and to the people's view of what the relations should be.

This book is concerned with the fact that governments must make decisions about how, when, and where to produce what services; which services should be provided to specific constituents; and how to finance the services that government provides. Whereas in the private sector supply and demand of goods and services are integrated by the workings of the market, in the public sector public officials are called upon to make such integrating decisions. Under federalism, however, one additional set of decisions must be made: which level of government is to provide constituents with specific classes of services, which level should finance services offered by lower levels, and to what extent should they do so. Because we are concerned with expenditures and receipts of all three levels of government under federalism, intergovernmental relations deserve special attention.

Conventionally, public finance texts have one or more chapters on intergovernmental fiscal relations or transfers. The emphasis is on the role of higher levels of government as a source of revenue for state and local governments. The concern, therefore, is to determine how the higher level of government can influence the actions of the lower levels of government. However, federalism covers a much broader scope than merely the transfer of funds from higher levels of government to lower levels. Economic analysis can be used, for example, to estimate the consequences of alternative arrangements for supplying public goods and services by various levels of government and for financing them in various ways.

Federal, state, and local governments relate and interact in numerous ways; some are formal or even codified, some are informal, some are institutionalized and continuing, others are ad hoc. Some are horizontal, between governments on the same level; some are vertical, between levels of government. Most are managed but some are beyond the control, and in part even beyond the knowledge, of governments. Although emphasis is often on fiscal intergovernmental relations, we must recognize that they are only part of a more inclusive set of relationships between local, state, and federal governments. Many are not fiscal in nature and do not involve the transfer of funds. For example, direct nonfiscal intergovernmental relations specify the powers and authority that local governments derive from the state.

A host of indirect nonfiscal intergovernmental relations also affect local government through the environment in which they operate. For example, a federal-state highway program can reduce the amount of taxable property and displace businesses and people. A federal program can train young adults and help them find jobs; as one result, local welfare payments to these persons will decline.

Nonfiscal governmental relations often take the form of mandates and constraints. Joseph Zimmerman defines a mandate as a "legal requirement—constitutional, statutory, or administrative—that a local government must undertake a specified activity or provide a service meeting minimum standards."[1] We differentiate between mandates and constraints (or restraints). If mandates involve coercive provisions that require local governments to take specific affirmative steps, constraints involve coercive provisions by higher levels of government that prohibit lower levels from specified activities. Thus local school districts may not raise sales or income taxes, local governments may be required to make purchases only after formal competitive bidding,[2] or local governments must comply with the equal employment provisions of the 1965 Civil Rights Act.[3]

Some mandates, particularly those issued by the federal government, involve financial transfers. In extreme cases, higher levels of government can assume the entire cost. Consequently, we can point to an entire spectrum of intergovernmental relations from those that involve no financial transfers to those that involve very large ones.

---

[1] Joseph F. Zimmerman, "State-Local Relations: The State Mandate Irritant," *National Civic Review* 65 (December 1976), p. 548.

[2] Ibid., p. 548.

[3] *Federal and State Mandates: Their Impact on Local Governments*, Research Monograph #7, Governor's Task Force on Local Government, Idaho (December 1977), p. 2.

If we focus on the flow of funds from the federal and state governments to local governments, we can see an intricate pattern of inducements intended to influence local government resource allocations. However, a meeting of a city or county council or of a school board reveals that local government is not a passive body but one that makes important choices about policy issues as well as about narrow management issues. It would be wrong to assume that local governments merely respond to such offers of intergovernmental aid or never react to change them. In most instances local governments actively lobby for intergovernmental transfers of funds.

Under the impetus of social and political forces such as increasing urbanization, mobility, and local government "fiscal crises," federal-state-local government relations have undergone major changes. For most of our history, the federal government had little direct influence on local government and maintained a fairly clear separation of functions with state governments. However, by the end of 1965 the federal government was administering more than seventy-five grant programs for urban governments, and more than three-quarters of these were authorized after 1950.[4]

After 1965, federal aid to state and local governments continued to increase at an unprecedented rate. From 1964 to 1979 federal aid doubled approximately every five years:[5] from $10 billion in 1964, to $20 billion in 1969, to $43 billion in 1974, and to $83 billion in 1979. It rose to $117 billion in 1988. Whereas inflation distorts these numbers, note that federal aid to state and local governments rose from 1.6% of GNP in 1964 to over 3% of GNP in the late 1970s, before starting its drop to around 2.5% of GNP in 1988. State aid to local governments has also increased at a rapid rate. It grew from $13 billion in 1964, to $25 billion in 1969, to $46 billion in 1974; by 1979, it amounted to $74 billion and by 1986 to $130 billion.[6]

But the changes in intergovernmental relations are not all financial. The scope of mandates and restraints imposed by states on local governments and of mandates with partial reimbursements imposed by the federal government has also undergone changes in the last fifty years. Especially in the 1970s many states imposed limits on taxes that local governments can raise. The 1980s also have seen reductions in the financial aid, i.e., subsidies, provided by the federal government to compensate lower levels for carrying out their mandated activities.

---

[4] For example, congressional enactments in 1965 alone included grants for basic water and sewer facilities, advance aquisition of land, open space for urban beautification, neighborhood facilities, code enforcement assistance, demolition of unsafe structures, rent supplements, and support for councils of locally elected officials—all as parts of the Housing and Urban Development Act of 1965.

[5] Advisory Commission on Intergovernmental Relations, *Significant Features of Fiscal Federalism, 1988 Edition*, vol. 2, M-155 II (Washington, DC: July 1988), pp. 26 and 35.

[6] Ibid., p. 83.

/// LEGAL FOUNDATION

Key guidelines to U.S. federalism are given in the Tenth Amendment to the Constitution. This amendment provides that all powers not specifically delegated to the federal government are "reserved to the States respectively, or to the people." Accordingly, the right of the federal government is limited in mandating the actions of state and local governments.

Compared to the federal government, states are much less restricted in mandating the behavior of local governments. The doctrine of state supremacy over local governments provides the legislature and the courts with authority to issue directives to local governments. In 1868 Judge John F. Dillon held that

> municipal corporations owe their origin to, and derive their powers and rights wholly from, the legislature. It breathes into them the breath of life, without which they can not exist. As it creates, so may it destroy. If it may destroy, it may abridge the control. Unless there is some constitutional limitation . . . the legislature might, by a single act, if we can suppose it capable of so great a folly and so great a wrong, sweep from existence all municipal corporations of the state, and the corporations could not prevent it.[7]

In 1923 the United States Supreme Court refused to recognize an inherent right of local self-government.[8] However, some states adopted constitutional amendments prohibiting enactment of special laws affecting specific local governments in response to unpopular actions by state legislatures.

Sources of Local Government Power

The ability of a government to influence the economy depends substantially on the scope of powers available to that government. It is inherent in federalism that some conflicts will develop regarding the proper activities of the various levels of government. The states receive their power from the Constitution, but local governments are all created by state actions. Although the common perception is of all-inclusive state power in contrast with inherent local powerlessness, the relationship was never quite so lopsided and it surely is not so today. The rights of local governments have been strengthened by a number of devices: states granting "home rule" to certain cities, constitutional limitations on state mandates, as well as some recent constitutional rulings by state courts allowing greater local autonomy and restricting federal guidelines.

Many states offer their local governments some form of home rule. While there are different versions, home rule generally entails the state granting

---

[7] *City of Clinton v. Cedar Rapids and Missouri Railroad Company*, 24 Iowa 455 (1868).
[8] *City of Trenton v. New Jersey*, 262 U.S. 182 (1923).

local governments the privilege of managing their own affairs.[9] However, the state legislature normally retains some powers to impose actions on local governments. The scope of these powers is limited by three state constitutions, those of Alaska, Louisiana, and Pennsylvania, and it is limited by court decisions in a number of other states.[10] In particular, local governments historically have been treated as having no right to challenge the actions of state governments in court since the local governments are created by the states; however, in recent cases the courts have recognized the rights of local governments to challenge state actions.[11] Thus, the relationship between the state and local governments varies from state to state and has been changing over time.

/// **THE ECONOMICS OF FEDERALISM**

De Tocqueville thought that "the federal system was created with the intention of combining the different advantages which result from the magnitude and the littleness of nations."[12] Although economic considerations most likely played only a minor part in favoring a federal system, federalism is a political institution with economic ramifications. For the political scientist federalism means the existence of different levels of government, each possessing an explicitly independent scope of responsibility and authority.[13] For the economist, however, the emphasis is on the allocation of resources and the distribution of income within the federal system. More specifically, for the economist federalism entails a multitier public sector that has both centralized and decentralized levels of decision making, where public service provision is greatly influenced by demands of residents of the different jurisdictions. Thus, a major focus for economists is on the responsiveness of jurisdictions to the demands for services by their constituents and on the efficiency with which those demands are met.

Microeconomic theory can be applied to analyze not only the public sector, but also public decision making in general and under federalism. Federalism makes contributions to efficiency when it leads to a matching of individual

---

[9] For a more complete discussion, see Advisory Commission on Intergovernmental Relations, *State Mandating of Local Expenditures*, A67 (Washington, DC: July 1978), pp. 17–18.

[10] *Constitution of the Commonwealth of Massachusetts*, art. LXXXIX, 7 of the Articles of Amendment; *Constitution of the State of Alaska*, art. II, 19; *Constitution of the State of Louisiana*, art. VI, 14; *Constitution of the Commonwealth of Pennsylvania*, art. VIII, 2(b).

[11] *Midwest City v. Cravens*, 532 P. 2d 829 (1975); *City of Hermiston v. Erb*, 27 OR. App. 755 (1976); *Town of Blackbrook v. State*, 363 NE 2nd 579 (1976); *Kennecott Corporation v. Salt Lake County*, 702 P. 2nd 451 (1985). See also Michael E. Libonati, "Local Governments in State Courts Call on a New Chapter in Constitutional Law?" *Intergovernmental Perspective* (Summer–Fall 1987), p. 17; and Richard Briffault, "State-Local Relations and Constitutional Law," *Intergovernmental Perspective*, op. cit., pp. 10–14.

[12] Alexis de Tocqueville, *Democracy in America*, quoted in Wallace E. Oates, *Fiscal Federalism* (New York: Harcourt Brace Jovanovich, 1972), p. 3.

[13] Oates, op. cit., p. 17.

preferences for public goods with a decentralized supply and when it improves the efficiency of provision of publicly provided output. At the extreme each jurisdiction would consist of one person or family (or business), and the decisions about level of provision of service and financing would all be made at this level. However, externalities and economies of scale in production and consumption make such an approach inefficient in practice. Yet most externalities do not spread over the whole country and most economies of scale are limited in scope. Hence, it is possible to have a small group share in the production of this good or service. Further, it is possible for the level and quality of provision to vary from group to group. As we showed in the previous chapter, the ability to differentiate the level of provision in response to variations in demand leads to more efficiency.

In the extreme, federalism would require that every publicly provided good or service should have a separate set of jurisdictions to provide that good or service.[14] The match between those who benefit from a good and those who pay for it is important if incentives for efficiency are to exist. Yet the geographic boundaries that are ideal for one set of goods or services are unlikely to be ideal for another; and some goods and services might best be provided by a governmental unit whose boundaries are not necessarily geographic. For example, services that require some fee for usage are in some sense not available to those residents of an area who do not pay the fee; but more frequently, the ideal boundaries simply differ. Thus, the lowest cost per person for provision of one service might occur at a population of 50,000, while it might occur at a population of 250,000 for another.

Based on the above argument, a great diversity of small, local governments can establish marketlike conditions in public services as each jurisdiction competes for resident taxpayers through its offering of services and its rate of efficiency and taxation. However, other issues are also important. Countervailing forces favor larger governments, among them the existence of scale economies. Also, government fragmentation may undermine citizen understanding and participation in government, creating high information and transaction costs. Finally, the administrative cost of all these jurisdictions is likely to be quite high.

A discussion of the economics of federalism must look at the issue of what missions and functions, respectively, should be assigned to what government. We cover these issues next.

Mission Assignments

Our economic analysis of federalism draws heavily on Wallace Oates's path-breaking *Fiscal Federalism*.[15] Oates follows Richard Musgrave's view

---

[14] Mancur Olson, Jr., "Strategic Theory and Its Application–The Principle of 'Fiscal Equivalence': The Division of Responsibilities among Different Levels of Government," *American Economic Review* 59 (May 1969), p. 483.

[15] Oates, op. cit., p. 256.

that government has three overriding objectives or missions, i.e., efficient resource allocation, appropriate distribution of burdens and gains, and stabilization of the economy.[16] Accordingly, from an economic point of view there is the question of what form of government promises to best advance a nation's allocation, distribution, and stabilization objectives, while reconciling possible conflicts among them.

We can visualize two extreme forms of government: a highly decentralized system in which the central government is almost completely devoid of economic responsibility, and a highly centralized one in which virtually all economic power rests with the central government. In relation to the three earlier mentioned objectives of government, a highly centralized government has certain efficiency advantages. It is able to internalize all externalities associated with the actions taken within the country, can take advantage of all scale economies (though it may suffer from diseconomies), and requires only one administrative structure. However, it is likely to be less innovative and less efficient in production and delivery of services. It is unlikely to benefit from the competition that results when there are many small governments. Further, it will be less responsive to differences in preferences and service conditions than would local governments.

Distributional objectives are much more easily obtained by centralized than noncentralized governments and the same holds for stabilization. Only the federal government has the fiscal and monetary policy tools needed to affect the business cycle; and redistribution carried out at the local level can create incentives for people to move to another jurisdiction in order to avoid the redistribution or to receive benefits from it. Such moves are not likely to promote efficiency in location decisions. However, there may be some benefits to local discretion. People seem to be much more inclined to help the needy in their geographic area than they are to help the needy elsewhere. If this is true, then even some components of distributional policy might best be left decentralized. Any benefits from such an arrangement would have to be balanced against any efficiency costs generated by the ability to move in response to redistribution.

Oates has summarized the advantages of a decentralized public sector:

> First, it provides a means by which the levels of consumption of some public goods can be tailored to the preferences of subsets of the society. In this way, economic efficiency is enhanced by providing an allocation of resources that is more responsive to the tastes of consumers. Second, by promoting increased innovation over time and by providing competitive pressures to induce local governments to adopt the most efficient techniques of production, decentralization may increase both static and dynamic efficiency in the production of public goods. Third, a system of local government may provide an institutional setting

16 Richard A. Musgrave, *The Theory of Public Finance* (New York: McGraw-Hill, 1959).

that promotes better public decision-making by compelling a more explicit recognition of the costs of public programs.[17]

Thus, the major mission of state and local governments is to provide specific goods and services to residents in an efficient and responsive manner. All other missions of government are reserved for higher levels of government, particularly the central government in a federal system. This may not work in practice. However, the economic analysis of federalism is largely limited to the provision and financing of publicly provided goods and services. Issues related to economic stabilization and distribution are largely the province of the central government. The economic analysis of federalism, then, focuses on which of the goods and services provided by government can best be provided by which level of government. Further, the method of finance for each good and service is also important both for efficiency and equity reasons.

Function Assignments

A major concern in a federal system is determining the most appropriate level of government to provide a particular government service function. The allocation of functions among levels of government is not, however, clear cut. Frequently there will be overlap in the areas of concern for different government units, so the appropriate degree of overlap and the method of coordination among the government units are of interest as well.

Among the considerations in determining both the appropriate degree of decentralization and the assignment of responsibilities to specific levels of government, the following are important:

Scale economies

Internalization of externalities

People-government proximity, which affects the responsiveness of government to individual preferences

Redistributive goals

Benefits that accrue from multipurpose jurisdictions

Before we take up these issues in turn, it is important to recognize the fact that the five considerations are of different importance to specific societies. In some, redistribution is of overriding concern and in others, efficiency. Also, the goals are often in conflict with each other. For example, the welfare gain associated with matching preferences must be measured against economies of scale and centralized coordination.

---

[17] Oates, op. cit., p. 13.

Scale Economies   The evidence suggests that major scale economies are likely to be enjoyed by such government services as air pollution control, sewage disposal, public transportation, power, water, public health services, hospitals and planning, which often are the domain of local government. Moreover, certain specialized higher education and library facilities can incur scale economies. However, there are few services presently provided by local governments whose average unit cost functions will continue to decline once communities have populations in excess of a quarter million.[18] This means that selected services of small communities could be consolidated and provided by a district form of government or assigned to county government. Alternatively, some large jurisdictions might find that some decentralization offers benefits. In few instances will scale economies favor assigning local government services to the state or federal government.

Externalities   In a highly urbanized, industrialized, and mobile America, externalities (defined in Chapter 2) abound. The problem is how to measure these externalities and determine the geographic delineation of benefits and costs. Many externalities do not stop at the boundaries of a local jurisdiction and some not at the boundaries of a state. Services with major geographic externalities include air pollution control, sewage disposal, transportation, public health services, planning, higher education, and specialized hospitals. Transportation, planning, and air and water pollution are good examples of activities that could internalize a significant portion of the externalities under a consolidation scheme of local governments or by assigning responsibilities to higher levels of government.

One way to maintain the benefits of small-scale government in the presence of externalities is suggested by Mancur Olson. "The necessary condition for Pareto optimality is then local governments of a size that minimizes unit costs, and central government grants to these local governments that are just large enough to compensate the local government for the external benefits of its expenditures."[19] Alternatively, if externalities are negative, higher levels of government could impose costs on the lower levels to internalize the externality or provide some other method to control the external effect rather than assume all responsibility for the activity or service.

People-Government Proximity   Proximity has a bearing on the responsiveness of governments to individual preferences. This consideration tends to favor relatively small government units. However, the people-government proximity issue is not unambiguous. In a democracy, we are concerned both with active participation of citizens in the operation of government and with the need to obtain a consensus that leads to action. These two considerations can be inconsistent. A good example is planning. Although an effective di-

[18] Werner Z. Hirsch, *The Economics of State and Local Government* (New York: McGraw-Hill, 1970), p. 183.
[19] Olson, op. cit., p. 485.

alogue between citizens and officials can make for enlightened and responsible government action, it can also lead to chaos and often has led to inaction.

Proximity of people to government can help prevent or expose graft. It can promote new avenues of operation, improve management practices, and bring about greater efficiency and better services. It can contribute to evolutionary rather than revolutionary change. In short, effective people-government feedback can produce better services for the same expenditures than could be obtained in its absence.

Opportunities to participate in government, or at least to perceive that such participation is possible, are important in a democracy. Large governments rendering services can contribute to the alienation so common in many American communities. However, government fragmentation can also undermine citizen understanding and interfere with citizen participation in government, resulting in significant information costs. Contrary to the objective of the supporters of decentralized governments, the actual locus of power resulting from functional and territorial fragmentation of authority might be to stimulate the transfer of decision-making authority away from the electorate and popularly elected officials to professional and bureaucratic interests.[20]

People-government proximity appears to be important in relation to such services as education, libraries, public housing, public welfare services, police protection, and fire protection.

Redistributive Goals   An important social objective relates to redistribution of service delivery and tax burdens. When public goods fail to affect a well-defined territory, the gains from decentralization decline, and an unintended byproduct of isolation may be the erosion of the ability to sustain desired redistribution.

Some jurisdictions are havens for industry, others are homes for the rich, and still others for the poor. The tax bases of these jurisdictions tend to differ greatly and therewith their ability to equitably distribute services. As long as there are many jurisdictions, location decisions can be made that permit wealthy residents and industrial and commercial activities to escape high taxes by moving to low-tax jurisdictions.

This is not merely inequitable, but it might also prove inefficient because of the resulting distortions of the locational choices. But it is not clear why redistribution should be limited by the confines of a metropolitan area, a district, or over a county. If redistribution were to take place over an entire state, state tax and spending programs could be tailored so as to deal effectively with redistributional aspects. Redistribution, as we stated earlier, is best considered the responsibility of higher levels of government.

Multipurpose Jurisdictions   Finally, there is the issue of multipurpose jurisdictions. Clearly, jurisdictions that perform several functions can be

---

[20] Advisory Commission on Intergovernmental Relations, *The Condition of Contemporary Federalism*, A78 (Washington, DC: August 1981), pp. 14–15.

inconsistent with the criterion of scale economies, since in the abstract each and every service is likely to favor operation at different scales. Further, different operations are likely to have different geographic benefits and spillovers. Likewise, there can be some inconsistency with the consideration of closeness of people to their government since a multipurpose government is likely to be larger and more bureaucratic than a single-purpose government for only one of the services covered. These disadvantages must be weighed against the administrative and other conveniences arising from having one government rather than many.

In addition to administrative costs, a proliferation of single-purpose districts may lead to voters being less well informed simply because there are more agencies to gain information from. One of the benefits of representative government is to have one person make choices about trade-offs for his or her constituency. The range of issues considered by any representative is much greater in a multipurpose jurisdiction since trade-offs can be made between functions.

These are some of the considerations that should enter into the determination of what service functions should be assigned to what government. Clearly, there is no one correct assignment. However, we can use the tools of economic analysis to gain insight into the effects of particular assignments. Before we turn to the fiscal issues that arise in studying government, we briefly discuss some of the other ways in which governments interact.

/// NONFISCAL INTERGOVERNMENTAL RELATIONS

The Constitution calls for a separation of government powers between the states and the federal government. However, this separation has many ambiguous areas, and there are substantial areas of disagreement between the states and the federal government concerning what states should do about particular issues. Further, states and the federal government interact with local governments. While the relations between the state and local governments differ across states, the presumption is that the state has substantial powers over its local governments. The relation between the federal government and local governments is much more ambiguous, but there are substantial areas where the federal government has attempted to control the behavior of local governments.

There are two principal nonfiscal methods that one level of government can use to alter the behavior of a lower level of government. The first is to *mandate* that the lower level of government do something. This can require that some action be taken or it can mean setting minimum standards of quantity and quality for a good or service. The other method is to *constrain* the lower level of government from doing something. While the distinction between these actions may sometimes blur, a mandate usually requires an expansion of activity and responsibility on the lower level of government while a constraint usually reduces or limits the activities and powers of the lower level of government.

Since in relation to many services states look upon local governments as direct extensions of their own powers, states can order them to take or not take certain actions. Compensation, even partial compensation, is not legally required when states force local governments to meet specific performance standards, undertake certain actions, and/or abstain from taking certain actions. Whereas there are few, if any, constitutional obstacles for states to order mandates or constraints without compensation, the federal government is significantly less free to do so. Instead, the federal government must enter into some sort of contractual relation with lower levels of government, often involving financial arrangements.

We first consider state mandates that are binding on local governments, the reasons for them, the types in use, and the economic analysis of their effects. Thereafter, we briefly analyze state constraints, and finish with a discussion of the federal activities relating to mandates and constraints. While both mandates and constraints can be constitutional, statutory, judicial or administrative in origin, all forms are similar in that they impose costs on the governments that must honor them.

Reasons for State Mandates

In relation to certain public (or quasi-public) goods, state governments may decide to require all their local governments to provide services of a minimum standard, or to perform a specified function. This action may stem from a decision by the state that the activity or service is of sufficient general importance that its provision cannot be left to the option of each individual local government. Also, the state may consider some uniformity in the provision of the service essential for the well-being of its people. In short, the state may be concerned with promoting the achievement of a desirable economic or social objective throughout its jurisdictions.

Zimmerman has given five reasons why states mandate minimum service standards or specific activities:[21]

(a) Some activities should be undertaken statewide and the decision cannot be left to local governments.

(b) Statewide uniformity may be considered essential, e.g., equal education opportunity.

(c) Current mandating may simply be a continuation of a historical requirement that is no longer justified.

[21] Zimmerman, op. cit., pp. 548–549.

(d) State governments might try to achieve a budget surplus by mandating local government performance of former state activities.

(e) The transfer of functional responsibility may be an attempt to make the provision of services more responsive to citizen needs and desires.

Types of State Mandates

A 1978 study by the Advisory Commission on Intergovernmental Relations identified four distinct types of mandates.[22] They clearly do not exhaust the range of state mandates, nor are they devoid of overlapping; still, they are illustrative.

Rules of the Game Mandates They relate to organization and procedures of local governments, including form of government, holding of elections, designation of public officers and their responsibilities, and safeguards to protect the public from malfeasance by local officials. They also encompass the requirement of due process with regard, for example, to the administration of justice and tax laws, and provisions of the criminal justice code that define crimes and mandate punishments.[23]

Mandates Related to Services with Significant Externalities These state mandates cover new programs and the enrichment of existing programs of local governments. They are found particularly in the areas of education, health, hospitals, welfare, environment and transportation.

Interlocal Equity Mandates Local governments under these mandates are required to act in a manner that avoids injury to or conflict with neighboring jurisdictions. Such mandates include regulatory and supervisory state roles in relation to local land use, tax assessment procedures and review, and environmental standards.

Personnel Mandates Such mandates (1) prescribe personnel standards with regard to educational training, licensing, and certification of local employees who carry out state-aided programs, (2) affect personnel benefits, where the state sets salary or wage levels, hours of employment, or working conditions, and (3) affect retirement benefits.

Economics of Mandates

When a state imposes on local governments legal requirements to undertake specified activities or provide services of a specified minimum standard,

---

[22] Advisory Commission on Intergovernmental Relations, *State Mandating of Local Expenditures*, op. cit., pp. 5–6.
[23] Ibid.

changes in public and often private actions tend to occur. These changes can result in costs and benefits, both direct and indirect. Direct costs are incurred by lower levels of government as they seek to comply with the mandate, and direct benefits are created for a variety of constituencies both inside and possibly outside the jurisdiction responding to the mandate. Direct benefits and costs are given primary attention; however, indirect costs and benefits, which tend to follow as economic and social adjustments to changes in government policy are made, can also be significant and lasting.

It may seem that mandates from higher levels of government should require that the higher level also assume responsibility for funding the mandated activity. While mandates ensure that a specific governmental activity is carried out, they also result in a loss of local autonomy, impose costs on local governments that they may be hard pressed to finance, and can lead to inefficiencies when the state acts without being sufficiently aware of cost implications. However, state funding of an activity can reduce local pressures to use funds wisely and also reduce the tie between taxes and benefits. Further, where the mandate offsets the actions of a negative externality, e.g., when sewers are mandated, the local assumption of cost comes closest to internalization of the cost of the externality created. Also, if costs differ across jurisdictions there may be some efficiency gains in forcing the local government to absorb the cost of achieving the objective. Thus, having local governments incur the cost of meeting fire safety objectives gives the correct incentive to avoid building in high-risk areas; however, absorption of the cost by a higher level of government would lead to excess building in risky places since the local decision maker would not be faced with the cost of providing protection.

A disadvantage of higher levels of government not having to finance their mandates can be their disregard for the costs they impose on others. At times, for example, special interest groups succeed in pressuring state legislatures to issue mandates to local governments. Legislatures sometimes respond positively since most, if not all, of the costs are transferred to local governments. In the process, the concept of home rule can be undermined, local accountability compromised, and the fixing of responsibility impeded. At the same time, mandates impose costs on local governments, which at times can be significant.

Moreover, the state government can issue mandates without much information as to the costs being passed on to local governments and the tax burden necessary to finance them. Under these circumstances the balancing of costs and benefits at the margin is likely to be carried out in a cavalier manner, and all too often by underestimating costs. Also, local officials on whom the mandates are imposed are often unenthusiastic about assuming this responsibility and do so poorly. Finally, in some instances, a state mandate can place a financial burden on a poor local government, which may be forced to reduce already low service levels in nonmandated areas. The result is an inefficient allocation of resources.

The overall benefits associated with mandates are related to the reasons for mandates, stated earlier. They include the establishment and enforcement of uniform standards for crucial services when the state determines that they cannot be left to the option of each separate local government. Uniform standards may become particularly important in the presence of externalities. Thus, certain mandates can force local governments to take into consideration externalities produced in their jurisdictions that otherwise would be neglected.

Efficiency Effects of Mandates   When local governments produce the correct amount of a good or service in the absence of higher level intervention, the mandate will impose an efficiency cost on society. This cost is analogous to the cost of a price ceiling or a minimum wage law. The mandate, of course, must be meaningful in the sense that the quantity of the good or service mandated (and thus its cost) is in fact above the level that otherwise would have been supplied by the local government.

In the following discussion, we assume for convenience of analysis that mandates take the form of minimum quantity restrictions. We also assume that there are no intergovernmental grants since these are analyzed in a later chapter.

The optimal level of provision of service by a local government would be where the marginal benefit equals the marginal cost of additional service. Thus in Figure 4-1 the optimal quantity of provision is given by Q^*. There is no reason to expect a local government to choose this level of service. It may choose to produce this amount, more, or less. Further, if a user price is charged, say the efficient price P^*, there is no guarantee that the revenue raised will exactly cover the cost of provision. It may be either more or less than the cost. Thus, we must address both the methods of paying for the service and the level of provision.

If the government starts by providing the optimal level of output, Q^*, and a higher level of government mandates an increase in service to Q_2, then there will be an efficiency loss associated with the overprovision of the good. This is because the additional output does not generate benefits sufficient to cover the additional cost. However, if the local government had started at Q_1 and the higher level government had mandated an increase to Q^*, then there would be an efficiency gain. The additional output would generate benefits that are greater than the additional cost. Even if the movement created by the mandate is in the right direction, it may be inefficient. For example, the higher level of government may mandate an increase from Q_1, which is less than needed to get to Q^*, or it might mandate an increase all the way to Q_2.

In assessing the impact of a mandate, it is also important to consider the funding source. The two most important cases are user fees and general revenues. For most services financed by user fees, we expect to find that the marginal cost of providing additional output is positive, and often it will be greater than the average cost. The local government may be able to finance a

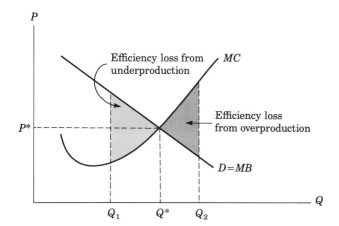

Figure 4-1 / **Efficiency and Levels of Public Provision**

mandated increase in the supply of a service by raising the user fee charged to constituents. However, this leads to a decrease in the quantity of the service demanded and therefore a decrease in the quantity actually consumed by constituents, not an increase, as the higher level government wanted. For example, if a mandate forces the local government to keep the community pools open twelve hours a day, rather than eight hours as it used to do, the increase in the cost of keeping the pools open longer hours will be translated into higher user fees if the revenue during the additional hours does not cover the cost of operation. Presumably the cost of operation during these additional hours would be greater than the benefits since the government was assumed to be operating at an efficient level.

If the demand curve for use during regular hours is fairly inelastic, it may be possible to find some price that will allow the government to recover these higher costs; but an extreme outcome might be the closing of the pool entirely. Even if it does not close, there will be an efficiency loss associated with the reduced usage during the times the pool was previously open. To actually increase the quantity demanded to the higher level specified by the mandate, the local government has to rely on other sources of revenue. If diverting this revenue to keeping the pool open causes other distortions, the total efficiency loss associated with the mandate may be greater than the direct efficiency loss associated with the pool.

In the absence of user fees, a mandate to increase some activity can only come at the expense of some other service or higher local taxes. Each of these sources is likely to add an efficiency cost above and beyond any associated with providing the wrong quantity of the mandated good or service.

Of course, not all mandates mean additional costs. One mandate may relieve local governments of other mandates, thereby resulting in a cost neutralization or savings; or a mandate may alter only a procedural requirement.

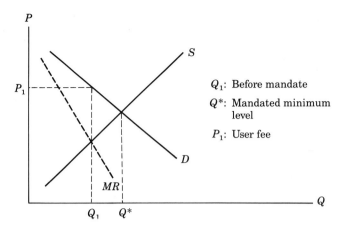

Figure 4-2 / **Efficiency Improvement from a Mandate**

Benefits of Mandates   Mandates provide for minimum levels of services or standards that otherwise might not be honored by local governments. This is particularly important in relation to police, fire fighting, environmental protection, social services, and education, where the welfare of the community is directly affected. Such mandates requiring minimum services or standards can be consistent with efficiency if there is reason to suspect that local governments would provide too little in the absence of the mandates.

There are a variety of reasons why local governments might produce too little of a good or service. Since local governments are de facto monopolists of specific goods, local constituents might have been getting less than the right amount of a certain service. Consider the situation where the local government can charge user fees for the specific activity under analysis (Figure 4-2). It can maximize its "profits" by equating marginal returns (MR) to marginal costs (S), analogous to a private monopolist. Then the level supplied would be Q_1, which is less than the efficient level. The mandate can be used to bring up the level supplied to Q^*.

Can a mandate increase social efficiency when it necessitates a supply of a certain government service in excess of the requirements of a community? For example, a fire district that takes only its own fire fighting requirements into consideration might provide a level of fire fighting services that seems inadequate to adjacent districts, which would suffer from fires spreading into it from the undermanned neighboring district. If negative externalities are involved, an across-the-board minimum standard enforced by higher level governments might be socially efficient. We could even imagine a case where one district might want to have a "free ride" on the service efforts of other districts. For instance, a district situated up the river could have limited regulations regarding waste disposal in the hope of inducing factories to locate there; and the district located downstream would incur excessive costs to clean up its water supply. When high transaction costs exist in negotiating between equally potent local districts, government implementation of a unilateral standard could increase efficiency by economizing on transaction costs.

In the case of positive externalities, however, it is difficult to justify mandates without fiscal support. Since the higher level government is the pooling and distribution center for funds, it should be able to absorb the overall benefits accruing from mandates with positive externalities and to redistribute the corresponding gains to each district. This alleviates the necessary sacrifices a local district must make to supply the mandated service.

In some cases, mandates can provide legal support for some groups or persons that might be underrepresented or at a bargaining disadvantage. A minority group working in a predominantly white district would be one example. Another example might be a state mandate requiring a minimum number of school days. The mandate can balance the otherwise unequal bargaining power of a nationwide union of schoolteachers who favor a small number of school days and a single school district that seeks a longer school year.

There may also be some indirect benefits from mandates. It is likely that some administrative capabilities are actually enhanced indirectly by the requirement associated with state mandates. For example, state requirements regarding employee qualifications and training may lead to the development of an improved local government administrative infrastructure. Also, the decision-making process might be formalized to a greater extent and the openness accompanying mandates might increase citizen involvement in the political process.

A Broader Evaluation of Mandates   So far we have not looked at mandates that are the results of and responsive to constitutional requirements, such as equal rights. Mandates that give expression to constitutional concerns seek to enforce values that the nation has deemed paramount and enshrined in the Constitution. Such lasting values often involve intangibles with major and far-reaching externalities. In the civil rights area, early examples are the Civil Rights Act of 1866 and 1871 and, more recently, the Civil Rights Act of 1964, especially its Title VII. For example, the 1866 Act provides that, "All persons . . . shall have the same right . . . to make and enforce contracts, to sue . . . and to the full and equal benefit of all laws . . . as is enjoyed by white citizens."[24] Since these constitutional values are mainly intangibles, these mandates' effects are difficult, if not impossible to estimate.

These Constitution-linked mandates must be differentiated from mandates that are the direct result of lobbying efforts by special self-serving interest groups. Such mandates can have significant redistributionary effects, which should be considered together with efficiency. The overall utility of the

[24] Act of 1866, Ch. 3151, 14 stat. 27.

local constituents might be increased through a redistribution resulting from such mandates, but the pure economic costs, such as distortion in government spending that we examined above, are likely to be exacerbated.

An important factor that should also be scrutinized is the informational asymmetry between higher and lower governments. In most cases, the local governments have a better idea of the demands of their constituents and their own cost functions. In this case, a mandate imposed on them by a higher government is likely to be inefficient. Furthermore, there is an inherent hazard because of this informational asymmetry. Local governments have an incentive to "shirk" on the mandated activities, regardless of whether mandates are financially supported by higher governments or not.

To summarize, the cost associated with implementing mandates should be compared with hoped-for benefits. The costs of mandates depend on whether

(a) Mandates regulate quantity or minimum standards.

(b) The objective is increasing efficiency or redistribution.

(c) Funds for the activity are obtained through user charges.

(d) Informational asymmetry is significant.

(e) Effective monitoring is carried out by higher governments.

The benefits can be direct and indirect. Mandates can improve efficiency if there is a significant undersupply in the absence of the mandate. Mandates are more beneficial when the positive externalities that arise from them are greater and the transaction costs of separate negotiations between individual districts are higher.

Constraints

Constraints or restraints can be understood as directives preventing local governments from doing certain things; a lack of authority to do so also falls into this category. A lack of constitutional or statutory authority for local school districts to levy a tax other than a property tax, a lid on local property taxes, or a cap on state expenditures are examples illustrating constraints as distinct from mandates. As in the analysis of mandates, a distinction needs to be made between constraints arising from voluntary participation of local governments, with or without fiscal support, and those that are unilaterally imposed on the local governments.

Although states can impose a variety of constraints on local governments, perhaps the most important ones are lid laws designed to restrict local tax and spending powers. In recent years, many states have coerced local governments to accept limits on their tax and spending powers, mainly as a result of the taxpayers' revolt of the 1970s. (For example, fourteen of the fifteen jurisdictions that in 1977 had limits on local taxing and spending powers had enacted them since 1972.) In late 1985, twelve states had overall property tax rate limits, thirty-one states specific property tax rate limits, twenty-one states property tax levy limits, and six states general revenue limits. In addition, six states had general expenditure limits.[25]

The controls that began to be imposed in the 1970s differ significantly from those that existed earlier. Conventional restrictions prevented local governments from relying on certain tax sources, e.g., school districts could only tax property. Moreover, the property tax rate could not exceed a certain limit. However, old and new controls stem from similar concerns about high property tax burdens and the growth of local government expenditures. New levy limits generally restrict the growth of property tax levies to some specified annual increases. While relief from these limits can be obtained from the electorate, conditions often are prohibitive. For example, under California's Proposition 13, increases in property tax rates are permitted only if approved by a two-thirds majority of the jurisdiction's voters.

Local property tax limits have produced a number of important results. They have been associated with a lower level of local, own-source per capita expenditures than one would expect given the levels of income, state and federal aid, urbanization, and centralized expenditures in the state. States with limits were found to be associated, on average, with a 6–8% lower level of local own-source per capita expenditures, *ceteris paribus*.

Because Chapter 20 focuses on revenue limitation measures, we concentrate here on constraints that take the form of expenditure limitations. As mentioned earlier, in 1986 six states had general expenditure limits. One such limit, Proposition 4, was passed in 1979 by California's voters as a constitutional amendment. It constrains the growth of expenditures by limiting the annual growth of the state budget to a formula based on year-to-year increases in the California population and one of two inflation indices—the U.S. Consumer Price Index or the California Per-Capita Income, whichever is lower.

The limitations make sense only if one believes that in their absence the state and local governments spend too much money. The constraints force a more restricted budget on these governments and force them to weigh their expenditures more carefully. To the extent that such constraints on state expenditures attain their objective, they do so at a cost, which under certain circumstances can be quite high. The budget limit may result in a significant number of citizens not being able to match their preferences for public services with actual supply; moreover, special groups of citizens who greatly value certain services which the state is forced to cut back may be forced to do with a substantially reduced amount of the service. Expenditure constraints constitute a drastic measure, one that is not fine-tuned to different and changing circumstances.

---

[25] Advisory Commission on Intergovernmental Relations, *Significant Features of Fiscal Federalism*, op. cit., p. 102.

Reasons for Constraints

The more important justifications for states to impose constraints on local governments can be summarized as follows:

(a) To implement limits on taxing and spending powers of downstream governments.

(b) To prevent local governments from engaging in activities that would either bring direct injury to or conflict with other jurisdictions, or cause negative externalities.

(c) To prohibit certain local activities that might jeopardize efficient achievement of nationwide or statewide goals.

(d) To exempt specific categories from local taxation.

Types of Constraints[26]   Constraints placed by states on local governments can be categorized as:

Lid laws: States can place ceilings to restrict local tax and spending powers.

Interlocal equity constraints: States can coerce local governments to refrain from taking steps that would bring injury to or conflict with neighboring jurisdictions.

Loss of tax base restraint: Such constraints remove property or selected items from the local tax base, e.g., exemption of business inventories from the local property tax base, exemption of food and medicine from the local sales tax.

Economics of Constraints

Assuming once again that the local government was supplying an optimal amount of certain services before a lid law was enacted, we can analyze the economic effect of a lid law type of constraint that limits local spending (Figure 4-3). The constrained level of expenditure falls short of the amount needed to supply the efficient amount. The loss in efficiency results from the gap between what constituents would like to have supplied by local government and what the constraint permits it to deliver.

A beneficial effect of such a constraint occurs if, before the lid was imposed, government was overspending. The lid prevents the local government from overspending in general or on certain activities. Overspending might have occurred because of imperfections in the market for local public goods, e.g., externalities, or because of the influence of strong interest groups in a local

---

[26] Advisory Commission on Intergovernmental Relations, *State Limitations on Local Taxes and Expenditures*, A-64 (Washington, DC: February 1977), p. 16.

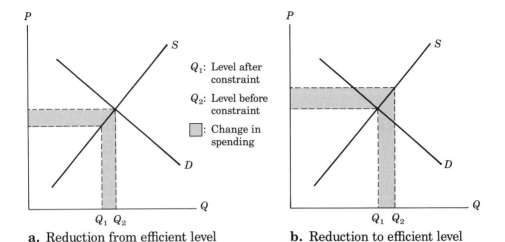

a. Reduction from efficient level   **b.** Reduction to efficient level

Figure 4-3 / **Constraints**

district. Under such circumstances constraints, which act as a lid on spending, do force financial responsibility on the local government and reduce the oversupply of certain public services. Since local governments often can divert funds from one category of expenditure to another, imposing a constraint on a certain activity might induce the local government to improve efficiency in other areas as well, to free more funds for the constrained activity.

So far we have not looked at constraints that are the results of constitutional requirements. As pointed out earlier in the case of mandates, the economic effects of these constitutional constraints are difficult to estimate because they entail intangibles. There are also redistributionary effects depending on what kinds of spending are limited. This fact should be considered along with efficiency considerations. The overall utility of some of the local constituents affected might be decreased because of redistribution working through constraints; but the externalities generated by constraints, such as tightening of the government spending process, might be beneficial for the whole community.

As with mandates, the informational asymmetry between higher governments and lower governments should be considered. In most cases, local governments have a better idea of the demands of their constituents and their own cost functions. Thus, a constraint imposed by a higher government might be inefficient.

/// FEDERAL NONFISCAL INTERGOVERNMENTAL RELATIONS

Whereas states have few constitutional limitations on their right to mandate or constrain actions of local governments, the federal government is much more restricted in its behavior toward state and local governments. Specifically, as we discussed earlier, the Constitution imposes limitations on the rights of the federal government to mandate or constrain the actions of state and local governments. As a result, most federal mandates take the form of contractual agreements in conjunction with grants.

Mandates Based on Court Orders and Federal Statutes

Federal mandates and constraints can come from any of the three branches of government. They can be based either on federal statutes or on the Constitution. Some are directed at state and local governments exclusively, while others apply to both the public and private sectors. Most federal mandates that apply only to state and local governments are the result of judicial interpretation of the Constitution, specifically the Bill of Rights and the Fourteenth Amendment.

Although court rulings commonly apply to specific jurisdictions, the principles articulated in the rulings usually have wide applicability. Thus while the court ordered Topeka, Kansas, in *Brown* v. *Board of Education* to desegregate its schools, the decision signaled all school districts to end *de jure* segregation of public schools. Other major court rulings involve redrawing of electoral districts, providing free counsel for indigents, reforming juvenile court procedures, and upgrading prisons and mental institutions.[27]

Congress, in its determination to achieve social and economic objectives that it considers meritorious, often uses its regulatory powers. While most of these mandates and constraints are directed toward the private sector, many concerning the environment and civil rights also affect state and local governments. The following are examples of federal mandates affecting state and local governments:[28]

> The Clean Air Amendments of 1970 (Public Law 91-604) require states to develop plans acceptable to the Environmental Protection Agency (EPA) to attain federal air quality standards. The EPA can require states to plan changes in state transportation policies (for example, by giving additional support to mass transit) as well as to regulate the pollution-creating activities of private persons (by establishing, for example, emission-control requirements and inspection programs for private cars).
>
> The Federal Water Pollution Control Act of 1972 (Public Law 92-500) requires state and local governments to adopt better methods of treating sewage in order to curb the discharge of pollutants.

---

[27] Congressional Budget Office, *Federal Constraints on State and Local Actions* (Washington, DC: Congress of the United States, April 1979), p. 6.
[28] Ibid., p. 7.

The Safe Drinking Water Act of 1974 (Public Law 92-523) requires all suppliers of drinking water (including, but not limited to, publicly owned systems) to test their water regularly for impurities. If "maximum contaminant levels" are exceeded, acceptable treatment processes must be introduced or another source of potable water used.

The Equal Employment Opportunity Act of 1972 (Public Law 92-261) prohibits state and local governments from discriminating in their employment practices on the basis of race, color, religion, sex, or national origin.

The Age Discrimination in Employment Act of 1967 (Public Law 90-202) prohibits discrimination in employment practices on the basis of age.

These regulations are based on various parts of the Constitution,[29] but the Constitution also places limits on the actions of the federal government that affect lower levels of government. For example, in 1976 the Supreme Court restricted the regulatory power of the federal government with regard to state and local governments. Specifically, in *National League of Cities* v. *Usery*, the Court invalidated the 1974 amendments to the Fair Labor Standards Act (Public Law 93-259) that extended minimum wage and overtime pay protection to nonsupervisory state and local government employees. According to the court, the extension of these provisions impermissibly interfered with the integral functions of state and local governments and threatened their "separate and independent existence."[30]

Contractual Arrangements

In pursuit of specific national policy objectives, Congress often enters into voluntary agreements with state and local governments in the hope of affecting their behavior. These contractual arrangements between the federal government and state and local governments often provide the latter with some benefits, usually (but not always) in the form of financial assistance. In return, state and local governments agree to act in a manner consistent with federal regulations. The grants thus provide a "carrot" to assure performance consis-

---

[29] These regulations are based on the "Commerce Clause," the "Necessary and Proper Clause," and the Fourteenth Amendment of the Constitution. The "Commerce Clause" and the "Necessary and Proper Clause" are both part of article I, section 8 of the Constitution. It reads, "The Congress shall have the power . . . [3] to regulate commerce with foreign nations, and among the several states and with the Indian tribes . . . [18] to make all laws which shall be necessary and proper for carrying into execution the foregoing powers and all powers vested by this Constitution . . . ." Additional authority is granted in the Fourteenth Amendment. Section 1 reads: " . . . No state shall make or enforce any law which shall abridge the privileges or immunities of citizens of the United States; nor shall any state deprive any person of life, liberty or property without due process of law; nor deny to any person within its jurisdiction the equal protection of the laws." Section 5 reads: "The Congress shall have power to enforce, by appropriate legislation, the provisions of this article."

[30] *National League of Cities v. Usery*, 426 U.S. 833 (1976).

tent with federal objectives. Conditions can be (1) "program specific," i.e., specify when and how money for a certain program is to be spent, or (2) generally applicable to grant programs. In the second case, the purpose is to ensure that all federally funded activities are consistent with broad national goals, particularly in the environment and nondiscrimination areas.

However, not all contractual obligations stem from grant-in-aid programs. Some have their origin in federal regulatory programs. One example is the occupational safety and health program giving states the option to assume administrative responsibility, provided they agree to specified federal standards and guidelines. Since most of these contractual arrangements involve grants, we discuss them in detail in Chapter 13, which deals with fiscal intergovernmental relations. This discussion includes reasons for federal grants-in-aid and a typology of grants; however, to illustrate some of the issues that arise we consider some of the cost and benefits related to Public Law 93-64, the Federal Aid Highway Amendments of 1974, which required states to adopt the 55 miles per hour speed limit.

Adopting the speed limit was a precondition for the receipt of federal highway aid.[31] To meet the requirement states immediately incurred a direct, one-time cost of altering or replacing speed limit signs. Continuing direct costs included additional police patrol and court costs as the speed limit change induced more people to violate the limit. A further financial cost would be reduced revenues from gasoline taxes if compliance led to better fuel efficiency and fewer gas purchases. To the extent that fewer accidents occurred as a result of lower driving speeds, a reduction in traffic police and court costs would also result. Direct private costs include those associated with the fact that lower speed limits force travelers to spend more time getting from one place to another. Likewise, the time it takes to transport goods increases. Direct private benefits associated with the lower speed limits include energy conservation and fewer accidents.

There are also a variety of indirect costs that result as production and consumption patterns change in response to price changes. For example, some companies may find their markets contracted, while others may be forced out of business when added transportation costs significantly reduce their competitiveness. Firms and locations with good access to rail transportation may benefit as railroads gain business while interstate trucking firms lose out. These indirect or second-order effects are important to a particular individual, business, or location. However, from a national point of view, indirect gains and losses tend to offset one another; their impact on efficiency is likely to be small. Yet gain and loss patterns are often very important in the evaluation of whether a given mandate is fair and equitable.

---

[31] Congressional Budget Office, op. cit., pp. 21–22.

/// SUMMARY

The United States has a highly fragmented government structure. Although the federal government dominates most discussion of government, the states have constitutionally protected obligations and rights. Further, local governments often stand separately from the state governments that created them. This may be from rights granted in the state constitution or from legislative or possibly other sources; but the separation creates both problems and opportunities. While government close to the people is expected to be more responsive and may in many cases be more efficient, there are problems with decentralized government. One response from a higher level of government is to address the problems through mandates and constraints on local governments.

The effectiveness of mandates and constraints from higher levels of government generally depends on the specific issue being addressed. If there is reason to expect lower levels of government to produce too little of a good or service, then mandates to increase provision may substantially improve efficiency in the system. However, not all mandates accomplish this objective; and even where the general idea is correct, the same mandate must be applied uniformly to all lower levels of government. Thus, some may be forced to improve efficiency, but others may find that the mandated level is either too high or too low.

Another issue is financing of mandated activities. While it may seem fair to make the state or federal government pay for the activities they impose on other governments, there are two problems with the approach. First, local governments are more likely to attempt to be efficient if they must raise funds themselves; second, the efficient way to internalize a negative externality is to impose the cost on the parties who are generating the externality. Payments to mitigate negative externalities that come from higher levels of government often do not create appropriate incentives to stop generating the externalities.

When higher levels of government do impose mandated activities on lower levels of government and do not provide funding, they may create distortions in the allocation of the lower government's funds. This is particularly a problem when there are constraints on the ability of the lower government to generate additional revenue. In this case, funds for a mandated activity may have to be diverted from other high-priority areas. Such constraints are becoming more common over time. While they may succeed in reducing government expenditure, they may also create substantial distortion in the allocation of resources. These distortions can then be exacerbated by mandates.

There still remains the question of what services under federalism should be performed by what governments and under what, if any, direction by higher levels of government. While it is useful to look at intergovernmental relations in terms of their fiscal attributes, nonfiscal issues, often neglected, are of great importance in a federated United States.

Part Two ///

Funding Government

Governments need money to operate; however, the methods they use to raise money have both efficiency and equity effects. This section shows how economists analyze these effects for the various methods of funding used by government. These methods range from the obvious use of taxes to borrowing and even setting prices on some goods and services. Governments also get money from other governments. Each source of revenue has different efficiency and equity effects. They also differ in the costs of administration, problems in enforcement, and the stability and growth of revenue. For these reasons, economists disagree about which sources of revenue are better. Further, most sources of revenue are used by more than one government unit; the interaction of the tax effects may be quite different from the effects of each in isolation.

We start by setting out some basic terminology, and we define and explain some of the key concepts used in the analysis of revenue sources. Then we turn to the major tax forms. Sales and excise taxes are presented first because they offer the most straightforward introduction into tax analysis. We then turn to income taxes, the most important revenue source. There are three chapters on income taxes. The first is a general introduction into the issues that arise when trying to tax income. We then present the income tax as it is used in the United States, and we end the discussion by looking at the corporate income tax. The final major form of taxation used in the U.S. is the property tax. It is the mainstay of local government finance, but it is probably the most controversial in terms of its ultimate impact, partly because of the various ways in which the tax can be analyzed.

The other revenue sources available to government close out the section. User charges have gained in importance with limits on the other sources of revenue available to local governments, and there is also concern with the ability to use such charges to promote efficiency in government. Governments at all levels seem to have problems with the amount of debt they carry, although the deficits of the federal government have received the most attention in recent years. Hence, it is important to determine when debt financing is likely to be beneficial and when it is likely to lead to problems. Finally, intergovernmental grants are used largely by higher levels of government to influence the behavior of the lower levels of government. We end the section by considering the impact of such grants on the recipient government. ///

Chapter 5   //////

Tax Concepts

It is important to understand exactly what is meant when discussing taxation. People often have different definitions for key terms and different objectives for the tax system, and these viewpoints color their evaluation of different taxes. We start our discussion of taxation by developing some important concepts and terms.

The first things to clarify are the objectives of taxation. Certainly a prime objective is to raise revenue; however, taxes are used for many other purposes. A second objective is to change the distribution of income. A third is to make the recipients of certain benefits pay the cost of generating those benefits. A fourth is to change people's behavior, for example, to discourage smoking by making it more expensive. In addition, taxes can foster or impede economic efficiency. Thus, economists often favor the use of taxes to charge people the "full cost" when they generate negative externalities so that they consider these externalities in making decisions. A final objective is to try to minimize the cost of running the tax system and enforcing the collection of taxes.

Often these objectives are in conflict; and the issues become even more complex when jurisdictions are either competing for a tax base or taxing the same base. Yet it is hard to find a tax base in the United States that is not taxed by more than one jurisdiction. Most sources of income are subject to federal taxation, but they may also be subject to state and/or local taxes. For example, personal and corporate income is often subject to taxation by the federal government and one (or even more than one) state and perhaps a local government. Cigarettes are taxed by most states as well as the federal government. So is gasoline. Property in an urban area is seldom, if ever, taxed by only one government.

Next we should clarify some of the key terms used in discussing taxes. The tax base refers to whatever is being taxed, i.e., on what the tax is levied. With an income tax, the base is the amount of income (as defined by statute); with a property tax, the base is the value of the property. For a cigarette tax, the base is the number of packs of cigarettes sold. The base can be measured in physical units or in dollar value. When the base is measured by a dollar value, the tax is called an ad valorem tax. The tax rate is the amount per unit to be taxed. For an ad valorem tax it is expressed as a percentage of a dollar value, such as a 2% property tax rate. However, a tax rate can also be expressed in other units, such as five cents per gallon of gasoline or sixteen cents per package of cigarettes. The rate will often vary over the number of units taxed, so it is necessary to have a rate schedule or tax table.

We should also be clear on the difference between the marginal tax rate and the average tax rate. The marginal tax rate is the tax on the last unit. For example, the marginal income tax rate would be the percentage of the last dollar that goes for taxes. The average rate is the total tax divided by the total base. The marginal rate and the average rate frequently differ. For example, suppose that a property tax is levied on residential units at a rate of 2% of the value of the house; however, there is a homeowner's exemption of $25,000 if you own your home. A person living in a $50,000 house would pay a tax of $500. This is only 1% of the value of the house; and 1% is the average tax. However, if the house were to increase in value by one dollar, the tax would increase by two cents. This is the marginal tax rate, 2%. In general, the average tax is a measure of the tax burden; but the marginal tax is an important determinant of how people respond to the tax. It is the marginal tax that determines how their taxes change in response to small changes in the base.

The tax rate is multiplied by the base according to the tax schedule to determine the tax liability. The tax liability is what is owed to government. This amount may be determined by self-assessment and reporting to the government, as with the federal income tax; or it may be assessed by government, as with most property taxes. Where self-assessment is used, the government often has ways of checking directly on some of the reported items. Thus, employer reports of earnings are checked against earnings reported on an employee's income tax returns; however, the taxpayer is obligated to report all income, whether or not it can be directly verified. Where the government determines the assessment, there is usually some form of appeal procedure in case the government makes a mistake; but the individual is not usually obligated to tell the government if it appears that the tax is being underassessed.

After the tax liability is determined, the government becomes concerned with the collection of the tax. Collections seldom come close to 100%. For example, property tax collections are often short because of property being abandoned as well as because of delays in payment. One author reports that the average uncollected property tax payments in a sample of forty-eight cities varies from 0.2% to 11.0% over the period 1950 to 1974.[1] Governments also

---

[1] Robert W. Lake, *Real Estate Tax Delinquency: Private Disinvestment and Public Response* (New Brunswick, NJ: The Center for Urban Policy Research, 1979), p. 56.

conduct audits of the taxpayers to determine if they are reporting their tax liabilities honestly and correctly. Associated with the audit is an enforcement mechanism to collect taxes from reluctant taxpayers. The costs that governments incur in monitoring the tax system and enforcing the collection of taxes are generally called the administrative costs of the tax.

Related to the audit and enforcement mechanisms are the compliance costs. These are costs imposed on taxpayers above and beyond the taxes themselves. They usually take the form of record-keeping requirements, but they can go substantially beyond simple record keeping. For example, the many hours that individuals spend on preparing their tax returns or the expenditures for expert help are part of the compliance costs of the federal income tax.

The eventual impact of a tax is often quite different from its initial impact. This final impact is called the economic incidence of the tax as opposed to the statutory incidence. Because people change their behavior to avoid taxes, they may not bear the full burden of a tax that they are legally required to pay. Thus, a tax imposed on gasoline wholesalers is likely to cause them to reduce the amount they are willing to sell at any given price; this reduced supply causes the market price to rise. The rise in market price causes at least some of the tax burden to be shifted to the users of gasoline. Hence, part of the economic incidence of the tax will be on the users even though the legal incidence is placed on the wholesalers. Because of these changes in behavior, there is often an efficiency cost to the economy over and above the amount of tax collected by the government.

Finally, we should note that some people consider the amount of tax collected by the government to be a poor measure of the government's taxing of the economy. They argue that the true amount of taxation is the amount of resources the government uses. To them the value of these resources is a tax even if the government does not levy any taxes explicitly, because those resources are not available to be used for other purposes. Alternatively, high tax collections coupled with low expenditure would overstate the tax burden, since government would not be taking resources away from other uses. We discuss this concept in more detail when we talk about government use of debt financing in Chapter 12.

/// FIGURES AND TRENDS

The amount of taxes collected can be expressed in a number of ways. The dollar amount is perhaps the simplest way to describe tax collections. Unfortunately, as we discussed earlier, dollar amounts suffer from several shortcomings. First, the aggregate dollar amounts are often quite large; many people have trouble comprehending these amounts. Second, the changes over time reflect not only changes in government collections but also changes in the price level. Third, even the changes in collection over time are somewhat misleading because of changes in the size of the economy over time. Hence, it is often desirable to make the comparisons in terms of per capita tax collections or taxes as a percentage of the GNP. These latter measures are easier to comprehend and provide rough adjustments for changes in the size of the economy.

Thus we find that the total amount of taxes collected by all levels of government is reported by the Advisory Commission on Intergovernmental Relations (ACIR) to have risen from just over $51 billion in 1948 to about $845 billion in 1986.[2] This is a 1557% increase in tax collections. However, expressed as a percentage of GNP, in 1986 the total of federal, state, and local collection of explicit taxes for general purposes was just under 20% of GNP, approximately the same as the percentage in 1948.

Despite this similarity, the total impact of government was much larger. This is because the ACIR tax totals do not include payments to insurance trusts, nor do they include new debt. Thus, the more than $266 billion paid in Social Security taxes is not included in the above total, nor is the approximately $220 billion in additional federal debt for that year. After these adjustments the government share of GNP goes well over 30%, and some people argue that even this is an understatement of the true situation. They are concerned about increasing liabilities of the Social Security system and other obligations of government whose funding is not growing as rapidly as their commitments, as well as about the many government enterprises that do not show up in budgets.[3]

Looking at the individual taxes, we find that in 1986 the property tax was about 2.5% of GNP, the same percentage as in 1948; the individual income tax had risen from 7.9% at the federal level to 8.2% of GNP; and the state individual income tax had risen from 0.2% to 1.6% of GNP. Offsetting the rising personal income tax was a decline in corporate income tax from 4.1% to 1.9% of GNP when the state and federal collections are combined.[4]

There have been ups and downs in these percentages over the intervening time period; but on the whole they have remained remarkably stable. Looking only at the amount that the various governments collect for general purposes in relation to GNP, it appears that the government is not growing. To the extent that the growth is occurring it appears to be in the area of social insurance and transfer payments. Thus, Social Security taxes have grown from close to zero in 1948 to $266 billion in 1986. Of course, taxes alone ignore the impact of increasing debt.

Even where deviations have occurred in the percentages of GPN going to

---

[2] Advisory Commission on Intergovernmental Relations (ACIR), *Significant Features of Fiscal Federalism, 1985–86 Edition*, M-146 (Washington, DC: 1986), Tables 29 and 31; and *1988 Edition*, M-155II (1988), Tables 61 and 62.1.

[3] For example, see James T. Bennett and Thomas J. DiLorenzo, *Underground Government: The Off-Budget Public Sector* (Washington, DC: Cato Institute, 1983).

[4] ACIR, op. cit., Table 61.

various taxes, we find evidence that the tax codes are being changed to offset this. While no one knows yet what the exact impact of the tax code revisions under the Tax Reform Act of 1986 will be, it is clear that one impact will be to shift part of the tax burden from the personal income tax back onto the corporate income tax. In historical perspective, the personal income tax has increased relative to GNP while the corporate income tax has shrunk as a percentage. Thus, the new law appears to be an effort to move back to the historical relationship.

There are no obvious theoretical reasons why the relationships should stay so stable; and one can never rule out the possibility that they are just a statistical artifact of little significance. However, the apparent stability is worth thinking about in terms of some of the theories put forth about the various taxes and the behavior of government. For example, the constant percentages may represent something like the maximum amount of revenue that government can appropriate from the system. More likely, they are accidental or are kept at the given levels by politicians (and their staffs) who are anxious not to deviate too much from the historical levels of these taxes. Another possibility is that the percentages remain constant from simple inertia and the high political cost of major tax changes. Finally, it is important to bear in mind that we are only discussing explicit taxes; there are many reasons why these taxes do not represent a comprehensive measure of government activity.

/// EQUITY

The most basic distinction in the equity dimension of public finance is the one between ability to pay and benefits received as the basis for setting and judging taxes. The ability-to-pay principle is concerned only with raising revenue, and it focuses on a fair way to accomplish this. This view looks at taxation as largely distributive in nature and seeks to make the redistribution conform to certain principles. The benefit principle is concerned with expenditures and so focuses on a fair way to pay for the benefits government provides. Because of the different values people place on the activities of government, the benefit principle would have them taxed on the basis of the benefit received. An alternative view of equity, related to the benefit principle, is the principle of marginal cost pricing. For many government activities, there is a specific cost involved in serving one more person. Economic efficiency requires that the recipients pay the marginal cost in most cases. Many people also see this as an equitable way to distribute the tax burden for goods or services where income redistribution is not an important issue. We consider each of these views in turn.

Ability-to-Pay Principle

The ability-to-pay view of taxation has two specific equity principles. The first principle is horizontal equity. This says that equals should be treated equally. The second principle is vertical equity. This says that those who are better off should pay more in taxes than those who are not as well off.

Horizontal equity is perhaps the easiest principle of taxation to justify. Virtually everyone agrees that equals should be treated equally under the tax system. The problem arises when we try to specify equality. The usual method is to look at either income or wealth and use this as the base for measuring equality. For example, if income is used, the argument is to tax those with the same income by the same amount. However, many practical problems arise in implementing this principle. One is the treatment of different-sized households. Should a family be treated as a group of individuals with income for each equal to the total family income divided by the number of family members? Another problem arises in terms of individual choice. Suppose that two people are identical in terms of ability, schooling, and so on; yet one chooses to be a beachcomber while the other has a high-paying job. Are they equal even though they have very unequal incomes? What if one earns income by investing inherited wealth while the other must work very hard? What about people who have very high medical expenses? In practice, the attempt to maintain horizontal equity can be extremely complex, since it is hard to get agreement on what constitutes equality. The current U.S. tax code tries to adjust for some of the issues raised here, among others; that is one factor contributing to its complexity.

Vertical equity assumes that those with more income should pay more in taxes since there is greater ability to pay. This appears to be straightforward at first glance; but problems arise when we try to specify things more exactly. The statement that those with more income should pay more in taxes is virtually unopposed. Further, there are few taxes in the U.S. that do not meet this criterion. The question is how much more should be paid in taxes. The concepts of progressive and regressive taxes were developed to help address this issue.

The standard measure of progressivity or regressivity is made by comparing income with taxes paid.[5] If tax payments go up faster than income, the tax is called a progressive tax. If tax payments go up less rapidly than income, the tax is called a regressive tax. If the tax payments are a constant percentage of income, the tax is called a proportional tax.

It should be clearly understood that many regressive taxes would meet the

---

[5] An alternative definition is that a tax is progressive if the marginal rate is above the average rate, regressive if the marginal rate is below the average rate, and proportional if the marginal rate is equal to the average rate. These two definitions are equivalent if the base is income; but they can vary when other bases are used. For example, a tax on diamonds that is 10% for the first $10,000 and 5% for the remainder would be regressive by the rate definition; but since diamonds are not often purchased by low-income people, the incidence would be progressive by the income definition.

ability-to-pay criterion. Those with more income could easily pay more in taxes while paying a smaller percentage of income in the form of taxes. For example, if someone earning $10,000 paid $1,000 in taxes while someone earning $20,000 paid $1,600 in taxes, the tax would be regressive. This tax would indeed require that the person with the higher income would pay the higher tax. However, the higher-income person's tax would be a smaller percentage of income (8% rather than 10%).

As we discuss in Chapter 6, the progressivity or regressivity of a tax depends on many things, such as the final incidence of the tax. One recent study concludes that the entire tax system in the United States is somewhere between slightly progressive and mildly regressive.[6] However, a number of arguments suggest that this study understates the progressivity of the U.S. tax system; we discuss some of these arguments when we cover the particular taxes in later chapters.

While our tax system tends to be progressive, there is no general principle that says how progressive it should be. Rather, the degree of progressivity is part of the political decision on how much income redistribution should take place. Attempts to develop an economic theory to justify a specific progressiveness of the tax system as part of the economic function of government have floundered on the difficulty of making interpersonal comparisons. For example, it is argued that the marginal dollar of income is worth less to the rich person than it is to the poor person. Hence, it is in some sense less costly to take the dollar from the rich person than from the poor person. While most people would agree with this statement, there are interesting philosophical problems in trying to make an interpersonal comparison of well-being; and this is ruled out in modern economic theory.[7] Despite the theoretical problems, most people seem to think that the tax system should be progressive; and often taxes are judged at least partially on their progressivity. However, there is much disagreement about just how progressive the tax system should be.

Issues of horizontal and vertical equity become even more complex when people live in different areas. For example, does the horizontal equity principle require that people earning the same income in Alaska and Texas pay the same amount of federal income tax? What about state income tax? There is general agreement that people in different states should pay the same amount of federal tax, though the income taxes of the various states differ greatly. It might seem that the equity issue can be treated as applying only to people within the same state; but important problems arise in the context of these

---

[6] Joseph Pechman, *Who Paid the Taxes, 1966–85* (Washington, DC: The Brookings Institution, 1985), p. 4.

[7] Thus, we might find that the rich person is rich precisely because that person enjoys the things that money can buy. Hence, he or she may be willing to make great sacrifices in other aspects of life in order to accumulate money. The poor person may be poor at least partly because he or she does not enjoy the things money can buy and thus chooses not to work as hard. To the extent that this happens, income redistribution might lower the overall level of satisfaction. See S. J. Chapman, "The Utility of Income and Progressive Taxation," *Economic Journal* 28 (March 1913) and Elmer D. Fagan, "Recent Theories of Progressive Taxation," *Journal of Political Economy* 46 (August 1938), both reprinted in Richard A. Musgrave and Carl S. Shoup, eds., *Readings in the Economics of Taxation* (Homewood, IL: Richard D. Irwin, 1959).

state differences. People in one state may have to pay higher tax rates to get the same level of service as people in another state or their higher taxes may be offset by getting more services through the public sector. The issue leads us into the other major equity criterion in public finance, the benefit principle.

Benefit Principle

The benefit principle states that people should be taxed on the basis of the benefits that they receive. Those who get more benefits should pay a larger share of the tax burden than those who get fewer benefits. Again, the principle is easier to state on an abstract basis than it is to apply in realistic situations. The complications primarily revolve around measuring benefits and around the difference between marginal and average benefits. However, there are also problems in applying this principle for goods and services that are essentially intended to redistribute income. Thus, it would not make much sense to apply the benefit principle in trying to generate funding for food stamps.

On an equity basis, the benefit tax should be proportional to total benefits; but in practice this would be almost impossible to determine. Different people would get different amounts of consumer surplus even if they did not get any other differences in service. Also, most benefit taxes are levied on the basis of some form of usage, and benefits and usage are not necessarily related. For example, it is fairly clear that automobile and truck users are the primary beneficiaries of the road system. The interstate highway system and parts of other roads are financed by taxes on motor fuels. Yet these taxes are levied largely in proportion to miles driven rather than to the benefits each person gets from the system. The assumption is that the number of miles driven is a rough measure of the benefits received; but this may in fact be incorrect. For example, an extra mile of urban freeway may reduce a person's commute significantly. The benefit of this may be very high despite the low number of miles driven. Alternatively, someone may choose to drive across the country because of the interstate highway system, but they may be almost indifferent to the choice of driving or flying. Hence, there may be a great deal of driving with relatively little benefit to the driver.

The benefit principle becomes much more relevant when people must essentially choose a tax in order to get certain benefits. For example, Charles Tiebout argued that the taxes paid to a local government can be thought of as a price for living in that community and receiving the benefits that the local government provides in the way of goods and services.[8] Viewed this way, all local taxes become benefit taxes to some extent. Of course, there are problems with this view of local taxes since there is not always a clear relationship between tax burden and benefits received; however, this distinction between local taxes and federal taxes is a key one in terms of the analysis of the equity

---

[8] Charles M. Tiebout, "A Pure Theory of Local Expenditures," *Journal of Political Economy* 65 (October 1956), pp. 416–424.

of specific taxes. It is much more difficult to treat a local tax in isolation since the tax is usually tied to local benefits.

Marginal Cost Principle

The other major way to view the equity of a tax is to consider it in relation to the cost of providing a good or service to someone. If the cost and the tax are the same, the person is essentially paying for what is received. In competitive markets, each price represents the marginal cost of providing the particular good or service. Hence, the person only buys something if it is worth more to that person than the cost of providing it. Similarly, if a tax represents the cost of providing a good or service in the public sector, people would be paying this cost and hence covering the cost of providing themselves with the good or service.

This may not be equitable if a person has no choice in what is provided. For example, it would not be equitable to tax some people the marginal cost of providing them with local strolling musicians if they in fact do not like to listen to strolling musicians. However, if these people have the choice of whether or not to listen, the tax would induce them to listen only if they valued the music at least as much as the cost of providing it. Further, no one else would have to be taxed to allow for the provision of the service to these people.

/// EFFICIENCY

Both the benefit approach to equity and the marginal cost approach can be related to the market price system and to efficiency. In the competitive market, the price represents the marginal cost to producers of producing one more unit and the marginal benefit to consumers of consuming one more unit. Thus, the price serves to provide substantial information as well as specific incentives for efficiency. Consumers only consume items that generate at least as much benefits as they cost to produce, and they consume all units that generate more benefits than costs. Similarly, producers only produce items that cost less to produce than the amount of benefits they generate, and they produce all units that generate more benefits than cost.

Taxes that act as prices serve both to provide information about the efficient level of output and to provide incentives for allocating the output. When goods are provided with no explicit price, people tend to want to consume up to the point where their marginal benefit is zero. However, this level of consumption is inefficient. The use of taxes as prices can in principle get people to reveal how much they value increments to public output. This preference revelation problem is associated with the benefit tax approach to the analysis of public goods. Recall that a pure public good is defined as a good that can be consumed by all at the same time, with no one's consumption interfering with anyone else's consumption. It can be shown that the optimal amount of such a good is determined by adding the marginal benefits each person receives and comparing this sum with the marginal cost of providing one more unit of the public good. Thus, if the government could charge each person a tax price equal to the marginal benefit received from the last unit at the efficient level, everyone would want to buy that level of output. No one would want more because the tax price would exceed the benefit received from the additional unit. However, no one would want to reduce the quantity because the tax savings would be less than the benefit reduction (see Box 5-1). Thus, in the pure public good case, the benefit tax would have certain desirable properties aside from its equity consideration.

The major problem with this perception of benefit taxes is that it requires the government to know the benefits that each person receives before it sets the taxes. If it did know this, it could simply choose the correct level of output and set taxes according to other criteria. The more useful approach to benefit taxation is to use the tax system to get information about how much individuals value particular goods or services. This can be accomplished, in principle, by setting taxes as prices and letting people consume what they want. Their behavior with respect to consumption reveals how much they value additional units of the good. It also limits consumption of the good or service to those who value it at least as much as the cost.

The other advantage of using taxes as prices is that they could be set to make the consumer aware of the full cost of providing a good or service. The use of taxes that equal marginal cost forces the consumer to choose only those levels of consumption for which the net benefits exceed the net costs. In the absence of such prices, the consumer has an incentive to consume up to the point where the marginal benefits of additional consumption are zero, and the government has no easy way to determine the efficient level of output.

Under this type of tax system many of the efficiency considerations that are relevant to private markets would be met in the provision of goods and services by the public sector. Again the key is the ability to decide whether or not to participate in the activity. This decision may be made either by choosing to participate directly or by choosing to move to a community with the particular good or service. If there is no choice, the efficiency and equity benefits would disappear. Hence, this type of consideration is more applicable to local taxes than to federal taxes, and it is particularly inappropriate when the intent is to aid the poor. In addition, administrative costs are likely to be a major problem for taxes that are tied to the cost of providing service.

Pricing Externalities

Another use of a marginal cost type of tax is to internalize the cost of a negative externality. Remember that the existence of a negative externality creates an efficiency concern because the generator of the externality does not take into account part of the cost of production. Thus, the activity that gener-

Box 5-1

////// **Benefit Pricing**

In the case of a pure public good, the demand curves of individuals are added vertically to get the "market" demand curve. This is because each person who "buys" the public good must consume the same quantity as everyone else. Thus, the willingness to pay for one more unit is a measure of the marginal benefit a person receives from the last unit of the public good. Hence, it is argued that charging a tax price equal to this would leave each person in equilibrium with respect to the public good. This can be seen in Figure 1. There are two individuals with demand curves D_1 and D_2 which add up to the market demand curve D_m. The quantity Q_1 is the efficient quantity because it is where total willingness to pay for one more unit is exactly equal to the cost of providing one more unit. Then, if person 1 were charged a "tax price" equal to P_1 and person 2 a price of P_2, each would want exactly Q_1 units, and this would be both efficient and fair. This pricing scheme is called a Lindahl price; but it is a fiction since no government could ever determine what price to charge each person. Even if the appropriate price could be determined, it is unlikely that it would be legal for government to set taxes in this manner. Nevertheless, this type of argument forms an important basis for the benefit principle of taxation.

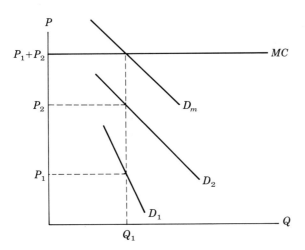

Figure 1 / "Pricing" Public Goods

ates the externality is carried too far. For production, this results in too much output relative to the efficient level of output. In general, if the externality can be measured and the negative effect evaluated, it would be possible to improve the allocation of resources by charging the creator of the externality a tax varying with the level of externality and the amount of damage it creates.

For example, if a factory generates smoke when it operates, it would be desirable to charge it a tax equal to the value of the damage that the smoke creates. Thus, the factory would take the cost of such damage into account both in deciding how much output to produce and also in deciding how to produce any given amount of output. This is preferable to regulation requiring specific types of pollution control devices, because the use of such devices does not induce polluters to weigh the damage done by the production of one more unit nor does it provide any incentive to find less polluting methods of production.

Efficiency Costs of Taxes

When taxes are used to collect general revenue, a cost is imposed on the economy in addition to the amount of tax revenue raised. This additional cost is the efficiency loss to the economy associated with distorting the price signals that allocate resource in a market economy. Each buyer responds to the total price he or she must pay for a good or service, and each seller responds to the net price received. As taxes are added to or subtracted from these prices, the net amounts paid or received no longer represent true marginal benefits or opportunity costs. These distortions create a net cost to the economy over and above any amount collected by the government. We spend considerable time on this topic in the next chapter, but it is important to remember when trying to evaluate a tax. Often the efficiency costs of a tax may be quite high, yet be ignored in terms of discussion of the tax because no one has a direct interest in them. The difficulty in quantifying them and allocating them to specific parties makes it hard to generate interest in them, but the efficiency costs can become quite large in a poorly designed tax system. One recent study concluded that the efficiency cost of taxation in the United States amounted to between 30% and 40% of the taxes collected at the margin.[9]

/// INCIDENCE

While taxes are almost always levied in such a way that a particular person or firm is responsible for paying them, e.g., writing a check for them, economists argue that the legal liability for taxes is not what determines who

---

[9] Edgar K. Browning, "The Marginal Cost of Raising Tax Revenue," in Phillip Cagan, ed., *Essays in Contemporary Economic Problems* (Washington, DC: American Enterprise Institute, 1986).

pays a tax. When a tax is levied, people seek to change their behavior in response to the tax. To the extent that this effort succeeds, it reduces the negative effects of the tax on those who pay it and shifts some of the tax burden to others. The incidence of the tax is determined by looking to see who is made worse off because of the tax and by how much. For example, the federal gasoline tax is levied on wholesalers. However, if an increase in this tax simply results in all wholesalers raising their prices by the full amount of the tax, then it would be the consumers who pay the tax rather than the wholesalers. They would pay a price higher by the full amount of the tax than they would have paid in the absence of the tax. Even if the tax is not fully passed on to the consumer, it is not necessarily the case that the wholesalers would pay it. For example, the wholesale price of gasoline might drop because of the tax. In this case, the tax would be partially shifted to the refiners or to owners of oil. It might even result in the reduction of wages in the industry, causing workers in the industry to pay part of the tax.

The determination of who is made worse off by a tax is called incidence analysis. The analysis is conducted by looking at changes in behavior that lead to changes in prices. These changes in prices then make various people better or worse off than they would have been in the absence of the tax, and the people who are worse off may not be the people legally responsible for paying the tax. For example, suppose that the gas dealers try to raise the price of gas by the full amount of the tax and this leads to a reduction in sales. They lower their prices in response to the reduced sales and absorb part of the tax. This also reduces the part of the tax paid by consumers. However, the reduced sales also reduce the demand for workers in the industry, and so on. Hence, a variety of people may be made worse off by the tax.

However, suppose that the government used the proceeds of the tax to buy gasoline. Then the reduction in sales due to the tax might be offset by the government's purchases, and there might be a net increase in sales. Since there is always some alternative form of tax or some expenditure that will be affected simultaneously with any tax, some people argue that tax incidence analysis must be done by taking into account all the interactions within the economic system. This is called general equilibrium tax incidence analysis. However, incidence analysis is often limited to the specific tax under consideration because the general equilibrium effects are thought to be small compared to the direct effects, and general equilibrium models are very complex.

There is seldom widespread agreement about the incidence of taxes. As we will see, differences in assumptions about the incidence of various taxes leads to widely different conclusions about the equity of the tax system. Further, to the extent that benefits can be shifted, we might also want to look at the incidence of the benefits from government expenditures. For example, the benefits of many government expenditures are capitalized into property values, so the property owner receives the benefits rather than the person who actually receives the direct goods or services. Thus, if a particular community provided exceptional schools and allowed someone to build a few small apartments within the school district, the rents on those apartments would be bid up by parents anxious to get their children into the good schools. The higher rents could offset most of the benefits that the families get from the better schools. If they did not, assuming perfect knowledge, then other families would offer still higher rents to live there. Hence, most of the benefits would accrue to the owner of the apartment building rather than the families living in it. Thus, the benefits would be shifted to the building owner, who may in turn have had to pay a premium for the building and passed the benefits on to someone else. Because of tax and benefit shifting, therefore, the study of the equity of government actions is far more complex than it appears to be.

/// ADMINISTRATIVE AND COMPLIANCE COST

It is common to ignore the cost of administering a tax system by a government and of complying with it by its citizens. Yet all taxes impose some costs on the economy so that the revenue raised is not simply a transfer from citizens to their government. The most obvious types of administrative costs are the costs associated with actually collecting the taxes. In order to collect taxes, government must hire people to keep track of what is owed and to verify that each person is paying the appropriate amount. Further, individuals incur compliance costs because they are required to keep track of how much money they owe the government and to see that appropriate payments are made. Both types of activity can become substantial relative to the amount of money collected by certain taxes. The more complex the tax code, the higher the cost of both administration and compliance.

Because administrative costs tend to be relatively fixed in nature, it would seem to be better to raise existing taxes rather than introduce new ones. We shall see, however, that the higher the rate for most taxes, the greater the efficiency cost to the economy. Hence, there is some tradeoff between efficiency and administrative cost in terms of a few taxes with high tax rates and many taxes with low tax rates. Further, it may make sense to use many taxes so as to make avoidance less rewarding. For example, it may not be worth the trouble to try to avoid a 1% sales tax, but it may be deemed much more worthwhile to avoid a 10% tax.

In fact, one reason why President Reagan made tax reform a major priority was the belief that tax rates had become so high that they encouraged an inordinate amount of tax avoidance behavior. This behavior (avoidance but not evasion) is perfectly legal; however, it does not necessarily promote a useful reallocation of resources. Further, significant resources may be required to accomplish tax avoidance. For example, someone may decide to use a trust to shift income to children so that it is taxed more lightly. This shift in income requires the efforts of a number of people to set up, execute, and monitor. Yet it provides no increase in output for the economy. All of these people are involved in simply trying to redistribute income by allowing some to pay less taxes. Of course, if everyone is doing the same thing then the net tax burden of everyone would stay about the same; but all of the resources involved in tax avoidance would have been wasted from the aggregate perspective of society as a whole.

Complex tax codes also make it more difficult for the taxpayer to keep appropriate records. These bookkeeping costs are often not considered when evaluating specific types of taxes and specific exemptions to those taxes. For example, many states exempt food purchased for home consumption from their sales taxes. This requires that retailers keep records of the types of goods they sell and the taxable category for them. Further, taxable goods must be separated from tax-exempt goods at the time of sale so tax is only charged on the taxable goods. Where the tax exemption is very detailed, this may create a significant problem. In addition, the retailer may have to maintain very detailed records of sales to be able to provide information for audits related to the breakdown between the types of sales.

There may be legitimate reasons to have complex tax codes and to accept high administrative and compliance costs. However, it is important to recognize the costs of such complexity. In addition, high tax rates and complex tax codes encourage tax evasion.

/// ENFORCEMENT

Frequently people calculate the incidence of a tax as if everyone pays according to the law. Unfortunately, not everyone does. Tax evasion results in both revenue loss to the government levying the tax and the need to devote resources to reducing the amount of evasion. Without the enforcement mechanism of an IRS audit, many more people would cheat on their income taxes. As things stand, the IRS estimated the federal income tax loss from illegal tax evasion at $95 billion in 1981 for the personal income tax alone as compared with tax collections of $286 billion in that year. Other estimates are even higher.[10] Some of this evasion is associated with people who conduct illegal activities and simply do not report their income from these activities to the government. This is itself illegal. (The notorious gangster Al Capone was convicted on charges of tax evasion rather than directly convicted for any of his other crimes.) Other people earn income in legal ways but simply fail to report the amount when figuring their taxes. Still others engage in illegal tax-sheltering schemes.

Tax evasion is not limited to the income tax. Some states have very high cigarette taxes, while others have very low ones. Thus, it can be very profitable to buy large quantities of cigarettes in low-tax states and then sell them in high-tax states without paying the tax required. Similarly, some states have

---

[10] Bennett and DiLorenzo, op. cit., p. 2.

high vehicle registration fees while others have low fees. Some people illegally register their cars in the low-fee states to avoid the higher fees in their home states. People have also been known to cross state lines to purchase goods in states with low or zero sales taxes or lower liquor taxes. This activity is sometimes legal and sometimes illegal, but it is always very hard to prevent. Nevertheless, states devote considerable resources to trying to limit the scope of such revenue-reducing activities. In some low-tax states, for example, police occasionally sit outside liquor stores and note the license numbers of cars in the parking lot. They then send the information on ahead to other police who stop the car as it enters its high-tax home state. The amount of additional revenue collected is only part of the reason for such activities. The existence of penalties serves as a deterrent to other potential tax evaders.

Most significant tax cheating occurs with the larger taxes. The greater the amount of revenue involved, the more incentive there is to try to avoid paying the tax. A large, complex tax becomes even more tempting. Consider again the exemption of various items from state sales taxes. While there is often good reason for these exemptions, they increase the compliance costs and make it easier for people to cheat on the tax. For example, retailers can say that more of their sales were in exempt categories and thus send less money on to the state. It might take a very careful audit to discover the discrepancy, and such audits can be very expensive.

The implications of this for determining the incidence of the tax depend on whether there is any pattern to the tax avoidance behavior. For example, if only high-income or low-income families were engaged in illegal tax avoidance, the reports of income tax by income group would be misleading. Further, the costs of legal tax avoidance are in some cases a form of tax themselves. Thus, if a high-income taxpayer chooses to invest in municipal bonds with a yield of 8% rather than corporate bonds with a yield of 12%, he or she will pay no federal taxes on the interest income. However, the person has implicitly paid a tax of one-third on this income by avoiding the higher yielding investment. Thus, taxpayer behavior must be analyzed carefully to determine the exact distribution of tax burden and the total cost to the economy of having a particular type of tax.

The issues of compliance and administration as well as the issue of enforcement are particularly vexing under federalism. They become more complex as more jurisdictions are involved. It is usually the responsibility of the taxpayer to determine the amount of money owed to each jurisdiction, but this may be quite a complex undertaking. For example, consider a person who lives in one state with an income tax, works in another with an income tax, and spent part of the year working in a third state with an income tax. First, this person would have to file a total of four income tax returns: one for each state and a federal one. Second, there is little likelihood that the four jurisdictions define taxable income in the same way. Third, each state probably has some rules about who has first claim on the person's tax payments, but the rules may be conflicting. Fourth, the taxpayer may be tempted to claim that income is earned in such a way as to minimize the potential tax.

The issues with a personal income tax are almost minor compared with the ones for corporate income taxes. This is especially true for corporations with plants in more than one state that all work toward producing one product. Suppose that state A has an effective tax of 10% on corporate profits while state B has an effective tax of only 1% on corporate profits. The company has a strong incentive to make it seem that most of its profits are earned from the plant in state B so as to reduce its tax liability. In response to these incentives states have set up more complex rules, which increase the compliance costs and may have their own problems.

/// REVENUE ELASTICITY

We can define revenue elasticity as the responsivness of tax collections to changes in economic activity, while tax base elasticity is the responsivness of the tax base to changes in the tax rate. Each type of elasticity has important implications for a government's ability to raise revenue.

Tax collections respond to changes in economic conditions over time and over the business cycle. The more responsive the tax collections are, the more elastic the tax is said to be. Thus, the progressive income tax is a very elastic tax. As income grows, the tax collections grow even more rapidly, because more of the earnings are taxed at high rates. Hence, a larger percentage of changes in earnings are taxed than the percentage of earnings as a whole. In the past this growth has been offset by tax reductions, but the trend has been quite clear. It partly explains why the percentage of tax showing up as personal income taxes has been creeping up over time.

Income taxes also are said to be elastic because they are responsive to changes in economic activity. As economic activity goes up, the tax base increases and so does the tax collected. However, some taxes are either not responsive to economic growth or have only a minor relationship. Thus, a head tax (a tax that is a given dollar amount per person) would not be a very elastic tax. Economic activity increases because of both increases in the number of people in the economy and increases in income per person. The head tax would only increase because of the first source of growth. Further, if the tax is levied in a dollar amount, then the real value of the tax will be eroded by changes in the price level due to inflation. The one disadvantage of an elastic tax base is the fact that such bases are also very responsive to the business cycle. Thus, the government levying such a tax is likely to see its revenue dropping during a recession.

Tax base elasticity relates to how the total tax collection changes in response to a change in the rate of the tax. It might seem that the tax collection should be proportional to the tax; but this is not correct. The higher tax encourages greater tax avoidance, and this leads to a reduction of the base on which the tax is levied. The higher rate times the lower base then determines the total tax collection. If the base is very responsive to changes in the tax rate, it is even possible for the total tax collected to decline as the tax rate is increased. This is not likely to happen for taxes at the federal level, but it becomes more likely when we look at lower levels of government. This is because the ability to avoid a tax is greater at the lower levels of government. Thus, if a local government raises its income tax, some of the residents may choose to move outside the jurisdiction to avoid the tax increase. If enough people do that, the total tax collected may actually decrease.

The question of tax base elasticity is affected by the time frame under consideration: the longer the time frame, the more people can adjust to the change in taxes. Thus, the reduction in revenue is likely to take some time to occur. For example, Grieson estimates that the wage tax in Philadelphia is already so high that any further increase will eventually lead to so much loss in employment that the city will see a reduction in revenue.[11] The loss in employment would only occur over a period of years, so it would not be apparent at the time the tax was raised.

/// SUMMARY

Raising revenue is only one of the objectives of taxation. Other objectives include: changing the distribution of income, making the recipients of certain benefits pay for them, or giving people incentives to alter their behavior. In addition, it is important to consider the administrative costs, the compliance costs, and the enforcement costs associated with a tax. Further, most taxes create an efficiency cost for the economy by distorting people's incentives. This is an amount lost to the private sector above and beyond the amount collected by the public sector. These factors should all be taken into account when evaluating a particular tax structure.

If we look simply at the major taxes, we find that they have grown in absolute size by a very large amount over the last forty years. However, if we consider them as a percentage of GNP, they are largely the same as they were forty years ago. The growth in government has shown up in increased taxes for transfer payments and social insurance, particularly the Social Security tax, and in the growing debt of the federal government. When these items are included, government is indeed growing as a percentage of GNP.

A variety of equity concepts are used in evaluating taxation. The ability-to-pay concept focuses on the revenue raised by taxation. The basic proposi-

---

[11] Ronald Grieson, "Theoretical Analysis and Empirical Measurements of the Effects of the Philadelphia Income Tax," *Journal of Urban Economics* 8 (July 1980), pp. 123–137.

tions are that equals should be treated equally and that those with more ability to pay should indeed pay more. With respect to the latter evaluation we define a tax as regressive, proportional, or progressive depending on whether the percentage of income paid for that tax declines, stays the same, or increases as income increases. The benefits concept focuses on the benefits created with public expenditure. Taxes are considered equitable under this concept if they are related to the benefits received. Finally, the marginal cost pricing concept focuses on the cost of providing government services to specific individuals; this requires that the tax reflect marginal cost as closely as possible.

It is also important to remember that the incidence of a tax is not necessarily on the person or firm on which it is levied. Some taxes are meant to be shifted to others; but all taxes could be shifted under the appropriate circumstances. Thus, it is important to determine the final incidence of the tax in evaluating it from the equity perspective.

Analysis of taxation is complex. The issues that must be addressed when considering a tax can be broadly broken down into considerations of the revenue raised, the equity of the tax, and the efficiency of the tax. As we will see in looking at specific types of taxes, these issues have somewhat different importance for each revenue source.

Chapter 6 //////

Sales and
Excise Taxes

Everyone is familiar with a sales tax. It is widely used at the state level, with forty-five of the fifty states levying a retail sales tax as of 1987,[1] and more than 97% of the population of the United States living in states that levy sales taxes.[2] In 1986, various forms of sales taxation generated around $182 billion when aggregated over all governments in the U.S. At the state level, the total was about $112 billion; this was almost 50% of total state tax revenue.[3] The predominant form of the retail sales tax appears to have originated in the United States during the Depression. Mississippi first enacted the tax in 1932, and several other states followed shortly thereafter.[4] The tax was viewed as a relatively painless way to generate revenue for state governments faced with increasing demands for services coupled with declining revenues. The tax remains a mainstay of state government revenue and is also used for local government finance in many states, with close to 7,000 local governments levying sales taxes in 1987.[5]

The sales tax is intended to be a tax on consumer expenditures, and items purchased for resale are often exempted from taxation. While most people believe that the base is the actual retail sale, this is not always true. The tax can be levied on the gross receipts of retail sellers; it is often legally imposed on the seller with the requirement that it be passed on to the consumer.[6] It is

---

[1] Advisory Commission on Intergovernmental Relations (ACIR), *Significant Features of Fiscal Federalism, 1988 Edition*, M-155 (Washington, DC: 1987 and 1988), Table 22.

[2] John F. Due and John L. Mikesell, *Sales Taxation: State and Local Structure and Administration* (Baltimore, MD: Johns Hopkins University Press, 1983), p. 2. This book is an exceptionally detailed study of the current state of sales taxation in the United States.

[3] Advisory Commission on Intergovernmental Relations, *Significant Features of Fiscal Federalism, 1985–86 Edition*, M-146 (Washington, DC: 1986), pp. 40–41; and ACIR, *1988*, op. cit., Tables 62.1 and 62.3.

[4] Due and Mikesell, op. cit., p. 2.

[5] ACIR, *1988*, op. cit., p. 57.

[6] Due and Mikesell, op. cit., pp. 23–25.

always levied as an ad valorem tax and stated as a percentage of the sale amount. In may cases, retailers are not allowed to state that they are paying the tax for the consumer, and they are required to list the tax payment separately. The base is almost always reduced from its broadest coverage by exempting items from coverage. For example, twenty-eight states exempted food in 1987 and forty-five exempted prescription drugs.[7]

An excise tax is a tax levied on a single type of good. For example, cigarette and gasoline taxes are excise taxes. Excise taxes are usually levied as a fixed amount per unit sold; however, they may also be levied as a percentage of an item's value. In the latter form, they function as selective sales taxes. All levels of government use excise taxes, but they are most heavily used by the federal and state governments.

/// THE ECONOMICS OF EXCISE TAXES

While excise taxes are far from being the most important taxes levied by any level of government, we treat them first because the economic analysis yields the most insight into how taxes affect the economy. We start our analysis with the most simple type of excise tax, a per unit tax rather than an ad valorem tax, and then look into the various complications that occur when using excise taxes.

Excise Tax on Sellers

Consider a very simple economy in which there are only two goods, X and Y. For simplicity you can think of Y as money, for it represents all the goods in the economy except X. The demand and supply curves for X are given in Figure 6-1. Recall that the demand curve tells us how many units of good X consumers will offer to purchase at each price. Similarly, the supply curve shows the amount that producers will offer for sale at each price. The equilibrium at P^* and Q^* is efficient if all markets are competitive. Now suppose that the government has decided to impose a tax of T per unit of output on this good only. Initially, let us consider a tax on the producers of good X. For each unit they sell, the producers must pay the government T dollars.

The effect of this tax is to increase the cost of production as perceived by the producers. It will cost them an additional T dollars per unit to produce good X for sale. From the producers' perspective it does not matter that the money goes to government rather than providers of inputs. It is still a production cost. Hence, the producers must receive T dollars more per unit to induce them to produce any given level of output. For example, if a price of $.50 would generate a total quantity supplied of 1,000 units and a tax of $.05 per unit is

[7] ACIR, *1988*, op. cit., p. 54.

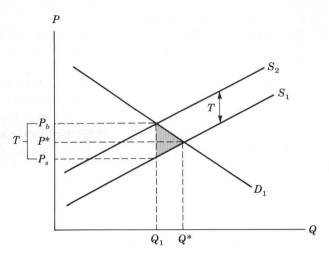

Figure 6-1 / Excise Tax on Seller

added, then the companies that sell X would have to receive $.55 in order to retain $.50 after the tax. Hence, the effective price to generate output of 1,000 units would have to rise to $.55. However, this will be true for all levels of output. Therefore, the supply curve would have to rise by the full amount of the tax. This is shown in Figure 6-1 as the supply curve S_2.

The new supply curve intersects the demand curve at the quantity Q_1. However, at this quantity the new market price of P_b represents the amount the buyer pays but not the amount the seller keeps. The seller receives P_b from the buyer but must give an amount T to the government. Hence, the seller only gets to keep the amount P_s. This is a market equilibrium because the amount the buyers want to buy at the price P_b is just equal to the amount the sellers want to sell at the price P_s. At this new equilibrium, the price to buyers is higher than it was in the absence of the tax and the price the sellers keep is lower than it was in the absence of the tax. Further, the differences of each of these prices from the zero-tax equilibrium must sum to the amount of the tax. Hence, these deviations from the zero-tax equilibrium are a measure of the incidence of the tax on buyers and sellers.

If P_b is very close to P^*, the tax has primarily affected the price received by the sellers, and it is the sellers who are said to bear the burden of the tax. However, if the price P_s is close to P^*, it is the buyers who are said to bear the burden of the tax. In the general case, the tax is shared by the buyer and the seller, with the buyer paying more and the seller receiving less than was true in the absence of the tax. This is despite the fact that the tax is levied on the sellers by the government. In other words, the sellers have managed to pass part, but not all, of the tax on to the consumers.

The second important point is that the quantity sold is lower in the new equilibrium. Thus, there has been a change in consumption patterns in response to the tax; this means that resources are being allocated inefficiently. In particular, consumers value another unit of this product at the price of P_b while it only costs producers an amount P_s to produce the additional unit. Hence, the economy is not taking advantage of an opportunity to increase net satisfaction.

The loss to the economy as a whole is called the deadweight loss or efficiency loss associated with an excise tax. It is represented by the shaded triangle in Figure 6-1. This loss represents a reduction in the net satisfaction of individuals in the economy over and above any losses associated with the tax collections themselves. Further, the tax collections are less than the amount that would have been calculated by taking the initial sales equilibrium and multiplying it by the amount of the tax. Thus, the tax collection is $T \times Q_1$ rather than $T \times Q^*$. Both the efficiency loss and the reduction in revenue are due to people responding to the economic incentives that they face. When the incentives change, so does behavior. We turn shortly to the analysis of these responses, but first we look at an excise tax imposed on the consumer rather than the producer.

Excise Tax on Buyers

Most actual excise taxes are in fact imposed on the seller for administrative convenience; but this just makes it more important to see if there is any economic reason why it would matter how the tax were imposed. Consider a tax of the amount T imposed on consumers of the same product discussed earlier. Figure 6-2 reproduces the original supply and demand curves from Figure 6-1. How does a consumer respond to an excise tax? From the consumer's perspective the tax is simply part of the price of the good. It does not matter to the consumer whether he or she pays the money to the producer or to the government. Hence, the original demand curve represents the consumer's demand in response to total price. On the other hand, producers only respond to the amounts they actually receive. Producers, in deciding how much to produce, do not take account of the amount that consumers pay the government. The amount the producers receive is determined by taking the tax away from the total amount the consumers pay, as shown on their demand curves. This is effectively the same as shifting the demand curve down by the amount of the tax.

In Figure 6-2 we see the downward shift in the demand curve producing an equilibrium at a price of P_s and a quantity of Q_1. The quantity is the same as when the tax was imposed on the sellers, but the market price is P_s rather than P_b. However, in this case the seller gets to keep the market payment and the consumer must pay an additional amount T to the government. Hence, the total price to the consumer is P_b. Thus, the payment by the consumer and the amount received by the seller are the same as they would be if the tax were levied on the seller rather than the buyer. This is an important result of the economic analysis of excise taxes; and it is somewhat counterintuitive. It says

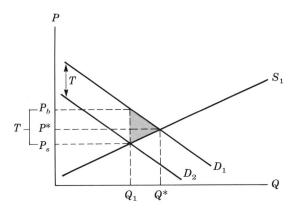

Figure 6-2 / **Excise Tax on Buyer**

that, in equilibrium, it does not matter whether the tax is levied on the buyer or the seller. The economic effects of the tax are the same in either case. This fits well with the notion that the tax is simply passed on to consumers by the producers; but our analysis shows that such a simple result is not correct either. The tax is shared by producers and consumers. Further, the deadweight loss or efficiency loss associated with the tax is the same in either case.

The incidence of the tax is the same no matter who nominally bears the burden of the tax because the tax drives a wedge between the payment by the buyer and the receipt of the seller. This wedge is equal to the amount of the tax and it is independent of who nominally pays the tax. If we start at the initial equilibrium of demand and supply and look to the left until we find the quantity where the vertical distance between the demand and supply curves is equal to the tax, we would again reach quantity Q_1. This is the only quantity where the tax can be subtracted from the amount consumers pay to give the price suppliers must receive to offer that quantity for sale. Hence, it is the only quantity consistent with equilibrium given the tax.

The equilibrium results which we just derived do not mean that it never makes any difference how a tax is levied. To begin, the administrative and compliance costs may differ depending on who must make the actual payments. For example, the federal gasoline tax is often thought of as a tax on consumers and is usually listed on the pump; however, it is actually a tax on wholesalers. The same is true of the federal cigarette tax. It is levied on wholesalers because the record-keeping and compliance costs are lower than if the tax were the responsibility of the individual.

Short-Run Incidence

In some cases, the distinction of who pays the tax is more than one of convenience. When tax rates change, the persons who nominally pay the tax often bear a larger share of the tax in the short run than they do in the long run. This is because it takes time for the market adjustment that shifts the tax to occur. One example is Social Security, which can be thought of as an excise tax on labor. The tax is partly levied on workers and partly levied on employers. In equilibrium, most economists conclude that it is primarily paid by workers; however, an increase in the tax is initially paid by whoever is specified in the law. Most labor contracts do not specify anything about Social Security taxes. Thus, the party specified by the law will absorb any unexpected changes in such taxes until such time as wage rates adjust to the new situation. Hence, it may take a long time for the full shifting of this tax to occur. Thus, the short-run incidence may in fact be altered by the specification of who pays the tax, although there is little evidence that it affects the long-run incidence. Unfortunately, in cases such as Social Security where it may take time for the tax to be shifted, people often misperceive the true incidence of the tax.

It is important to understand that this analysis is only relevant for one market in isolation. It is called a partial equilibrium analysis since the changes in output produced and consumed are likely to cause other changes, which may allow further shifting of the tax incidence. For example, the producers require fewer inputs because they are producing less output. Hence, the reduced demand for inputs could cause the price of those inputs to decline. In effect, the producers would then be further shifting the incidence of the tax (see Box 6-1). Alternatively, the consumers may decide that they no longer want certain goods that are complementary to the taxed good. The reduced demand here might also lead to a price reduction and, hence, a further shifting of part of the tax incidence.

Efficiency Cost

While the shifting of a tax may create problems in terms of evaluating its equity, the actions that lead to this shifting create an uncompensated loss in the economy. In other words, the losers when the tax is imposed lose more than the gainers gain. This loss is known as a deadweight loss or efficiency loss to the economy. The amount of this loss is tied to the change in quantity bought and sold in the market.

When competitive markets are in equilibrium, the marginal unit has a value to consumers that is just equal to the opportunity cost of producing it. If it is not produced and sold, the loss to consumers in satisfaction is just about exactly offset by the savings of resources that would have been needed to produce the output. As the quantity gets lower and lower, the losses to consumers in terms of satisfaction get larger for each additional unit reduction in output. At the same time the savings to producers in terms of resources not used get smaller with each additional unit reduction in output. Thus, the difference between loss in consumer satisfaction and resource savings per unit gets larger as the quantity is reduced. The sum of the losses on each unit is the deadweight loss. We have shown this as a shaded triangle in Figure 6-1.

Box 6-1

/////// Backward Shifting of Tax Incidence

It is common to study the shifting of tax incidence between the buyers and sellers in a market, but the shifting may go much farther than this. In particular, the shifting from a supplier backward to factors of production is likely whenever there are factors specific to a particular industry.

Consider an imaginary new agriculture product, oilgrass, which can only be grown on a certain plot of land. Further, the land has no other productive use and the only other input is fertilizer, which is readily available. Thus, the supply curve for the land as an input to this production process will be very inelastic. Suppose that there was some equilibrium in the market represented by the price P_{L1} and the quantity Q_{L1} in Figure 1. Next suppose that an excise tax is imposed on this item and at least part of the incidence is on suppliers. Given the reduced quantity sold, the suppliers can be expected to

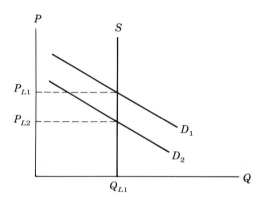

Figure 1 / Backward Shifting with Inelastic Supply

Strictly, this shaded triangle is only an approximation to the true deadweight loss, but it will suffice for our purposes.

An important point can be made with this interpretation of the deadweight loss. As the figure shows, the deadweight loss tends to get larger per unit as the deviation from the market equilibrium gets larger. This is frequently used as an argument that higher tax rates create larger efficiency losses. Figure 6-3 shows the effect of doubling a tax rate when the demand and supply curves are linear. The initial tax raises the supply curve to S_2, which

Box 6-1 *(continued)*

reduce their demand for the inputs needed to produce oilgrass. Thus the demand curve will shift to D_2 in the figure. As we see, there is no decrease in the quantity of land used for oilgrass production; but the price paid to the owners of this land for its use has dropped to P_{L2}. Thus, part of the incidence of the tax has been shifted back to the owners of this land.

Figure 2 shows the market for the fertilizer used in growing this product. The supply of this product is very elastic. Again the reduction in output leads to a reduction in demand for the input; but in this case, the effect is that less quantity of fertilizer is used. The quantity demanded falls

from Q_{F1} to Q_{F2}, but the price that the growers pay for the fertilizer is not affected by the reduction in demand. Hence, none of the incidence of the tax can be shifted back to the producers of fertilizer. These examples simply show that the ultimate incidence of a tax may be hard to determine. In particular, the part of the tax on suppliers is seldom actually paid by suppliers unless they are also owners of resources that are in relatively inelastic supply to the particular industry. Further, it is not generally possible to shift the tax to resources that are in elastic supply to the industry.

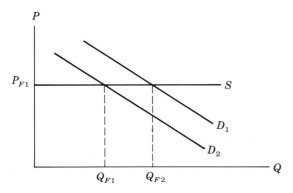

Figure 2 / **Backward Shifting with Elastic Supply**

creates a deadweight loss equal to the lightly shaded triangle. Doubling the tax rate raises the supply curve to S_3 and adds the heavily shaded area to the deadweight loss. In the linear case, it is easy to see that the heavily shaded area is larger than the lightly shaded area. Thus, the deadweight loss has more than doubled with the doubling of the tax rate.[8]

[8] In fact, the area of the triangle is given by the formula Area = (1/2) × Base × Height. The base of the triangle is the change in quantity as compared to the efficient level, and the height is the amount of the tax. Doubling the tax also causes the change in quantity to double, so the efficiency loss would increase by a factor of four.

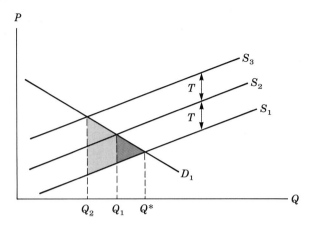

Figure 6-3 / Deadweight Loss with Linear Demand Curve

The larger increases in deadweight loss with each increment to the tax rate serve as the basis for the general argument against high marginal tax rates on specific goods or services. However, there are a number of complications in this general statement. First, the deadweight loss is not the same for all goods and services. A high tax on one good may generate less deadweight loss than a low tax on some other good. In particular, we show in the next section that the deadweight loss is smaller when demand or supply of a good is inelastic and larger when both are elastic. Second, the linear demand case is not necessarily descriptive of all goods and services. If the reduction in quantity is smaller for the second increment of the tax than for the first, the deadweight loss may actually be less than doubled when the tax rate is doubled. This is illustrated in Figure 6-4. The heavily shaded area associated with the doubling of the tax is smaller than the lightly shaded area associated with the lower tax. Thus, the total deadweight loss goes up but by less than double. This, however, would be rather unusual; it is more often the case that higher tax rates result in more than proportionately higher efficiency losses.

Elasticity and the Shifting of an Excise Tax

So far we have determined that an excise tax will be partly paid by the consumer and partly paid by the producer. It is tempting to conclude that each simply pays half the tax. However, this simple conclusion is almost invariably wrong. The amount of shifting is determined by a somewhat more complex set of conditions: the relative elasticity of supply and demand.

Generally, the more elastic a curve, the more the tax is shifted away from that curve and the less elastic the curve, the more the tax is shifted to that curve. Further, the more elastic the curves are, the greater the deadweight loss will be and the less elastic, the smaller the deadweight loss will be from a

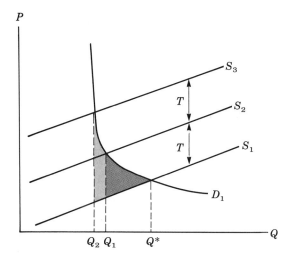

***Figure 6-4* / Deadweight Loss with Nonlinear Demand Curve**

given tax rate. Finally, the quantity sold and, hence, the tax revenue will be reduced the most if the curves are relatively elastic and reduced the least if the curves are relatively inelastic.

Figure 6-5 shows four of the extreme cases of elasticity. In Figure 6-5a, the demand curve is perfectly elastic. When the supply curve is shifted up by the amount of the tax the new equilibrium's price is at exactly the same level as before the tax. Hence, the net return to the producer is reduced by the amount of the tax. Thus, the tax is paid entirely by the supplier. This is the case whether the tax is nominally placed on the supplier or not. The reason is fairly clear. A perfectly elastic demand curve implies that consumers will purchase as much as suppliers want to sell at the given price, but they will purchase none at any higher price. Of course few goods have a perfectly elastic demand; but the demand for many goods is very elastic. These would be goods for which there are excellent close substitutes. For example, if the government were to levy a special tax on one brand of gasoline, either the producer would absorb most of the tax or stop selling gasoline. For most brands of gasoline, other brands are a very close substitute. Hence, the buyer would not normally be willing to pay much of a premium for a particular brand. Note that this also creates some deadweight loss. If supply and demand are both every elastic, then the deadweight loss is fairly large. Essentially, the producer with the tax would be forced out of business. Of course, the government does not levy taxes on individual businesses; but the example illustrates why a tax on a good with easy substitutes is likely to be paid by the producers.

Figure 6-5b shows a case of perfectly inelastic demand. In this case, the upward shift of the supply curve causes the equilibrium price to rise by the full amount of the tax. The buyers bear the full burden of the tax. The inelastic demand means that the consumers will purchase a given quantity no matter

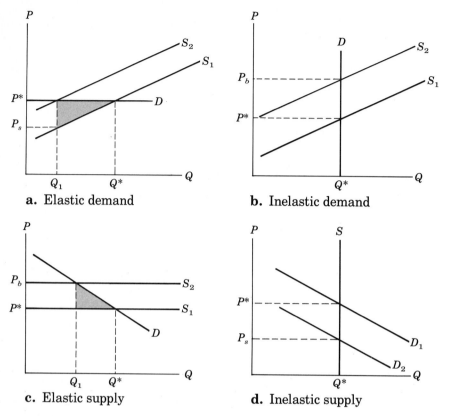

a. Elastic demand

b. Inelastic demand

c. Elastic supply

d. Inelastic supply

*Figure 6-5 / **Elasticity and Incidence***

what happens to the price. Hence, they absorb the full price increase with no reduction in quantity purchased. Also, there is no deadweight loss associated with this tax. The quantity produced and consumed remains unchanged. There are not many good examples of goods with perfectly inelastic demand curves, but the demand for many goods tends to be very inelastic. Table salt is one possible example. A tax constituting a large percentage of the price of this commodity would not be expected to cause many consumers to alter their use. Thus, the consumers would end up paying the tax.

Figures 6-5c and 6-5d show the cases of perfectly elastic supply and perfectly inelastic supply. With the elastic supply the tax is shifted to the consumer and with the inelastic supply it is absorbed by the producer. In general, an elastic supply results when there are no specialized resources used in the production of the good or service. Thus, producers would readily shift into the production of some other good or service if the price they received in this market were to fall. An inelastic supply is associated with resources that are specialized to the industry. Since they have no alternative uses, the price paid for these specialized resources falls as the price of the output falls (see Box

6-1); and the lower price of inputs allows production to continue at relatively high levels. Note again that the deadweight loss is greater the greater the elasticity; there is no deadweight loss with the perfectly inelastic supply.

In terms of tax policy this implies that it is better to levy excise taxes on goods that are either in inelastic supply or inelastic demand to minimize the efficiency losses; however, this also implies that the group with the inelastic curve is likely to bear a large part of the tax burden. This latter point may make the tax undesirable from an equity standpoint. For example, many food staples are believed to have an inelastic demand; but they are considered poor choices for excise taxes because the tax tends to be regressive. The inelastic demand for some goods, however, leads to a fairly heavy reliance on excise taxes. Liquor and tobacco products are examples of goods where a heavy tax on users is generally considered acceptable and where significant excise taxes exist.

Another factor to consider with respect to both revenue productivity and efficiency is the geographic area covered by a tax. The smaller the geographic area, the higher the elasticity of both supply and demand are likely to be. Hence, a tax imposed on a small area will generate a larger efficiency loss and a smaller amount of revenue than would occur in the same area if the tax were imposed at a higher level. This is because some consumers will look outside the jurisdiction to make their purchases and some sellers will make more of their sales outside the jurisdiction. This option is limited if the tax covers a larger area.

/// SALES TAXES

A sales tax is a generalized form of excise tax. It covers a wide variety of goods and is specified as some percentage of the retail value of the goods or services. Sales taxes are most often levied on retail sales for final consumption. Final consumption means that the item will not be resold; however, it does not have to be consumed by an individual. Many of the items subject to sales taxes are used by businesses, and most states make no distinction between final use by a business and final use by an individual. In principle, any sale to a business results in an item that becomes part of the production process; but few states see it that way. However, many states do exempt items that will be directly resold or that will become part of the item to be sold. Thus, office supplies and machinery would not be exempt from the sales tax but intermediate goods would be. The tax is often confused further because sales to nonprofit organizations or to government units may also be exempt.

Turnover Taxes

The retail sales tax should be carefully distinguished from gross taxes on all sales. The latter are known as turnover taxes because they are levied each time an item turns over from one producer to another. Such taxes usually have very low rates; but this disguises the magnitude of the tax. Because the tax may be levied at several stages of the production process, it tends to be cumulative so that the total tax on the final item may be many times the nominal rate. Since the retail sales tax is largely aimed at items being sold for final consumption, it is levied on a much smaller base than a turnover tax. However, it is sometimes difficult to distinguish the retail sales tax on items sold for final consumption to a business from a turnover tax. The tax that the business pays on the items it consumes becomes part of its cost of doing business; this cost is likely to result in higher prices charged for the firm's output. Further, to the extent that the tax is levied on business consumption, it does create an incentive for the firm to become its own supplier of the input. This may not be an issue for paper clips, but it may be an important determinant of whether the firm hires an outside accounting firm or law firm rather than using its own accountants or lawyers. The turnover tax has not been used extensively in the United States although it has been used in other countries. We discuss it further when we talk about value-added taxes, and we reserve the term sales tax for the retail sales tax.

Sales Tax on Seller

Generally, sales taxes are expected to be passed on to the buyer, although they are often levied on the seller. Even when the tax is imposed on the buyer, the government essentially appoints the seller as its tax collector. Thus, individuals are not expected to keep track of their purchases subject to taxation and then mail a check to the government every so often. Clearly such a tax would be very difficult to administer and enforce; but it represents the intent of the sales tax.

Sales taxes are usually thought to be regressive taxes. The actual incidence depends on a variety of conditions, the most important one being the coverage of the tax. Virtually all sales taxes exempt some items from the tax, and many have significant exemptions. The pattern as well as the level of exemptions can alter the final incidence pattern; we discuss this issue shortly.

Efficiency

Recall that the analysis of the excise tax showed that it could lead to important efficiency problems. In particular, levying a tax on one good caused people to substitute away from that good in consumption. This substitution was inefficient because the rate at which consumers were willing to trade off one good for another in consumption was no longer the rate at which they could be traded off in production. Hence, it would be possible in principle to change the production and consumption patterns and make someone better off without making anyone worse off. This incentive to distort between different goods is eliminated by a comprehensive general sales tax.

The effect of a single excise tax is to make the taxed good relatively more expensive than other goods. This causes people to reduce their consumption of this good relative to other goods, and that is the source of the efficiency loss. Suppose that there were only one other good in the economy. Then relative consumption of this other good must have increased. If a tax is imposed on the second good, the resulting reduction in the consumption of the second good would not result in an efficiency loss. Rather, it would result in an efficiency gain. People would move back toward consuming the two goods in proportions representing their relative values and production costs.

The difference when an excise tax is imposed on the second good is that the economy does not start from a position of pure competitive equilibrium. Once a distortion is introduced into the economy, the theorems associated with a purely competitive economy may no longer hold true. This is itself a theorem, known as the theorem of the second best. Essentially it says that movements that would move you toward efficiency if the economy were in competitive equilibrium (except for the issue under study), would not necessarily do so if the rest of the economy also suffers from distortions. Thus, our partial equilibrium analysis of a single excise tax is only directly applicable if this is the only distortion in our system. (See the appendix to this chapter for an analysis in a simple general equilibrium case.) When this analysis is applied to a second or third distortion, the results are not necessarily correct.

While it is important to recognize the theorem of the second best and its related warnings, it is also important not to get carried away with it. Many people consider this theorem as a statement that nothing can be analyzed because there is never a pure competitive equilibrium. In a sense this is true; but we never have anything that fits our models exactly. Rather, we try to understand what the models can teach us about a particular situation. In most cases, the models can provide important insight and policy direction. The key is determining which is the more appropriate model in a particular context.

The general sales tax could in principle be levied so as not to change the relative prices of any goods or services in the economy. In this case it would not show any of the efficiency losses associated with the individual excise taxes. Rather, it would function as a general tax on consumption. We consider the efficiency problems of such general taxes at length in the next chapter. In this chapter we consider some of the issues that arise when the sales tax is not levied uniformly within the economy.

Multiple Jurisdictions

Suppose that the economy has two political jurisdictions and that only one chooses to impose a sales tax. It is fairly clear that the residents of both jurisdictions would be better off personally by making their purchases in the nontaxing jurisdiction. Only if the cost of transporting the commodity were large would it make no sense to purchase outside the jurisdiction levying the tax. The smaller the jurisdiction, the easier it is for people to shop outside to avoid the tax. Thus, local governments would have the most trouble with a sales tax; this helps explain why only large jurisdictions tend to have them. However, even states have problems at their borders.[9] For example, the state of Washington recently tried to raise its sales tax for all counties except those that bordered Oregon. Oregon does not have a sales tax, and Washington merchants on the border complain about Washington residents who cross over to do their shopping. This border differential was struck down by the courts, but it does show the perception of the problem even at the state level.

In response to this incentive to purchase outside the jurisdiction, most governments that levy a sales tax also levy a use tax. A use tax is levied on the market value of goods purchased outside the jurisdiction but then brought into the jurisdiction for consumption or use. It is intended to prevent people from avoiding a sales tax by shopping elsewhere. In practice, such taxes are difficult to enforce. It is usually possible to collect use taxes from individuals only on major purchases like automobiles. Even here it is only because the vehicle must be registered that the jurisdiction can realistically levy such a tax.

The ability to avoid sales taxes is greater when the jurisdiction levying the tax is small in geographic area. Hence, cities that levy sales taxes face more serious problems with avoidance than do states. Nevertheless, more than half of the states have authorized at least some of their cities to levy sales taxes, and more than half of municipalities with populations greater than 100,000 levy such taxes.[10] Some of the problems are avoided when the state levies the tax and remits the collections to local governments, but this is not really a local tax. Further, a uniform state levy for local purposes may give some jurisdictions with high concentrations of retail sales large amounts of revenue. If the state is going to collect such taxes, there is often a good case to be made for distributing the revenues on some basis other than the place of collection. Alternatively, if the local government has some discretion in determining the amount of the tax but has the state collect the tax, there is likely to be an administrative advantage. Further, the local discretion makes the tax more of a local tax. However, differences between jurisdictions still create incentives for activity to shift. Such local uses of the sales tax are largely restricted to the bigger local governments.

/// EQUITY AND INCIDENCE

The notion that excise taxes are often regressive is tied to the income elasticity of demand for various goods. Taxes on goods used in essentially equal amounts by all income groups or used relatively more heavily by low-

---

[9] For example, see John L. Mikesell, "Central Cities and Sales Tax Rate Differentials: The Border City Problem," *National Tax Journal* 23 (June 1970), pp. 206–213.

[10] Due and Mikesell, op. cit., p. 266. They also note (p. 4) that cities in Alaska levy sales taxes at rates that rival most states. This is probably possible because of the relative isolation of those cities.

income groups tend to have a regressive incidence if the tax is shifted to consumers. Taxes on goods that have a high income elasticity of demand are likely to have a progressive incidence. Thus, an excise tax on salt would probably be passed largely to the consumer since the demand tends to be inelastic. Further, salt consumption does not seem to increase in proportion to income. Hence, a tax on salt would not tend to increase in proportion to income, and it would therefore be regressive. A tax on diamonds, however, would be expected to be a fairly progressive tax since diamonds are not consumed in great quantities by low-income groups. Generalizations about the equity impact of the taxes becomes much harder when the tax is shifted backward to producers and factors of production or when there are other types of shifting.

Despite the possibility of an excise tax having a progressive incidence, excise taxes are generally thought of as regressive taxes. This is because most such taxes are levied on items that are consumed by a large percentage of the population and that tend to have inelastic demand. Both factors are important in terms of the revenue raised by the tax. Goods sold in small volumes do not raise much revenue; and if the demand is elastic, the decline in volume of sales both limits revenue collections and creates a reaction from sellers.

There are a variety of reasons why the sales tax is often characterized as a regressive tax. The most important issue is the incidence of a general sales tax. It is common to treat such a tax as having a final incidence on consumers. A sales tax covering all items is necessarily proportional to consumption since it is levied as a percentage of sales price. Thus, it would be a proportional tax if everyone consumed the same proportion of their income. However, there is some evidence that higher income households tend to save a larger percentage of their income. Hence, they would pay the tax on a smaller percentage of their income and the tax would decline as a percentage of income.

If this were the major factor, there would probably be little concern about the regressivity of the tax. Most of the problem disappears if income and consumption are averaged over long time periods (see Box 6-2). However, almost no sales tax covers the entire potential tax base. Many governments exempt some services from the base, and some exempt all services.[11] Since services tend to make up a larger percentage of consumption as income rises, the percentage of consumption that is not taxed would also tend to rise as income rises. This creates a tendency for the sales tax to be regressive. However, there are a variety of reasons why the tax is not extended to services (see Box 6-3). In the past, the tax was also deductible in figuring federal income taxes, and this made it more likely to have a regressive incidence (this is discussed further in Chapter 7).

Rather than extend the tax to more comprehensively cover services, most jurisdictions seek to reduce the regressivity by exempting certain goods that

---

[11] ACIR, *1988*, op. cit., pp. 54–55, identifies only four states in 1987 as having general taxation of most services.

Box 6-2

////// **The Relationship between Annual Income, Average Income, and Housing Expenditure**

Think of a society in which there are three types of people: low income (Lows), middle income (Mids), and high income (Highs). Each person goes through a three-stage life cycle, with earnings starting low and increasing over the life cycle; but the housing consumed is the same in each time period. Lows have an income pattern of $8,000, $10,000, and $12,000; Mids have $10,000, $12,000, and $14,000; and Highs have $12,000, $14,000, and $16,000. In the first time period, each person accurately estimates average income and chooses to spend 20% on housing. Thus, Lows spend $2,000, Mids spend $2,400, and Highs spend $2,800. Each income level and stage of the life cycle are equally represented. In any given year, then, we would observe the following relationship between income and rent:

	L_1	L_2	L_3	M_1	M_2	M_3	H_1	H_2	H_3
Income	$8,000	$10,000	$12,000	$10,000	$12,000	$14,000	$12,000	$14,000	$16,000
Rent	$2,000	$ 2,000	$ 2,000	$ 2,400	$ 2,400	$ 2,400	$ 2,800	$ 2,800	$ 2,800

Now we want to look at the relationship between income and average rent paid. Assuming equal numbers of people in each classification, the relationship would be:

Income:	$8,000	$10,000	$12,000	$14,000	$16,000
Rent:	$2,000	$ 2,200	$ 2,400	$ 2,600	$ 2,800

If we fit a line through these points, we find the equation to be $R = \$1,200 + 0.1I$ even though we know that the average relationship is $R = 0.2I$. Thus, the estimated relationship shows rent expenditure to be

---

are viewed as being necessities. Such items tend to be goods that are thought to have a low income elasticity of demand as well. This tends to make the tax more progressive, but it can have a significant effect on revenue from the tax. As noted earlier, the usual exemptions include food purchased for home

Box 6-2 (continued)

much less responsive to differences in income than in fact it is (see Figure 1).

The difference between the estimated relationship and the actual relationship is caused by a form of measurement error. In each year we are only measuring each person's earnings for that year, but the housing consumption decision is based on their average earnings. Thus, when we compare the variation in annual earnings to the variation in rent, it appears that the rent varies less in response to changes in earnings than in fact it does.

Another way to look at this is that when we observe someone with high earnings, the probability is rela-

tively high that this person is in the high part of their earning pattern. Thus, when we observe someone earning $12,000 it is equally likely that this is high, average, or low earnings for that person (since people in each of our three groups can earn this amount). However, when we observe an amount of $14,000 it can only be average or above average, and $16,000 can only be above average. Similarly, the low earnings are more likely to represent being in the low part of one's earning pattern. Because of these factors we tend to associate low earnings with relatively high consumption and high earnings with relatively low consumption if we ignore the average over time.

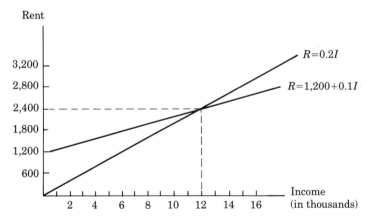

Figure 1 / **Current versus Average Income**

consumption and prescription medicines. The final result differs significantly from state to state.

While such tinkering with tax coverage may make the tax more equitable, it also tends to make it more costly to administer and harder to enforce.

Box 6-3

////// Sales Tax on Services

A variety of reasons are offered for not taxing services more inclusively in sales taxes. The first reason is that medical, dental, and legal services are a substantial part of personal expenditures on services. Many people feel that it would be unfair to add a sales tax onto large medical or legal fees, which are usually also unexpected, so it would appear inappropriate for government to add to financial burdens at such times.

The second problem is in the distinction between business and consumer taxation. While the retail sales tax is thought of as a tax on consumers, it is paid by businesses on many items that they use. Many services that would be subject to taxation are ones used heavily by businesses. Thus, the tax would either become more of a business tax or it would become more difficult to enforce if business use of services were exempted. Further, a tax on business services would create an incentive for firms to hire service providers directly rather than hire firms that provide a service. This would probably be inefficient.

The third major problem is that many services are hard to evaluate or the payment would be hard to monitor. For example, many financial services are provided as compensation for deposits in financial institutions. Such transactions would be hard to tax. Further, there are substantial services provided directly to households, and since the household has no reason to report the transaction, the tax would be hard to enforce.

A good example of the difficulties in extending the tax to services is given by the state of Florida. In 1987, the state passed a law extending its sales tax to a variety of services, "including advertising, legal fees, construction, accounting, pest control and architecture."* Many of the service industries mounted a public relations campaign against the tax and others threatened to stop doing business in the state. This, coupled with normal taxpayer resistance to new taxes, led the legislature and governor to repeal the tax within two months of its going into effect.

* Florida May Repeal New Tax on Services," *Oregonian* (September 20, 1987), p. A20. For a thorough discussion of this unusual incident see Walter Hellerstein, "Florida's Sales Tax on Services," *National Tax Journal* 61 (March 1988), pp. 1–18.

Further, it is likely to exempt much of the consumption of higher income households as well. For this reason, most analysts conclude that the better approach to equity with respect to the sales tax is to offer an income tax credit or direct rebate to low-income households. The net result of such exemptions and exclusions is that it is difficult to make generalizations about the level of tax burden as a percentage of income. However, sales taxes are still widely perceived as being regressive.

The revenue generated per 1% sales tax also differs widely across states because of differences in coverage. In 1980, yields per capita for each percentage of sales tax varied from $31 in Massachusetts and Rhode Island to $141 in Hawaii.[12] Aside from differences in the coverage of food and services, states differ in their ability to "export" the tax. Some states with large amounts of tourism, such as Nevada and Hawaii, would generate a larger amount per capita from a given sales tax. Finally, the average income in the state affects the amount of purchases and the amount of sales tax collected for a given rate.

/// OPTIMAL EXCISE TAXES

Recall that an excise tax creates a deadweight loss when imposed on only one commodity. This deadweight loss is reduced if the tax is made more general. However, even the most general form of the excise tax, the general sales tax with no exemptions, does not eliminate all deadweight losses. A person can escape part of the tax by reducing consumption relative to leisure or by reducing market transactions in favor of home production. However, it has been argued that a set of excise taxes could be devised to minimize the deadweight losses associated with excise taxes or even those associated with income taxes. This set of taxes improves economic efficiency by recognizing the distortions created by having some items exempt from taxation. Further, it draws on the fact that not all items create the same amount of deadweight loss when an excise tax is placed on them.[13]

The problem with any form of the sales tax is that it cannot tax leisure. Hence, the trade-off between leisure and goods is distorted by even the most comprehensive of sales taxes. Recognizing that the sales tax is simply a comprehensive set of excise taxes, some economists have argued that the distortion could be minimized by taxing those goods that contribute to the enjoyment of leisure time relatively more heavily than other goods. Thus, if people tend to drink beer and play tennis during their leisure, a tax system that encourages leisure would also tend to encourage the consumption of beer and tennis rackets. Hence, if beer and tennis rackets are taxed relatively heavily, they will be consumed in lower amounts. This reduced consumption of goods complementary to leisure makes leisure less valuable to the individual and offsets some of the distortion created by the general sales tax system.

Another set of criteria comes from recognizing that the goods with rela-

[12] Due and Mikesell, op. cit., p. 9.
[13] For a discussion of the various views on optimal taxation see Agnar Sandmo, "Optimal Taxation: An Introduction to the Literature," *Journal of Public Economics* 6 (1976), pp. 37–54.

tively inelastic demand have the least deadweight loss associated with an excise tax. Thus, it is argued that since any set of excise taxes is composed of a series of individual excise taxes, it would be possible to minimize the deadweight loss by taxing those goods with inelastic demand relatively more heavily than those goods with elastic demand. In fact, generalized problems requiring the minimization of deadweight loss in using excise taxes conclude that this is correct. In other words, the efficiency of the allocation of resources can be improved by setting excise taxes in relation to the elasticity of demand for the product. Those goods with relatively inelastic demand would be taxed more heavily while those with relatively elastic demand would be taxed more lightly. Unfortunately, this general conclusion seems to place efficiency directly at odds with equity, for it is generally accepted that the goods with the most inelastic demand tend to be consumed relatively more heavily by low income families.

For practical purposes, the taxing of goods associated with leisure activity is more acceptable than is the general setting of tax rates on the basis of elasticity of demand. While such results are appealing in theory and can offer some guidance on practical applications, they suffer from serious administrative and equity drawbacks. The administrative drawback is most easily seen. Imagine a sales tax in which you were faced with a different rate on every good or service you purchased! The complexity and administrative cost of such a system would create costs of their own. And it is by no means clear that the improvement in the allocation of resources in the economy would offset the loss associated with more complexity in administering and enforcing the tax code.

/// ADMINISTRATION AND ENFORCEMENT

General sales taxes create a variety of administration and enforcement issues. These issues are related to the scope of the tax and the liability of collectors of the tax to the jurisdiction for which they are collecting it. When the tax is levied on only some subset of goods and services, someone must keep track of the sales of taxable and tax-exempt goods and services. Further, the state must keep track of those who sell goods and services subject to the tax. Both collection and auditing are more complex when there are many exemptions to a tax. The retailer is left with the necessity of separating the taxable and nontaxable items involved in a sale. The auditor is left with verifying that the breakdown is correct and that the correct amount of tax was collected and then turned over to the taxing jurisdiction.

While the administrative cost of sales taxes seldom goes much above 1% of revenue collected, the compliance costs can be quite high. One study estimated them at almost 4% of the revenue collected from the tax.[14] These

---

[14] Cited in Due and Mikesell, op. cit., p. 325.

administrative costs are probably declining with more computerization of sales, but they are still at least partially absorbed by the retailer.

The issue of tracking taxable sales and collecting the tax due becomes even more of a problem when the taxing jurisdiction is small. If the tax is viewed as a use tax, the jurisdiction should try to collect the tax on purchases made by its residents outside the jurisdiction. Many states do indeed make such collections, but most local jurisdictions find such attempts to be too costly. Hence, a local government is more likely to tax the sale rather than the use of a good or service while the state government is more likely to try to tax both the sale and the use of the good or service.

Enforcement of sales and excise taxes is usually done through audits of those establishments required to collect the tax. Some enforcement issues occur at the federal level, e.g., the interstate smuggling of cigarettes to avoid state taxes; but most enforcement is done by the states. Often sales from outside the jurisdiction are simply ignored, such as those from mail order outside the state. The states are definitely interested in finding a way to tax such transactions, but it is difficult to enforce any such taxes.

Another problem with enforcing sales and excise taxes is the amount of illegal or underground activity. Services by individuals directly to consumers, such as home repairs, would be particularly hard to monitor for sales taxes. Illegal activity also creates obvious problems for tax collection. One interesting variation on the enforcement of excise taxes is the levying of such taxes on illegal drugs. Minnesota and several other states have started levying taxes on marijuana and other drugs (see Box 6-4). Anyone caught with the substance and no tax stamp is subject to fines associated with tax evasion as well as any other penalties.[15]

/// THE VALUE-ADDED TAX

One form of sales tax which has received a lot of attention in the U.S. in the recent past is the value-added tax. A value-added tax is levied on the net sales of a firm, i.e., gross sales minus purchase of inputs from other firms. The value-added tax is widely used in Europe, and generates large amounts of revenue with relatively low rates.[16] In many ways it resembles a uniform sales tax on all goods and services sold for final consumption; however, the various methods of implementing the tax can make it look like other types of broad-based taxes. Before we go into the complications of the tax, let's consider the basic form of the tax and a simple analysis.

Suppose that we start with a turnover tax on all sales of goods and services

---

[15] See Philip M. Dearborn and Robert D. Ebel, "Minnesotans Decide If You Can't Beat Pushers, Tax Them," *Oregonian* (November 28, 1986), p. D17; and "Tax Report," *Wall Street Journal* (December 10, 1986), p. 1.
[16] See Henry J. Aaron, ed., *The Value-Added Tax: Lessons from Europe* (Washington, DC: The Brookings Institution, 1981).

Box 6-4

////// **If You Can't
Beat Them, Tax Them**

The tax on marijuana is simply the latest wrinkle in the taxation of items that some people think others should not consume. Such taxation is called sumptuary taxation. The intent is both to discourage the use of the item and to punish those who insist on continuing its use. We have already mentioned the taxes levied on cigarettes and liquor. Other types of "immoral" behavior, such as gambling, are also subject to large taxes in many places where they are legal. In other places, the government itself sells the good or service and charges a high tax by keeping the price high and absorbing the resulting monopoly profits. Thus, lotteries have become a popular form of revenue raising for states. In principle, there is no reason why the states could not just legalize this form of gambling and place a high tax on tickets. The effect is very similar. Other states reserve for themselves the right to sell some or all alcoholic beverages. The high prices in such states represent a form of taxation of the item. There is some evidence that this "tax" does not all end up in the public treasury since costs would likely be higher in states with no competitive pressure; but the effect of discouraging consumption or punishing it is the same no matter what the reason for the high cost to the consumer.

Many economists believe that taxing pollution would be a far more effective way to control this type of externality than would the current system of regulation. In addition to any improvement in the allocation of resources which would result, this form of controlling pollution would generate revenue for government. The combined appeal of generating revenue and discouraging undesirable behavior would appear to be a strong reason for adopting such taxes; but so far, taxes on pollution are much less popular than lotteries and taxes on specific consumption items.

in the economy. This tax generates a series of distortions in the way in which goods and services are produced. Such a tax compounds as goods or services are processed at various points in the economy.

Consider bread as a simple example. When the farmer grows wheat and sells it to the miller, the farmer must pay a tax on the value of the wheat. When the miller mills the wheat and sells the flour to the baker, the miller must pay a tax on the value of the flour. Finally, when the baker sells the bread to the consumer, the baker pays a tax on the bread. This differs from a retail sales tax in that there are taxes on the intermediate steps. Thus, a company that owns a wheat farm and a mill as well as a bakery would not have to pay taxes on the intermediate sales; this vertically integrated firm would have an advantage over the independently organized set of producers. This advantage comes solely from the way in which the tax is levied and has no relation to a true economic advantage in the form of more efficient production.

The compounding feature of the tax and the incentive for vertical integration are eliminated by allowing each firm credit for the tax paid on its purchased inputs. Hence, it is only taxed on the value that it added to the value of the inputs it purchased. There is no incentive to vertically integrate firms simply for a tax advantage. In this case the tax would be the same for the vertically integrated firm and for the baker who purchased inputs from other merchants. Thus, the value-added tax is clearly superior to the cascading turnover tax. It is very similar to a general sales tax. The general sales tax is levied only at the point of final sale; but there is no deduction for the taxes paid on inputs.

The method of implementing such a tax can best be described by a simple example. Let us go back to our baker. The baker must have an oven, workers, and ingredients to make the final product. The ingredients are clearly purchased inputs and the value of these inputs can be subtracted in determining the amount of value-added tax due. The tax due on them was paid when these inputs were sold to the baker, and it is only by allowing their cost to be deducted that it is possible to avoid double taxation. Just as clearly, the workers have not been produced by some other firm and, hence, there has been no value-added tax paid on their services. If we ignore the oven for the moment, we see the value-added tax as equivalent to a sales tax. The tax is levied on the bread when it is sold, but credit is granted for all taxes paid on inputs to that point, so there is no double taxation. This would be equivalent to taxing the bread at the full rate and not taxing any of the inputs.

Because it is so similar to a sales tax, the value-added tax is subject to many of the same problems and objections. For example, because it is largely a tax on consumption, many people worry that it has a regressive incidence. In practice, European countries that use the tax tend to use differential rates or outright exemptions in order to make it a more progressive tax. This obviously creates some administrative, compliance, and enforcement costs.[17]

Differences do exist between the value-added tax and the sales tax. For example, the treatment of the oven, which we skipped over above, becomes an important issue in influencing capital formation. Clearly this is a purchased input used in the production of bread. However, the oven is not entirely used up when the loaf of bread is baked. So how much of the cost of the oven should be allowed against the sale price of each loaf of bread? If the baker gets credit for the tax paid in the year the oven is purchased, there would be more of an incentive for using capital goods than would be the case when the oven must be depreciated over time or if no credit for the tax paid is allowed at all.

---

[17] Ibid., pp. 9–12.

The incentives for capital formation are just one of the issues that arise in considering this tax. Other issues include the use of the tax as a tool for international trade, the interaction with the general sales tax at the state level, and, since the tax is usually discussed as a replacement for the corporate income tax, the different effects of the corporate tax versus a value-added tax. So far, only one state in the U.S. has experimented with this tax and that was as a replacement for a state corporate income tax.

The international trade issue is tied to the replacement of the corporate income tax with a value-added tax. A value-added tax can be rebated to the producer of goods sold outside a country's boundaries. A corporate income tax cannot be rebated in such a way since it is not as clearly tied to the specific goods. Thus, most European countries rebate this tax to exporters and impose the tax on all imports. Some people argue that this gives those countries an advantage in world markets. Many economists dismiss this argument. They point out that the balance of trade between countries is determined by a wide variety of factors and that relative taxes and subsidies should not affect the total volume of trade between countries. Rather, the exchange rates between the two countries would adjust to offset any net subsidy. Despite the logic of this argument, the trade issue is considered to be an important factor in practical discussions of the value-added tax.

Even with the trade arguments in favor of this tax, it is viewed as unlikely for the United States to adopt such a tax in the near future. The major arguments against it at the national level are that it would preempt state value-added taxes and make the federal government compete with states in the sales tax area. Further, there are differences in the incidence and economic effects between a value-added tax and a corporate income tax.

There is moderate agreement that at least some of the incidence of the corporate income tax is on suppliers of investment funds and that this segment of the tax has a progressive incidence. However, it is widely believed that the value-added tax would be largely passed on to consumers and hence would be somewhat regressive in incidence. Finally, a switch from a corporate income tax to a value-added tax would significantly shift tax burdens among industries and would alter the relative prices of different goods and services under almost any shifting assumptions. The corporate income tax is nominally levied in proportion to the level of prosperity of a firm. Thus, less prosperous firms receive a respite from the tax collector. This would not happen with a value-added tax. Each firm pays, no matter what its situation. Even if the tax is largely shifted to others, this feature strikes many as being undesirable.

The similarity of the value-added tax and the general sales tax also makes the tax somewhat unpopular at the state level. Since such a large percentage of the states levy sales taxes, it would seem that a value-added tax would simply be an indirect way to raise the sales tax rate. Further, if the value-added tax is levied by the federal government, it would be in competition with the states for this tax base. This looks plausible on the surface; however, it does depend on how the tax is implemented and how the base is defined.

Thus, it does not seem probable that the value-added tax will be widely adopted in the United States. Nevertheless, its widespread use in Europe and its high revenue potential keep it under discussion.

/// SUMMARY

A single excise tax on one good will be partly shifted to parties other than the nominal taxpayer. This shifting of taxes is likely to be true of all taxes. Thus, it is important to study the incidence of a tax. Because of the actions that lead to shifting, we find that taxes have an associated efficiency loss. This is due to the distortion of relative prices caused by the tax. When the tax base is broadened the efficiency loss is likely to be reduced. Nevertheless, no one tax scheme is likely to eliminate all the efficiency problems.

The broadening of the excise base to include all retail sales generates large amounts of additional revenue. However, most sales taxes have significant exemptions or exclusions. Some items, like services, are excluded because of the perception that they would be difficult to tax. Others, like food for home consumption, are excluded because their consumption tends to go up by much less than income as income goes up. The exemption of services tends to make the tax more regressive while the exemption of "necessities" tends to make it more progressive.

It is possible to improve the efficiency of sales taxes by taxing different items at different rates. One approach looks to minimize the deadweight loss associated with specific excise taxes by taxing goods with relatively more inelastic demand more heavily. This tends to run counter to equity considerations since goods with very inelastic demands tend to be consumed relatively heavily by lower income groups. Thus, we are more likely to find low rather than high tax rates on such goods. Another approach is to try to tax goods that are complementary to untaxed goods more heavily. This approach is more acceptable on equity grounds, but it is likely to have high administrative costs. In practice, equity and administrative issues seem to be more important determinants of differences in tax rates and coverage than are efficiency concerns.

Value-added taxes are common in Europe but not in the United States. Such taxes are levied at each stage of production but allow for deductions of taxes paid in earlier stages. Ultimately the tax is similar to a sales tax although treatment of depreciation can alter this similarity somewhat. The value-added tax is under consideration in the U.S. because of its high revenue potential, but it is not likely to be enacted at the federal level. There is some possibility that states will make more use of such a tax, but at the state level it

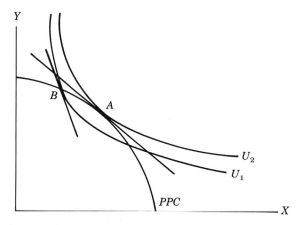

Figure 6-6 / **Excise Tax Distortion**

would likely replace some form of business tax. The substitution of a business tax with a tax widely known as a consumption tax is generally politically unpopular, so it appears unlikely that many states would seriously consider such a tax.

Appendix   //////

Excise Tax Distortion

The easiest way to show the difference between a single excise tax and a general sales tax is through the use of a production possibility curve. Figure 6-6 shows such a curve for goods X and Y. Assume that all consumers are identical so that we can draw a set of indifference curves. The efficient level of output is determined by the tangency of the indifference curves and the production possibility curve. In an unconstrained competitive economy, a price ratio arises such that maximizing profits subject to production constraints results in exactly the efficient level of output. Further, maximizing satisfaction for consumers subject to their income constraints results in their choosing to consume this level of output. This is illustrated by the price line drawn tangent to each curve at their point of tangency with each other. This is point A in the figure, representing an efficient allocation of resources.

The effect of an excise tax is to alter the ratio of prices between the goods in the economy. The economy as a whole, however, is still constrained by the production possibility curve. We assume that the government simply uses tax proceeds to purchase some amount of each good and give a share to each consumer. Thus, the only effect of the tax is the effect on relative prices. Suppose the tax is on good X. This causes the relative price of good X to rise and the budget line facing consumers to become steeper. Thus, the tangency with indifference curves occurs to the left of point A. However, at the new tangency there is still production efficiency. The tangency must occur on the production possibility curve. This is illustrated by point B. This new tangency is at a lower indifference curve than the one at point A. Hence, the economy is worse off.

Next consider a tax on good Y that exactly restores the original price ratio. Again, production efficiency requires that output be on the production possibility frontier, and the equilibrium is back at point A. Thus, the general excise tax in this case would have no efficiency cost. The problem with this illustration is that it does not take into account the possibility of other, untaxed goods. If we were to treat X as all goods that could be taxed and Y as all goods that could not be taxed, we see that we are back at point B. The general sales tax can reduce distortions between taxed goods, but it cannot remove the distortions between goods that are taxed and those that are not.

Chapter 7 /////

Analysis of Personal Income Taxation

Taxation of personal income generates large amounts of revenue in the United States, and personal income is considered a very desirable tax base because it grows with the economy. Both increases in economic growth and increases associated with inflation show up rapidly in income. Thus, tax collections are automatically adjusted for both real growth and price level changes. Further, if the tax is progressive, the additions to income tend to be taxed at higher rates. Thus, tax collections often rise more rapidly than the economy grows. Alternatively, tax collections tend to decline in business downturns. At the federal level, this is often considered an advantage because it creates an automatic offset to changes in the economy, but it creates problems for state and local governments, especially since most have balanced budget requirements.

Income taxes are usually progressive, but they can be proportional or regressive as well. The taxes are characterized by differences in what is defined as income as well as by differences in the rate structure. Labor earnings are often treated differently from returns on savings and investments. Further, the definition of income can be quite complex. Administrative feasibility and equity are two of the major reasons to carefully define income; but a variety of other issues arise in specifying income and the taxes on it.

We devote this chapter to a consideration of the issues of incidence and efficiency which arise with taxes on personal income; we discuss some real tax systems in the next chapter.

/// TYPES OF PERSONAL INCOME TAXES

Personal income taxes are generally categorized as taxes on earned income or comprehensive income taxes. An earned income tax is one on labor earnings. The Social Security tax is an earned income tax, as are most of the income taxes levied by local governments. A comprehensive income tax is one on both labor and nonlabor income. Nonlabor income is frequently referred to as unearned income; its major component is the returns to savings and investments. The federal personal income tax and most state income taxes are comprehensive income taxes.

Personal income taxes are also classified by whether they are proportional taxes on all earnings or progressive taxes in which those who earn more face a higher tax rate on their additional earnings than those who earn less. The federal personal income tax and many of the state income taxes have progressive rate structures.[1] This is usually achieved by exempting some amount of income from any taxation and then having all increments to income taxed at higher and higher rates. Note that it is only the increments to income that are taxed at the higher rates. This prevents the possibility that some income would actually be taxed at rates above 100%.

For example, in 1987 Louisiana had a tax rate of 2% on taxable income up to $10,000; 4% on taxable income above $10,000 and up to $50,000; and 6% on taxable income above $50,000.[2] Thus, a taxable income of $20,000 would be subject to a tax of $600: $200 on the first $10,000 and $400 on the remaining $10,000. If the rate were to change on all income as total income increased, then the tax on some small increments would be very high. Suppose that Louisiana had the tax jump on all income rather than just on the increments to income. Then a person faced with income going from $9,990 to $10,010 would have taxes increase from $199.80 to $401.40. The tax increase would more than offset the income increase. Hence, the $20 income increment would be taxed at 1000%, and a person earning $9,990 would have more after-tax income than a person earning $10,010. This result is clearly undesirable. Obviously it would create a disincentive to earn that additional income. While no tax code acts in this manner, many people still seem to think that the federal code does. They worry about the effects of being in a higher tax bracket. In fact, the only effect of being in a higher tax bracket is that each *additional* dollar is taxed at a higher rate.

The confusion about the effect of tax brackets is associated with the difference between the marginal tax rate and the average tax rate. The average tax rate is determined by dividing taxes paid by total income; the marginal tax rate is determined by the amount that taxes increase when income increases by a small amount. Effectively, it is the tax rate on the last dollar earned. Our example yields an average tax rate of 3% compared to a marginal tax rate of 4% for a person with $20,000 of taxable income. In progressive tax structures, the marginal rate is often much higher than the

[1] Many states with progressive structures achieve their highest rates at fairly low levels of income. Thus, the taxes are not really very progressive. See Clara Penniman, *State Income Taxation* (Baltimore, MD: Johns Hopkins University Press, 1980), pp. 32–43.

[2] Advisory Commission on Intergovernmental Relations, *Significant Features of Fiscal Federalism, 1988 Edition* (Washington, DC: 1987 and 1988), Table 16.

average rate. This insures that those with more income pay a larger percentage of their income in taxes, but it also has some efficiency problems, as will be shown shortly.

While states and some cities also levy progressive, comprehensive income taxes, most local governments rely on a proportional tax on earned income if they use an income tax. Further, the Social Security tax is largely a proportional tax on earned income. Local wage taxes are usually set at a fixed percentage of all earned income. The Social Security tax is a fixed percentage of earned income in most forms of employment, but it is zero for income earned above a certain amount. This ceiling amount varies from year to year. It was set at $43,800 in 1987, and income earned above that amount was not subject to additional Social Security taxes. Hence, viewed solely as a tax, the Social Security tax is a regressive tax. The tax would fall as a percentage of income for incomes above the ceiling since the fixed minimum tax would be divided by a larger income.[3]

Taxes on Earned Income: Incidence

One of the most controversial issues with respect to a tax on labor income is whether or not it induces people to work less. If we think about the tax in the same way we modeled an excise tax, we could draw a market diagram for labor services, such as Figure 7-1. This figure shows a market clearing amount of labor services, L_1, and a market clearing wage, W_1, in the absence of any tax. Because the workers are the suppliers in this market, a tax on the workers causes the supply curve to shift upward. Note that in the diagram the new supply curve S_2 has a steeper slope than the original supply curve. It is steeper because the tax on wages is an ad valorem tax rather than a per unit tax. Hence, the difference between the original supply curve and the new supply curve is larger for higher wages because the tax is also higher. Imposing the tax would be expected to generate a new equilibrium at a wage of W_2 and a quantity of services L_2. The worker would get W_3 as a net after-tax wage.

Unfortunately, this analysis does not work as well for the labor market as it does for most goods and services. The problem is that the analysis ignores the income effect of a change in price. As we stated earlier, ignoring the income effect is acceptable for most markets since people spend relatively little of their income on most specific goods and services. However, the income effect of a change in the wage rate can be substantial and we cannot ignore it in this case. In fact, the income effect can be so large that it causes people to work more when the tax is levied rather than work less. We will analyze this shortly, but intuitively we can think about people trying to maintain their standard of living and still pay the tax. If they are unwilling or unable to cut their other consumption, then the only way to pay for the tax is to earn more rather than less.

---

[3] See Chapter 16 on transfers for a more complete discussion of the Social Security system.

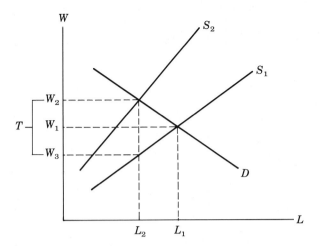

Figure 7-1 / Wage Tax

If the tax results in a labor shift such as that shown in Figure 7-1, the incidence of the tax is distributed as shown by the diagram. The workers receive a lower after-tax wage of W_3 and the difference of this from W_1 is a measure of the incidence of the tax on workers. Alternatively, employers will be paying more for labor by the amount of $W_2 - W_1$. This amount could be further shifted to customers, and so on. If workers choose to work more when their after-tax wage decreases, it is possible that the wage before taxes would decline as well. Workers could conceivably bear more than the full burden of the tax. They would have lower market wages and would have to pay the tax from these lower wages. However, this result appears very unlikely.

Taxes appear to have little effect on the hours worked by an individual. Most studies find the supply curve of labor to be positively sloped, but fairly inelastic.[4] Hence, it is expected that workers bear most of the burden of the earned-income portion of the federal income tax. However, the supply curve of labor within small geographic areas tends to be much more elastic. It is more likely that the local wage tax will be shifted at least partly. The exact incidence of such taxes becomes very hard to determine. Viewed strictly as a tax, a local wage tax makes the region less attractive relative to other areas. Ultimately, this lowers the returns to immobile resources, mostly land. However, it would not be correct to treat such taxes without considering the alternatives. The use of a local income tax allows either higher spending by the local government or a reduction of other taxes. Depending on how the money is spent and which other taxes would have been raised, the incentives to avoid

---

[4] Jerry Hausman, "Labor Supply," in Henry J. Aaron and Joseph A. Pechman, eds., *How Taxes Affect Economic Behavior* (Washington, DC: Brookings, 1981), pp. 27–83, also concludes that hours worked are not affected much by taxes, but his results indicate that the efficiency losses from a progressive tax system may be quite high.

working in the jurisdiction may be partially offset. Further, many people will be able to deduct the local tax when figuring their federal or state taxes; hence, part of the cost will be shifted to some other level of government rather than being paid by the individual. The few empirical studies done of local income taxes seem to confirm that the supply of labor tends to be fairly elastic and that the tax results in a decrease in employment within the jurisdiction.[5]

Taxes on Earned Income: Efficiency

To analyze the efficiency effects of taxes on labor income we must model the choice of how much to work. Each person is viewed as having a certain amount of time that can be devoted to either leisure or to generating market income. Further, we can envision the person's indifference map between money income and leisure. The more time the person spends working, the less time is available for leisure activities, but the indifference curves show us the rate at which the person is willing to trade off such leisure for income.

This is illustrated in Figure 7-2. Each indifference curve shows the rate at which a person is willing to give up leisure to gain income and become neither better nor worse off. The higher indifference curves represent higher levels of satisfaction for the person. The nonlabor income is given by the amount NL_0 and the amount of time the person has available is given by L_{max}. If no market work is performed, the nonlabor income and the maximum amount of leisure are consumed. However, the person has the option of giving up some leisure for money income by working. The trade-off is given by the budget line shown in

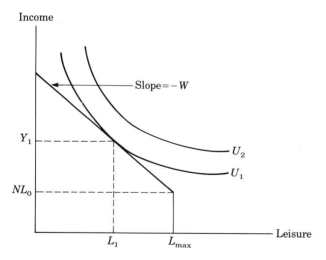

Figure 7-2 / Leisure or Income Choice

[5] For example, see Ronald E. Grieson, "Theoretical Analysis and Empirical Measurements of the Effects of the Philadelphia Income Tax," *Journal of Urban Economics* 8 (July 1980), pp. 123–137.

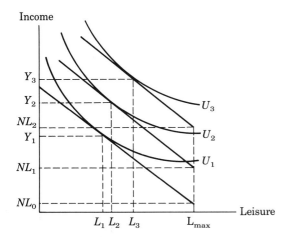

Figure 7-3 / Effect of Nonlabor Income on Hours Worked

the figure. A higher wage creates a steeper line since the slope is given by $-W$, where W is the hourly wage the person could earn by working. The utility maximizing point is given by the tangency of the budget line and the indifference curve. Thus, in the figure the person would choose to work $L_{max} - L_1$ hours and earn $Y_1 - NL_0$ in wages to yield Y_1 in total income and L_1 in leisure. At higher or lower wages the person's choices would be different.

Leisure is usually considered to be what economists call a "normal good," something whose consumption increases as income increases. Thus if we were to raise the initial income from nonlabor sources we would expect the person to choose to work less. This is illustrated in Figure 7-3. Higher levels of nonlabor income are represented by NL_1 and NL_2. Holding the market wage fixed, the person chooses to work less as nonlabor income increases and consumes L_2 and L_3 of leisure, respectively.

Higher wages have two opposing effects on a person's consumption of leisure. The first effect is as mentioned above. A higher wage leads to higher income and this tends to increase the consumption of leisure time. However, the wage increase also means that the person is giving up more in terms of money income when leisure is consumed. Economists say that the opportunity cost of leisure has increased. Since more money income must be given up for each additional hour of leisure, there is a tendency to consume less leisure. We normally expect that the wage effect dominates the income effect and that people tend to work more as wages rise; but this is certainly not a foregone conclusion. In particular, if a person must make an investment in education in order to get the higher wages, the likely effect is an increase in hours worked (see Box 7-1).

Proportional Wage Tax   The simplest type of income tax to analyze is a proportional tax on money wages. The analysis of the labor market indicates

Box 7-1

////// Investment and Earnings

One issue that arises in the context of the labor-leisure trade-off is the treatment of investments in earnings ability. One of the largest costs of an education is the earnings that the person foregoes while in school. In principle the person could have worked and taken the earnings and invested them. This plus any out-of-pocket expenses create an investment pool, which can be viewed as generating nonlabor income. In Figure 1 we see the two possibilities for a person just indifferent between going to school and going to work. If he or she goes to school, investment income is the lower NL_1, but the higher wage allows the person to achieve total income Y_1. Not going to school produces nonlabor income of NL_2, which is higher, but total income is only Y_2.

Before you conclude that the person is better off with the education, remember that both situations are on the same indifference curve. The person feels that the higher leisure in the no education case just offsets the higher earnings in the education case. However, in the education case, the person works more. This is because the problem has been set up so as to remove any income effect on the demand for leisure. This shows that higher wages, all else equal, lead to more work effort.

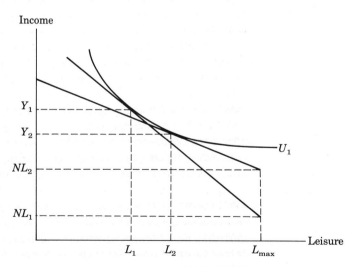

Figure 1 / Education Investment and Hours Worked

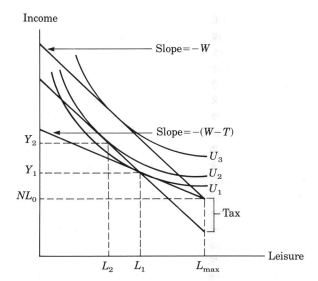

Figure 7-4 / Proportional Wage Tax

that such a tax may be shifted if imposed on labor earnings; but we analyze it as if no shifting takes place. Thus, we can derive the supply response to the tax, and this could be incorporated into a market analysis to determine the full effect. In addition, we have already noted that empirical studies find that workers are likely to bear most of the burden of the tax. The effect of such a tax is to reduce the effective wage rate by the amount of the tax. Using the diagram in Figure 7-4 we can show that the income tax creates an inefficiency as compared to the same revenue generated through a lump-sum tax. A lump-sum tax is defined as an obligation set in advance, which cannot be changed by the actions of the individual. Obviously, a wage tax would not meet that criterion because the person affects the tax by the amount of time worked. In Figure 7-4 we see the initial equilibrium given the wage rate W. The wage is then reduced by the amount of the tax. The new equilibrium is given by the tangency of the lower wage line and an indifference curve.

The higher efficiency of a lump-sum tax can be seen by comparing the revenue collected and the level of satisfaction achieved by the individual in the two cases. The revenue received by the government in the wage tax case is given by the difference between the original budget line and the after-tax wage line at equilibrium. The original budget line shows the amount of wages actually earned by the worker. The new budget line shows the amount the worker gets to keep. The difference must be the revenue to the government. Now suppose the government chooses to levy a lump-sum tax equal to this amount. The new budget line goes through the budget line with the tax at the point of equilibrium, but it is parallel to the original budget line. As can be seen in the figure, this budget line is tangent to a higher indifference curve.

Thus, the government collects the same amount of revenue, but the individual is better off with the lump-sum tax.

One interesting point of this analysis is that the worker may actually work more hours under the tax on earned income and still be working too little. Remember that there is an income effect associated with the amount of leisure chosen. To the extent that an income tax lowers a person's net income, the income effect would lead that person to work longer hours. This income effect could offset the substitution effect toward leisure associated with the tax. Nevertheless, the person would be working too little compared with a neutral tax. Point A in Figure 7-5 shows the income-leisure combination the person would choose if there were no tax. The move to point B associated with the income tax actually increases the number of hours worked.

The person is working more to offset part of the reduction in money income. However, at this lower standard of living, the person would work even more if allowed to keep the entire amount of marginal earnings. Thus, it is not sufficient to look at the number of hours worked in trying to decide whether a given tax affects economic efficiency. In particular, increases in taxes in the short run are not likely to cause people to reduce their number of hours worked. Many have relatively fixed expenses and would find it hard to adjust their living pattern in a short period of time. This, coupled with the offsetting effects of lower net income and lower net returns to working, makes it unlikely that significant reductions will occur in actual hours worked. Nevertheless this is a reduction from what people would work if income were lowered by this amount in a lump sum and the workers could keep all their additional earnings.

Essentially, the individual would have chosen to work even more hours because of the reduction in income, but the deterrent of the tax prevented this

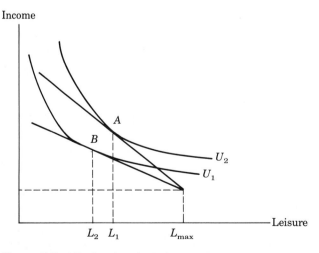

Figure 7-5 / Reduction in Leisure with a Wage Tax

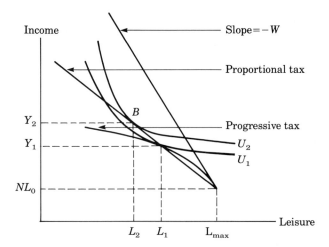

Figure 7-6 / **Progressive versus Proportional Wage Tax**

from happening. Since the wage represents the value of the additional output, which would be created if the person worked one more hour, we see that this person values the additional hour of leisure less than the additional value of output. However, the distortion created by the tax prevents this transaction from taking place. Hence, the economy as a whole gives up the more valuable output in exchange for the less valuable leisure. This is true even if the person is now working more than before the tax. It is important to keep in mind the income effect of the tax. Because of the substantial reduction in income the person would have chosen to increase work hours even more if the tax were not also creating a distortion. This is why we cannot rely on simple analyses of whether people work less or not in evaluating the efficiency of income taxes.

Progressive Wage Tax   With a progressive wage tax, the tax increases in rate as income increases. This is shown in Figure 7-6. The effect of the progressive tax is to cause the budget line to curve as the tax rate increases. The slope of the after-tax budget line shows the marginal benefit of working one more hour; this marginal benefit declines with additional hours worked because the tax rate increases. In practice, this budget line would be composed of discrete segments corresponding to the effective range of specific marginal tax rates; but the continuously increasing marginal tax rate is the most general presentation.

The progressive tax generates an equilibrium at a point of tangency between the after-tax budget line and the indifference curves. The difference between the original budget line and the new line again represents the amount of revenue collected for the government. It is now possible to see that even the proportional wage tax is clearly superior to this tax in terms of the efficiency of the tax. It is possible to find a proportional wage tax that generates a budget line that cuts through the point of tangency for the progressive tax. This new budget line is tangent to a higher indifference curve to the left of the intersection. This is shown as point *B* in Figure 7-6. At this point the person works more but has a higher income. The person is clearly better off by being on a higher indifference curve, and the government gets a higher level of tax revenue than would be collected with the progressive tax structure.

From the efficiency perspective there is a clear ranking of the types of taxes on earned income. The progressive tax generates the lowest level of consumer satisfaction for a given amount of government revenue. The proportional tax generates a higher level of satisfaction, but it is still below what could be achieved with a lump-sum tax. Essentially, the higher the marginal rate of taxation the individual faces, the lower the incentive to work additional hours; and for a given amount of revenue raised, the progressive tax has a higher marginal rate than a proportional tax, while both have a higher marginal rate than a lump-sum tax. All but the lump-sum tax create a difference between what a worker produces by working an additional hour and the increment to income that is received. This difference leads to the efficiency loss.

Since the lump-sum tax is clearly superior to the proportional and progressive wage taxes in terms of efficiency, it is worthwhile to consider why we do not see such taxes in practice. The major reason is equity.

The taxes we considered were designed to raise the same amount of revenue from the same person. Any realistic lump-sum taxing system would not be able to generate the same tax distribution as a proportional or progressive tax system. The tax would have to be based on something other than a person's behavior or wealth. Simply charging everyone the same amount of tax either would not generate much revenue or would be a major burden on a large part of the population. Most equity considerations suggest that those with greater ability to pay should pay more in taxes. Yet any attempt to incorporate this concern means abandoning the lump-sum tax. Nevertheless, we continue to make reference to such a tax as an optimal point in terms of efficiency.

Taxes on Nonlabor Income: Efficiency

People receive nonlabor income mostly by saving and investing. The alternative to saving and investing is to use the money for current consumption or to work less. An analysis similar to the one we did for the labor-leisure choice could be done for the saving versus current consumption choice. The results are the same. Progressive taxes on the returns to savings lead to too little savings from an efficiency perspective. Proportional taxes have less of an efficiency loss for a given amount of revenue raised, but there is still some efficiency loss. Only lump-sum taxes remove all efficiency losses.

Despite the efficiency losses and the incentive to save less, there may be an increase in savings associated with a tax if people decide that they have to save more because of the reduction in the after-tax pool of savings in the future.

Nevertheless, reductions in savings appear to be the more likely outcome. This is because the income effect of the tax is likely to lower the amount of savings, so the income and substitution effects would both be working in the same direction; lower income would reduce the ability to save for the future and a lower after-tax return on savings would make it appear less attractive. (See the appendix to this chapter for a detailed discussion.)

Another way of looking at the savings issue is to consider savings as a payment for future consumption. Taxes on the return to savings are the same as taxes on future consumption. Thus, the price of future consumption increases. This leads to a reduction in the quantity of future consumption; but total expenditure on future consumption may increase if the demand for future consumption is inelastic. Since expenditure on future consumption is the amount of savings, savings could increase if the return to savings is taxed.

The effect of taxes on the amount of savings is even more complex than this analysis indicates. We have ignored the determination of retirement. One effect of lower returns to savings may be to delay retirement. Thus, yearly savings may decline while lifetime savings increase. We return to some of these issues shortly. However, it is important to understand that the effect of a tax on level of work or level of savings is not necessarily the same thing as its effect on efficiency. More work or savings is not necessarily a good thing. The problem is to find the level of work where the additional production just offsets the loss in value of leisure or where the additional value of savings just offsets the loss in current consumption. Alternatively, even when the response to taxation is an increase in work or savings, the efficient response to higher taxes may be even more of an increase in work or savings than the tax actually induces.

Taxes on Nonlabor Income: Incidence

Most people believe that a tax on nonlabor income is primarily paid by the owners of savings and investments. Since the ownership of savings and investments is a form of wealth, the incidence of such taxes are larger on the relatively wealthy if they are not shifted. This would make such a tax relatively progressive in incidence.

Most studies of savings behavior conclude that the supply of savings by individuals is relatively insensitive to the rate of return on savings. Thus, the supply is fairly inelastic. If this is the case, then the tax would be borne by the owners of wealth. This is not by any means an unchallenged conclusion. Some researchers argue that various forms of taxation have significantly reduced the amount of savings in the United States, and that this reduction has lowered the economy's rate of growth.[6] Hence, these people favor changes in the tax system which would be more favorable to savings.

---

[6] A summary of some of the literature on the effect of taxes on saving can be found in George M. von Furstenberg, "Saving," in Aaron and Pechman, op. cit., pp. 327–402.

The basic conflict with respect to taxation of savings is that the tax on "unearned" income is believed to have a very progressive incidence and it is also believed to deter savings. The trade-off between the taxation of wealthier individuals and the encouragement of savings is one that seems to generate more than the usual amount of controversy. One reason for this controversy is widespread disagreement about both the incidence of the tax and its effect on savings.

To the extent that savings are reduced in response to the income tax, the lower capital stock could lead to lower wages and higher consumer prices. Thus, the tax would be at least partially shifted to consumers and labor. In addition, the rate of investment is likely to affect the rate of growth of the economy, so the reduced capital formation might lead to lower income for everyone in the future.

The changes in behavior associated with the use of an income tax can lead to important efficiency losses as compared with a lump-sum tax; however, these losses are only part of the efficiency cost of such taxes. There are major distortions associated with the definition of taxable income.

/// IDENTIFYING INCOME

It seems easy to define income. Everyone knows what it is, and extensive records are kept of people's earnings. Yet the usual definitions create problems for economic analysis because they are not representative of the concept. For example, suppose that two jobs each pay an equal hourly wage but that one requires the worker to purchase special clothing and expensive tools. Would you consider the equal wages as representing equal income? What if one job offers extensive fringe benefits while the other has none? Suppose that two families have identical money income but that one owns its own home while the other must pay rent. Do they have the same income? These and other problems arise when we have to define income in an economic analysis.

The economist sees income as a measure of consumption or potential ability to consume. Hence, the economic definition of income focuses on the actual amounts of consumption and the changes in ability to consume in the future. The ability to consume in the future is measured by the value of assets owned by an individual or family. Thus, in principle a person's income would be found by adding the value of consumption and the net change in asset value over a given time period. This total represents income during that time period, while the net value of assets is a measure of wealth. Another way to say this is that income represents consumption plus net changes in wealth. In practice, we settle on much less theoretically correct measures of income.

Measuring Income

Leisure or Nonmarket Work   Many issues arise in terms of measuring income. Consider two people with the same wage opportunities and the same nonlabor income; however, one has a much greater taste for leisure than the other. For any given wage rate, the second person maximizes utility by choosing to work less than the first person. Each has the same opportunity, yet one has a higher money income than the other. This is offset by more hours of work. Should they be treated as having the same income or not? On a practical level, they are of course treated as being different; but from an economic perspective they are the same. The fact that one consumes in the form of leisure while the other consumes in the form of market goods and services does not change their similarity.

A more practical problem arises when work is done in a manner that does not generate market income. For example, farmers who grow food for home consumption have a form of income from that consumption. Yet this income is not taxed. However, if the food is sold on the market instead of being consumed directly, measured income increases. Similar issues arise for many types of activity that are not compensated through the market. For example, the person who does repairs around the home rather than hire an outside contractor is implicitly generating income. The same is true of people who trade services. For instance, if an automobile mechanic took care of a barber's car in exchange for haircuts, there would be no market income for either.

Consumer Durables   Other problems arise when income comes from the use of a consumer durable good. Consumer durables are defined as relatively long-lived articles of consumption. Because they provide service over a long time period, they have some aspects of an investment as well as some consumption aspects.

A house is the major form of consumer durable; but automobiles, furniture, even clothing can generate benefits over long periods of time. This is important because the return to such investments should properly be treated as income. However, the difficulty in measuring such returns means that this form of income usually is not counted. Yet it is clear that if we have two identical families, except that one owns a very nice house while the other does not, the family with the house will have a higher level of consumption each year. The income from consumer durables is called imputed income. It is essentially the income a person would have to pay him or herself to use the consumer durable if it were being offered for rent on the open market. Thus, if you live in a house that could be rented for $10,000 per year net of expenses, then you would have an imputed rent of $10,000 per year from the house. This imputed rent is included in the tax base for some countries, such as Switzerland, but it is not calculated in the United States.

In-Kind Income   A similar problem arises when some people receive goods and services from others rather than money income. These goods and services make the recipient better off, yet if we only measure money income they are not counted. Consider a person whose employer provides free housing. This person is clearly better off than an employee receiving the same money wages but not the housing. While housing is a relatively rare fringe benefit and would be subject to taxation in many circumstances, medical insurance is a common tax-exempt fringe benefit. Many other items are provided by some firms but not others.

The issue of in-kind benefits also arises when considering the actions of the government. It provides various goods and services to large segments of the population. These goods and services make people better off; but they may not show up as income to the recipient. Thus, many of the antipoverty programs appear to have had little effect on the number of people in poverty. This is because they provide direct consumption items rather than money income to the recipients, and the number of people in poverty is determined by the money income that people have.[7] Similarly, when income is calculated to determine taxes and to determine the progressivity of the tax system, the consumption value of these items is not generally included.

The exact value of these in-kind benefits is very hard to determine. Since the recipient often has no choice about the form or amount of benefit, it may be valued at much less than the cost of provision. For example, it may cost the government $500 per month to provide housing for a poor family; but that family may feel that they would be better off if they had $400 per month in cash income and had to find their own housing. Similarly, an employee may value the health benefits provided by his or her employer at much less than the cost of providing them. Thus, in many cases it is difficult to determine the income represented by in-kind transfers.

Numerous other issues arise in terms of what constitutes income and what does not. For example, when a person receives a monetary gift from someone else, our definition of income would treat it as income for the recipient and a reduction of income for the giver. The federal tax code, however, treats it as a gift by the giver and then subjects it to potential gift or estate taxes for the giver. The recipient is not treated as having any additional tax liability.

Adjusting Income

Cost of Generating Income   Another important issue in determining income for tax purposes is the cost of generating income. If you need special tools in order to do your job, the cost of those tools is not part of your consumption. Thus, according to our definition of income, the amount spent on such tools should be deducted from income. If it were not deducted, the expenditure would show as an item of consumption.

A problem arises in determining exactly what is an expenditure required for a job and what is simply consumption occurring at the workplace. The three-martini lunch is a classic issue in terms of consumption versus work. Many business executives take others out to lunch or simply charge their own

---

[7] For a discussion of some of these issues, see Morton Paglin, "Poverty in the United States: A Reevaluation," *Policy Review* (Spring 1979), pp. 7–24.

lunches as a business expense. They argue that they are conducting business during these meals. Even when legitimate business is being conducted, it would appear that some part of the expense should count as consumption for the person eating the meal. Yet the tax code would be inordinately complex if it tried to make such distinctions as the percent of a meal that goes for business and the percent that could count as an expense of generating income. The 1986 tax reform reached a compromise by allowing only 80% of such expenses to be deducted in computing taxable income.

Some distinctions become even more difficult when the item is used both for consumption and to earn income. For example, a car might be used partly for personal matters and partly for business. It is not clear how the allocation should be made between business expenses and consumption. Should the person be allowed to deduct the full fixed costs as part of the business portion or should this be treated as part of the consumption? The tax code allows this to be separated on the percentage of usage, but this increases the record-keeping and enforcement costs of the tax and may still miscount income.

Depreciation   Not all work-related items will be used up within one year. Many have useful lives that extend for long periods. Allowing a person to deduct the full cost of such equipment in the year of purchase tends to understate income that year. Thus, taxes for that year are reduced, and postponing taxes is a benefit even if the same amount is eventually paid. Instead, such items should be treated as declining in value each year, and this reduction in value, or depreciation, should be allowed as a deduction for the cost of earning income each year. However, most assets do not have a readily determined market value at each point in time. Long-lived assets tend to be kept for many years. Hence, the change in value each year is not accurately known.

In practice, capital assets can be thought of as having a certain useful life. At the end of that time they have either lost all value or have some small scrap or resale value. If the asset declines in value in equal increments each year, the owner could calculate the expected total decline in value and divide by the number of years of use the asset has. This number would represent the annual depreciation of the asset, and this is the simplest type of adjustment to make. There are many different ways to calculate depreciation in practice. Some of them tend to understate the true loss in value, but most tend to overstate the true loss in value to the owner of the asset.

Depreciation is only allowed on goods used to produce income. Hence, it is not allowed on goods that produce only imputed income. This reduces the tax advantage of consumer durables somewhat, but does not fully offset the fact that the imputed rent is not taxed.

Capital Gains   Some items held for the purpose of producing income may have unexpected increases or decreases in value. Thus, if they are sold before they wear out, the taxpayer may achieve a windfall gain or loss. The same thing can happen with respect to assets held as part of a savings or investment plan. In addition to paying dividends, or interest, or rent, the market price of the asset may go up or down in response to economic conditions. This change in market value generates a windfall type of gain or loss. These changes in value are known as capital gains or capital losses. In principle, they should be treated as part of a person's income, either positive or negative. However, in practice, the treatment has been far from uniform.[8]

First, the changes in value of assets should be calculated each year for all assets and treated as part of income in that year. However, for many assets this would create substantial problems since there is no readily determined market price. Further, the tax due on the appreciation of a capital asset may create liquidity problems for its owner. While the person may have an asset that has increased greatly in value, until such time as it is sold the person may not have sufficient cash to pay the taxes due. For example, a retired person may live in a house which is appreciating rapidly in value. Taxing the person on the income associated with this increase in value may force him or her either to sell the house or to borrow against the increase in value. Many people would consider this to be an unfair imposition on the homeowner. Thus, the law does not require any payment of taxes on the income associated with capital gains until the item is sold.

While this rule alleviates some problems, it creates new ones. The first is that under a progressive tax system, any lump-sum distribution tends to be taxed at a higher rate than a similar amount spread over a number of years. The second is that some of the increase in value of an asset is likely to be associated with inflation, and this does not represent a real increase in income. Offsetting these two is the third issue, which is that any system allowing the deferral of taxes creates a tax benefit. As a practical matter the federal tax code provided very preferential treatment of capital gains for items held over relatively long periods by allowing only part of the gain to be taxed. Prior to the 1986 tax revision, only 40% of the long-term capital gain was subject to taxation. This provision was eliminated in 1986, but there is constant talk about Congress replacing it. We discuss the issues we just raised and look at how the timing of income receipts can affect one's tax burden after we analyze how the definition of income affects efficiency and tax incidence.

/// **THE INCOME TAX BASE**

The particular treatment of specific types of income can have a significant impact on both the equity and efficiency of the tax system. If some type of income is treated particularly well in the tax code, many people will try to earn that type of income. This partly offsets the tax advantage since the

---

[8] For a discussion see Joseph Minarik, "Capital Gains," in Aaron and Pechman, op. cit., pp. 241–281.

competition is likely to lower the return for that type of activity. However, the effect of the tax advantage will be more people engaging in the tax-advantaged activity. This may be desirable if the activity generates some type of positive externality, or if it is expected that there will be too little of this activity for some other reason. However, many people believe that tax shelters do little to promote efficiency and create significant incentives to use resources to take advantage of the tax code rather than to do something productive. This is the type of argument that proponents of less complex tax codes offer; the tax reform of 1986 was intended to greatly reduce such incentives. Nevertheless, there are still many provisions in the tax code that favor particular activities. Further, the difficulty in measuring certain types of income remains.

These problems in measuring income create distortions in the economy. Lightly taxed goods or services receive more attention than those that are heavily taxed. This creates inequities in the amount of tax paid by different taxpayers who are otherwise identical; and it creates inefficiencies as people try to take advantage of the lower taxes associated with certain types of consumption or investment.

Efficiency Effects of Income Definition

It might seem that the decision as to what should be included in taxable income would have little effect on the efficiency of the tax system. Small exclusions from the tax base would not appear to create much distortion. Yet when enough small distortions are added together, the effect can be quite large. Each untaxed item becomes a preferred form of compensation. People are willing to take amounts for which their additional satisfaction is less than the cost of provision as long as the tax savings offset the difference. Thus, an employee who asks for health benefits rather than more money wages wants to increase those benefits to the point where the value of the additional unit of benefits is equal to the cost of provision minus the tax savings. For example, if each unit of health insurance costs the employer \$1, the employee will prefer additional units as long as the value to the employee is equal to $\$1 \times (1 - t)$, where t is the employee's marginal tax rate. Thus, if the employee has a marginal tax rate of 28%, he or she would prefer an additional dollar spent on health insurance as long as the insurance is worth at least \$0.72 to the employee because the employee is only giving up \$0.72 in after-tax income. The employer is indifferent to a dollar spent on wages or a dollar spent on medical insurance because both are treated as expenses in determining business taxes. This is equivalent to the government subsidizing the consumption of health insurance and would lead to overconsumption relative to the efficient level. This overconsumption of fringe benefits creates a deadweight loss to society as well as revenue losses to the government.[9]

[9] See Werner Z. Hirsch and Anthony M. Rufolo, "Effects of State Income Taxes on Fringe Benefit Demand of Policemen and Firemen," *National Tax Journal* 39 (June 1986), pp. 211–220.

Tax Expenditures

The term *tax expenditure* is used to describe the equivalence between a government tax to finance certain subsidies and the achievement of the same effect with a tax exemption. One reason why tax exemptions are a popular way for a government to subsidize certain activities is that the subsidies never show up in the budget. Instead of collecting taxes and appropriating funds for a subsidy, the tax exemption provides the subsidy by not collecting the taxes that are otherwise due. The term *tax expenditure* is a relatively recent one;[10] however, tax expenditures are now reported by the federal government and seventeen state governments.[11]

When the federal government allows a taxpayer to deduct charitable contributions from income or gives a tax credit for child care expenses, it is subsidizing these activities. The effect is to lower their price for taxpayers. The system differs from a direct subsidy because the amount of subsidy is closely related to one's tax status and because it never shows up in the budget totals.

It is important to understand that there is no clear method to calculate tax expenditures. The concept requires that the analyst estimate the amount of tax the government would have received in the absence of a specific exemption, exclusion, or credit. To calculate this would require knowledge of the tax brackets for everyone claiming the special benefits. In addition, it is usually necessary to assume that people do not in fact change their consumption because of the tax preference. Further, if we are working with a progressive tax system, we calculate the amount under the assumption that the other tax expenditures are left alone. However, there is an interaction effect since each tax expenditure that affects a person can put that person in a different tax bracket. Hence, the net effect of all tax expenditures is likely to be different from the sum of each individual item.

There are two views on what constitutes a tax expenditure. In one view the tax expenditure arises over any deviation of tax liability from that determined by the best definition of tax base and rate for the tax in question. The alternative view takes the broad legal definition of rate and base as the starting point, and only counts deviations from the base and rate as specified by the tax law. The latter view excludes many of the tax expenditures made because of administrative difficulty in implementing taxation on these items. The tax expenditures are generally broken down into those associated with administrative convenience, equity, and special incentives.

The area of administrative convenience is an important one for tax purposes because there is some presumption that if the administrative issues could be overcome, there would be an opportunity to broaden the tax base. For example, we noted earlier that the income base used for the income tax differs

---

[10] See Stanley Surrey, *Pathways to Tax Reform* (Cambridge, MA: Harvard University Press, 1973).
[11] Karen M. Benker, "Tax Expenditure Reporting: Closing the Loophole in State Budget Oversight," *National Tax Journal* 39 (December 1986), pp. 403–418.

in many important respects from the ideal definition. Many forms of income production do not generate a market transaction and, hence, are not taxed. Thus, the farmer growing food for home consumption does not pay any tax on the value of that food. This form of tax expenditure does not have a specific purpose. Rather, it is simply too difficult to determine the market value of work performed in the home. Further, it is not counted as a tax expenditure in actual studies even though it would fit as one under a strict definition.

The second major type of tax expenditures are those intended to promote equity. For example, certain medical expenses are deductible, not because the government wants to encourage medical usage but because it is felt that heavy medical expenses represent a burden on the individual; on the basis of horizontal equity, the person with the burden should be granted some tax relief. This is also the reason for allowing deductions of business expenses. The person with large expenses for earning income is not really as well off as the person with the same income and no such expenses. Of course, it is often hard to determine exactly where the distinction between necessary business expenses and personal consumption occurs; however, the principle is a fairly clear one.

The special-incentives type of tax expenditures is intended to encourage some type of activity. These are the closest to pure subsidies that exist in the tax expenditure area. The clear alternative in these cases is to explicitly subsidize certain behavior. For example, the various energy tax credits were specifically a subsidy for that type of behavior. The intent was to encourage people to do more energy conservation. It is in this type of usage that the tax expenditure is most clearly an attempt to evade being accountable for additional expenditures.

Most tax expenditures relate to income taxes, and this is where they were first analyzed. The analysis usually focuses on the federal law, but it is equally applicable to state income taxes and to other taxes. In fact, it is estimated that while federal tax expenditures in 1981–82 totaled $253.5 billion, or 8.3% of GNP, those for the state of California amounted to about $9 billion in 1983–84.[12] The tax expenditures for equity and to encourage specific actions are usually in the form of deductions or tax credits. The distinction is important for two reasons. A deduction is only applicable to those who itemize deductions, although a few deductions are allowed outside the itemization restrictions, e.g., the deduction for moving expenses when changing jobs was outside the itemization restriction until the 1986 tax reform. Further, a deduction is worth more to those in higher marginal tax brackets. A $1,000 deduction will result in a $280 tax savings for someone in the 28% tax bracket, while it would result in only $150 in tax savings for someone in the 15% tax bracket and no savings for someone with no tax liability. A tax credit, on the other hand, results in the same savings to all eligible people. The earned income tax

---

[12] "Governor's Budget 1983–4" (Sacramento: State of California), p. A-110.

credit can even result in negative tax payments. Thus, the tax credit is much closer to being a direct subsidy.

Tax expenditures for taxes other than income taxes are usually designed to meet some equity concern rather than to alter behavior. Often the argument for such exemptions from a sales tax is based on the inelastic demand people are likely to have for the exempt goods or services. Thus, it is argued that food is a necessity and hence would have an inelastic demand curve. Exempting food from the sales tax thus would not be expected to induce people to eat a lot more. However, it would be expected to have a greater impact on low-income familes than on high-income families. Thus, the exemption would make the sales tax a more progressive tax.

There are a few major exceptions to this equity concern in the non–income tax expenditures. For example, many states or localities offer reduced property taxes for land used in farming. This may partly reflect an equity concern since farm taxes may not be as closely related to benefits received as are residential and commercial property taxes. However, the more common reason is to encourage the continuation of open land because of its external benefits.

The use of tax expenditures to internalize externalities has both advantages and disadvantages. It is good because the subsidy is generally open-ended. This is how an internalization subsidy should be. As we shall see in Chapter 13, however, many explicit subsidies have an arbitrary limit. They act more as a lump-sum grant than as a guiding mechanism to encourage a certain activity and internalize the relevant externality. This use of tax expenditures is bad because it is often not visible as a subsidy and it differs across taxpayers, as noted above.

Finally, we must note that despite these various rationales for tax expenditures, in practice they are frequently targeted at special interest groups as a hidden payoff for political support.[13] They are particularly attractive for this purpose because they do not show up in the government budget.

Revenue Impact of Tax Expenditures

Tax expenditures lower the tax base and hence revenue. The resulting revenue losses then create the need to raise the tax rate to generate the same amount of revenue from the smaller tax base. This rise in the tax rate creates further efficiency losses in the comparison of taxable and nontaxable forms of consumption. For example, the higher tax rate might induce people to work less.

One effect of the higher tax rates associated with a smaller base is the possibility that rates could get so high as to actually reduce the amount of revenue raised. It is easy to provide examples of such situations with respect to excise taxes on goods that have a very elastic supply or demand. Figure 7-7

[13] Information on special exemptions for groups as diverse as chicken farmers and steel companies is reported in *Newsweek* (December 29, 1986), p. 22.

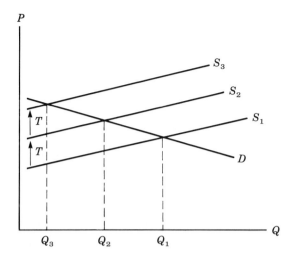

Figure 7-7 / **Higher Tax Rates May Reduce Revenue**

shows such a good. With no tax the equilibrium is at Q_1 and there is no tax revenue. With a tax of T per unit, the equilibrium is at Q_2 and the revenue is $T \times Q_2$. However, raising the tax to $2 \times T$ results in quantity falling to Q_3, which is less than half of Q_2. Thus, $2 \times T \times Q_3$ actually generates less revenue than does $T \times Q_2$. The higher tax would cause such a decrease in the volume of sales that the revenue from the higher tax would be lower than the revenue from the lower tax rate.

In principle there is always some tax rate that causes revenue to decline. Revenue collected at a zero rate would be zero since people would get to keep all they earned. However, revenue at a 100% tax rate would also be zero. People would have no incentive to work if the government simply took everything they earned, so no one would earn anything. Somewhere between the rates of zero and 100% there is a rate that would maximize the government's revenue.

Some people argued that rates on income in the U.S. were getting to this point. Thus, when President Reagan asked for major tax reductions in 1981, there were predictions that the total amount of revenue collected by the federal government would increase because of the additional activity. This in fact did not happen; however, tax collections from people in the very highest brackets apparently did increase. This is probably associated with reductions in tax-sheltering activity rather than with more hours worked; but it is a significant indication that very high tax rates can induce major tax avoidance behavior.

This also points out a further difficulty in determining the incidence of taxes. It is frequently assumed that the total tax liability of a family is the amount that it pays to the government. This amount is compared with before-tax income to get a measure of the progressivity of the tax system. However, this is not likely to be a meaningful measure because part of tax avoidance behavior can be considered as a tax. Consider a person who is in a 50%

marginal tax bracket. Thus, half of any additional income will go for taxes. If this person could invest in corporate bonds yielding 16% before taxes, the tax would be half of the money received, and the investor would end up with an 8% return on the investment. Now suppose that this person is given a tax-exempt alternative that yields a 12% return. Since the latter return is tax exempt it is more attractive, but the investor does not really escape all taxes. Implicitly some taxes are being paid in the form of accepting a lower return on investments. A tax rate of 25% on the taxable investment would leave the investor with a 12% after-tax return. Thus, the investor is implicitly paying a tax of 25% in the form of a lower return on investment. However, this will never show up in any comparison of the person's tax bill and income. Rather, it will simply show up as no taxes paid. This lower return has some of the same effects as government collecting a tax and using the proceeds to subsidize certain types of activity.

Tax Expenditure Incidence

Tax expenditures reduce tax liability but they do not make the taxpayer better off by the full amount of the reduction. Part of the difference is the efficiency loss, which we have already discussed, but part of the benefit of a tax expenditure will also be shifted just as a tax might be shifted. To the extent that the tax expenditure is designed to subsidize a particular activity, this shifting is desirable. However, the tax expenditure may not be an efficient form of subsidy because the shifting is not complete. The exemption of interest on state and local debt from federal income taxation is very much like a direct subsidy. It offers a good example of why such subsidies are not very efficient. In this case, state and local governments can pay a lower interest rate because the recipients do not have to pay any federal income tax on the interest received. Thus, a person in a 50% marginal tax bracket would be indifferent between a municipal bond paying 5% and a corporate one paying 10%. With the corporate bond, half of the interest would be paid to the federal government in the form of taxes for a net return of 5%. This is equivalent to the local government paying interest of 10% and the federal government reimbursing them for half of their interest expenses.

Unfortunately there is a large amount of leakage in this system of subsidies. State and local governments float a large amount of debt; and they must appeal to investors below the top federal tax bracket. Suppose that on the margin they must appeal to investors in the 25% tax bracket. Then if the corporate rate is 10%, the state and local governments must offer 7.5% to attract sufficient investors. For the marginal investor, the tax reduction exactly offsets the savings to the local government. However, the person in the 50% bracket also has to receive the 7.5% return. Thus, in this case, the federal government is giving up 5% in order to benefit state and local governments by 2.5%. The other 2.5% is a net gain to the high-tax investor. This example highlights one of the major problems with tax expenditures as a form of subsidy. Much of the benefit may not reach the intended beneficiary.

It is also important to note in this example that the tax "loophole" is not entirely a benefit to the investor. In fact, the marginal investor finds that the lower interest rate exactly offsets the tax savings; and even the high-bracket investor is accepting a lower return than was available on taxable investments. Thus, these "loopholes" do not have as much of an effect on tax avoidance as might appear. Rather, they are a relatively inefficient form of subsidy that allows some people to reduce their income taxes; but the reduction in tax collections is not all benefit for the taxpayer.

Tax credits are very close to a direct subsidy. For example, the tax credit that was available for home insulation essentially lowered the price of such insulation to eligible homeowners. The tax credit was 15% for all homeowners. Thus, the price reduction was the same for all. If the subsidy were set so as to exactly offset the external benefits from home insulation, it would have been efficient. One can question whether this was indeed the case or not, but it did have the result of encouraging more use of insulation.

/// ISSUES IN THE TIMING OF TAXATION

While we have identified a number of complex problems that arise in a tax system when viewed at a point in time, other problems arise when we try to look at how taxes are treated as spread over time. In particular, several deviations from the preferred treatment of income can lead to either higher or lower real taxes.

Tax Deferral

Any postponement of a tax liability is a form of interest-free loan to the person postponing the taxes. The money that should have been paid in taxes could be deposited in a bank. When the tax is actually paid, the person must pay the tax on the original amount of income and must pay tax on any interest earned. However, by postponing the tax, the person gets to keep the interest left after paying taxes. Suppose you bought a stock that went up in value by $1,000 in each of two years and the relevant tax rate is 20% for all income. If the stock were reevaluated after the first year, you would have to pay tax on that $1,000 of income. However, the stock will not be reevaluated unless you sell it. The tax would have been $200, and you deposit this money at 10% interest in anticipation of the tax payment. At the end of the second year, you sell the stock and withdraw the deposit with interest. You have $2,000 in gains plus the $20 in interest, so you pay taxes of $404. This leaves you with $1616 after taxes. Alternatively, if you had paid the $200 in tax at the end of the first year and the $200 at the end of the second year, you would end up with $1600 as your after-tax return. The difference of $16 represents the value of deferring the tax.

The effect of not having to pay the tax on the part of the capital gain that occurred in the first year was to get an interest-free loan of the amount of the tax for one year. While it was necessary to pay the tax on the interest earned, the person is still better off by $16. The longer the gains are sheltered and the higher the tax rates are, the more significant this postponement of the tax becomes.

Uneven Income

A progressive tax structure tends to penalize any type of income that is paid out in lump sums rather than evenly over a number of years. Each additional dollar received in a given year is taxed at the highest rate reached for that year. Hence, if you take two years' worth of income and lump them into one year, the total tax paid would probably increase. A simple example would be if the tax were 10% of income up to $10,000 and 20% of the amount over $10,000. A person earning $10,000 in each of two years would pay $1,000 per year in taxes. However, a person who earned $20,000 the second year and nothing in the first year would pay $3,000 in taxes the second year and nothing the first year. The total tax bill would be higher for the person with unequal income from year to year. This also tends to discourage risky investments (see Box 7-2).

The federal tax code used to take partial account of the higher tax on uneven income "streams" by allowing people to use income averaging. Income averaging is only a limited method to deal with this problem. Under such a system a person with a large increase in income could reduce the taxes due by essentially shifting some of the income back to the previous low-income years and having it taxed at the marginal rates for those years. However, a person with a decrease in income could not reduce taxes paid in previous years on higher income. Further, the time limit for averaging was the previous four years; and income had to be at least 20% above the average for those four years. Hence, the averaging option did not fully offset the effect of a progressive tax on uneven income flows. Since capital gains can represent a very uneven income flow, this presents one possible reason to give them favorable treatment. In any case, income averaging is no longer allowed for individuals under the federal tax code. The general reasoning appears to be that the marginal rates are levied over broad ranges, and they are not as high as they have been in the past, so the disadvantage of uneven income streams is not as great as it once was.

Inflation

Inflation creates problems in the taxation of both labor and nonlabor income, but the problem is greater for the taxation of nonlabor income. For

Box 7-2

////// Taxes on Risky Investments

Suppose that the tax structure is 10% of all income up to $10,000 and 20% of all income over $10,000. For simplicity consider a person earning wages of $9,000 per year and having $20,000 to invest. The tax on labor income will be $900.

One option for the investment is to put the money in a bank and receive 5% interest per year. Thus, at the end of the year the bank balance would be $21,000 and the person would have $1,000 of investment income to add to wages. This would bring the person's total income to $10,000, and the tax would be $1,000. The other option is to invest in a project that will yield $22,000 if it is successfuly but only return the $20,000 if it is not successful. In other words, it will yield a 10% return if successful but a zero percent return if not. Further, each outcome is equally likely, so the investment has the same average return as the bank. Half the time the person would receive $2,000 and half the time nothing for an average return of $1,000. However, when the investment is successful, taxes are paid on an income of $11,000; this amounts to $1,200. When the investment is not successful, income is only $9,000 and taxes are $900. Thus, the average tax would be $1,050 instead of $1,000. We see that a progressive tax system tends to penalize risky investments.

labor income, the problem only arises with a progressive tax system. As income increases to adjust for inflation, the increments to income are taxed at higher and higher rates; this amounts to an increase in effective tax rates. Consider again a simple progressive system that levies zero taxes on the first $10,000 of income and a 10% tax on all income above $10,000. Now allow prices and wages to increase by 10% per year. Initially a person earning $10,000 does not pay any taxes. After one year, income has adjusted to $11,000 but this does not represent any increase in purchasing power. Nevertheless, the amount above $10,000 is taxed and the person is paying a higher effective tax rate. If the inflation continues, nominal income would rise to about $20,000 after seven years. This would still represent the same purchasing power as in the initial period, but taxes would have risen to $1,000.

This inflation-induced rise in income taxes explains why the government could continue to increase spending over the inflationary 1970s and still give large tax "cuts" occasionally. The solution to this problem for labor income is simply to allow the tax brackets to adjust for inflation as well. In the above example, if the tax brackets adjusted for inflation, then the zero income point

Box 7-3

////// Inflation and Assets

Both depreciation and capital gains and losses are complicated by inflation. When prices rise, depreciation based on the original purchase price of an asset understates the loss of value of the asset. Similarly, the calculation of capital gains overstates the increase in income associated with an increase in market price. Consider depreciation first. Suppose that prices rise at 10% of the base year's price each year (inflation is normally measured on a year-to-year basis, but the resulting compounding of rates simply complicates the analysis). Then we would observe that prices double after ten years.

Now consider a machine that sells for $10,000 in the first year and has no scrap value. The owner is treated as having a reduction in income of $1,000 per year for depreciation in each of the ten years the ma-

chine is used. Suppose that gumdrops sell for $1 apiece when the machine is purchased, and the machine produces 1,000 gumdrops per year. The owner is then foregoing 10,000 gumdrops in order to purchase the machine. The next year, the owner is allowed to treat the machine as having declined by $1,000 in value and count this as negative income. However, the $1,000 would only purchase 909 gumdrops at the price of $1.10 each. Hence, the depreciation understates the actual loss in consumption opportunities. In this example, the depreciation each year should exactly offset the production of gumdrops; however, the value of gumdrop production is now $1,100, so the depreciation does not offset this income. If you calculate the depreciation in gumdrops over the ten-year lifetime of the machine, you will find

would have also moved up to $20,000 after seven years, and the person would still owe no taxes. Current tax law calls for brackets to start adjusting for inflation again in 1990; but some members of Congress would prefer to delay the adjustment as a form of tax increase.

A more intractable issue arises when we consider savings and investment with inflation. Inflation distorts the taxes of both debtors and creditors and it increases the taxes on most investments. The basic distortion comes from the rise in nominal value of goods over time. Since income is measured in dollars, the increase in dollar value looks like income even though there is no commensurate increase in consumption opportunities. For example, if you bought a painting for $10,000 and sold it one year later for $11,000, it would appear that you are better off by $1,000. You would have income of $1,000. However, if the prices for all goods and services had increased by 10% over the same time period, the actual income would be zero since it would cost $11,000 this year to

Box 7-3 (continued)

that the owner gets to reduce income by much less than 10,000 gumdrops.

Because inflation reduces the real benefit of depreciation, which is based on original purchase price, the amount of income a person receives is overstated. Our gumdrop producer will get $1,000 from the sale of gumdrops in the first year and will be able to deduct $1,000. Thus, the producer is seen to have no net income, as money assets increase by just the loss in value of the machine. In the second year, the producer receives $1,100 from selling gumdrops and again deducts $1,000. Now it appears that the ability to consume has gone up, since there is $100 in income; but loss in value of the machine is actually $1,100. Another way to look at this is to consider what would happen if the investor in our gumdrop machine set aside $1,000 per year to replace the machine when it wears out. At the end of ten years the investor would have $10,000; but the new machine

would cost $20,000.

The increase or decrease in value of an investment item affects income in terms of potential consumption. Thus, in the absence of inflation, if an item increases in value it can be sold for more money and the additional money could be used to purchase additional consumption goods. However, when the increase in value is due to a price change, the additional money would only compensate for price changes in consumer goods and consumption could not be increased. Thus if our gumdrop machine did not wear out, its value after ten years would be the same as when it was first purchased. However, if there is inflation over this time period, the price of the machine rises from $10,000 to $20,000. This price does not represent an increase in income in terms of purchasing power, but $10,000 would be treated as income if the price level change were not taken into account.

---

purchase the same things $10,000 would have purchased last year. Thus, it would be an error for government to tax the $1,000 in nominal capital gain. Yet government does indeed do this. The best response would be for the value of the good to be adjusted for inflation in figuring depreciation and capital gains; but it is often very difficult to determine the change in value of such assets that is due entirely to inflation. Inflation also distorts the value of depreciation allowances to offset the income that the assets produce (see Box 7-3 for further examples).

Inflation does not necessarily raise tax burdens for everyone. People who are paying off debts with lower valued dollars are receiving income in the form of reduced liabilities. The reduction in their liabilities should be counted in determining taxable income each year. Yet they do not have to take account of this reduction. Hence, they would have a lower tax burden than they should. In the private sector, the reduction in the value of the debt to one party is offset by the reduction in the liability of the other. Ignoring this factor does not appear to have a significant effect on total taxes paid; however, it could cause significant shifting of the total tax burden among borrowers and lenders.

The increase in net taxes associated with borrowing and lending arises from the fact that the federal government is a major net borrower from the rest of the economy. The higher taxes induced by inflation are not offset within the private sector for the interest received from government. Further, the taxes associated with returns to investments are still subject to the higher real taxes. In addition, the different expected lives of various investments make some lose more from the tax effects than others. Hence, the indirect effect of inflation acting through the tax code is to alter the pattern of investment. This altered pattern is likely to generate a deadweight loss for the economy as a whole. In particular it creates a relative premium for short-lived rather than long-lived investment goods, and this distortion creates efficiency costs for the economy.[14]

The net result is that inflation greatly increases the real taxes on savings and investment. This largely explains many of the steps taken by Congress to try to encourage savings and investment during the 1970s and early 1980s. However, the lower recent rates of inflation have made this appear to be a less significant problem; and this probably explains why these tax advantages for savings and investment were significantly reduced by the tax reform of 1986. The issue will certainly arise again if the rate of inflation should start to rise significantly.

/// TAX COORDINATION

Most of the previous discussion in this chapter is concerned with the federal government and its personal income tax. Yet most states levy some form of income tax as well; there are only six exceptions. This proliferation of income taxes creates problems of coordination among the states and coordination with the federal tax system. Further, some local governments levy forms of personal income tax. The issues that arise are mostly related to determining who gets to tax what; but there are also significant problems with the administrative and compliance costs of the various sytems, as well as equity concerns.

If various levels of government are all going to tax income, it might appear to be advantageous to simply have the lower level of government levy a surcharge on the income tax collections of the federal government. However, this method is only followed by a few state governments, and not by any local

---

[14] For an extensive discussion of the issues and some proposed solutions, see Charles R. Hulten, ed., *Depreciation Inflation and the Taxation of Income from Capital* (Washington, DC: The Urban Institute, 1981).

governments. Local governments tend to be more cautious in defining their tax bases because of the possibility of people moving outside their jurisdictions. States also take account of taxes paid to other states in determining tax liability.

Another major problem is that the states do not agree with each other or with the federal government about what should be taxed. For example, the federal government may decide to encourage investment by offering tax credits or faster depreciation for certain types of investment. States might not be interested in offering the same type of incentives. However, if their tax liability were just some percentage of the federal tax due, there would be some additional incentive for this type of activity associated with the state tax.

Another problem from the state's perspective is that rapid or major changes in how the federal government handles certain items could have a significant impact on the state's revenue for a given year. Thus, states are somewhat reluctant to tie themselves directly to the federal tax system. Nevertheless, a variety of states do try to adhere fairly closely to the federal definition of income. This is done to reduce the compliance and record-keeping costs for taxpayers.

If each state defines income differently, taxpayers have to calculate a different income figure for each state. This becomes a large record-keeping and filing burden for either companies or individuals, and it makes auditing more difficult for the state. Further, it creates opportunities for taxpayers to shift income into the state that taxes it less heavily. This shifting can occur purely as a record-keeping device or it may result from the actual movement of activity between states. Both issues are more important for business taxation than for personal taxation, so we will treat them in that context; but the analysis also holds for personal taxes.

Tax Avoidance and State Income Taxes

People and businesses do many things to avoid taxes. Some of these things are legal and some are not. All taxes allow for some deductions and exemptions, and people use these characteristics to influence their tax payments. This is usually the intended effect of such tax preferences. However, when several jurisdictions claim the right to tax the same income, additional methods of reducing the tax burden become possible. These methods are associated with either actual or apparent movement of activity between taxing jurisdictions.

Income Tax Interactions The federal code allows deductibility of state and local income taxes at least partially to prevent very high marginal tax rates. If neither the state nor the federal government allows deductibility of taxes paid to the other jurisdiction, it might be possible to end up with marginal tax rates that exceed 100%. This becomes even more of a problem when two states claim the right to tax the same income or when municipalities also tax income. For example, if a person lives in one state and works in another, both states may claim the right to tax the person's earned income, and either the municipality of residence or that of the workplace may also claim a tax. When the combined taxes are added to the federal tax and Social Security tax, the marginal tax rate could be quite high. Thus, most states allow some credit for taxes paid to other states and may allow deductibility of federal taxes in computing income.

Related to this is a question of the likely equity created by uncoordinated interaction of income taxes. The federal income tax is a progressive ability-to-pay tax. Many state taxes are also progressive. Subjecting the same income to several ability-to-pay taxes could violate some equity principles. The resulting tax might be more progressive than one jurisdiction intended, and the question of horizontal equity arises because of people earning the same income and residing in different states. Deductibility addresses both of these concerns.

Deductions as Subsidies   Once the federal tax code allows for the deductibility of one form of state tax, there is an argument for allowing the deduction of all state taxes. If one tax is deductible and the other is not, the state has a clear incentive to use the deductible tax for its residents. Thus, the federal tax code influences the choice of tax systems for lower levels of government. Further, the deductibility lowers the net cost of state taxation to the residents of that state. Some argue that this is a desirable subsidy of the activities of state and local governments, while others believe that it leads to too much taxation at the state and local level. However one views it, the effect of the deductibility is to lower the net cost to residents of a particular state of their own state's taxation. One of the arguments agains the property tax limitation movement in California was that lowering property taxes would result in increases in federal tax payments by California residents of over $1 billion per year.

This form of state and local government subsidy has a number of problems. One problem is that it encourages tax financing of state and local government activities even if some form of user financing might be better. User charges paid to state and local governments are not deductible in figuring federal tax liability. Thus, a given amount of money paid in the form of user fees costs the resident more on average than does the same amount collected by taxation. For example, if your municipality finances a pool out of tax receipts, each person who itemizes can deduct those expenses in figuring federal tax liabilities. However, if the same pool is financed by entrance fees, none of the expenses are deductible. In some cases user fees may be the more efficient and more equitable way to finance certain government services, but they are more costly to the residents.

Another issue is that state and local governments that engage in more activities than the average are partially funded by taxpayers in the rest of the country. For example, New York City has its own university, which had no tuition for many years. The costs were paid by local taxes. Thus, part of the costs were paid by the country at large. Of course, to the extent that all jurisdictions do the same thing there is no net subsidy, but there is a lower "price" for government activity at the state and local level.

The Reagan tax reform plan for 1985 called for the elimination of this deductibility. Such elimination was strongly opposed by high-tax states like New York. The result was an elimination of the deductibility for state sales taxes but not for income and property taxes in the 1986 tax bill. It will be interesting to see if any states decide to eliminate their sales taxes because of this (see Box 7-4).

The change in net tax burden has more than an equity dimension. The net tax burdern in a state is likely to affect its overall attractiveness to residents and to businesses. For example, the oil boom in Alaska led to that state making a net tax payment to its residents. The payment as well as normal state activities were funded by severance taxes on oil. This made Alaska more attractive to potential residents and probably added to the growth rate in the state. Similarly, any net changes in tax distribution across states is likely to result in incentives for activity to shift. Those areas where net federal burdens decline would be expected to have slightly higher growth rates, and those where net taxes increased would be expected to have somewhat slower growth rates.

/// SUMMARY

Income taxes are widely used at the federal and state levels. Both personal and corporate income is taxed by the federal government, forty-four states, and a number of local governments. Serious issues arise in terms of the efficiency effects of income taxes and in terms of the definition of income for tax purposes. Income taxes, and particularly progressive income taxes, create an incentive not to earn income. This can lead to inefficiently low levels of work effort or of savings. In particular, the distortion that a tax is likely to cause is related to the marginal tax rate and the marginal tax rate will be higher for a progressive tax structure than for a proportional tax structure raising the same amount of revenue. Thus, there is a trade-off between the redistributive effects of the tax system and efficiency since the progressive tax will place more of the tax burden on higher income people.

There are many problems in trying to define the tax base for an income tax. Some items are not included in the base because of administrative difficulty in measuring them, others are not included because of equity consid-erations, and still others are excluded in order to subsidize certain activities. The items may be excluded by never counting them, by allowing exemptions or deductions for them, or by allowing a tax credit for qualifying expenditures. Excluding items from the tax base is a form of subsidy. The term "tax expendi-ture" refers to these exclusions and deductions.

Box 7-4

////// **Deductibility of Sales Taxes**

The tax reform of 1986 eliminated the deductibility of state and local sales taxes in calculating income for the federal income tax. This leaves income taxes and property taxes as deductible items. This situation does not satisfy those who believe that no state and local taxes should be deductible nor those who believe that all such taxes should be deductible. Rather, it is a compromise that takes account of several specific items regarding the sales tax.

Perhaps the most important characteristic of the sales tax deduction was that it was most blatantly a simple reduction in the rate at which people in a given state were taxed by the federal government. Most deductions require that the individual produce some evidence that the deductible expense actually occurred; but to do this for a sales tax would require that people keep detailed receipts for all their eligible expenditures each year. Since this was not considered feasible, the IRS allowed taxpayers to deduct a certain amount of money from their income based on their level of income. Hence, for most people the deduction was determined by income level rather than actual expenditures on the sales tax.

The second problem with the deduction was that it was more likely to be taken by higher income families since they are more likely to itemize their deductions. Further, the deduction lowered federal tax liabilities more for those in high tax brackets than it did for those in lower tax brackets. Thus, a person facing a 50% marginal tax rate would have federal taxes reduced by half of the amount of sales taxes paid while someone in the 25% bracket would only have the federal taxes reduced by one-fourth of the tax paid even if both itemized. This characteristic tends to make the sales tax more of a regressive tax by reducing its real cost to higher income taxpayers.

The problem with eliminating deductibility for this tax only is that it treats residents of states with a heavy reliance on sales taxes differently from residents of states that rely on other taxes. It also creates an incentive for such states to shift to some other form of taxation. Unless the deductibility status of the various taxes is changed, it is likely that the sales tax will be relied on less heavily in the future.

Tax expenditures both reduce revenue and can create efficiency costs by distorting behavior. Income that is not subject to taxation is relatively more attractive than taxable income. This can lead to excess emphasis on these forms of income. Also, expenditures that generate tax advantages may be similarly overused. The tax expenditure form of subsidy partly benefits taxpayers and partly benefits the subsidized activity. In general a tax subsidy is less efficient than a direct subsidy, but a tax expenditure may be favored because it does not show up as a direct government expenditure.

Because income is taxed by a variety of government units, there are problems with coordination of taxes. Generally, every state with an income tax taxes income earned in the state as well as all income of its own residents. Most states then give residents credit for taxes paid to other states. The federal government allows a deduction for income taxes paid to other governments for taxpayers who itemize deductions. This can serve some equity considerations by reducing the cumulative taxation on income, but it also serves as a subsidy to state and local income taxes. This encourages the use of tax financing by the lower levels of government as compared to user charges.

Inflation and depreciation of capital goods create additional problems for the tax code. Capital goods should be treated as being consumed as they wear out. However, difficulty in measuring real economic decline for goods held for long periods of time has led to various rules for depreciation. Sometimes these rules are overly generous and at other times, e.g., in periods of high inflation, they tend to penalize long-lived investments. At the same time inflation can cause significant increases in the percentage of income going to taxes in a progressive tax system. Various reforms have attempted to deal with these issues in the last few years, but none have met with universal approval.

Appendix   //////

Effect of Taxing Interest on Savings

The effect of taxation on savings is complicated by the fact that savings is not itself a good or service to the consumer. When a person saves, there is usually some other objective; the savings are a means to achieve this other objective. Most people save to increase future consumption or security. Both of these goals are dependent on the amount of savings accumulated. Yet the amount that is available in the future is affected by both the amount set aside in the present and the rate of interest on those savings. With higher interest rates, the individual does not have to set aside as much money today to have a given amount in the future. However, any amount set aside will grow into a larger future total. The effect of taxes on savings depends on how these two factors work out for both individuals and for the economy as a whole.

Not all individuals save in any given time period. Some will be net borrowers. The analysis we conduct could be generalized to consider borrowing as well as saving, but the complication does not add much to the conclusions. Hence, we only consider the savings decision for now.

The analysis for individuals can be seen in Figure 7-8. On the vertical axis we represent present consumption; on the horizontal axis we represent future consumption. Think about there being only two possible time periods, today and next year. Income can be consumed today or saved for next year; saved income earns the prevailing rate of interest. Thus, the future prices would have to be discounted to be comparable to present prices. All future prices are therefore equal to the future amount times $1/(1 + r)$, where r is the relevant interest rate.

If all income is spent today, there is none available for future consumption. This corresponds to the vertical intercept in the figure. Alternatively, if all income is saved, there would be no current consumption; this corresponds to the horizontal intercept of the budget line. The intermediate points on the budget line correspond to some amount of savings. Any increase in current consumption will mean a decrease in savings. The equation of the budget line is

$$Y = P_c \times C + \frac{P_f \times F}{1 + r}$$

where Y is income, C is current consumption, F is future consumption, and r is the interest rate. If we assume that there is no inflation, then the P's can be eliminated from the equation. We can rewrite it as

$$C = Y - \frac{F}{1 + r}$$

Thus, the slope of the budget line is

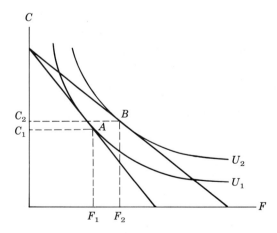

Figure 7-8 / **Higher Interest Rate with Reduced Saving**

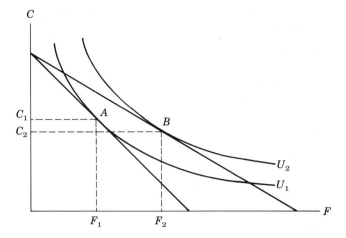

***Figure 7-9* / Higher Interest Rate with Increased Saving**

$$\frac{-1}{1 + r}$$

and the slope becomes flatter as the interest rate rises. Figure 7-8 shows one possible effect of a rise in the interest rate. The equilibrium shifts from A to B. Future consumption shifts from F_1 to F_2; but current consumption increases as well from C_1 to C_2. Thus, the increase in interest rates could cause a decrease in savings.

Figure 7-9 shows the outcome most people would expect: an increase in savings in response to the increase in the interest rate. For borrowers, the increase in interest rates results in a reduction in current consumption. This reduced borrowing also shows up as an increase in net savings. Thus, there is a good possibility that any increase in net interest rates would result in an increase in aggregate savings and that a decrease in net interest rates would result in a decrease in net savings. However, some people could be expected to have the opposite behavior; this would dampen any impact of interest rate changes on savings.

One further issue complicates the theoretical analysis of the effect of changes in interest rates on savings. As interest rates fall, the present value of future income rises relative to the value of current income. Hence, a person might change his or her expected lifetime work pattern. In response to lower interest rates, it may make sense to plan to work longer and retire later than would be the case with high interest rates. This would also affect savings behavior.

Chapter 8 //////

Income Taxes in the United States

Is the tax code an "important vehicle for social engineering," or should we have "a neutral tax code that would tax all activities roughly the same way and have a minimum impact on private financial decisions"?[1] Both positions were presented during the debates over the 1986 revisions to the federal income tax code; they represent the fundamental conflict over how the tax code should be structured. Those who favor a neutral system want a tax code in which few items receive preferential treatment, and they usually prefer to minimize the progressivity of the tax system because of the efficiency effect of high marginal tax rates. On the other side, many legislators see the power of tax preferences for achieving specific goals, and they are unwilling to give up that power. The issues that arise in terms of specifying an income tax code are often shaded by these fundamental disagreements over what the tax code is expected to accomplish.

The income taxes used by states and some local governments must take account of the dominant federal presence with respect to this tax base. The levying of taxes by a variety of jurisdictions leads to cumulative marginal tax rates that can be much higher than any individual marginal tax rate, yet the interactions among the tax codes mean that simply adding the different rates usually overstates the true marginal tax rate. The possibility exists for substantial coordination of the income taxes levied by different levels of government, but there are a variety of reasons why this does not happen. Differences in outlook about the uses of the tax code for nonrevenue purposes is one reason for lack of coordination. The substantial number of changes that have been made in the federal code over time also makes states wary about relying on the federal tax code when planning state tax collections.

---

[1] Laurie McGinley, "Treasury's Plan to Overhaul Tax Code Sparks Heated Debate," *Wall Street Journal* (January 3, 1985), pp. 1 and 25.

/// THE ISSUES OF TAX REFORM

The Tax Reform Act of 1986 has been viewed by many as a fundamental change in federal income taxation. The top marginal tax rate was nominally lowered from 50% to 28%; the 50% rate was itself a reduction from a top 70% rate in 1980. The number of marginal tax brackets was nominally reduced from fourteen to two, so that the progressivity of the rate structure was substantially lowered. At the same time the base of the tax was broadened by removing a substantial number of tax preference items from the tax code. Thus, more income is taxed, but generally at a lower rate. While the top rates were reduced, the personal exemptions and standard deductions were increased, so that taxes on most low-income families were eliminated altogether. Thus, many of the changes in exemptions and deductions made the income tax relatively more progressive and at least partially offset the reduced progressivity of the rate structure.

Both the flattened rate structure and the broadened tax base are expected to reduce the efficiency costs that the income tax imposes on the economy. The flatter rate structure and lower maximum rates mean that most income will be taxed at a lower marginal rate. As we showed in the last chapter, generating the same amount of revenue with a lower marginal rate reduces the efficiency loss associated with the tax. Further, the removal of many tax preference items means that there is less distortion in the relative attractiveness of different types of income or expenditure. This reduces the efficiency loss associated with distorted spending or earning patterns.

The drastic revision of the federal tax code forced many states to revise their own tax codes, since these state codes are closely tied to the federal code; this again raised the issue of whether or not the states should adhere closely to federal practices. In general, the states have looked at income taxes more as methods to raise revenue than as methods to achieve other objectives, but many have adjusted their codes to conform to federal definitions while others have added their own incentives to the tax code.

The debate about federal tax reform had been building for some time prior to 1986. There were a variety of proposals, which were jointly debated as "flat taxes."[2] Effectively, they were all proposals to replace the progressive income tax structure with its complicated series of exemptions, deductions, and credits with a much less complicated tax having a broad base. Much of this movement was in response to a perception that the federal tax code was becoming both unwieldy and unfair. A poll by the Advisory Commission on Intergovernmental Relations in 1983 found that 35% of respondents singled out the federal income tax as the least fair of all major taxes, and a *Newsweek* poll in 1985 found that 60% of respondents classified the federal income tax as

---

[2] Joint Committee on Taxation, *Analysis of Proposals Relating to Comprehensive Tax Reform*, JCS-35-84 (Washington, DC: U.S. Government Printing Office, 1984).

either "mostly unfair" or "very unfair."[3] Further, this perception of unfairness was apparently leading to increases in tax evasion.[4]

The problems had developed over a long time period. The progressive tax structure would have generated large increases in the real tax burden during the inflation of the 1970s. At the time, the brackets of the federal income tax did not adjust for changes in the price level. Thus, as incomes increased they were taxed at higher rates, even though the increases in income were largely offset by increases in the price level. Hence, the percentage of income being paid in taxes was increasing. Congress reacted by passing a number of "tax reductions" to keep collections from rising too rapidly; but many of these reductions were in the form of deductions, exemptions, and tax credits designed to achieve specific goals. However, as people took advantage of these tax preference items, the horizontal equity of the tax system was placed in serious question. Many people perceived that others were not paying their fair share of taxes. Thus, the reform issue became one of trading off the uses of tax preferences against high marginal tax rates.

As we discussed in the previous chapter, tax preferences are roughly equivalent to a subsidy for the activity generating the preference. Thus, it would be possible to revise the tax code and vote for explicit subsidies; but few believed that many of the items receiving tax preferences would be offered funding if the tax preference were eliminated. One member of the House said specifically, "I know what I want to accomplish. If I can't do it directly through a spending program, I'll do it indirectly through the tax code."[5] One positive argument for the use of tax preferences in favor of direct subsidies is that they do not require a separate form of administration; but this must be balanced against the fact that they potentially affect everyone's tax calculations.

The widespread use of tax preferences and the accompanying high marginal tax rates create a substantial incentive to avoid taxes. A person with a 50% marginal tax rate would find that a dollar's worth of tax savings would be equivalent to two dollars' worth of extra income. However, some proponents of the higher rates see this as a benefit. They clearly acknowledge that the major reason for retaining high marginal tax rates is to maintain substantial progressivity in the income tax system. Some also recognize that the high tax rates indeed make tax preferences more worthwhile. One commentator went so far as to write, "Perhaps Congress will wake up in time to realize that the 27% top bracket is too low and could severely damage the ability of the tax system to properly encourage social policies."[6] When the tax revisions left top marginal rates of 28% and 33%, there was significant consternation among the representatives of the beneficiaries of some of the tax preference items.

---

[3] Advisory Commission on Intergovernmental Relations, *Changing Public Attitudes on Governments and Taxes, 1983*, S-12 (Washington, DC: 1983), p. 1; and "Newsweek Poll: Cheers," *Newsweek* (June 10, 1985), p. 22.

[4] Shlomo Maital, "The Tax-Evasion Virus," *Psychology Today* (March 1982), pp. 74–78.

[5] McGinley, op. cit.

[6] Robert C. Taylor, "Low Marginal Rates Could Backfire," *Wall Street Journal* (June 10, 1986), p. 32.

There was recognition that even those who retained tax preferences would find them less valuable than in the past. Whether this is good or bad is open to discussion; but most people seem to believe that the reformed tax system is an improvement over the old one. Despite this consensus, substantial controversy remains about the use of tax preference items.

Lest one believe that the reform really did eliminate the use of the tax code for influencing the private sector, we should note that even the reform bill itself was reported to have over 360 tax preference items with an estimated value of about $10 billion. They are as diverse as special accounting rules for poultry farmers (worth an estimated $1 billion over five years) to investment tax credits for the steel industry (refundable if the net tax is negative) and a proposed $5 million tax reduction for an "old college classmate of one Senator."[7] While it is not clear that the last item made it into the final law, the others appear to be part of the tax code, and Congress has been busy with other "adjustments" to the tax code ever since. These loopholes in the original bill and the rapid move to make other changes lead many to expect that large numbers of tax expenditures will start creeping back into the tax code over time.

Major changes in the tax code create substantial changes in the tax burden for many people. Those who have made important commitments on the basis of the existing tax code are at a disadvantage if the code is changed suddenly. In particular, people who have made investments or taken other actions largely because of the tax benefits could see major increases in their tax bills. For example, some people are likely to have borrowed more money because interest payments were tax deductible than they would have in the absence of the deduction. Sudden loss of this deduction would impose a cost on people in excess of what they may have anticipated when they undertook the debt. Because of the burden that such unanticipated changes can create, many of the provisions of the new tax code were phased in over several years. Thus, the 1986 tax reform phased out the deduction for interest on consumer debt over a five-year period. These transition rules create some of the complexity that appeared in the tax process after "tax simplification" was completed, and they will disappear after the code has been fully phased in. Other issues which were not anticipated in the tax reform act itself have been addressed in subsequent legislation. However, attempts to legislate either equity or special favors both lead to increased complexity in the tax code; and there is little evidence that Congress has stopped making such changes.

/// FIGURES AND TRENDS

Income taxes are the mainstay of the tax system in the United States. There are essentially two different taxes on personal income at the federal

---

[7] "Tax Reform: Congress Hatches Some Loopholes," *Newsweek* (September 29, 1986), p. 22; and Alan Murray, "Lobbyists and Chums from College Leave Imprint on Tax Bill," *Wall Street Journal* (May 16, 1986), pp. 1 and 19.

level: the personal income tax, a comprehensive income tax with a progressive rate structure; and the Social Security tax, a tax on earned income, which is proportional for most earnings. The revenue from the personal income tax goes into the general funds of the federal government and can be used for any purpose. However, the revenue from the Social Security tax goes into a trust fund and can only be used to pay the benefits of the Social Security system.

The federal government collected $472 billion in tax revenue in 1986. Of this amount it received $349 billion, about 74% of its general tax revenue, from the personal income tax. In the same year, the federal government received $267 billion for its social insurance trust funds, and almost all of this came from Social Security and related taxes. While Social Security is often treated as a form of benefit tax, many people consider it when evaluating the progressivity of the federal tax structure. In addition, forty states levied reasonably substantial personal income taxes, from which they received about $67 billion in 1986. This was almost 30% of all state tax revenue. Finally, many local governments also receive revenue from personal income taxes of one sort or another. In 1986 this amounted to $6.9 billion, which is substantial even though it represents less than 5% of local tax revenue.[8]

The widespread use of income taxes is primarily due to their ability to generate large amounts of revenue while allowing the taxing government to tailor the tax to particular notions of equity. The large revenue potential also makes it the tax that is used most often to encourage activities through tax exemptions. These exemptions, deductions, exclusions and tax credits originate for a variety of reasons; but they create a tremendous amount of the complexity in the income tax codes. Further, they are likely to generate significant efficiency losses to the economy as a whole.

While the hodgepodge of loopholes in the federal income tax was a prime factor in the movement for tax reform in 1986, it is instructive to consider what the "tax simplification" in 1986 actually accomplished. First, there is widespread agreement that it did not in fact simplify the personal income tax code. Second, while the tax base was broadened and the marginal rates lowered, this was not as much of a fundamental restructuring of the tax system as many people seem to believe. For example, total tax expenditures associated with the federal budget were estimated to have an outlay equivalence of $337 billion in fiscal 1982; despite tax reform, they grew to an estimated outlay equivalent of $361 billion in fiscal 1988.[9] To understand the issues raised by the tax revision, it is helpful to look at the major structure of the federal tax code and some of the sources of controversy about how the tax is levied.

Once we have reached some understanding of how income is taxed at the federal level, we turn to state and local income taxes. We consider general

---

[8] Advisory Commission on Intergovernmental Relations (ACIR), *Significant Features of Fiscal Federalism, 1988*, vol. 2, M-155 II (Washington, DC: 1988), pp. 60–61.

[9] Joseph A. Pechman, *Federal Tax Policy*, 4th ed. (Washington, DC: Brookings Institution, 1983), p. 342, and 5th ed. (1987), p. 356.

issues such as administrative costs and equity, viewing each tax in isolation and also looking at the interaction among the different taxes. Finally, the efficiency effects of income taxes can be quite significant. We treat these from the different perspectives of the various levels of government.

/// DEFINING INCOME FOR FEDERAL TAXATION

The definition of income for tax purposes addresses many of the issues we discussed in the previous chapter. However, the general approach can be broken down into several basic areas: (1) a definition of income; (2) exclusions or exemptions from this definition; (3) deductions and items of tax preference that are subtracted from income; (4) items of tax credit that directly reduce the tax due on income. Some of the specific items within this broad classification were altered or moved to other classifications in 1986, but the broad classifications were not changed.

For the federal personal income tax, the basic definition of income is all money payments for labor, plus the interest and dividends received on savings and investments, plus the net gain on assets sold during the accounting period and any profits from running a business. Most items of consumption that are not received as monetary payment are excluded from the income base. For example, employer-paid health care benefits are not treated as taxable income; however, free housing provided by an employer is.

Most income received from pensions is treated as earned income to the extent that it is paid from untaxed contributions. If the employee made any after-tax contributions to the retirement fund, part of the payments will be treated as a tax-exempt return of contribution. Social Security payments were completely tax free until recently. Now half of the payments are taxable for single taxpayers with income above $25,000 and for married taxpayers with income above $32,000. Essentially, the part of the Social Security tax paid by employees comes from after-tax income and the part paid by the employers is not taxed. Thus, about half of the contributions are not taxed, so the current system taxes half of the benefits, but only for higher income taxpayers. Certain other types of money income have also been excluded in the past, such as some unemployment compensation and some disability compensation, but the tax reform of 1986 made unemployment compensation part of the tax base. The exact specifications could easily take up several pages, but this gives the broad nature of the definition.

Once total gross income is calculated, the tax code allows the taxpayer to reduce this income for a variety of reasons. When adjustments have been made, the remaining amount is the *adjusted gross income* for the taxpayer. The most basic reduction is for the cost of earning income. In the past adjustments for the cost of earning income were relatively widely available; but one of the effects of the base broadening of the 1986 tax revision is to make this item a deduction rather than an adjustment for taxpayers who are employed by others. It is now deductible only if it exceeds 2% of the adjusted gross income. Certain moving expenses were also allowed as an adjustment to income prior to the 1986 change and are now allowed only as an itemized deduction. The distinction is an important one because most people do not itemize. Also, certain tax calculations depend on adjusted gross income, so a higher number here might increase taxes even if the deduction is allowed somewhere else.

The taxpaying unit may be either an individual or a family. Filing as a family allows a one-earner household to spread the income over more people and thus reduce the progressivity of the tax; however, households with more than one income-earner may pay more tax as a family than the total of the individual tax liabilities. The income of the second earner is taxed at the higher rates for the total family income. Essentially, the federal code allows some benefits for joint returns by making the income brackets wider for them, but they are not twice as wide as the ones for individual returns. Thus, two-earner families might find themselves with higher taxes as a married couple than they would if they added their individual taxes as singles. The tax code has been changed for such concerns a number of times in the past. Just prior to the 1986 revision, married couples were allowed a tax credit on the income of the lower paid person. This was used to offset the "marriage penalty" for those with two incomes; but it is no longer available.

Most people file on a calendar year basis. In certain circumstances, however, it is possible to have a tax year that does not correspond to the calendar year.

Personal exemptions are allowed for each family member. In 1986 the amount allowed was $1,080 per person; this was to be indexed for inflation under the old law. The new law raised the deduction to $1,900 in 1987, $1,950 in 1988, and $2,000 in 1989. It is supposed to be indexed to the rate of inflation after that. In addition there is a standard deduction for each taxpaying unit. The combined effect of the standard deduction and the personal exemptions is to try to exempt from tax the amount of income that a person or family needs for minimal subsistence. This objective had been somewhat eroded over time, and the revisions of the code in 1986 have significantly altered the direct taxation of low-income persons. The changes in the exemptions and in the standard deduction when coupled with the earned income tax credit (which we come to shortly) have greatly reduced the number of poor families paying federal taxes.

Standard deductions have been increased somewhat under the new law. This is the amount that a taxpayer can deduct from adjusted gross income to determine taxable income even if there are no itemized deductions. Itemized deductions are various expenses such as mortgage interest, state and local income taxes and property taxes, medical expenses, charitable contributions, costs of earning income, and certain other expenses. Under the new tax law some of these items can be only partially deducted. If the allowable deductions exceed the standard deduction, this amount is deducted from adjusted gross income to determine taxable income.

The standard deduction went from $2,540 in 1987 to $3,000 in 1988 for singles and from $3,760 for married couples filing jointly in 1987 to $5,000 in 1988. The option of itemizing deductions is still attractive for many taxpayers; however, the reduction in itemized deductions along with the increase in the standard deduction makes itemization less attractive for a large number of people. Preliminary estimates for the 1987 tax year indicated that about 15% fewer taxpayers were itemizing as compared to 1986 and the full adjustment had not yet taken place.[10] One benefit of having people using the standard deduction is reduced incentives to take advantage of the tax expenditures available through deductions. Those who take the standard deduction get no benefit from small increases in the amount of itemized deductions.

The major changes in itemized deductions were to eliminate the deduction for state and local sales taxes and to phase out the deduction of interest expenses other than those for home mortgages. Other important changes were to limit medical deductions to amounts greater than 7.5% of adjusted gross income and miscellaneous deductions to amounts greater than 2% of adjusted gross income. The effect of these limits is both to increase taxable income even for those who use the deductions and also to discourage most people from using them at all.

Taxable income is then taxed at either the 15% or 28% rate associated with the new tax code. The new law creates a rather strange quirk in tax rates by phasing out personal exemptions and the "preferential" tax rate of 15% for higher income individuals. Thus, there is a range where the 28% tax rate is effectively a 33% tax rate. Once the "preferences" are taxed at the 28% rate, the marginal rate drops back down to 28%, so that there is no possibility of paying more than the 28% on average, although there is a range where the marginal tax is above this. The old tax law allowed additional personal exemptions for the aged or blind, but these have been converted to additional standard deduction amounts. Hence, they are not available to people with large amounts of itemized deductions.

There are alternate ways for people to calculate their tax liability. For example, those who make extensive use of tax preference items may have to pay the alternative minimum tax. This tax is intended to reduce the incentive to use tax preference items by reducing the possibility that high-income households will be able to pay zero taxes.[11] The specifics are fairly complex, but the effect is to reduce the value of tax preference items for some taxpayers by assuring that all high-income families pay at least some tax. Another form of alternative tax calculation, income averaging, was eliminated by the 1986 revisions. Remember that income averaging was supposed to reduce the effect of a progressive tax system on unusually large income years. The extra tax

---

[10] "Fewer taxpayers itemize – as planned," *Oregonian* (May 5, 1988), p. D9.
[11] For example, 325 individuals and couples with income over $200,000 paid no federal income taxes in 1985. See Jim Luther, "Fewer Wealthy Americans Escape Taxes," *Oregonian* (March 25, 1987), p. D13.

was associated with the higher marginal rates applicable to high income versus lower incomes. Congress apparently felt that the lower marginal rates and wider brackets made this a less important concern under the new tax code and eliminated the possibility for individuals.

Once the tax has been calculated, a number of tax credits directly reduce the amount of tax owed. These credits were greatly reduced by the tax reform act of 1986 except for the earned income tax credit, which is available for income earned by low-income families with children. It is only applicable to earned income, and it is phased out for higher incomes. The maximum credit rate is 14% for income up to $6,225, for a maximum credit of $874, and this is reduced until it reaches zero for income above $18,576 in 1988. The applicable ranges were adjusted for inflation each year. It is the only widely available credit that can result in a negative tax liability. This credit will be refunded to the taxpayer even if the federal government ends up refunding more than was actually paid in taxes. To a large extent this reflects a concern that low-income households pay Social Security taxes even if they have no personal income tax liability. Other credits cannot reduce the tax liability below zero.

/// PAYING FEDERAL TAXES

The actual payment of taxes is done largely over the year in which the income is earned. Wages and salaries are subject to withholding by the employer. Essentially, the employer uses information furnished by the employee to determine how much of the wages are likely to be needed to pay federal taxes. This amount is withheld from the employee and sent to the IRS instead. People with income from other sources, such as interest or self-employment, are required to submit estimated taxes to the government each quarter. Many people believe that without the use of withholding the income tax system would not be feasible at its current level. Withholding allows the government use of the money over the year, but it also allows the individual to avoid having to make one very large payment once a year. For a variety of reasons people would probably spend more during the year rather than setting aside the money needed to pay their tax bill when due. Thus, they would be faced with either a significant reduction in their other savings at tax time or the need to borrow money for taxes. It is widely believed that people would resent either of these approaches much more than they do the current approach. In addition, as noted earlier, the fact that the government already has a substantial amount of tax money induces people to file returns. This greatly reduces the amount of tax evasion.

Once the taxpayers' income tax liability is calculated, they compare this to the amount that was either withheld or paid in quarterly estimated payments. If the liability is greater than the amount paid, another check is due to the government. If the tax liability is below the amount already paid, a refund is due. When the tax return is sent to the IRS, all returns are checked for certain frequent errors, and some are selected for audit. An audit simply means that the IRS wants to verify the accuracy of the return; it usually does not want to do that unless there is some reason to suspect that the taxpayer owes more to the government than the return shows.

The IRS gets independent reports of wages and salaries from employers and reports of many sources of interest and dividends from the payers. These are compared to the amounts shown on a return to see if all income is being reported. In addition, the IRS has certain guidelines regarding reasonable levels for certain deductions and preference items. Returns that fall outside of these guidelines might also be selected for audit.

The IRS has much better information about income for most people than it does about their allowable deductions. Thus, these are the areas where there is likely to be the greatest uncertainty and where people are likely to try to interpret things in their favor. Further, the complexity of the tax code can lead to many honest errors.

/// SELECTED ISSUES IN FEDERAL INCOME TAXATION

Deductions

Items may be deducted from income because they are costs of earning that income, are themselves taxes, or have been granted special status by Congress. Generally, items are allowed as deductions either because they represent lowered real income, such as medical costs, or because Congress believes people should be encouraged to do more, such as giving to charity. Many of these deductions are now limited to amounts above a certain percentage of income. For example, we already mentioned that many of the business expenses for employees could only be deducted if they exceed 2% of adjusted gross income. Similarly, medical expenses can only be deducted if they exceed 7.5% of adjusted gross income. Interest expenses can be deducted for most mortgages and for loans used for investment. However, interest for consumer items is being phased out as a deduction.

To help raise the rate of savings in the U.S., Congress created the individual retirement account. The Pension Reform Act of 1974 established the individual retirement account and the 1981 Tax Act substantially increased eligibility. Under this provision, each worker could set aside up to $2,000 per year of earned income for retirement. The amount could then be deducted in figuring taxable income. As part of the base broadening in 1986, this deduction was limited. It is allowed for most single taxpayers with adjusted gross income below $25,000 and married taxpayers with adjusted gross income below $40,000. For those covered by pension plans this deduction is phased out for incomes above these limits.

These limits and phase-outs for deductions can increase effective marginal tax rates above the published level, and they make the tax code more complex. Consider as an example a married couple, each of whom earns $21,000 per year with no adjustments to income. Imagine that they also have medical expenses above the 7.5% limit and miscellaneous deductions above the 2% limit. Finally, imagine that they each contribute to an IRA for $2,000 per year. If either of these people were to increase earnings by $1,000 their taxable income would rise by $1,495. This is because they would lose $400 in deductions for the IRAs, $75 in deductions for the medical expenses, and $20 in miscellaneous deductions. The increase in tax would then be $419 or about 42%. This shows that there are at least some cases where the marginal rates are going to be substantially higher than was originally intended.

The intent of the minimum amount needed to get a deduction was both to reduce the amount deducted and thus raise the tax base and also to reduce the negative incentives associated with the use of these deductions for normal expenses. However, the above example illustrates that these goals have been achieved at a cost. Whether they are worth the cost or not is open to debate. In particular, the information on how many people are caught in situations like the above will be necessary to determine if it creates a significant problem.

Another area of some controversy related to deductions is the elimination of the deduction for sales taxes. There is disagreement about whether state and local taxes should be deductible in figuring federal income taxes. The basic justification for such deductibility in the past was that it prevents the levying of a tax on a tax. In particular, it prevents the interaction of state and federal income taxes from creating a rate above 100% at the margin. With the lowering of federal rates, this particular concern is less relevant; but there is still controversy regarding the issue. One could justify the elimination of the sales tax deduction on the technical grounds that this was the only tax deduction for which there was no requirement to verify expenditure. Because it was deemed unreasonable to expect individuals to save all receipts showing sales tax payments, the IRS essentially adopted a rule allowing people in sales tax states to take a deduction of a given percentage of their income. Thus, the effect was in practice a lowering of the federal marginal rate for those who itemized.

There are several arguments for allowing the deduction of such taxes. They all relate to a form of subsidy of the state and local sector by the federal government. Perhaps the most plausible argument is that state and local governments levy taxes that are only loosely related to the services they provide to any particular taxpayer. Hence, there is incentive for some tax-payers to move to low-tax states. However, the deductibility of these taxes for federal tax calculations reduces this incentive and, in particular, reduces it more for higher income individuals. They are more likely to move in response to such differences and they receive the greatest benefits from the deduction since they have the higher marginal tax rates. The other side of this argument is that the residents of the taxing jurisdiction do not bear the full costs of the taxes raised. Rather, part of the tax burden is shifted to taxpayers in the rest of the country. Hence, there may be an incentive for the state and local governments to expand excessively. In either case, the controversy is likely to continue for some time.

The treatment of interest has also created significant controversy. Under the old income tax laws, all interest payments were deductible as an itemized deduction. Many people felt that this led to excessive use of credit, since the federal government was effectively subsidizing borrowing. This was also associated with the argument that there is too little saving in the U.S. Attempts to exclude all interest payments from deduction were thwarted by strong support for continued deductibility of the interest on home mortgages. In addition, it was recognized that if interest and dividend income were going to be taxed, it would create problems not to allow a deduction for loans used to buy these investment instruments. If the deductions were not allowed, people would have a strong tax argument against borrowing to make such investments, and this was not considered desirable.

The issue with respect to home mortgages is also related to the imputed rent on home ownership. Essentially, it is possible to make the case that the major tax benefit to home ownership is that the rent on imputed income is not taxed. This benefit will always be available to those who can purchase their homes outright. However, it can also be made available to less wealthy taxpayers by allowing the deductibility of the home mortgage interest. Thus, the deductibility of interest on home mortgages could also be considered as an equity issue given that the imputed rent on home ownership will not be taxed (see Box 8-1 for an example).

Tax Exemptions

As we have just argued, the lack of tax on imputed rent is a major tax advantage, but it is not likely to be altered in the United States in the near future. Other forms of tax-exempt income are subject to discussion even if the probability of changing their status is fairly low. For example, there have been proposals to tax the value of major fringe benefits to workers, but this does not appear likely to happen in the near future. The exemption of interest on state and local bonds has also been discussed, but this also does not appear likely to become a taxable item very soon. Rather, the 1986 reform placed limits on how much tax-exempt debt could be issued, in particular, on the amount of private purpose tax-exempt debt.

/// STATE AND LOCAL INCOME TAXES

Many states define their income bases essentially the same way that the federal government does. However, others deviate significantly from the federal treatment. There are several reasons why a state might want to define

Box 8-1

/////// Mortgage Deductibility

Consider the following example. The Smiths and the Joneses each receive $30,000 per year in wage and salary income and each couple has a net worth of $100,000. The Smiths own a $100,000 house while the Joneses own $100,000 worth of stock. Each year the Joneses receive a $10,000 dividend on their stock and use it to rent a house identical to the Smiths'. For all intents and purposes, these families are identical in income, wealth, and housing consumption, yet the Smiths will have a lower tax bill. Their tax will be based only on their $30,000 income, while the Joneses' tax is based on their income plus the $10,000 dividend received. Clearly, the Joneses have a strong incentive to sell their stock and buy the house that they have been renting.

Although economists recognize imputed rent as the major tax expenditure associated with home ownership, most people focus on the deductibility of mortgage interest. The deductibility of interest does indeed make home ownership more attractive to many, but this particular deduction has a strong equity component. Consider a third family, the Does, who also have an annual income of $30,000 but who have no savings. They also rent a home identical to the Smiths' for $10,000. They pay the same taxes as the Smiths, but the Smiths are clearly better off. Suppose that the Does decide to borrow $100,000 to buy their current home. For simplicity assume that the interest payments on this loan are also $10,000 per year. If interest is not tax deductible, the Does find no tax advantage to ownership. However, if they can deduct the interest, they get the same advantage that the wealthier families do. Thus, if the deduction for mortgage interest were to be eliminated, it would have little impact on those wealthy enough to own their homes outright. They could simply sell off income-earning assets to pay off any mortgage they might have. In this way they would reduce their income through lower investment returns rather than mortgage deductions. But others would simply lose their deductions.

This type of argument probably helps explain why the 1986 tax reform continued to allow deduction of mortgage interest but does not allow the deduction of interest on consumer loans.

the income tax base differently. One is that there are many things that the federal government wants to encourage with tax breaks that the state governments would not want to encourage. For example, federal tax credits for energy conservation or preferential treatment of capital gains to encourage investment may be areas that some state governments do not want to subsidize. Further, a state tax that is simply defined as the federal base suffers from possible severe jumps in tax revenue as the federal government redefines its base. Thus, such states saw their tax bases increase significantly when the federal government eliminated the preferential treatment of capital gains along with many other tax preferences in 1986.

Since 1972, the option has existed for states to "piggyback" on the federal income tax. If they were willing to define their tax base as the federal tax base with a few minor modifications, the federal government would collect the tax for them and absorb the administrative costs. Despite the seeming attractiveness of the offer, no state has ever been willing to do this.

In 1985, three states simply levied an income tax that was a stated percentage of the federal tax liability. This type of state income tax obviously has the least amount of taxpayer compliance cost associated with it. Another seven states started with federal taxable income and then essentially applied their own rate structure to the taxable income. This allows the state to make its tax code either more or less progressive than the federal code. One state allows its residents to choose between the two options. Twenty-four states and the District of Columbia start with federal adjusted gross income and have their own rules for deductions, exemptions, and so on. Several states only tax "unearned income" or tax this at a higher rate than earned income. Only six of the states do not start the calculation of state tax liability from some part of the federal tax calculation.[12]

Finally, most local governments that use an income tax either rely on a wage and salary tax or specify their tax as a levy on the state tax base. It is much easier to administer and enforce a wage and salary tax than a comprehensive income tax. Also, labor earnings are less geographically mobile than are other assets. Hence, local governments may actually be better off using the less comprehensive base because it is a much harder tax to avoid by moving. Those who want to avoid it must usually both live and work outside the taxing jurisdiction, whereas the tax on unearned income usually can be avoided by simply living outside the jurisdiction.

/// THE MAGNITUDE OF TAX EXPENDITURES

When the government does decide to specifically encourage some form of activity, a tax expenditure can be a powerful incentive. In some extreme cases, the government pays close to the full cost of the activity. For example, both the federal government and the state of Oregon used to allow 50% tax credits against political contributions up to $50 for a single taxpayer or $100 for a married couple filing jointly. Thus, Oregon residents paid little of the first $50 of political contributions. They got a $25 credit against their federal tax and a

---

[12] Advisory Commission on Intergovernmental Relations, *Significant Features of Fiscal Federalism, 1985–86* M-146 (Washington, DC: 1986), p. 90.

$25 credit against their state tax. This does not reduce the tax burden by the full $50 because many people itemized state taxes in computing their federal tax and the state allowed everyone to deduct federal taxes in computing state income. Thus, the reduction in federal taxes raises state taxes and the reduction in state taxes may raise federal taxes. Nevertheless, the net cost of the political contribution was fairly low. When the federal government eliminated its 50% tax credit in 1986, the state of Oregon raised its credit to 100%. Thus, except for the time between payment and reimbursement, the state is paying the full cost of this activity.

The magnitude of these tax expenditures gives some idea of how significant the effects can be. The federal government publishes a series of Special Analyses of the federal budget. Special Analysis G is an estimate of the outlay equivalents for major tax expenditures.[13] The estimated outlay equivalent under the heading "Commerce and housing credit" for 1987 is $41 billion for corporations and $180 billion for individuals. Because of the changes in the tax laws and the reduction in marginal tax rates, this falls to an estimated $35 billion for corporations and $89 billion for individuals in 1989. Thus, there is a reduction of almost $100 billion in these incentives, but the total is still substantial. While this is the largest subtotal in the section, several others have amounts in the tens of billions of dollars; for example, the subtotal under "Income security" is $80 billion for 1989, down from $96 billion in 1987.

It may be helpful to look at some of the biggest tax expenditures individually to get some idea of where the tax breaks are greatest. For example, the deductibility of mortgage interest on owner-occupied homes is estimated to have an expenditure equivalence of $32 billion in 1989. Deductibility of interest on consumer credit fell from about $12 billion in 1987 to $3 billion in 1989 and should fall to zero since this deduction is being phased out. Special treatment of capital gains had an equivalence of $98 billion in 1987, which fell to zero in 1989. It is interesting to note that the 1987 figure is high because many people "cashed in" their capital gains before the special treatment expired. Exclusion of interest on public-purpose state and local debt had a combined individual and corporate amount of $14 billion in 1987, which rose to $15 billion in 1989 despite the reduction in tax rates. In contrast, tax incentives for preservation of historic structures had a combined impact of only about $220 million in 1987, which fell to $170 million in 1989.

At the state level the magnitude of the tax expenditures is not as great, but there are a large and growing variety of them. California provides estimates of the annual cost of certain tax expenditure items associated with either the personal income tax, the bank and corporation tax, or the sales and use tax.[14] The state estimated that tax expenditures associated with the state personal income tax totaled $7.5 billion in 1987–88. For example, the solar energy

---

[13] U.S. Office of Management and Budget, *Special Analyses: Budget of the United States Government, Fiscal Year 1989* (Washington, DC: U.S. Government Printing Office, 1988).
[14] "Governor's Budget Summary 1987–8" (Sacramento: State of California, 1987), p. 110.

credits cost about $45 million per year and the capital gains exclusion cost about $770 million per year. Alternatively, the exemption of bottled water from the sales tax cost about $25 million per year.

The tax reform of 1986 was largely a response to the perceived unfairness of the many deductions and exemptions in the federal tax code. By eliminating many of these tax expenditures, the tax base was broadened. This allows the same amount of revenue to be raised with lower marginal tax rates. Thus, the maximum effective tax rate when the new system is fully phased in will be 33% rather than 50%. Despite this drop in the marginal rates, the reduction in tax expenditures means that the average tax paid will go down by much less than the reduction in marginal tax rates.

/// ISSUES OF STATE AND LOCAL INCOME TAXES

As noted earlier, most states tie their income taxes to that of the federal government. The four that specify state taxes as a percentage of the federal personal tax liability saw their potential tax decline as a result of the 1986 tax revision. Personal taxes, on average, were reduced and corporate taxes increased to offset the revenue decline. Alternatively, those states that based their income tax on the federal definitions of income found that they would receive increases in their collections. In all, twenty-two states would have received substantial increases in revenue if they had maintained their relationship to the federal tax base and used their existing rates.[15] Most of these states then revised their own tax codes in response to this stimulus.

Many of these individual states obtain substantial amounts of their total state revenue from the income tax. For example, Oregon obtained 61% of all state tax revenue from its income tax in 1986; New York and Massachusetts each received about half of their state tax revenues from income taxes.[16] Raising this amount of revenue from the tax that the federal government relies on has aroused some concern over efficiency. Remember that it is the marginal tax rate that creates the efficiency cost of a particular tax. The marginal rate can be substantially increased if the state is taxing the same income as the federal government. Similarly, the use of the same deductions and exemptions creates a compounded effect on the incentive for such items. This is further exacerbated where cities add on to the state tax. For example, New York City levies a city income tax, which is simply a surcharge on the state income tax. The combined effect of these rates can be a marginal rate substantially above the marginal rate reported in any one of the tax codes. Thus, the maximum state tax rate in New York in 1987 was 8.5%, but a person living in New York

---

[15] Steven J. Gold, "The State Government Response to Federal Income Tax Reform," *National Tax Journal* 40 (1987), p. 434.

[16] Ibid.

City could be subject to an additional 4.1% for a true state-local marginal rate of 12.6%. This would be in addition to any federal income taxes or Social Security taxes.[17]

Part of this problem is offset by the use of mutual deductibility. Thus, the state and local taxes might be itemized in the calculation of federal tax liability. Hence, a person subject to the New York state and city taxes and also subject to a 28% federal marginal rate would have the federal taxes reduced if the state and local taxes were itemized. This would make the state-local tax rate an effective marginal rate of 9% rather than the nominal cumulative rate of 12.6%. New York does not allow the deductibility of federal taxes, but some other states do, and this further reduces the cumulative marginal rates.[18] The federal government allows the deductibility of state taxes largely for this reason. In addition, sixteen states allow either full or partial deductibility of the federal tax in calculating state liabilities.[19] This does indeed reduce the problem; however, it does not eliminate the issue of very high marginal tax rates.

Perhaps in response to the federal initiative to broaden the base and lower rates, many of the states appear to be reducing their use of tax expenditures and their highest tax rates. The increased conformity is likely to reduce the administrative and compliance costs that the taxes generate. It will be some time before the transitional issues and responses to the changes have settled out of the system and the new tax code can be fully evaluated.

/// INTERACTION

There is an important issue regarding the income that a state can legally tax. The state clearly cannot tax the income of nonresidents earned in other states. Thus, California cannot arbitrarily tax the residents of Massachusetts. Generally, the courts have allowed the states to tax all income of their residents no matter where it is earned and they allow the states to tax all income originating in the state whether or not it accrues to residents. This clearly allows for some overlapping. Thus, a Massachusetts resident who worked in California for a while might find that both states wanted to tax the income earned in California. Most states take the position that they can indeed tax all such income; however, they recognize the double taxation problem by allowing the person to take a credit for any taxes paid to other states. Nevertheless, an individual might find that there is substantial complexity related to the state

---

[17] ACIR, *1988*, op. cit., Tables 16 and 20.

[18] The deductibility of federal taxes on state returns is a form of subsidy to the federal government by the states. See Roger H. Bezdek and Ernest M. Zampelli, "State and Local Tax Expenditures Relating to the Federal Government," *National Tax Journal* 39 (December 1986), pp. 533–538.

[19] Gold, op. cit., p. 435.

income taxes if income is earned outside the state of residence and the various states have substantially different tax codes.

Progressivity in State and Local Income Taxes

State and local taxes that are modeled after the federal tax also tend to have a progressive tax structure. While the degree of progressivity is usually lower in the state and local taxes, it does raise a controversy. The major element in the controversy is the extent to which these levels of government should be engaged in redistributive activity. The use of a progressive tax is almost certainly intended to be of a redistributive nature. Yet the greater mobility at the state and local level leads many analysts to conclude that attempts to redistribute at this level will create inefficient migration incentives. In particular, there is concern that relatively high-income families will move out of states with substantially progressive tax systems.[20]

There are several interesting responses to this argument. One is that some amount of redistribution is required at levels other than the national one to take account of differences in cost of living among regions. Thus, any set federal redistributive program is either going to give too little to low-income people in high-cost areas and take too much from high-income people in such areas or it will give too much to low-income people in low-cost areas and take too little from high-income people in such areas. Another argument is that the local community is better able to assess the desire for redistribution and that people are far more concerned about the income distribution in their immediate area than they are about the distribution in the nation as a whole. Thus, local redistribution is likely to be more acceptable.

There is much controversy about the above views, but there is another issue relating to our discussion of the interaction of taxes. The fact that people can itemize their state taxes when calculating their federal taxes creates an opportunity for the state to export part of its tax burden. Essentially, the state tax is lowered by the federal reduction for those who itemize. Further, high-income families are more likely to itemize and they will face higher federal tax rates. For example, in 1980 the percentage who itemized climbed from less than 10% of those with adjusted gross income of less than $14,000 to over 90% of those with adjusted gross income above $80,000.[21]

One author calculates that if the state of Minnesota had used a flat-rate tax to generate its state income in 1980 instead of its progressive tax, the reduction in federal taxes for the state's residents would have been $239 million rather than the estimated $306 million. Thus, the use of the progres-

---

[20] One study finds that such incentives might be very significant at the local level. See Henry W. Herzog, Jr. and Alan M. Schlottmann, "State and Local Tax Deductibility and Metropolitan Migration," *National Tax Journal* 39 (June 1986), pp. 189–200.

[21] Joel Slemrod, "The Optimal Progressivity of the Minnesota Tax System," *Final Report of the Minnesota Tax Study Commission: Vol. 2, Staff Papers* (St. Paul, MN: Butterworth Legal Publishers, 1986), pp. 127–138.

sive system led to an increase of almost $67 million in the amount of tax exporting by the state.[22] Hence, the state faces a trade-off in terms of the amount of tax it can export and the incentives to move it gives higher income people. This trade-off is likely to get worse with the reduction in the highest federal marginal tax rates; but it is also likely that the percentage of low-income people itemizing will be further reduced relative to higher income people. This is especially true since the number of low-income families paying any federal income taxes has been reduced with the tax reform.

One final issue with respect to progressivity is that many of the states use their personal income tax code to offset the regressivity that may exist in other major taxes. For example, we have discussed that the sales tax is often regressive as it is actually administered. One approach to this issue is to make substantial adjustments in the coverage of the tax. Thus, many states exempt food to try to reduce this regressivity. However, a state income tax credit is likely to be a more efficient way to offset this type of regressivity. It certainly will have lower administrative and compliance costs than the direct attempt to alter the coverage of the sales tax. The ability to make such adjustments is another reason why states appear to be unwilling to "piggyback" on the federal tax code.

/// SUMMARY

The federal tax reform of 1986 created substantial changes in the way the federal government collects income taxes. The structure of the tax was made flatter but the base was substantially broadened. Despite the lowering of the tax rates for higher income families, most calculations find that they are likely to face higher rather than lower taxes under the new system. Thus, the system has changed to look more like a flat-rate system and act more like a progressive system. Many of the changes in the use of deductions and other tax provisions have increased the complexity of the code substantially. Part of this is due to the many transition rules, but it is likely that the new code will remain a complex one. The importance of this complexity will be largely determined by the number of people who choose not to itemize or take advantage of other tax preferences because of the changes. One aim of the revisions was to induce more people to file simple tax returns, and this may reduce the overall complexity even if the code itself has become more complex.

Despite the reduction in the use of tax preferences, many remain in the tax code. Further, many legislators still view tax preferences as a useful tool to accomplish their objectives. Hence, it is likely that additional tax preferences will continue to be added to the tax code and some of the ones removed may be resurrected. Part of the reason is that the tax code does have substantial

[22] Ibid.

incentive effects, and the importance of particular incentive effects changes over time.

Most state income taxes were affected substantially by the changes in the federal code. This is because most states either calculate their taxes as a percentage of the federal liability or they use the federal base as a starting point in calculating their taxable base. The interaction of federal and state-local taxes can create relatively high marginal tax rates. These rates can in turn create high marginal efficiency costs in the collection of revenue. However, the use of a progressive income tax system can appear to be beneficial to a state government because the deductibility of state taxes in calculating federal income tax liabilities allows more of the state tax to be exported to the rest of the country. This occurs because a progressive tax structure requires larger state payments from higher income families, who are also more likely to itemize and will have higher marginal federal rates. Thus, they get a greater reduction in their federal taxes for each dollar paid to the state. Offsetting this advantage is the possibility that the higher marginal rates will discourage some higher income families from living in the state.

Chapter 9 //////

Corporate Income Taxation

Many people question why there is a separate tax on corporate income. All other sources of income are taxed under the personal income tax system. Profits from businesses that are run by one person or by a set of partners are taxed as part of the owners' income. Indeed, the dividends that a corporation pays to its shareholders are also taxed under the personal income tax system. So why is corporate income subject to an additional tax?

From an economic perspective, the corporation could serve as a tax shelter under current treatment of its activities and earnings. Corporations are legal entities, which are in some sense separate from their owners. The owners have clear rights to the returns that the corporation earns; however, the shareholders only receive this money when it is paid out as dividends. Until such time as the corporation pays a dividend to its owners, no income is created for the owners under current federal definitions of income.

In practice, many corporations pay out very little of their net earnings in the form of dividends. Rather, they use this money to expand or to make other investments. Thus, the value of the company increases over time, but the owners are not subject to any personal income tax. In the limit, the corporation would never have to pay any dividends and the owners could get their investment returns in the form of increases in the value of the stock. Whenever they wanted to convert this increase in value into income, they could sell off some of their stock. In this way the income tax would be postponed until such time as the person chose to convert the stock to cash. Further, the increase in stock value would be treated as a capital gain rather than as ordinary income. Under the current tax law this makes little difference; however, when capital gains were receiving preferential treatment, this resulted in a favorable tax situation as well.[1]

---

[1] The tax changes did not eliminate all the favorable treatment that capital gains receive. In particular, all

Since postponing taxes creates a net benefit for the taxpayer, the ability to use a corporation to postpone taxes on business profits could generate a substantial tax advantage. Further, if preferential treatment of capital gains is reinstated, the income from the corporation could largely be taxed at the favorable capital gains rate rather than the rate of ordinary income. Both of these advantages associated with the returns to corporate investment warrant some method to maintain equitable tax treatment between individuals who invest in corporate businesses and others who do not. The corporate income tax is a tax on the net earnings of corporations. Thus, it does prevent the earnings that are not paid out as dividends from being completely untaxed. However, many argue that it results in overtaxation of this form of income and leads to substantial distortions within the economy.

/// FIGURES AND TRENDS

The corporate income tax is a tax on all earnings of corporations minus the expenses of generating those earnings. However, as we discuss shortly, the treatment of various types of expenses can have a substantial impact on how the base is defined in practice. In particular, the treatment of expenses for capital goods has been very important in determining the actual tax base. Both the federal corporate income tax and most state corporate income taxes have progressive rate structures; but the federal tax and most state taxes reach their maximum marginal rates at relatively low values of corporate income, so they are often treated as flat-rate taxes. In many ways, the concept of ability to pay does not apply to corporations, since there is no reason to expect a correlation between the income of the corporation and the income of its shareholders. For example, the shares of an unprofitable corporation might be owned by very high-income individuals while the shares of a very profitable one might be owned by lower income individuals. Further, the distortion caused by the tax will be higher if marginal rates are above average for a given revenue yield. Hence, there is little rationale for having a progressive rate structure for the corporate tax.

Starting July 1, 1987 the federal rate was 15% on earnings to $50,000; 25% on earnings to $75,000; and 34% on amounts above $75,000. Further, there is a surcharge on amounts above $100,000, up to $335,000, to offset the preferential treatment of the tax for lower incomes. This amounts to an effective marginal tax rate of 39% over this range. The highest state marginal tax rate was 12% for Iowa in 1987, but this rate was not reached until taxable

---

assets left as bequests are revalued at the giver's death and there are no capital gains taxes. There are also other methods by which a person can escape some or all capital gains taxes; and even if taxes are paid, the ability to set the timing of the taxes provides some benefits. For example, a person may sell a capital asset when other income is low and he or she is in a relatively low marginal tax bracket, e.g., after retirement.

income exceeded $250,000.[2] Further, the effective rate was only 7.9% because of the interaction with the federal tax.[3] New Mexico did not impose its highest tax rate until taxable income went above $1,000,000; many other states have only one rate for all levels of taxable income.[4]

The federal corporate income tax generated $63 billion in 1986, around 13% of the total tax revenue collected from general sources. Meanwhile, states collected another $18 billion from corporate income taxes, close to 8% of total general tax revenue at this level. Finally, local governments collected almost $1.6 billion from this source, but this was almost exclusively collected by the cities of New York and Washington, DC.[5] As noted earlier the federal tax had been going down relative to GNP over the last few years. However, this should change with the new code. In fact, a substantial part of the revenue needed to make the 1986 tax reform generate the same amount of revenue as the tax code it replaced is associated with this shift from the personal to corporate tax.

The expected corporate tax payments to the federal government are higher despite the rather large decline in the highest tax rate because the decline in rate is accompanied by a substantial increase in the base on which the tax is levied. Many tax preferences have been either eliminated or made less generous. We discuss the reasons for such changes and their impact in more detail shortly, but the effect is an increase in corporate tax payments. Some analysts have criticized the tax reform for promising lower taxes to most people and then making up the difference with a "hidden" increase in the corporate tax. One problem with the tax is that there is little agreement on its final incidence. However, some people are going to end up paying higher hidden taxes to offset some of the reduction in the more visible personal income taxes.

/// **INCIDENCE**

From an economic perspective, a corporation cannot bear the final incidence of a tax because it does not consume. Hence, its final consumption cannot be affected by the existence of the tax. The tax must be paid by the owners of the corporation, the customers of the corporation, or the suppliers of inputs to corporations, if we are to look at the direct shifting possibilities. The shifting of this tax may lead to many other incidence possibilities.

First, it is important to understand exactly what the corporate income tax taxes. It is specified as a tax on corporate profits. However, these profits are generally the return on investments made by the company. They differ little

---

[2] Advisory Commission on Intergovernmental Relations (ACIR), *Significant Features of Fiscal Federalism, 1988 Edition*, vol. 1, M-155 (Washington, DC: December 1987), pp. 50–53.

[3] Joseph A. Pechman, *Federal Tax Policy*, 5th ed. (Washington, DC: Brookings, 1987), p. 398.

[4] ACIR, op. cit.

[5] ACIR, op. cit., vol. 2, pp. 60–61.

from the interest earned on savings by an individual or the return to any other investment made by a person or business. Since the personal income tax code taxes these type of earnings, there is nothing unusual about their inclusion in the tax base. The problem as seen by the critics of the tax is that this return is taxed once at the corporate level and then again when the corporation either forwards the net earnings to the owners as dividends or when the owners sell part of their appreciated stock and receive capital gains.

Some of the support for the tax is associated with the belief that its incidence is very progressive. This conclusion stems from an assumption that the tax is paid by the owners of the corporation. If this assumption is accepted, the tax is indeed quite progressive. Stock ownership increases substantially with income. Fewer than 20% of all households in the United States own any corporate stock; those with incomes above $96,000 in 1983, about 2.4% of all households, owned almost two-thirds of all stock held by households.[6] Thus, the incidence of the tax on the direct ownership of stock would be very progressive. This is somewhat offset by the fact that pension funds own about half of all corporate stock, and thus the ultimate ownership is not clear. The incidence in this part would depend on whether companies would have to pay more into the pension plans to offset lower returns or whether workers would have to accept lower pensions. In any case, this simplistic view of the incidence of the tax is not widely accepted.

In part, the problem is a confusion between the short-run incidence of the tax and its long-run incidence. In the very short run, companies cannot do much in response to changes in the tax laws. Hence, the changes in tax rates or the tax base do lead to changes in net income, which largely affect the owners of the company. However, these short-run changes lead to changes in behavior for the owners, and the compound effect of many people taking the same type of actions causes at least some shifting of the tax.

For the owners to completely absorb the corporate income tax, the rate of return for investing in the corporate sector would have to be lower than the rate of return for other types of investment. This would be an unlikely situation in a free market. Rather, the lower rate of return would induce people to shift some of their investments out of the corporate sector and into other types of investment. Of course, any such incentive has to be considered in relation to the potential tax advantages of corporate investment relative to the personal income tax. To the extent that investment in corporations provides a personal income tax benefit, this reduces the effect of the corporate income tax. However, the analysis is simplified if we treat all corporate income as being taxed again as personal income. The corporation would have to earn as much after taxes as other forms of businesses do before taxes in order to equalize the return to investment for the two types of businesses. This is because the

---

6 F. Thomas Juster, "Stock Prices and Consumer Spending: An Appraisal of the Great Crash," *Economic Outlook USA* 14 (Winter 1987–88), pp. 17–18.

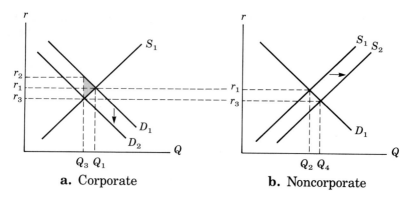

Figure 9-1 / Corporate Tax Incidence: Inelastic Supply of Funds

returns to other forms of business are only taxed once as part of the personal income of the owners.

Fixed Supply of Investment Funds

The long-run incidence of the corporate tax, then, depends on the elasticity of supply of investment funds. Two extreme cases generally represent the way the tax tends to be discussed. The first view takes the total supply of investment funds as given and assumes that they can be invested only within the national economy. As you might guess, the inelastic supply of funds leads to the suppliers accepting a lower rate of return on their investments after the tax is imposed. This creates no distortion between saving and spending.[7] However, it does create an efficiency cost associated with the difference between the two types of investment. If we treat the total supply of funds as being fixed there is still an upward-sloping supply of funds to either the corporate or the noncorporate sectors, since differences in the rate of return cause the funds to be shifted between the sectors. Hence, the supply curves are linked to each other because the two quantities must add up to the total amount available. Consider Figures 9-1a and 9-1b. In the first we have equilibrium in the corporate sector between the supply and demand for funds. The equilibrium rate of return in the absence of any tax is r_1 and the sector gets the quantity Q_1 of funds. In the rest of the economy, the rate of return should be equal to that in the corporate sector at the margin, so the marginal rate of return is also r_1, and the quantity Q_2 when added to Q_1 equals the amount of investment funds available to the economy.

If we now impose a tax on the return to investment in the corporate sector, the effective demand for funds curve shifts down to reflect the tax. This is

---

[7] While the amount of saving and investment may not be changed, there may still be an efficiency cost. See the appendix to Chapter 6 for a complete discussion.

shown as the demand curve D_2 in Figure 9-1a. The lower rate of return after tax is associated with a higher rate of return to before-tax investment. Thus, r_3 is below r_2 by the amount of tax paid and r_2 is the actual return earned on the marginal investment. The reduction in funds from Q_1 to Q_3 also generates an efficiency cost associated with the shaded triangle. This is due to giving up investment possibilities with higher returns because the after-tax return is not high enough.

By assumption, the total amount available for investment is fixed, so the reduction associated with the drop from Q_1 to Q_3 is now available to invest in the noncorporate sector. This results in the rightward shift of the supply curve in Figure 9-1b to S_2. The figure shows that this results in an equilibrium with the new rate of return also at r_3, the same as the after-tax rate of return in the corporate sector. In addition, the amount of increase in investment in the noncorporate sector just equals the amount of reduction of investment in the corporate sector. If this were not the case, adjustments would continue in the two sectors until it were true.

This result shows that all investors are made worse off by the corporate tax. They all receive the rate of return r_3 on their investments in the new equilibrium whether they invest in the corporate sector or not, and this return is lower than the old r_1. Thus, in this analysis, the tax is largely paid by all investors and the incidence would be expected to be fairly progressive. Note that the analysis does not end here. The higher required rate of return in the corporate sector would presumably lead to higher prices for corporate output and the lower rate of return in the noncorporate sector would lead to lower prices for its output. Thus, consumers who used the output of the corporate sector relatively heavily would be worse off and those who used the output of the noncorporate sector relatively heavily would actually be better off because of the lower prices. However, these effects are generally expected to be small and the incidence impact is uncertain.

The final incidence in this analysis is on the returns to investment or, more generally, the returns to savings. The result depends on the assumption that the amount of funds available is determined by the savings rate and that this rate is insensitive to the generated rate of return. If this incidence analysis is correct, it would argue that the same results as for the corporate income tax could be achieved by a general tax on savings, without the efficiency cost caused by the distortion in investment patterns. Effectively, since it is the amount of savings that is in inelastic supply, the incidence is shifted to savings.

One of the more important forms of noncorporate investment is the investment in housing and other consumer durables by individuals. Since the corporate tax causes a shift of resources away from the corporate sector, one effect would be an increase in the amount of housing and other consumer durables. While this might seem desirable, it is inefficient. It would mean giving up relatively more productive investments in plant and equipment for relatively less productive investments in housing. This is only one of several ways in which the tax code favors housing over other forms of investment, but empirical studies do seem to support the conclusion that there is too much investment in housing in the U.S. relative to other forms of investment.[8]

Incidence: Elastic Supply of Savings

The assumption that the supply of funds available for investment is fixed depends on two important arguments. The first is that the supply of savings in the U.S. is indeed fixed. There is substantial disagreement about this assumption. Empirical work on the determinants of savings does not seem conclusive regarding the sensitivity of net savings to the interest rate paid on it. The second important assumption is that only savings originating in this country can be used for investment in this country and that it cannot be invested outside of the country. This is not a very realistic assumption in the current financial markets.

Available investment funds appear to move fairly readily between countries depending on where the best investment opportunities exist. Thus, it may be that the supply of investment funds to the corporate sector is fairly elastic even if the supply of savings in the U.S. is fixed. With lower rates of return to corporate investment, the funds may go to investment overseas rather than investment in the noncorporate sector. This is illustrated in Figure 9-2. With the corporate tax, the demand curve again shifts down. However, in this case there is no additional investment until the after-tax return is again up to r_1. There is still an efficiency cost associated with the shaded triangle, but there is no impact on the noncorporate sector. The incidence now shifts fully away from investors and on to either customers or other factors of production. In this case, the tax is not likely to have a progressive incidence and might have a regressive incidence.

The shifting to either customers or factors of production is easier to visualize by considering a corporate income levied by a state. The investment in a corporation will have to generate the same after-tax return as either noncorporate investment in the state or corporate investment in a state without a corporate income tax. This leads to reduced production in the state, and the most likely impact would be a reduction in the demand for factors of production in that state. While labor is likely to be in fairly elastic supply in the long run, land and natural resources would not be. Thus, there is a strong possibility that the tax would be shifted backward to the factors of production in inelastic supply. Part of the tax could also be shifted forward to consumers if some types of output are in inelastic demand and can only be produced by corporations operating in the state. It is harder to come up with specific examples of such services, but certain types of banking services might provide a reasonable example.

---

[8] See Edwin S. Mills, "Has the United States Overinvested in Housing?" *American Real Estate and Urban Economics Journal* 15 (Spring 1987), pp. 601–616.

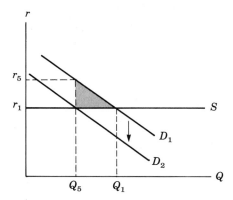

***Figure 9-2* / Corporate Tax Incidence:
Elastic Supply of Funds**

It seems only fair to emphasize again that there is no consensus on the incidence of the corporate income tax.[9] In fact, some analysts have gone so far as to argue that one reason the corporate income tax is popular with politicians is because no one is sure who ultimately bears the tax burden.

/// THE EFFECTIVE TAX RATE

Whichever view one takes of the supply of savings, the tax on corporate returns does appear to have an efficiency effect, and the magnitude of this effect depends on the effective tax rate. Thus, it is useful to consider some of the factors that determine what the effective tax rate will be.

There are several possible definitions of the effective tax rate.[10] In general, it refers to the actual tax paid divided by the amount of income. However, there are various ways to identify both income and taxes. For example, the most comprehensive measure of effective tax rate would be one that relates all taxes paid by both corporations and individuals to the earnings of the corporation, but this is seldom done. Rather, the effective tax rate is determined by the corporate taxes paid relative to corporate earnings. We can further identify a marginal effective rate and an average effective rate.

In practice, the factors affecting the corporate tax also affect other types of business tax, so we start by discussing the impact of various investment incentives on effective tax rates in general. Then we consider some of the

---

9 For a good discussion see Arnold C. Harberger, "The State of the Corporate Income Tax: Who Pays It? Should It Be Repealed?" and the comments of the discussion participants, particularly the comment by Joseph A. Pechman, in Charls E. Walker and Mark A. Bloomfield, eds., *New Directions in Federal Tax Policy for the 1980s* (Cambridge, MA: Ballinger Publishing, 1984), pp. 161–184.

10 For example, see Don Fullerton, "Which Effective Tax Rate?" *National Tax Journal* 38 (March 1984), pp. 23–42.

issues associated with the effective tax rates on investment in the corporate sector.

Investment Incentives

The federal tax code has frequently contained substantial incentives for additional investment. The impact of these incentives has been to reduce the effective tax rate on all investment. This would be important if, for example, there is too little investment because of tax-induced distortion away from such investments. However, the incentives that have been used are generally not neutral with respect to either type of investment or industry. Different incentives offer varying benefits, depending on the type of investment. These variations in tax benefits create distortions in the return on investment and they create divergences in the effective tax rates by type of investment. Because industries differ in their use of capital assets, the differences in returns by type of asset create differences across industries.[11] In particular, incentives for investment in plant and equipment favor heavy manufacturing industries relative to other businesses.

The most important type of investment incentives are those associated with depreciation of capital investments. Recall that depreciation is the part of an asset's value that is lost in a given year. This means that if an asset loses 10% of its value, that amount should be subtracted from any income earned to reflect the cost of using the asset. A neutral tax system would allow for depreciation equal to the loss in economic value for each item each year. No system can do this effectively. Different goods depreciate at different rates, and even within broad classifications, the rate of depreciation depends on intensity of use, maintenance, and many other factors. Aside from differences between goods, there can be broad efforts to allow depreciation to be taken for tax purposes either faster or slower than it actually occurs.

In general the tax system has been tilted toward allowing depreciation to be treated for tax purposes faster than it in fact occurs. However, other factors may work to offset this tax advantage. In particular, as we discussed, there is a tendency to overtax investment income during inflationary periods. The response of the federal government has been a long series of incentives to invest. These have the impact of effectively reducing the tax on investment returns, but they also distort investment incentives.

The simplest type of investment incentive is to allow for depreciation to be claimed more quickly than the item actually declines in value. Since the depreciation is treated as an offset against current income, the effect of rapid depreciation is to defer taxes. As we showed earlier, deferral of taxes is equivalent to an interest-free loan of the amount of taxes deferred. The benefit

---

[11] Various estimates of effective tax rates by category of investment and by industry are reported in Pechman, op. cit., p. 163; Charles R. Hulten and James W. Robertson, "The Taxation of High Technology Industries," *National Tax Journal* 37 (September 1984), pp. 327–345; and Fullerton, op. cit.

of the deferral makes the investment look more appealing. In the extreme, the investment might be expensed; that is, the investor is allowed to treat the good as if it were used up in the first year. This shelters the largest amount of income.

Rapid depreciation for tax purposes distorts the investment incentives for assets with different expected lives. Accelerating the depreciation on a short-lived object does not provide much tax benefit; but accelerating depreciation on a long-lived asset can provide much more tax benefits. For example, if an asset has an expected life of twenty-five years, allowing it to be expensed would take the tax savings for the next twenty-five years on the asset and bring them into the present. The owner of the asset could simply put these tax savings into a bank and make withdrawals as the higher future taxes became due. At the end of the process, any interest earned would be the net benefit of being allowed early depreciation.

Another method which the federal government has used to try to encourage investment is the investment tax credit. This is a direct tax credit equal to some percentage of the cost of eligible investments. Thus, the most recent credit was for 10% of the amount invested (although this was eliminated in 1986). Under this credit, the investor simply reduces his or her tax bill by 10% of the amount of the investment in the first year. The credit was largely invariant with respect to the expected life of the investment; hence, it created incentives to use many short-term investments rather than one long-term investment. Since each of the short-term investments would be eligible for the credit, a series of investments would receive a much greater total tax advantage than one long-lived investment.

These items can all be viewed as ways to offset some of the effects of the tax system on the return to investment, particularly during highly inflationary periods. While this was desirable given the unintended increases in tax on investments, the distortions created efficiency costs of their own. In particular, the system as a whole was criticized for favoring investment in old, declining industries rather than encouraging new, growing industries.[12] Most of these investment incentives were removed or reduced with the 1986 tax revision, but many people expect them to return should high levels of inflation raise the real tax on investment again, or if there are other reasons to suspect that the country is investing too little.

Effective Tax Rates on Corporate Investment

As we already noted, certain aspects of corporate investment make it appear attractive relative to other types of investment. In particular, the ability to delay paying taxes is a benefit to investors. If this could be done perfectly, the corporate tax would simply substitute for the shelter that the

---

[12] See Hulton and Robertson, op. cit.

investor gets on the personal tax. Of course, this is not done perfectly; but the relatively low rate of dividend payout indicates that some substantial part of the net return is probably sheltered in this way.[13] Thus, a low effective tax rate may induce too much investment in corporations relative to other types of investment.

Inflation tends to increase the tax on all real assets, as we discussed in Chapter 7, and this is directly applicable to corporations. An increase in the value of an asset owned by the corporation is subject to taxation when the asset is sold even if the increase is caused solely by inflation. Alternatively, the assets used by a corporation have insufficient depreciation to fully offset the impact of inflation. These effects are identical for the corporate tax and the personal income tax. However, increases in the value of the corporation's stock which are also associated with inflation will be taxed again as capital gains for the investor when the stock is sold. For example, suppose a corporation is formed, sells $1,000 worth of stock, and uses that money to buy a machine. The machine makes neither profit nor loss each year but eventually doubles in price purely because of inflation. The corporation still pays a tax on the $1,000 in capital gains if it sells the machine. The value of the corporate stock is then the after-tax amount left from the sale, say $1,660 (subtracting the 34% in tax from the $1,000 gain). If the stockholders sell the shares for this amount, they will be subject to capital gains tax on the $660 increase in value, even though this represents a loss when adjusted for inflation and has already been subject to taxation at the corporate level.

It is clear that the effective rate of taxation on the corporate sector cannot be determined by simply looking at the corporate tax rates. The effective rate is also affected by the actions of the corporate stockholder. In particular, the effective tax is likely to be reduced by holding stocks for long periods of time since the buildup of nondividend earnings is not taxed until the stock is sold.

If large amounts of the investors' return to investment have been converted to capital gains, investors effectively become locked into a particular investment. If the investment is liquidated, taxes are due on the capital gains; however, if the investment is retained, the investors may continue deferring taxes. This is perhaps one of the strongest arguments in favor of some form of preferential treatment for capital gains income, and there is still disagreement about whether an increase in capital gains tax rates will increase revenue for the federal government or decrease it because it will induce people to hold their investments longer.[14]

---

[13] Such sheltering may have its own efficiency costs. Corporations would have an incentive to grow well beyond the point where they would if there were no tax consequences to the investor associated with cash payouts. In trying to shelter the investor from the taxes associated with dividends, the corporation may become very inefficient and make poor investment choices. See Robert J. Samuelson, "Subsidized Mega-Companies," *Newsweek* (March 19, 1984), p. 76.

[14] See Eric W. Cook and John F. O'Hare, "Issues Relating to the Taxation of Capital Gains" and Lawrence B. Lindsey, "Capital Gains Taxes Under the Tax Reform Act of 1986: Revenue Estimates Under Various Assumptions," *National Tax Journal* 40 (September 1987), pp. 473–504.

/// PROPOSALS FOR REFORM

There seems to be a very wide range of analysts who conclude that the federal corporate income tax results in excess taxation of corporate income. The overtaxation is alleged to occur because firms do pay out some dividends and these dividends are then taxed as personal income. Hence, the current system taxes the profits to corporations both when they are earned under the corporate tax and when the investor realizes the return by receiving either a dividend or a capital gain from the sale of stock. In either case, the investor pays a direct tax in addition to the indirect tax paid by the corporation.

There are a number of complications to this simple analysis, but they do not change the general view. As we have discussed, there are benefits associated with the ability to defer taxes and with some of the depreciation rules. However, these are often offset by further disadvantages associated with inflation and with the distortions created by the tax advantages.

One suggested reform is to have all corporate profits credited to the shareholders each year and to eliminate the corporate income tax. Thus, all corporate profits would be subject to income taxes based on stock ownership, and the corporate sector would be treated just like other business sectors in the personal income tax. All profits, whether realized in cash payments to the owners or not, would be subject to taxation as if they had been received by the owners. This solution might create cash-flow problems for stockholders who receive a tax bill but no dividends, and it might also be difficult to implement.

Further, all corporations do not generate profits each year, so a corporation incurring losses would be able to pass the losses on to its owners.[15] This would allow investors to essentially buy and sell tax losses through the shares of such firms. A person with a high marginal tax rate would be willing to pay a premium over the actual value for a stock that would reduce his or her tax bill by more than it would reduce the initial owner's tax bill. For example, suppose that a person in the 15% marginal tax bracket owned stock that had a $1,000 loss for the year. This loss by the corporation would reduce the owner's tax bill by $150. However, a person in the 33% marginal tax bracket would save $330 in taxes with this same loss. Hence, the higher tax person would be willing to pay a premium above the market value of the stock to get the additional tax savings. This transaction would simply generate another form of tax avoidance. Also, much stock is currently held by pension funds, which do not pay taxes on their income, and this reform would allow them to sell any tax advantages from stocks that incurred losses. Consequently, substantial amounts of corporate earnings would still escape taxation for long periods of time while losses would be used to offset current tax bills.

A more promising reform would be to allow corporations a deduction for

---

[15] In 1984, 44% of corporate tax returns showed no net income. This number was somewhat high, but the percentage in previous years did not fluctuate greatly. See Tax Foundation, *Facts and Figures on Government Finance, 1988–89 Edition* (Baltimore, MD: Johns Hopkins University Press, 1988), p. 135.

dividends paid. Thus, earnings passed directly to others would be taxed at their ultimate destination, while earnings retained by a corporation would be subject to the corporate tax. The major objection to reforms like this, aside from any loss of tax revenue, is that they tend to encourage more payment of dividends by corporations. This might reduce the total amount of investment, since a very large percentage of all investment is financed by retained corporate earnings.

States also face serious issues with respect to corporate taxation. It is much easier for a state to identify operations within the state than it would be to try to tax all stockholders of corporations doing business there. Further, the number of state tax returns that would be required by owners of stock in large corporations could be unreasonable. Thus, states would almost certainly retain their corporate taxes as taxes on the business rather than on its stockholders. States also find that there are difficulties in levying a corporate income tax, even as a tax on business operations. The basic problem is apportioning the profits of firms that do business in more than one state or country.

Although a variety of reasons can be generated for having special taxes on corporations, the consensus among those who study them seems to be that the corporate income tax at the federal level is not a very efficient way to raise revenue because it creates serious distortions in the economy. However, these claims rest on a number of controversial assumptions, and the conclusions are not universally accepted.

/// STATE TAXATION OF CORPORATIONS

States have corporate tax systems for reasons similar to those of the federal government. In the absence of such taxes, there is the substantial possibility that much of the income earned within the corporate sector would escape taxation indefinitely. This is a particular problem for a state since many of the stockholders do not reside in the state. However, this type of taxation creates substantial problems in defining taxable income for firms that do business in more than one state.

One issue that arises in terms of tax avoidance is that each state may tax income at different rates. Consider a corporation active in each of two states. State A has a high corporate tax rate, whereas state B has a low corporate tax rate. The firm has a parts manufacturing plant in state A and an assembly plant in state B. Since the parts plant only makes parts for the use of the assembly plant, the parts do not have a readily determined market price. However, the company must determine some price for the parts because it must allocate its profits among the two states. Given that state A has a relatively high tax rate, the company has an incentive to declare a low price for the parts. If the sales price of the parts are low, the plant will account for little of the company's profits. Hence, only a small amount of the overall profits would be taxed at the higher rate. Because the price of inputs would be low for the plant in state B, its profits would be higher and they would be taxed at the lower rate.

Suppose that the location of the plants were reversed. Now the parts would be produced in the low-tax state and assembled in the high-tax state. Declaring a high price for the parts makes the parts production plant appear very profitable while the assembly plant would appear to generate little in profits. Thus, more of the company's overall profits would be declared in the low-tax state.

The above example may appear simplistic, but it is representative of the problems a state faces when it tries to tax business profits for companies that do business in more than one state. Because companies have incentives to carry out these bookkeeping reassignments of profits, states use some apportionment formula to determine the tax liability for each state. Essentially, this method takes the company's total profits for all operations and assigns them on the basis of relative activity. For example, our parts and assembly plants might be allocated shares of profits for state tax purposes based on their relative employment ratios. If the parts plant had twice as many employees as the assembly plant, it would be assigned two-thirds of the company's profits, no matter what the company claimed as the sales price for the parts. In practice, most states allow the firm to use an equal weighting of the percentage of its sales, property, and employment in that state as compared to its total operations. However, many states allow the firm the option of choosing other types of apportionment if they wish. For example, Minnesota allows the firm to use a 70% weight on sales rather than equal weight on all three items.

This approach certainly limits the amount of bookkeeping adjustments that a company can make. However, many companies argue that it is an unfair way to allocate taxes and may cause distortions where companies choose to expand.

From the business perspective, some operations of any large company are not going to be as profitable as other operations. Also, a new operation may not generate profits for a number of years. Yet, if these activities are located in a state that uses a formula apportionment of profits to determine taxation, the company may still end up paying significant taxes to that state on the basis of its profitability of operations in other states or other parts of the world. There is, therefore, a significant conflict between states that worry about companies avoiding taxes and firms that worry about states taxing them unfairly.

Regional Growth   The equity of treatment for taxpayers who earn income in different jurisdictions is only one part of the issue. The other part is the mobility of resources across jurisdictional boundaries. If state A has higher taxes than state B, there would appear to be some incentive for firms to migrate from A to B. Even if firms did not migrate, the lower taxes in B would make firms located there more profitable than firms located in A. Hence, the firms in B would expand more rapidly over time. With these considerations in mind, many states offer tax breaks or other inducements to firms. However, empirical work on the effect of state taxes on the location decision of firms tends to find that taxation makes little difference in these decisions. The attention taxes receive in this context and the potential resource allocation effects make it important to consider these issues in more detail.

The first item to consider is what happens to the tax revenue. Part of the revenue goes to provide services for the company that pays the taxes. As activity increases new roads will have to be built, more employees hired, and so on. Generally, these costs are not perceived to be as large as the revenues generated. Hence, most states view businesses as net revenue enhancers. However, the revenue that is collected will be spent somewhere. Even if it is not spent on direct services for business, the money can finance additional services for residents of the state or allow the state to lower other taxes.

Most uses of the revenue would make the state more attractive to workers. Because the service level is higher or other taxes are lower, individuals who might want to live in the state would be willing to work there for a slightly lower wage than they would otherwise require. Thus, some of the effect of higher business taxes is likely to show up as lower wages for the employer. To the extent that this happens, the high-tax state may remain competitive with other states.

Federal-State Tax Interaction   A further issue arises here in terms of interaction of state and federal taxes. Businesses can treat all state taxes as expenses in figuring their federal tax obligations. Hence, if they pay a high state tax, they essentially receive part of the money back from the federal government. In Chapter 7 we discussed the possibility that shifting taxes to high-income taxpayers assisted in exporting the tax burden to the rest of the country. Individuals who itemize also can deduct state taxes when figuring their federal tax; higher income taxpayers are more likely to itemize and will tend to have higher marginal tax rates. However, taxation of business could be even more effective in exporting taxes. Many people do not itemize and hence get no credit for state taxes paid, and those who do itemize generally face a lower marginal tax rate than do businesses. Thus, by taxing businesses within the jurisdiction fairly heavily as compared to individuals, the state can shift more of its overall tax burden to the federal government.

A simple example may help to clarify this. Assume that businesses pay a 34% tax on profits to the federal government and that individuals pay a 28% average marginal tax to the federal government, but that only half itemize. The state is considering raising an additional $1,000 in taxes. If business taxes are raised by this amount, then business federal taxes would be reduced by $340, creating a net cost of $660 within the state. If the same amount is raised by taxing individuals, about half would get no federal offset and the other half would have only their federal tax reduced by 28% of the tax they pay. Thus, the federal tax reduction would only be $140, and the net cost within the state would be $860. Alternatively, if the money is raised using a sales tax, which is no longer deductible for any individuals, the total cost would be paid by residents in the state. Thus, the federal tax code affects both the net cost of state taxes and creates incentives to use certain types of taxes to fund state and local governments. These taxes may still create significant distortions, but they are more likely to be used because more of the cost can be shifted to other governments.

One effect of the deductibility of state taxes when figuring federal taxes is to mitigate the incentive for movement which differences in tax rates across states would be expected to create. This also creates incentives to tax corporations more heavily because this allows for greater tax exporting. As noted when we discussed personal income taxes, there is some belief that removing the deductibility of state and local taxes when figuring personal income taxes would create some improvement in the efficiency of the overall tax system. However, such a change would probably create even greater incentives for state and local governments to rely on business taxes, because they would still be deductible in figuring federal taxes for the businesses.

/// **SUMMARY**

The federal government treats corporations as legal entities and subjects them to tax. Many people argue that this is an unfair and inefficient tax because the earnings of the corporation are taxed directly and are then taxed again when they are paid out as dividends to stockholders. Countering this is the ability of the corporation to retain much of its net earnings and thus defer the tax that stockholders would have to pay on dividends.

The incidence of corporate tax is subject to considerable controversy. If the supply of investment funds in the U.S. is fixed, the tax is largely paid by investors and would have a progressive incidence. However, if the supply of investment funds is very elastic, the tax is not paid at all by investors. In this case it would be shifted either to customers or to other factors of production, and its incidence would be difficult to determine.

Taxation of corporations at the state level is often difficult because many companies have operations in more than one state. Thus, most states treat the company as a single operation and apportion its profits based on certain formulas. It is argued that these formulas create distortions of their own, but a better alternative does not appear to be available. Further, the deductibility of state taxes when figuring federal tax liabilities reduces the impact of interstate differences in the taxes levied.

Chapter 10 //////

Property Taxes

The property tax is the largest tax in the United States which is not levied on the basis of a transaction. Income taxes are levied on the basis of income earned during a year; sales and excise taxes are based on the value of a particular sale or the number of units sold. In contrast, the property tax is levied on the value of property at a particular point in time. Thus, it is a "wealth" or "stock" tax rather than a "flow" tax. While property taxes represent only about 13% of all taxes collected in the U.S. in 1986, they represent 74% of the taxes collected by local governments and about 31% of total expenditures by local governments in 1984.[1]

In contrast, the property tax represented 87% of local tax revenue in 1955 and 53% of expenditures. By 1970, this tax was still 85% of tax revenue but only 40% of expenditures; and by 1975 it was 82% of tax revenue and 35% of expenditures. Thus, while the property tax has declined relative to expenditure by local governments, it has remained the mainstay of local tax revenue. Further, if we were to delete a few large cities, the importance of the property tax to local government would become even more evident.[2]

The property tax always seems to be under attack, yet it endures as a major source of funding for local governments. Perhaps some of the controversy can be understood when it is realized that, when viewed from different perspectives, the property tax has been found to be a regressive tax,[3] a progressive tax,[4] and a benefit tax.[5] The ambiguity in our expectations of the

---

[1] Advisory Commission on Intergovernmental Relations (ACIR), *Significant Features of Fiscal Federalism, 1988 Edition*, M-155 (Washington, DC: 1986), Tables 44 and 62.1.

[2] ACIR, op. cit., *1985–86 Edition*, pp. 24 and 41.

[3] See Dick Netzer, "Is There Too Much Reliance on the Local Property Tax?" and John Shannon, "The Property Tax: Reform or Relief?" in George E. Peterson, ed., *Property Tax Reform* (Washington, DC: Urban Institute, 1973), pp. 13–52.

[4] Peter Mieszkowski, "The Property Tax: An Excise Tax or a Profits Tax?" *Journal of Public Economics* 1 (April 1972), pp. 73–96; reprinted in W. Patrick Beaton, ed., *Municipal Expenditures, Revenues and Services*

tax best explains the ongoing controversy over the tax and the variety of reforms that have been proposed. In this chapter we present each view of the property tax along with proposed reforms.

The other major issue is whether the property tax should be deductible in figuring federal income taxes. The tax reform of 1986 eliminated the deduction for sales taxes but retained the deductions for state and local income taxes and property taxes. However, many economists do not believe that the property tax should be deductible.[6]

/// WHAT IS A PROPERTY TAX?

The property tax is a tax on the ownership of assets. The traditional view is that the ownership of assets represents wealth; hence, the tax on property is a tax on wealth. In practice, property is broken into two broad classifications: real property and personal property. Real property is defined as land and immovable structures; personal property includes everything else and is further divided into tangible and intangible personal property. Tangible personal property includes furniture, machinery, and inventories for business, and household effects, jewelry, and related items for individuals. Intangible personal property includes stocks, bonds, bank balances, and other forms of financial assets.

Most local jurisdictions tax real property, and this is the tax most often associated with the term "property tax." Further, most property tax revenue comes from the tax on real property. Hence, this chapter focuses on the tax on real property. However, many local and state governments do tax businesses' tangible personal property. Relatively few tax individuals' intangible personal property or tangible personal property, and revenue from these sources is usually small. As we shall see, the mobility of the tax base is a significant reason for this breakdown.

The mechanics of the property tax are also of interest. This is an ad valorem tax which is levied as a percentage of the value of the property. Value is determined by an assessment procedure. The assessed value is normally related to market value, but this is not necessarily the case. Particularly when market value is difficult to determine, assessments may be based on replacement cost or the income generated by property. When market value is used, the assessor considers the actual transaction price if the property were recently sold in a free market exchange. The assessor also considers the prices at which comparable properties have recently sold. Once the market value is

(New Brunswick, NJ: Center for Urban Policy Research, 1983), pp. 37–59.

[5] Charles M. Tiebout, "A Pure Theory of Local Expenditures," *Journal of Political Economy* 65 (October 1956), pp. 416–424.

[6] For a presentation of the arguments see John M. Quigley and Daniel L. Rubinfeld, "Budget Reform and the Theory of Fiscal Federalism," *American Economic Review* 76 (May 1986), pp. 132–137.

determined, an assessment value is generated, which may be equal to or less than market value. For example, since 1978 California has had legal restrictions on how rapidly the assessed value of property that does not change hands can increase, although there are no such limits on the market value. Hence, the relationship between assessed value and market value can change over time. Finally, the assessed value is multiplied by the tax rate to determine the tax liability. Since assessed value can differ from market value, the effective tax rate can differ from the nominal tax rate.

/// THE "OLD" VIEW OF THE PROPERTY TAX

Until about 1970, the property tax was widely viewed by economists as a regressive tax. This conclusion was based on a set of reasons that we summarize briefly as follows: (1) The property tax can be treated as an excise tax and the supply of property in a community is very elastic, hence the tax is paid by users of property; (2) property consumption increases relatively less rapidly than does income, so (3) the tax paid increases less rapidly than income. It is necessary to examine these arguments in more detail to understand the areas of controversy.

Property Taxes as Sales Taxes

The property tax is explicitly a tax on a form of wealth, so how can it be treated as equivalent to a sales tax? The answer is that it is an annual tax on wealth, equivalent to a tax on the usage value of property. Since the usage value of property is simply rent, the property tax can be viewed as an excise tax on the rental value of property. An example may help to clarify this. Suppose that a house worth $50,000 rents for $5,000 per year. Further, a 2% property tax is levied on the market value of the house; hence, the property tax is $1,000 per year. While this is indeed only 2% of the value of the house, it is equal to 20% of the annual rent. Thus, in many ways the 2% tax on property value is the same as a 20% tax on the rental value.

It is common to treat the market value of property as simply the present value of the anticipated stream of future net revenues. The market value is then given by the simple formula $MV = R/i$ where MV is the market value of the property, R is the rent received each year net of all expenses, and i is the market rate of interest. Thus, the formula says that the market value is equal to the net rent divided by the interest rate; or, alternatively, it says that the net rent is equal to the market value times the interest rate. The latter interpretation makes important intuitive sense. With i as the rate of interest, if you invested MV in an interest-bearing account, at the end of each year you would get $i \times MV$ in interest. The principal would not be changed by your withdrawing the interest. Hence, you would expect net rent to be at least equal to the

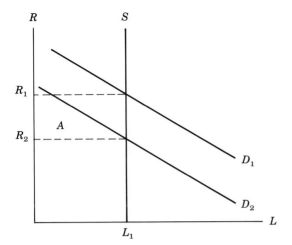

Figure 10-1 / Property Tax on Land

interest you could earn in the bank on the same dollar investment. On the other hand, the return could not be much above the market return because other potential buyers would start bidding for the property. This would push up the property's price until this relationship between market price and net rent held once again.

Given this relationship, define the tax rate as t. Hence, $T = t \times MV$ shows the relationship between the tax, the tax rate, and market value, but MV is approximately equal to R/i, so $T = (t/i) \times R$. If i is about 10%, the effective tax rate as a percentage of rent is about ten times the rate as a percentage of market value. Thus, a tax rate of 2.5% of market value is a tax rate of 25% of annual rent. Further, the tax on annual rent is essentially an excise tax on the sale of housing services. One benefit of levying a property tax rather than an excise tax on rental units is that it is paid on both rental units and owner-occupied units (as well as vacant units).

Once we see that the tax can be treated as an excise tax, we can also see one reason why it may be unpopular. Few items have excise taxes approaching 25% of their value, but this is about average for property tax as a percent of rental value. Now let's look at the incidence analysis.

Incidence

The incidence analysis of the property tax is usually separated into two sections: the incidence of the tax on land and that on improvements. The incidence on land is fairly straightforward. Land within a community is generally fixed, hence the supply of land is perfectly inelastic. In such a situation the tax is borne by the owner of the land. In Figure 10-1 we see that changes in demand from D_1 to D_2 lead only to a price change. There is no change in the quantity of land. Recall that, in equilibrium, it does not matter whether an excise tax is levied on the buyer or the seller. Thus, we can treat the property tax as causing an effective reduction in demand and therefore a shift of the demand curve from D_1 to D_2 in the figure. The amount that the renter actually pays is unchanged at R_1. The amount that the landlord receives is R_2, which is equal to the amount paid by the renter minus the property tax payment. The government receives $(R_1 - R_2) \times L_1 = t \times L_1$ in property tax payments (this is equal to area A in the figure), and there is no distortion in the market.[7] The fact that there is no distortion (or deadweight loss) associated with a land tax is the reason that some argue that land is the most appropriate source of local tax revenue. Unfortunately, separating land value from improvements value is no easy task.[8]

The incidence of the tax on improvements depends on the elasticity of supply of nonland improvements. If the amount of improvements is fixed, just as the amount of land is, then the incidence of the tax will be on owners again. This assumption is appealing because structures are so immobile once they are in place; and, in fact, it is reasonable for short-run analysis of the incidence of changes in the property tax. However, taxes are one of the costs of owning property, and in the long run the amount of property on a parcel of land can vary. First, the landlord can choose not to build or to build a less valuable building in response to property taxes; second, the landlord can let existing buildings deteriorate. The incidence thus hinges on the elasticity of supply for property improvements.

If supply of improvements is perfectly elastic, as shown in Figure 10-2, then the incidence of the property tax is on the users of property. In the absence of the tax the market rent is R_1 and the quantity is Q_1. The tax effectively shifts the supply curve up to S_2 in the figure. The new equilibrium quantity is Q_2 and the new market rent is R_2, but the amount T goes to the government, and the net rent for the supplier remains at R_1. Note that government receives the area A in tax revenue, $(R_2 - R_1) \times Q_2$, but that this is also associated with a deadweight loss equal to area B.

It is generally argued that the long-run elasticity of supply of property improvement is very high. If the net return to new buildings is higher in one community than it is in another, builders will shift their activity until the after-tax return is equalized. This forms the basis for the argument that users bear the burden of the property portion of the property tax.

---

[7] We are treating the property tax as a tax per unit of land rather than as a tax per dollar of land value. This simplification makes the presentation easier without distorting the results.

[8] Aside from any difficulties in determining what land value would be if there were no structures on the land, land could not be shifted without cost into its most profitable use. Thus, the existing use of the land influences its value. Land with a building on it would not be as valuable for creating a new building as would vacant land, because the old building would have to be demolished before the new structure could be built.

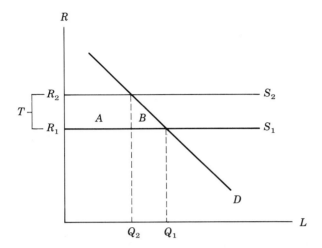

Figure 10-2 / **Property Tax on Improvements in One Community**

Income and Consumption

The next significant part of the old view is the argument that property consumption increases less than proportionately to income. Consider residential consumption first. Cross-section evidence shows that even people with zero (or negative) income tend to live somewhere.[9] Thus, the percentage of income used for housing is fairly high for low-income families and the percentage declines as income increases, even as actual expenditures increase. In Figure 10-3, the equation $R = C \times Y$ indicates a situation in which rent is strictly proportional to income, with net rent being C percent of income. As income goes up by 10%, housing expenditures also go up by 10%. The equation actually found in cross-section empirical studies resembles the other equation in the graph, $R = A + B \times Y$. This equation shows rent increasing as income increases, but not by the same percentage. Because of the A term, rent is always a higher percentage of income than B; but rent comes closer and closer to B as a percentage of income as income rises. Hence, rent as a percentage of income falls as income rises.

In practice, the value of improvements on property is substantially greater than the value of the land, so the incidence of the property tax is largely determined by the incidence of the tax on improvements. According to the old view, therefore, the incidence of the property tax must be regressive. The tax is assumed to be paid by the user of property and, hence, to be proportional to rent; and rent increases less than proportionately to income.

---

[9] While there are homeless people in the United States, many people with zero reported income nevertheless do have homes. In fact, many own their homes. For an example of this type of analysis, see Shannon, op. cit., p. 27.

Therefore, the tax payment increases less than proportionately to income and this, by definition, is regressive.

/// THE "NEW" VIEW OF PROPERTY TAX INCIDENCE

The old view of property tax incidence has been criticized on a variety of grounds. Going through these criticisms reveals many of the problems of trying to determine tax incidence in practice. The criticisms of the old view are: (1) It is a partial analysis, when in fact virtually all property is subject to the property tax. Hence it is necessary to consider the incidence of a tax on all property as well as one on property in only one community. (2) Even within communities, the analysis is based on a faulty interpretation of the data. Housing expenditure is approximately proportional to income if the relationship is averaged over time. Finally, (3) much of the tax is levied on business, and the business portion of the tax is more likely to have a progressive incidence.

Under the old view, each community is examined in isolation; hence each community faces a very elastic supply of property. However, the supply of capital to build property within the nation is much less elastic. Thus, while suppliers of capital may move from a particular community to escape property taxes, they cannot find any community in which they escape all property taxes. Therefore it is argued that the average value of property taxes is a tax on all property in the nation, and this tax is largely borne by the owners of capital.

As shown in Figure 10-4, it is assumed that the supply of capital is fairly inelastic; therefore, when the tax shifts the supply curve up from S_1 to S_2, the

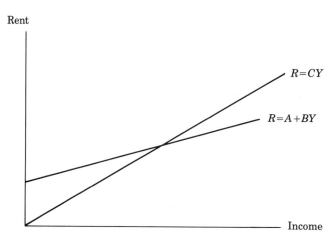

Figure 10-3 / Rent versus Income

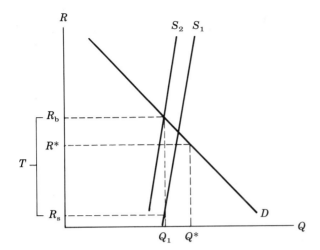

Figure 10-4 / **Incidence of a National Property Tax**

new equilibrium rent, R_b, is only slightly above the old equilibrium rent, R^*. Thus, the net amount received by suppliers falls by almost the full amount of the tax to R_s. Since suppliers of capital tend to be higher income families, this part of the tax incidence is progressive.

The second objection to the old view is based on a general problem with cross-section consumption studies. Consumption patterns do not change dramatically from year to year in response to fluctuations in income. In particular, people do not move each year so as to maintain the ideal level of housing expenditure given that year's income. Thus, the relationship between income and consumption in a given year may not reflect the general pattern of income-consumption over a lifetime. This would not create statistical problems if the deviations averaged out within a given year, but in fact they do create a bias. A person with low measured income has much more than a 50% chance of that income being below their average income, whereas someone earning a high income in a given year has better than a 50% chance of that income being above average for them. The analysis in Box 6-2 of Chapter 6 is relevant to this point. The box shows the effect of this averaging on cross-sectional estimates. It leads to an underestimate of the responsiveness of housing consumption to changes in income. Studies that correct for this bias tend to find a proportional relationship between income and housing expenditures.[10] Hence, it is argued that even the portion of the tax borne by users of property may be more proportional than regressive.

The third objection centers on the property tax levied on business. If the tax is treated as being shifted to users of property, the business users of

---

[10] For example, see Henry Aaron, "A New View of Property Tax Incidence," *American Economic Review* 64 (May 1974), pp. 212–221.

property would bear the business portion of the property tax. If it is shifted to either owners of the business or the suppliers of capital, it is likely to increase the progressivity of the tax. Only if it is shifted to consumers is it likely to be regressive. This would occur if the demand for the firm's output is inelastic. For example, the portion of the tax on grocery stores has the potential to be shifted to customers, since demand for local grocery stores is probably inelastic.

Even this amount of shifting to customers may not occur. If the demand for property in a community starts to decline, it is expected that land prices will fall. The reduction in land prices means that land owners would bear part of the tax on reproducible property. To the extent that land owners are relatively wealthy, this portion of the tax would be progressively distributed also.

For these reasons, proponents of the new view tend to believe that the property tax is proportional or even progressive in its aggregate incidence. Nevertheless, deviations from the average for a particular community will be less progressively distributed within that community. There is thus a difference between its local incidence and its aggregate incidence[11] (see Box 10-1).

/// PROPERTY TAX AS A BENEFIT TAX

The question of tax incidence is particularly important when the tax is judged on the ability-to-pay principle; but it is not at all clear that ability to pay should be the judgment criterion. Rather, many experts argue that the incidence of the property tax cannot be judged in isolation. They see it as a form of price for receiving the goods and services provided by a local government. In this context, the tax should be analyzed as a benefit tax; on that basis the incidence issues must be balanced against the benefits which the tax finances. Viewed as a benefit tax, the property tax becomes a price for services. The equity concern of ability to pay is of little relevance if the tax is a payment for services. In fact, attempts to alter the incidence pattern of the tax may work to the detriment of low-income households by seriously reducing their access to services funded from the property tax.

Higher taxes would normally be used to fund more or better local services. Thus, people have some choice between high-tax and high-service or low-tax and low-service communities. The key to this view of the property tax is to look at a house as much more than a residence. Each house comes with a set of local services and a set of local taxes. Few people would want to live in communities with high taxes and low service levels, while many would want to live in areas with low taxes and high service levels. However, if the taxes are used to finance the services, then high taxes and high service levels will go together as will low taxes and low service levels. To the extent that services are financed by the property tax and the value of services increases property values, the two offset

[11] Mieszkowski, op. cit.

Box 10-1

////// Local versus Global Incidence of a Property Tax

Using some fairly extreme assumptions, we can offer an example of the difference between the local and national impacts of a property tax in one community and then compare that with the aggregate effect of all communities having such taxes.

Suppose that community A is one of ten similar communities in the country and it has 10% of the property in the country. Throughout the country the rate of return on capital invested in property is 10%. Now community A imposes a 1% property tax. Because of the tax some investment is shifted out of A until the return to investment in the community is 10.9%; but the increased investment in other areas causes the rate of return outside the community to fall to 9.9%. Users of property within the community are now paying more for property compared to the situation before the tax. In comparison to other communities, users are paying more by the full amount of the tax. Despite this, owners of capital as a group pay the full amount of the tax through lower investment returns. All owners of capital are receiving a reduction of 0.1% in their investment return, no matter where their investment is located. When this is aggregated over all property, the reduction in return is approximately equal to the amount collected in community A.

However, users of property in other communities are paying less for property. Thus, the effect is to lower the return to owners of capital everywhere; but this primarily shows up as reductions in cost of capital outside the community. Those inside the community still end up paying higher prices by about the amount of the tax.

Now assume that all communities impose the same tax. Since the same impact is expected, the tax causes the rate of return in that community to rise by 0.9% and the rate in all others to fall by 0.1%. As each community adopts the tax, it finds that viewed in isolation its residents are paying the full tax. When all communities have adopted a property tax, the gross return on capital is back at 10%, but the net return is 9%. Hence, owners pay the full tax and users pay the same cost as if there were no taxes.

one another and the tax is simply the price of the services that the community offers.

We can see this effect with an idealized example in Figure 10-5. The property tax causes the supply curve to shift up as in the usual excise tax case. However, if the tax revenue is used to finance desirable service, it leads to an

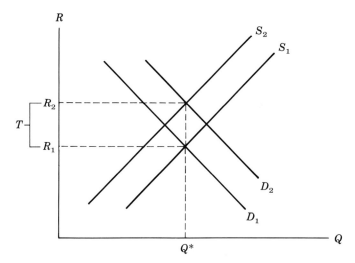

Figure 10-5 / Taxes and Services

increase in the demand to locate in the community. In the figure demand rises from D_1 to D_2 and this exactly offsets the tax effect. The quantity stays at Q^* and the market rent increases from R_1 to R_2. This higher rent is exactly enough to allow the seller to pay the tax and retain the same amount as before the tax. The buyer is just as well off with the higher rent because of the services received. Thus, the property tax has been converted into a price, or alternatively, it is a benefit tax that relates taxes to evaluation of services.

Clearly, there are limits to which this view can be pushed. Many services are financed by intergovernmental grants rather than local property taxes, some services have almost no relationship to property, and there are restrictions on household mobility. Nevertheless, there is empirical support for the benefit-tax view; and a better linkage between the tax and property-related services is likely to improve the allocation of resources in the public sector.[12]

Consider an extreme case as an example. There are two communities with identical houses and all other features are the same. In one community the tax is very low and only minimal services are provided. In the other, the tax and services are higher. Those families who place a very low value on public services would go to the first community. They would not mind the low service level because they pay little in taxes. Families with a high demand for public services would go to the second community and pay the higher tax price to receive the desired services. If there are a wide variety of communities with different service packages, each family would choose the one that best

---

[12] Anthony M. Rufolo, "Efficient Local Taxation and Local Public Goods," *Journal of Public Economics* 12 (December 1979), pp. 352–376.

matched their demand for public services. In the extreme case, this would essentially convert the provision of local services into the equivalent of a private market. Those wanting more services and willing to pay the additional cost could move to a community that provided more services; but they would have to pay the cost through higher taxes. Those who want to keep their tax payments low could move to a community providing fewer services and levying lower taxes.

The problem with this view is that the property tax payments are not the same for everyone in a community. Rather, they vary with the amount of property consumed. Thus, each person in a given community would have an incentive to reduce his/her consumption of housing so as to reduce tax payments while receiving the same level of service. Clearly, if everyone does this, then either tax rates must go up or service levels down. For example, if everyone in the community reduced their property consumption by 10% and the administrator raised tax rates to offset the decline in revenue, no one would have lower taxes but everyone would have a deadweight loss because of the underconsumption of property. Further, no individual family would have any incentive to move their property consumption back to the optimal level because this would raise their taxes without any offsetting increase in services.

Fiscal Zoning

It is only a minor step from this relationship to one in which communities try to set minimum standards for property per family in order to prevent low property consumers from enjoying the service benefits that everyone else receives without paying the same taxes. One way of restricting access to the community is with zoning laws. For example, by insisting that all housing in a community have at least a half-acre lot, the community places an effective floor on the tax contributions that each family in the community will make. This practice is referred to as "exclusionary zoning," and it has a fiscal objective.[13] Such zoning laws are not intended to prevent incompatible land usage; rather they are intended to prevent differences in the tax payments generated.

The only time such distortions would not be generated is when the costs and benefits of the services are closely related to the amount of property consumed. For example, if the cost of providing fire protection services is roughly proportional to the amount of property that must be protected and people view property as being more valuable because it has such protection, it can be shown that the property tax is an efficient method of finance with few distortions.[14]

---

[13] William A. Fischel, "A Property Rights Approach to Municipal Zoning," *Land Economics* 54 (February 1978), pp. 64–81; and Werner Z. Hirsch, "The Efficiency of Restrictive Land Use Instruments," *Land Economics* 53 (May 1977), pp. 145–156. Both are reprinted in Beaton, op. cit., pp. 216–255.

[14] Rufolo, op. cit.

A major use of the property tax is to fund local schools. This usage of the tax does not meet the criterion of being related to property consumption on either the cost or benefit side. A four-bedroom house could be occupied by a childless couple, a family with six children, or any combinations in between. Hence, the cost of schooling is not directly related to property amount. Further, the benefits received will depend largely on the number of children, not the size or value of the house. A two-child family living in an apartment gets the same school benefit as they would if they lived in a four-bedroom house; this creates an incentive for the community to try to keep out the apartment dwellers with children.

To the extent that zoning laws set a minimum amount of property tax for each community resident, the tax still serves as a price. However, the effect in this case is usually to discriminate against those with a higher preference for public services and a low preference for housing consumption. The average expenditure on schooling is highly correlated with expenditure on housing. There are families with a preference for high levels of schooling who cannot afford to also consume high levels of property, but they will be unable to find communities with their preferred combination because it is fairly unusual. Hence, they will be unable to get the high level of schooling.

/// **TAX BASE MOBILITY**

Each of the views of property tax incidence that we have reviewed – the old view, the new view, and the benefit-tax view – accepts that the supply of property, other than land itself, is highly elastic for each community. This assumption is based on the small amount of property in any one community compared to the nation or even to most regions. If the return to investment in any one community goes above average, many people would want to invest in the community. Similarly, below-average returns would deter future investment and lead to a decline in the property base. While this analysis is relevant for long-run considerations, it is much less applicable to short-run variations. In the short run the amount of real property in a given community is fixed.

The demand for property in a given community is also thought to be elastic in the long run. Over time, people choose either to move out or not move into a community that has very high taxes relative to the services provided. Thus, it is argued that the tax payments must finance benefits or taxpayers will desert the community. As Figure 10-6 shows, if both supply and demand are very elastic, a property tax simply leads to nothing to tax. The tax raises the supply curve from S to $S + T$, and this causes the equilibrium quantity to fall from Q^* to zero. Clearly, this does not happen for entire communities; but it could happen for specific types of people within communities. For example, if taxes are raised to finance better schools, childless couples may choose to leave the community. Differences in demand can cause some people to move when-

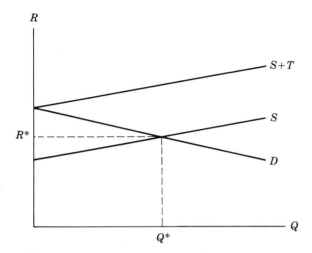

Figure 10-6 / **Elastic Supply and Demand**

ever tax and service levels go either up or down. However, the more common problem is associated with income redistribution within the community.

Few communities make any explicit attempts to redistribute income among their residents. Most of the explicit redistribution programs are funded by the federal and state governments, but local governments undergo a form of implicit redistribution. In principle everyone in a community is entitled to the same level of public services, but everyone does not pay the same amount for those services. Rather, the tax payment is tied to the amount of property the person consumes. Hence, high property consumers tend to subsidize low property consumers indirectly. Further, if the property tax funds services like education, businesses in a community tend to subsidize individuals living in the community.

Such subsidies can create incentives to move. Suppose that a high-tax, high-service jurisdiction is funded by a property tax on expensive, single-family homes. A developer builds a condominium complex where the tax per person is much less than the average for the community. Further, suppose that the cost of providing a given level of services is a fixed expenditure per person. Then the new taxes collected do not cover the cost of the services provided. Other residents find either their taxes rising or the level of services declining. This gives the old residents an incentive to move.

It is interesting to examine the extent to which such mobility can occur. Consider a homeowner who suddenly faces an increase in taxes with no offsetting increase in benefits. This individual is unable to escape the tax increase. All other potential buyers reduce their bid for the property in light of the higher tax payment. This is called capitalization of the tax; in the extreme case, the change in market value of the property is the equivalent of setting aside enough money to pay the increase in tax forever (see Box 10-2). Hence, it

---

Box 10-2

/////// Property Tax Capitalization

Suppose market value is given by the formula $MV = R/i$, where $R =$ net rent and i is the interest rate. We could define $R = P - M - T$, where P is the annual payment, M is the maintenance expenditure required to keep the property in an unchanged condition, and T is the tax payment. Hence, $MV = (P - M - T)/i$. Now consider what happens if you raise T while holding P, M, and i constant. For example, $P = 12,000$; $M = 2,000$, $T = 1,000$, and $i = 0.1$ implies $MV = (12,000 - 2,000 - 1,000)/0.1 = \$90,000$. If T is raised to $\$2,000$, $MV = (12,000 - 2,000 - 2,000)/0.1 = \$80,000$. Thus, if every-thing is expected to stay the same, the owner of the property takes a capital loss equal to the capitalized present value of all future tax payments, since $1,000/0.1 = \$10,000$. This means that there is no way the owner can escape the tax by selling the property and leaving the community. However, there is no requirement that M be kept constant. The owner can lower the value of the property by allowing it to deteriorate and thus escape some of the future tax burdens. Alternatively, P may rise over time as less property is made available in the community.

---

would not be possible to sell the property at its old market value. This in turn makes the area less attractive for new investment, since the new property would also be less attractive and generate a lower market price. The initial effect would be reduced over time but only insofar as the supply of property is adjusted. The argument that the taxpayers will flee is not correct in the short run. However, the long-term effect will indeed be to reduce the number of taxpayers, either through a reduction in construction or deterioration of existing property.

The issue specifically arises when low-income families move into a community and/or high-income families move out. As the composition of the community changes over time, the cost-revenue balance also changes. The low-income residents tend to require more services relative to their tax contributions. The community must either lower service levels or raise tax rates for existing residents, and this creates additional incentive for higher income residents to leave. Capitalization can slow the rate at which it occurs, but it does not change the long-term implications.

This leads us to several important observations regarding the property tax. One is that it is popular at the local level because the base is rather immobile. Hence, it is really not possible for property owners to escape the effects of tax changes in the short run. The controversy over incidence relates only to the long-run incidence. However, this multiplied impact through capitalization also helps explain why property owners are very sensitive to changes in tax rates. There is an old saying that "an old tax is a good tax" and the capitalization phenomenon helps explain why. People can be expected to have fully adjusted to an old tax, but a change in the tax can affect behavior for a number of years. Even a movement toward equity may backfire. For example, suppose a community raises property taxes substantially for some reason. Because of this the value of a particular house falls from $90,000 to $80,000. Then the house is sold. Several years later, the community decides the tax is unfair and again reduces it. The new owner gets a windfall gain of $10,000 without in any way offsetting the harm done to the original owner when the tax was raised.

/// ASSESSMENT PROBLEMS

Since the property tax is not directly based on a transaction each year, the specification of the tax base depends on the assessment of property value. For a long time, economists viewed property assessment as the major problem in property taxation. In particular, infrequent assessment, especially in periods of inflation, greatly distorted the tax. Many jurisdictions have made major improvements in their assessment procedures, but problems still exist. Since any biases in assessment will affect the distribution of tax burden, it is worthwhile to consider some of these issues.

Assessment practices tend to undervalue high-valued property relative to low-valued property. A number of reasons have been proposed to explain this phenomenon. The first is that assessors recognize the greater mobility and fiscal contribution of high-income households and try to make the city more attractive to them or, alternatively, the assessor may be biased against minorities, who primarily reside in low-value housing. Such practice if it occurred would clearly be illegal. Further, the owners and occupiers of a building, especially a low-income one, are not necessarily the same people (although ownership wouldn't matter if the tax were passed on to renters).

A more plausible explanation for the observed differences in assessment-to-sales-price ratio is that institutional factors create them. A major institutional factor is the appeals board. If a property owner feels that his or her property is assessed at a rate above that of equivalent property, it is possible to appeal the assessment. Yet the appeal can be costly in terms of time and documentation. For example, one way to appeal is to bring in a professional appraisal of the property to show that the stated market value is incorrect. Even this approach is difficult in areas where the assessment is typically made below the market value of the property and only the assessed value is part of the public record. In this situation, the appeal becomes even more difficult because the property owner must show that his or her property is assessed at a higher value than similar property even though the assessed value is below market value. Again, the use of expert witnesses may be highly desirable.

Given the potential costs of an appeal, it has been argued that only those with relatively valuable property are likely to appeal. For others, the tax saving would not offset the cost of the appeal. Suppose that a $200,000 home and a $40,000 home have each been overassessed by 10% and that the tax rate is 2%. The potential savings from an appeal by the owner of the more expensive home is $400 per year, while the potential savings on the lower priced home is only $80 per year. Further, the owner of the higher cost house is more likely to be familiar with appeals procedures and less likely to be intimidated by the process.

Another assessment problem is probably even more important in this regard. In many jurisdictions, reassessment takes place infrequently. Hence, assessed value tends to lag behind market value. A home that has a low value in a given year is unlikely to have increased greatly in value in the recent past. Rather, it probably stayed the same or declined in value. Alternatively, a home that has a high value in a given year is unlikely to be one that suffered a decline in value in the recent past. It is likely to have increased in value at above-average rates. Thus, the ratio of assessed to market value will be lower for the higher valued home if it has been several years since the last reassessment. One study found that this lag in assessment procedure was a major explanation for assessment ratio differentials.[15]

Even communities that try very hard to maintain accurate assessment practices may find that changing markets create problems (see Box 10-3). Yet inequities in assessment continue to be a problem with the property tax, and assessment is a major cost in the administration of the tax.

/// POLICY ISSUES

Numerous proposals exist to reform property taxation. We present some of them and consider the reasoning underlying them. We also try to evaluate them from various perspectives.

---

[15] Robert F. Engle, "De Facto Discrimination in Residential Assessments: Boston," *National Tax Journal* 28 (December 1975), pp. 445–451. Whatever the incidence of a proportional property tax, the fact that low-valued homes tend to have higher assessment-to-sales-price ratios than do higher valued homes makes it a more regressive tax. Countering this effect is the fact that property tends to constitute a larger percentage of housing expenditure for higher valued property than for lower valued property. This is primarily because maintenance expenses do not increase proportionately with house value; and housing expenditure includes both payment for property and maintenance costs. Since the tax is only on property value, it tends to increase more than proportionately to housing expenditure.

Box 10-3

////// "Incorrect" Market Prices and Assessment

Another problem that has cropped up since 1979 is the issue of reliability of market price in measuring true market value. The problem arose because many sellers were not getting cash for the sale of their homes during periods of very high mortgage interest rates. Rather, they were financing the sale at concessionary terms. This effectively lowered the price for which the home sold. Hence, a number of analysts have argued that the market price in these transactions overstated market value because the home would have sold at a lower price if the seller had not offered such concessions.

A typical sale of a home requires that the buyer pay the full amount to the seller at settlement. This is normally arranged by the buyer taking out a mortgage on the house to finance the sale. However, high interest rates deter buyers, and many sellers offered to finance the sale themselves at lower rates. Yet, if a seller lends a buyer $80,000 at 10% interest when the market rate is 15%, the seller is providing more than just a house. The seller, in essence, is offering to provide a new car along with the house in order to close the deal. The price on the house overstates its true market value.

Tax Relief

Recall that the property tax is probably proportional or slightly progressive when compared to life-cycle or average income, but that it is regressive when compared to current income. This distinction between life-cycle or "permanent" income and current income is especially important for the property tax. That is because it is such a large tax on a large part of annual expenditures. It is not uncommon for property tax payments to amount to 5% of average income. Thus, when a person retires, for example, and current income falls, the tax can loom very large indeed. It is for this reason that many states have enacted some form of property tax relief for the elderly and/or for low-income homeowners.

The tax relief for low-income or elderly homeowners is known as circuit-breaker relief. The analogy is to a circuit breaker in an electrical system, which turns the current off when there is an overload. Proponents of circuit breakers see them as relieving poor and elderly homeowners of unconscionable property tax burdens. Opponents see them as misguided efforts that tend to help those who are least needy within any given group.

The simplest form of circuit breaker is one that exempts elderly house-holds from some of the property tax. Normally, the tax payments are made by the state on behalf of the homeowner; however, it is also possible for the local jurisdiction to simply forego the tax collection. This form of circuit breaker has received the most criticism. Remember that property is an important compo-nent of net wealth. To the extent that tax relief is granted to all elderly homeowners, the greatest relief is granted to the wealthiest families in the group while the least relief is granted to the poorest. To the extent that the property tax is passed on to renters and the very lowest income elderly rent, the tax relief is not granted to the most needy elderly at all.[16]

Certainly, even relatively wealthy families may have trouble paying prop-erty taxes out of current income, but this is a liquidity problem. It is often possible for such families to borrow against the value of their house to pay such taxes, although this approach may eventually force them to sell the house. An extreme example of the problems with targeting property tax relief to all elderly occurred in Atlantic City, New Jersey, when gambling was legalized. Almost immediately property values in some neighborhoods went up by a factor of ten. Assessors soon raised tax bills by an equal ratio. Many of the elderly homeowners saw tax bills that were a large percentage of their fixed incomes, and there was a movement to grant them tax relief. This might seem desirable until one realizes that these families had received a windfall of higher property values amounting to close to half a million dollars apiece.

From an ability-to-pay standpoint, circuit breakers for the elderly do not appear to be desirable since they make no distinction on the basis of ability to pay. Rather, circuit breakers for all low-income families meet this goal. Many jurisdictions now use this type of property tax relief. However, on the benefit principle, circuit breakers for the elderly make much more sense. To the extent that local property taxes finance education and the elderly have no children in school, they get little benefit from the spending financed by the tax. It would make sense to exempt them.

The problem with the benefit argument is that logically it should be extended to all property owners who do not have children in the local schools. In fact, many people believe that funding for schools should be shifted away from the property tax. Those who view it as a benefit tax find the relation between schooling and property value to be too tenuous, and those who see the property tax as a regressive ability-to-pay tax would generally prefer to shift the funding to a more progressive source.

Another issue that arises in this context is the exemption of most govern-ment and nonprofit organizations from property taxation. This can result in more than half of the property in some cities being exempt from taxation.

---

[16] See Henry Aaron, "What Do Circuit-Breaker Laws Accomplish?" and Mason Gaffney, "An Agenda for Strengthening the Property Tax," in Peterson, op. cit., pp. 53–84.

Many question whether this is desirable.[17] If the goal is to aid certain organizations, it seems foolish to tie the aid to the amount of property owned. For example, a well-funded organization with a plush headquarters building would be receiving far more in implicit aid than an organization that kept its administrative costs small and used rented offices. In fact, the latter would not receive any property tax relief. On a benefit basis, the exemption still does not make sense. It is true that these organizations do not use schools, but they do use other services and, again, one may question why they should be singled out for exemption as compared to other property owners. In fact, some municipalities now collect payments in lieu of taxes from some of these organizations to help cover the cost of services provided. However, these payments are usually much less than property taxes would be.

Tax Interactions

In a federal system, we should also consider the interaction of the property tax with other taxes. The major interaction occurs because the property tax can be deducted from income for property owners who itemize deductions. This amounts to an additional subsidy toward home ownership, and one that increases with income (see Box 10-4). It was estimated that the federal government tax expenditure for this deduction amounted to almost $11 billion for 1987. Many states also have substantial tax expenditures because property tax payments are deductible in figuring state income taxes.[18] Viewed on either an ability-to-pay basis or a benefit basis this deduction makes little sense.

From an ability-to-pay basis, the property tax deduction is seen as a method of preventing double taxation. Thus, income that has already gone to pay taxes is not subject to further income taxation. However, as we saw earlier, the property tax can be viewed as a tax on imputed rent, which normally escapes income taxation. In this context, the argument for a deduction is questionable. Alternatively, if the ability-to-pay argument is made on a liquidity basis, e.g., that it helps keep the elderly from being saddled with very high total taxes relative to current income, then it should be in the form of a tax credit rather than a deduction. The deductibility gives the biggest tax break to those with the most income.

From a benefit standpoint, deductibility makes even less sense. If the tax is indeed a price for services rendered, then deductibility merely offers an incentive to have more services provided through the local public sector. For example, if a wealthy community has a local golf club and virtually all

---

[17] Taxation of one government by another would raise serious constitutional issues; however, the federal government does make payments in lieu of taxes to many jurisdictions as do many state governments. See Advisory Commission on Intergovernmental Relations, *Payments in Lieu of Taxes on Federal Real Property*, Appendices, A-91 (Washington, DC: 1982).

[18] *Budget of the United States Government, Fiscal Year 1987, Special Analysis*, p. G-28.

Box 10-4

////// Property Tax Deduction for Homeowners

The property tax is deductible from income for homeowners who itemize. Hence, their federal (and often state) income tax liability declines by their marginal tax rate times the amount of property tax. This means that a homeowner in the 33% marginal bracket receives federal tax relief equal to one-third of his or her property tax payment. Someone in the 15% marginal bracket would receive relief equal to only 15% of property tax payments. Renters receive no relief. Thus, the property tax biases the decision between owning and renting even more toward ownership, especially for higher income families.

To see that the tax biases toward ownership, consider a tax increase of $1,000. The itemizing homeowner pays the additional $1,000 and deducts it from income in computing federal income taxes. The renter pays an extra $1,000 in rent (assuming the tax is fully passed on in equilibrium) and gets no additional deduction. It is true that the landlord can deduct the $1,000 in tax when calculating business income; but this deduction is exactly offset by the $1,000 in additional rent received. Hence, there is no reduction in federal taxes.

---

residents belong, they can lower the costs to themselves by having the local government buy the club and charge membership fees through the property tax. This may not be a significant effect, but it shows why deductibility makes little sense on this basis. The one argument that could be made for deductibility on a benefit basis is that the property tax is used for implicit redistribution at the local level. Deductibility then offers partial compensation to the higher income families for their subsidy to lower income families. Unfortunately, this does not differentiate between high-income families living in high-income communities and those living in low-income communities. Hence, it would not be an efficient method to achieve the desired effect.

The argument for deductibility that makes the most sense is that it is an indirect subsidy to local governments from higher levels of government. As we saw earlier, such indirect subsidies tend to be very inefficient. Hence, there do not appear to be any good reasons for maintaining deductibility other than the "old subsidy is a good subsidy" argument. Since so many homeowners are accustomed to this deduction, repeal would be politically unpopular; repeal would also redistribute tax burdens. In addition, many people might make other choices with respect to housing and local government services if they were faced with paying the full cost of their property taxes.

/// REVENUE ELASTICITY

Does property tax revenue keep pace with economic growth and inflation? Many local government officials believe that it does not. It is argued that property values lag behind in inflationary periods and that property is a declining percentage of wealth in the United States. Neither claim appears to be true. The lag in property values in inflationary periods appears to be due to lagging assessment rather than an actual lag in property values.

From 2.4% of GNP in 1948, property tax collections rose to 3.4% of GNP in 1970 and peaked at 3.7% of GNP in 1972. Collections rose less rapidly than GNP over the remainder of the 1970s; they were down to 3.4% of GNP by 1978. They then fell, to hover around 2.5% of GNP through the first half of the 1980s. Despite the decline as a percentage of GNP, actual property tax collections only fell in 1979. Every other year since 1948 shows an increase in dollars collected.[19] The decline in 1979 is almost certainly caused by property tax limitations rather than any failure of the tax base to keep up with growth in GNP.

The real issue for many local governments is that their property tax base does not grow as rapidly as the rest of the economy. In most cases, this is consistent with slow growth in the entire local economy. Many areas have slow growth or decline, while others are booming. Since the disparities in growth rates are much greater at the local level and the property tax is primarily a local tax, it is the tax most associated with slow growth. However, slowly growing areas would find that their revenues did not grow at the national average no matter which base they taxed.

The other reason why property tax collections may not keep up with expectations is that the property tax does not have a progressive rate structure. Thus, as the value of property increases tax collections only increase proportionately. With progressive tax structures, such as that for the federal income tax, the tax collections increase more than proportionately because increments to income are taxed at higher rates.

Another issue is the cyclical sensitivity of tax revenue. Most tax sources provide collections that head down during a recession and then jump back up during a recovery. This can create serious instability in funding for governments that rely on such tax sources. The property tax is one of the least variable of broad-based taxes. Property values simply do not change much in response to the business cycle. Hence, tax obligations tend to stay the same. To be sure, there are cyclical increases in delinquent payments, but that is not the

---

[19] ACIR, *Significant Features of Fiscal Federalism, 1985–86*, op. cit., p. 43.

same thing as a reduction in tax liability, since most such payments will be made eventually and the government can borrow against these expected future payments. The reverse side is that tax obligations remain the same for those who become unemployed or face other financial hardships. This may be offset to the extent that circuit breakers exist.

/// SUMMARY

The property tax is the only major tax in the United States that is levied on the basis of ownership of a form of wealth rather than on the basis of a transaction. Despite its appearance as a relatively straightforward tax to analyze, it is a complex phenomenon with many interesting features. Under certain circumstances it is a benefit tax. When viewed as an ability-to-pay tax, it is sometimes regressive and sometimes progressive. Despite its short-comings it is likely to stay with us for some time, though its importance has been declining. From an economic perspective, it might be best to say it is a benefit tax to finance services directly related to property. There appears to be no good economic reason for the many exemptions that are granted nor for the deductibility from federal income taxes. Improved assessment procedures are curing many of the problems associated with assessment, but there is still much room for improvement. Means-tested circuit breakers are useful to the extent that the tax is an ability-to-pay tax.

Chapter 11 //////

User Charges

In their most common form, user charges are simply prices. When your local government sends you a water bill or charges a fee to inspect your home or record a deed, it is imposing a user charge on the service. Similarly, when you pay an entrance or camping fee at a state or national park, your government is acting like a private business and charging for some of the goods or services provided. Although such charges are imposed at all levels of government, they are most important as a revenue source for local governments. In 1986 they accounted for 13.2% of all local general revenue and ranked second only to property taxes as a source of locally raised revenue. However, they amounted to only 7.6% of state general revenue.[1] The states varied substantially in their reliance on such charges. Combined state and local amounts ranged from a low of $209 per capita in Connecticut to $766 per capita in Alaska, with a national average of $334 per capita.[2]

Throughout the United States reliance on user charges has been increasing, particularly since many state and local governments are now operating under tax limitations. For example, in 1970 user charges accounted for 7.9% of all government revenue, but this increased to 8.6% in 1980 and 9.6% in 1985.[3] Further, there is evidence that the public favors a continuation of this shift. One opinion survey found that more than half of the respondents favored charges for local services as the best way to raise more local revenue.[4]

The amount of user charge revenue would be much greater if we included the operation of the various publicly owned or regulated utilities, but these are

[1] Advisory Commission on Intergovernmental Relations, *Significant Features of Fiscal Federalism, 1988 Edition*, vol. 2, M-155 II (Washington, DC: 1988), Tables 64 and 65.
[2] Ibid., Table R-7.
[3] Tax Foundation, *Facts and Figures on Government Finance, 1988–89 Edition* (Baltimore: Johns Hopkins University Press, 1988), p. 15.
[4] Advisory Commission on Intergovernmental Relations, *Changing Public Attitudes on Government and Taxes* (Washington, DC: 1982).

usually treated as separate entities. However, both forms of provision provide insight into the issues raised by the use of pricing for government provision of services. Hence, we consider both the direct pricing of such services by government and the effect of government regulation on the pricing done by regulated private firms.

User charges perform many of the functions that prices perform in the private sector. These functions include rationing the use of a good or service, providing government with information on its value to consumers, and providing financing for the production of the good or service. This provision of financing is frequently the most attractive feature of a user charge from the politician's perspective; from the economic perspective, the other two functions are equally important.

/// THEORY OF USER CHARGES

Our discussion of revenue to this point has frequently addressed the ability-to-pay or benefit principle in evaluating a tax. User charges are also considered under the benefit principle since there is a rough equity in having those who benefit from a public service pay for it. However, the analysis of user charges from an economic perspective focuses more on the use of such charges to promote efficiency.

The price in an efficient market will be equal to the marginal cost of producing one more unit of the good. The consumer must then decide whether or not the additional unit is worth the cost. To achieve the same type of allocation in the public sector, the public sector price should also be set equal to marginal cost. Where the item is a good or service that can be used in variable amounts, such as water, the price should reflect the marginal cost of providing additional units of water. Where the service is provided at the same level to everyone who chooses to participate but the cost varies depending on the number of participants, the price should be set equal to the marginal cost of serving an additional person. This pricing method insures that people only use an item up to the point where the value to them of an additional unit is at least as great as the cost of providing it, which is necessary for an efficient allocation of resources.

Although economists almost uniformly agree that marginal cost pricing is very desirable when the public sector uses prices, it is hardly used at all in practice. Rather, most of the pricing in the United States, whether for regulation or direct charges by a government, uses the principle of "normal rate of return" or effectively of average cost pricing. For the privately owned but publicly regulated producers, the normal rate of return amounts to a target rate of return on investments in the company. Since this return is set equal to the return that a similar investment would have received in other possible uses, it is part of the opportunity cost of using the investment funds. Consequently, earning a normal rate of return is the same as earning zero economic profits. For a publicly held company, the interest cost on debt is treated as part of the cost of operation. This interest cost replaces the return to investment in the cost structure, and the pricing system is essentially the same. This is again similar to an average cost pricing system.

The information on how consumers value additional units of output can also be very important for a government provider. As we shall see when we discuss expenditures, determining just how much voters value additional output is often a perplexing problem when the price is not tied to consumption. People have a tendency to overstate the value they place on more of a good or service if they do not believe that they will have to pay the cost of providing it. Further, if they are not charged an explicit price for consuming more, they have a tendency to increase consumption until the marginal benefit of an additional unit is zero. If the good or service is costly to provide, the government must usually set an arbitrary limit on how much will be provided and find some other method of rationing the amount provided. For example, the city of New York found that welfare patients would frequently call an ambulance to go to the hospital for minor illnesses. From their perspective, the service was less expensive than alternative means of transportation; but the city was finally forced to place significant restrictions on the use of ambulances because of the high cost.

If the government does choose to produce less than is demanded at a zero price and provide it on first-come, first-served basis, then it essentially forces people to wait in line for the service. This causes the recipients to waste some of their time in order to gain the benefit provided, but this lost time does not in any way benefit the government. If the rationing device is money, the government has the money received to help offset its costs while time spent in line is simply lost. Of course, for many types of services the use of money as a rationing device would be inappropriate because the intent of the service is to redistribute income. For example, charging for "free" clinics would be contradictory. However, in other instances some form of pricing would lead to an improvement in the allocation of resources.

Another area where user fees could be expanded is in the control of negative externalities. The appropriate price would be one equal to the marginal cost generated by the externality. Negative externalities exist where private costs are less than true social marginal costs. In such cases, a price or tax on the generation of the externality equal to the marginal cost imposed outside the market mechanism would internalize the externality. In addition, the fee would raise revenue for the government.

Price and Revenue

We begin the analysis with the simple case in which the government faces a constant cost for providing additional units of the output. This might correspond to inspection services, for example. Given the constant cost for addi-

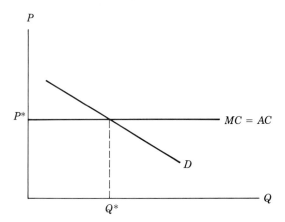

Figure 11-1 / Constant Cost Pricing

tional output, the situation can be modeled as in Figure 11-1. In this figure, the marginal cost (MC) is equal to the average cost (AC); the appropriate price is fairly clearly the one that is equal to both. This is shown as P^* and leads to consumption of Q^* units of the output. Most people would find this equitable, and it is also efficient. The level Q^* is the efficient level of output because it represents the point where the marginal benefit to consumers of one more unit is exactly equal to the marginal cost to the government of providing an additional unit. If more is produced it will be inefficient because the additional output is not worth the additional cost; and if less is produced, consumers would value the additional output at more than the cost savings to government from not producing it.

The revenue generated from the sale of this service is equal to the cost of providing it. Hence, there are no issues of budget shortages or surpluses for the provider of the good or service. If the cost of provision should differ for different customers, the agency is faced with a problem of charging some people more for the service or of overcharging some customers in order to subsidize others. For example, if it is more costly to inspect custom-designed homes than it is to inspect tract dwellings, the marginal cost principle would argue that the fees should differ. The average cost pricing principle would lead to this conclusion as well if the average cost were calculated separately for the various groups of customers, but not if the government is constrained to charge the same price to all. The latter principle is fairly common in the public sector; however, it can lead to large efficiency distortions. In particular, Figure 11-2 shows that the common pricing would lead to overconsumption by the high-cost users and underconsumption by the low-cost users. A number of other possibilities exist, and efficiency becomes harder to achieve while respecting the various other constraints usually placed on pricing (see Box 11-1 for another example).

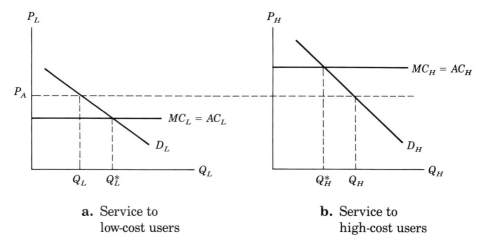

a. Service to
low-cost users

b. Service to
high-cost users

Figure 11-2 / Different Cost of Service

Returns to Scale and Pricing

In the private sector, competition between firms keeps each one earning zero economic profits. However, there is no particular reason why the marginal cost price will generate revenue exactly equal to the cost of production in the public sector. In other words, the marginal cost may be above or below average cost, so the revenue associated with this price would also be above or below total cost. This is associated with either increasing or decreasing returns to scale. In the increasing returns case, the average cost goes down as more is produced; in the decreasing returns case, the average cost goes up as more is produced. These situations are usually associated with large fixed costs and some form of capacity restraint, respectively. This can be illustrated by considering the analysis of the pricing of government utilities.

Start by considering the case of natural monopoly. A natural monopoly is a production situation in which there are very large fixed costs and fairly low marginal costs. For example, most of the items we think of as public utilities have this characteristic. The fixed cost is associated with the distribution network that must be established to get the service to where it is required. Once the distribution network is established, the cost of hooking up another customer is likely to be relatively low. Thus, the marginal cost is below the average cost for the entire feasible range of output. This is illustrated in Figure 11-3. The optimal output is Q^* units at an average cost of C^* per unit. However, if two firms each produce half of Q^*, they incur an average cost per unit that is higher than C^*. This is because each would have to incur the fixed cost of providing the service but they would only be able to spread this fixed cost over a smaller customer base. If there were two firms the situation would be unstable. Each would have to charge at least average cost to stay in

Box 11-1

////// Equitable and Efficient Pricing?

The text shows the case in which a requirement of uniform pricing creates inefficiency when marginal cost differs among users. However, the requirement for uniform pricing can have a number of different efficiency problems. Consider the case in which people who live far from a water line can get adequate water service only if a pipe is run to their homes. Once this is provided, the marginal cost of providing water is the same as it is for everyone else, but the average cost differs. If we go simply by the marginal cost pricing rule, everyone should pay the same price for water; but if they do not have to pay the full cost of providing the service, people might choose to build houses too far away. Use of average cost pricing might discourage them from building in the first place; but once they were there it would distort their consumption choices. The better solution would be to move away from a single price as the method of funding. The builders of the isolated houses should be charged a fixed fee equal to the additional cost of serving that area, and then the users should be charged a variable fee based on usage for the water itself. The use of such fee systems is increasing as many communities recognize the large capital costs they must incur to provide service to new developments.

Although such fees must be carefully reviewed to be sure that they do not distort choices, they offer a significant improvement in the allocation of resources.

A similar problem arises with first class mail service. The postal service still is constrained to charge the same price for a piece of first class mail, no matter where in the country it is going. The price is supposed to cover the average cost of operations, but there is no differentiation among users or uses. For example, distance would be expected to affect the cost of providing mail delivery, as would origin and/or destination in rural areas rather than urban areas. The latter in particular is cited as an example of an implicit subsidy from urban to rural dwellers since the average cost of rural mail delivery is far greater than the average cost of urban mail delivery; but it is not at all clear that the marginal cost is any different. It may indeed be best to continue the current system if there is to be a single price per letter; but it would probably be more efficient to have people charged a fixed fee per month for postal delivery associated with the difficulty of providing them with service. The problems with such a system would be the administrative costs and the various perceptions of equity associated with mail delivery.

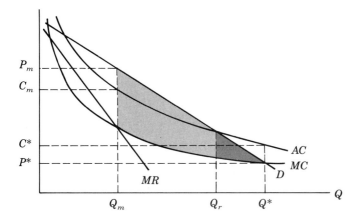

Figure 11-3 / Natural Monopoly

business in the long run, but each would recognize that it could charge lower prices if it could expand its customer base. The result would be a price war until only one firm was left providing the service.

When the remaining firm is left alone, it would be expected to react as would any monopolistic firm and reduce output to the point where $MR = MC$. This is shown as Q_m in Figure 11-3 and the corresponding price is P_m. Hence, the private market would not reach an efficient level of output. The efficiency loss would be equal to the entire shaded area in the diagram. In contrast, if the government decides to provide the good and charge no price, it will have to produce out to the point where the demand curve hits the horizontal axis, which is clearly a point of overproduction.

The efficient solution is to set a price equal to P^*. This will induce consumers to purchase the optimal quantity. Unfortunately, in this situation the total revenue is less than the total cost: in the figure, C^* is above P^*. Since the average cost times quantity equals total cost and average revenue times quantity equals total revenue, the multiplication of each by quantity shows that there is a loss. The best that can be done in the form of a self-financing project with a uniform price per unit is to produce at Q_r, where price is set equal to average cost. In this case the revenue generated is exactly equal to cost. This is not an efficient solution, because the marginal cost of additional units is lower than the value to consumers that those additional units would generate. However, if the price is lowered to allow those additional units to be sold, revenue no longer covers total cost. The efficiency loss has been reduced from the lightly shaded area associated with the monopoly output to the smaller heavily shaded area, but there is still an efficiency loss.

Some people believe that the efficiency cost associated with deviations from marginal cost pricing is quite high. One study illustrates the impact marginal cost pricing could have on efficiency by estimating the efficiency gains from instituting marginal cost pricing of business telephone service.

The finding is that under reasonable assumptions, the efficiency gain would be about 65% of revenue.[5]

If we drop the constraint of uniform pricing, it may be possible to get to the efficient level of output and still cover all costs. For example, it may be possible to charge each person a fixed fee to cover part of the fixed cost and then charge a price equal to marginal cost for all units. For most utilities, this is unlikely to cause people to drop the services. However, the fixed fee component serves as a form of lump-sum tax, and many people object to this as being a regressive method of financing the service. Other issues are also raised when we consider that there are likely to be many other factors affecting the cost of service; but the basic analysis is largely unchanged when these complications are added.

Not all of the goods and services which government provides fit the natural monopoly model. Many of them have marginal cost above the average cost, just as the standard private firm would. This is illustrated in Figure 11-4. This could be a utility where the marginal cost curve has started to turn up. It would still be inefficient to have more than one firm, and an unregulated firm would try for the monopoly price and output. However, in this case the efficient output of Q^* is achieved with a price of P^*, so average revenue is above average cost. Thus, total revenue is above total cost and the efficient level of operation would generate a profit. In fact, however, a government providing this good or service would generally charge the price P_2, which generates revenue exactly equal to cost. Similarly, the government regulation of a utility would lead to the utility setting this price.

At the price P_2 more than the efficient amount is produced and sold. This overproduction has an associated efficiency cost as shown by the heavily shaded triangle. As drawn, the efficiency loss associated with government pricing is less than the efficiency loss associated with monopoly pricing, but

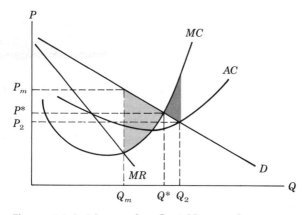

Figure 11-4 / **Increasing Cost Monopoly**

[5] Stephen J. Brown and David S. Sibley, *The Theory of Public Utility Pricing* (New York: Cambridge University Press, 1986), pp. 50–51.

Box 11-2

////// Electricity Pricing under Increasing Costs

A typical "natural monopoly" is the distribution of electricity. The distribution network constitutes a large fixed cost. The cost of serving an additional customer is relatively small, but the cost of creating a second distribution network is quite large. However, in many areas this is now an increasing cost natural monpoly.

For example, in the Northwest a large amount of electricity is generated by public hydroelectric projects. The cost of generating the electricity can be less than one cent per kilowatt hour (kwh). Yet this electricity is no longer sufficient to satisfy the quantity demanded at that price. Hence, higher cost nuclear or fossil fuel plants are used to generate the additional electricity. The marginal cost of using these plants is more than seven cents per kwh. Since this represents the resource cost of producing the last kwh of electricity, it should only be produced if consumers value it at more than the cost of production. However, consumers only have to pay about four cents per kwh and will use electricity up to the point where the last unit is worth only four cents. The electric utilities are essentially using their profits on the hydroelectric plants to subsidize the more costly fossil fuel or nuclear plants.

there is no particular reason why this must be true. It is interesting to consider why the government pricing solution, which has a lower price and higher quantity than the optimum, is inefficient. In terms of marginal cost and marginal benefit, it is easy to see that the cost of the additional output is greater than the benefits it generates. At the optimal price, the enterprise would be generating an economic profit. This profit is then being used to subsidize the overproduction (see Box 11-2 for an example). At the optimum, the profits from the enterprise could be used for other purposes.

The ability of the government to divert profits to other uses might help explain why there is reluctance to allow profits to be generated. If the government is allowed to keep the profits from an operation, there is the possibility that it will start to act like a monopolist itself and use the extra profits for other purposes. In particular, it may be very difficult to determine the true marginal cost for additional output, which leads to the possibility of the price being manipulated. Thus, a government faced with a budget deficit might find it more expedient to raise the price of water than to raise other taxes or to cut spending. However, if they raise the price above the efficient price they are creating the same type of distortion that a monopolist would. Whether this is the reason or not, most governments that operate public utilities in the United States have significant restrictions on the ability to divert funds to other purposes.

This situation is worth emphasizing because it is a very clear example of a case where a market failure creates an opportunity for government intervention to improve the allocation of resources but where the government intervention is also imperfect. Thus, it is necessary to compare the actual allocation of resources under realistic government intervention with the allocation if the market is left alone. It also illustrates that often much can be done to improve the activities within the public sector.

Peak Load

Another area where pricing differences are likely to be important is where the demand for a good or service has clear patterns. Generally, the capacity provided by government is strongly influenced by the highest level of demand. However, this level may occur infrequently. Thus, the marginal cost of providing service may be quite high at times of peak demand and much lower at other times. The appropriate response to such demand swings would be to charge a higher price at the peak times than at the off-peak times. Thus, some utilities charge lower prices for electricity based on the season or the time of day.

Peak price differentials are not widely used in the United States. There are, of course, some government recreation facilities that charge higher prices during the summer and on weekends, but this tends to be a relatively minor issue. One area where the peak demand is a significant issue is transportation. Both the public transportation system and the roads suffer from clear peak demand problems, yet neither is generally observed to use higher prices during peak times. For example, a mass transit system must determine its need for capital equipment and drivers on the basis of rush hours. An increase in rush hour demand requires that more resources be used to maintain the same level of service. Alternatively, most transit systems have large amounts of excess capacity at nonpeak times. Thus, the efficient solution would be to charge higher prices at the peak time and lower prices at the off-peak times. While a few systems do follow such pricing schemes, most do not. In fact, many systems charge lower fares at peak times by offering discounts to frequent users, many of whom are rush hour commuters.

Externalities

Internalization of externalities is another area where government could use pricing to offset the inefficient allocation of resources associated with some market failure and also generate revenue. The principle is simply to charge the person generating the externality the cost that is imposed on others. This makes the external cost one of the factors the person takes into account in

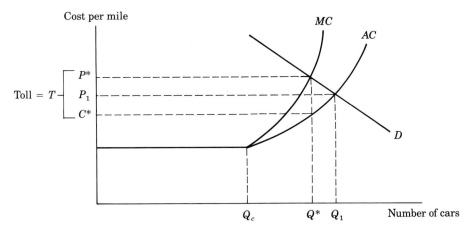

Figure 11-5 / Congestion

determining behavior and it leads to a more efficient allocation of resources. This issue can be combined with the peaking issue by looking at highway congestion.

When a car enters an unused roadway, it generates virtually no cost other than its own operating costs. However, a car entering a congested roadway does generate an external cost. This car slows the journey fractionally for many other drivers. It is an extremely tiny cost for any one auto, but when you consider that each car may indirectly influence thousands of others, even this very tiny cost per car can become substantial. Economists argue that highways and many other roads tend to be overutilized because the individual users of the congested facilities do not consider the cost that they impose on others. In such cases, user charges set equal to this cost would force each individual to face the full cost of utilizing the facility. If this were added to the cost of driving, some drivers would decide to take the bus, form carpools, or not commute at peak times. This would allow others to reduce their trip time, in partial compensation for the tolls paid. Further, this would also generate revenue for government, which could be used to reduce other taxes.

These arguments are illustrated in Figure 11-5. The average cost curve, AC, shows the cost to the individual in terms of his or her own expenditures and the value of the time used in commuting. Beyond Q_c cars at a time, congestion causes a reduction in average speed. This results in an increased time cost to all drivers, and the average cost curve starts to turn up. However, if the average cost is turning up, then the marginal cost must be above it, and marginal cost shows the change in total cost associated with one more person using the road. Consider a simple numerical example. Suppose that the average cost just before congestion starts to affect speed is $3 per car, including both monetary and time costs. Further, suppose that 1,000 cars are using the road at this point. Now if one more car wants to use the road, the effect is that on average everyone is delayed for a few seconds and the average cost goes up to $3.01. Total cost has gone from $3,000 to $3,013. Thus, the marginal cost is way above the average cost. Each driver is only going to consider the $3.01 that it costs to use the road. But total costs would decline by $13 if one of them were to choose not to use it.

In the figure, the average cost determines the actions of the drivers, so the equilibrium is at Q_1. This represents overusage of the roads. The efficient level is at Q^*, but this could only be achieved if the government charged a toll of T per car to use the road. Each driver would be worse off facing the toll. Those who continue to drive pay P^* instead of P_1; those who have stopped driving have lost some consumer surplus. Yet society as a whole is better off. This is because the loss to the individual drivers is a gain to the government rather than a consumption of resources. The government gets T times Q^* in revenue; this money can be used for productive purposes or to reduce other taxes.

Other User Charges

A large variety of the services provided by local governments are potential areas for user charges. Many of the services are used in different amounts by different people and the cost of providing them depends on the amount of usage. Nevertheless, governments traditionally have been reluctant to place too much emphasis on these charges. Some of this reluctance is reduced by the need to generate revenue; and in some cases, the entire activity can be removed from the government budget by making it a fee-financed activity. For example, most local governments pay for trash collection from general revenues. However, it is certainly possible to give a contract to a private trash collector and have that company charge directly for trash collection. This is done in some areas. Yet it is also important to be cautious about what the repercussions of the fees might be. In many cases, government provides a service because there is a substantial externality to be offset. Thus, trash is collected because burning it or dumping it creates substantial problems. When a fee is set some people may be tempted to avoid the charge by disposing of their trash in undesirable ways. Thus, the enforcement costs would be expected to increase.

There are fewer opportunities for user fees at the state and federal level than there are at the local level, but they are coming under increased consideration. For example, the Coast Guard might charge for some of its services to boaters, and the fees to enter national parks are expected to cover many of the operating costs. While the potential benefits of increased use of fees are clear, there are some concerns as well.

/// OBJECTIONS TO USER CHARGES

There are two major areas of objection to the imposition of user charges. One is the cost of administering the collection and the other is the equity impact of such charges.

Returning to the automobile example, several problems with administering such fees can be readily identified. First, there are the actual expenses of monitoring auto traffic, determining the correct fee, and collecting the fee. Second, if the fees are not universal, traffic will be diverted to unpriced side roads and cause congestion there. Finally, the motorist must devote some effort to determining what the charges are, select and then pay the appropriate one. These efforts can reduce the attractiveness of a fee option.

The major objection to such tolls appears to be an assertion that they would be very costly to administer. This objection is probably overstated since systems are being tried at least on an experimental basis in a number of countries.[6] As the congestion problem in our major cities increases we may yet see the resistance diminish.

The problem of equity is potentially more serious than the problem of administrative costs. In the case of administrative cost it is possible to balance gains against losses in terms of efficiency. Trading gains to one person for losses to another is considerably more difficult. Yet the apparent redistribution and equity effects of user charges are frequently exaggerated. Further, the redistribution attributed to a lack of user charges often is not targeted very effectively.

The specific argument is that pricing the use of public facilities or services discriminates against the poor. In a very broad sense, this is true. Use of the price system invariably gives more options to those with more money. But the relevant question should be whether the poor would be hurt relatively more by the imposition of a fee than would higher income individuals. Often this is not the case; and when it is, the additional revenue raised could be targeted toward aiding low-income individuals.

In the congestion example, low-income drivers are more likely to forego the road during high-fee times; but this is hardly a compelling argument for not imposing fees. First, the usage of congested roads by low-income groups is likely to be small relative to their number in the population. They are less likely to own automobiles, less likely to live in the suburbs, and so on. Second, most of the revenue will be collected from high-income groups whether the low-income groups avoid the roads or not. Hence, this may be a very progressive tax. Third, the proceeds might be used to reduce reliance on registration fees or other taxes, which are likely to be regressively distributed. Looked at another way, a general subsidy of any good or service is seldom a target-efficient method of aiding the poor. Most of the benefits spill over to other groups.

---

[6] Hong Kong has considered a complex set of congestion tolls, and Singapore uses a licensing system to limit use of downtown roads during rush hours. In the United States, there are no user charges to control congestion; however, automatic vehicle identification systems are being tested for collection of tolls. These systems allow a driver with an identification tag on the vehicle to pass through toll stations without stopping. In some of the systems, trucks are weighed as they drive through. Tolls are then charged against the vehicle's account or a check is made to see that fees have been paid in advance. See Charlotte F. Ahern, "California Tests High-Tech Tolls," *City & State* (July 4, 1988), pp. 1 and 28.

One final issue with respect to user charges at the local level is the interaction with other levels of government. As already noted, user fees are not deductible when paying federal taxes although many other types of taxes are. The same is true for many state income taxes. Hence, the community that relies on user fees is giving up some of the ability to export its taxes through the various income tax systems.

/// **SUMMARY**

User fees are an important part of government revenue, particularly at the local level. They represent the areas of government activity where overlap with the private market is greatest. The actual use of user fees is primarily in the funding of utilities, but additional opportunities appear to exist in a variety of areas. Even where such fees are used, they do not always mimic the market solution. Most government agencies set price to cover average cost and this may not be efficient. The efficient price is set at marginal cost. This price may generate either too little or too much revenue. Too little revenue is a problem because of the need to divert revenue from other areas. Too much revenue is likely to be a problem because government may be tempted to act like a monopolist if allowed to keep the profits from one of its enterprises. Also, there tends to be substantial political pressure to keep prices as low as possible. Use of nonuniform pricing could alleviate many of the efficiency problems while still generating enough revenue to cover costs, but such systems are not widely used.

The use of fees to reduce congestion would likely generate substantial revenue and improve the allocation of resources. It is very unpopular in the U.S. but other countries are starting to experiment with such systems. Periods of budget stress frequently bring out more discussion of user fees, and they appear to be expanding as a revenue source at the local level. However, they tend to be of little consequence at the higher levels of government.

Chapter 12 //////

Government Borrowing and Sale of Debt Instruments

Governments borrow to finance part of their expenditures. The effect of such borrowing often depends on how the funds are going to be used. Borrowing to finance the purchase or construction of capital assets is not likely to create serious problems, unlike borrowing to finance current consumption or transfers. Governments that borrow to fund current expenditures have a future obligation to pay interest and possibly part of the principal without having any additional services or assets to offset this expenditure. There is also a substantial difference in the ability of different levels of government to borrow. The federal government has such vast powers of taxation and monetary control that its obligations are treated as being virtually free of any risk. However, other governmental units can much more easily become unable to make interest payments or redeem bonds. Hence, they are judged individually and they sometimes have difficulty in borrowing.

Through borrowing, governments can obtain funds without imposing current-period tax liabilities on individuals and firms. Such borrowing is appropriate if benefits also occur over a number of years. In theory, only physical capital creation should be financed through the sale of debt instruments, but few governments have separate capital and operating budgets. Nevertheless, state and local governments consistently tend to use such instruments to finance capital construction.

Matters are very different in relation to the federal government. Historically, budget deficits were associated with financing wars or other unforseen problems. This position has been altered by consideration of the use of debt for the purpose of adjusting macroeconomic policy or achieving other objectives. We do not consider such use of debt policy, but we note that the issues are still strongly debated.

In addition to their direct borrowing, governments are increasingly active in the area of private debt. Thus, the federal government guarantees loan repayments for a variety of borrowers, and state and local governments borrow money at tax-exempt rates and relend it to various private borrowers. These activities can both increase the debt burden of the government that guarantees the repayment and distort private borrowing and lending patterns. In addition, the hidden cost to government from such involvement in the debt markets can be quite large.

/// MAJOR PUBLIC DEBT INSTRUMENTS

A brief review of the most commonly used debt instruments is in order. Debt instruments issued by the federal government differ from those of state and local governments; the latter tend to be much more innovative. In particular, the variety of debt instruments used by state and local governments has become quite large, especially since some now pay taxable interest and others do not. We focus on the major classes of such debt instruments.

The federal debt can be subdivided into marketable and nonmarketable issues. The former, accounting for about three-quarters of the total, are in the form of Treasury bonds, notes, and bills, which basically differ in terms of maturity. Bonds run longer than ten years, notes from one to ten years, and bills have maturities of up to twelve months. While notes and bonds carry an annual coupon payment (interest) and are redeemable at par (face value) at maturity, bills are sold at a discount (less than face value) and pay no interest; the appreciation in value to maturity represents the investor's return. Nonmarketable issues include savings bonds, notes, and various government account series, i.e., debt held by United States agencies and trust funds.

State and local government debt instruments are of many types, both long-term and short-term issues. All the instruments used by subnational governments tend to be grouped as "municipals." Let us first examine long-term financing techniques. The major long-term debt instruments are general obligation bonds and revenue bonds. The purpose of general obligation bonds is to finance public facilities at the lowest cost to the taxpayer. Public facilities in this instance are defined as those from which benefits accrue in significant amounts to both users and nonusers in the community, i.e., law enforcement, fire protection, schooling, and public health. Bonds are sold by a public entity, e.g., a state or city, which has pledged its full faith and credit for the principal and interest on the bond. The public entity is authorized by state law to levy on all real property such ad valorem taxes as may be necessary to pay the bonds and interest thereon without limitation as to amount.

In many states, approval by two-thirds of those casting a vote on the specific measure is necessary to authorize a general obligation bond. Clearly, the security on general obligation bonds tends to be of the highest quality, including both the pledge of all general revenues as well as the legal means to raise the tax rates to cover debt service. Because of this superior security, interest rates on these bonds tend to be the lowest of any municipal bond. The legal general obligation bonding capacity of a city is often limited, for example to 15% of its gross assessed valuation in California.

Revenue bonds encompass a broad category, including general revenue, parking revenue, lease revenue, mortgage revenue, residential rehabilitation, historical rehabilitation, and industrial development, the latter of relatively recent vintage. In general, revenue bonds are serviced from income generated by the facilities they are issued to finance. This usually entails the levying of user fees, which then become the source of servicing the bonds. It is essential that the facilities financed with revenue bonds provide benefits to a group of readily identifiable users. This makes it possible to levy fees on specific users. In some instances charges other than conventional fees are levied, i.e., tolls, stand-by charges, leases, and even rent. Once a revenue bond program has been established, in many states bonds are issued without voter approval.

Short-term financing techniques are used for meeting anticipated cash-flow deficits, interim financing of a project, and project implementation. These techniques involve the issuance of short-term notes or commercial paper; voter approval is not required. All short-term financing techniques have strong similarities, differing mainly in the source of revenues pledged for repayment. Some of the major techniques are discussed next.

Bond anticipation notes (BANs) are used to obtain financing in conjunction with a project for which bonds are authorized but not yet issued. BANs permit the issuance of debt in increments as work on a project progresses, before some or all of the bond proceeds are available.

The legal basis for issuing BANs prior to the issuance of bonds is contained in the various laws authorizing specific types of bonds. The issuer can be any public entity eligible to issue long-term bonds, including cities, counties, redevelopment agencies, and other special districts. BANs are secured by pledges of, and have a lien on, the bond proceeds and other revenues or assets from which the long-term bonds are intended to be supported. Moreover, insurance during construction of the facility is a requirement.

The ability to issue BANs periodically permits use of temporary financing not only to initiate but also to complete the project. Once a project is completed, long-term bonds tend to be issued promptly to pay off all outstanding BANs as well as any outstanding project costs.

Grant anticipation notes (GANs) may be issued to eliminate cash-flow deficits in conjunction with a secured federal or state grant or loan. For example, in order to receive federal and state grants to comply with the Federal Water Pollution Control Act, Amendments of 1972, a local public entity must comply with federal grant regulations. These regulations require that applicants possess the legal, institutional, managerial, and financial capability to assure adequate construction, operation, and maintenance of the grant-funded project. The issuance of GANs in this instance assists the public entity to meet all project requirements and to cover cash-flow deficits that may result from delays in the receipt of reimbursements for grant-eligible costs.

GANs may be issued for a term not to exceed thirty-six months from the date of issuance. They may be sold either publicly or privately, with the interest rates not to exceed 12%. Issuers may be cities, counties, special districts, school districts, community college districts or any other municipal corporation. The issue size must conform to IRS regulations on the basis of a cash-flow analysis of the project, the anticipated receipt of grant funds, and costs of issuance. Security for the GANs is provided by a first lien on the grant proceeds, project revenues, and investment income.

Tax and revenue anticipation notes (TRANs) are issued in order to reduce and possibly eliminate cash-flow deficits in the general fund and other unrestricted funds of a public entity prior to receipt of taxes and other revenues during a given fiscal year. In order to issue TRANs, a cumulative cash-flow deficit must be projected. The maximum size of the issue is computed by adding the largest cumulative cash-flow deficit in all identified funds to the projected expenditures for the following month. A repayment fund must be established for the deposit of pledge revenues as they are received during the year to repay principal and interest.

TRANs can be issued by cities, counties, school districts, community college districts, or any other municipal or public corporation or district. Most TRAN issues are secured by a combination of property tax and non–property tax revenues that are not less than four times the amount borrowed.

A TRAN is a unique short-term instrument, very similar to a general obligation bond. TRANs may be issued year after year, as long as the public entity is eligible on the basis of unrestricted funds and projected cash flows. Money raised through the issuance of TRANs can in turn be reinvested until it is needed. Because the interest on TRANs is exempt from federal taxation, the interest rate paid is usually less than can be received on other short-term investments. Hence, the issuing government can earn a net profit by borrowing and relending money. Interest income from the investment of TRAN proceeds can become a sizeable addition to general fund revenues, depending on the interest rates at which the TRANs are issued and the interest rates at which the TRAN proceeds can be invested.

/// FIGURES AND TRENDS

Total government debt has grown almost continuously over time. It amounted to close to $3 trillion when aggregated over all governments in 1987 or well over $12,000 per person in the country.[1] About three-fourths of this debt is issued by the federal government; it owed over $2.3 trillion in 1987 or over $9,500 per person. The federal debt in 1851, the earliest date for which data

---

[1] Advisory Commission on Intergovernmental Relations (ACIR), *Significant Features of Fiscal Federalism, 1988 Edition*, vol. 1, M-155 I (Washington, DC: December 1987), p. 8.

are readily available, amounted to $68 million. It surpassed the $1 billion mark for the first time in 1863, hovered around $1 to $2 billion until the end of World War I, and had reached $250 billion by the end of World War II.[2]

Although the public debt has grown rapidly, its ratio to GNP has not. For example, the federal debt as a percentage of GNP was 46% in 1941, increasing to 123% at the end of World War II in 1946.[3] There were no substantial attempts to reduce the federal debt, but it grew much more slowly than the economy through the 1970s, so that it had fallen as a percentage of GNP to about one-third.[4] The large increases of the 1980s left it slightly above half of GNP by 1987. Viewed in this context, the debt does not seem so troublesome, but many are worried by the trend.

Most of the federal debt is in marketable form, i.e., it can be sold by one holder to another without the government redeeming it. Marketable debt takes the form of bills, notes, and bonds. These amounted to $882 billion on December 31, 1982. At that time, the nonmarketable debt amounted to $314 billion.[5] This consists of savings bonds and various amounts issued to other government agencies or to other governments.

Who holds the debt? At the end of 1987, $457 billion was held by the federal government itself, whereas $1.63 trillion was held privately in the United States and $267 billion by foreigners.[6] The federal debt holdings by the federal government are investments by the federal trust funds. For example, the surplus of the Social Security Administration is invested in federal debt. This trust fund revenue cannot be used for general purposes, but it is used to offset some of the net borrowing that the federal government must do. The importance of foreign lenders has greatly increased in recent years. In 1986 alone, $43.6 billion was added to the net holdings of federal debt by foreigners. While the increase in 1987 was a greatly reduced $13.9 billion, the total volume of purchases each year is much larger because of refinancing of maturing issues.[7]

A major shift in the maturity of marketable debt has taken place. In 1950 only about 27% of the debt had a maturity of less than one year, but that percentage had increased to 46% in 1982. At the same time the percentage of debt maturing in more than ten years had decreased from 53% to 10%.[8] There has been some movement back toward longer maturities in recent years. The average maturity of marketable federal debt declined from about five years in

[2] U.S. Bureau of the Census, Historical Statistics of the United States, *Colonial Times II, 1957* (Washington, DC: U.S. Government Printing Office, 1961), pp. 720–721.

[3] *Economic Report of the President* (January 1983); and Federal Reserve Bulletin (1983).

[4] ACIR, op. cit.

[5] Federal Reserve Bulletin (April 1983), pp. 17–33.

[6] Office of Management and Budget, *Special Analyses: Budget of the United States Government, Fiscal Year 1989* (Washington, DC: U.S. Government Printing Office), pp. E-15 and E-24.

[7] Ibid.

[8] *Federal Reserve Bulletin* (March 1979); and *Economic Report of the President* (February 1983), p. 256.

1967 to about two and one-half years in 1975 before increasing again to close to six years in 1988.[9]

State and Local Government Debt

State and local governments have been issuing debt to fund projects for public purposes, e.g., fire stations, city halls, schools, hospitals, police buildings, and so forth, ever since the 1820s. These debt instruments are the traditional "municipals." In general, they share the characteristic that the interest paid on the debt is exempt from federal income taxes. A setback caused by the panic of 1873 slowed down debt financing, but it increased again thereafter, and by 1900 it totaled more than $2 billion. The depression years and World War II reduced the growth in the issuance of municipal bonds; however, by 1950 the value of such bonds had reached $24 billion and by 1986 $659 billion.[10] The levels and trends in new issues can be seen in Figure 12-1. The growing use of revenue bonds contributed to the swelling municipal debt during the 1960s and '70s. By 1979, the volume of new revenue bonds exceeded general obligation bonds by almost a two-to-one margin nationwide. The 1970s saw the use of tax-exempt revenue bonds to finance such diverse facilities as housing, hospitals, industrial pollution control equipment, public power projects, sports stadiums and convention centers, all of which led to further increases.

The uses of debt financing vary substantially across states. For example, guaranteed long-term debt per capita varied from $157 in South Dakota to $8,084 in Alaska in 1986. Nonguaranteed long-term debt varied from $820 per capita in Wisconsin to $13,948 in Alaska, and short-term debt varied from $0.80 per capita in Wyoming to $250 in New York.[11]

/// THE USES OF GOVERNMENT BORROWING

Governments basically borrow funds for two main purposes—to fund capital investments and to meet operating expenditures. The federal government does not normally make a distinction between its expenditures for capital improvements and its other expenditures. In addition to its own borrowing, the federal government guarantees the repayment of debt for a substantial number of other borrowers. While this guaranteed debt is not technically federal borrowing, it has the potential to create repayment obligations; hence, it is worth looking at the guaranteed debt a little more closely. In addition, the federal government creates obligations to make payments at some time in the

---

[9] Office of Management and Budget, op. cit., p. E-14.

[10] ACIR, op. cit., p. 8.

[11] Ibid., p. 127.

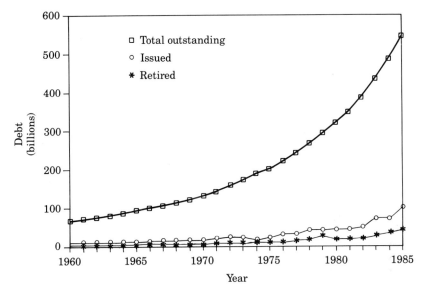

***Figure 12-1* / Long-Term State and Local Debt**

(Source: Tax Foundation, *Facts and Figures on Government Finance, 1988–89 Edition* [Baltimore: Johns Hopkins University Press, 1988], p. 199.)

future. These obligations are known as unfunded liabilities; they have many of the same characteristics as outright debt obligations. We consider these as well.

State and local governments are more constrained in their borrowing than is the federal government. Much of their long-term borrowing is constrained to be for capital expenditures. Nevertheless, in recent years increasing amounts of the borrowing have been for purposes other than traditional public infrastructure. In addition, state and local governments have also indulged in the creation of unfunded liabilities (such as pension promises) and off-budget agencies (such as housing authorities) to float debt.

Public Physical Infrastructure

The provision of roads, sewers, and other items of physical capital for use by the public as well as the buildings and related items used in serving the public are the public infrastructure. In many instances the cost of individual items is far in excess of the ability of a governmental unit to raise taxes at a given time. However, the long life of these items means that they will provide benefits over time; hence, it makes sense to spread the cost out over time as well. Despite this rationale, many government units finance their capital stock from current revenues. In addition, the federal government has offered grants to cover large parts of the cost of many capital projects by state and local governments. Thus, debt financing plays an important role in the provision of public infrastructure, but there is no clear relationship between debt and infrastructure development.

Some public sector investment projects generate revenues while others result only in nonmarketable benefits. The difference is crucial in considering the taxation consequences of borrowing associated with public investment schemes. Investing in a power station, for example, should generate sufficient revenues to cover interest and debt repayment. Servicing the debt associated with such nonmarket public services as are generated by prisons or police cars, however, must be done through taxation. There are some intermediate cases, such as roads, which should raise GNP and yield additional revenue at existing tax rates. But where projects do not yield direct benefits and are not funded by user charges, additional public sector revenue is usually small in relation to overall benefits, thus necessitating higher tax rates.

When projects do not generate revenues, borrowing is simply deferred taxation, whether or not it is perceived as such by citizens. Thus, before deciding about debt issuance, government should in principle weigh the disincentive effects of taxing now or taxing later.

When other sources of funds are not available, debt may be used for the funding of infrastructure. In general, infrastructure should be built if the benefits it will provide over time are greater than the cost of building it. However, the method of financing is often as important as the net benefits in determining whether or not it will be built. Borrowing allows a government to build infrastructure that it might not be able to fund with current revenues; but it also places a repayment obligation on that government in the future. Thus, the capital financing must be balanced against other future obligations. Further, a capital item often carries implications for operating expenses in the future, e.g., a new road will require maintenance, a fire station will require equipment and personnel, and so on. These factors may influence the decision to borrow in order to build infrastructure.

In the early 1980s, America discovered an alleged physical infrastructure crisis. Academics and practitioners sounded warnings about the nation's crumbling roads, bridges, public buildings, and the like. A variety of inventories of infrastructure condition and of dollar estimates for new construction and previously deferred maintenance made their appearance. Concern about the financing of the needed rebuilding and repair became commonplace, and new financing mechanisms were discussed.

It is not altogether clear why this interest in America's physical infrastructure surfaced in the early 1980s. Perhaps it happened because of a few dramatic, even tragic events such as the collapse of an interstate highway bridge in Connecticut, a broken water line in New York City's garment district, and the ever more frequent breakdowns of New York City's subways. Perhaps too, the passage of Proposition 13 in California and similar initiatives in other states contributed to the concern. The dramatic reduction in local government funding options led to the fear that governments would be unable to repair and maintain, let alone rebuild their infrastructure. Finally, the aging of much of the nation's public physical capital, whether schools, buildings, streets, dams, water and sewer lines, subways or roads, particularly in the older parts of the United States, gave further impetus to this concern.

Capital investment in government infrastructure, measured in 1972 dollars and on a per person basis, rose rapidly after World War II, from $106 in 1950 to a high of $207 in 1968. Thereafter per capita capital investment declined steadily to about $120 in 1982. At that point, the new investment was just about equal to estimated depreciation on the existing capital stock, so the value of the capital stock leveled off and started to decline slightly.[12] The pattern of expenditure is not necessarily any indication of a problem in the investment in infrastructure. The need to build schools and the movement to the suburbs following World War II as well as the interstate highway system could easily have led to investment at above long-term rates. The key question is whether the change in investment is indicative of a change in the need for new investment or of a changed attitude toward such investment.

No crisis in financing for infrastructure needs to occur. The life expectancy of many physical structures such as the above can be forecast and demand estimated. However, there are a variety of reasons why government might not make appropriate investments or might defer repair and maintenance, leading to inefficient decline in the capital stock. It is also important to recognize that many of the "needed" capital stock items are the result of the perception of zero price for the goods. If the people making the estimates do not expect to pay for any of the capital items, they are going to look at the expansion of the stock to the point where the marginal benefit is zero. Much of the complaint about the existing capital stock may simply result from the differences in quantity demanded at zero price and the quantity demanded at marginal cost. For example, road capacity estimates are often made on the basis of providing some predetermined level of service in all areas even if this level of service may not be the efficient level in all areas. Faced with financing the level of service, voters may choose a lower level of service and leave the capital stock at an "inadequate" level.

The federal government does not differentiate between current expenditures and capital stock expenditures. Because of this it is not often clear what percentage of the budget goes to capital creation. Some people have argued that the federal deficit should be compared to net capital creation to determine if there is a real problem associated with the deficit. They look at the new roads being built along with other new capital and argue that a deficit is just a way of financing this capital. Unfortunately, such a view is open to the major criticism that it is ignoring the depreciation of the existing capital stock. If one takes the view that the borrowing is acceptable if it offsets capital creation, then the existing debt must be paid off along with the capital depreciation.

---

[12] Advisory Commission on Intergovernmental Relations, *Financing Public Physical Infrastructure* (Washington, DC: June 1984), pp. 8 and 11.

Looking only at new capital formation without considering depreciation on existing capital stock would give a very biased view of government net capital formation. Since it would be difficult to generate widely accepted estimates of such depreciation, it does not appear to be feasible to create a realistic capital budget for the federal government. One corollary of this is that the sale of assets to balance the federal budget does not in fact improve the net fiscal position. Thus, the federal deficit can have a variety of interpretations; but it is probably best to simply accept it as a current account deficit until there is a better way to account for changes in the capital stock of the country.

Other Uses of Debt and Debt Instruments

Public sector balance sheets often do not include all debt items. For example, the federal government's guarantees of Lockheed Corporation's and Chrysler Corporation's debt issues — steps designed to rescue these companies from bankruptcy — created liabilities that were close substitutes for public sector debt. Yet this debt did not show up as an obligation of the federal government. Similarly, when the federal government guaranteed repayment of some of New York City's debt, it was creating a potential federal liability, but this did not show up as debt for the federal government.

In the United States, in addition to direct Treasury borrowing, the federal government guarantees and sponsors borrowing by various federal agencies which, in turn, lend out the proceeds to private borrowers. By the end of 1987, guaranteed debt amounted to $507 billion, mostly covering issues of the Federal Housing Administration and the Veteran's Administration. In addition, there are a variety of other types of indirect debt obligations for the federal government. These obligations arise from federal insurance programs or from federal guarantees. In total, it is estimated that the contingent liability of the federal government in 1987 amounted to $3.6 trillion.[13]

Although there is some reason to argue that these debts are not equivalent to direct government borrowing, it is also not correct to ignore them entirely. The federal government is responsible for the payments in the event of default. The potential impact of all such guarantees is quite large, as we shall see in Chapter 21 when we discuss fiscal crises.

State and local governments do not use guarantees to extend their presence in the bond market. Rather, they borrow directly for some private purposes and they also offer "moral obligations" to repay some debt for which they cannot offer guarantees. The effect of the moral obligation is that the sponsoring government is expected to make good on any defaults while not obligating itself in a way that would violate restrictions on the amount of general obligation debt it could offer. Again the full treatment of the impact of these developments is given in Chapter 21; here we focus on the impact on the debt markets.

---

[13] Office of Management and Budget, op. cit., pp. F-9 and F-34.

Municipal financing encountered a setback when in 1975 New York City defaulted on a note issue and the value of other New York City obligations held by investors declined substantially. The financial difficulties of New York City and of the state of New York to no small degree were the result of "backdoor borrowing." During the reign of Governor Nelson Rockefeller, public authorities were used to finance activities that the state could not fund from its conventional revenue sources. The authorities were to pay their own way, with the state having only a moral obligation to stand behind them. But when the public authorities ran into financial trouble, they had to be bailed out. This was one of the precursors to the default by New York City, which in turn made it much more difficult for any subnational government to borrow for some time.

Industrial development revenue bonds (IDBs) are designed to assist private firms and corporations in the construction, expansion, and relocation of commercial or energy-related facilities. Effectively the sponsoring government enters into an agreement with the private party in which a building or other security is pledged as collateral and the private party agrees to make interest and principal payments to the government to repay a specific debt. The government then uses these promises of future payment and the collateral offered as security for a revenue bond. Since the bond is offered by a government, the interest payments are exempt from federal income taxation. Thus, the lender charges the government a lower rate than it would on a direct loan to the private borrower. The effect is to make the loan to the private borrower a tax-exempt bond.

These bonds are used by individual governments to provide an incentive for private firms to locate in specific places. However, since most governments now use them, it is not clear that any one government could gain a competitive edge from this mechanism. The rapid growth in the use of these private-purpose bonds is shown in Table 12-1. In any case, the tax reform act of 1986 placed substantial limitations on new issues of such bonds and the volume, while still substantial, has declined. Some of the movement against continuance of the industrial development bond tax-exempt financing program is based on the opinion that the bonds do not serve a public purpose.

Another form of debt which exists at all levels of government is the unfunded liabilities that the governments generate. The term refers to a promise to make payment in the future which does not show up as a current obligation of the government. The largest source of such liabilities is the pensions of public employees. When a pension is promised, money should be set aside to make the payments for current employees when they come due. For example, the federal government has required that private companies set up such payment systems to guarantee that workers would not lose their pensions if a company went bankrupt. However, governments themselves are not subject to such requirements.

Most state and local governments now set aside at least partial funding for their pension obligations. However, a number face substantial problems in the

Table 12-1 / Tax-Exempt Financing (in billions of dollars)

	Actual									Preliminary 1987	Estimated	
	1978	1979	1980	1981	1982	1983	1984	1985	1986	1987	1988	1989
Private-purpose tax-exempts	19.7	28.1	32.5	30.9	49.6	57.1	74.0	121.6	29.9	31.0	28.8	27.4
Housing bonds	6.9	12.1	14.0	4.8	14.6	17.0	20.5	41.5	7.7	8.4	6.5	4.5
Single-family mortgage subsidy bonds	3.4	7.8	10.5	2.8	9.0	11.0	12.8	14.3	5.1	6.2	4.2	2.0
Multifamily rental housing bonds	2.5	2.7	2.2	1.1	5.1	5.3	5.5	25.0	2.2	1.9	1.8	1.9
Veterans general obligation bonds	1.2	1.6	1.3	0.9	0.5	0.7	2.2	2.2	0.3	0.3	0.5	0.6
Private exempt bonds[1]	2.9	3.2	3.3	4.7	8.5	11.7	11.7	38.2	6.2	12.3	13.1	14.0
Student loan bonds	0.3	0.6	0.5	1.1	1.8	3.3	1.2	4.0	2.0	1.8	1.8	1.8
Pollution control industrial bonds	2.8	2.5	2.5	4.3	5.9	4.5	8.1	7.7	2.4	2.5	1.6	1.2
Small-issue industrial development bonds	3.6	7.5	9.7	13.3	14.7	14.7	18.3	17.8	7.8	2.8	2.8	2.8
Other industrial development bonds[2]	3.2	2.2	2.5	2.7	4.1	6.0	14.1	12.3	3.9	3.2	3.0	3.0
Public-purpose tax-exempts[3]	29.3	20.3	22.0	24.2	36.3	36.2	41.7	99.6	115.5	68.8	72.0	77.0
Total new issues, long-term tax-exempts[4]	49.1	48.4	54.5	55.1	84.9	93.3	115.7	221.2	145.4	99.8	100.8	104.4

[1] Private exempt entity bonds are obligations of the Internal Revenue Code Section 501(c)(3) organizations, such as private nonprofit hospitals and educational facilities.

[2] Other IDBs include obligations for private businesses that qualify for tax-exempt activities, such as sewage disposal, airports and docks.

[3] While most of these are commonly referred to as governmental bonds, some may be nongovernmental.

[4] Includes long-term refunding bonds including advance refundings.

(Source: U.S. Office of Management and Budget, *Special Analyses: Budget of the United States Government, Fiscal Year 1989*, p. F-60.)

future because they promised very generous pensions without setting aside any money to pay for them. The various pension programs of the federal government also have substantial unfunded liabilities. If the Social Security system were treated as a private pension, it would have unfunded liabilities that are far larger than all the existing government debt in the United States–exceeding $4 trillion. However, there is substantial disagreement about whether or not this should be counted as part of the federal debt.

In any case, these unfunded liabilities have another important effect on the debt markets. The money that governments set aside for such trust funds is treated as budget revenue in the national income accounts. Thus, if a state contributes $10 million to its pension trust fund, that amount shows up as part of the budget surplus for state and local governments. Similarly, the increases in the trust fund for Social Security are currently used to mask part of the federal deficit.

/// BURDENS OF GOVERNMENT DEBT

Common concerns, particularly in periods of rapidly rising public debt, center on the possibility of fiscal bankruptcy and on the burden placed on future generations. An analysis of these concerns clearly emphasizes the effects of debt creation on future economic conditions rather than on the current effects.

Fiscal Solvency

When governments sell debt instruments year after year, a proper question clearly is whether adequate allowance for repayment is made and, if not, whether bankruptcy can result. Looking at the huge federal debt, it is easy to worry about the nation's ability to pay it. However, even in the light of this huge and rapidly increasing national debt, federal bankruptcy is not in the cards. The ability to raise taxes is coupled with substantial ability to monetize the debt if necessary. Thus, the federal debt can usually be rolled over and refunded with relatively little difficulty.

Still, interest payments have a major effect on the economy. The large and increasing interest costs that have become so common in recent years bloat the budget and substantially affect the credit markets. Taxes must be raised in order to pay the interest, and they impose a burden on the economy. Like all taxes, those that have to be raised to finance interest payments carry a deadweight loss. These effects become more burdensome as the tax revenue needed to service the debt rises relative to GNP. For example, while the total federal debt declined relative to GNP for many years and is still well below its peak, the interest payments on the debt have almost continuously increased as a percentage of GNP. They stood at 1.34 percent of GNP in 1955 and climbed fairly steadily to peak at 3.76 percent of GNP in 1985, before starting a slight decline to an estimated 3.4 percent of GNP for 1989.[14]

There are a variety of ways in which government can address such increases in the debt burden. One is to effectively reduce the debt through inflation. With the par value of outstanding debt fixed in dollar terms, its value in real terms is reduced by inflation. To the extent that the inflation was not anticipated, interest payments do not cover the loss in value of money to be repaid. Therefore, losses can accrue to investors who hold long-term debt instruments. This in turn constitutes gains to the taxpayer who benefits when interest payments and repayment are made in cheaper dollars. Over time, however, the amount of inflation becomes part of the calculation relating to the borrowing and lending of money, and the government must pay higher and higher premiums because of the additional risk as well as the expected loss in value of the repayments. Even when inflation is lowered, there is likely to be a residual effect on future long-term borrowing. Thus, the government can make clear short-term gains in reducing the real value of its debt by creating inflation; but this is generally not a viable long-term solution to debt.

A number of steps have been taken, all ineffective, to rein in the public debt and interest rates. Thus, for example, Congress sets a debt limit which the Treasury cannot exceed. Whenever current operations require increases in government borrowing beyond this ceiling, the Secretary of the Treasury is required to appear before Congress and plead to raise this ceiling. Clearly, this method of establishing debt ceilings is a futile gesture to keep the size of the debt under control. The procedure is particularly inappropriate since the Congressional Budget Act of 1974 requires that Congress annually pass the Joint Budget Resolution, which basically determines the size of the new public debt.

Congress also has interfered with the interest payments that the Treasury can make. Thus, toward the close of World War I, it enacted an interest ceiling of 4.25% on securities in excess of five years, excluding those issued by government agencies. While this interest ceiling was, by and large, effective until the second half of the 1960s, at that time long-term bonds began to yield increasingly large interest rates. Actually, the law could have been circumvented by selling bonds with a 4.25% coupon rate at a price below par. The Treasury did not use that route, fearing that it would violate the congressional intent. Starting in 1965, Congress responded to requests from the Treasury and authorized a limited issue of Treasury bonds at above their ceiling yield. By 1983 Congress had authorized $150 billion in such long-term bonds. Since the ceiling has no obvious effect on the rate that the Treasury must pay on its long-term bonds, the effect of the interest ceiling is simply to limit the amount of long-term debt issued.

Matters are very different for debt by state and local governments. These governments cannot always roll over their debt, a fact exposing them to the

14 Ibid., p. E-12.

possibility of insolvency. Revenue bonds must be backed by receipts from the investment financed by the debt instrument, and general obligation bonds by the general tax base of the government. Moreover, local governments often face legal obstacles, e.g., they cannot issue debt instruments in excess of a fixed percentage of their assessed valuation.

The burden of interest payments by state and local governments also can be different from that of the federal government. If the interest is fully covered by fees paid by beneficiaries of the facility financed by the debt instrument, no deadweight loss will result. Finally, since a large portion of state and local debt is long-term, major debt repudiation through inflation can readily occur even though these governments cannot directly affect the rate of inflation. Also, they too face higher interest rates on new debt issues because of past inflation.

While state and local governments can indeed default on debt and a few have done so in the past, the general perception is that this is a fairly safe form of debt; indeed, the level of default is generally low. However, there have been several major defaults in the recent past, including New York City and the Washington Public Power Supply System, both of which were defaults on bonds with values into the billions of dollars. Because of these widely publicized defaults, the municipal bonds are not considered as safe as they once were.

Burdening Future Generations

When expenditures are financed with loans rather than taxes, there is a shift in the nominal payment responsibility from current taxpayers to future ones. However, this shift may or may not occur in practice. According to one view of public finance, the method of finance between taxes and debt is not relevant. According to this view, the true tax on the economy is the amount of resources diverted from the private sector. Whether it is diverted by taxes or by borrowing would appear to make no difference since the amount of resources left for the private sector is the same. The problem with this argument is that it ignores the different sectors in the private economy. In particular, private resources can be used for consumption or for investment; it is likely that the choice of financing will determine something about where the private sector resources are diverted from.

Suppose for simplicity that everyone saves a fixed percentage of after-tax income. Then a dollar collected in taxes mostly reduces consumption. However, a borrowed dollar does not affect consumption at all. Hence, the borrowed dollar must come from the net savings available. This means that it effectively reduces the amount of private investment by one dollar. This can be seen in Figure 12-2, where the amount of savings available for investment is given by the supply curve S. The private demand for funds is given by the demand curve D_p. When government demand for funds D_g is added to D_p to get D_m, the market clearing interest rate goes up from i_1 to i_2. The total amount of lending

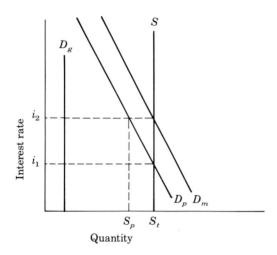

Figure 12-2 / **Government Borrowing with Fixed Supply of Savings**

remains the same, so the government borrowing must be exactly offset by the reduction in the private borrowing from S_t to S_p.

If the investment is reduced, future generations will end up with a smaller capital stock. Thus, they would be made worse off because total future output would be lower than if the present expenditures had been financed by taxes instead of borrowing.

Suppose that the amount of money available for investment is not fixed but is rather very elastic. This appears to be the case because the world market for funds allows them to be diverted from many other countries. Hence, even if the domestic supply of savings is inelastic, the supply to the country could be very elastic. This situation is depicted in Figure 12-3. In this case, when the government enters its demand for funds, the interest rate remains unchanged as does the amount of private borrowing. Instead, the money that the government borrows is offset by an increase of that amount in foreign lending. In the future, the country will have the higher capital stock associated with the use of taxes; however, the interest payments are made to foreigners. The payments of principal and interest reduce the amount available for domestic consumption. Thus, future generations again bear the burden of the borrowing.

One effect of the rise in federal debt has been a substantial increase in the amount held by foreigners. Some people worry that this increase in foreign debt is bad for the country, whereas the problem would not exist if the debt were held domestically. The fallacy of this view can be seen by considering the two cases discussed above. If there were no foreign lending, the effect of large federal borrowing most likely would be to crowd out private investment. The reduced private investment would affect the growth of the economy as well as

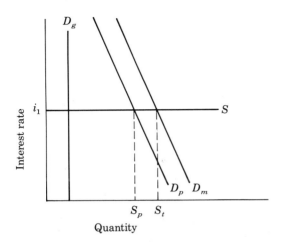

Figure 12-3 / **Government Borrowing with Elastic Supply of Savings**

the payments on the debt. By lending the money, foreigners allow the United States to continue to grow even though it is not setting aside enough domestically to finance its growth. The interest payments are a drain on the economy, but this drain is offset by the productive assets financed by the loans. The real problem is the amount of borrowing, not the specific identity of the lenders.

According to the above analysis, borrowing rather than taxing must make future generations worse off; but this is only true if the economy is working at something close to full employment and if the supply of savings is inelastic. To the extent that people increase their savings in response to more borrowing, the crowding-out effect would not take place; however, it seems unlikely that the typical person would respond to an increase in federal borrowing by increasing his or her savings.

The choice of debt would then depend on whether it is desired to pass the cost of government on to future generations. The benefit principle argues that it is proper for citizens to pay for government goods in line with the benefits that accrue to them. Applying the benefit principle, each generation should pay for its own share in the benefits received from the capital investment. Accordingly, as long as benefits extend into the future, intergenerational equity requires an appropriate burden transfer into the future.

The federal government, which in recent years has incurred increasingly large debts to finance budget deficits, has a distinctly different burden transfer problem than do state and local governments who use debt instruments to finance specific capital projects. When, for example, a local government builds a sewer line with, let us say, a forty-year life expectancy, financing methods are available—and often used—which assure intergenerational equity. As was argued earlier in this chapter, it would be improper to use taxes to finance this long-term capital investment. Moreover, a sharp, if temporary, increase in the tax rate would be required. More significantly, such a procedure would place an unfair burden on those who pay taxes at the time construction takes place. But since the sewer line will be used for more than forty years, it is proper to spread the burden across successive generations of users who will benefit from its services. Thus, the benefit principle of taxation can be applied in fairly allocating the burden between generations. Toward this end, the capital project should be financed by debt issuance. Annual tax payments, in addition, should be used to tax users in accordance with their current benefit shares. By this method, the debt is amortized by the time the useful life of the facility has come to an end. By each generation paying for its own benefit share, intergenerational equity is assured. Thus, a local government that finances its sewer system by borrowing and properly amortizing the debt over the system's expected life assures an equitable burden distribution pattern, equitable not only among age groups but also among changing groups of residents who may move in or out of the jurisdiction.

/// GOVERNMENT BORROWING UNDER FEDERALISM

Federalism poses some unique problems for debt financing. Not only do governments on different levels compete for money with one another but, since municipal bond interest is exempt from federal income taxes, state and local borrowing reduces revenue to the federal government. Thus, it is estimated that in 1989 the U.S.Treasury lost about $20 billion from tax exemptions of interest on state and local securities.[15] Further, state income tax revenue is reduced because of interest paid by the federal government that is not taxed by the states. It is much harder to determine the magnitude of this reduction in revenue because of the differences in state tax codes and rates; however, one study estimates that the loss in revenue amounted to about $2 billion in 1982.[16]

The federal tax exemption of interest on bonds issued by states and localities stems from a doctrine known as "reciprocal immunity." Between 1819 and 1895 the Supreme Court established this doctrine, which holds that states are immune from federal interference just as states may not interfere with federal government affairs. This has been interpreted as states not being able to tax the obligations of the federal government and of the federal

---

[15] Ibid., pp. G-41–G-45.
[16] Roger H. Bezdek and Ernest M. Zampelli, "State and Local Tax Expenditures Relating to the Federal Government," *National Tax Journal* 39 (December 1986), p. 535.

government not being able to tax the obligations of states.[17] In this legal environment, the types of capital projects state and local governments have financed in recent years have grown greatly in scope. Thus, while the traditional public purposes were education, transportation, water and sewers, and public power, lately various types of housing, industrial development, pollution control, hospitals, and student loans were added to the list. As can be seen from Table 12-1, there was a very large increase in the issuance of long term tax-exempt bonds through 1985, followed by a fairly large drop in response to the tax reform of 1986. While tax reform placed restrictions on many forms of tax-exempt financing, it focused more on the private-purpose use of tax-exempt financing; these private-purpose uses show the greatest decline. Borrowing for nontraditional purposes was only $800 million in 1970, less than 5% of the total of $18.1 billion issued that year.[18] Yet Table 12-1 shows that private-purpose borrowing virtually exploded and surpassed public-purpose borrowing in 1979. It stayed above the public-purpose totals until the tax reform of 1986.

It is not easy to justify why tax-exempt status should be given to interest on bonds that finance private industry in their housing, industrial development, and pollution control activities. Starting in 1978, the practice of issuing mortgage subsidy bonds to provide low-cost mortgages for single-family housing became so widespread that Congress enacted the Mortgage Subsidy Bond Tax Act of 1980 to limit its use. Likewise, in 1975 government funding of industrial development took off at an amazing speed, forcing the federal government to rein in this activity by passing, among others, the Tax Equity and Fiscal Responsibility Act of 1982. Pollution control bonds have been extensively used by private firms to meet federal pollution control requirements. Finally, tax-exempt bonds for hospital facilities, first issued in 1971, skyrocketed to $9.5 billion by 1982.[19] Remember that these bonds are not issued to finance state or locally operated hospital facilities, but instead to aid in the financing of private hospitals.

Before examining some side effects of these large increases in state and local government borrowing, let us briefly examine what caused the extraordinary growth in tax-exempt bonds for the financing of private purposes. Reasons frequently given are wholesale expansion in perception of the role of state and local governments in providing tax-exempt financing; a desire to offset cuts in federal programs; avoidance of constitutional and statutory debt lim-

---

[17] *McCulloch v. Maryland* in 1819 established that states could not tax federal obligations; *Pollock v. Farmers' Loan and Trust Company* in 1895 applied the converse immunity to obligations of states. Some argue that reciprocal immunity was overturned or at least weakened by the Sixteenth Amendment to the Constitution, giving Congress the right to collect taxes on income "from whatever source derived." The Supreme Court affirmed the right of Congress to tax the interest on municipal debt in 1988.

[18] Advisory Commission on Intergovernmental Relations (ACIR), *Strengthening the Federal Revenue System: Implications for State and Local Taxing and Borrowing*, A-97 (Washington, DC: 1984), p. 117.

[19] Ibid.

itations and referendum requirements; a desire by state and local governments to assist private industry in financing federally mandated functions,
particularly pollution control facilities; and promotion of a potent tool in
interstate and interjurisdictional competition for jobs and industry through
stimulation of industrial development and diversification.[20]

The effect of the spread of these bonds is to cause interest rates to rise for
public-purpose municipal bonds and to increase the loss in tax revenue to the
federal government. Figure 12-4 shows an elastic supply of funds at the
corporate rate for taxable bonds. This is reasonable since the municipal bond
market is still fairly small relative to the total bond market. The tax-exempt
supply curve starts out at an interest rate below the taxable supply curve.
People in the highest tax bracket would be willing to purchase municipal
bonds as long as the return is at least as much as the after-tax return on
corporate bonds. However, such people will purchase only a limited amount.
For larger quantities, the interest rate must be raised to make the bonds
attractive to those in lower marginal tax brackets. Thus, as the demand
increases from D_1 to D_2, the interest rate rises from i_1 to i_2. This causes a
reduction in some of the original public-purpose issues from Q_1 to Q_2 and
forces a higher interest rate for the remaining ones of i_2 instead of i_1; but it is
still attractive from the private borrowers' perspective since the interest rate
i_2 is below the taxable rate i_c. Note that the difference between what the
federal government foregoes in tax collections and the benefit to the state and
local governments gets bigger with the increased demand. The loss to the
federal government can be thought of as the difference between the two supply
curves up to the quantity of loans. The gain to the state and local governments
is simply the reduction in the interest rate for the amount that they borrow
directly. As the volume of private-purpose tax-exempt borrowing rises the cost
to the federal government increases, while the benefit that the state and local
governments receive in the form of reduced interest payments actually decreases. A report by the Advisory Commission on Intergovernmental Relations concludes that,

> The ever-increasing volume of tax-exempt bonds drives up interest rates for all
> tax-exempt bonds and makes it more expensive for states and local governments
> to finance traditional government functions such as streets, sewers and school
> buildings. Although the proliferation of private purpose bonds is only one cause
> of increased tax-exempt interest rates . . . it is a significant cause.[21]

Finally, there is the issue of inefficiency. One inefficiency is allocational in
nature, relating to the diversion of scarce capital resources from some private

---

[20] Examples of studies that have shown the effectiveness of tax-exempt financing for private capital projects
include Norman B. Ture, *Industrial Revenue Bonds: Estimates of Employment Effects and Size of Benefiting
Companies* (Washington, DC: September 8, 1983); and Massachusetts Industrial Finance Agency, *Economic
Growth and Industrial Revenue Bonds* (October 1981).
[21] ACIR, A-97, op. cit., pp. 115–116.

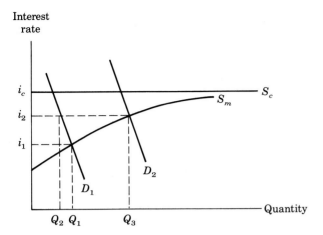

Figure 12-4 / Tax-Exempt Interest Rate and the Demand for Funds

sector projects to other projects funded by tax-exempt bonds, with subsidies often overshadowing relative economic merits. A second inefficiency is the fact that not all of the federal income tax savings go to the beneficiaries of bond financing. Much is diverted to upper-income holders of the bonds, who may receive higher interest rates than those necessary to induce them to purchase tax-exempt bonds, and to bond lawyers and salespeople, as well as financial institutions. A further source of inefficiency is the random nature of the federal aid, because the assistance is triggered by state or local activities without regard to federal economic development policies, federal standards, or other factors.

In contrast to what takes place under a centralized form of government, federalism allows types of debt financing by a multitude of governments to proceed with hardly any coordination.[22] At times, serious conflicts arise, for example, when governments on all three levels borrow heavily. Then they compete for funds and drive up interest rates. Partly in this connection, there is a keen interest in whether state and local government surpluses can be considered to offset federal deficits.

On a national income accounts basis, state and local government surpluses were between $27 and $57 billion during the years 1980–86.[23] However, most of these surpluses were in social insurance funds and therefore belong mostly to present and future retirees, not to state and local governments. For example, while in 1982 the total state and local government surplus was about $35 billion, operating and capital accounts ran a deficit of $1.7 billion.

Another debt concern under federalism relates to the burden issue. In a

[22] Wallace E. Oates, *Fiscal Federalism* (New York: Harcourt Brace Jovanovich, 1972), p. 154.
[23] Tax Foundation, *Facts and Figures on Government Finance, 1988–1989 Edition* (Baltimore: Johns Hopkins University Press, 1988), p. 10.

certain sense, local government debt must be paid by whoever is living in the community when the debt becomes due. In this sense it places a real burden on future residents, for they will have to repay the loan whether or not they receive any benefits. Matters are somewhat complicated on the local level by the fact that, particularly in relation to small jurisdictions in a highly mobile and industrial economy, much movement into and out of the community takes place. It thus appears that current residents will be able to finance current services with debt financing and then shift the cost to future residents by moving. However, market mechanisms limit the ability to do this.

When households move they take account of differences in taxes and in benefits among communities. If one community has used much debt financing, local taxes will be higher to make the necessary payments. In equilibrium, this differential becomes capitalized in the form of lower local property values in the particular jurisdiction. Lack of demand for residences in such a jurisdiction bids down the value of local property until it is lower than the value of similar properties elsewhere by the present discounted value of a future stream of additional payments, which must be made by a resident of this jurisdiction. Under these circumstances, fiscal disadvantages of the jurisdiction are offset by the lower prices for housing, eliminating any inducement for any further locational adjustment.[24] However, the higher tax rates make the community less attractive for new development and might hinder its future growth.

An individual who moves away from a jurisdiction and sells his or her property there stops paying taxes and also stops receiving benefits. According to Oates, the new resident of the community is compensated for any differentials between the remaining tax liability and the residual stream of benefits from the project by offsetting adjustment to the price paid for the local property. In this model there is a payment in accordance with fiscal benefits received. It occurs regardless of whether the jurisdiction uses bond finance or current taxation to meet the costs of the project.[25]

Finally, we must point to the great diversity of rules under which the fifty states and tens of thousands of local governments issue debt instruments. This is of major concern to investors who would benefit from greater uniformity. Thus, regulation of specific aspects of the municipal bond market by the federal government is of great interest. No doubt the establishment of some uniformity across states, particularly regarding disclosure of information and penalties in case of abuse, would have a positive effect on bond markets and would be welcomed by investors.

//// SUMMARY

Governments borrow large amounts of money each year, some to roll over existing debt as it matures and some to finance new expenditures. A general

---

[24] Oates, op. cit., pp. 154–155.
[25] Ibid., pp. 156–157.

principle for government is that the use of borrowing should coincide with the benefits that the borrowing will be used to finance. Thus, long-term borrowing is most appropriate for financing large capital expenditures. Most state and local governments try to adhere to this principle, but the federal government does not. Federal borrowing more closely resembles borrowing to finance current consumption, but it is very hard to accurately determine what is happening to the nation's capital stock of public infrastructure.

Borrowing generally places a repayment burden on future taxpayers. If the borrowing is all from domestic sources, the capital stock is likely to be smaller than it would have been if the same amount were financed with taxes; hence, future generations will have a lower capital stock. If the borrowing is financed by foreigners, future generations will have the same capital stock, but they will be obligated to send some of the proceeds to the foreigners because of the debt. Hence, borrowing generally makes future taxpayers worse off.

Borrowing by state and local governments is possible at interest rates that are below other levels because in most cases the interest payments are exempt from the federal income tax. The attractiveness of this exemption has caused many government units to borrow for private purposes and to relend the money to selected private borrowers at the tax-exempt rate. This practice drives up the cost of borrowing for all state and local governments, causes distortions in the private allocation of credit, and creates a larger loss of tax revenue to the federal government. The Tax Reform Act of 1986 made such private-purpose borrowing more difficult, and there has been a reduction in the volume of such borrowing.

Chapter 13 //////

Intergovernmental Transfers

The more than 80,000 governments in the United States generate revenue through taxes or fees, but they also transfer revenue. The single largest transfer is from the federal government to state and local governments, about $100 billion per year in the 1980s. In addition, states transfer funds to their local governments, and a significant amount of money moves between local governments. This chapter looks at these movements of money and the effect of the availability and distribution of such funds on the actions of both the receiving and the giving government. It also considers the related issue of the link between financing and provision of particular services.

/// FIGURES AND TRENDS

It is sometimes thought that intergovernmental aid is a product of the Great Society programs and that it did not really develop in the United States until the 1960s. Yet although there was a clear increase in the amount of aid given during the early to middle 1970s, such grants developed long before then. For example, in 1955 local governments received $368 million directly from the federal government and states received about $2.8 billion. The states in turn sent close to $6 billion to local governments. Even then, much of the aid was earmarked for school districts. While municipalities received aid of over 20% of the general revenue that they raised themselves, school districts received revenue equal to over 70% of what they raised. By 1960 states were receiving federal grants equal to 31% of the revenue they raised themselves.[1]

Although federal aid continued to increase beyond this point, it grew

---

[1] Advisory Commission on Intergovernmental Relations (ACIR), *Significant Features of Fiscal Federalism, 1988*, vol. 2, M-155 II (Washington, DC: 1988), p. 81.

relatively more rapidly in the form of direct aid to local governments. The absolute number of dollars going to the states increased more than the absolute dollars going directly to the local governments, but in percentage terms, direct aid from the federal government increased substantially for the local governments. Spurred by the money coming from the federal government and by a variety of other reasons, the states also increased their aid to local governments substantially. The dollar volume of aid has grown almost constantly, but it reached a peak as a percentage of state revenue around 1976. At that time the federal government was providing states with aid equal to almost 40% of the money they raised themselves. Both federal and state aid to local governments continued to increase as a percentage of local revenue until 1979, when local governments were receiving aid equal to about 80% of what they raised. Federal aid to state and local governments combined peaked in 1978 both in inflation-adjusted dollars and as a percentage of state and local revenue.[2]

Since 1978, the growth in state and local revenues was faster than the growth in intergovernmental aid, so even though such aid has been increasing it has decreased as a percentage of expenditures. Since that time, the amount of aid has not even grown as rapidly as the price index, so the real amount of money has declined: in 1982 constant dollars, from a peak of $109.7 billion in 1978 to $90.6 billion in 1987. Further, much of this has been a decline in the more general type of grants, so that the grants for payments and services to individuals have grown as a percentage of the total.[3] This can be seen in Figure 13-1. Perhaps the biggest contribution to this shift has been the phase-out and cancellation of the general revenue-sharing program. The latter was never very large compared to total federal grants, but it was highly important to local governments because it came with no strings attached.

The Advisory Commission on Intergovernmental Relations finds that federal aid has declined from a peak of over 26% of state-local outlays in 1978 to less than 17% in 1988. The commission projects the possibility that by 1998 this will again decline to the 11% it achieved in 1958.[4]

/// REASONS FOR GRANTS

The U.S. Constitution makes a fairly clear distinction between the functions of the federal and state governments. The federal government is supposed to handle large-scale concerns and the state governments, local issues. Thus, the federal government has control of national defense and foreign relations. It also coordinates some activities of the states. However, the fra-

---

[2] Ibid.

[3] Robert Gleason, "Federalism 1986–87: Signals of a New Era," *Intergovernmental Perspective* 14 (Winter 1988), p. 9.

[4] Ibid., p. 13.

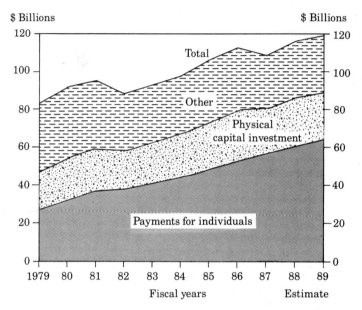

Figure 13-1 / Federal Grants to State and Local Governments

(Source: U.S. Office of Management and Budget, *Special Analyses: Budget of the United States Government, Fiscal Year 1989*, p. H-3.)

mers of the Constitution were wary of concentrating too much power in one place. Their solution was to leave the states with the responsibility for all government functions not specifically assigned to the federal government. It was generally accepted that smaller government would be more responsive to citizens than larger government. Further, restrictions on the powers of the central government would prevent many of the abuses that the colonists were trying to escape.

The economic view of government has some clear parallels with the division of functions found in the federalist tradition. Generally it is believed that a local government would know more about the preferences of its residents and would be more responsive to those preferences. Thus, the smaller a unit of government, the better able it is to serve its constituents. However, we have already seen that there are a number of problems with small governments. It is easier to avoid taxes levied by small governments. This can lead to efficiency costs, which are large relative to the tax collected. Smaller units are more likely to have externalities associated with their actions, and they are less likely to be able to take advantage of economies of scale in production or in administration. Finally, the existence of large numbers of governments is likely to make coordinated action more difficult.

If many people outside a jurisdiction receive benefits from the activities of that jurisdiction, government service will tend to be underprovided. The local government may be very responsive to the preferences of its residents, but there is no reason to be responsive to the preferences of those outside the jurisdiction. Hence, the benefits to those outside the jurisdiction are not considered in determining how much to provide. This may be the equitable thing to do; however, it is not likely to be the efficient thing. A government that encompasses all of those affected by its actions is more likely to take all benefits into account and can spread costs over the wider group as well.

When the actions of a local government have a negative impact on those outside its jurisdiction, these negative effects also are likely to be ignored. Thus, if prevailing winds carry smoke and air pollution from one community to others, it is not likely to be of much concern to the polluting community. The desires of the downwind residents have little influence on the actions of local politicians. Hence, the level of negative externalities is likely to be unduly high.

If there are important economies of scale in providing a good or service and each small jurisdiction tries to provide the activity by itself, unnecessarily high costs will be involved. For example, if one water reservoir is sufficient for an entire metropolitan area but each municipality decides to build its own reservoir, the total cost of the many small reservoirs will almost certainly exceed the cost of the one large reservoir. Thus, it may be better to have the service provided by a higher level of government. In practice, specialized governments to provide such services constitute a large number of the governments in the U.S., but they acount for only a small percentage of government expenditures. For example, in 1982 there were 28,588 special districts and 14,851 school districts out of a total of 82,341 government units in the U.S.[5] Yet in 1986 special districts other than school districts spent $23.5 billion, and this was only 1.8% of all government spending.[6] In addition, such services are often provided by regulated utilities or by off-budget government agencies.

Finally, let us consider the problems small governments face whenever they try to tax a mobile base or fail to match benefits and taxes for residents. The problem is associated with the mobility of people within small geographic areas. If a local government tries to tax an activity that can easily be moved a short distance, the consumer is often given an incentive to shift the place of the transaction so as to avoid the tax. For example, a local retail sales tax may look as if it would generate large amounts of revenue; but in the presence of the tax, people may start buying more goods outside the jurisdiction. For a small jurisdiction this may be quite significant and lead to a large loss in the property tax base or to some other negative consequences. As we saw in the discussion of the excise tax, such changes are associated with efficiency losses for the economy as a whole. The more elastic the demand and supply curves are, the more significant the losses are expected to be. Yet the curves are more

---

[5] Tax Foundation, *Facts and Figures on Government Finance, 1988–89 Edition* (Baltimore: Johns Hopkins University Press, 1988), p. 4.
[6] ACIR, op. cit., p. 40.

elastic for a small jurisdiction, especially in an urban area, since people can travel to other jurisdictions to carry out transactions. They can shop outside the city limits and do so if the tax savings offsets the cost of the trip. This type of avoidance is eliminated if the tax is levied by a jurisdiction that includes all the potential competitive jurisdictions. Then the resident must travel far to look for other places to provide an untaxed service, and the amount of travel associated with tax avoidance is substantially reduced.

There is also likely to be actual moving if the benefits and costs of living in an area are very different. If the town you now live in does not provide you with as much service per dollar of taxes as you could get in the next town, you have an incentive to move. This may work to the disadvantage of both towns. The town you leave may have been collecting more in taxes from you than it cost to provide services; the town you move to may have to pay more for the services it provides than it collects from you in taxes. Thus, in both towns the other residents will find themselves either paying higher taxes or receiving lower levels of service than before you moved. To the extent that you move merely because of these transfers, there is a misallocation of resources.

Redistribution between residents in a community occurs because of the divergence between the source of funds and the benefits provided whenever taxes rather than user fees are used to fund services. The most important example involves local school financing. Education is the largest expenditure at the local level. The cost of provision is clearly related to the number of children in a family. Yet the major source of local revenue for education is the property tax. Thus, a childless couple living in a large house may pay more for education than a large family living in a small house in the same community. This creates an incentive for the childless couple to find a community with low taxes and poor schools.

The decision of which level of government should provide a particular service depends a lot on the nature of the service. Generally, there is a tradeoff between the responsiveness of local provision and the problems associated with spillovers, economies of scale, and implicit redistribution. In addition, some specific measures can be taken other than changing the level of government that provides the service. One of these is the intergovernmental transfer of money. Others include mandating actions for lower levels of governments and contracting services between different government units.

/// INTERGOVERNMENTAL GRANTS

When most people think about intergovernmental grants, they tend to think about the general revenue-sharing program. Under this program the federal government provided state and local government with money that could be spent any way that the recipient government desired. The money was distributed by a complex formula which tried to take account of differing financial conditions between government units but which was constrained by floors and ceilings on the amount of money any government could receive. The result was that the revenue-sharing system was a curious cross between an attempt to target aid to certain local governments and a general attempt to simply share the revenue that the federal government received from its income-elastic tax base. The revenue-sharing system is one of the programs that the Reagan administration tried to phase out almost from the beginning and that finally ended as part of the response to the massive federal deficits. However, the state and local governments fought hard to retain this source of funds.

Despite the press attention to revenue sharing, it represented only a small fraction of all intergovernmental transfers. At its peak it was only 13% of all federal grants and just over 3% of the expenditures of state and local governments.[7]

Most grants, called categorical grants, are given for a specific purpose. Categorical grants are often further classified by whether there are matching requirements by the recipient government, whether they are open-ended or have a maximum amount, and whether they are automatic grants or must be awarded only after a competitive application process.

Automatic grants are often associated with the use of federal funds to provide some minimum level of redistributive activity at the state and local level. The major open-ended matching grants are Aid to Families with Dependent Children (AFDC) and Medicaid. The federal transfers for 1989 are estimated at $11 billion and $33 billion for these two programs respectively.[8] These grants are primarily intended to ensure a minimum level of income and health care to certain groups. In some ways it would be more efficient for the federal government simply to provide the aid directly; however, the current method allows state and local governments to decide something about the level of aid to be given in their areas. Further, local administration of the programs may improve their responsiveness to local conditions.

Education and transportation are two other areas of major federal and state grant activity. These grants are usually closed-end grants, often with some matching requirements. The federal government provides funding for a variety of education programs; the state governments are more likely to provide general support for schools within the state. Thus, the federal government would fund a program like Head Start but a state government would be unlikely to do so. Transportation grants from the federal government fall into two distinct categories: road funds come from dedicated revenues largely collected from excise taxes on motor fuels; mass transportation funds come primarily from general revenues. The first priority for the road funds is the

---

[7] Robert Reischauer, "Fiscal Federalism in the 1980s: Dismantling or Rationalizing the Great Society," in Marshall Kaplan and Peggy Cuciti, eds., *The Great Society and Its Legacy* (Durham, NC: Duke University Press, 1986), p. 186.

[8] U.S. Office of Management and Budget, *Special Analyses: Budget of the United States Government, Fiscal Year 1989*, p. H-33.

interstate highway system. Mass transit funds are primarily used for the purchase of capital equipment. These funds all require some matching by the recipient state or local government, but the percentage match is usually fairly small.

The major set of other grants are project grants, which are awarded on a competitive basis, usually for some sort of public works or some experimental program. For example, most of the federal funds for sewage treatment plants were allocated on the basis of competitive proposals. In some instances this may mean that the federal administrators simply determine when the applicant governments will get the money and in other cases there is real competition with many applicants being turned down.

A recent addition to the grant picture is the use of block grants. A federal block grant is intended to take many of the federal grants in a particular program and tie them into one grant. This grant then goes to the state government, which is restricted to use it in the general program area, such as health, but is otherwise unrestricted. In 1989, the broad-based grants are expected to account for a total of $12.6 billion of the $119 billion in intergovernmental aid from the federal government.[9]

The intent of block grants is to reduce the amount of federal intervention and the complexity of the grant system. Offsetting this intention toward less intervention is the tendency for Congress to be more specific about how grant money can be used:

> Included in the [1987 highway reauthorization] bill were 120 "demonstration" projects for specific undertakings. This had the effect of dictating priorities for certain roads and bridges, and superseded the discretion of state highway administrators. In essence, this is a new way for members of Congress to get credit for their spending.[10]

Economics of Intergovernmental Grants

Intergovernmental grants can be viewed as either increasing the income of the recipient government or as reducing the price to the recipient government of some particular service. Thus, we can apply standard economic analysis of the effects of increases in income or decreases in prices to get some idea of how the recipient government would be expected to respond.

We start by treating the government as having a set of preferences and a budget constraint, or as an individual in terms of decision making. In Figure 13-2 the horizontal axis represents the quantity of all programs other than the one we are examining. The vertical axis represents the amount of the target program (*TP*). Each indifference curve shows a higher level of satisfaction, moving northeast. These can be thought of as some form of social indifference

---

[9] Ibid., p. H-23.
[10] Gleason, op. cit., p. 12.

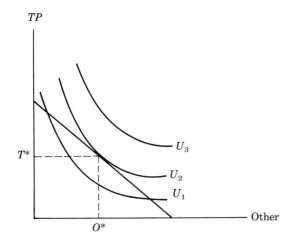

Figure 13-2 / Budget Equilibrium

curves or as the indifference curves of the local decision maker. In addition, there is a budget constraint. Given the prices of the various services that the government can provide, the budget constraint shows the trade-off between services available to the local government. Even tax cuts can be included in the analysis by thinking of the budget constraint as showing the maximum amount of revenue that could be raised and thinking of a tax cut as one of the services included in the "all other" category.

Each type of intergovernmental grant has a particular effect on the government's budget constraint. An unconstrained transfer, such as revenue sharing, shifts the budget line out by the amount of the transfer. Thus, if the government has $10,000,000 to spend before the intergovernmental grant and we adjust the units so that one unit of each output costs exactly one dollar, the budget line would intercept each axis at the 10,000,000 point. This represents the maximum amount of each output that the government could purchase if it spent all its budget on that good. Each unit of one good that is not purchased allows for one additional unit of the other good to be purchased. This is illustrated in Figure 13-3. The consumption point in the figure is for 3,000,000 units of the target program and 7,000,000 units of other programs, i.e., $3,000,000 will be allocated to the target program and $7,000,000 will be allocated to the other programs.

Now suppose that the federal government provides $1 million in revenue sharing funds. The intercept on each axis moves up by this amount. Thus, the budget constraint runs from 11 million units of the target program to 11 million units of the other programs. This shift is also illustrated in Figure 13-3. In the figure, expenditure on each program is increased by 500,000. However, this is a purely arbitrary increase. It is possible to get much more or less than this increase in the target program. If it is a program which the government feels has to be provided at some minimum level but which does not have a high priority for expansion, it may get none of the new funds. Alternatively, it may get all of the new funds if it is a high-priority area for the government. In practice, we would not expect either of these extremes. Rather, the increase in income would lead to a small increase in each of the programs the government undertakes.[11] Since we are treating local tax cuts as one of the "other" programs, it is likely that the increase in intergovernmental aid would reduce the amount of local taxes raised, so the increase in recipient government spending would be less than the full amount of the grant.

A program-specific grant has the effect of increasing the amount of money available for that specific program, but it does not guarantee that the level of spending on the targeted program will increase by the full amount of the grant. Figure 13-4 shows the effect of a grant for $1 million that can only be spent on the targeted program. The maximum amount that can be spent on other programs remains $10 million. However, this amount is available until spending on the targeted program hits $1 million. Beyond that amount, the local government must decrease its own spending by one dollar for each additional dollar spent on the target program. Hence, the budget line starts at

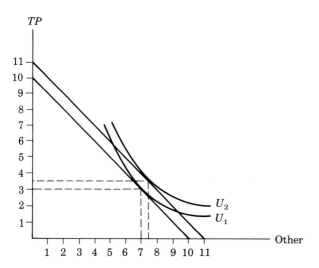

Figure 13-3 / **Lump-Sum Grant**

[11] It is probably worthwhile to point out that the increase can be more than $1 million or the program could actually see a decrease in its funding. These actions depend on the relation of the program to the income of the government. For example, a school district may provide a variety of special programs. Some of these programs may be viewed as providing experience that is desirable for all students but that is restricted because of limited resources. The increase in income may allow for the material to be incorporated into the regular curriculum, thus causing a reduction in funding for the target program. Alternatively, more of the student's time may be shifted into the target program because of the higher level of funding. This may reduce expenditures in other areas and allow for an increase of more than $1 million in the funding for the target program. However, in most cases we expect that each program will receive some part of the additional money.

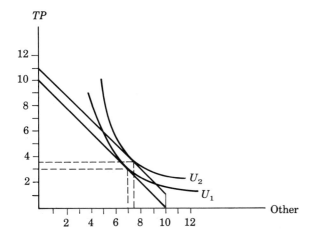

Figure 13-4 / Targeted Grant

$10 million on the horizontal axis and goes up for the first million dollars. Then it goes back to its original slope and intersects the vertical axis at $11 million.

In the figure we see that the effect is exactly the same as an unconditional grant in terms of the spending decisions of the local government. This is because this particular local government would have spent more than the $1 million on the program in the absence of the federal grant. Hence, the grant simply substitutes for the first million dollars of local expenditure and frees that amount for the general budget. The targeted grant would have the same effect as a general grant if the recipient government chose at least the minimum desired by the higher level of government, even if the grant were unconstrained. For example, if the local government would have chosen to spend nothing on the targeted program in the absence of the grant, the grant effectively guarantees at least $1 million of expenditure on the targeted program. Few governments would turn down the "free" part of the program even if they would not spend any of their own money on it. This is illustrated in Figure 13-5. The local government chooses to spend nothing on this program given its preferences. A grant of another million dollars would still cause no spending on this program; but a categorical grant for $1 million is accepted. Note that the government has not reached as high an indifference curve as it would have with the cash transfer. However, there is some presumption that preferences of others should be taken into account or there would be no reason to use anything other than a cash grant. For example, the expenditure may generate spillover benefits in other communities.

This analysis shows that the nonmatching categorical grant can guarantee some minimum level of expenditure, but that it otherwise may not affect the expenditure on the targeted program any more than would a general revenue-sharing grant of the same amount. To offset this ability to shift the

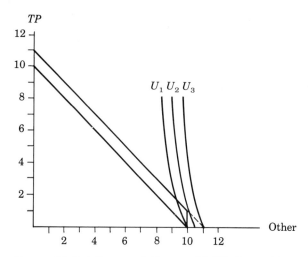

Figure 13-5 / Targeted Grant with Minimum Expenditure

money out of the targeted activity by reducing its own expenditures, some categorical grants have a "maintenance-of-effort" provision. According to this provision, the local government can only receive the federal grant if it is used in addition to the amount the local government would have spent in the absence of the grant. This type of grant is illustrated in Figure 13-6. The local government with some expenditure on this good is now facing a different opportunity set. If this is a categorical grant for a fixed amount, the new level of expenditure is likely to be higher by the amount of the grant. A community like the one in Figure 13-5 has no effort to maintain, so the analysis is not changed by a maintenance-of-effort provision.

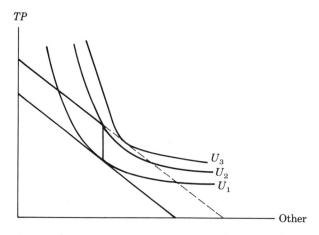

Figure 13-6 / Maintenance-of-Effort Provision

The maintenance-of-effort restriction sounds effective, but it has a number of problems. The most important problem is figuring out what the level of expenditure would have been in the absence of the grant. In practice, some historical level is usually treated as the minimum amount, which must be maintained to be eligible for the grant. Governments can change their spending patterns from year to year. Thus, a maintenance-of-effort provision may be ineffective if the program would have increased anyway. Alternatively, it may be particularly troublesome for a local government that was planning to reduce its expenditures on the targeted program. This may lead to loss of federal assistance for a declining community while a rapidly growing one receives the assistance. In addition, inflation tends to water down the effectiveness of maintenance-of-effort provisions over time since they would usually be specified in dollar amounts rather than level-of-service amounts.

Another way to discourage the diversion of local funds from targeted programs is to use a matching grant. With such grants the local government receives grant money in some specified proportion to local spending. For example, the federal or state government may match local expenditures on a dollar-for-dollar basis. This is illustrated in Figure 13-7. The local government faces a budget that allows expenditure of up to $10 million on other expenditures or up to $20 million on the target program. For each additional dollar spent on the targeted program the local government must only reduce spending on other programs by $0.50 since the federal government pays half the cost. In the figure, this leads to expenditure of $12 million on the targeted program and $4 million on the other expenditures. As can be seen, a lump-sum grant of $6 million would not have led to as large an increase in the expenditure on the targeted program. The lump-sum grant would lead to expenditures of $8 million on each category.

The figure shows an open-ended matching grant. In practice, most such grants have a limit on the amount of the match. These close-ended matching grants function more like lump-sum grants with some minimum local expenditure because the match often ends at a low level compared to the desires of the local government in response to the match. To the extent that the local government spends more than the match amount, the grant acts like an unrestricted lump-sum grant since the local government must pay the full cost of the expenditure beyond the match amount.

Uses of Grants

The flow of funds from one government to another raises some serious issues regarding the purpose of such funding. Why should one level of government raise money and give it to some other level of government to spend? It would seem to make more sense to let the spending government be responsible for raising the funds as well. There are essentially six reasons why a higher level of government funds a lower level. The first is to account for redistributional goals. If a local government tries to redistribute, it creates incentives for

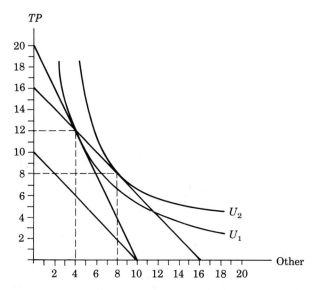

Figure 13-7 / Matching Grant versus Lump-Sum Grant

the losers to leave its jurisdiction and for gainers to enter. This is not efficient and does not seem to promote equity, either.

Why should the residents of one community have to pay more toward the services provided to low-income families than the residents of another community? There may be some reasons why a federal program would not take sufficient account of the differences among areas in the desired amount of redistribution or of the differences in cost of living or support for redistribution. Also, some services must be provided equally to all residents of a community regardless of their ability to pay, and this amounts to redistribution within the community. Intergovernmental grants can offset some of the incentives created by redistribution if the funds are targeted at communities with a high percentage of low-income residents; however, the use of grants allows for local variation in levels of service or amount of redistribution. For example, the grants for direct redistribution often leave some leeway for the state or local government to allow for differences from the national average. This resulted in the state-local per capita expenditure for public welfare ranging in 1986 from a low of $141 in Texas to a high of $625 in New York.[12] Obviously one reason for such a difference is a much higher level of benefits in New York.

A second reason is for the higher level of government to set a uniform tax standard for the lower levels of government so as to prevent some of the distortions associated with competition for the tax base. Thus, if the state sets a sales tax, which is then distributed back to the local governments, there is no incentive for people to move around among the local governments to avoid the

[12] ACIR, op. cit., p. 124.

local sales tax. They must pay it in all the jurisdictions within the state. However, if only one local government did not have such a tax, it might be able to attract large amounts of retail sales business. This might seem very desirable to the one local government, but its gains are at the expense of other local governments. If they then responded by removing their own local sales taxes, there would be little net effect on the total amount of retail sales activity or on its distribution; but the local governments would not have the tax revenue. For this reason, the state collection with a formula redistribution to the local governments may be an efficient way to raise local taxes. In practice we have already noted that a substantial part of state aid is targeted at schooling. In particular, the weak relationship between local benefits from schooling and local taxes makes the problem of competing for a tax base a substantial one.

A third reason for the grants could be to internalize the externalities associated with small communities providing a good or service whose benefits are shared by many people outside the community. For example, the residents of an inner suburb may find that their roads are used extensively by people traveling from more distant suburbs to the central city. These people receive benefits from the roads but do not help finance them directly and do not have any direct voice in determining the level of service the roads should provide. Thus, the road decisions made by the residents of the inner suburb would not take into account the benefits to others, and roads would tend to be underprovided.

A matching grant from a higher level of government is one way to internalize this externality. Residents are likely to want more road services if the direct cost to them of providing the services is reduced. If the matching grant is designed to represent the amount of services received by nonresidents, it would lead to the appropriate level of road service. Of course, there are other ways of achieving this result; but a matching grant has the advantage of leaving most of the decisions at the local level where the information is likely to be best about how residents value additional road services.

The fourth major reason for the use of intergovernmental grants relates to the fund-raising ability of different levels of government. In the 1960s, it was generally accepted that the federal and state governments had access to the most income-elastic source of revenue, the progressive income tax. Because each additional dollar of income is taxed at a higher rate than the average dollar of income, the revenue from the tax goes up more than proportionately with rises in income. This is further augmented by the effect of inflation pushing income into higher tax brackets. At the time, many people were worried about the ability of the federal government to spend this additional revenue effectively. They thought the surpluses would create a "fiscal drag" on the economy which could not be offset by simply reducing taxes. At the same time, the riots in a number of central cities and the difficulties many growing cities had in financing the infrastructure needed for development created an argument for simply passing this federal surplus on to the state and local governments. This showed up most clearly in the form of general revenue sharing, but it also gave rise to many of the other grant programs.

With the federal deficit problem the country now faces, such concerns may seem to have been foolish, but they were widely held at the time. Now that the local governments have come to rely on these grant programs, it is difficult to get agreement on their reduction or elimination.

A fifth argument for intergovernmental grants is that they are required to get local governments to do certain desirable things that they have no incentive to do on their own. These may relate to externalities or to merit goods. We have already seen how the use of a matching grant can get a local government to internalize the benefits that its activities generate for others. However, there are some activities that may be desired at the national level but that local governments have no incentive to provide. For example, a national policy to provide additional education for disadvantaged children would be difficult to implement directly; however, a grant from a higher level of government may induce the local communities to take the desired action. Even if the higher government has the authority to order the local government to implement the program, substantial hardships may be imposed on the local community because of the expenditure, so a grant may be an equitable way to achieve the goal even if it is not required.

The final major reason for a higher level of government to provide funds to a lower level of government is to fund an activity that is the appropriate responsibility of the higher level government but that can be better administered at the local level. This is the case for many of the program grants to local governments. For example, the federal government may want to increase the amount of energy conservation in the country, yet a federal program may not be sensitive to regional differences in energy usage. Instead the federal government may decide to provide grants for local governments to offer such programs. Then the local governments essentially become agents of the federal government in conducting the programs.

State aid to local governments is more closely tied to a combination of issues regarding which level of government should raise funds for specific purposes and how much state interest there is in the provision of these services. For example, the Serrano-Priest decision in California was a ruling that the exclusive use of the property tax as a source of funding for education violated certain principles of the California constitution. The ruling regarded the funding for education rather than the actual provision of education. Hence, the state chose to address the funding issue without altering the education system by providing a larger share of the cost of education. In this way the state could meet its role in terms of the access to education for students in all communities in the state without eliminating the local control over education, which many people see as very desirable. While this ruling applies only to California, other states have moved to greater reliance on state financing of education for similar reasons; they virtually all use grants rather than direct state control. Similar arguments could be made for the role of state financing of local roads.

State intergovernmental grants are more likely to be made on a formula basis than are federal grants. States seldom sponsor competitive project grants. Presumably the state government is more interested in the actual operations of local government and their funding problems while the federal government is more interested in innovation and testing of new programs.

The Flypaper Effect

Our analysis of how local officials are likely to react to the incentives offered by intergovernmental grants is not completely supported by the empirical evidence. Although there is evidence that the money targeted for specific purposes is often equivalent to general revenue sharing, other evidence shows that the level of spending on targeted programs is higher than would be the case if the grant were treated purely as an income transfer. This has been called the "flypaper" effect – the money sticks where it lands. This phenomenon has led to a number of hypotheses about the likely causes. One is that the citizens of a community are less aware of intergovernmental grants than they are of local taxes. Hence, an increase in intergovernmental aid would not be offset by a decrease in local taxes because the citizens generally would not be aware of the federal money.

A more plausible explanation is that the distribution of federal funds is somewhat conditional on the desire to spend the money. A community that wants to carry out a specific project would be more likely to apply for a grant. If the project is funded by the federal government, the money is indeed likely to be spent in the targeted area. When such a community is compared to others without the grant, it appears that the grant stimulated the specific expenditure. However, it was really the desire to make the expenditure that stimulated the application for the grant. In addition, recipients of competitive project grants may be inclined to spend the additional money in the target area so as to improve their chances of receiving future grants. If a city is perceived by the grant administrators as simply trying to get additional funds rather than meeting the objectives of the grant program, that city would not be likely to get additional money in the future.

A final reason why project grants may have more impact on the target program than general grants is the time needed for a local government to change its budget. If the money from the federal government cannot be counted on in a particular budgetary cycle, it is not likely to enter into the decisions about allocations to other programs. Money that becomes available after the budget is set could only be used on the target project. Thus, it may take time for the local government to react to the change in funds. This is consistent with research that finds that large percentages of the intergovernmental grants are diverted to other purposes over time.

It thus appears that the economic analysis can show us the tendency of a local government to spend money received in intergovernmental grants, but the slow reaction time of the local government, the desire to get future grants, and the tendency for those with greatest desire to make a specific expenditure to apply for a grant all temper our ability to make predictions using the model.

/// REDISTRIBUTION

Many of the grants from the federal and state governments are intended to equalize resources across jurisdictional boundaries. Thus, state governments tend to provide equal amounts of school aid to all areas while collecting different amounts from different areas. This redistributes some money from richer school districts in the state to poorer school districts. The federal government provides some aid directly tied to redistributive programs; but it goes further by having many of its formula grants give more money to districts with either lower tax bases or higher concentrations of the poor. The redistributional effect of the latter grants has been questioned in terms of both ability to aid the poor and the efficiency of the method.

Consider a city and its suburb. Suppose that there is a difference of 20% in per capita income and per capita property tax base between the two communities; the suburb would be able to raise the same amount of revenue per capita with a lower tax rate or could raise more revenue with the same tax rate as the city. Many people would argue that this is inequitable and that intergovernmental grants should be used to offset the differences. They argue that the federal government should provide more assistance to the central city than to the suburb. However, others question the effectiveness of such policies in helping low-income families.

Suppose that the central city of an urban area does indeed have more low-income residents and a lower tax base than its surrounding suburbs. It seems tempting to conclude that a grant to the city will help offset the disadvantage of having a large low-income population and allow the city to provide better services to its residents. However, if residents are freely mobile between communities, the grant is likely to aid landowners in the central city rather than low-income families. We can see this by imagining what the rent differential would have to be between the city and the suburbs. Presumably the suburb would provide a higher level of service and/or a lower tax for a given house. However, if this is the case, the price of the house in the suburb would have to be higher than the price in the city. If it were not, city residents would want to move to the suburbs. In equilibrium, the city residents and the suburban residents with the same income would have to be equally well off or there would be additional movements between the city and the suburbs. Providing funds to the central city would allow it to raise its level of service or reduce its level of taxation. This would make it more attractive relative to the suburbs; but if suburban families tried to move back to the city, they would bid up the price of city housing relative to suburban housing. The beneficiaries of the grant would be property owners. Similarly, renters would bid up the rents in the city relative to the suburbs, and the beneficiaries of the grant would be landlords.

Since low-income families are more likely to rent than to own, they are not likely to share in the benefits of the grant as much as might be supposed. Further, the existence of differentials between taxes and services is one reason why suburban communities often try to keep out low-income households. However, a grant to a city would not change those incentives. Both the city and the suburbs would find that it is still in their best interest to try to encourage high-income families to locate within their boundaries and to discourage low-income families from locating there. The result is that there is little in the way of benefit to low-income families because of the grants.

There would be some benefit to the recipient community in that the increase in property values would induce more building in that community. To the extent that fiscal redistribution was previously leading to underinvestment in the community, the redistributional grant would tend to offset the negative effects. However, there are likely to be more effective ways to offset such impacts (see Box 13-1).

/// GRANTS AND REGULATION

States have significant control over all the local governments in the state since they are all formed under state laws. There is ample precedent for the states to make rules and regulations that restrict the behavior of local governments. For example, many states have limits on the tax authority of local governments. The state is also likely to set minimum standards for school districts, limits on local borrowing, and so on.

The federal government has a much more limited role in influencing the activities of the states and their local governments. The Constitution sets clear limits on the functions of the federal government and reserves all other powers for the states. However, the Constitution does not limit the restrictions that the federal government can place on money it is giving to a state or local government, and the federal government has found that it can enforce many regulations which it is not authorized to issue by threatening to cut off one form of funding or another. For example, the 55 MPH speed limit was a requirement set by Congress. However, the federal government has no authority to set speed limits. Rather, it simply threatened to withhold all federal highway funds for states that did not set a maximum 55 MPH speed limit. Many states were not pleased with this restriction; some even considered repealing this limit and accepting the reduction in federal funds. However, none have yet done so, and the recent increase in the permissible limit to 65 on parts of the interstate system seems to have reduced the conflict.

Box 13-1

////// Example of Grant Capitalization

One way to see how the effect of a grant can be different from what was intended is to work through an example. Suppose that there are only high-income and low-income groups. Each family in each group is identical. The suburb has 90% high-income families and the city has 90% low-income families. Taxes are the same in the two communities but services are higher in the suburbs. Each high-income family would be willing to pay $1,000 per year for the additional services in the suburbs and each low-income family would be willing to pay $200 for the additional services. If everyone is thought of as renting their residence, the rent in the suburbs would have to be $1,000 per year higher for the high-income residences and $200 per year higher for the low-income residences. If the difference were less than this, some of the city residents would try to move to the suburbs and would bid up rents. If the difference were more than this, some of the suburban residents would try to move to the city and would bid up the rents there relative to the sub-

urbs. This is the only differential that can be maintained over long periods of time.

Now suppose that the federal government gave the city a grant allowing it to increase its level of services to the level in the suburbs. The rent differential would have to disappear. Thus, either rents would go up in the city or go down in the suburbs. To the extent that they go up in the city, they do not aid the city renters. Renters could have achieved the same level of services before the grant by moving to the suburbs. Further, the benefits are spread over all city property owners; so even if the low-income families own their own homes, the benefits of the grant are not targeted at them.

The desire to help specific groups in a community may be one reason why many of the federal grants are project grants rather than general grants. But even in these cases, the benefits are likely to be capitalized into property values and to benefit owners of property rather than the targeted group.

The threat to cut off funds has been used in many instances for the federal government to impose its will on lower levels of government. Some view this as an unwarranted usurpation of power. Others consider it a necessary means to control otherwise irresponsible lower levels of government. However, the situation will remain as long as the federal government continues to disburse large amounts of money to lower levels of government. Unless the Constitution is changed or the Supreme Court significantly alters its interpretation of the

Constitution, the federal government will continue to use the powers that come with the purse.

Dramatic reductions in the level of federal grants would also significantly reduce its ability to influence these lower levels of government. However, the outcry arising from the recipients whenever there is a threat of such reductions makes it fairly clear that those in charge of the lower levels of government would rather have the money with all its strings than raise the money themselves.

The other problem associated with these grants is the difficulty in reversing expenditures when the source of funds dries up or of coming up with funds to operate a facility built with federal money. The former problem is tied in with the discussion of the nature of such grants. If the federal government is trying to provide funds for experimental projects or to allow a local government to meet high start-up costs, it is entirely appropriate for the funds to disappear at the end of the start-up period. However, if the intent is to cause the local government to internalize an externality or to provide some merit good, there is no justification for the funds to be withdrawn. This is especially true if the local government was led to expect the funding to be ongoing. Many times a local government will start a program in order to receive the federal funds that support it, and when the federal funds are stopped they find that there is an established constituency for the program. Those who use the program and those who provide the service become an organized special interest in favor of its continuation. This must then be financed by state or local funds. The desirability of this outcome depends on one's view of the appropriate scope of government and the relationship between its different levels.

A related problem is associated with the use of federal funds for capital expenditures but local funds for operating expenses. Many of the federal programs provide funds for capital expenditures only. This removes the need to float bonds to fund a large expenditure; however, the additional burden of operating the project may be much greater than was anticipated while it was being built. Also, the free capital funds create a bias toward capital-intensive project designs. This may lead to systems that are either too large or simply inefficiently designed. Most local governments would gladly spend $10 of federal money to save $1 of local money, and if the federal government will pay for replacement of capital equipment, the local government may have poor incentives for maintenance of the equipment.

Finally, there is one kind of intergovernmental grant that tends to flow from the local governments to higher levels of government. As was discussed in the sections dealing with the property tax, state and federal governments are exempt from local property taxes. Hence, the local governments tend to subsidize them to some extent by providing services that are not paid for. This is offset in some instances by payments in lieu of taxes. For example, the federal government will make such payments to a local government to offset the costs of schooling for children of workers at a military base; however, such payments are only made on a small percentage of all such property.

/// **SUMMARY**

Intergovernment grants make up a large percentage of the expenditures of local governments. This amount grew rapidly during the late 1960s and early 1970s. The rate of growth has fallen in recent years and the total amounts may start to decline. General revenue sharing by the federal government is one of the best known intergovernmental grant programs, but it was actually only a small percentage of even the federal grants. It may be more indicative of the general situation with respect to intergovernmental aid than important by itself, for the rise and fall of general revenue sharing is closely associated with the general level of aid from the federal government. Most grants are for specific purposes; however, there has been some attempt to consolidate grant programs by the creation of block grants. States also provide significant amounts of grant money to their local governments. Most of this money is provided on a formula basis, so there is less discretion in how it is allocated.

The major reasons for grants are to get the recipient government to do something it would not otherwise have done or to redistribute money. There are criticisms of grants on both counts; but the existing grant system is likely to be a major source of funds to local governments for the foreseeable future. One major side effect of the intergovernmental transfer of funds is that it has significantly increased the centralization of power. Because they control the purse strings, higher levels of government can impose standards on lower levels of government, which can be enforced by the threat to withhold funds. Whether this power will decrease in line with the decrease in federal funds remains to be seen.

Part Three ///////////////////////////////////////

Services and Expenditures

Governments both spend money on goods and services and give money away. Each activity has an impact on how people behave, and these expenditures can also have both efficiency and equity effects on the economy. We start this section by identifying some of the key issues in evaluating government expenditure, such as the difficulty in measuring the output of government activities. Then we turn to budgeting, the means by which government sets its spending decisions. The budget process is important both in terms of setting incentives and constraints on government behavior and in terms of identifying the goals of government action.

While governments spend large amounts of money on direct purchase of goods and services, transfers of money have been the fastest growing part of the budget. Some transfers are made as part of the social insurance programs, such as unemployment compensation or Social Security; others are intended to assist low-income families, such as food stamps and Aid to Families with Dependent Children. Both types of transfer have important efficiency and equity effects.

The remainder of the section is devoted to an

analysis of three major areas of expenditure which have different patterns of provision and financing. National defense is the sole responsibility of the federal government, and we analyze it as both a major expenditure item and as the standard example of a public good. However, the difficulties in determining the specific goals and resources needed to achieve them make the process of determining expenditures extremely complex. Further, the major impact of such large expenditures means that other factors are also important in determining expenditure patterns. Primary and secondary education is mostly provided by local governments, but funding is provided by all three levels of government. This is an important area of government expenditure where criticism of the existing system is extensive but where there is little consensus on how reform should proceed. Finally, fighting crime has become a major concern, but the predominant efforts at crime fighting are still local and most of the funds for fighting crime originate at the local level as well. The economic analysis of crime provides some insights into methods to deter criminal behavior; but again there is little consensus on how best to proceed. ///

Chapter 14 //////

Introduction to Services and Expenditures

Without doubt, total government expenditures have been increasing as a percentage of GNP for the past 30 years. Yet the nature of that expansion could be interpreted in a variety of ways. First, it is important to separate the growth of the federal government from that of the state and local governments. Second, it is necessary to look at the division between actual purchases of goods and services and the transfer of money from government to people or from one level of government to another. Third, there may be a distinct difference between spending more money on goods and services and getting more goods and services. It is necessary to look at the production process and the relation between inputs and outputs for government. This chapter sets out the basic trends in government spending and separates the transfers from the purchases. Then we look at the issues that arise in trying to evaluate government output and spending and their effect on the economy. Finally, we look at the production of goods and services by government. A variety of issues are raised in this context with respect to cost, efficiency, and the allocation of resources.

Government expenditures are a significant part of the gross national product (GNP). The public sector accounts for more than one-third of GNP. If we look at direct expenditures, the importance of the federal government is almost twice as large as that of state and local governments combined, i.e., accounting for 61% of all government expenditures in 1987.[1] Over the last sixty years, total government expenditures as a percent of GNP have been increasing (see Figure 14-1).

An analysis of government services and expenditures is possible only if we master a number of key concepts, techniques, and theories. Among the most

---

[1] Advisory Commission on Intergovernmental Relations (ACIR), *Significant Features of Fiscal Federalism, 1988*, vol. 2, M-155 II (Washington, DC: 1988), p. 24.

important are the concepts of output, production and production functions, and cost and expenditure functions. These concepts make it possible to test hypotheses about the presence or absence of scale economies in the operation of the public sector and the merits of consolidating or breaking up governments. Demand for public services is another important concept. Its determination is made much more difficult in the public than the private sector, because in the public sector, all too often few if any demand signals are given.

/// FIGURES AND TRENDS

To determine the magnitude and significance of government in the national economy, the following numbers are instructive. In 1987, all government expenditures were estimated to have amounted to $1,571 billion, of which $964 billion was spent by the federal government and $607 billion by state and local governments.[2] As a percentage of GNP, the share of the public

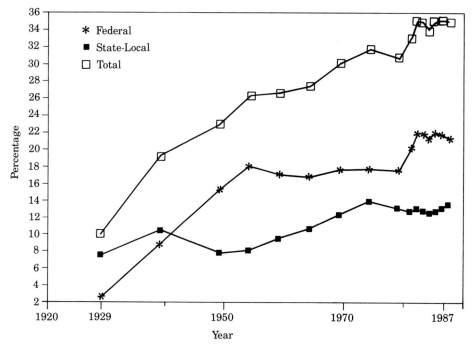

***Figure 14-1* / Government Expenditure as Percentage of GNP**

(Source: Advisory Commission on Intergovernmental Relations, *Significant Features of Fiscal Federalism, 1988 Edition*, vol. 2 [Washington, DC: July, 1988], M-155 II, pp. 24–25.)

[2] Ibid.

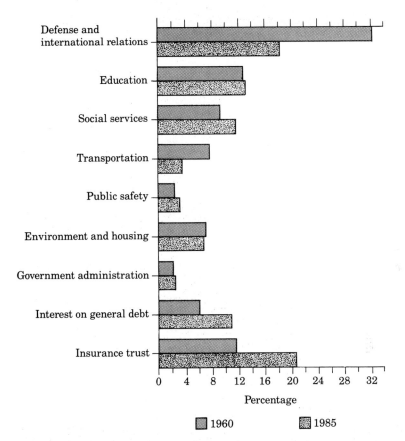

Figure 14-2 / Selected Percentage Distribution of Expenditures

(Source: Tax Foundation, *Facts and Figures on Government Finance, 1988–89* [Baltimore: Johns Hopkins University Press, 1988], p. 10.)

sector was 35%, that of the federal government alone 21.5% and that of state and local governments 13.5% (see Table 14-1). Measured in 1982 dollars, government spending amounted to $5,481 per capita, of which the federal government alone spent $3,363 per person.

Figure 14-2 indicates some of the items on which governments spent money and the relative expenditures for 1960 and 1985. It shows that in 1960 the largest budget item was national defense followed by education and insurance trust expenditures. However, in 1985, the insurance trust expenditures took the largest percentage, followed by defense and education.

Spending on major functions by federal, state, and local governments in 1960 added up to $151 billion, of which 32.3% was spent on national defense and international relations, the single largest budget item. Interestingly enough, while total spending reached $1.4 trillion in 1985, the share of expenditures for national defense and international relations had declined to

Table 14-1 / Government Expenditures, After Intergovernmental Transfers,[1] Selected Years 1929–87

Calendar Year	Total Public Sector	Federal Government	Total State-Local Government	State Government	Local Government
Amount (in billions of current dollars)					
1929	$ 10.4	$ 2.6	$ 7.8	$ 2.2	$ 5.6
1939	17.6	8.0	9.6	3.0	6.6
1949	60.0	39.8	20.2	7.7	12.5
1954	97.6	67.4	30.2	10.7	19.4
1959	131.9	84.9	47.0	16.7	20.3
1964	177.9	109.1	68.8	23.9	44.8
1969	290.3	171.0	119.3	43.1	76.3
1974	467.5	261.6	205.9	76.7	129.2
1979	768.3	440.6	327.7	125.6	202.1
1981	1,006.8	615.4	391.4	154.0	237.5
1982	1,111.6	697.3	414.3	163.4	250.8
1983	1,189.9	749.7	440.2	173.6	266.6
1984	1,277.9	803.8	475.9	191.9	284.1
1985	1,401.4	887.1	516.5	209.2	307.3
1986	1,487.0	928.1	561.9	227.5	334.5
1987	1,570.8	963.7	607.1	245.8	361.3
As a percentage of GNP					
1929	10.0%	2.5%	7.5%	2.1%	5.4%
1939	19.3	8.8	10.5	3.3	7.2
1949	23.0	15.3	7.8	3.0	4.8
1954	26.2	18.1	8.1	2.9	5.2
1959	26.6	17.1	9.5	3.4	6.1
1964	27.4	16.8	10.6	3.7	6.9
1969	30.1	17.7	12.4	4.5	7.9
1974	31.7	17.8	14.0	5.2	8.8
1979	30.6	17.6	13.1	5.0	8.1
1981	33.0	20.2	12.8	5.0	7.8
1982	35.1	22.0	13.1	5.2	7.9
1983	34.9	22.0	12.9	5.1	7.8
1984	33.9	21.3	12.6	5.1	7.5
1985	34.9	22.1	12.8	5.2	7.7
1986	35.1	21.9	13.2	5.4	7.9
1987	35.0	21.5	13.5	5.5	8.0
Per capita, in constant (1982) dollars					
1929	$ 585	$ 146	$ 439	$124	$ 315
1939	1,059	481	578	180	397
1949	1,711	1,135	576	220	357
1954	2,276	1,572	704	250	452
1959	2,440	1,570	869	309	560
1964	2,818	1,728	1,090	379	710
1969	3,599	2,120	1,479	534	946
1974	4,048	2,265	1,783	664	1,119
1979	4,343	2,491	1,853	710	1,142
1981	4,654	2,845	1,809	712	1,098
1982	4,781	2,999	1,782	703	1,079
1983	4,878	3,073	1,804	712	1,093
1984	5,006	3,149	1,857	752	1,113
1985	5,267	3,334	1,933	786	1,155
1986	5,394	3,367	2,027	825	1,213
1987	5,481	3,363	2,118	858	1,261
Percentage distribution, by level of government					
1929	100.0%	25.0%	75.0%	21.2%	53.8%
1939	100.0	45.5	54.5	17.0	37.5
1949	100.0	66.3	33.7	12.8	20.8
1954	100.0	69.1	30.9	11.0	19.9
1959	100.0	64.4	35.6	12.7	23.0
1964	100.0	61.3	38.7	13.4	25.2
1969	100.0	58.9	41.1	14.8	26.3
1974	100.0	56.0	44.0	16.4	27.6
1979	100.0	57.3	42.7	16.3	26.3
1981	100.0	61.1	38.9	15.3	23.6
1982	100.0	62.7	37.3	14.7	22.6
1983	100.0	63.0	37.0	14.6	22.4
1984	100.0	62.9	37.1	15.0	22.2
1985	100.0	63.3	36.7	14.9	21.9
1986	100.0	62.4	37.6	15.3	22.5
1987	100.0	61.4	38.6	15.6	23.0

[1] Federal aid to state and local governments spent by state and local governments counted as state and local government expenditure. State aid to local governments counted as local government expenditure.

(Source: Advisory Commission on Intergovernmental Relations, *Significant Features of Fiscal Federalism, 1988 Edition*, vol. 2, M-155 II [Washington, DC: July 1988], pp. 24–25.)

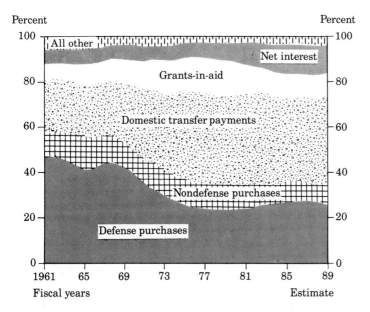

Percent

Percent

Figure 14-3 / Distribution of Federal Sector Expenditures by Category

(Source: U.S. Office of Management and Budget, *Special Analyses: Budget of the United States Government, Fiscal Year 1989*, p. B-6.)

18.3%. Looking at the detailed information in the figure we see that education was about 13% in both 1960 and 1985 whereas social services showed an increase from 9.3% to 11.6% of expenditures. Transportation showed the largest relative decline, going from 7.7% of expenditures in 1960 to 3.6% of expenditures in 1985. Insurance trust expenditures increased the most, from 11.6% in 1960 to 20.8% in 1985. It is clear from the fairly substantial differences in distribution between the time periods that government expenditure patterns are not fixed. Figure 14-3 shows the relative shares for federal government spending in six broad categories over the period 1961 to 1989. Although we seldom see reductions in expenditure on major categories, expenditure on some items grows faster than on others; and when expenditure grows less rapidly than inflation, there is a real reduction in expenditure.

Figure 14-4 shows the spending patterns of the different levels of government for various functions. Of course, only the federal government spends money on national defense and international relations, but virtually all other categories have some expenditure at each level of government. It is interesting to note that local governments spend the most for education and police while the state governments are responsible for the largest share of expenditure on public welfare. Much of the state expenditures on welfare, however, are financed by the federal government through intergovernmental grants. Finally, we note the large amount spent by the federal government under the category

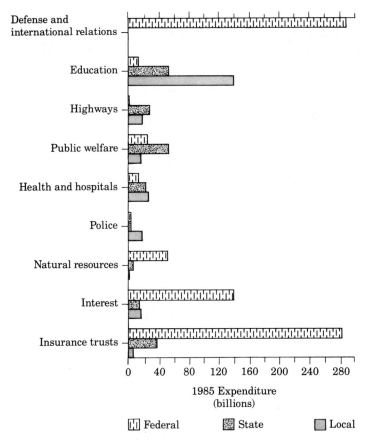

**1985 Expenditure
(billions)**

[:] Federal   State   Local

Figure 14-4 / **Expenditures by Function and Level**

(Source: Tax Foundation, *Facts and Figures on Government Finance, 1988–89* [Baltimore: Johns
Hopkins University Press, 1988], p. 8.)

of insurance trusts, which includes Social Security, as well as the large
amount of interest which it pays.

We can undertake a long historical review as well. According to Table 14-1,
over the last sixty years or so the public sector in the U.S. has grown rapidly.
Total public expenditures in 1929 amounted to $10 billion, in 1954 to $97
billion, in 1974 to $468 billion, in 1979 to $768 billion, and in 1987 to $1.57
trillion. As a percentage of GNP the major change took place between 1929
and 1939, with growth during this period from 10.0% to 19.3%. By 1982 it had
reached 35.1% and from then it varied very little, staying between 34% and
35% for the next five years.

On an overall basis, the role of the three levels of government has undergone significant changes. World War II left the federal government with a very
large share, i.e., 66% in 1949, which slowly declined to 56% in 1974. Since

then, the share has slowly increased to about 61% in 1987.[3] The share of state governments has increased from 11% in 1954 to a high of 16.4% in 1974, to decline to 14.6% in 1983 and then increase to 15.6% in 1987. In a similar manner the share of local governments increased from 20% in 1954 to a high of 28% in 1974, to decline from that date to 22% in 1985 and increase to 23% in 1987.

Much additional insight into the public sector and its spending is gained by separating government spending into two distinct categories: government spending for goods and services, i.e., resources consumed by government, and nonpurchase spending involving income redistribution by government.

When government purchases goods and services, part of the economy's total output of goods and services is allocated to the operation of government programs, be they national defense, the criminal justice system, education, or research and development. These expenditures include paying government employees and purchasing goods and services for direct government use. In theory, these resources could have been used by the private sector of the economy and these total purchases are indicative of the size of government in economic terms.

Governmental nonpurchase spending is very different from the first type of spending. It transfers dollars to individuals as additions to their income in the form of Social Security and Medicare payments, welfare payments, and civil or uniformed service pensions. Additionally, there are transfers to businesses as subsidies, e.g., water delivery, agricultural prices and housing, and to holders of the national debt who are paid interest. There is some disagreement over what constitutes a transfer and what constitutes payment for services. For example, the interest paid by the government is a payment for the use of money. This is different from a welfare payment, which is based on the low income of the recipient. There is even some disagreement about the Social Security system since the recipients' benefits are at least loosely tied to the taxes paid. However, in these cases, the government does not directly use up resources; rather, it transfers the ability to use resources to others.

When we divide spending into purchase and transfer categories and trace them over time, some interesting facts are revealed. First, Figure 14-5 indicates that between 1954 and 1984 spending on purchases of goods and services by all three levels of government has been relatively stable at about 21% of GNP. Thus, ever since the end of the Korean war, the share of government purchases in the national economy has remained stable. However, in 1954, while 13.1% of GNP was accounted for by federal spending on purchases, 7.6% was spent by state and local governments. The share of the latter increased during the next twenty years to 14% of GNP in 1975, growing almost twice as fast as the economy as a whole. The reason was the postwar baby boom, which required significant increases in education. These increases were offset by declines in the defense share, which fell in the same period from 11.2% to 5.4%

3 Ibid., p. 25.

of GNP. However, since 1974, the defense share has slightly risen from 5.4% to 6% in 1984. During the same period, the demand for education associated with the postwar baby boom declined and with it the share of state and local government spending declined from 14% in 1975 to 12.4% in 1984.

With the share of total government purchase spending stable, yet the overall share of government spending increasing during this period, non-purchase spending must be the villain and indeed it is. As can be seen in Figure 14-6, transfer payments alone increased from 4.6% of GNP in 1954 to 11.1% of GNP in 1984, thus growing about two and a half times as fast as the economy during that period. For the first half of the period 1954–84, non-purchase spending grew at a rate that added less than 0.2% of GNP every year. In the next fifteen years, this rate of increase accelerated. Governments at all levels, but especially at the federal level, each year added an average of nearly 0.4% more of GNP to spending on income redistribution. Reasons include large-scale increases in Social Security payments, indexing for inflation of most retirement and welfare spending, and higher interest rates, together with an enlarged national debt. Note that much of the responsibility for this development rests on the federal government. We can also compare the total of 0.6% added to the defense purchases share of GNP with the 0.4% of GNP

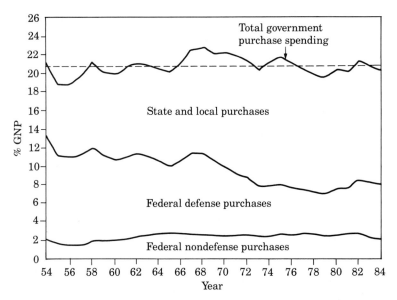

Total government purchase spending stays around 21% of GNP

Figure 14-5 / **Spending on Goods and Services by All Levels of Government**

(Source: Donald B. Rice, *The Battle of the Budget Deficit* [Santa Monica, CA: Rand Corporation, 1985], p. 4.)

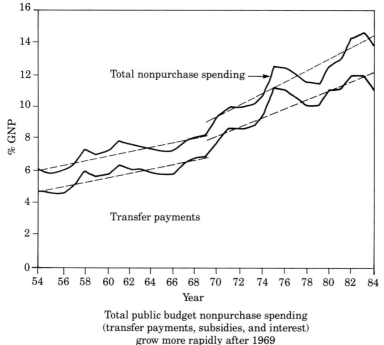

Total public budget nonpurchase spending
(transfer payments, subsidies, and interest)
grow more rapidly after 1969

Figure 14-6 / **Increase in Nonpurchase Spending**

(Source: Rice, op. cit., p. 6.)

added each year for fifteen years to nonpurchase spending, mainly on transfer payments, especially entitlement programs.

/// EXPENDITURE ANALYSIS

When government spends money, a variety of issues can be raised regarding equity and efficiency. For example, what should determine how much a government spends on different citizens? Should expenditure be equal across all individuals or should it be set in some relationship to their contribution to the public treasury? Also, it is possible that the behavior people exhibit in response to the actions of government causes benefits to be shifted in much the same way that taxes are shifted. The final incidence of a government benefit may be very different from the initial allocation of the expenditures. Finally, the cost of production can differ for different methods of production.

When we discussed the uses of taxes we looked at the various definitions of equity with respect to the revenue raised. Each of these has a counterpart with respect to expenditure policy. For example, the benefit principle of taxation says that people should be taxed according to the benefits they receive from the public sector. However, we could look at the issue from the opposite side and argue that the benefits a person receives from the government should be related to the amount he or she contributes to the public coffers. This argument has been used to try to explain why higher income families in a city are likely to get more of certain types of services than are lower income residents. These higher income residents have the option of moving out of a jurisdiction, and they generally require less in the way of demand for services relative to their contributions than do lower income residents. Thus, most local governments would like to keep such residents to reduce budget strain. For example, if the city were to spend $500 per family in one part of the city but $1,000 per family in another, this might be justified if the city received revenue of $300 per family associated with the low-income area but revenue of $1,200 per family from the high-income area. From the city's perspective it may be necessary to spend more on the high-income family to offset some of its incentive to move to the suburbs. Even with this higher expenditure it may be difficult to convince the higher income residents to stay. If enough such families leave, the tax base may decline to the point where the level of service per household in the low-income community may have to be further reduced.

Another way to look at the equity issue is with respect to the ability-to-pay principle. Remember that under the tax analysis, ability to pay is an evaluation of the tax treatment when there is no clear-cut relationship between revenues and expenditures. There is a similar issue with respect to the requirements for service on the expenditure side. No matter what they contribute to the government, there are a number of people who are eligible for various government goods and services, so we can take an analogy with the revenue side and look for principles of horizontal and vertical equity in expenditures. Horizontal equity would be the equal treatment of equals, suitably defined; vertical equity would be the provision of more government services to those judged to require them.[4] Hence, just as we would expect that the government would collect higher taxes from those with more ability to pay, we would expect it to provide more services to those with greater requirements for assistance. The different principles would be expected to be applied in different circumstances. In particular, the requirements principle would be of more relevance in the direct redistribution programs than it would in the service provision programs; but there are many cases where they cannot be easily separated.

Another issue arising in this context is the meaning of the term equality. Equality of taxation is a relatively simple concept since taxes are usually paid in money. However, equality of services might be defined in a number of ways. It might mean equality of expenditure on services, it might refer to equality of

---

[4] For some reasons why government redistribution may be desired see Harold M. Hochman and James D. Rodgers, "Pareto Optimal Redistribution," *American Economic Review* (September 1969), pp. 542–557; reprinted in William Breit, et al., *Readings in Microeconomics* (St. Louis: Times Mirror/Mosby), 1986.

service provided, or it might refer to equality of results in the service provision. The requirements principle would argue for the equality of output as the goal. However, the benefits principle would argue for better schools in the more affluent neighborhoods since they contribute more to the tax base.

Similar issues arise when considering many of the services that government provides. For example, should the IRS try to provide good service to higher income taxpayers with large tax bills, or should it direct its resources to the lower income taxpayer? The former clearly pays a larger share of the cost of government and is more likely to have technically complex questions. The latter, however, is not as likely to have access to professional assistance or other sources of aid. So how should the resources be allocated?

The relationship between inputs, service levels, and results is an important issue from the efficiency perspective for two reasons.[5] First, it may relate to the way in which inputs are converted to outputs, i.e., the production function; and second, the choice of which to equalize could have important efficiency effects. Consider the following example. In neighborhood A a given level of fire protection can be achieved by having an assignment of one station per 1,000 residents, while in neighborhood B one fire station per 10,000 residents is required to maintain the same level of protection. Now suppose that the city decides to equalize the protection provided. People who were previously deterred from locating in B because of the fire danger may now choose to do so. If 10,000 people move from A to B, the fire damage rate would stay the same only if the city were to provide additional fire stations. This would qualify as an inefficient incentive from the perspective of setting incentives, but it may be viewed as very desirable from an equity and other perspectives. In any case, the attempt to equalize results is likely to lead to some inefficiency; and this means that there tends to be a trade-off between equity and efficiency on the expenditure side as well as one on the revenue side.

The shifting of benefits may occur just as the shifting of taxes occurs. For example, suppose that several businesses renting space in a small shopping mall are concerned about poor traffic flow on surrounding streets, making it hard for customers to reach the center. They convince the city government to improve the nearby streets. One effect of this is to increase the demand by other merchants to locate in the center. This increased demand should lead to a rise in rents in the center. In this way, the benefits to the merchants would be shifted to the owners of the center through higher rents. This can be seen graphically in Figure 14-7. The increase in the number of customers is shown as an increase in demand for the output of each store. The higher demand then leads to higher prices and higher profits, and we expect to see an increase in demand for those locations, as in Figure 14-8. Thus, the rent is bid up as a means of rationing the sites and making merchants once again indifferent between these sites and other available locations.

---

[5] Werner Z. Hirsch, *The Economics of State and Local Government* (New York: McGraw-Hill, 1970), pp. 155–158.

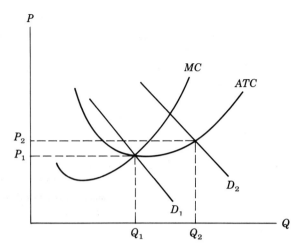

Figure 14-7 / **Demand and Store Profit**

The capitalization of these benefits into land values is a useful illustration of why the decisions on where and how to spend public money are not neutral. A new military base or a new school may serve the general public purpose in a variety of locations; however, the location that receives the facility will also see some rise in private land values and other forms of private benefits. These changes in private benefits make it almost impossible to keep the efficiency issue separate from the distribution issue. It is because of these potentials for major changes in private wealth that so many resources are spent on trying to influence public decisions. In principle, it would make sense to spend additional private resources on trying to get a favorable outcome as long as the expenditure raises the probability of success by a sufficient amount. Thus, it might make sense for a private firm to spend $1 million on trying to influence

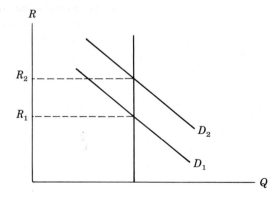

Figure 14-8 / **Demand for Sites and Rent**

a public decision if the firm believed that the expenditure would raise the probability of a decision in its favor from zero to 10% and the value of a favorable decision is greater than $10 million. If the firm followed such behavior consistently, the benefits from the 10% of the time in which it was successful would offset the costs of all of the efforts to change the outcome. However, from the efficiency perspective, the resources devoted to changing the public decision in favor of the firm are likely to represent a waste, since there is likely to be no greater value to the economy from this firm getting its outcome than if the decision went against it.

/// GOVERNMENT PRODUCTION DECISIONS

It is important to separate government production and expenditure decisions. In principle there could be two possible extremes of government involvement in the production and distribution of goods in an economy. The first extreme is for government to organize all production and distribute all of the product. In this case there are no private markets or ownership of productive resources. Until recently such a system, which makes no distinction between what we have identified as public and private goods, was approached by China and the U.S.S.R. For example, both national defense and steel are directly produced and allocated by government. While in practice all economies have some market transactions, in the extreme there is not even a need for markets as we know them. The government simply determines what each person gets.

At the other extreme is a system in which government has no responsibility for either production or distribution. All production and distribution occur through some form of market arrangement. In this extreme, government still sets up the rules of the economy and arbitrates disputes, but all production and distribution of both public and private goods is done through markets.

While no nation can be characterized as purely government or purely market, there are many dimensions of the involvement of government in the economy. For example, the degree of regulation that a government practices can be a major determinant of how much the market influences the allocation and distribution of resources. However, regulation would not show up as much in the way of taxes and expenditures. Government macroeconomic policies also have significant effects on the private sector.

Even when we focus on the level of government production and spending as measures of government activity, we find that there are several dimensions to the issue. A government that spends money by purchasing goods and services from the private sector under a competitive bidding system is quite different from a government that produces its output directly by hiring workers and purchasing inputs. One difference is in the incentives that exist within the two organizational structures. The company providing output to the government still has the profit incentive. This means that the company has more incentive to keep costs down than does a direct public producer. This is likely to result in more efficiency, but it also may result in reduced quality of output.

There are a variety of possibilities in between the government directly producing output itself and purchasing the output from the private sector. The government may use a variety of privately produced outputs in its production process or may be involved with the private sector in jointly producing an output. For example, many local governments have their own road maintenance facilities, but they may contract with the private sector to supplement their efforts at various times. Defense is provided by the government, but the production of the various systems used in the process is done largely through the private sector.

The rest of this chapter presents concepts and methods relevant to the production of the output distributed by government and its cost. We pay special attention to what has come to be known as "privatization" and we discuss some issues that arise when considering government production as compared to government distribution or allocation, as well as privatization.

/// PRODUCTION CONCEPTS AND METHODS OF ANALYSIS

It is important to have command of some key concepts and tools helpful in measuring and evaluating government output and in making production decisions.

Output

Output, which is the key to evaluating any production process, is more difficult to measure for services than it is for goods, and it is often more difficult to measure for government services than for private services. Goods can be defined by certain physical characteristics.[6] These characteristics can include both the features that define the good and others, which are usually considered as measures of "quality." The quality of a good would include its likely service life and other beneficial characteristics. Most of these characteristics can be described in a fair amount of detail so that someone other than the consumer could determine the level of each such characteristic. Services tend to have more intangible characteristics and are usually harder to evaluate than physical goods. In addition, the output of the service is likely to interact with the environment in which it is provided. Thus, fire protection is more difficult to provide to a building on an isolated hilltop than on a level area near a fire station.

Despite the difficulty in determining output, it is the concept on which we should focus in evaluating government production. Since this often cannot be

---

[6] Ibid., pp. 147–155.

measured we are forced to turn to other techniques. These techniques rely on using proxies, which can be weak on both the relationship between the proxy and the actual output and on the valuation of the output. For example, inputs are often used as a proxy for output, but if the production process is inefficient, this will overestimate the output. Also, the recipients of the output are not likely to turn it down as long as it has some positive value to them, but this may be much less than the value normally assigned to the output. For example, recipients of public housing may value it at much less than the rent for equivalent housing; but they accept it because they pay only a fraction of its cost. Thus, its true value to recipients may be very hard to determine.

Production Functions

Inputs are related to outputs by means of a production function, and for any given level of inputs, a particular level of output could be produced.[7] In the private sector it is common to relate the cost of inputs to the value of output. This is because competition tends to force those using the wrong combination of inputs or using their inputs inefficiently to change their actions or be driven out of business. The same pressures do not exist in the public sector; however, many people still equate the value of the inputs with the value of the output. This can be erroneous for several reasons. First, the inputs may not be used efficiently. Second, the combination of inputs may not be the most efficient for the output being produced. Third, the inputs may be receiving too high a price. For example, the government may be paying a wage that is too high for a particular type of labor. Using this wage as a measure of the value of the output produced would be a serious error.

Inputs also differ from outputs when service conditions differ. This is a frequent occurrence in the public sector. Further, the government manager is unlikely to have much control over the service conditions, which are likely to have a major impact on the output created. For example, fire departments are mandated by law to protect each person and structure in their area. Yet such areas may differ significantly in the ease with which such protection can be provided. A hilly area with low water pressure, poor access, and much dried brush could pose a significant challenge to a department. It would affect the perception of output. A department faced with these conditions might do a much better job than a nearby department in an area with modern subdivisions, yet the department with the easier conditions would appear to be providing better output by most measures.

Even when the relation between inputs and outputs could be measured effectively, changes in technology may leave a unit operating very inefficiently if it does not adapt to the new technology. Thus, a manager may appear to be doing an admirable job considering the service conditions, capital, and labor

---

[7] Ibid., pp. 155–159.

resources available, yet the overall effect may not be efficient production because there are better methods available. Failure to choose such methods would again make the relationship between input and output a poor method of measuring output.

When output measures are available, it is also possible to have some trade-off between the quantity and quality of output. Since quality is often much harder to measure than quantity, there is some incentive for managers to make sure that they meet their quantity objectives even if it means a significant shortfall in the quality dimension. This is particularly true when the quantity is specified by law but the quality is not.

Cost and Expenditure Functions

True social cost of a government project is determined by the opportunity cost of the resources used in the process. However, budget makers are concerned with what government spends on the project rather than the opportunity cost. Even here there are likely to be differences depending on the perspective taken. Some costs of local projects will be paid by higher levels of governments. These costs may not be counted by the local government. Similarly, some costs may be paid by local residents. Often these indirect costs will be left out of the calculations. For example, a new highway may be eligible for federal subsidies. These subsidies might not be counted as part of the cost at the local level. Further, the disruptions caused when construction takes place will create costs for local residents, which are unlikely to show up in any calculation relating to the project.

A true cost function is one that takes into account the quality of the output as well as the quantity. It is adjusted for the service conditions, factor prices, and costs imposed on others.[8] Because of the difficulties mentioned above, we almost never see a true cost function for government output. We are much more likely to be able to determine the expenditure function for government.

An expenditure function is a relationship between the expenditures of a government unit and various explanatory variables.[9] These variables are often a mix of true cost factors and demand factors since expenditure is determined by both. The problem with an expenditure function is that it is often difficult to sort out the effects of changes in cost factors and changes in demand factors. For example, the observation of a negative relationship between population and per-capita service expenditure is taken to imply the existence of economies of scale, and vice versa. The reasoning implicit in associating a negative relationship between population and per-capita expenditure with economies of scale is that population size is a good proxy for output. Such reasoning is clearly wrong, however, because the assumed proxy relationship is, for the most part, invalid. If scale economies related to city size

[8] Ibid., pp. 167–169.
[9] Ibid., pp. 172–174.

do exist, expenditures may well increase with output; this would indeed be the case whenever the elasticity of demand for services is greater than unity. Although expenditure determinant functions cannot be used to test hypotheses about economies of scale, they are quite useful for short-run expenditure projections.

Scale Economies, Consolidation, and Breakup

The issue of optimum size units is important to all three levels of government, but particularly important at the local level. Here the main concern has been whether the government provision of services would be more efficient if the government units were larger or smaller. A good example is the quest for metropolitan consolidation, which was on the front burner in the 1950s and 1960s. Today the issue more frequently is whether a particular urban government or school district may not be more efficient if broken into smaller units.

The basic issue in the size category is one of economies of scale in production coupled with fewer administrative units versus the diversity and responsiveness that smaller units bring. There is also the question of whether competition among government units producing the same good or service is desirable or not. Some argue that it keeps cost down as governments compete with each other to attract activity. Others argue that it requires much greater coordination among government units and this is costly and inefficient when they are fragmented.

The optimum size issue also pertains to federal and state departments. An example is concern about the size of the Defense Department, where a compromise solution has been adopted. Today we have separate Air Force, Army, and Navy secretaries, who for most purposes report to the Secretary of Defense.

/// RISING GOVERNMENT BUDGETS: REASONS

Table 14-1 testifies to the fact that expenditures by all levels of government have been increasing over time. Why? The level of service may be higher, the cost of providing a given level of service may be higher, or the amount of redistribution may have increased. Further, if the cost is higher, it may be higher because of changes in the circumstances of production, it may be higher because of higher costs of inputs, or it may be higher because of lower efficiency in production.

Another explanation is that the demand for government services has been increasing over time, which could occur if the demand for such services is income elastic and income has been rising. In fact, there is evidence that the overall demand for services *is* income elastic, i.e., people tend to spend a larger percentage of their money on services as their income rises. There is little reason to suspect that government services are treated differently from other services, and there is evidence that real income in the U.S. is rising over time, although there may be some disagreements about its rate of increase and its distribution.[10] Thus, one reason for government spending to increase is to provide for the larger amount of service that people demand.

For example, one author argues that a clean environment is a good with an income-elastic demand.[11] Hence, government is called upon to do more and more to clean the environment as income increases. In poor societies, raw sewage may be dumped in open rivers or streams. Burning coal may create killer fogs. In wealthier societies, such externalities are controlled by government expenditures and regulations. At the same time, advances in technology may create new types of externalities, such as toxic wastes. As government is asked to control more and more of the externalities created, the cost of government tends to increase. In addition, people want higher quality levels of the services, e.g., better schools, more rapid police response, more frequent collection and delivery of mail, and so on. If government responds, its costs rise.

Related to the income elasticity of demand argument is the argument that society will redistribute more as it becomes more wealthy. With increased redistribution, government expenditure for this purpose will also increase. There is some evidence that this has happened in the United States and other Western countries.

The demand for public services will also increase because of the host of interactions created by urbanization.[12] As people come together in urban areas, the externalities they create affect more and more people. Since many of these are negative externalities and need to be offset by government, demand for government activities tends to increase with urbanization. For example, as long as families lived on large farms, the use of septic tanks and the burning or burying of trash had little impact on others. However, when someone in an urban environment does this, it affects others. As the population increases more people are affected, and the absorptive capacity of the environment is further strained. These negative interactive effects are likely to increase much more than proportionately with population. Similarly, the cost of providing such services may increase more than proportionately with population. For example, it may be necessary to transport water from greater distances and sewage is likely to need more treatment to prevent the greater volume from exceeding the absorptive capacity of waterways.

Offsetting part of the costs of greater density can be some real reductions in the cost of providing certain services because of economies of scale. For

[10] ACIR, op. cit., p. 25.
[11] Larry E. Ruff, "The Economic Common Sense of Pollution," *The Public Interest* 19 (Spring 1970), pp. 69–85; reprinted in Edwin Mansfield, *Microeconomics: Selected Readings*, 3rd ed. (New York: W. W. Norton, 1979).
[12] A number of the arguments in the next few pages can be traced to William J. Baumol, "The Macroeconomics of Unbalanced Growth: The Anatomy of Urban Crisis," *American Economic Review* 57 (June 1967), pp. 415–426.

example, a local government may decide to open a community museum or zoo after the population has reached a certain size. Both the reduced costs of some services and the greater requirement for others are likely to lead to increases in the amount of government spending as the population urbanizes.

A further consideration is productivity. Increasing productivity in the private sector may cause the cost of government output to rise relative to the cost of private output if the government does not maintain the same rate of productivity improvement. The cost of inputs could rise in the private sector over time and output price could still decline if the productivity improvement allowed more output to be produced by a given level of inputs. If real wages are rising over time because of increases in output per worker throughout the economy, they will rise at approximately the same rate in all sectors. However, if the government does not have the same rate of productivity increase, the higher wages are passed through as a higher cost per unit of output (see Box 14-1).

Government services do not show major productivity improvement over time.[13] To the extent that there are productivity increases in the private sector, the cost of government services relative to the cost of other goods and services would be expected to rise over time. This could lead to either an increase or a decrease in expenditure depending on how people react to the higher cost. The normal reaction to a higher price is to consume a smaller quantity. Thus, as the price of government goods and services rises relative to the cost of private goods and services, there should be some substitution effect toward the private goods and services. If the substitution is small, the total expenditure will still increase. The higher price will more than offset the lower quantity in terms of expenditure. Only if the reduction in quantity is large relative to the price increase will total expenditure on the government goods and services actually decline. Essentially, if the demand for the goods and services provided by government is elastic, the expenditure will decrease. If the demand is inelastic, and as was argued earlier this appears to be the case, the expenditure will increase. Hence, a rise in the cost of the inputs shows up as higher expenditure.

Despite the various complaints about rising government expenditures, only two of the above factors warrant concern about the trend—the relatively small productivity improvement in the public sector and the rise in wages.

Government Productivity

Several arguments exist about why government production tends to show relatively minor increases in productivity. For example, government provides goods and services that are inherently unsuited for productivity improve-

---

[13] Charles R. Hulten and James W. Robertson, "Labor Productivity in the Local Public Sector" in Werner Z. Hirsch and Anthony M. Rufolo, eds., *The Economics of Municipal Labor Markets*, Monograph and Research Series 33 (Los Angeles, CA: Institute of Industrial Relations, University of California, 1983).

Box 14-1

////// Productivity and Cost

In a very influential article,* William Baumol argued that economic growth will almost necessarily increase the cost of some goods and services relative to others. His argument is associated with the relative rates of productivity improvement in different sectors of the economy. Suppose that we want to compare two segments of the economy. In one section, the rate of productivity improvement is very high, while in the other there is no improvement in productivity. Finally, to keep the analysis very simple, assume that the price of output is simply wage divided by output per worker. In Table 1 we see that the output per worker and price of output are the same for each industry in the first time period. However, in the second time period output per worker has doubled in industry B and so have wages in both industries.

The wages in both industries must be the same in a competitive economy. Otherwise, either workers would be unwilling to work for the lower paying sector or the higher pay-

ing sector would not be hiring workers for the lowest wage they could pay. The effect of the equal wages and the unequal increases in productivity are unequal prices in period 2. In the example, the price of output in industry A has doubled. Thus, the cost of a given amount of output in industry A has also doubled. Note, however, that since wages have doubled, the people in this society can afford to buy more of both goods even with the higher cost of the first one. Thus, it is possible to have one sector absorb a larger and larger proportion of the economy's resources over time and still have the standard of living in that economy increasing over time. The choice of output depends on the preferences of the consumers. It is possible for the output of industry A to increase if the income elasticity of demand is high enough. However, the most likely outcome is for a reduction in output in this industry but an increase in total expenditure.

* Baumol, op. cit.

Table 1 /

	Industry	Output per Worker	Wage	Price
Period 1	A	20	10	0.50
	B	20	10	0.50
Period 2	A	20	20	1.00
	B	40	20	0.50

ments. Most of the services provided by government are labor intensive. Because of this, there may be relatively little room for use of capital to improve productivity. Thus, teachers, police, and firefighters can be aided by improvements in technology, but the basic service requires that one or more people be available to provide the service. Further, having one person serve more people is almost always equivalent to a reduction in service. Hence, it is argued that low rates of productivity improvement are not a result of any inefficiency on the part of government or its workers.

There are a number of reasons to fault the above conclusion. The first is that even if there is no increase in productivity over time, there may still be inefficiency in the way a good or service is provided. The second is that there *are* ways for government to improve productivity. For example, many of the services provided in the private sector show productivity improvements over time, far in excess of those for government. This is supported by a number of studies which find, for example, that private sector providers tend to innovate more readily and tend to have lower costs than public sector providers of the same good or service.

One reason government tends to be slow to innovate is that there appears to be little incentive for managers in the public sector to take risks. Ideally, in a private firm a change will be made if the benefits from an increase in productivity are likely to compensate, on average, for the situations in which a change is costly. Private managers are likely to be more generously rewarded for taking the risks than are public managers. In fact, it is sometimes argued that the public sector manager is likely to be penalized for successful improvements in productivity. This is because the salary of many public sector managers is determined by the size of their departments. If they find a way to reduce the number of workers needed to produce a given output, there is likely to be a reduction in the work force, which may then lead to a reduction in salary for the successful manager. Alternatively, someone who does not improve productivity but manages to get additional workers may see a rise in pay. For example, at one time postmasters' salaries were determined by a formula that included the number of workers and trucks.[14] Thus, a postmaster who managed to get the mailed delivered with fewer people or trucks would be likely to see a reduction in salary as a reward.

A related issue is the reward to workers in the public sector for their productivity. Most government agencies have some form of civil service system. Under such a system, workers tend to be rewarded for their seniority on the job rather than their performance, and it may be extremely difficult to fire unproductive public sector workers. The original intent of civil service was to isolate the provision of services from politics. Winning politicians used to reward their followers by giving them public sector jobs. If necessary, other workers were fired to create the vacancies. The use of civil service prevents this

---

[14] For example, see Charles Wolf, Jr., "A Theory of Non-Market Failures," *The Public Interest* (Spring 1979), pp. 114–133.

type of abuse. Yet many argue that the protection is too strong and prevents the firing of incompetent workers.[15] Further, if salary increases and promotions occur on the basis of seniority, there is little incentive for workers to exert themselves. Even dedicated workers could become indifferent about their jobs if they see fellow workers doing little but getting the same raises and promotions.

The separation between production and compensation is likely to be much greater in the public sector. The difficulty in even measuring the output of a public agency makes it hard to determine how valuable the output is or how each worker contributes to the total production process. There is no feedback from profits or other forms of competitive pressure. In addition, the manager in the public agency often has no real incentive to evaluate his or her workers. If an employee gets a bad evaluation, working relations may be strained with little chance that the employee will be fired. It is only when the reward for the job is closely tied to the effort of the employee that there is an incentive for the employee to exert the appropriate amount of effort.[16] However, the nature of the output and incentives make this much less likely to happen in the public sector.

Government Wages and Salaries

In recent years the public sector has appeared to pay wages that are high relative to the equivalent private sector wage. In the past, employment in the public sector was often viewed as very safe but with little monetary reward. The safety factor is now lower than in the past but the level of compensation is higher.

Wages alone are not always a good way to make comparisons between workers doing the same job; it is often difficult to determine if jobs really are the same. Items that should be considered in addition to wages are fringe benefits, job security, and opportunities for advancement.

Studies of public sector workers conclude that they are generally paid more than equivalent private sector workers if you look at the lower paid part of the spectrum.[17] While the value of the fringe benefits in the public sector is usually greater than it is in the private sector, opportunities for advancement seem to be more limited in the public sector. At the higher paying management positions, the public sector seems to pay less than the private sector.

---

[15] Georgina Fiordalisi, "Incompetent Instructors Costly to Fire," *City and State* (December 1986), pp. 2 and 48, reports that it costs an average of $56,000 to fire an incompetent teacher with tenure in New York City. Other jurisdictions may not find it quite as expensive, but it is usually costly. In addition, given the high cost, only the most blatant cases are likely to be addressed.

[16] For a more detailed discussion see Werner Z. Hirsch and Anthony M. Rufolo, "Monitoring Costs and Labor Productivity in Municipal Labor Markets" in M. B. Ballabon, ed., *Economic Perspectives*, vol. 2 (New York: Harwood Academic Press, 1981).

[17] Werner Z. Hirsch and Anthony M. Rufolo, "Determinants of Municipal Wages: Some Tests of the Competitive Wage Hypothesis" in J. V. Henderson, ed., *Reserach in Urban Economics*, vol. 2 (New York: JAI Press, 1982).

However, once the characteristics of the worker are taken into account, the differences are either less notable or may actually reverse.

In general, workers with more skills or training are more productive than similar workers with less skill or training. Education and years of work experience are the most typical measures of training. When these factors are taken into account, the wages in the public sector do not seem as high. This is because the worker in the public sector appears to have more education and/or years of job training than the equivalent private sector worker.

Whether public sector wages are higher than necessary to attract workers of appropriate qualifications is a debatable point. There are examples of positions that pay more than is necessary to get qualified workers. This is obvious from the long lists of qualified applicants for many positions.[18] However, this is not evidence of consistently high wages unless it is found for large numbers of positions; and it is not evidence of high wages in most government employment unless it is found in most government employment. It does raise the question of how such wages might exist.

Since the demand for the output of government tends to be somewhat inelastic and there appear to be limited possibilities of substituting capital for labor in production, high wages are not likely to have much impact on total employment. Hence, if public sector workers do succeed in getting higher wages, they are unlikely to face the loss in jobs that often occurs in the private sector. Further, workers do not have to worry about some other producer offering the same goods or services for a lower price. The government is a monopolist for most services it produces. Hence, it is certainly possible that wages are higher than would be set in competitive markets.

The most compelling evidence that workers in the public sector tend to receive wages that are higher than market wages comes from comparison studies of public and private production. These studies tend to find both higher cost and higher wages in the public sector.[19] It is these higher costs that create the incentives for government to contract with the private sector for production. However, public sector workers frequently oppose such moves because they anticipate that it will lead to a reduction in both wages and job security. Thus, it is useful to know exactly what benefits and problems are likely to arise with contracting out or privatization of public production.

The combination of a high income elasticity of demand for government services, a low price elasticity of demand, low productivity growth, rising wages, and the effects of increased urbanization all work to increase the share

[18] For example, in 1984 6,118 people signed up to take an examination to qualify for a machine clerk job with the U.S. Postal Service, down from the 18,000 applications in the prior examination, even though there were expectations of only 150 to 200 openings over the next three years. People were even reported to have taken tutoring courses for the exam. Phil Manzano, "6118 Sign Up to Take Postal Test," *Oregonian* (May 12, 1984), p. C1.

[19] For example, see Daniel S. Hamermesh, "The Effect of Government Ownership on Union Wages" in Daniel S. Hamermesh, ed., *Labor in the Public and Nonprofit Sectors* (Princeton, NJ: Princeton University Press, 1975).

of GNP that goes to government. In addition, as incomes rise, there appears to be some tendency to increase the amount of income redistribution that the government does. This too shows up as an increase in government expenditure.

/// RISING GOVERNMENT BUDGETS: REMEDIES

In the preceding pages, we pointed to a tendency of government to achieve relatively small productivity increases while wages appear to increase more than those in the private sector. When these conditions exist or are perceived to exist, it is easy to see why there emerge advocates of the privatization of select government activities. Ronald Moe has even suggested that "when administrative historians some years hence will study the 1980s, they are likely to conclude that 'privatization' was the single most influential concept of the decade."[20]

Privatization can take two major forms: (1) permanent transfer, i.e., sale of government-owned assets to private owners, or (2) temporary transfer of rights and obligations to private firms for the delivery of goods and services formerly carried out by governments themselves. Most common under the second heading is contracting out, although there is also the possibility of leasing government assets or government providing private service firms with franchises.

In recent years, quite a few industrial countries have sold government assets (in part or in total) to private firms. Examples are the sale of publicly owned British Telecommunication and Jaguar in the United Kingdom and of the publicly owned National Railroad and Nippon Telegraph and Telephone in Japan.

Supporters of private ownership of such industries argue that the private sector is better able to allocate resources efficiently; that there is nothing wrong with such industries making profits, as merely the return to ordinary investment; and that where the public sector will find it difficult to close inefficient operations, private firms can do so more easily. They point to nationalized industries in such countries as Great Britain and France, which historically have incurred large wage increases and many work stoppages. Organized labor has looked on government as "deep pockets," and forced government to provide significant subsidies to the nationalized industries. This not only has been very costly to government, but also has led to rigid work rules, distorted prices, and other inefficiencies. Advocates of private ownership expect public enterprises to be inefficient and argue that government enterprises are no more immune from the corrupting influences of power than are private ones.

We next turn to privatization in the form of contracting out, i.e., the

---

[20] Ronald Moe, "Exploring the Limits of Privatization," *Public Administration Review* (November/December 1987), p. 453.

signing of contracts from governments for private firms to deliver specified services during an agreed period. Examples in the United States range from contracts from the Department of Defense to the Northrop Corporation to build a specified number of stealth bombers to contracts from Los Angeles County to a private firm to perform data processing functions. Los Angeles County, for example, as of March 1986 had signed 175 contracts amounting to $47 million on an annualized basis.[21] Production of the same services by county employees were estimated to have cost $70 million, so contracting generated a savings of about 33%.

A study by Borcherding, et al. reviewed fifty empirical studies of cost reductions by contracting out, surveying nineteen different services by governments in the United States, West Germany, Switzerland, Australia, and Canada.[22] In forty of the fifty case studies private supply was less costly than government supply services. In only three cases (electric utilities, veterans' hospitals, and garbage collection) private firms were more costly than public ones. Furthermore, a study by Stevens (see Box 14-2) found that public production usually was more costly than private production.[23]

While these figures are impressive and the reported cost reductions are substantial, at least two qualifications should be considered. First, we must remember that government, even if totally committed to privatization, only contracts out when bids with costs lower than government's have been obtained. Second, contracting out amounts to a very small percentage of the government's budget. For example, the annual budget of Los Angeles County in 1986 was about $7 billion, most of it not involving transfer payments and therefore, in theory, eligible for contracting. Yet, in this multibillion dollar budget, services that were contracted out amounted to a mere $47 million (or would have amounted to $70 million if produced in house). Thus a county which, for the last six years, has had a government totally committed to contracting out, succeeded in doing so for only 2% of its budget.[24] Third, lower cost can result from paying exploitative wages, as is done in the case of undocumented aliens.

Efficiency

Efficiency concerns clearly dominate the argument that contracting out can be an antidote to ever rising government expenditures.[25] Efficiency consid-

---

[21] James C. Hankla, *Report on Board Awarded Privatization Contracts* (Los Angeles, CA: Chief Administrative Offices of Los Angeles County, May 2, 1986), p. 3.

[22] Thomas E. Borcherding, et al., *Comparing the Efficiency of Private and Public Production: The Evidence from Five Countries* (Zurich: Institute for Empirical Research in Economics, University of Zurich, 1982).

[23] Barbara J. Stevens, "Delivering Municipal Services Efficiently: A Comparison of Municipal and Private Service Delivery," U.S. Department of Housing and Urban Development, HUD-0003744 (June 1984).

[24] In some instances not a single lower cost bidder could be found, as in the case of efforts to contract out for the repair and maintenance of the county's fleet of cars, trucks, and buses.

[25] Werner Z. Hirsch, *Production by Government vs. Contracting Out to Private Firms* (Paris: 43rd Congress of the International Institute of Public Finance, August 24–28, 1988, mimeographed); and Werner Z. Hirsch and Robert Harding, *Contracting Out: A Literature Review*, Working Paper no. 446 (Los Angeles, CA: Department of Economics, University of California, 1987).

Box 14-2

////// Municipal versus Private Production

The issues of the relative cost of government versus private production of goods and services is sufficiently important that the federal government funded a study of it.* The findings of this study are informative.

The objective was to find if the private sector could provide the same quality of service as the public sector but at lower cost. The comparison was done over eight services: street cleaning, janitorial services, residential refuse collection, payroll, traffic signal maintenance, asphalt overlay construction, turf maintenance, and street tree maintenance. Clearly, the scope of the study is not as wide as might be desired, but a larger scope is precluded by lack of data on private production of many services. Further, it is easier to control for possible differences in output if the service is relatively straightforward.

The general findings were that the municipal service delivery is on average significantly more costly than the private contractor service delivery. For seven of the eight services, the study found municipal provision to be between 37% and 96% more costly. Only for one service, pay-

roll, did they find little difference in average cost. These differences were not caused by differences in the quality of service provided or in wages. Rather, they appear to be caused by differences in the use of labor and capital.

Private sector contractors required the workers to work more for their salaries. They were less liberal with vacation and other leave. In addition, they tended to use the least qualified workers who were able to do the job and they used relatively more part-time labor. The mangers of the service department were more likely to be directly responsible for capital equipment, and the production process was less labor intensive. This was in contrast to the public sector, where capital equipment was more likely to be the responsibility of some central equipment department.

The study does indicate that some of the municipal producers were as efficient as the private producers, but that the averages were clearly in favor of the private producers in terms of cost.

* Stevens, op. cit.

erations encompass both incentives to minimize costs and institutional constraints on the public sector production process.

The incentive issue relates to the degree to which producers are pushed toward a purely competitive output and pricing structure. Private sector firms seek profits, and the degree to which their pricing and output levels approach purely competitive ones depends on the market structure. Although firms with significant monopoly power tend to earn substantial profits by restricting output to suboptimal levels, firms in highly competitive markets tend to have output and pricing structures that approach socially optimal levels.

In addition to the structure of output markets, the composition of input markets confronting producers, particularly the labor market, affects firms' pricing and production decisions. The existence of unions, for example, can increase costs and thus prices. Conversely, if there is an abundance of labor of a certain skill level, wages may be low. Consequently, private sector firms may be able to produce at lower costs, even with the same production technology. In this case, the lower private sector costs would not reflect a more efficient use of resources but rather a lower wage structure, which may or may not be socially desirable.

Hypothetically, public sector producers should be driven toward an efficient production process regardless of the market structure, since taxpayers want to minimize tax liabilities for any given level of service provision. In reality, elected officials' political considerations can prevent government producers from acting in a socially optimal manner. Yet the market can provide incentives to drive public sector producers toward the least-cost method of production. When an agency does not have exclusive rights to provide services in its jurisdiction and the government is likely to consider contracting out in the future, managers are likely to have an incentive to minimize costs. Without the presence or at least the threat of competition, managers do not have to worry about being "put out of business." Under these circumstances, managers have little incentive to innovate or generally minimize costs. Instead, government managers not closely constrained by the performance of their operations may pursue objectives incompatible with efficient production. This pursuance of "internal objectives" is thought to be a major problem in the public sector.[26] Government managers are often thought to maximize expenditures or staff employment; consequently, they may seek to rationalize costs instead of minimizing them.

In this vein, Courant, et al. have argued that municipal employees seek not only to raise public sector wages but also to increase the demand for public sector services.[27] In their public sector model, municipal employees seek to increase both wages and employment. As the number of municipal workers increases, their political influence rises and they are more successful in attaining their objectives. However, municipal employees are restrained by the fear that unduly burdened taxpayers will vote with their feet, thereby reducing the tax base and the demand for public services. Therefore, "the

[26] Charles Wolf, Jr., *Markets or Governments: Choosing Between Imperfect Alternatives*, N-2505 SF (Santa Monica, CA: RAND Corporation, 1986).
[27] Paul N. Courant, et al., "Public Employee Market Power and Level of Government Spending," *American Economic Review* 69 (December 1979), pp. 806–817.

ability of public employees to convert their power into high wages will be attenuated both by the mobility of the private sector and by the simple arithmetic of 'dividing up the pie.'"[28]

The ability of municipal employees to influence wage and employment levels is limited even further if they must compete against other public and/or private sector producers. Actual competitive bidding need not occur; the mere threat that the service may be contracted out, should productivity remain low, may suffice. This threat tends to be particularly persuasive if a government has already experimented successfully with contracting out services.

In general, the lack of competition rather than the inherent nature of the public sector probably bears the main responsibility for the greater efficiency in the private sector, although as we discuss below, rigidities associated with the public sector may also decrease its efficiency.[29]

Finally, we turn to the incentive for technical change in the production process. The incentive to innovate tends to increase as more firms compete to provide the service; and the more freedom firms enjoy in determining their own production technologies, the more creative they will tend to be. Clearly there exists a direct trade-off between efficiency and accountability, an issue we take up below; but as long as firms are monitored such freedom is important in order to provide services more efficiently. Since public sector producers tend to have a more rigid hierarchical structure, especially in the absence of competition, the decision not to permit competition will probably reduce the potential for technological improvements over the long term.[30]

Besides incentive-related problems, at least three institutional arrangements may constrain public sector managers from utilizing efficient production technologies: scale, constraints on raising capital, and labor relations.

The scale of public firms is not determined by economic criteria, but rather by the size of the municipality. Therefore, it is unlikely that government enterprises are optimal in size unless the industry in question is characterized by constant returns to scale. In many instances, municipalities are either too small to reap the advantages of scale economies, or are so large as to be confronted with scale diseconomies. In both cases, private firms may have a competitive advantage over public enterprises, since they have the flexibility to adopt a size that is favorable under existing production technologies. The magnitude of the advantage to private firms varies depending on the shape of the cost function and the difference between optimal scale and size of munici-

---

[28] Ibid., p. 816.

[29] This view is consistent with the findings of a study of the Canadian railroad system, which concluded that "public ownership is not inherently less efficient than private ownership—that the oft-noted inefficiency of government enterprises stems from their isolation from effective competition rather than their public ownership per se." Douglas W. Caves and Laurits R. Christensen, "The Relative Efficiency of Public and Private Firms in a Competitive Environment: The Case of Canadian Railroads," *Journal of Political Economy* 88 (October 1980), pp. 958–976.

[30] Harvey C. Mansfield, "Independence and Accountability for Federal Contractors and Grantees," in Bruce Smith ed., *The New Political Economy* (London: Macmillan, 1975), pp. 319–335.

pality. If the cost function is sharply U-shaped, efficiency losses to the government may be significant.

Restritcions on borrowing for capital investments are a second set of institutional constraints facing municipal governments. Many states have laws requiring that major capital expenditures be approved directly by a referendum. In addition, a municipality with weak financial conditions faces high capital costs when seeking financing. These difficulties in raising capital force municipalities to use fewer capital-intensive production technologies than they otherwise would. Consesquently, they produce less efficiently in the long run.

Public sector labor relations probably constitute the most important institutional issue for efficiency. Civil service provisions based on the merit principle provide guidelines intended to compensate and promote workers according to their productive contributions rather than political, racial, or other noneconomic factors. Yet in securing equal treatment for all workers, these guidelines are often too rigid and unyielding to allow management the flexibility necessary to produce most efficiently. Over the years, the positive aspects of civil service provisions have been overshadowed by abuses and rigidities, so that today these provisions may be counterproductive.

In relation to cost comparisons, we would like to make one further point. If everything else is equal, the government is going to find that its own direct cost of production is lower than the price that it can receive from a private firm. This is because of taxes. A private firm must make some profit to stay in business, even if this profit is simply the return to equity investment. The firm may pay federal and possibly state or local corporate income taxes. In addition, all firms pay local property taxes. Furthermore, a public agency that borrows to finance capital equipment can borrow at a low rate because its interest payments are tax exempt to the recipient. A private firm must pay the higher rate associated with taxable interest. Thus, the dollar outlay should be lower for the same service if produced directly. Other types of tax considerations also may enter into the calculation, depending on the level of government. If the federal government leases part of a building from a private firm, that private firm must pay property taxes on the building. Presumably, that cost is passed on to the federal government in the rent charged. However, if the federal government owns the building directly, it is exempt from local property taxes. A number of other types of taxes and tax exemptions can affect the relative costs of doing business. While these are really just transfers from one government unit to another, taxes do enter into the cost as perceived by the paying government.

Accountability

It would be a serious mistake, however, to make a decision to contract out based entirely on efficiency considerations, even though they are likely to dominate the decision. A second consideration relates to the quality of the output produced. A variety of government services have characteristics that society values highly and/or deems crucial; legislating, judging, and providing personal and national security are examples. Assuring that society receives the desired and agreed-upon output characteristics of these activities involves very high transaction costs and resources. This issue can be discussed under the heading of accountability. We must worry whether government can meet its accountability obligation better, and in extreme cases at all, if it is not directly responsible for the production and delivery of a specific service. When accountability is important, contracting out tends to involve significantly higher transaction costs than does government in-house production. When a service, such as the protection of the civil rights of minorities, involves major difficulties in measuring output and/or performance, it is costly to carry out the accountability task.

Distributional Aspects

In addition to efficiency and accountability, contracting out also has distributional implications, which tend to be highly complex. There are two distributionary aspects of the choice between public and private service provision: allocation of output and distribution of revenue generated from service provision.

As to the distribution of services among constituent groups, government in some instances has a compelling stake in making sure that a "proper" distribution indeed takes place. This responsibility looms larger for some goods and services than for others. When meeting this responsibility is difficult and yet deemed crucial, government might prove to have advantages over private firms.

Turning to how total costs of in-house government compared to contracted production is distributed, there are two major concerns: the share of revenue between labor and owners of capital, and the fact that public enterprises do not pay taxes. If, for example, private firms have significant monopoly power, they are likely to earn substantial profits from government contracts while paying competitive wages. On the other hand, if government production faces no competition, bureaucratic prerogatives are likely to emerge and public employees may not be paid according to their productivity levels. Workers with political connections may end up with secure jobs at inflated wages. This outcome is reinforced, as public sector unions are stronger than their private counterparts.

We now turn to taxes, which are paid by private but not public firms. Since taxes, particularly on the local level, are payment for services, e.g., police and fire protection, public enterprises are subsidized while private firms are not. The nature of the subsidy is not easy to estimate, since private firms pay a variety of different taxes to a variety of governments, some of which are nearby while others are far removed.

In summary, contracting out, though often invoked as a remedy to alleged inefficient governments and rising public expenditures, is not necessarily always more efficient;[31] and if it is, it may not assure constituents that appropriate quality levels are attained. Moreover, the distributional implications of moving from public to private production must be taken into consideration. This evaluation is affected by value judgments and politics.

/// SUMMARY

Government produces a large amount of output in almost every country in the world. In the U.S. most of this output is associated with the provision of goods and services. It is possible to evaluate this output in different ways. It might be distributed according to people's perceived need, according to how much they contributed to the public revenues, or some other criteria. It is also difficult to evaluate government activity and output for a variety of reasons. These include differences in the conditions under which services are provided and difficulty in measuring the output.

There is much evidence that government expenditures have been increasing rapidly over time. A variety of reasons have been offered to explain this phenomenon together with select remedies. The emphasis has been on privatization, particularly in the form of contracting out. It has been argued that the determination of the advantages of contracting out over in-house government production requires an analysis of efficiency, accountability, and distributional implications of shifting from one mode to another. Although there are limits on the benefits of such contracting and its scope, the current trend is toward more contracting of services by government, and the evidence is that in many cases it does indeed produce lower cost and better service.

---

[31] For a review of the case for and against privatization, see Steve H. Hanke, ed., *Prospects for Privatization*, Proceedings of the Academy of Political Science, vol. 36 (1987).

Chapter 15   //////

Budget Concepts

Government intervenes in the economy in a variety of ways. First, it sets the rules by which the economy operates. By specifying rights and obligations for different individuals under different circumstances, the government largely determines what type of economy a country will have. Second, government collects revenue from its citizens; we have seen that the manner of collection as well as the amount of revenue collected affects economic activity. Third, government owns and manages resources; its decisions on how to use such resources and whether to add to or sell off its assets affect the economy. Fourth, government gives money, goods, and services to some of its citizens to change the distribution of income. Finally, government provides certain goods and services directly to its citizens. These may be goods or services that would not have been provided by the private sector, or the level or distribution of such goods or services may have been considered undesirable. We are not going to spend much time on the first issue and we have already covered the second in some detail. So now we turn to the analysis of government expenditure.

Government units operate by spending money. The decisions about how much to spend and how to spend it have important effects on the economy. Just as taxes may not have the impact that a superficial analysis would indicate, so too expenditures may have indirect or hidden effects. Because government spends so much money, it is important to evaluate both how desirable its spending is and how effective that spending is in achieving its goals.

People respond to incentives from government expenditures in much the same way that they respond to the incentives from the tax system. Expenditures create direct benefits by providing goods and services or by providing a transfer of money. People are likely to expend resources in trying to gain part of what government is spending or giving away. This has an impact on the economy as people try to become eligible for the money, or try to direct where or how it will be spent. Thus, a giveaway may induce many people to wait in line for long periods to get a share, or a lucrative government grant or contract may induce people to spend large amounts of time and money lobbying to get the grant or contract. From the economic perspective, such waiting or lobbying is a loss of valuable resources.[1] Each minute spent in line cannot be spent doing something else. Similarly, resources devoted to lobbying cannot be used for other purposes. Other activities designed to get a share of the government's expenditure may also create inefficiencies in the economy. When the government is the primary distributor of output, it makes sense to devote time and resources to getting it to give more. However, this is not a productive activity and it reduces the net output available in the economy.

Government expenditure also creates a movement of economic activity in response to the expenditure. Thus, a military base or other federal project creates much activity in its area. The spillover of this activity may be important for the economic well-being of many people. At the local level, the opening of a new school may cause significant new residential development in the area served, or the closing of an old school may accelerate the conversion from residential to other land uses. In other cases, people may refuse jobs to retain their eligiblity for transfer benefits; or they may consume relatively large amounts of some good or service because "the government is paying for it." Other effects may be fairly indirect. For example, the construction of the interstate highway system is credited with at least facilitating the decentralization of population that has harmed many of the older central cities. Thus, it is important to analyze the impact, both direct and indirect, of government expenditure on the economy.[2]

The methods by which the government plans its expenditures are associated with budgeting. One aspect of budgeting is to analyze each type of government expenditure in isolation to determine its value and its cost. These types of analyses can take a variety of forms. One form is the program budget or cost-benefit analysis, an attempt to determine whether the program or project generates economic benefits in excess of its economic costs. Economists place great emphasis on cost-benefit analysis, but the goals of many programs are not related to economic efficiency. Economic analysis can still be useful in such situations to determine if a program is likely to be successful in achieving its stated goals. For example, many economists have been skeptical of the public housing program because they believe that public housing displaces low-income private housing, which otherwise would have been made available. The analysis of such programs highlights the important issues in determining their effectiveness; we turn to some of these issues later in the chapter.

---

[1] See Yoram Barzel, "A Theory of Rationing by Waiting," *Journal of Law and Economics* (April 1974), pp. 73–95; reprinted in William Breit, et al., *Readings in Microeconomics* (St. Louis: Times Mirror/Mosby, 1986), pp. 218–231.

[2] The impact of the federal government on urban areas became such a large issue under the Carter Administration that the federal government began doing Urban Impact Analyses for many activities. See Norman J. Glickman, ed., *The Urban Impact of Federal Policies* (Baltimore: Johns Hopkins University Press, 1980).

However, the first item to study in determining the impact of government expenditure on the economy is the budget.

/// BUDGET CATEGORIES

It is only when a program gets through the budget process that it will actually be implemented. The budget process itself is an opportunity for the use of expenditure for purposes other than the provision of goods and services. For example, a congressional representative may arrange to have a particular item purchased from within his or her district. This may be viewed as a benefit to that representative's constituents; but it is likely to mean that the total cost will be higher than if the item were purchased from a low-cost producer.

The budget is the means by which a government unit specifies where it will get its revenue and how it will spend the money. A budget usually covers a fiscal year. For example, the federal government uses a fiscal year that starts on October 1 and ends the following September 30. Most state and local governments use one that starts on July 1 and ends the following June 30. A number of other starting and ending times are used and some states operate on a biennial budget. The budget is named for the year in which it ends; thus, the federal budget for fiscal 1990 ends on September 30, 1990. All prospective revenues are specified as are all anticipated expenditures. Because the anticipated revenues and expenditures may differ from those that actually occur, the budget can serve both as a planning document and as a means of monitoring status during the budget period. It is also possible that the final budget figures will differ substantially from those used during budget planning.

Capital Budget

There are a number of ways to consider budgets and a number of functions that they serve. For example, a capital budget is concerned with expenditures for long-lived assets. Clearly, there is a different effect when a government spends $10 million to buy a new building than when it spends $10 million on labor costs. The building will continue to provide services for a long time while the services provided by the labor are provided in the current time period. Thus, it makes sense that the capital expenditure should be paid for partly by future citizens rather than totally by current citizens. Most governments make distinctions in practice between capital expenditures and current expenditures, but this does not always show up in budget documents. Those that do use the capital budget often use some form of borrowing to finance capital expenditures and then use taxes levied over the expected useful life of the item to pay off the bonds. This is typical at the local level but it is less common at the state level and virtually nonexistent at the federal level.

A number of people have asserted that the federal government should use a capital budget in determining its true deficit position.[3] For example, they believe that many of the expenditures of the federal government are for capital items, and if we exclude the building up of capital, we overstate the extent of the budget deficit. This is only partly correct. If we recognize the existence of a capital stock, we would also have to recognize deterioration of capital as part of the analysis of the capital budget. Each year part of the existing stock deteriorates. This depreciation must be offset by some gross investment in order to have the same amount of capital stock at the end of the year that existed at the beginning. The real problem with a capital budget at the federal level is making estimates of the amount of deterioration.

If we look only at gross investment by the public sector, the evidence is that the level of investment has started to decline. This means that the gross additions to the capital stock each year are less than they have been in the past.[4] Further, the estimates by the federal government of the public capital stock show that it seems to have either stopped growing or started to decline. This is not necessarily bad, although many view the trend with alarm. For example, if local governments are closing down unneeded schools or the federal government has stopped investing in wasteful dams, the reduction in capital stock may be beneficial. However, if the reduction in stock represents roads and buildings that are wearing out or water systems on the verge of collapse, then the reduction may be a serious matter.

There can be no doubt that some forms of capital stock have been allowed to deteriorate in response to short-run budget pressures. Local governments faced with budget pressure frequently look first to capital items and then to maintenance in attempting to balance the budget. In a certain sense these savings represent false economies; but the savings are usually viewed as better than the alternatives by hard-pressed city officials. Some indications of the effect of the neglect can be determined by looking at some results. In 1973 a truck fell through an overpass on the Westside Highway in New York. More recently, a number of bridges have collapsed. *Newsweek* made the deteriorating public capital stock in the United States its cover story in one issue.[5] It is not hard to find other tales of deterioration, lack of maintenance, or new capital "requirements." Many of these items reflect local deterioration rather than a national problem; there is clearly a difference among various areas in how much decline has occurred in the capital stock.

At the federal level, there has been an attempt to sell off assets to reduce the deficit. This does not in fact reduce the operating deficit, but it does reduce

---

[3] There are also issues with respect to inflation and its effect on the real value of the deficit. For a discussion of these issues see Robert Eisner and Paul J. Pieper, "A New View of the Federal Debt and Budget Deficits," *American Economic Review* 74 (March 1984), pp. 11–29; also see Edward M. Gramlich, "How Bad Are the Large Deficits?" and the comments by discussants in Gregory B. Mills and John L. Palmer, eds., *Federal Budget Policy in the 1980s* (Washington, DC: Urban Institute Press, 1984), pp. 43–78.

[4] Advisory Commission on Intergovernmental Relations, *Financing Public Physical Infrastructure* (Washington, DC: 1984), p. 8. See also U.S. Office of Management and Budget, *Special Analyses: Budget of the United States Government, Fiscal Year 1989*, Section D and especially the chart on p. D-12.

[5] *Newsweek* (August 2, 1982).

the need to borrow through the use of bonds. Virtually all analysts agree that selling assets or allowing them to deteriorate does not in fact solve any deficit problems, but it is a widely used procedure by many government units. Thus, if a true capital budget is to be used, there must be some way to take this deterioration or sale of assets into account. It would be a serious error to credit all capital formation as being "costless" in terms of the money spent. About the only way in which this can be accomplished is to use the bond financing method of local governments. Here the borrowing is not treated as a current cost, but both the principal and interest payments needed in the future are treated as costs. Thus, the bonds actually end up being paid off as the asset wears out. If the bonds are simply refinanced, as the federal government does, we cannot realistically separate capital expenses from current expenses.

Trust Funds

Another budget distinction is often made between trust fund items and general budget items. A trust fund represents money collected for a specific purpose and then set aside until needed for that purpose. For example, the federal government collects money from gasoline taxes and related sources and places the money into a fund for road building, road repair, and mass transit. The money can only be used for those purposes. The money set aside in this way is a trust fund. Other examples of trust funds include aviation at the federal level and employee pension programs at lower levels of government. There is a fairly clear distinction between money collected for a trust fund and money available for general purposes. Nevertheless, most trust fund accounts are lumped in with general budgets. This makes it look as if the state and local governments are running large surpluses. The money in the trust funds for pensions is treated as being available to spend, and as governments build up their pension funds in anticipation of future benefits, the contributions are counted as revenues but not as expenditures.

The budget treatment of trust funds can create misleading measures of the financial condition of a government unit. It can hide some deficit financing or make it appear that a budget is running a surplus when it is not. This can lead to some unusual behavior. For example, it is asserted that the federal government does not use some of the money in the aviation trust fund because it would make the federal deficit look worse, despite the fact that the money cannot be spent for any other purpose.[6] Hence, it appears that the government is using an accounting gimmick to reduce apparent expenditures.

The Social Security system has a trust fund. This fund is small compared to the benefits the system pays and the obligations it has, but it does vary over time. These variations have little to do with the general budget of the United States government. In fact, the Social Security system is supposed to be

---

[6] Andy Oakley, "Fed Hoards Funds, Airports Say," *City & State* (December 1986), pp. 3 and 42.

separated from the unified budget in 1990; but any increases in its net trust fund surplus before it is separated are counted as reducing the federal deficit.[7] To the extent that this happens, it violates the very reason for having the trust fund. The trust fund is currently being built up because it is expected that the Social Security system will have expenditures exceeding revenues in the not too distant future. A substantial trust fund would allow for those benefits to be paid without either raising taxes or cutting benefits. To the extent that the trust fund is treated as offsetting other current federal expenditures, the money will not be there for its intended purpose. Reductions in the trust fund would then be adding to the federal deficit and would require offsetting increases in taxes or reductions in other expenditures at that time.

Off-Budget Activity

The final budget distinction which is often made is that between the official budget and the so-called "off-budget" accounts. An off-budget account is one associated with an agency of the government in question. Usually, the agency has the power to issue debt and to raise revenue to pay off that debt; however, the agency also usually has the actual or implied guarantee of the sponsoring government. Because of this guarantee, any losses sustained by the agency will affect the sponsoring government. Either the sponsor will have to make good on the losses or the sponsor's credit rating will be affected. Where the guarantee is explicit, the sponsoring government has no choice but to make up the shortfall. For example, the federal government required that all private firms put aside enough money to fund their pension obligations starting in 1976. Prior to that time there was no such requirement; many workers lost their pensions when their employers went bankrupt. Since many of the programs required substantial amounts of money to be adequately funded, the employers were given up to forty years to make up for any existing shortfalls, and the government set up an insurance fund to protect workers who might be harmed by a company going bankrupt before it fully funded its pension obligations. Unfortunately, more companies are likely to go bankrupt than the federal government anticipated, and billions may have to be paid from general revenues to meet the government's promise.[8] Because these off-budget enterprises have the potential to require large expenditures on the part of the sponsoring government some people have argued that they should be recog-

---

[7] Jodie T. Allen, "Trust Fund Surpluses Help Make Possible Fiscal Irresponsibility," *Oregonian* (April 28, 1987), p. B9.

[8] J. Ernest Beazley, "Bankruptcy Filings in Steel Overwhelm U.S. Pension Insurer," *Wall Street Journal* (May 21, 1987), pp. 1 and 12. See also U.S. Office of Management and Budget, op. cit., p. F-35, which shows an estimate of $3.8 billion for the contingent liability of the federal government for the Pension Benefit Guarantee Corporation in 1987. The same source provides estimates of the federal government's potential liability for a variety of activities. Others argue that at least some of these estimates are too low. For example, another estimate of the funding deficiency for the pension guarantee program is $21 billion. See Federal Reserve Bank of New York, "Estimating the Funding Gap of the Pension Benefit Guarantee Corporation," *Quarterly Review* 13 (Autumn 1988), pp. 45–59.

nized in some way as part of the budget process. In addition to the potential payments that government might be liable to, these agencies often borrow under the auspices of the sponsoring government. If the sponsor is a state or local government, the borrowing is done at the preferential rate associated with tax-exempt interest, and if the federal government is the sponsor, then the rate is still below that of other borrowers because of the security that the federal government can provide against default on the bonds.

Cash versus Accrual Accounting

The federal budget and most state and local budgets are cash budgets. In other words, they look at the actual amount of money collected and the actual money spent. Most private companies are required to use accrual methods of budgeting. Under the accural method, the revenue is counted when it becomes owed to the government, while an expenditure is counted when a commitment is made. The differences can be quite substantial. For example, a government unit may make a purchase of some item and the bill may be presented. Under a cash accounting system, this expenditure is not counted until the bill is actually paid. If payment is postponed until the following fiscal year, it will be counted as an expenditure in that fiscal year. Alternatively, if next year's revenue is paid early, it can be counted toward the current budget. Governments at all levels have used such gimmicks as methods to make budgets look better. For example, if a city offers a tax reduction for early payment of taxes, then any taxes collected can be counted for the fiscal year in which they are received. However, if the city were to pay an equivalent amount in interest to borrow against the next year's taxes, this would leave the budget unbalanced. The potential for such gimmicks is very large when a cash accounting system is used. There have been a number of proposals for reform and some state and local governments have adopted more reliable accounting systems. However, most government units still use systems that would never be allowed for a private company or individual.

There is not likely to be agreement on what would constitute an ideal budget procedure; but one can make a case for using accrual accounting and keeping the capital budget, the trust fund budgets, and the off-budget budgets separately. The potential liabilities from the other budgets should then be noted on the general fund budget. In practice, some of these procedures may be followed, but no government follows all of them.

/// BUDGETING

The executive and legislative branches of government have the responsibility to formulate a budget policy. The resulting budget is in many respects a detailed statement of that government's socioeconomic program and its fiscal implications. The budget is a detailed expression of what government intends to do during a prescribed period and its cost; the procedure used to prepare the budget is referred to as budgeting. It is a formalized routine involving both the legislative and executive branches of government, determining what government services will be provided, by whom they will be produced, who will receive them, and how they are to be paid for. The public sector must make these decisions, which in the private realm are made by the workings of the market.

At least three steps are involved in what is basically a continuous budget cycle. First, the executive branch formulates a budget establishing priorities for public expenditures. The executive budget represents a summation of plans for the provision of services and the raising of revenues. It contains a comprehensive listing of the costs of various planned activities in association with statements of how to finance them. After the executive branch has prepared its annual budget, which takes many months, it submits it to the legislative branch for review. Legislative action ultimately culminates in authorization and appropriation. Authorization allows a program to exist while appropriation actually provides funding. After the budget legislation is signed into law by the chief executive he or she, with the aid of the executive departments and agencies, implements the legislation. Finally, at the end of the budgetary period, an independent audit usually follows.

The legislative process is different on the federal, state and local levels. Throughout the nineteenth and early twentieth centuries, the federal government had few budget responsibilities. Government departments took their fund requests directly to Congress. In order to make sure that the president controlled requests for funds and proposed a budget that represented his priorities, Congress passed the Budget and Accounting Act of 1921. Under this act, the Bureau of the Budget, later renamed the Office of Management and Budget, was created for the purpose of reviewing requests from departments and agencies and providing the president with information on which he could base his budget proposal.

The Employment Act of 1946 created the Council of Economic Advisors. It was given responsibility for forecasting economic developments, assisting the president in formulating fiscal policy, and making an annual economic report to Congress. During the 1960s and 1970s, much progress was made by the executive branch in efforts to evaluate government programs systematically; to anticipate demands for government activities; to estimate costs, benefits and distributional effects of alternative spending or taxing programs; and to put the budget decision-making process on a more or less firm schedule. Efforts to systematize and improve the budget-making process included the introduction of program budgeting into the Defense Department in 1961 and the Presidential Directive of August 25, 1965 to employ program budgeting throughout the federal government, which however was only in effect for a few years.

The Congressional Budget Act of 1974 created budget committees in each house charged with formulating an overall budget policy, culminating in a budget resolution that would serve as a controlling framework within which individual taxing and spending measures would have to fit. It also created the Congressional Budget Office to give Congress an objective, nonpartisan source of budget analysis and information. With the creation of the Congressional Budget Office, Congress has been placed on a more equal footing with the executive branch and its Office of Management and Budget.

Specifically, the budget reform legislation passed in 1974 provides for the executive budget to be received by the Congressional Budget Committee, flanked by corresponding committees in the House and Senate. Each of these committees must prepare a Concurrent Resolution by April 15. It sets overall levels of expenditures, provides a division among major functional categories, and indicates required revenue levels. By May 15, this legislative process must be completed and the various appropriation committees begin their work, which culminates in Congress passing a second Concurrent Resolution on the budget by October 1.

There is no doubt that the intent that led to the budget reform legislation of 1974 was praiseworthy. Likewise, there is no doubt that it has not worked as well as its architects had hoped. All too often there are deadlocks, and virtually always there are delays in passing budget legislation. Almost every new fiscal year begins without a budget having been passed, making it necessary for Congress to enact makeshift budget legislation; usually this is in the form of a continuing resolution which provides for funding levels that existed in the previous fiscal year.

One of the most qualified practitioners, Alice M. Rivlin, who served as the first director of the Congressional Budget Office, offered the following evaluation:

> The 1974 law gave Congress a . . . mechanism for making overall budget decisions. . . . it also made . . . the process still more complicated and time-consuming. The new procedure . . . added yet another layer: the budget committees. The resulting schedule of . . . decisions . . . was impossibly demanding, even if reasonable agreement existed on overall budget policy.[9]

Still, Rivlin looked with favor on the process, saying,

> The new decision process established by the Congressional Budget Act of 1974 accomplished its major purpose. It gave Congress a forum for deciding fiscal policy. The new procedures were expected to strengthen Congressional power at the expense of the President.[10]

The budgetary process on the state and local level is different from that on the federal level. Although there is no universal pattern, most states have

---

[9] Alice M. Rivlin, "The Need for a Better Budget Process," *Brookings Review* 4 (Summer 1986), pp. 5–6.
[10] Ibid.

finance departments that help the governor prepare a budget. Once submitted to the legislature, specific budget items go to relevant appropriation committees. For new programs with direct budget implications it is necessary to have legislative sponsorship, so that a specific bill can be placed before the relevant committee for action. After positive action by committees of the lower and upper houses, a positive vote by both houses and, if need be, a reconciliation of differences between the two versions, the legislation is incorporated in the total package to be voted on in terms of the overall annual budget. Then, after receiving a positive vote in each house, it is submitted for signature to the governor.

States differ widely in the extent of professional capability and insight that is brought to bear during the budget process. In California, for example, the Office of the Legislative Analyst reviews the governor's proposed budget and submits its report to the legislature. Moreover, the legislative analyst sits with the relevant committee as it considers specific legislation and comments on the legislation's likely fiscal implications, if any.

In California, also, the governor is not faced with an either-or proposition when considering the legislature's budget. He or she can eliminate select items from the budget, i.e., "blue pencil" them, leaving it up to the legislature to overwrite the line item veto by a two-thirds majority.

Local governments also vary greatly in their budgeting process. Larger governments have budgetary experts whose title may be chief administrative officer, city or county manager, or legislative analyst. In most instances, the chief executive's budget proposals go to the local legislative body as a whole and are transferred to a Finance or Expenditure and Revenue Committee. The committee's recommendations are then voted on by the entire legislative body and sent on to the chief executive. He or she in turn has an opportunity to accept or veto the budget as it is returned by the legislative body.

Budget execution and control is the implementation of the legislation by the executive branch. This operation is perhaps most sophisticated on the federal level where the Office of Management and Budget appropriates funds to individual departments and agencies on a quarterly basis. In this manner the Office of Management and Budget exercises a significant degree of oversight and control, not only over the specific expenditures but also their timing.

Finally, the audit function is designed to make sure that the individual departments' or agencies' monies have been properly spent. This means that expenditures must encompass only those that have been specifically authorized. Most higher governments have an Office of the Auditor General, which at the end of the fiscal year conducts an audit of the financial records of departments and agencies and reports its findings to the legislature. Most local governments do not have this highly formalized audit procedure.

Budget making is inherently difficult, whether it is undertaken by a household, business, nonprofit organization, or government. What makes it so hard is the existence of unlimited demands in the face of limited resources. Government budgeting is especially complex and requires difficult decisions about who is to benefit and who is to bear the burdens. It is particularly difficult if the collection of individuals affected is large and heterogeneous, if there exist numerous decision makers with different values and agendas, if the organization has access to credit, and if uncertainties about the future make estimates about the costs and revenues associated with different decisions difficult and unreliable. Clearly, in line with these considerations, the federal government, more than any other, faces complex budget-making decisions, though those of states and large cities and counties are not to be underestimated.

What makes further demands on budget making is that in any one year expenditures and receipts depend heavily on laws enacted in the past. Thus, budget makers never start with a clean slate but must estimate the implication of past legislation and seek to add to it, or subtract from it, a select number of programs.

Controllable versus Uncontrollable Expenditures

When Congress and the president are arguing over ways to balance the budget we frequently hear that there is little room for discretion because much of the budget is "uncontrollable." It is important to understand what such terms mean. An uncontrollable expense is one that the government is obligated to make unless it changes the law, while a controllable expense is one that requires a law before any money can be spent. In particular, uncontrollable expenses are largely items like interest on the debt and the various entitlement programs. An entitlement program is one where the government is obligated by law to provide benefits to anyone meeting the specified requirements. Previous laws required that money be budgeted to meet such expenditures, and the budget will reflect this unless the law is changed. Thus, many of the uncontrollable expenditures are uncontrollable simply because a decision has been made not to try to change the law.

For some expenditures, such as interest on the national debt, there does not really seem to be much that the government could do to alter the law and change expenditures. However, for many other expenditures the choice not to try to change the law is purely a political decision. For example, many of the entitlement programs at the federal level are set to increase at the same rate as the cost of living. These cost-of-living adjustments (COLAs) are an innovation of the mid-1970s. Before that time few government programs had benefits that increased without some explicit action. Now many increase by formula each year. While this is certainly a way to protect the beneficiaries from the impact of inflation, it has also taken much of the discretion away from the budget process. Further, there are those who argue that the increases have made the recipients better off in real terms.

Two specific items are associated with increases in real benefits. First, the Social Security program had an accidental double indexation feature for the period from 1972 to 1977. During that time the benefits increased at double the rate of inflation. The indexation feature was corrected in 1977 but the level of benefits was left permanently at the higher level. The other major issue is that the Consumer Price Index was overstating the rate of inflation for much of the late 1970s. The index has since been corrected to give a more accurate measure of the rate of inflation, but the real increase in benefits has not been adjusted for the programs that had cost-of-living increases. Finally, many people wonder whether the general level of inflation is an accurate measure of the rate at which certain benefits should be adjusted. For example, should food stamp benefits be adjusted by the CPI if food prices are falling while other prices rise?

Many of the so-called uncontrollable expenditures are there because it was politically convenient to promise benefits at some time in the past and to push the costs off into the future. While these costs are now becoming more apparent, the political calculations do not seem to have changed. Thus, one of the areas that is frequently cited for potential reform is the military retirement system. It is much more generous than any equivalent private system, but it is difficult to reform because many people see these high benefits as a trade-off for lower pay. Whether or not this is true, many people have come to plan on these benefits and any changes would have to be phased in over a long period of time. For precisely this reason, the short-term benefits are small but the political opposition is intense. Hence, it is difficult to alter the program.

Budgeting under the Balanced Budget and Emergency Deficit Control Act of 1985 (Gramm-Rudman Law)   Elected officials are supposed to make the hard choices in relation to policies affecting all members of society; however, in late 1985 the Congress and president joined forces in assigning the task to a robot. Huge annual deficits in the order of $200 billion made it difficult, if not impossible, for politically sensitive elected officials to prepare a budget that would meet the demands of citizens and reduce the deficit, and do all this without tax increases. Legislation was enacted and signed which placed a mandatory ceiling on the federal budget deficit, starting with $171.9 billion in fiscal year 1986. The ceiling was to be reduced by $36 billion each year until it reached zero in fiscal year 1991. Specifically, the president is required to submit a budget and Congress is required to pass a budget resolution within the deficit target. If the regular budget and appropriations actions fail to reach the specified deficit target, the automatic suspension of certain cost-of-living adjustments and sequestering of other funds is to take effect. Court rulings have altered the specific process but have not changed the targets.

The legislation precisely specifies what items in the budget are to be reduced. Budget reductions under the sequestering provisions must be shared equally between defense and nondefense items. A specified group of programs, mainly those that directly affect the elderly and needy, are protected from reduction. Presidential discretion is severely limited, since the legislation requires conformance to cut levels for each program as determined by the General Accounting Office, based on information in required reports supplied by the Congressional Budget Office and the Office of Management and Budget. The legislation, called the Gramm-Rudman Deficit Control Act, was passed by large majorities in both the senate and the house and signed on December 12, 1985 by President Reagan.

What makes Gramm-Rudman particularly burdensome is that about 41% of all budgeted authority is exempt from reductions. When those programs granted limited protection are added to this total, about 55% of the budget is exempted from cuts, which must be made by reducing about equally the remaining 45% of the budget.

As to the first year, the act required that on January 15, 1986 the Office of Management and Budget and the Congressional Budget Office release their estimate of the budget deficit for fiscal year 1986. They estimated it to be $220.5 billion and called for a sequestering of $11.7 billion. The cuts included 4.3% for nondefense programs and 1% for five protected health programs, including Medicare and Community Health. In late 1986, Congress conformed to these requirements.

In the second year, the budget again was made to fit the general limits of the act, although it did not meet the precise target; however, in 1987 the targets were revised upward. In addition to the continuing possibility that the targets will be adjusted, many critics of the act argue that it encourages the use of fiscal gimmicks to make the budget look balanced when in fact it is not. For example, the sale of assets does not actually improve the budget balance, but this is one way to meet the deficit targets.[11]

State and local programs may also be seriously affected by the act, though there are uncertainties because of difficulties in forecasting the deficit. However, the following is clear. Quite a few federal aid programs to states support individuals in need, and they are largely protected under the act. Specifically, Aid for Dependent Children, the food stamp program, Medicaid, and child nutrition programs are exempted from sequestering. Moreover, cost-of-living adjustments and certain health programs are limited in their reductions under the special health category. Therefore, about one-third of the grants to state and local governments will receive some kind of protection. Since most aid to local governments is directed at economic development and general fiscal assistance, many of their progams could be subject to sequestering.

Outlays mainly involve cash transfer programs and their cuts have an immediate effect in the same fiscal year. Outlay cuts tend to be taken almost in their entirety in the year in which they are made. Budget authorization relates to the funds that, for example, a state agency has been given the authority to spend over a number of years. These funds are mainly for construction and capital acquisition programs, investments that take many years to be brought to completion. Therefore, authority cuts are very different from outlay cuts. Thus, for example, in terms of outlays, Gramm-Rudman is estimated to have

---

[11] For example, see David Wessel, "Gramm-Rudman Fails to Shrink Deficit Much, Causing Pressure to Use Gimmicks to Meet Targets," *Wall Street Journal* (December 29, 1988), p. A8.

reduced federal grants to California in fiscal 1987 by about half a billion dollars or 5.7%. Yet the effect in terms of budget authority is estimated to be much larger, i.e., a reduction of about $1.25 billion or 10.1%.

Not all states, however, incur equal cuts in federal aid. This is because of the varying composition of grants. For example, California and New York have relatively high AFDC benefits and large Medicaid populations and therefore will be cut less compared to states receiving a smaller share for these exempt programs. In many southern states, food stamp programs constitute a large proportion of welfare benefits, and therefore they will not incur a large reduction in federal grants. On the other hand, Alaska, where airport and other assistance make up a large proportion of federal grants, and the District of Columbia and Puerto Rico, both of which receive high levels of special payments, will be hit the hardest.

Thus, while Gramm-Rudman has the worthy aim of seeking to restore the federal government's fiscal integrity, it does so in a mindless manner. The resulting cuts would seldom make much sense viewed in isolation. There should be a better way for government to bring its expenditures and revenues in line with each other.

Budget Process Reform

Improvements in the budget process are constantly being demanded. This is easily more true for the federal than state and local government budgets. A major reason is the huge size and complexity of the federal budget. Moreover, it covers a much larger percentage of capital investments, particularly in the area of national defense. Consequently, as we discuss in Chapter 17, budgeting is a continuous process and often five or more years elapse from the time when planning for a major budget item starts and the date the final dollar is spent for the procurement of the end-product.

A reviewer of the federal budget process cannot help but be impressed by its shortcomings. There are signs of it breaking down of its own weight. There are complaints about the length of time spent on each budget—at least six months for preparation of the president's proposal and at least nine months for Congressional decisions. Others complain that deadlines are missed regularly and continuing resolutions are becoming more and more frequent. There are complaints about the multiplicity of congressional committees with overlapping jurisdictions, and about the fact that Congress becomes increasingly immersed in details of programs and less with the overall policy direction of the federal government.

A variety of proposals have been advanced to correct some of these problems. In the eyes of Alice M. Rivlin three types of reform would be especially appropriate: utilizing a multiyear budget in place of the annual budget, reducing the number of congressional committees by consolidating the authorizing and appropriating processes, and simplifying the budget itself by reducing the number of accounts and line items.[12]

Multiyear budgeting would have the advantage of reducing the time spent by the executive and legislative branches of government on the budget process; managers of federal programs and recipients of grants could then spend more time on managing and less on preparing and defending budgets. Also, longer funding periods are likely to improve the effectiveness of program operation. An admitted disadvantage relates to those programs that are greatly affected by the state of the economy and for which, therefore, longer run forecasts are unreliable. Still, at least some programs could be moved to a multiyear basis.

Consolidating the authorization and appropriation functions should not be difficult, in principle. In recent years, the distinction between the two has tended to blur. Moreover, with two-fifths of the budget spent for entitlements, there is little scope for appropriations committees. Still, representatives are reluctant to give up membership, let alone the chair, of a committee.

Congress could reduce the number of accounts and line items that it considers and thereby reduce its micromanagement. At present, the executive branch is given very detailed line item budgets and is seldom permitted to shift funds among items. Congress could seek to function more like a board of directors that makes major policy decisions, leaving detailed operations to the executive branch.

There is one further potential improvement. Congress could change its ways and vote on the entire expenditure package. This would require that committees hold all spending and tax bills for final vote at the same time, possibly in the form of a single bill. In this manner, not unlike most state and local governments, Congress would vote on a budget for the entire government and forward the budget to the president in one package. The problem with such large bills is that they become so complex that no one really understands them; and there is much more room for special interest provisions to be hidden in the bill.

State and local governments also have sought to improve their budget process. They have done so mainly by developing specialized capabilities to assist the chief executive in the preparation of the budget and the legislative body in reviewing and possibly revising the proposed budget. To accomplish this objective, many governors, mayors, county supervisors, and school superintendents have set up offices that, though on a much smaller scale, tend to emulate the federal Office of Management and Budget. This function is carried out in many states within the Department of Finance on the chief executive's side. On the legislative side, a growing number of states, cities, school districts and county governments have set up offices of legislative analysts. Their role is to analyze the proposed budget and assist the legislative body in its evaluation.

---

[12] Rivlin, op. cit., p. 8.

/// EVALUATING EXPENDITURES

Before most programs become part of the budget, they are supposed to be evaluated on their merits. Those that promise to be beneficial are supposed to be funded and those that are not should receive no funding. Programs that are not meeting their goals over time or that have had changes in costs or benefits are supposed to be reevaluated. This seldom appears to happen for existing programs, but new programs are often subjected to some form of formal analysis to determine their impact on the economy. The formal analysis most recommended by economists is cost-benefit analysis. This is simply a formal way of trying to look at both the benefits that a program generates and the costs that it imposes on society.

Cost-Benefit Analysis

One goal of every economic system is to make the best use of the resources available. Any action that increases benefits by more than it increases costs would move the economy toward more efficient use of resources. This is the basis for the economic analysis of many activities. Of course, there are numerous complications in actually doing a study of costs and benefits, but the basic principle is very simple.

One of the more intractable problems is the issue of who receives benefits versus who pays the cost. In market exchanges, the recipient of the benefits pays the cost of providing them; however, this seldom happens with government provision. Hence, some people will almost always be made worse off by any single government action. Even if there are no direct losers, the taxpayers at large have to come up with the funding. The widely used approach to this dilemma is to evaluate whether the winners could in principle compensate the losers and still be better off. This is justified by two arguments. One is that government could indeed see to it that the losers are compensated; the other is that if there are enough beneficial projects, the redistribution should work out so that in fact everyone is better off when the whole group of projects is considered. Despite the general acceptance of this criterion by economists, the actual distributional impacts tend to be very important in the choice of new projects. Nevertheless, an understanding of cost-benefit analysis allows us to determine something about the efficiency costs of various government policies so that these costs can be weighed against any distributional gains caused by the policies.

A cost-benefit analysis, then, is an attempt to determine if the total value of benefits created by a project is greater than the total value of the costs that the project imposes on society. Further, there is an attempt to determine what level of activity or which alternative form of implementing a program will yield the greatest net benefits. One attempts to find the benefits by estimating willingness to pay for output, and the costs by estimating the true opportunity costs of government actions.

The major difficulty with the analysis is the determination of the benefit and cost information. In competitive markets, people reveal their preferences and hence their willingness to pay for various goods and services by their actions. If they buy something, they believe it is worth more than the price, and if they do not, they believe it is not worth the price. Hence, the market demand curve can be estimated, and these estimates give a means to calculate the total benefit. However, when people will get the benefits whether they must pay for them or not, they do not give such clear signals about their willingess to pay for output. Even if they have no reason to hide the information, it would be costly to collect; but often they have little incentive to provide the correct information and they may even have a positive incentive to lie. For example, if your answer determines whether or not government will do something you want done, you have an incentive to overstate the value of the benefits you expect to receive. This incentive does not exist if the people receiving the benefits have to pay the additional cost, but it does exist if they perceive that their share of the cost will be much less than their share of the benefits.

Similarly, the fact that producers produce a given amount at a particular price is an indication that this is the marginal cost of producing the last unit. If it were not, various producers would either expand or contract production. The estimates of the supply curve can then be used as the basis for estimating the opportunity cost of production. However, the cost may not be accurately estimated if a direct market price is not paid for the resources. For example, both the government and private firms may treat the cost created by pollution as zero. This is an error from the opportunity cost perspective because clean air or clean water does have an opportunity cost.

Estimating Costs   It might seem that estimating the cost of government actions would be fairly straightforward, but this is often not the case. Remember that the economist's definition of cost is often different from the accountant's definition. For an economist the cost is the highest valued alternative use of resources. For goods and services produced in a competitive market with no externalities, this is simply the market price for that good or service. However, there are important exceptions to this rule. When a particular market is not in a competitive equilibrium, the market price may not reflect true opportunity cost. Further, if there are market imperfections such as monopoly or externalities, the price may not reflect true opportunity cost (see Box 15-1).

A common example of a market cost that may not represent an opportunity cost is the case of labor that would otherwise have been unemployed. In a competitive labor market, the wage represents the marginal product of labor. Hence, when a particular project uses labor, the wage paid represents the opportunity cost of that labor. It represents the value of the output that worker would have produced in the next best employment opportunity. However,

Box 15-1

////// Opportunity Cost with Monopoly

The differences between price and opportunity cost can be illustrated easily with respect to monopoly. Suppose that the government wants to purchase an amount Q_G; the initial equilibrium is at price P_1 and quantity Q_1 (see Figure 1). When government enters the market, the market demand curve shifts to the right to D_2. The new equilibrium is at P_2 and Q_2. The opportunity cost is determined by looking at the source of the units used by government. Part of this comes from new production and the opportunity cost is determined by the resources used. However, part comes from deterring other purchasers and the opportunity cost is the value of the output to them. In the figure, the opportunity cost of new production is the area under the marginal cost curve from output Q_1 to Q_2. The opportunity cost of displaced consumption is the area under the private sector demand curve from Q_3 to Q_1. Thus, the relationship between opportunity cost and price depends on where the government units come from. If primarily from new production, the opportunity cost may be considerably below price for a monopolist.

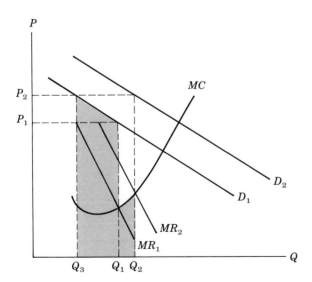

Figure 1 / Opportunity Cost of Monopoly Output

wages are often slow to adjust downward so that there is the possibility that people will be unemployed at the current market wage.[13]

When people would otherwise have been unemployed, the market wage is an overstatement of their true opportunity cost. The opportunity cost would not be zero, since they presumably could do something with their time, but it would not be the full wage, either. A similar issue arises when the government pays a wage above the market wage. The workers will be happy to receive this bonus, but the cost would be the value of the workers in their next most valuable use. This would be the market wage, not the actual wage paid.

While the opportunity cost principle is sometimes used to justify a lower value for labor used in a project, it is difficult to justify such a reduction in many cases. In particular, it is necessary to show that the person would have remained unemployed over the life of the project or that someone else would have been unemployed. In other words, it is necessary to show that the project caused a net reduction in the total amount of unemployment and that this had no other resource effects. Even then the reduction in total unemployment is not likely to be equal to the total employment on the project. Hence, there would still be some opportunity cost.

Another problem with opportunity cost estimates concerns the use of resources already owned by the government. The opportunity cost is again the value of these resources in their next highest valued use. But this is often ignored in decision making. For example, if a government owns a parcel of land that could be used in building a school, there is a tendency not to count the land as part of the cost of the school. This is clearly a mistake since the land does have other uses. Its market value or value in some other use should be included as part of the cost of the project even if there is no direct expenditure involved.

Other issues arise when we talk about projects by different levels of government. It may be clear that a particular cost is miscounted by some state or local government, but that government may not be concerned. For example, a local government is likely to be concerned only with the costs and benefits to its own constituents. Thus, if labor that would otherwise have been unemployed is used on a project, but those workers live outside the jurisdiction of the government paying for the project, the government is not likely to be very concerned. It will consider the salaries as a cost since it must pay them. Even if the workers lived inside the jurisdiction, the local decision maker is faced with an actual outlay of funds and would find it hard to ignore such costs in making a final decision.

---

[13] Not all unemployment is caused by problems in the labor market. Some unemployment, necessary to the proper functioning of the labor market, is associated with people looking for the best job or waiting for a job to begin. Such unemployment is not associated with a low opportunity cost since the searching is actually a productive activity. For a more detailed discussion of the concept see Julius Margolis, "Shadow Prices for Incorrect or Nonexistent Market Values," in Robert Haveman and Julius Margolis, eds., *Public Expenditures and Policy Analysis*, 2nd ed. (Chicago: Rand McNally College Publishing, 1977).

Thus, it should be clearly understood that many government officials are not inclined to do the kind of cost-benefit studies that economists would recommend, and in some cases it is not clear that they should. In a federalist system, each level of government has certain concerns of importance. Issues such as unemployment can seldom be addressed at the local level and so it is not clear that local governments should consider them in making decisions. Often, at the local level, governments do a fiscal impact study rather than a cost-benefit study. The fiscal impact study simply tells what the costs and benefits of a project will be to the local community. If higher levels of government take action to offset any externalities occurring between local governments units, this may be efficient. However, if the higher levels of government do not take this into account, the results of such decision making may be inefficient allocation of resources. This is often alleged to be a problem when there are externalities between communities (see Box 15-2).

Benefit Concepts   The problem of estimating the benefits of government actions largely revolves around determining who benefits and by how much. Many of the things often treated as benefits by politicians are not treated that way in the economic analysis. Rather they are redistributional concerns, which do not represent any net improvement in the allocation of resources in the economy. For example, many people consider the creation of jobs as a benefit of certain government actions, but this is really a cost. When the government creates a job it is diverting a person from producing some other output. Hence, the person with the new job is causing society to forego some other benefit. The person with the job may consider it better than any other job available and may be happy to have the job; but this is a redistributional concern, not a production one. Hence, we have to be careful to separate these distributional considerations from actual resource issues.

The benefit from a government action should be addressed by looking at the productive or consumptive output arising from the activity. A consumptive output is anything that directly makes someone better off in terms of their perceived level of consumption. This may occur as a recreational benefit, better health, or any other method that directly increases welfare. The measure of the benefit would be the amount the person would be willing to pay to have the results of the government action rather than do without them entirely. This would be equivalent to measuring the area under the demand curve for this activity.

Some benefits do not directly create improvements in the well-being of consumers. These benefits show up as reductions in the cost of producing certain other goods or services. These cost reductions are only benefits insofar as the reduced costs create a net benefit to consumers or free other resources, and they would be valued in terms of the net benefits to consumers or the value of the resources freed for other uses.

Where there are direct benefits to consumers we are interested in their willingness to pay for those benefits. This is often quite different from any

Box 15-2

////// Externalities and Local Cost-Benefit Studies

A true cost-benefit study looks at all costs and all benefits no matter who pays the costs or receives the benefits. Local governments often ignore the costs and benefits that occur outside their boundaries. For example, suppose that one city upstream on a river takes water from the river for drinking and dumps sewage. The sewage affects a second city downriver, which also uses the river for drinking water and sewage disposal.

If the first city is considering building a sewage treatment plant, it is unlikely to consider the benefits that will occur downstream in making its decision. However, those downstream benefits may be the most important of all the benefits created by the treatment plant. Thus, the first city is not likely to voluntarily build a sewage treatment plant when the local cost and benefits do not warrant it even though the total benefits from the plant may be much greater than the costs.

Situations like this are one reason why the federal government may become involved in the building of sewage treatment plants. It may be in a position to cause the local governments to internalize the externalities in the decision process. A cost-benefit analysis done from the federal level would include not only the benefits to the first community but also those to the second community since both are in the federal government's jurisdiction.

market price or other information that is readily available. For example, the price paid reflects the value of the last unit to consumers; however, it is usually not a good measure of the total value of the output to consumers. Figure 15-1 shows that at a price of $0.50 people in the community will purchase 100 units of output. This might represent the admission price for a swimming pool and the number of people who use it on an average day. The revenue raised by the pool is thus $50.00 per day (area *A* in the figure), but this is not a measure of the benefit that the pool generates. The demand curve in this case is not perfectly elastic. Hence, some people receive consumer surplus from the provision of the pool.

The total benefit of the pool would have to take this consumer surplus into account. The consumer surplus is shown as area *B* in the figure, and it can be calculated as the area of a triangle in this case. Area *B* is equal to $(1/2) \times 0.50 \times 100$ or $25.00. Thus, the total benefit from having the pool used by 100 people is $75.00 rather than $50.00. This is an important point that

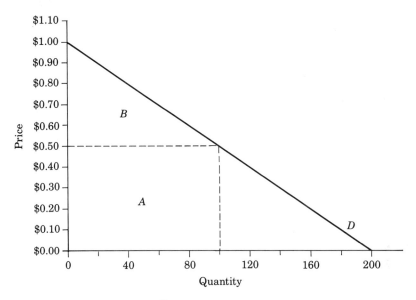

Figure 15-1 / **Total Benefit**

warrants further clarification. In the competitive market, we usually treat the benefit of a firm's output as being simply the price paid times the quantity delivered. Why should the benefits of public activities be treated differently?

The answer is that they are not. In a competitive market, the output of any one firm is sold in response to a perfectly elastic demand curve, as in Figure 15-2. In such a market, the price times quantity calculation will indeed give us the total benefit of one firm's output since there is no consumer surplus associated with the output of any particular firm. There is no consumer surplus because customers of any one firm can simply switch to the output of some other firm if the first firm goes out of business. Thus, from the customer's perspective, the output of any specific firm has very close substitutes, and the customer gets very little consumer surplus from the output of the particular firm. Since government seldom produces an output for which there is a perfectly elastic demand or for which there are many competing suppliers, the issue of consumer surplus is almost always important.

Another common practice in government is to treat the cost of a program as a measure of the benefits it generates, since the latter are so difficult to estimate. The fallacy of this approach can be seen in Figure 15-3. At the market clearing price of $.50, 100 units of output are produced and sold to consumers. If there are no fixed costs, the cost of the first 100 units is $35 (the area under the marginal cost curve). The value of the first 100 units is $75, which is simply price times quantity plus consumer surplus. However, for the next 100 units the benefit is only $25 while the cost is $85. Thus, the project would go from a net benefit of $40 at the optimum level of output to a net loss of

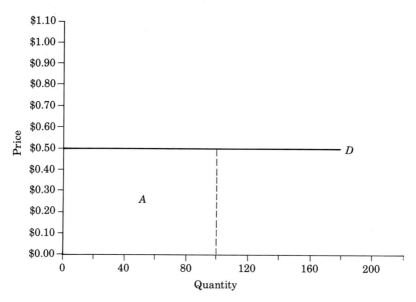

Figure 15-2 / Elastic Demand

$20 at the maximum output used. Further, if the output is evaluated at the cost of production, it will look as though it is producing far more benefits than it actually is.

Estimating Benefits Since there is seldom information on the demand curve for government output, it is often necessary to find some way to estimate willingness to pay. There are a number of ways in which this could be done. For example, the demand curve might be estimated by looking at how much people actually spend to gain access to a similar project. Thus, if different people face different costs to gain access to a recreation area, the percentage of those who go can be used as a measure of quantity demanded if that expenditure were the price. If 600 out of 1,000 people go to the recreation area when the access cost is zero, 400 out of 1,000 go when the access cost is $1.00, 200 out of 1,000 go when the access cost is $2.00, and none go at $3.00, we can draw the demand curve in Figure 15-4 as the demand per 1,000 people. The argument is that if all groups of people view the recreation area as being equally desirable, then 200 of those who spent zero to get there would have been willing to spend at least $2.00, and another 200 would have been willing to spend at least $1.00. Thus, the amount above what they actually spent could be treated as consumer surplus.

Notice that in this case only the consumer surplus counts as a benefit of the project. That is because the people actually used up resources to gain access to the recreation area. The net benefit from the recreation area is the amount of benefit generated minus the cost of the resources used to gain

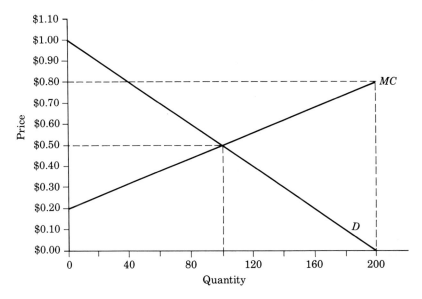

***Figure 15-3* / Net Benefit**

access. This point often causes confusion and should be understood. From an economic perspective, the net gain from the project counts as a benefit, and any costs incurred to gain the benefit must be subtracted from the gross benefits. This would seem to argue that the consumer surplus is the only

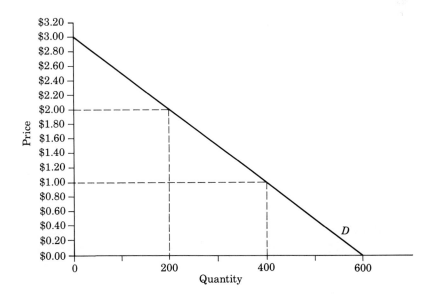

***Figure 15-4* / Demand per Thousand**

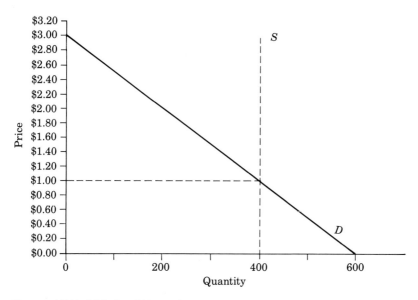

Figure 15-5 / Limited Quantity at Zero Price

benefit ever to be counted, but that is not the case. A person who pays money for a good or service is not actually using up resources to get that good or service. The money is simply a transfer from one party to another. It is not used up in the process. However, if someone uses gasoline and time to gain access to a recreation area, that is a real use of resources. The gasoline and time are gone; they have not been transferred to someone else to use.

Rationing   This brings us to another point regarding the measurement of benefits from government output. Frequently, government produces less than would be used at a zero price but still charges a zero price for using the good or service. Since there is excess demand at the zero price, the government rations the output on a first-come, first-served basis. It is tempting to treat the benefit of such activities as the area under the demand curve at a zero price, but this would be an error. In such cases, the price is a time price rather than a money price; however, it is a price. Further, the government does not get the time which those waiting are spending, so this is an access cost, not a transfer. In Figure 15-5 we see that at a zero price, 600 units would be demanded. However, the government is only providing 400 units. Thus, people wait in line to get the limited number available. They will wait until, at the margin, the time cost is $1.00. As an approximation, around $400 worth of time is spent on gaining access to the "free" good. This use of resources should be deducted from any willingness-to-pay measure in determining the net benefits of the government output.

Capitalization   Another method used to determine the value that people place on a government-sponsored project is to look at changes in property values near the project. If property values increase or decrease, it may be possible to use this information to estimate some of the value of the project. Such changes in property values in response to changes in the benefits or costs associated with a location are called capitalization (this was discussed in more detail in Chapter 10). It is important to stress that the rise in property value is not in itself a benefit of the project; rather, it is a way of finding out what net benefits, if any, the project generates.

Suppose that we reconsider the information in Figure 15-4. The people with the lowest access cost get the greatest net benefit from the recreation opportunity. Suppose that the access cost is proportional to distance from the site; then those living nearest the site get the largest net benefit from it. Hence, people compete for those sites and thus bid up their price. This shows up as an increase in the property values near the recreation site as compared to other property values. However, the increase in property values generates no net gain. Instead, the owner of the property gets an increase in wealth from the rise in value while the buyer gets an offsetting decrease in wealth.

The buyer is willing to accept this decrease in wealth because of the net benefits received from the recreation area. However, the effect is to transfer the net gains from the user of the recreation site to the owner of the property around the recreation site. Because of the greater value that people place on the areas near the recreation site, we have a measure of how much they value this access. The value should show up as being very similar to what we would have calculated on the basis of the information in Figure 15-4. The two methods hold the same information, and counting the benefits from each would be double counting.[14]

Similar information on the costs of some government activities can be generated using decreases in property values. For example, an estimate of the cost of airplane noise or of having a garbage dump nearby can be generated from property value declines near the airport or the garbage dump.

Other examples of property values responding to government activity can be found by looking at transportation infrastructure. When government builds a new road or provides some other form of transportation improvement, it is providing a service to people near the road. The service is faster access to other places. The value of this service is often capitalized into property values as people compete for the property with this enhanced service.

All the methods of calculating the benefits of government actions have some shortcomings. More advanced knowledge is required to use the information available to generate these benefit estimates, but it is useful to know that such methods exist. Sometimes the output of a government project is the same

---

[14] See a detailed discussion of these points in A. Myrick Freeman, III, *The Benefits of Environmental Improvement* (Baltimore: Johns Hopkins University Press, 1979).

as a private good sold in a market. In these cases, it is tempting to simply value the good at its market price. This is usually misleading in terms of the willingness-to-pay criterion. If the government output simply displaces private output, the price is indeed the relevant measure; however, it is unusual for government to be involved in such production. Rather, when government does produce what are essentially private goods, it does so to distribute them on a nonmarket basis, usually as a method to aid "deserving" service demanders.

While it may be desirable, for example, to aid low-income people in a particular way, such as by providing medical care, such aid often would not pass the willingness-to-pay cost-benefit test. This is because many of the recipients of the care would prefer to take the money the government spent on the care rather than the care. They may not be given such a choice, for a number of reasons. For example, the government may have a paternalistic attitude that the poor underconsume health care. Alternatively, the givers may get some satisfaction from seeing health care provided that they would not get if the money were spent on clothes or recreation. These items certainly affect the final decisions on many programs, but they are almost impossible to include in a benefit-cost analysis.

A final problem with measuring the value of the output of government activities is that of measuring the output itself. When a factory produces cars or soap, it is reasonably easy to measure the output of that factory. When a person cuts someone else's hair there is still some measure of output. However, how do you measure the output of a police department? Is it the number of arrests made? Many factors, as we see in a later chapter, affect the provision of police services, but a major goal is to deter crime. The number of arrests may in fact be a measure of failure in the deterring of crime. A police force able to deter crime completely would make no arrests! Unfortunately, many of the things government does have this problem. Nevertheless, it is possible to make estimates of the value of output in many cases by the indirect methods mentioned above.

Decision Rule   Once estimates have been made of the costs and benefits of the various options available, it is necessary to decide whether to go ahead with a project. It may also be necessary to choose among various options in terms of the scope or size of the project. The rule is very simple: choose the combination that gives the greatest net benefit. Despite the simplicity of this rule, people use others that may lead to incorrect decision making. Perhaps the most common error is to try to maximize the ratio of benefits to costs.

It is not uncommon to see the ratio of benefits to costs listed with a recommended project. Many analysts see this as a method of showing the effectiveness of expenditures on a given program. However, it is a misleading number when used to determine the size of a project. Figure 15-6 shows the marginal cost and demand curves for a given project. As the figure shows, at an output of 1, the benefit is 10 while the cost is 1. The ratio of benefits to costs would therefore be 10. If one more unit is produced, the total benefits climb to

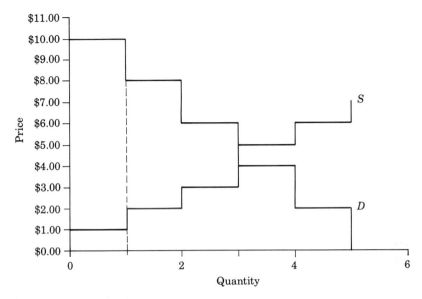

Figure 15-6 / Ratio of Benefit to Cost

18 but the total costs only increase to 3. Clearly there has been a net gain in the expansion of output; however, if we look at the ratio of benefits to costs we find that it has declined to 6. Thus, maximizing the benefit-cost ratio would lead to stopping production at 1 even though there is room for significant increase in output for which the benefits exceed the costs.

Discounting   A major problem associated with cost-benefit studies is the comparison of costs and benefits that occur at different times. It is fairly common for a government construction project to generate large costs as it is being built and then to generate benefits for long periods afterward. The costs and benefits that occur now are of greater importance than those that will occur later. This is because of interest. A dollar now will grow to one dollar plus interest if deposited in a bank for a year. The bank can pay the interest because other people or firms pay the bank interest. Some people pay the bank interest because they value current consumption more heavily than they value future consumption. Firms are willing to pay interest because they can use the borrowed money to make investments, and they expect the investments to return enough to at least pay off the loan and interest.

Because of this general preference for current as opposed to future use of resources on the part of both firms and people, it is necessary to discount future amounts to find the current amount to which the future amount is equivalent. This is done by looking at what a dollar now will grow to in the future at a given interest rate. Suppose that the interest rate is simply i. Then one dollar deposited in a bank today will grow to one dollar plus interest in one year. Similarly, A_0 dollars deposited today would grow to A_0 plus $i \times A_0$. If we denote the amount in one year as A_1, we have $A_1 = (1 + i) \times A_0$. If we denote the future value of one dollar as A_t where t is the number of years ahead we are looking, we can see that the future amount is given by $A_t = (1 + i)^t \times A_0$. If we knew that the amount A_t were going to be available in t years, we could express its current value as $A_0 = A_t/(1 + i)^t$. This is because the amount A_0 will grow to A_t in t years. Finding the present value of a future amount is called discounting. If we discount all future amounts, we have a reasonable basis for comparing projects with different streams of costs and benefits.

An important problem with discounting is the choice of a discount rate. There are many different interest rates: the rate a bank pays on deposits, the rate firms and consumers pay on loans from the bank, the rate government pays. For each of these purposes there are likely to be many specific differing rates. Thus, short-term borrowing is usually done at a lower rate than long-term borrowing, and some companies can get much more favorable rates than others. The general rule is that the appropriate discount rate is determined by where the funds came from. For example, if government borrows money to build a project, it would seem that the interest rate that government pays on the loan would be appropriate. Generally this is not true, because government borrowing is likely to crowd out some private borrowing. Government can pay a lower interest rate than private borrowers because of tax exemptions or perceptions of the safety of government as a creditor. In either case the true opportunity cost of the borrowing is the return on the investment that would have been made if the government had not borrowed the money. This is usually the borrowing rate for the private sector.[15]

If money is raised through taxes, some consumers will save less and others will borrow, but most will primarily cut back on their current consumption. In most cases, the opportunity cost is reduced consumption and the appropriate discount rate is the rate at which consumers are compensated for their postponement of consumption. This is approximately the interest rate on savings.

The choice of the correct discount rate has received a lot of attention because there has been a tendency to use rates that are too low. When costs occur in the present and benefits occur in the future, a low discount rate makes the project appear to have a higher net benefit than it really does. For example, a project that costs $10,000 to construct now, which would return $11,000 worth of benefits in ten years, is not likely to be desirable under a cost-benefit study. At an interest rate of even 5% the benefit has a present value of only $6,753. However, if the future benefit is not discounted at all, the project has costs of $10,000 and benefits of $11,000. Thus, it appears to be worthwhile if the timing of the benefits is not taken into account.

[15] See William J. Baumol, "On the Discount Rate for Public Projects," in Haveman and Margolis, op. cit.

One way to determine if the project decision hinges on the choice of discount rate or not is to do a sensitivity analysis. In this procedure, the project is evaluated using a variety of different discount rates and other assumptions. If the project is desirable under all conditions or undesirable under all conditions, there is no need to agonize over the appropriate choice of assumptions. It is only when the choice of assumptions matters in determining the outcome that it is really necessary to be careful about the choice. Then it may be necessary to determine exactly how the project is to be funded, for example, in choosing a discount rate.

Shortcomings   Cost-benefit analysis is often attacked as an analytic tool for two reasons. The first is that it can be manipulated by choice of assumptions. The analyst can make projects look more attractive by ignoring or understating certain costs, or the project can be made to look worse by doing the same for benefits. It is also possible to manipulate the outcome by the choice of discount rate or other matters. The second criticism is that the technique does not take into account distributional issues that are likely to dominate actual decision making. Thus, politicians may vote for an inefficient project because it will benefit deserving people. In some cases this means the poor or others that the society as a whole wants to aid; however, in many cases it simply means the local constituents or political contributors.

Both of these criticisms miss the main point of cost-benefit analysis. It is a technique to evaluate the efficiency of a proposed project; and like all techniques, it must be applied properly and not misused.

Yet efficiency, while an important factor, is only one of the many factors that enter into a decision. The possibility of an analyst biasing a study should indeed be recognized. However, the fact that the study is based on a specific technique means that others can determine whether or not they agree with the assumptions. By altering the assumptions it is possible to see if the conclusion is indeed sensitive to the choice. Thus, someone who wants to challenge a project can do so in a meaningful discussion of the study. This is almost impossible if there is no basis for the decision other than that someone thought it might be a good idea. Further, the fact that distributional issues enter into government decision making does not invalidate the importance of the efficiency effect.

If redistribution were all that the government were concerned with, there would be no need to alter things through large-scale projects, and politicians could simply vote to give some people money and collect it from others. It is the combination of distribution and efficiency concerns that should and indeed does affect political decisions. Those who argue that government should not be concerned strictly with efficiency considerations should recognize that government also should not be concerned strictly with redistributional considerations.

/// PROGRAM EFFECTIVENESS

In many cases the objective of cost-benefit analysis is rejected as too narrow. The political process specifies certain goals, which the economic analysis finds to be inefficient. For example, the political process specifies that housing is a preferred item and that there should be government programs to foster housing consumption. One economist estimates that the overconsumption of housing since World War II has led to a standard of living about 25% lower than it would have been if all investment were made efficiently.[16] Despite this disagreement about the desirability of certain goals, the economic analysis can be used to determine if they are being met effectively by a particular program.

We use housing to illustrate how the economic analysis can be used to evaluate effectiveness of a program. We compare a public housing program and the use of rent subsidies as means of increasing the housing consumption and well-being of low-income households. The main objective of the program is assumed to be the increase in housing consumption; hence, direct income redistribution is ruled out. However, given the increase in housing consumption, an increase that leaves more benefit with low-income households is preferred to one that allows the benefits to be diverted in some way.

Consider the situation illustrated in Figure 15-7. In this case we are assuming that there is some fixed quantity of low-quality housing available in a given market. Government wants to evaluate the effectiveness of public housing and rent subsidies as means of achieving the increase in housing consumption. If the government builds Q_G units of housing, it is added to the private supply and the supply curve shifts to the right. The net result is given by the new equilibrium, which shows a larger quantity of housing consumed and a lower net rent paid by the low-income households that do not reside in public housing. Thus, even though the public housing would only serve a subset of the eligible population, all low-income households would benefit. Now consider a subsidy in the same diagram. This would result in an upward shift of the demand curve by the amount of the subsidy. The new result would be a rent R_2, which is higher than the old rent by exactly the amount of the subsidy. In this example, the subsidy would be shifted to landlords and the net benefits to low-income families would be zero. They have the same number of units to consume and the net rent they pay is unchanged.

Now consider a situation like that in Figure 15-8. Here the supply of low-income housing is perfectly elastic. When the government builds public housing units, the supply curve again shifts to the right, but this shift results in no change in the total number of units available. The increase in government units is exactly offset by a decrease in private units. The people living in the public housing may be better off because they pay less than a market rent, but

---

[16] Edwin Mills, "Has the United States Overinvested in Housing?" *American Real Estate and Urban Economics Journal* 15 (1987), pp. 601–616.

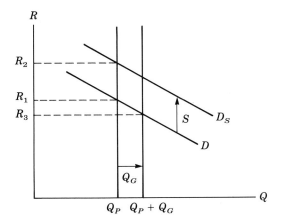

Figure 15-7 / Fixed Quantity of Housing

there is no spillover benefit to other low-income residents. Further, the residents of the public housing may not value it at its cost to the government, so even this part of the transfer may be overstated. Compare this to a rent subsidy. In this figure, the upward shift of the demand curve results in a new equilibrium at Q_2 units of housing. Further, the market rent has not changed, so the net rent to low-income households is lower by the full amount of the subsidy.

Clearly, the desirability of the two approaches to the issue depends on the elasticity of supply of low-income housing. We would expect that the elasticity is fairly low in the short run but fairly high in the long run if the housing market is relatively free. In fact, the little empirical evidence that we have finds that there was no noticeable effect of the subsidies on market rent even in

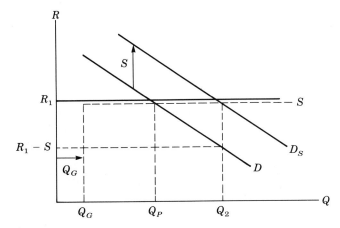

Figure 15-8 / Elastic Supply of Housing

the short run, although that experiment was not one of generally used rent subsidies. This implies that the public housing approach is likely to look good compared to the subsidy approach in the short run but that the subsidy approach is likely to have a better effect in achieving the objective in the long run. This may help to explain the relative political popularity of public housing since the short-run results are often asserted to be all that matters in evaluating government programs.

/// SUMMARY

Budgeting is the process by which a government specifies how much revenue it expects to receive and how this revenue will be spent. There are many possible ways to organize budgeting. Most governments operate under a unified, cash-flow budget. Thus, all their receipts are counted when received and all expenses are counted when paid. This can be misleading because of the opportunities to shift revenues and expenditures over time or to buy or sell assets. Other types of budgets would account for capital expenditures or trust funds separately from the main budget, and it may be better to account for general revenues and expenditures on an accrual rather than cash basis. These issues are more important for state and local governments than they are for the federal government, but the concepts are applicable at all levels of government.

The federal budget process has become slow and unwieldy. There have been numerous attempts at reform, but little success so far. Nevertheless, the process has been improved, with much better ability to determine the long-run implications of budget changes.

Cost-benefit analysis is a method for determining whether a particular government action improves the allocation of resources in the economy in terms of economic efficiency. It requires that the opportunity cost of the action be determined and compared with the benefits generated in terms of people's willingness to pay for those benefits. The costs and benefits are often difficult to quantify; however, there are a variety of techniques to accomplish this objective. Once the amounts are determined, discounting is used to make the amounts comparable on a current term basis.

The information from a cost-benefit study is only part of the decision-making process since efficiency is only one of the goals of government. Nevertheless, the use of cost-benefit studies can allow government to achieve many of its objectives with the least use of resources. At the very least it can give politicians some idea of the efficiency loss generated by certain types of redistribution.

Chapter 16 //////

Transfer Programs

Income distribution is an important issue in any economy, yet there is relatively little agreement on whether any given distribution should be changed or by how much. At one extreme are those who argue for complete equality of income. Aside from the problems with defining equality, any system that guarantees that everyone ends up with the same amount of income destroys many of the incentives which exist to get people to work at undesirable or unpleasant jobs (or even to work at all) and to make efficient use of other resources. At the other extreme are those who believe that the outcome of the market is the most desirable and that there should be no redistribution from the market outcome. This view is inconsistent with widespread feelings that everyone should receive at least minimal food, housing, and shelter if they cannot care for themselves. Further, many believe that too great an inequality is not conducive to a harmonious and stable society.

As we discussed earlier, economic theory has relatively little to say about what constitutes a desirable distribution of income. The economic efficiency criterion simply says that a given distribution of income is not obviously inefficient if there exist no changes in the allocation of resources that could make at least one person better off without making at least one other person worse off.[1] Yet there are infinite possible allocations of resources that meet this criterion. In the absence of other criteria, there is little guidance on redistribution. Rather, we end up with the somewhat negative statement that, given the initial distribution of resources, most attempts to change the distribution of income will result in efficiency losses to the economy. This means there is a trade-off between efficiency and equity. As we have seen, under most circum-

---

[1] If interdependent utility functions are assumed, then economically efficient transfers are possible. Many high-income people vote to support transfers, give to charity, and so on, which suggests that such interdependence does exist. See Harold M. Hochman and James D. Rogers, "Pareto-Optimal Redistribution," *American Economic Review* (September 1969), pp. 542–557.

stances when government raises taxes, there is some efficiency loss to the economy. Similarly, when government spends or gives away money, there are likely to be some efficiency costs to the economy. Hence, taking from one citizen to give to another is likely to have efficiency costs on both sides of the transaction. Economists usually end up saying that issues of income redistribution are outside their domain and must be settled by the political process.

The other methods of determining how much income redistribution should occur also have problems. For example, we have seen that there is likely to be either indeterminancy or other problems in the political decision-making rules. Despite these problems with the theory of income redistribution, we find in practice that the political system has resulted in substantial attempts to change the final allocation of resources. These programs are broadly characterized as forms of social insurance and pure redistributive programs. The social insurance programs are meant to tide people over periods of low income and the redistributive programs are intended to aid those with chronically low income. This distinction tends to blur in practice, but it is important in classifying programs.

Debates on income redistribution are complicated by the indirect effects of government actions on income. It would be impossible for government to operate and not affect the distribution of income in society, at least indirectly. Purchases of goods and services and distribution of benefits all affect the well-being of various people, and governments finance these activities with taxes, which often have no relationship to the benefits provided. For example, various states spent tens of millions of dollars trying to qualify as the location of the federal government's proposed superconducting supercollider, because the increase in demand for workers and resources was expected to make many people in the chosen state better off than they would be without the expenditure. Yet their efforts were largely intended to attract a potential windfall rather than to lead to a better allocation of resources for the economy, and these issues have no clear relationship to the ultimate use of the facility. More mundane examples of the effect of government expenditure are fairly easy to find. Even at the local level, it is often very difficult to get agreement on closing superfluous schools or other facilities because the location of the nearest facility determines much about the value a person receives from government activity. And we have already discussed the effects of property tax financing on the incentive to allow or not allow certain types of development.

Any attempt to look at the distribution of income also has to grapple with the issues associated with defining income and with the tax system. Many of the things that individuals consume are not paid for explicitly, yet they are part of income as measured from the economic perspective. For example, one criticism of the government's poverty measures is that they ignore the value of in-kind transfers such as food stamps, Medicaid, and housing subsidies, which government provides for low-income people.[2] The effect of this method is to overstate the number of people in poverty using the official estimates.

We endeavor in this chapter first to provide some descriptive material on how income and wealth are distributed in the United States. We then offer a brief review of the analysis of the determination of wages and hours for workers. Next we turn to the issue of determining the level of poverty and the various policies directly intended to alleviate poverty. After this we look at the various social insurance programs and their effect on the distribution of income. Finally, we raise some of the issues that occur because government actions can have a substantial impact on income for many people.

/// INCOME DISTRIBUTION

There are many ways in which one could look at the distribution of income to determine something about how equal or unequal it is, but most policy discussions start by looking at some fairly simple comparisons. For example, the top 20% of income recipients in the United States receive more income than the lowest 70% of income recipients, and the gap between higher income and lower income recipients appears to be widening.[3] In 1985 the top fifth of the family income distribution (those with income of $48,000 or above) received 43% of all family income, while the bottom fifth (income less than $13,200) received only 4.7%. These percentages represent the highest share for upper-income families since World War II and the lowest share for low-income families since 1960.[4] Nevertheless, money income distribution has stayed remarkably stable over this time period, with the upper fifth never getting a share less than 40% and the lower fifth never getting a share more than 5.6% over the last forty years, despite large changes in the economy and in transfer programs.[5] Further, the number and percentages of people living below the poverty level showed substantial increases from the middle 1970s to the early 1980s before turning down again, but this percentage has also remained fairly stable over the last twenty years.[6]

The differences show up across various categorizations, as one might

---

[2] See Morton Paglin, *Poverty and Transfers In-Kind: A Reevaluation of Poverty in the United States* (Stanford, CA: Hoover Institution Press, 1980); and Timothy Smeeding, "The Antipoverty Effectiveness of In-Kind Transfers," *Journal of Human Resources* 7 (Summer 1977), pp. 360–378.

[3] Cited in "Rich Man, Poor Man," *Wall Street Journal* (November 28, 1984), p. 32; and David Wessel, "U.S. Rich and Poor Increase in Numbers; Middle Loses Ground," *Wall Street Journal* (September 22, 1986), pp. 1 and 20.

[4] Ibid.

[5] Frank Levy, *Dollars and Dreams: The Changing American Income Distribution* (New York: Russell Sage Foundation, 1987), pp. 13–15.

[6] Tax Foundation, *Facts and Figures on Government Finance, 1988–89* (Baltimore: Johns Hopkins University Press, 1988), p. 57.

expect. For example, in 1985 median family income (half of families earned more while half earned less) was at $27,735; but families headed by college graduates had a median of $46,423. Male-headed families with no wife present had a median income of $22,622; female-headed families with no husband present had a median of only $13,660; and married couples in which both work came close to a combination of these two with a median income of $36,431. White families had a median of $29,152 compared to a median of $16,786 for blacks.[7] Certainly we would expect college graduates to earn more than less educated people to make up for the expense and foregone earnings of a college education; the reported difference also reflects the fact that college graduates are likely to marry other high-earning college graduates. Many factors contribute to the lower earnings of blacks, and some minority groups have higher median earnings than whites. While the causes of these differences are open to some debate, their existence alone is the reason for many of the redistributive transfer programs.

Wealth

The differences are even more pronounced if wealth distributions are examined. Only 0.4% of households have stock holdings of greater than $500,000 in value; yet these households own 54% of all individually owned stock. Further, close to 80% of all households have no direct ownership of stock.[8] Distribution of many other forms of wealth show similar patterns. While many households do have some indirect ownership of wealth through pension programs, it is clear that the wealth distribution is even more skewed than the income distribution. In 1983, almost 4% of the population had a net worth of over half a million dollars while about 8% had a net worth of zero or less. Median net worth was about $25,000; a large percentage of this represented equity in houses and cars.[9]

Geographic Differences

The dispersion of income also shows geographic dimensions. For example, the average annual earnings of workers in Alaska in 1986 ($28,442) was almost double that of workers in South Dakota ($14,477).[10] Although Alaska is something of an outlier (New York had the second highest average at $23,200), there is a very clear difference across states in average earnings. Is this an issue that should be considered in looking at income distribution? Some argue that poor states like South Dakota should receive more help from

[7] *Wall Street Journal*, op. cit.
[8] F. Thomas Juster, "The Distribution of Wealth in the U.S. Economy," *Economic Outlook USA*, Part 1, vol. 14 (Summer 1987), pp. 16–19; and Part 2, vol. 14 (Spring 1988), pp. 9–12.
[9] Ibid., Part 1, p. 17.
[10] Employment Division, Department of Human Resources, State of Oregon, *Portland Metropolitan Labor Trends* (April 1988), p. 12. Note that data is for workers covered by unemployment compensation.

the federal government to offset the relatively low income while others argue that the poor in Alaska and New York need additional assistance because part of the wage differential is associated with the higher living costs in these states.

Other geographic differences occur within urban areas and within states. Often the urban areas of a state have higher levels of income (and living expenses) than the rural areas, and the suburban parts of urban areas have higher levels of income than the central cities. Should these differences be taken into account in determining redistribution policies? As we shall see, they are not taken into account for most purposes of explicit redistribution as conducted by the federal government. However, they are of some importance when it comes to issues such as the financing of certain types of public services. In particular, a number of court rulings have the effect of forcing some states to use statewide redistribution to maintain some minimum standard for public schools in lower income communities.

/// **POVERTY**

The method by which poverty is defined is obviously an important determinant of how much poverty exists. Some view poverty as an absolute standard determined by some minimal level of food, clothing, transportation, housing, and so on. Others view poverty as a relative situation, determined by the difference between available consumption opportunities relative to the average for the nation.[11] Under the latter view, a poor person in the United States has much higher levels of consumption than someone in a developing country because the comparison level of average consumption is much higher. While there is no doubt that the level of consumption for poverty families in the United States is considerably higher than it is in many other countries, the United States uses a form of absolute standard in defining poverty. Essentially, the poverty level in the United States is defined as income that is less than three times the cost of an adequate diet. This definition has been used since the 1960s and is based on the finding that in 1955–61 middle-income families spent about one-third of their income on food. The level of income needed to achieve the poverty cutoff varies over time with changes in price levels and some other factors, but the basic definition has not been changed.

Under the relative consumption definition of poverty, a person who cannot come close to the consumption levels of most people in the country would be considered poor even if there were adequate food, shelter, and so on. For example, poverty might be defined as being in the lowest 20% of the population with respect to income. The major problem with such a definition is that it

[11] See, for example, Harold Watts, "Have Our Measures of Poverty Become Poorer?" *Focus* 9 (Summer 1986), pp. 18–23.

becomes almost impossible to eliminate poverty or to measure progress in alleviating it. Poverty could only disappear if everyone had the same income.

Other possible definitions of poverty focus on the level of income relative to average income. Such measures of relative poverty react only to changes in the distribution of income. Thus, if the measure of poverty is determined to be half of median income, then poverty is only reduced by bringing up the percentage of income going to those in the lowest part of the income scale. With an absolute measure of poverty, an increase in average incomes would reduce the number of people in poverty if the distribution of income were unchanged. However, with a relative measure, the number of people in poverty would be unchanged no matter how much the average income went up. In fact, the poverty population would increase if the income of the lower groups went up less rapidly than average.

Measuring Poverty

The issue is further complicated by the methods used to measure poverty. Essentially, the definition is based on family income and family size. The Census Bureau conducts an annual survey of household income for a sample of the population. Those falling below the poverty line (or threshold) are counted as poor. This information is then used to estimate the totals for the country.

There are a variety of objections to this procedure. Perhaps the most important objection is that only before-tax money income is counted in determining who is poor. Thus, transfers in the forms of goods and services do not count, nor does a family's level of assets. Further, increases in the taxes paid by a low-income family or in the tax credits they receive would not affect the measure of poverty. Since in recent years over 70% of the welfare-type transfers by the federal government to low-income people has been in the form of goods and services, the failure to include this appears to overstate the amount of poverty. Similarly, ignoring a persons business and other assets in determining poverty is likely to overstate the number defined as being in poverty.[12]

While the dispersion of income and wealth is generally accepted as a reasonable measure of the divergence in economic status of different parts of the population, the notion that it is increasing over time is open to serious question. Part of the problem with family income as a measure of economic status is the changing composition of families over time. For a long time, the family consisted of a husband and wife with their children and the father was the principal source of money income. Older people often lived with their children, and more than 25% of the aged were poor in 1964. This pattern has changed substantially. Most women are now in the labor force, and there are

[12] Paglin, op. cit., reports that over one million of those counted as in poverty in 1976 were so because of losses associated with accelerated depreciation and related types of business losses. Many family farms and other family businesses have high permanent or long-run income but in some years show accounting losses and are counted as in poverty.

more households headed by women. The elderly have an official poverty incidence less than half of what it was in 1964; alternative estimates find the incidence even lower. By most measures, the standard of living achieved by retirees has soared in the last twenty years and this shows up as reduced poverty even though more are living independently. Even within the elderly population, much of the poverty is associated with the older cohorts which have not received as much benefit from higher Social Security payments and which consist disproportionately of widows who receive only dependents' payments.

The changes in the amount of poverty are often hard to document, but there seem to be some clear trends. The growth in the number of female-headed households has increased the incidence of poverty because of the high incidence of poverty within this subgroup. Some even refer to this as the feminization of poverty. This leaves many children in poverty as well. In fact, over half of all poverty households are headed by women with no husband present.[13] On the other side of the income distribution, the number of two-earner households is at historic high levels. The two-earner households are also responsible for much of the increase in the highest income-earner classes.

We still do not have good data and analysis on how much of poverty is caused by the breaking up of families, but this is a far different problem than one in which earnings are decreasing. It suggests that part of the solution may be to return more of the financial obligation of raising children to absent parents.[14]

The Haves and Have Nots?

The possibility that labor earnings are showing greater divergence than they once did is receiving substantial attention at the national level. Several influential studies have concluded that although the U.S. economy clearly created huge numbers of jobs during the 1970s, these jobs were low paying and unskilled.[15] Again, there is serious question as to the accuracy of this observation;[16] but there are a number of issues that should be addressed with respect to public policy, in particular, the concern that unskilled workers may find few job opportunities and low wages as a permanent condition.

---

[13] Wessel, op. cit., p. 20.

[14] See Daniel Moynihan, "Our Poorest Citizens – Children," *Focus* 11 (Spring 1988), pp. 5–6; Paglin, op. cit.; and Smeeding, op. cit.

[15] The best known is Barry Bluestone and Bennett Harrison, "The Great American Job Machine: The Proliferation of Low Wage Employment in the U.S. Economy," a study prepared for the U.S. Congress, Joint Economic Committee (December 1986). Also see Chris Tilly, Barry Bluestone, and Bennett Harrison, "What Is Making American Wages More Unequal?" *Proceedings of the 39th Annual Meetings* (Industrial Relations Research Association, 1986), pp. 338–348.

[16] For example, see Robert J. Samuelson, "The Myth of the Missing Middle," *Newsweek* (July 1, 1985), p. 50; M. W. Horrigan and S. E. Haugen, "The Declining Middle-Class Thesis: A Sensitivity Analysis," *Monthly Labor Review* 111 (May 1988), pp. 3–13; and Gene Koretz, "Is Upward Mobility Shrinking the Middle Class?" *Business Week* (August 15, 1988), p. 34.

The available information indicates that changes in position within the income distribution over time are fairly substantial. Although being born into a wealthy family makes it much more likely that a person will be wealthy, it is by no means a foregone conclusion. Similarly, receiving welfare benefits at some time does not mean that a person will be permanently dependent on welfare benefits. Whereas about 25% of one sample received welfare payments in at least one of ten years, only about 2.6% appeared to be chronically poor, and only about 2% of the sample received more than half of its income from welfare in at least eight of the ten years.[17]

This movement among income and wealth classes forms the basic criticism of some of the measures of disparity in the U.S. Because people do not have a steady income stream over their entire lifetime, they tend to use savings to smooth out their consumption over time. However, if we focus only on current income, we are likely to find great disparity, which simply reflects the different stages of the life cycle. People just entering the working years are likely to have substantial periods with low or zero income while they complete their education or learn skills on the job. This is often followed by fairly high income years in which there is substantial savings to build up wealth (particularly home ownership) or where participation in Social Security and private pension plans builds a claim to income during retirement. This wealth and/or pension is used after retirement to maintain consumption despite reduced earnings. Thus, if we simply look at the pattern of income associated with one family, we would likely conclude that it is very unequal over time. However, looking at different families in different phases of the life cycle creates the same problem. Looking only at differences in lifetime earnings for families reduces one measure of income inequality by as much as one-third.[18]

Adjustments for life-cycle differences in earnings and for in-kind transfers substantially reduce the number of people counted as being in poverty. Further, it is fairly clear that for most of those people, the condition is a temporary one. Thus, public policies to alleviate the problems associated with low income can generally be broken into two classes: the social insurance programs or the basic welfare programs. The social insurance programs are designed to address problems associated with an uneven income stream over a person's lifetime while the welfare programs are largely aimed at alleviating hardship for those unable to earn sufficient income for long periods of time.

The relationship between reward for effort and efficiency creates problems in attempts to redistribute income. It means that more redistribution tends to result in a less efficient allocation of resources. In particular, if taxes are very heavy on those who work while the financial support provided by government to those who do not work is substantial, then the incentive to work is greatly

---

[17] Greg Duncan, *Years of Poverty, Years of Plenty* (Ann Arbor, MI: University of Michigan, 1984), pp. 41–43 and 91.

[18] Morton Paglin, "The Measurement and Trend of Inequality: A Basic Revision," *American Economic Review* 65 (September 1975), pp. 598–609.

reduced. Worse, the incentive to make the investment of time and money needed to obtain education or particular skills could also be affected. The absence of these incentives not only lowers the value of output created in the present, it can also reduce the rate of growth of the economy. The latter ultimately reduces the effectiveness of redistribution programs.

To the extent that there is a trade-off between growth and redistribution, the result of more current redistribution would be to leave everyone worse off in the future. It is reasonably clear that to be poor in one of the industrial countries is far preferable to being poor in one of the developing countries. Further, there is fairly widespread agreement that the rate of poverty was falling in the United States prior to the War on Poverty because of the overall growth in the economy. Thus, while many things can be done to alter the distribution of income at any time, one should not lose sight of the importance of rising real per-capita income in the long-run fight against poverty.

/// SOCIAL INSURANCE PROGRAMS

There are several causes of poverty. Many people suffer times when the loss of a job or insufficient planning for retirement leave them among the ranks of the poor. Some people manage to save enough during working periods to alleviate the problems of the low-income periods, but many people do not. Two major programs at the federal level attempt to address this problems: unemployment insurance is intended to smooth over relatively short periods of job loss, and the Social Security system provides some insurance against income loss associated with old age.

Social Security

Social Security is now the second largest item in the federal budget and expenditures are expected to continue to grow over time. Many people pay more in Social Security taxes (especially if the employer portion of the tax is counted) than they do in federal income taxes; and these taxes have the potential to grow as the number of workers relative to retirees declines. The increase in benefits associated with Social Security since the late 1960s is an important factor in the substantial reduction in the number of elderly living in poverty, and a major factor in retirement planning for most people. Despite its billing as a retirement system, the Social Security system has many features of a transfer program. Current retirees get benefits financed by the taxes on current workers, and current workers will have their benefits financed largely by future workers. In addition, low-earning workers get a higher pension relative to their wages than high-earning workers.

Retirement systems fall into two basic categories: defined contribution and defined benefit. The defined contribution system requires that a certain amount of money be set aside each year a person is employed. This money is then invested in some manner so that it grows over time. The amount in the fund when the worker retires determines the amount of pension the worker will receive. Should the employer who promised the pension go bankrupt or otherwise cease operation, the fund set aside for the employee generally still belongs to the employee.

The defined benefit retirement plans call for a particular level of benefits to be paid in retirement, regardless of the amount that has actually been set aside. These defined benefit plans could be of the pay-as-you-go type or the trust fund variety. The latter type of plan requires that a certain amount of money be set aside each year that the person works. When the person retires, the trust fund should provide all of the money needed to pay out benefits. If there is any shortfall, the employer is required to make up the extra from current revenues. Under the pay-as-you-go system, the pension does not amass assets and must rely on the current financial situation to provide sufficient revenues to pay all current claims for pension benefits. Because of problems created when a company goes bankrupt or otherwise tries to avoid paying promised pensions, the government forced all the private-sector defined benefit systems to start putting money into trust funds to pay for expected costs of the program. Thus, virtually all the private pension programs are now at least partially funded.

The Social Security system is still funded largely on a pay-as-you-go basis even though it is a defined benefit pension program. Hence, Social Security is more accurately described as a system of transfers between current workers and current retirees than as a retirement system. If the program were to be canceled for some reason, there are virtually no assets with which to pay promised benefits. Of course, the federal government is not likely to cancel the program; but some people wonder if the increase in future demands on the system will force some cut in benefits as compared to the benefits promised under the current system.

Social Security also has an element of redistribution among contemporaries since higher income workers pay more in taxes and receive more in benefits, but lower income workers receive more benefits relative to the taxes they paid. For example, in 1987 the basic retiree benefit was figured as 90% of the first $310 of average indexed monthly earnings (AIME), plus 32% of AIME between $311 and $1,866, plus 15% of AIME above $1,866.[19] Since taxes are paid on the basis of AIME, the benefits are lower relative to taxes paid as income goes up. AIME is determined from earnings over a person's life adjusted for inflation.

When the system was first instituted, the number of workers was high relative to the number of eligible beneficiaries; hence, the taxes required were

---

[19] Merton C. Bernstein and Joan Brodshaug Bernstein, *Social Security: The System That Works* (New York: Basic Books, 1988), pp. 30–31. Note that the intervals change over time to reflect changes in average earnings.

low as well. While there are still more workers than retirees, the ratio is lower and the level of taxation is commensurately higher. In the future, the ratio of workers to retirees is expected to become even lower than it is now. Even if a substantial trust fund is built up, it is possible that future Social Security taxes might have to be set at a much higher level than they are now.

In contrast to the Social Security system, the federal government requires that private pension plans set money aside during each worker's working years to pay for any promised pension benefits. Thus, the pension program builds up a fund so that the retiree will get benefits even if the company is no longer in business. This system has the advantage of providing more security for the worker and of showing the employer just how much the pension program will cost. It is estimated that if the Social Security system were funded in the same way, it would require a trust fund of over $4 trillion. The actual trust fund was under $100 billion in 1987, or about one-quarter of 1% of what would be needed.[20] While the fund is growing over time, the difference between promised pensions and assets will remain huge.

Because of its nature, it is difficult to evaluate the Social Security system. Viewed as a welfare system, it provides too much money to those who are not low-income. However, viewed as a pension system, the level of benefits is not tied closely with contributions, and they are subject to political influence. Despite the ambiguity in terms of what it is intended to do, the increases in Social Security benefits over the last few decades are largely credited with the major reductions in the incidence of poverty among the elderly.[21] By one estimate the rate of poverty among the elderly has dropped from about 30% in the mid-1960s to less than 4% in 1983.[22]

Unemployment Compensation

Unemployment compensation is the other major form of social insurance. For male-headed families, more than half of the periods of family poverty are caused by a drop in the earnings of the head; and more than one-third of all periods of poverty for all household types are caused by such drops in income,[23] despite the existence of the current system of unemployment conpensation. In the absence of such insurance, there are other ways to provide for periods of unemployment, but it is likely that the overall amount of poverty would be higher than it currently is.

The unemployment compensation system in the United States is actually

---

[20] For a discussion see Martin J. Feldstein, "Social Security, Induced Retirement, and Aggregate Capital Accumulation," *Journal of Political Economy* 82 (September/October 1974), pp. 905–926.

[21] For example, see Gary Burtless, "Public Spending for the Poor: Trends, Prospects, and Economic Limits," in Sheldon H. Danziger and Daniel H. Weinberg, eds., *Fighting Poverty: What Works and What Doesn't* (Cambridge: Harvard University Press, 1986), pp. 18–49.

[22] Sheldon H. Danziger, et al., "Antipoverty Policy: Effects on the Poor and the Nonpoor," in Danziger and Weinberg, op. cit., pp. 50–77.

[23] Mary Jo Bane, "Household Composition and Poverty," in Danziger and Weinberg, op. cit., p. 223.

determined at the state level, but the federal government has provided a set of incentives, which induce states to have some unemployment compensation system and to have some uniformity across states. Essentially, the federal government levies a tax on labor payments made by firms and allows a credit for most of this tax if the firm makes payments to a state program that meets federal guidelines. Since the money is essentially "free" to the state, states generally collect at least the amount released by the federal credit. However, because of differences in the individual state programs there is no uniform unemployment compensation program. Most state programs are designed to replace some percentage of the lost wages up to a given maximum for a set period of time. If the worker finds alternative work within the stated time period, he or she is not eligible for continued payments; however, if unemployment extends beyond the time limit, there may be supplemental payments financed by the federal government.

Since a tax on labor payments by firms finances most of the unemployment compensation system, there appears to be little in the way of redistribution because of the system.[24] However, the loss of benefits associated with going back to work is credited with causing some increase in the measured unemployment rate.[25] In terms of the overall income distribution, the payments associated with unemployment compensation are more likely to affect short-term measures of the income distribution than to affect the overall distribution of income. In particular, very low-income workers are much less likely than higher income workers to have worked long enough to be eligible for unemployment compensation when they do lose jobs; however, when they collect, minimum payments usually result in some small transfer relative to the taxes paid by their employers.

/// POVERTY POLICIES

Aside from the social insurance programs, the major method of coping with the problems of low income are the various forms of redistribution programs.

The Existing Programs

There are a large variety of programs intended to aid low-income families; however, the major cash redistribution programs are Aid to Families with Dependent Children (AFDC) and Supplemental Security Income (SSI). AFDC, the largest of the cash transfer programs, accounted for transfers of $16.2

---

[24] Daniel S. Hamermesh, *Jobless Pay and the Economy* (Baltimore: Johns Hopkins University Press, 1977), p. 98.
[25] Hamermesh, op. cit., p. 100, estimates it at about .7 percentage points.

Table 16-1 / **Government Transfer Payments ($ Billions)**

	1929	1949	1969	1986
Federal Government	.7	8.7	50.8	385.9
Social insurance	.1	4.2	43.0	338.0
Veterans benefits	.5	4.2	5.8	14.9
Food stamps	–	–	.3	10.6
Other	.1	.3	1.7	22.4
State and Local Government	.2	3.0	16.7	110.1
Social insurance	.1	.5	4.4	34.1
Medical care	–	–	4.5	45.2
AFDC	–	.5	3.5	16.2
Other	.1	2.0	4.3	14.6
Total	.9	11.7	67.5	496.0

(Source: Tax Foundation, *Facts and Figures on Government Finance, 1988–89* [Baltimore: Johns Hopkins University Press, 1988], p. 31.)

billion in 1986.[26] This is in contrast to $45.2 billion for medical care alone in the in-kind redistribution category, which should give some idea of the relative weights for the two types of redistribution. Table 16-1 shows historical data for the various types of general public assistance programs. Note in particular the rapid increase in medical payments relative to money payments.

There are two basic issues in the attempts to alleviate poverty. One is getting basic items to people in time of need while the other is to find some way to treat the causes of poverty so as to allow a person or family to stay out of poverty in the future. The methods of achieving these goals are often incompatible. The easiest way to achieve the first goal is to provide food, housing and other resources to those in need. The long-range solution, however, rests on getting those who are capable into the work force. Yet the means testing done for the short-run approach becomes a deterrent to long-term solutions. It is possible for a person who is in the welfare system to find that he or she is made worse off by going back to work. Even when the person does not end up with less income, the increase in standard of living may be slight relative to the work effort; this is equivalent to a very high rate of marginal taxation on earnings. As earnings increase, the person loses eligibility for many of the transfers. The loss of these transfers can be of greater significance than the income earned, so the person may actually be worse off by working than by not working.

This problem is illustrated in Figure 16-1. The redistributive program is

[26] Tax Foundation, *Facts and Figures on Government Finance, 1988–89* (Baltimore: Johns Hopkins University Press, 1988), p. 31.

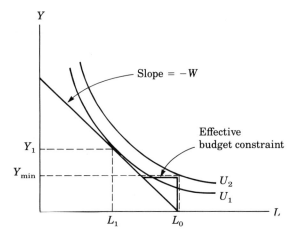

*Figure 16-1 / **Means-Tested Transfer and Work Effort***

represented as the amount Y_{min}. The person is eligible to receive this amount if there are no other sources of income. However, any earnings are offset by a dollar for dollar reduction in the transfer payments. Thus, the effective budget line starts at Y_{min} and is horizontal up to the point at which it intersects the earned income line. It is then the earned income budget line for any income above Y_{min}. Since there is likely to be some aversion to work, it is entirely possible for someone who could earn more than the welfare minimum to still choose to remain on welfare. This is shown with the indifference curve U_1 tangent to the earned income budget line at income Y_1, which is above the minimum, while the person still chooses to accept the minimum because it is associated with a higher indifference curve.

Obviously, not everyone who is eligible for welfare benefits would choose to accept them rather than return to work. As the wage available rises, the budget line rotates upward from L_0. The higher income associated with these opportunities will eventually induce the person to choose work rather than stay on welfare. Thus, in Figure 16-2, we see that the wage W_2 is just large enough to make the person indifferent between working and staying on welfare. Note that from the perspective of the individual, the earnings of Y_1 only result in an increase of income from Y_{min} to Y_1. Essentially, the loss of welfare benefits is equivalent to a tax on the worker; it is this "tax" associated with the loss of benefits that creates the work disincentive.

One approach to reducing the work disincentive associated with the loss of redistributive benefits is to lower the benefits at a rate of less than dollar for dollar. For example, the benefits might be reduced by only 50 cents for each additional dollar of earnings. This type of program would reduce the number of people who would choose not to work at all; but it would extend benefits to many who would not be eligible under the complete loss of benefits scheme. Thus, the cost of the program is likely to be considerably higher than one with

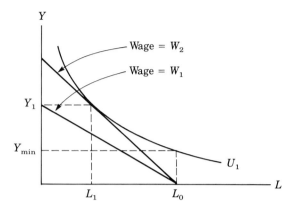

Figure 16-2 / **Effect of Rising Wages**

complete loss of benefits for those earning above Y_{min}. The first case is illustrated in Figure 16-3. It shows that the person would choose not to work at all under the complete loss of benefits scheme, but chooses to work some under the 50% loss sytem. The cost of the benefits this person receives is lowered because the person is working. Figure 16-4 shows a similar situation in terms of work and benefits for a person under the 50% reduction scheme except that this person would have chosen to work rather than accept welfare under the complete loss system. Hence, the cost of transfers to this person is higher than it would have been. If there are more people of the second type than there are of the first type, the total cost of the system will increase.

The expectation is that there are indeed more people of the second type than there are of the first type, and an increase in the level of income at which certain benefits are available would cause a substantial increase in costs. The

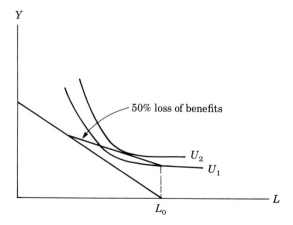

Figure 16-3 / **Some Work More**

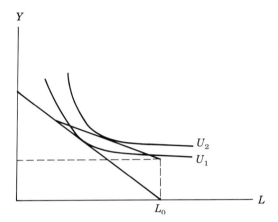

Figure 16-4 / Some Work Less

disincentive to work in the current welfare system must be traded off against the higher cost of an expanded system.

Negative Income Tax

A number of economists have argued that the replacement of the current system of welfare programs by a single cash transfer program would lead to a substantial improvement in the well-being of the poor and would eliminate many of the disincentive effects associated with the loss of benefits under the current system. The program they advocate is known as the negative income tax. The negative income tax is composed of a lump-sum grant to all tax-payers, which is reduced by some explicit tax on earnings. Thus, as earnings increased the net amount of the transfer to the recipient would decline and eventually reach zero. This is shown in Figure 16-5. The base amount, labeled B, is the minimum amount of income the recipient would receive under the program. As earnings increase, the after-tax and transfer amount will also increase, but by less than the amount of the additional earnings. The earnings will be subject to a tax in the form of a reduction in the transfer received. At earnings of Z, the person receives no net subsidy and pays no net taxes. Any earnings beyond Z would be taxed at positive rates.

The major benefits of the negative income tax program are that it removes many of the severe reductions in benefits associated with working under the current system of welfare payments and that it can be used to substantially increase the well-being of the poor. The major disadvantages are that it creates some work disincentives for many who are not currently eligible for any transfers and it is likely to be either very costly or provide only a minimal level of base benefits.

The problem with the system is that in order to keep the tax rate low,

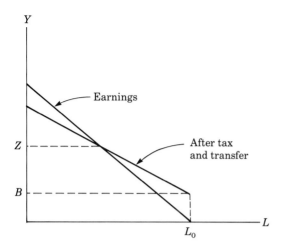

Figure 16-5 / **Negative Income Tax**

either the base amount will have to be low or the breakeven point will have to be high. The base amount is simply equal to the tax rate times the breakeven amount. Once any two of these amounts are chosen, the other is determined. Thus, if the tax rate is set at 50% and the base amount is chosen as $12,000 (close to the poverty level), the breakeven point would be $24,000 (close to median income). This means that in order to guarantee everyone at least the poverty level of income and a marginal tax rate no greater than 50%, it would be necessary to provide some grants to almost half the population. This is obviously very expensive, so realistic programs set the base amount well below the poverty line; but if this were the only transfer program, it would leave substantial numbers of people in poverty. In addition, experiments conducted to test the work effects of such a system conclude that it would reduce work effort among low-income households and might increase the rate at which low-income families break up.[27]

An alternative method to alleviate the work disincentive effects of the loss of benefits associated with working is to place stricter work requirements on those receiving transfers who are capable of working. This is the general direction of the changes in welfare policy in the 1980s. Rather than reduce the loss in benefits associated with working, there has been a tendency to target more of the benefits at those below the poverty line and provide for sanctions, such as complete loss of benefits, to those deemed capable of working who do not find suitable employment.

---

[27] There are a variety of reviews of the results of this research. A recent one is Alicia H. Munnell, ed., *Lessons from the Income Maintenance Experiments* (Federal Reserve Bank of Boston and The Brookings Institution, 1987).

Workfare

The policy of requiring welfare recipients to work is often referred to as "workfare" in contrast to "welfare." Some critics of the welfare system in the United States have argued that the system itself creates substantial work disincentives and that it has created at least some of the recent increase in the number of people in poverty.[28] A requirement that the able recipients of aid be willing to work is seen as a way of circumventing these incentives without the high cost and other problems of a general transfer program like the negative income tax.

Recently a number of states have instituted work requirements for recipients of AFDC since it is the largest source of money aid to families with limited income. The legislation to allow more substantial work requirements for AFDC recipients was contained in the Omnibus Budget Reconciliation Act of 1981.[29] Since that time Massachusetts and California have made some form of work effort or job search mandatory for certain classes of AFDC recipients. A review of one work-requirement experiment concludes that the program did indeed lead to more employment and earnings and less welfare than for a comparable control group. Further, the experiment results suggest that some recipients drop out of the program when there are work requirements. One hypothesis is that these are people who are working in the "underground" economy, although there is no direct evidence of this.[30]

Thus, a requirement that those who can work do so in order to be eligible for transfer payments appears to be a viable alternative to a program like the negative income tax in increasing the work incentives for transfer recipients. In principle, this system achieves a lower cost for the transfer without denying benefits to those in need. However, the system is likely to have much higher administrative costs than the standard welfare system. The administrators will have to determine which of the people collecting welfare payments could have had jobs and which are simply not able to find work and then enforce the programs' provisions. In practice, many programs have such requirements but they are only loosely enforced. Alternatively, the government could provide a guaranteed job for those who do not find private sector employment. The problem with such systems is that the guaranteed job would be unlikely to produce output equivalent in value to the wages paid. Hence, the government would be committed to an expensive jobs program rather than the welfare program, and the total costs net of benefits produced could easily exceed the total cost of the simple welfare program. Thus, while the limited information we have on such programs seems reasonably positive so far, it will be some time before they are clearly shown to have achieved their objective of providing both work incentives and a set of subsidies targeted very narrowly to the needy.

[28] Charles Murray, *Losing Ground: American Social Policy, 1950–1980* (New York: Basic Books, 1984).
[29] Michael Wiseman, "Workfare and Welfare Policy," *Focus* 9 (Fall–Winter 1986), p. 2.
[30] Ibid., pp. 4–5.

Past attempts to provide either job training or job search assistance have not been notably successful. In general, an employable person is likely to find a job even in the absence of any government assistance. Hence, additional training has only a small impact on either the time it takes to get another job or the salary that the new job pays. On the other side are those with serious skill deficiencies or attitude problems. Short training courses are unlikely to provide sufficient new skills to make such people employable in the private sector. Hence, the investment in such programs would essentially be wasted for those who do not find new employment. The trade-off between more work effort and program costs seems to be fairly substantial for some groups. Thus, the success of workfare requirements is likely to depend on how carefully they are targeted at people who could indeed be helped by relatively small amounts of training and job search assistance. If such requirements are used too broadly, the results may be too expensive to achieve.

Much of the thrust of the reforms of the transfer system under President Reagan were aimed at targeting more of the aid to the poor and requiring more work effort to be eligible for the aid. This has reduced the benefits going to the "working poor."[31] Since such efforts have increased the incentives not to work, these incentives are being offset by requirements that able-bodied recipients find work. These efforts are still in the experimental stage, so there is no clear evidence that the program is either working or not working. Only information on the net long-term savings associated with reduced welfare dependency for some subset of the population could be compared to costs in determining success or failure for these systems.

Some of the required information should become available over the next few years because the Family Support Act of 1988 requires that each state set up a Job Opportunities and Basic Skills program and enroll at least 20% of eligible participants by 1995. This program effectively requires that many welfare recipients enter job training programs in exchange for the benefits they receive. In addition, there are extensions of certain benefits to welfare families switching to employment for a period of twelve months to further encourage them to leave the welfare rolls.

In-Kind Transfers

We tend to think of welfare programs as providing money to the poor. However, the majority of aid to low-income families is now given in the form of goods and services rather than money. These are known as "in-kind" transfers. From the economist's perspective, each person is the best judge of what is good for that person; in-kind transfers distort consumption patterns in a way that makes the recipient less well off than if he or she had received the money

---

[31] John C. Weicher, "The Reagan Domestic Program Cuts: Proposals, Outcomes, and Effects," in Phillip Cagan, ed., *Essays in Contemporary Economic Problems* (Washington, DC: American Enterprise Institute, 1986).

Bread

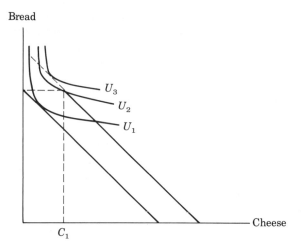

Figure 16-6 / In-Kind Transfer

needed to finance the transfer. The principle is the same as the one we noted when analyzing the use of intergovernmental grants by one level of government to influence the activities of another level of government. Briefly, Figure 16-6 shows that the person who receives the amount C_1 of cheese is able to move from indifference curve U_1 to U_2. This represents a clear improvement in well-being for this person. However, at the existing price ratio, the person would have preferred to receive the amount of money needed to buy the cheese. With cash rather than cheese, the person would have consumed less than C_1 of cheese, as shown by indifference curve U_3.

Clearly, if the person could use the money to purchase the cheese, he or she would be expected to do so if this were the form of expenditure that would raise utility the most. Why then does the government prefer to give many types of goods and services rather than cash? A variety of reasons might explain such behavior. One is that the government does not buy the good or service on the open market and in fact has a cost lower than the market price for the item. This has been true, for example, for the giveaways of surplus cheese by the federal government. While the cheese might have a nominal market value, the government ends up with it in the first place because it cannot be sold on the open market at that price. In addition, the government has storage costs associated with retaining the cheese. Hence, the option is not really between the money and the cheese, so an analysis like that in Figure 16-6 is somewhat misleading.

Another argument for the use of in-kind transfers is that the government does not want to subsidize just any kind of consumption. For example, most families that receive welfare payments contain children. The parents may not consider the welfare of the children as extensively as the government might like in making decisions about resource allocations. Thus, the parents might not provide breakfast or other meals to the children. If the government specifically wants to improve the nutrition of these youngsters, direct intervention in the form of meals or food subsidies might be much more effective at achieving this goal than would cash transfers. However, black markets sometimes develop which result in inefficient attempts to achieve consumption levels similar to the cash alternative. Similarly, the provision of housing would more effectively guarantee some housing services for the children than would the provision of cash, and in the housing allowance program the government transfers the cash directly to landlords so that the tenants are forced to "spend" it on housing that meets the government's standards.

In general, the view that the government should provide cash rather than goods and services is linked to the view that redistribution programs are methods to equalize the distribution of income rather than methods to alleviate inadequate consumption. The provision of goods and services is the only way to be sure that government transfers do indeed provide the minimal level of consumption. When cash is transferred, the recipient may choose to spend the money on items other than those which the giver would like to see consumed. Further, differences in prices over time or even in the ability of consumers to seek out the best price would make it difficult to insure that the cash transfer would just meet the stated requirements. If the amount of cash transfer is changed infrequently, there would certainly be times when it is either too high or too low relative to the prices available.

Another problem with provision of goods and services is the lack of market incentive to produce efficiently and to provide the appropriate mix of characteristics. For example, if the government is building housing to be provided at a subsidized price, it is unlikely that the units would go empty even if the cost of building them were very high relative to the cost of building comparable units. If a private company were to build inefficiently, the losses associated with rents that did not cover costs would soon force the company either to change its behavior or to go out of business. If the government is doing it, there is a wide range of potential inefficiency that would not prevent the subsidized unit from being filled. Thus, if the government builds a housing unit equivalent to one renting on the open market for $400 per month but will rent it for $300, it will be able to find tenants even if its cost is $500; but a private developer would only be able to get the $400 in rent and would lose money. Many people feel that something like this happened with the public housing program in the United States because most public housing units were built as new additions to the housing stock, while most private low-income housing is created by converting older housing stock. The latter approach appears to be much more cost-effective for low-income units, and this is one reason why the current trend is toward rent subsidies and away from direct public provision of housing. Even where the new building might be appropriate, it appears that the government costs are higher than those for equivalent private units.

Regulatory Approaches

In addition to direct transfers of money or goods and services to the poor, a variety of regulatory methods are used to try to change the distribution of income. For example, rent controls are used by a number of local governments in certain states, including New Jersey and California. A standard argument for such controls is that they keep rents low and therefore help low-income renters. However, economic analysis has shown that a likely long-run response to such controls is for landlords to reduce the number of available units, and this is likely to work against the poor since they are the least likely to get units when there is a housing shortage.[32] One study goes so far as to blame much of the homelessness in the United States on the existence of rent controls.[33]

The minimum wage is viewed by many as an antipoverty measure because it appears to raise the income of the unskilled. It is frequently stated that the minimum wage is insufficient to maintain a family of four at the poverty level; and it seems to be the goal of many of its proponents that it achieve this level of income for full-time work. Unfortunately, there are several problems with this view of the minimum wage. The most important problem is that it is likely to reduce the number of jobs available to low-skilled people. Thus, while some recipients of the wage are better off than they would be in the absence of this legislation, others have no jobs and are worse off.

This can be seen in Figure 16-7, where the reduction in labor demanded from L_e to L_{min} leaves fewer people employed or those employed working fewer hours. The increase in wages from W_e to W_{min} offsets this in terms of total earnings, but not by as much as would be assumed looking only at the level of wages. In fact, it is possible that the total amount of money going to unskilled workers would be reduced by the minimum wage. The total income received by minimum-wage workers would be given by the product of hours worked and wage. Thus, the product of $W_{min} \times L_{min}$ may be lower than the product of $W_e \times L_e$. This occurs if labor use is reduced by a greater percentage than the percentage increase in wages, i.e., if the demand curve for such labor is elastic. While this is unlikely to happen in the very short run, it is much more likely to happen over longer periods of time as employers adjust to the higher wages.

A recent report by the Congressional Budget Office was reportedly sent back by congressional supporters of the minimum wage because it indicated that as many as 500,000 jobs would be lost if the minimum wage were raised to $5.05 an hour.[34] This loss of jobs would offset most of the higher income of those working under the legislation.

In addition, Figure 16-7 shows that the number of people willing to work rises with the minimum wage. This means that low-skill workers face increased competition for the jobs available, and that those most willing to work may not be the ones who actually get the jobs. For example, many teenagers are willing to work for the minimum wage who might not be as anxious for a job at lower pay. Given the excess supply of potential workers, employers can be

---

[32] Werner Z. Hirsch, *Law and Economics*, 2nd ed. (Boston: Academic Press, 1988), pp. 44–50 and 82–87.

[33] William Tucker, "Where Do the Homeless Come From?" *Associates Memo*, no. 5 (New York: Manhattan Institute for Policy Research, 1987).

[34] Tom Seppy, "Raise Minimum Wage, Lose 600,000 Jobs, Aide Warns," *Oregonian* (May 19, 1988), p. D11.

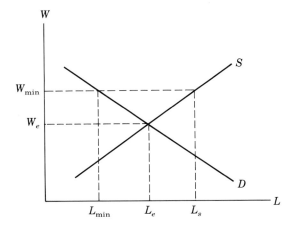

Figure 16-7 / Minimum Wage

selective about hiring. Thus, an employer faced with a minority teenager from an inner-city school in competition with a white, middle-class one from a suburban school is likely to go with the latter. Some researchers have concluded that this type of effect is responsible in large part for the high rate of unemployment among minority teenagers in particular. The conclusion of much of this research is that a minimum wage provides at best a small net benefit to low-income families and is likely to make many such families worse off.[35]

/// POLITICS AND INCOME

A final issue with respect to the redistribution of income is the extent to which the political process becomes the means to determine the arbitrary redistribution of income among those who are not poor. In the market economy the distribution of final product has at least some relationship to the value of the output produced by the person receiving the income. As we have seen, the value may fluctuate for some fairly random reasons and people may find that their incomes go up or down in an unpredictable way. However, within the bounds of uncertainty there are incentives to allocate resources and effort so as to produce something of value to others.

The political process also serves to allocate income. Unfortunately, many of the incentives given within the political process do not lead to the production of desirable goods and services. Rather, the political process leads to

[35] See, for example, William R. Johnson and Edgar K. Browning, "The Distributional and Efficiency Effects of Increasing the Minimum Wage: A Simulation," *American Economic Review* 73 (March 1983), pp. 204–211.

resources being devoted to the reallocation of existing goods and services among the various interested parties. Because there is no creation of value in this process, the resources are wasted in a certain sense. If the output of the political process is a more desirable allocation of output, it might be said that the process did indeed create value. However, the process often becomes one of determining who has the most political clout rather than one of determining who is most needy or deserving.

The importance of the political redistribution system can be seen by the efforts made to prevent various changes in government spending. For example, for many years the military had difficulty in closing bases in the United States. Every time it suggested closing bases, the congressional representatives from the affected areas made sure that the Defense Department received directions not to close the base. Certainly, many of the local merchants and workers would be worse off if a large base near them closed; but this is hardly a reason to keep open bases that are hard to justify for any other reason. The most recent attempt to get around the parochial interests of various elected representatives has been to form an independent commission to make recommendations on which bases should be closed. The commission provided a list of bases which Congress would have to vote on as a group to ensure that no one area was singled out. Even this has been opposed by some politicians, although it does appear that the eighty-six bases identified for closure by the commission will eventually be closed.[36]

A similar issue arises with respect to federal farm programs. There is little evidence that the billions spent by the federal government on farm subsidies is intended to do anything other than redistribute income to farmers. Yet the method chosen is a very inefficient way of accomplishing this objective. Many other examples could be found. The magnitude of the effort alone raises some serious questions about how important the political process has become in determining income for large parts of the population. In many ways, arbitrary changes in income for the nonpoor may have more of a long-run impact on the economy than the explicit redistribution programs aimed at alleviating the problems of the poor.

/// SUMMARY

The distribution of income in the United States shows substantial differences between the high and low ends of the scale. The distribution of wealth shows major differences as well. These differences are greatly reduced when some of the movement among income and wealth classes are averaged over a

---

[36] See John J. Fialka and John E. Yang, "Panel Backs Closing 86 U.S. Bases in Biggest Realignment Since 1940s," *Wall Street Journal* (December 30, 1988), p. A3; and "Armed Forces Agree in Spirit, Not Action," *Oregonian* (June 19, 1988), p. A12.

person's lifetime and when differences in consumption associated with non-monetary transfers are considered.

In response to these differences, government has a variety of programs aimed both at alleviating the problems associated with fluctuations within a person's lifetime and aiding those with chronically low income. The social insurance programs have grown substantially over the last thirty years, and they are responsible for much of the observed decline in the rate of poverty among some groups, particularly the elderly. The transfer programs aimed at alleviating poverty have a mixed record. Official poverty statistics do not show much of a decline in the rate of poverty in recent years, but these statistics only measure money income. When the growth in transfers in kind is taken into account, the reduction in poverty is substantial. Some people argue that the very success of the poverty alleviation programs has reduced incentives for people to escape poverty on their own. In particular, it is possible for some people to be better off staying on welfare programs than it is by working. Responses to this situation were to extend benefits to many of the near poor. However, the recent trend has been to reduce the benefits going to the near poor (often the working poor) and to impose more severe work requirements on welfare recipients. The initial response to such attempts has been fairly favorable, but the long-term effectiveness of such policies is still unknown.

In addition to direct social insurance and redistributive functions, government often affects income distribution through its actions. These may be intentional programs to aid some group, such as farmers, or they may be the unintentional side effects of various spending programs. In either case, they induce many people to look to government in attempting to change their share of the total income available. While this can change the distribution of income, it can also lead to a less efficient allocation of resources for the country.

Chapter 17 //////

The Provision of National Defense

National defense is the activity usually cited when economists are looking for an example of a public good. In effect no one consumes it directly, and the benefits to any one person are not changed as the country's population grows. Yet the very size of the expenditures involved means that the way national defense is provided has significant effects on the allocation of resources in the economy. Further, efficiency in setting and meeting the goals of national defense can be an important determinant of the overall cost of government. This chapter focuses on national defense because it is clearly an area of responsibility for the federal government; it has many characteristics of a public good; it is a large expenditure; and it illustrates how some of the issues associated with public choice affect what government actually does.

By any measure, the U.S. military budget is very large. For example, expenditure on defense was about $295 billion in 1987, or well over $1,000 per person for the country as a whole.[1] The defense budget showed rapid growth during the early 1980s, doubling in size between 1979 an 1985; and even in constant dollars, it increased on a per capita basis by more than 40% (see Table 17-1). In the mid-1970s defense was overtaken as the largest expenditure for the federal government by the Social Security system with its rapidly growing membership and, therefore, liabilities. However, defense retook the distinction of top expenditure program in 1985.[2] While the rate of increase in defense has slowed, it is still growing fast enough to maintain its share of GNP.

Historically, defense only took a substantial portion of GNP in the United States during wartime. Prior to World War II, the United States typically

---

[1] Advisory Commission on Intergovernmental Relations (ACIR), *Significant Features of Fiscal Federalism, 1988 Edition*, vol. 1, M-155 I (Washington, DC: 1987), pp. 12–14.
[2] Ibid.

Table 17-1 / Federal Government National Defense Expenditures 1954–1987

Calendar Year	Billions of Current Dollars	Percentage of GNP	Per Capita in 1982 Dollars	Percentage of All Federal Government Expenditures
1954	$ 41.6	11.2%	$ 971	59.2%
1959	46.4	9.4	859	50.6
1964	50.6	7.8	802	42.4
1969	79.1	8.2	981	41.4
1974	82.9	5.6	718	27.1
1979	122.5	4.9	692	23.5
1981	168.3	5.5	778	23.9
1982	194.7	6.1	837	24.9
1983	214.9	6.3	881	25.7
1984	235.1	6.2	921	26.3
1985	260.5	6.5	979	26.5
1986	279.6	6.6	1,014	27.1
1987	297.0	6.6	1,036	27.8

(Source: Advisory Commission on Intergovernmental Relations, *Significant Features of Fiscal Federalism, 1988 Edition*, vol. 1, M-155 I [Washington, DC: 1987], pp. 32–33.)

spent less than 2% of GNP on defense.[3] This jumped to about 40% during World War II, stayed at around 10% during much of the 1950s, and declined to less than 5% in 1979.[4] The much publicized Reagan defense buildup brought the percentage above 6% of GNP, where it seems to have stabilized, at least temporarily (see Table 17-1 and Figure 17-1). Among the countries of the NATO alliance, the United States devotes the largest share of its output to defense. For example, in 1984 the U.S. spent 6.9% of its gross domestic product (GDP); Greece spent 6.8% and the United Kingdom, 5.4%; Germany spent 3.3%, Norway 3.0%, Italy 2.8%, and Canada a mere 2.1%.[5]

Current levels of defense spending are neither inordinately high nor unusually low. There is room in the historical context for substantial movement either up or down and strong arguments are made for each of these changes. Critics of defense expenditures point out that resources used by the military are not available for other purposes. They look at the limited resources available and would like to divert them to redistributive policies or other domestic priorities. Supporters of defense expenditures see a hostile

[3] Charles J. Hitch, "The Military Budget and Its Impact on the Economy," in Joseph Scherer and James A. Papke, eds., *Public Finance and Fiscal Policy* (Boston: Houghton Mifflin, 1966), p. 88.
[4] ACIR, op. cit.
[5] "Defense White Paper," *The Economist* (May 4, 1985), p. 137.

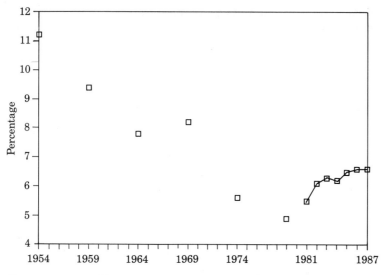

Figure 17-1 / Military Spending: Percentage of GNP

(Source: Advisory Commission on Intergovernmental Relations, *Significant Features of Fiscal Federalism, 1988 Edition*, vol. 1, M-155 I [Washington, DC: 1987], pp. 32–33.)

world with growing threats and believe that the increased expenditures are necessary to maintain the deterrent effect of our military forces. Each side has its estimates of the size and capability of the threat from the Soviet Union and other sources and each would like to change the level of our spending.[6]

Although serious concern for the country's safety underlies much of the controversy surrounding changes in defense spending, substantial other issues are tied to any changes in defense spending. The type of expenditure could affect certain aspects of military preparedness, such as the trade-off between conventional weapons and strategic nuclear weapons. Further, it is often important, at least to a few residents of an area, to have the government's expenditures targeted on specific locations. Finally, the ability to convert resources to "safety" is dependent on the efficiency of production of the output.

/// DEFENSE AS A PUBLIC GOOD

At first glance, defense is one of the best examples of a public good as defined in Chapter 2. It is available to all at the same time; one person's feeling of safety is not influenced by the number of other people who are protected by a

---

[6] See Richard A. Stubbing, "The Defense Budget" and Robert B. Pirie and Robert F. Hale, "Comments," in Gregory B. Mills and John L. Palmer, eds., *Federal Budget Policy in the 1980s* (Washington, DC: The Urban Institute Press, 1984), pp. 81–120.

given level of service. It would be virtually impossible to exclude residents of the country from being protected if they did not pay for service; because of this, there would be significant incentives for "free riders" if the financing were voluntary. Thus, in principle we could find the point where the marginal cost of additional defense would equal the sum of the marginal willingness to pay for more defense over the entire population. This would determine the optimal level of defense expenditures. Note that for any realistic tax price, some people will think that expenditures are too high while others will consider them too low. There may be some people for whom the additional expenditures have a negative benefit aside from any additional taxes they might have to pay. For example, they may think that too strong a defense induces other countries to spend more on defense and further destabilizes the world.

There are a number of problems with the public good view of national defense. First, there is little agreement on what the marginal cost curve looks like in terms of security. Information is available on the cost of specific defense systems and on the cost of personnel and supplies, but then it is necessary to determine how these items are converted into defense and how much each contributes to an improvement in the overall level of security. There is likely to be significant disagreement over how additional funds should be spent or over what should be cut first if funds are reduced.

The public good aspects of defense also spill over to other countries. Thus, the level of defense that the U.S. provides for itself affects the level available to many of our allies. Also, the placement of troops and materials alters the perceptions of protection that different areas receive. Even the type of equipment emphasized for development may influence perceptions of security. For example, money spent on improvements in tanks might be viewed as more oriented toward defending Western Europe than would money spent on improving submarines. Thus, foreign policy issues also enter into the decisions regarding defense expenditures.

From an economic perspective, the benefits of additional defense expenditures should be measured as the willingness to pay for the reduced probability of loss associated with hostile actions against our country. Yet there is virtually no way to determine the magnitude of such benefits. Rather, our leaders rely on the analysis of experts within the government and the military of resource requirements to meet specific goals, coupled with political indications that people want more or less defense spending. These considerations are further complicated by the fact that a country's military chiefs consider it their charge to assure survival and victory and therefore assume "worst case scenarios." Moreover, defense spending can have important implications for certain parts of the economy. An area with a defense base or a large defense contractor has a significant economic stake in certain defense decisions. These distributional effects are taken into account by the various politicians involved in the decision process.

Once the level of expenditure has been decided there is rivalry among the branches of the armed service in terms of sharing in those resources. Each branch may see itself in competition with other branches for a limited amount of resources rather than as parts of the same team trying to find the most efficient way to achieve a given objective. This competition can create problems such as lack of coordination or excess duplication of capabilities. Further, although the incentives that the managers of each lower level decision face should be ones that lead to efficiency, it is not at all clear that the system creates such incentives. Responses to these conflicting objectives have led to a fairly complex process of determining how much money is to be spent on defense and how it is to be allocated.

/// ALLOCATING RESOURCES TO NATIONAL DEFENSE

Defense is a good case study of the federal budget process because it is a large item that is exclusively a federal concern. In principle the production of national defense can be broken down into three distinct phases. In the first phase, the elected political leadership determines how much defense should be "purchased." In the second phase, the military leadership determines how the defense goals would best be met given the level of resources available. The last phase is to achieve the procurement of the required items at the least cost. In practice the three phases are not distinct, and many issues other than the optimal allocation of resources to defense arise.

Budgeting

Budgetary decisions about national defense are more complicated than those about most other government programs. There is great uncertainty about the nature and magnitude of future threats to our national security, and the implications of failing to meet those threats are enormous. Under these circumstances, civilians have a difficult time holding their own against services that can claim to know so much more. Defining and specifying the nation's defense goal and translating it into a set of quantifiable objectives is an almost superhuman task. Yet systems analysts and economists have made great strides in recent years.

In the abstract, budgetary decisions must be made to determine what the military requirements are and how to provide them efficiently. Conceptually, the determination of requirements involves the following steps:

1. Stating policy goals in the light of precisely defined enemy threats.
2. Determining the military capabilities that are required in clearly articulated circumstances to meet these goals.
3. Establishing a force structure to provide these capabilities.[7]

---

[7] Charles J. Hitch, "Cost Effectiveness," in Samuel A. Tucker, ed., *Decision-Making in the Department of Defense* (Washington, DC: Industrial College of the Armed Forces, 1966), pp. 133–158.

This process is beset with serious difficulties, starting with the problem of translating a statement of national policy into military strategy and requirements, though such steps have been quite effectively taken in some very difficult areas. For example, strategic nuclear policy has been translated into deterrence to be accomplished by Mutual Assured Destruction (MAD), which in turn has been translated into quantitative judgments of resource requirements.[8] It has proved much more difficult, however, to agree on a military strategy to defend the freedom of Western Europe, which is so vital to U.S. interests. Proposals have ranged from the immediate use of nuclear weapons in the event of any aggression to massive non-nuclear defense at the border. Even when agreement is reached on a strategy, it is difficult to translate it into U.S. force requirements, in light of the uncertainty about the level of support that will be given by our allies and the nature of the enemy's threat.

Executive Branch Actions   The Department of Defense has used a number of methods to bring order to the complex process of coordinating such a huge undertaking to achieve the country's goals in a reasonably efficient way. Prior to 1961, each military service received a budget of money and manpower, but each had much freedom to interpret foreign policy and to decide what was the most important military threat and how to meet it. The result was an unbalanced and often poorly integrated total force structure. The advantage was that the service rivalry over budgets led to some competition in the provision of defense services.

In the early 1960s, Robert McNamara introduced the Planning-Programming-Budgeting System (PPBS) and also centralized decision making in the Office of the Secretary of Defense. This was perhaps the first systematic attempt to analyze and plan the actions of a government department using sophisticated optimization techniques. The basic process continues to be important in defense budgeting although it has been modified extensively over time. We briefly review the process as it was practiced in the first term of the Reagan administration.[9]

The resource allocation process began with an annual preparation of a five-year Defense Guidance document. On the basis of information provided by the Joint Chiefs of Staff, threats to the country were defined against which programs could then be measured. The intent was to spell out national defense policy, objectives, and strategy. The prior year's document was reviewed each year to identify major changes in the global situation, policy, and strategy and to identify progress in achieving goals. This became the basis for planning documents that set objectives for force and resource planning, taking explicit account of fiscal projections.

Next the Armed Services and Defense agencies submitted programs de-

---

[8] Ibid., p. 199.

[9] The following material draws heavily from Vincent Puritano, "Resource Allocation in the Department of Defense," *Armed Forces Comptroller* (Spring 1984), pp. 4–11.

signed to meet the five-year objective of the Defense Guidance document and, at the same time, stay within the fiscal limits of the projected defense budget. The final internal phase was a program review with most of the major agencies in the Defense Department paying special attention to duplication, overlaps, and missed opportunities for economies and efficiencies. The remaining unresolved issues would be addressed during additional review as the administration's budget was completed.

Congressional Actions The congressional review process begins soon after the president submits the budget to Congress. In preparation for the congressional review, the department prepares congressional justification documents, testimony for the secretary and other DOD witnesses, and various documents in support of the budget. In 1983, for example, more than 21,000 pages of documents and exhibits were prepared for these congressional presentations.[10]

In the 1980s, the congressional budget process involves three distinct but somewhat overlapping phases. First, the Budget committees of the two houses set an overall ceiling for the defense budget as part of the first concurrent budget resolution, which is due in mid-May. Next, the Armed Services committees put together the Defense Authorization Act, which should be completed by middle to late summer. It specifies what the Defense Department is authorized to spend in the coming year. Finally, the Appropriations committees must pass a Defense Appropriation Act, usually in the fall, which appropriates the funds to pay for the expenditures that have been authorized. The actual outlay in a given year depends on the amount of new authorized spending that actually takes place in that year plus authorized spending from prior years that will take place in the current year. The latter is likely to approach 50% in any given year. For example, it has been estimated that only about 13% of new authorizations for procurement are spent in the year in which they are authorized.[11] The remainder is spread out over future years.

Because the national defense budget involves so many long-term commitments and because so few defense activities are set by statute, the budget is very much dependent on the annual authorization and appropriation process. Even programs with authorization may be stretched out to allow current expenditures on other programs; thus, even the ongoing programs may be in some sense dependent on current budget activities. Delays in the annual review process and its conclusion can cause serious problems and inefficiencies, and these delays have been worsening in recent years despite congressional efforts to improve the system. For this and various other reasons, biennial budgets have been urged on Congress, but so far without success.

The Budget and Impoundment Control Act of 1974 enacted reforms de-

[10] Ibid., p. 6.
[11] Commission on State Finance, State of California, *Impact of Federal Expenditures on California* (August 1986), p. 14.

signed to ensure that Congress completed all appropriations before the beginning of the budget (fiscal) year, changing the beginning of the fiscal year to begin three months later, to assure that this would happen. These reforms have not reduced tardiness: in six successive years (and in nineteen of twenty-one years), DOD has begun the fiscal year under a continuing resolution authority. For example, the FY 1983 DOD Appropriations Act was over three months late. Congressional budget tardiness creates much uncertainty and program instability, especially for procurements with long lead time or for ongoing procurement programs in which annual appropriations determine the number of items to be purchased each year.

Part of the problem in getting the budget passed on time is that Congress takes a very active role in managing the Department of Defense. A heated controversy exists over whether Congress interferes too little or too much in defense. One side would like to see more representatives acquire deeper knowledge about defense so as to be better able to make major defense decisions intelligently. The other side, particularly the defense establishment, is convinced that the congressional review of defense budgets is already far too laborious and often stifling. The constantly expanding number of congressional hearings each year, before more and more committees, forces top management to allocate a vast amount of time and resources to responding to Congress.[12]

Another complaint about the congressional role in budget making relates to overlapping jurisdiction of congressional committees and to the addition of legislative directives and restrictions for DOD. For example, the enactment of authorization provisions or limitations into appropriation bills, in direct violation of congressional rules, has grown considerably. In FY 1984, a total of 216 general provisions were directed to DOD. Many general provisions protect specific interests (see Box 17-1). For instance, DOD is forbidden by one provision from converting heating plants from coal to oil at defense facilities in Europe and by another from using European coal in European defense heating plants when U.S. coal is available. Other provisions prohibit DOD from buying aircraft ejection seats for the F-18 fighter from Britain.

/// THE WEAPONS ACQUISITION PROCESS

The military acquisition process is particularly complex because it involves the acquisition of items that are produced over long periods of time, have a relatively long life expectancy once completed, and often are at the cutting

---

[12] For example, in 1983 1,306 DOD witnesses provided 2,160 hours of testimony in hundreds of appearances before a total of 96 different committees and subcommittees. In addition, there were approximately 85,000 written inquiries and nearly 600,000 telephone calls from Congress during the year. In 1983, DOD provided Congress with 21,753 pages of justification documents in support of the FY 1984 budget request, a threefold increase over 1970. Puritano, op. cit., p. 6.

Box 17-1

////// Distributional Issues

The importance of distributional issues in the way Congress views the defense budget is well illustrated by the case of the T-46 trainer jet. This jet would be built by Fairchild Industries in Long Island, New York. The *Wall Street Journal* reported that the New York delegation managed to keep the trainer as an option by inserting certain requirements into the 1987 budget. However, the Air Force did not want to spend the billions needed for a new trainer at that time.*

While there can be differences in priorities between the president and Congress which may get Congress involved much more closely into the spending decisions of the Defense Department than might seem desirable, it is reasonably clear that this program was simply an attempt to increase defense spending in a particular geographic area. The billions of dollars spent on the plane would provide an economic boost to the area, and companies that produce military equipment often give large donations to political campaigns.

The logrolling model of public decision making sees the opportunity for trade-off among legislators as a means of improving efficiency. However, when the issues of most importance to politicians are related to directing federal expenditure to their region rather than enhancing programs that are important to their constituents, the efficiency effects of logrolling are at best problematic.

* *Wall Street Journal* (December 10, 1986), p. 4.

---

edge of science and technology. High-performance aircraft, missiles, ships and tanks, among others, are developed over many years before they enter into the military's inventory. Costs, therefore, are often significantly larger than initially visualized and so is the production period. Congress often finds itself with the difficult task of either significantly increasing appropriations for a project or terminating it. The latter decision is often hard to defend, since it is an admission of an earlier mistake made by Congress. There is little wonder, therefore, that the military and military suppliers try to understate acquisitions and maintenance costs, hoping to have Congress make an initial commitment. This can lead to what is often referred to as "foot-in-the-door financing."[13]

Certain types of cost increases can be the fault of Congress. For example,

---

[13] The B-1 bomber is a good example. For a discussion see Nick Kotz, "Money, Politics, and the B-1 Bomber," *Technology Review* 91 (April 1988), pp. 30–40.

Congress tends to change the timing of acquisitions and thereby causes cost increases. Binding multiyear contracts would reduce this problem.

At least in the abstract, there is some least cost acquisition timetable. This would be associated with a rate of production allowing producers to establish and sustain production rates at which unit costs are low and relatively stable. However, a desire to get a weapon into place more quickly or a need to stretch out procurement because of insufficient money appropriated can cause production to take place at rates that lead to higher overall unit costs.

The importance of program stability can be seen from the December 1980 Selected Acquisition Reports for forty-seven major programs. These reports show costs that are 129% greater than the original estimates.[14] Some of these cost increases can be directly attributed to items like inflation and quantity increases. However, of the forty-seven programs, nineteen actually had quantity decreases, and 15% of the cost increase could be attributed simply to changes in scheduling. It has been estimated that multiyear contracts could result in average dollar savings of 10% to 20% in unit procurement costs because of efficiency gains, scale economies, decreased financial borrowing costs, better utilization of facilities, and reduction in administrative costs.[15]

Part of the cost increases are associated with acquisition cost estimates, which are purposely low either because DOD has forced the program to fit available funding or because contractors lower their cost estimates to win a contract and hope to be made whole as the program proceeds. In both instances, ultimate costs are likely to be much higher than those contracted for; this may in turn force a stretch-out or other changes, which can further increase costs.

Some have argued that it would be possible to eliminate such problems by forcing producers to accept losses associated with cost overruns. This would require that the government leave the producer alone once an acquisition contract is signed. However, the actual production is often done with a large amount of government involvement. Because of this, there are likely to be numerous changes in a product as it is developed. These changes frequently raise the total cost of the system, but it is argued that they also make the system more valuable. The argument for allowing some design changes appears to be reasonably sound since there are always some problems with new weapons systems which no one could be expected to predict. However, these design changes then make it almost impossible to enforce the original price agreement. The effect of this practice is to turn many government procurement contracts into "cost-plus" contracts. In this situation the government agrees to pay the producer actual production costs plus some margin of profit.

---

[14] The following material draws heavily on Vincent Puritano, "Getting Ourselves Together on Systems Acquisition," *Armed Forces Comptroller* (Winter 1982), pp. 8–14.
[15] U.S. Department of Defense, *Selected Acquisition Reports* (December 1980).

Under such contract terms producers have little incentive to be efficient in production.

A related problem is that the armed forces often act as if all programs must be protected once they are started. This is related to the way in which defense appropriations are allocated. Once a system has funding, dropping the system would be expected to lead to a complete loss of the related funding, and the process of justifying an alternative would start again from the beginning. Thus, fixing up a flawed system often looks preferable to dropping the system altogether. For example, the Army spent $1.8 billion to develop a radar-controlled antiaircraft gun, the DIVAD; yet there is evidence that the Pentagon knew the gun did not meet specifications and rigged tests to ensure that it passed so it would continue to receive funding.[16] While this system was eventually killed, it is fairly clear that there has to be something very wrong with the procurement system. It might be more efficient to give each head of an armed forces unit the incentive to dump bad systems and develop new ones. This would require more emphasis on dollar totals for defense and less emphasis on the specific items that are being purchased. However, Congress tends to balk at allowing such flexibility. And there are reasons to suspect that the return to older policies might lead to the same problems that existed in the past, with the various branches of the armed forces not cooperating and with internal allocations of funds which would not necessarily promote efficient defense.

A related criticism of the armed forces is that they tend to want major jumps in the systems they use rather than incremental improvements in existing weapons. Totally new weapons systems have very long lead times and there is often great uncertainty about their final feasibility until prototypes have been built and tested. Thus, the cost per unit is likely to be quite high. Older models with some improvements might be more cost effective in some cases.

Even where new systems are much more effective than those that they replace, the total cost of defense is likely to keep rising because the opponents keep improving their systems in responses to changes made. Thus, the more effective item simply becomes the norm rather than allowing a reduction in the number of items needed to maintain the same level of security.

While there is general agreement about ultimate civilian control of the military, there is substantial disagreement on how to organize the chiefs of the different services in advising the secretary of defense and the president. For many years it was the combined Joint Chiefs of Staff who did so. In the mid-1980s Edward Luttwak recommended that the authority of the chairman of the Joint Chiefs be strengthened. Shortly thereafter legislation was passed making the chairman the principal military advisor to the president and secretary.[17]

---

[16] *Newsweek* (November 16, 1987), p. 14.
[17] Edward N. Luttwak, *The Pentagon and the Art of War* (New York: Simon and Schuster, 1985).

In recent years, a number of presidential commissions and task forces, including the Grace Commission and the Packard Commission, have labored to propose improvements in managing the Pentagon, though none had a major effect on the way the U.S. produces defense.[18] The concern has been heightened since 1987 when contracting scandals among the major multibillion-dollar defense companies were revealed and legal prosecution was initiated.

/// GEOGRAPHIC ISSUES

The spending patterns of the federal government are widely acknowledged to have at least an indirect effect on the well-being of many regions. In the geographic context, the location of a spending point is important because once money is brought to a location, it is likely to circulate at that location for a while before it moves on. Thus, if the federal government has employees at a particular location, the money to pay those employees comes from the country as a whole. This represents an infusion of cash into the local economy. As those employees spend that money on groceries, recreation and other items, it is indirectly supporting other employment in the region. Some cities and towns have been built up around military bases and other installations in response to the spending of the government personnel located there. Thus, the consternation when the federal government decides to close such a facility can be high. Nevertheless, closing may be the ideal thing to do for certain services. In the absence of market forces, the closing may never take place.

The problems of controlling cost for the military are complicated by the redistributional issues that arise in connection with military expenditures. It might seem that there are few distributional consequences associated with the output of national defense, since each person gets to consume it at the same time, and this is generally correct. However, there are substantial issues with respect to how this money is spent. For example, the state of California, in a report on the impact of federal spending in the state, requires the Commission on State Finance to "(a) develop and maintain an economic model capable of estimating the impact of federal expenditures on the state's economy and employment, (b) project federal spending coming into California and (c) estimate the impact of these expenditures on the state's economy and on General Fund revenues."[19] The report makes it clear that military spending is its primary focus, covering $48.5 billion in defense spending versus $8.9 billion in nondefense spending.[20] Even for a state as large as California, this amount of spending can have a large impact. The commission estimated that defense

---

[18] President's Private Sector Survey on Cost Control (Grace Commission), *Task Force Report on the Office of the Secretary of Defense* (July 13, 1983) and President's Blue Ribbon Commission on Defense Management (Packard Commission), *A Formula for Action: A Report to the President on Defense Acquisitions* (1986).
[19] Commission on State Finance, op. cit., p. 5.
[20] Ibid., p. 6.

spending would account for over 9% of total private output in the state in 1986 and more than 50% of the output in the aerospace industry.[21] Thus, the geographic implications of the expenditure patterns become very important, and this leads to much of the political pressure regarding where and how the defense appropriations are spent.

Another issue of somewhat less importance is the indirect effect of federal location decisions on state and local finance. For example, military bases are exempt from local property taxes. Yet many dependents of military personnel live near the bases and send their children to local public schools. This drain on the school finances is only partly offset by the property taxes on the residences, so the federal government makes payments in lieu of property taxes to many of these communities. Whether this appropriately compensates the communities, overcompensates or undercompensates them is unknown. Another issue of some concern to many state governments is the ability to tax the income of military personnel. While there have been agreements that make it possible to tax some of this income, the refusal of the federal government to institute any withholding of state taxes from military pay effectively precludes collection of much of the potential state tax revenue.[22]

/// SUMMARY

Decisions about national defense are the domain of a single government and are highly centralized. In contrast, for example, decisions on education involve all levels of government and are highly decentralized. National defense involves large expenditures and most of the decisions regarding it are complex. It involves procurement of costly weapons systems with long lead times, under conditions of great uncertainty about the nature and likelihood of the enemy threat as well as about weapons on the cutting edge of science and technology. We should therefore not be surprised about loud, almost continuous criticism of the Defense Department and efforts to improve it. The 1980s saw substantial changes in the way the military leadership interacts with the secretary of defense and the president, and various scandals regarding procurement practices have focused attention on the whole procurement process.

There is a further issue relative to national defense decisions. Substantial economic impacts are determined by the particular procurement decisions that are made. Since defense is close to a pure public good, its providers should be able to concentrate on allocating resources efficiently. However, the significant economic impact of such expenditures means that distributional issues are often key. In addition, great uncertainties surround defense, further complicating the decision-making process.

---

[21] Ibid., p. 27.
[22] Clara Penniman, *State Income Taxation* (Baltimore: Johns Hopkins University Press, 1980).

Chapter 18 //////

Education for America's Young

While education is a private good in many ways, it is also a merit good, i.e., society has decided to encourage its consumption regardless of the recipient's ability to pay. Moreover, because there are large externalities associated with education with the result that many parents underinvest in their children's education and because there are important market failures in terms of people being able to borrow to finance their education, government must play a major role.

Another reason for government intervention in the provision of education is that education is an important determinant of earnings. To the extent that poor families are unable to afford education for their children, lack of education would be a factor in extending poverty into another generation. Thus, the provision of education now is seen as a method of reducing the need for other types of redistribution in the future. Once government decides to provide education directly, there are also issues of horizontal and vertical equity in its provision. Should everyone receive the same educational services? Should the amount depend on the amount of taxes one pays? Or should the services be provided in some compensatory manner, with the most disadvantaged receiving the greatest amount? Issues such as these have an important part in the debate over the financing and provision of education.

The different reasons for financing education lead to different types of government intervention. They also imply differences in the level of government that should be responsible for the intervention. Further, the methods of financing and providing education create significant incentives for people to migrate among communities, and the heavy reliance on the property tax for elementary and secondary education can create important inequities in the way education is financed.

Finally, the actual production of education uses a large amount of resources. There are important controversies about how effectively education is provided and about what could be done to improve efficiency. Many of these controversies are centered in questions of defining how education is produced and how the output is supposed to be measured. Differences in family and neighborhood often appear to be more important than the actual efforts of the educational system, and this makes it even more difficult to evaluate the "production function" in this context.

Clearly the analysis of education is a complex one. Many of the issues related to the use of property taxes, which are the main source of financing for elementary and secondary education, were covered in Chapter 10; other finance issues are largely covered elsewhere. In this chapter we focus on analyzing a service that is important at all levels of government and for which the output is extremely difficult to measure. Hence the responsibilities of each level of government and of private citizens are not clearly delimited and the finance and provision mechanisms create substantial controversy.

/// BACKGROUND

At least since Adam Smith, economists have pointed to the importance of education, not only for its own sake, i.e., as a consumption good, but as a contribution to a person's future income and to economic growth, i.e., as an investment good. People have many motives for getting an education, but clearly when they take resources away from present consumption to spend on training and education so as to earn more income in the future, they are making an investment in themselves. This investment has many similarities to an investment in a plant or equipment. The higher value of the labor produced by an educated person appears to be a major factor in the determination of wage differentials. The higher level of education also partly explains why wage levels are much higher on average in developed countries than in others.

The benefits of education are generally believed to extend far beyond the person receiving the education. At the very least, a person's ability to participate in a democracy is affected by the amount of education he or she has. Our earlier analysis of benefit spillovers leads to the conclusion that private choices as to the provision of education would lead to individuals choosing less education than would be efficient. Each person would only invest in additional education to the point where the private value of the additional education was equal to the private cost; the person would not take account of the value that accrues to others because of the education.

The external benefits of education appear to fall off rapidly with distance from the student, e.g., people in New York are far less concerned about the education received by children in California than they are about the education received by children in New York. Thus, historically, education has been primarily a local concern. With the majority of the benefits accruing privately and with geographically limited spillover, local provision appeared to be the most efficient.

Interest in the general level of education in the country, however, is likely to be much larger. In the United States, with its great mobility, most Americans who are educated in one school district or one state university will move to different jurisdictions during their lifetime and contribute to that jurisdiction's economy. Because the education of many youngsters ultimately contributes to the income and wealth of some other community, there may be little incentive to fully internalize the externalities of education within the local community. This could prevent optimal financing of education by local jurisdictions.

In addition to the externalities that education may generate, it has been viewed as a component of the income redistribution system. In particular, the lower levels of education associated with low income were seen as causing perpetuation of poverty across generations. Thus, provision of education to the children of the poor can help to reduce the future level of poverty. Local financing of education is limited in its ability to generate such redistribution since it is constrained by both the level of the existing tax base and the possibility that higher taxes would cause part of the base to leave the jurisdiction in the future. Thus, a variety of issues have been raised about the appropriateness of the traditional financing mechanism for education.

The various arguments related to the public provision of education are associated with the educated person, not with the production of education. There appear to be only limited economies of scale in providing educational services. Clearly the joint consumption characteristic of education is limited. For example, the larger the class size the less attention an instructor can pay to any one student, and therefore the quality of education a student receives declines with class size. Hence, an increase in the number of students requires an increase in resources to maintain quality.

/// FIGURES AND TRENDS

Education can be divided into elementary and secondary education, and higher education. The former involves education from kindergarten through high school, i.e., K through 12, and is generally regarded as a government responsibility. It used to be predominantly the responsibility of local jurisdictions, mainly school boards. In recent years the states have increasingly prescribed the schools' role and responsibility and they have become the major funding source. The federal role has also increased but only in a minor way.

In the United States we have a prevalence of public schools, but we must remember that a substantial number of students receive their elementary and secondary education through private alternatives.

Higher education is provided by degree-granting colleges and universities to students who have satisfactorily completed their secondary education. In addition, there are a variety of vocational and professional schools. These schools provide education beyond secondary school, but they do not offer a formal academic degree. Such institutions are diverse and numerous, ranging from private aviation schools to schools for barbers and beauticians.

Education in the United States is a very large industry, whose units of production, i.e., schools, are extraordinarily decentralized. On the elementary and secondary school level, over 15,000 school districts and thousands of private schools make decisions year by year about what to teach, how to allocate students and teachers to classrooms and schools, what compensation to pay teachers and their support staff, and what capital improvements to make. Similar types of decisions are made by 3,270 colleges and universities. Teachers all over the United States (about 2.5 million in elementary and secondary schools alone) decide where to teach, how to teach, and whether to continue in the profession. The 45–50 million students in elementary and secondary schools and the more than 12 million students in colleges and universities attend classes and, particularly at more advanced levels, decide what to study and to what end. In short, in each class of those engaged in education, there are vast numbers of participants. They respond not only to laws specifying some of their obligations and rights but also to incentives that affect the type and quality of teaching and learning in classrooms.[1]

Elementary and Secondary

Spending on elementary and secondary education is about 4% of GNP, with 8% of the total spent in 1987 on private education.[2] Private enrollment, which is mainly on the elementary level, declined from 14% in 1960 to less than 11% in 1980; since then it has been increasing, to 12% in 1986.

In 1987, all public education expenditures in the U.S. amounted to $229 billion.[3] Elementary and secondary public education constituted the most significant expenditure items, amounting to $156 billion, while expenditures for higher education were $73 billion.

The funding of public elementary and secondary education has undergone major changes over time.[4] In the 1920s local sources provided about 83% of the funding for public schools and states the remaining 17%. The local share declined continuously until the early 1980s, while the state share was growing continuously and now constitutes the largest source of funding at this level. Federal contributions grew until the early 1980s and hit a high of 9.8% of the

[1] Richard J. Murname, "An Economist's Look at Federal and State Education Policies," in John M. Quigley and Daniel L. Rubinfeld, eds., *American Domestic Priorities: An Economic Appraisal* (Berkeley, CA: University of California Press, 1985), pp. 118–147.

[2] Bureau of the Census, *U.S. Statistical Abstract, 1988* (Washington, DC: U.S. Printing Office, 1988), p. 119.

[3] Ibid., p. 119.

[4] Advisory Commission on Intergovernmental Relations (ACIR), *Significant Features of Fiscal Federalism, 1988 Edition*, vol. 2, M-155 II (Washington, DC: July 1988), p. 58.

total; but the trend has been broken and the percentage share has been steadily declining to 6.5% in 1985–86.

State support for public education increased from $3 billion in 1954 to $27 billion in 1974, to $67 billion in 1984 and $82 billion in 1986. Some annual increases were small, e.g., 4% in 1983, while others were much larger, e.g., 15% in 1979.[5] Federal aid also increased from $0.5 billion in 1954 to $7 billion in 1974, to $14 billion in 1984 and $18 billion in 1986.[6] (Since 1979 increases were much smaller than before, and in three recent years decreases occurred.) One reason for the rapid increase in federal financing was the Elementary and Secondary Education Act of 1965. Title I of this act provided $1 billion to local school districts for compensatory education. Funding for these programs grew rapidly and reached $3.4 billion in 1980 (a 30% increase in real terms between 1966 and 1980). The thrust of Title I was to mandate that to receive funds, districts would have to spend as many non–Title I dollars on low-achieving children as they spent on other children. According to Goettel et al., this program was quite effective in improving the education of disadvantaged children and in reducing the achievement gap between black and white children.[7]

In 1986 the average state-local direct per capita education expenditure amounted to $874, of which $602 went for elementary and secondary education. The overall education expenditure amounted to 6.4% of personal income. But there were great variations among the states, from Alaska spending $2,273 or 12.8% of personal income, to Tennessee spending $652 or 5.8% of personal income,[8] to Connecticut spending only 4.1% of personal income.

Under the administration of President Ronald Reagan, the federal role in education greatly declined, consistent with his view that education is the responsibility of state and local governments. Specifically, the Educational Consolidation and Improvement Act of 1981 reduced federal funding by 24%.

Not many Americans realize that public school enrollment has declined in recent years. Thus, for example, between 1970 and 1980 enrollment in public elementary and secondary schools fell by 13%, from 45.9 million in 1970 to 41 million in 1980 and 40.2 million in 1987.[9] This significant decline in enrollment led to the closing of some schools and a reduction in employment, although such reductions were not as great as the decline in enrollment.

The public schools are also important as employers. In 1986, they employed about 2.2 million public elementary and high school teachers.[10] During this period of retrenchment they saw a decline in real wages from $25,963 in

[5] Ibid., p. 83.

[6] Ibid., p. 82.

[7] Robert J. Goettel, et al., *A Comparative Analysis of ESEA, Title I Administration in Eight States* (Syracuse, NY: Syracuse Research Corporation, 1977).

[8] ACIR, op. cit., p. 123.

[9] U.S. Department of Education, National Center for Education Statistics, *Digest of Education Statistics, 1987–88* (Washington, DC: 1988), pp. 46–47.

[10] U.S. Department of Education, *The Condition of Education 1988* (Washington, DC: 1988), p. 67.

1970–71 to $22,664 in 1980–81 (in 1986–87 dollars) followed by a return to about the 1970 level of $26,551 in 1986–87.[11] A positive effect was a decline in the student-teacher ratio from 22.3 in 1970 to 18.8 in 1980 and 17.4 in 1987.[12]

Employment and real income declines gave clear signals to college students as they made their career decisions. The evidence is convincing. In 1971, 177,000 students graduated from colleges and universities with degrees in education, but that number fell to 101,000 by 1982 and 87,221 by 1985–86.[13] The falling number of those fulfilling minimum requirements for certification was even more precipitous. Moreover, a serious shortage of mathematics and science teachers, so essential for the education of a sophisticated, science-oriented, high-tech society, has developed. One of the main reasons is low salary and the refusal of most school districts to pay different salaries to people teaching different subjects. In 1981 the average salary differential between business and industry, on the one hand, and teaching, on the other, was 61% for graduates trained in mathematics.[14]

Higher Education

Institutions of higher learning constitute a large industry. In 1982, America's colleges and universities numbered 3,340, 45%[15] of which were "public" (supported directly by taxes) and the rest "independent" or "private" (not supported directly or primarily by taxes).[16] Altogether, these institutions enrolled over 12,247,000 students in credit courses and spent $98.3 billion on all their activities, or 2.5% of the gross national product.[17] Table 18-1 highlights some of their other general characteristics. As it shows, the majority of institutions are independent rather than public; however, in 1985 the independent institutions enrolled only 22.6% of all students.[18] In part this is because the independent schools concentrate more on the highest levels of education. Relatively few independent institutions are two-year colleges; many of them are doctoral institutions.

States are the major source of funding for public higher education and were responsible for 76.6% of the public financing in 1985–86.[19] However, even public institutions rely on tuition, donations, and other sources of funds for a large part of their revenues. California is an example. The state has some 290 colleges and universities that offer degrees (see Box 18-1).[20] In 1985–86, they

---

[11] U.S. Department of Education, *Digest of Education Statistics*, op. cit., p. 72.
[12] Ibid., p. 67.
[13] Ibid., p. 231.
[14] Samuel B. Bacharach, *Paying for Better Teaching: Merit Pay and Its Alternative* (Ithaca, NY: Organizational Analysis and Practice, 1984).
[15] Bureau of the Census, op. cit., p. 141.
[16] U.S. Department of Education, *Digest of Education Statistics*, op. cit., p. 182.
[17] Bureau of the Census, op. cit., p. 141.
[18] Ibid., p. 141.
[19] U.S. Department of Education, *Digest of Education Abstracts*, op. cit., p. 259.
[20] Ibid., p. 187.

Table 18-1 / Characteristics of American Colleges and Universities 1985-86

Type of Institution & Characteristics		Numbers in 1986-87
Public		
Total no. of public institutions (incl. branches)		1,533
4 year		573
2 year		960
Doctoral granting		213
Total enrollment		9,726,168
	(1970	6,428,134)
Private		
Total no. of private institutions (incl. branches)		1,873
4 year		1,497
2 year		376
Doctoral granting		260
Religions affiliated		794
Total enrollment by attendance status		2,774,630
	(1970	2,152,753)

(Source: U.S. Department of Education, National Center for Education Statistics, *Digest of Education Statistics 1987–88* [Washington, DC: 1988].)

spent $12.2 billion.[21] The nine campuses of the University of California enrolled 134,608 students and spent $6 billion.[22] (This includes more than $1.5 billion for managing the Department of Energy's Los Alamos and Livermore National Laboratories.) However, only $1.1 billion came from state appropriations. The California community colleges enrolled over 1.2 million students and spent $1.8 billion of state appropriations.[23] In 1985–86 the 153 independent institutions in the state[24] enrolled 205,622 students[25] and spent $364 billion.[26] About $100 million of this came indirectly from the state and local governments through grants to students.[27]

Even though much of higher education is provided by public institutions, families pay about a third of the total instruction and living expenses, down

---

21 Ibid., p. 277.
22 California State Department of Finance, *Governor's Budget Summary, 1985–86*, p. 7.
23 California State Department of Finance, *Governor's Budget Summary, 1986–87*, p. 11.
24 U.S. Department of Education, *Digest of Education Statistics*, op. cit., p. 187.
25 Ibid., p. 154.
26 Ibid., p. 277.
27 Ibid., p. 264.

Box 18-1

////// Public Higher Education in California

It is useful if public institutions are properly structured and coordinated. One example is the California system of higher education.* According to the master plan, which has been in effect in California since 1960, higher education is provided by three types of institutions. The junior colleges are community based and locally controlled.** They are financed with state funds as well as locally raised property taxes. Junior colleges offer instruction through but not beyond the fourteenth grade level, including standard collegiate courses for transfer to higher institutions; vocational-technical fields leading to employment; and general, or liberal arts courses. Studies in these fields may lead to the associate in arts or associate in science degree.

The four-year state colleges, called the California State University Colleges, occupy a middle ground between the decentralized junior colleges and the centralized University of California. Their primary function is to provide instruction in the liberal arts and sciences and in professions and applied fields that require more than two years of collegiate education, and to teach education for both undergraduate and graduate students through the master's degree. The doctoral degree may be awarded jointly with the University of California.

The University of California,

from the two-thirds families paid in the 1930s. State governments pick up another third, while the federal government and philanthropic institutions share the final third about equally.[28]

The instructional costs of colleges and universities have grown between 2% and 2.5% a year above inflation, about keeping pace with the growth in family real income. However, since government subsidies have increased, on average family expenditures per student have actually grown somewhat less than their incomes.

/// POLICY ISSUES ABOUT EDUCATION PROVISION

The scope and complexity of the educational system precludes a comprehensive analysis of all issues regarding the production, finance, and distribu-

[28] Michael S. McPherson and Mary S. Skinner, "Paying for College: A Lifetime Proposition," *The Brookings Review* (Fall 1986), p. 30.

Box 18-1 *(continued)*

governed by a board of regents, provides instruction in the liberal arts and sciences and in the professions, including teacher education. It has exclusive jurisdiction over training for the professions, including dentistry, law, medicine, veterinary medicine, engineering and architecture. It has the sole authority in public higher education to award the doctoral degree in all fields of learning, except that it may agree with the state colleges to award joint doctoral degrees in selected fields. The University of California is the primary state-supported academic agency for research.

The great advantages of a three-tiered higher education system with close coordination are that it permits specialization and allows for numerous junior colleges in close proximity to students' homes. The latter feature greatly increases college accessibility for low-income groups. However, for such a system to be effective it is necessary that qualified students can readily transfer from junior colleges to state colleges and ultimately to the University of California. One way to achieve this objective is to insist that all three levels have a common core curriculum, an objective which in the past has been difficult to attain in California.

* California State Department of Education, *A Master Plan for Higher Education in California, 1960–1975* (Sacramento, CA: 1960), p. 230.

** While there has been much discussion about higher education and its financing, in general there has been relatively little attention paid to community colleges. An excellent book is David W. Dreneman and Susan C. Nelson, *Financing Community College: An Economic Perspective* (Washington, DC: The Brookings Institution, 1981), p. 222.

---

tion of education. Instead we focus on a sample of issues that relate to the equity and efficiency of the educational system and pay particular attention to the growing interrelationship between the various levels of government in funding and controlling the production of education. We start with some issues that are common to all levels of education and then turn to some that are very specific to the particular level of education analyzed. For example, any answer to the question of how to finance education bears on the efficiency with which education is likely to be produced and distributed.

How Much Education to Produce?

One of the major policy issues is how much education to produce and of what type. Part of the issue was resolved long ago when the people of the United States decided that everyone should be able to receive education through high school at no cost to the student. This still leaves open the questions of what quality of education should be made available; how much freedom should individual familes be allowed in choosing to support different levels of provision; and how many people are to get a college education and how much of it. These decisions are the result of both private and governmental actions.

The quality of education can vary significantly. This issue is complicated because of the difficulty of measuring output. Even with universal access to education, differences in quality yield vastly different results; quality is very often influenced by the environment even if the inputs are the same. This is particularly true in the lower levels of education where a number of researchers have concluded that the home and school environments are more important than input resources in determining the amount of education achieved.[29]

The school environment can also be influenced by attempts to maintain universal education. In many schools, a substantial proportion of the students create difficulties. These students not only require additional resources, but they create negative externalities when their disruptiveness reduces the educational opportunity of others in the classroom. Hence, there is a serious debate about when to expel such students. One principal started his tenure at a high school by expelling 300 hard-core troublemakers in the first week. The school has shown a substantial increase in educational achievement; but his action created a controversy about whether the expulsion of students is an appropriate response.[30] In other schools, the drain on resources for various special problems can be quite large. For example, New York City had a total enrollment of 939,142 in 1987. Of these students, 113,238 were handicapped or emotionally disturbed students in special education programs. Bilingual education was provided in nine languages for some of the 115,000 students for whom English was not the primary language.[31]

The decision structure is further complicated by the fact that individual families are much more open to paying higher direct costs or higher taxes for education for their own children than they are for the education of others. This private component of the education system makes it inefficient to impose equality of inputs on all students. When the public system does not provide enough quality for some families, they have the option of taking their children out of the public system; this usually leads to reduced support for public education in general. Thus, attempts to force everyone to consume the same level of education could ultimately lead to even greater disparities than exist under the current system.

There is little consensus about the appropriate level of public support for education beyond high school. Many people seem to see this as largely a private investment decision, especially since the direct monetary rewards to

---

[29] Eric A. Hanushek, "The Economics of Schooling," *Journal of Economic Literature* 24 (September 1986), p. 1155.
[30] *Newsweek* (January 18, 1988), pp. 80–81.
[31] Ibid.

additional education are fairly high. While the externalities associated with a college education do not seem to be as significant as those associated with lower levels of education, there seems to be a trend toward more state funding of this level of education. Aside from the issue of externalities there is the possibility of significant market failures in the provision of this level of education because of the difficulty in borrowing to finance such an investment. Partly in response to this concern, the federal government has a significant program of loan guarantees. However, the use of such guarantees has been associated with substantial default rates and the loan system has been subject to various types of abuse (see Box 18-2).

The Returns to Education as an Investment

If we know the value of education and its contribution to total output, we can make some estimates of whether the education is worth the cost. Ideally we would like to know the cost of the marginal unit of education and the benefits it would generate for each type of educational investment. In practice, we are often left with estimates of the average rate of return to investment in education. With this in mind we can look at the estimates of the rate of return obtained on investments in education and compare it with rates obtained on alternative investments. Notice that the profitability of higher education can be looked at from the point of view of the individual or of society as a whole. The individual's concern is the relation between the expected increase in his or her own income relative to the private cost of that education.

Schultz has pursued the cost of production approach in making estimates of gross investment in education in the United States in the period 1900–56.[32] His concern is formal education at the elementary, secondary, and college or university level. His estimates include the direct cost of education, e.g., outlays for teachers' salaries, books, equipment and maintenance of buildings, and the indirect cost of the earnings foregone by students who would have been working if they had not been attending school. According to Schultz's findings, since 1900 gross investment in education has been a significant part of total investment in the United States, growing rapidly relative to gross physical investment. Specifically, it rose from 9% to 34% of gross physical investment between 1900 and 1956.[33] Also, income foregone by students became an increasingly important part of total educational investment, since enrollment grew faster at the high school and college levels than in elementary schools.

The decision of whether it would be economically advantageous to increase the number of young people going to school must be based on the real

[32] Theodore W. Schultz, "Capital Formation by Education," *Journal of Political Economy* 48 (December 1960), pp. 571–583.
[33] Ibid., p. 583. These estimates have an upward bias since Schultz did not subtract the earnings of students attending college. However, they also have a downward bias since the estimates are based on the average earnings of college-age workers actually in the labor force. Yet college students have superior average earning ability and therefore would have higher earnings were they to hold full-time jobs.

Box 18-2

////// Loan Defaults

The ability to borrow funds to finance education is crucial for those without the resources to pay for it directly. Yet lenders have been reluctant to lend for this purpose. The problem is the difficulty in collecting on the loan if the person chooses not to pay it back. Most loans require some collateral, such as a house or a car, on which the lender can foreclose if the loan is not repaid. However, there is no such possibility with a loan for education. The problem is compounded because many college students move after graduation. Thus, a lender might have to search all over the country simply to find the borrower; then it would be necessary to take the person to court, get a judgment, and find some way to collect the money. The federal government has helped alleviate this problem by guaranteeing repayment of loans for large numbers of students.

One study concludes that the grant and loan programs available are such that low income does not seem to deter qualified students from aspiring to or entering college.* The federal government guaranteed over $8 billion in loans in 1985 and provided other loans and grants for a total of over $14 billion. The 1985 total is down somewhat from the $15.6 billion provided in 1980, but this is in contrast to total federal aid of only $594 million in 1963.**

With a federal guarantee, the government must make payments only if the student does not. Thus, if the student defaults for any reason, the lender can collect from the federal government. Lenders are usually happy to make such loans since the federal government is such a good credit risk. However, the federal government has indeed found that the default rates are quite high.

In many cases, successful students simply choose not to repay because they do not think that the federal government will be able to collect. Others do not complete their education and decide not to repay

cost to the economy, which includes the income foregone by attending college. But how should foregone income be measured? Schultz takes as his measure the income that an average person with the characteristics of a student can presently earn if he or she is not in school, multiplied by the number of students.

Box 18-3 presents some information about private and social rates of return to investment in higher education. These returns appear to be high enough to explain the investment in higher education.

Altogether there appears to have been a decline in recent years in the private rates of return, for a number of reasons. One is that increasing

Box 18-2 *(continued)*

either because they have financial difficulties or because they have complaints against the schools. Part of the latter problem arises because some schools view the federal money as an easy target even though the student ends up stuck with some obligation to repay the loan. These schools appeal to potential students with the promise of high-paying jobs. They encourage the students to get federal grants or loans to pay for tuition. If the school fails to provide the services offered, the student is still responsible for any loans and must seek legal action against the school to recover expenses. In 1985, there were more than 600 such schools with student default rates of 50% or more; a variety of them have been convicted of fraud and other illegal practices.† Yet the students remain liable for the loans and many of the companies continue in business.

The charges are most often made against schools that offer vocational education, but the default problem is certainly not limited to them. More than $1 billion in uncollectible loans is outstanding†† and the amount in default is far greater. It appears that the guarantees that come with the loans keep both the borrower and the lender from looking into the application to which the money will be put in as much detail as they would in other circumstances. For example, a person trying to get a loan for an overpriced house in serious disrepair would have substantial difficulty finding a loan; but the lender has no such incentive to be cautious about the purpose of the loan when it is guaranteed. Thus, while the loans do serve a valuable purpose, there are costs in terms of defaults and in terms of disillusioned students stuck with large obligations to the government and nothing to show for their investment.

* "Financial Aid for College Students: Have the Barriers to Opportunity Been Lowered?" *Focus* 10 (Fall 1987), p. 9.
** Ibid., p. 7.
† Henry Weinstein, "Disreputable Vocational Schools Take Students for a Ride," *Oregonian* (June 21, 1988), p. A2.
†† Ibid.

numbers of students have graduated from college and the general increase in the supply of college graduates has reduced the "price" for this type of labor. The other major explanation is that when very few go to college, only those who will get a high rate of return do so; however, when college is made available to many, some of the additional students would be expected to get a lower rate of return to their investment. This comparison reflects the differences between the average and the marginal rates of return.

Still, it appears that these private rates of return are high enough to encourage high school students to continue their education. From their point of view, college education appears to be cost effective. There is evidence that

Box 18-3

////// Returns to Education

Studies by Walsh and Friedman and Kuznets examined the profitability of various types of higher education from the point of view of the (average) individual. Walsh, using a 4% discount rate, found the average value of a college education, as well as of legal and business school training, to be considerably greater than the cost to the average recipient.* Friedman and Kuznets reached similar general conclusions, though their main emphasis was on explaining the existing income differentials between professional and other workers among the various professions.** They found training costs alone explaining only part of these differentials.

Estimates of rates of return on investment in higher education have been made by a number of scholars. Becker found rates of return of 14.8% in 1939, 12.4% in 1949, and 14.8% in 1956.† Hanoch, using data for 1959, found that white males in the northern United States had an average rate of return to investment in college (against high school) of 10%.†† Freeman found that the rate of return to college education had declined from 11.5% in 1969 to 8.5% in 1974.§

* J. R. Walsh, "Capital Concept Applied to Man," *Quarterly Journal of Economics* 49 (1935), pp. 255–286.
** Milton Friedman and Simon Kuznets, *Income from Independent Professional Practice* (New York: National Bureau of Economic Research, 1945), chs. 3 and 4.
† Gary S. Becker, *Human Capital* (New York: Columbia University, 1964).
†† Giora Hanoch, "An Economic Analysis of Earnings and Schooling," *Journal of Human Resources* 2 (Summer 1967), pp. 324–325.
§ Richard B. Freeman, "Overinvestment in College Training," *Journal of Human Resources* 9 (Summer 1975), p. 230.

students make well-informed guesses of expected earnings increases associated with college education. For example, McMahon and Wagner examined the expected earnings reported by a nationwide sample of college students and compared these student estimates across race and degree levels as well as the actual starting salaries earned by these individuals upon graduation.[34] They concluded that college freshmen quite accurately perceived the relative differences in earnings across fields. For example, those in health, technical, and science fields expected the highest salary, while those in education, liberal arts, and humanities expected the lowest future earnings.

Clearly, the conclusion that private returns to higher education are quite

[34] Walter W. McMahon and Alan P. Wagner, "Expected Returns to Investment in Higher Education," *Journal of Human Resources* 16 (Spring 1981), pp. 274–282.

high cannot answer the policy question of whether national income could be increased by raising levels of investment in higher education. To answer this question we need information on the rate of return that society as a whole is likely to earn on the resources devoted to higher education and how this compares with rates of return obtained on resources devoted to other types of investment. Social gains from education can differ from private gains because of differences between social and private costs and between social and private returns.

The other important issue in determining how much to subsidize higher education is a distributional one. Since education generally raises a person's earnings, subsidies to education increase the wealth of those likely to have relatively high earnings. This is particularly true if the demand for education is not price elastic. In this case, the subsidy merely lowers the cost to many who would have gone to college anyway while inducing relatively few additional people to go. This is a further problem because of the income elasticity of demand for education. In general, the higher a family's income, the higher the probability that children in that family will go to college. Hence, reducing the cost of college is often a subsidy to the higher income segments of society. This distributional concern could be addressed by targeting more of the aid directly to low-income students.

Some studies remind us of the difficulty of comparing rates of return in education and in business even if they were comparable in concept, since the education industry is not composed of profit-maximizing firms.[35] Forced to compete in the marketplace, firms in the manufacturing industry are likely to exploit many of the most profitable opportunities. Since educational institutions are heavily subsidized and are not forced to compete with each other to increase the economic benefits passed on to the student, they are likely to miss opportunities on which the rates of return are high.

Denison has looked at the contribution education can make in a different manner. He has studied the growth in U.S. productivity between 1929 and 1957 and has estimated that during that period 42% of growth in productivity resulted from improved education.[36] Another study by Denison shows that the incorporation of new knowledge into production was the major source of economic growth in the U.S. between 1948 and 1973, accounting for 45% of growth in national income per person employed.[37] Education was the second most important source, contributing 20% of growth in per capita national income. The other three sources of growth combined—improved allocation of labor, increases in amount of capital, and economies of scale—did not equal the contribution of research and education to the economy during that period.

That higher education generally pays off in higher earnings for the indi-

35 Alice M. Rivlin, "Research in the Economics of Higher Education," in Selma J. Mushkin, ed., *Economics of Higher Education* (Washington, DC.: U.S. Office of Education, 1962), p. 371.

36 E. F. Denison, *The Source of Economic Growth in the United States and the Alternatives Before Us*, CED Supplementary Paper No. 13 (New York: 1962).

37 E. F. Denison, *Accounting for United States Economic Growth, 1929–1969* (Washington, DC: 1974), p. 129.

vidual is widely accepted. More importantly, the return to society from investment in higher education is also substantial. Economists have calculated this rate of return on investment in human capital at 12% to 13%. This figure is determined by comparing the expected lifetime earnings of college graduates with non–college graduates, with adjustments made for the potential income lost while students attend college and for the tax dollars used to support education.[38]

Producing and Distributing Education

The production and distribution of education are closely tied because student characteristics and other environmental attributes have a substantial effect on the ability to produce educational advancement. This is usually discussed with respect to elementary and secondary education but it is also relevant for higher education. Further, attempts to stimulate more production of education are often more effective with respect to higher income households than they are to lower income households. For example, one study of the Marshall, Michigan, school district in 1979 found that the district's operating expenditures exceeded its estimated efficiency level and that the estimated distribution of perceived benefits, net of local tax payments, went disproportionately to the well-to-do households in the district.[39]

Allocating Resources to Schools   The textbook version of microeconomic theory assumes a known, deterministic relationship between inputs and outputs. In fact, this relationship in general, and with regard to education in particular, is unknown and indeed must be estimated by using inadequate and imperfect data. This input-output relationship is estimated with the aid of a production function which, because of data and specification problems, is subject to considerable uncertainty. All this is especially true for the education production function, where output is exceedingly difficult to quantify, as are certain input factors. Moreover, the educational process is cumulative, past inputs affecting students' current achievements.

For all enterprises, allocating resources efficiently is of major concern, and public education is no exception. Therefore, we are interested in education production as well as cost functions. In line with concepts developed in Chapter 14, we consider some of the more unique characteristics of education output and its measurement, as well as the specific input factors of education production and cost functions. This information is used in the next section to examine the shape of the average education cost function.

In the education production function, the output of the educational process

[38] Carnegie Commission, *Higher Education: Who Pays? Who Benefits? Who Should Pay?* (New York: Carnegie Commission, 1973), p. 73.

[39] R. Hamilton-Lankford, "Efficiency and Equity in the Provision of Public Education," *Review of Economics and Statistics* 67 (February 1985), pp. 70–80.

is the end result of combining amounts of a series of input factors in a prescribed manner. Because of its many complex dimensions, the measurement of education output poses especially serious difficulties. The output measure must be readily available, reasonably reliable, and closely linked to what we consider to be long-run goals of schooling.

Perhaps the best and most comprehensive output measure for public education is the discounted lifetime earnings associated with education. These earnings in a market economy, if properly adjusted for personal characteristics, can testify to the contribution eduation makes to a person's income during his or her lifetime. Discounting the value for consecutive years back to a single number permits comparisons among different people with different educational experiences.

But there exist also a few indirect output measures which, although inferior to discounted lifetime earnings, can be helpful. In the case of elementary and secondary education, such indirect measures include standardized achievement test scores, percentage of annual continuation rates among students (i.e., the converse of the dropout rate), and the percentage of graduating seniors entering college.

Service conditions turn out to be important because school officials must offer education in all sections of the community regardless of how difficult it is to overcome the service conditions they face. Public schools are mandated by law to provide education through high school for all school-age youngsters. A child's native ability, home environment, motivation, and desire to learn are human conditions over which school superintendents and principals have little control, yet these factors greatly complicate their tasks. Thus, for example, Stanley H. Masters has found that for children whose parents have little education or low incomes, the possibility of dropping out of school is more than twenty times greater than for children from well-to-do families where both parents have graduated from high school.[40] Likewise, school officials have virtually no control over funding laws that affect methods of teaching and discipline, or the political climate in which they must operate.

In 1986, Hanushek reported that he had found 147 separately estimated educational production functions in the published literature.[41] They clearly differ in quality and target population, but can nevertheless offer some limited insights. He finds that the empirical results are rather inconclusive.[42] For example, in 112 studies that estimate the effect of class size on educational outcome, only 23 have statistically significant relations, of which 9 are positive and 14 negative.

A similar picture emerges in relation to 106 studies that measure teacher education: only 11 find a significant effect, with 6 positive and 5 negative. In

[40] Stanley H. Masters, "The Effect of Family Income on Children's Education: Some Findings on Inequality of Opportunity," *Journal of Human Resources* 4 (Spring 1969), p. 158.

[41] Hanushek, op. cit., pp. 1159–1167.

[42] Ibid., pp. 1159–1167.

the 109 studies that include teacher experience, the effect is significant in 40, with 33 positive and 7 negative. Teacher salary is examined in 60 studies and found to be significant in 10, with 9 positive and 1 negative. Finally, per pupil expenditures are included in 65 studies and found significant in 16, with 13 positive and 3 negative.

Based on these summaries, Hanushek reaches the pessimistic conclusion that there is "... no strong evidence that teacher-student ratios, teacher education or teacher experience have an expected positive effect on student achievement... [and] no strong or systematic relationship between school expenditures and student performance."[43]

While these results are somewhat discouraging, they reflect our data and specification problems. Moreover, the Hanushek findings are not inconsistent with the arguments presented earlier in the chapter, that service conditions tend to overshadow factor inputs.

Let us next consider the importance of service conditions. Education cost functions estimated by Burkhead, Fox, and Holland[44] and by Kiesling[45] point to the importance of service conditions. To overcome difficult service conditions, resources must be invested. Some strategies are likely to be more cost effective than others. For example, we can point to at least two strategies to overcome service conditions associated with segregation in public shools: helping culturally deprived students interact with culturally more favored and strongly motivated students, for example, through busing; or placing more teachers, counselors, and so forth into schools in culturally deprived areas.

The 1966 Coleman Report concludes that simply equalizing educational inputs for all schools would do little to promote equality among the races in terms of educational attainment.[46] In fact, Coleman found smaller differences than expected between inputs devoted to predominantly white schools and those devoted to predominantly black schools.[47] A more important factor for educational achievement appears to be "attributes of a child's fellow students in school," which is a service condition and cannot be controlled in the way that the number of pupils per teacher or the existence and quality of science laboratories can.[48] Integrated schools enable black students to benefit from the presence of others with backgrounds that place greater stress on learning. If one accepts this logic, then desegregation aided by school busing may be justified.[49]

[43] Ibid., p. 1162.

[44] Jesse Burkhead, et al., *Input and Output in Large City High Schools* (Syracuse, NY: Syracuse University Press, 1967), p. 72.

[45] Herbert J. Kiesling, "Measuring a Local Government Service: A Study of School Districts in New York State," *Review of Economics and Statistics* 49 (1967), pp. 356–367.

[46] James S. Coleman, et al., *Equality of Educational Opportunity* (Washington, DC: U.S. Government Printing Office, 1966). The same general arguments are found in Christopher Jencks, *Inequality* (New York: Basic Books, 1972).

[47] This referred to physical quantities of inputs. Qualities were not necessarily similar.

[48] Coleman, et al., op. cit., p. 316.

[49] For a collection of articles on the Coleman Report, see Frederick Mosteller and Daniel P. Moynihan, eds., *On Equality of Educational Opportunity* (New York: Random House, 1972).

Bowles and Levin criticize the Coleman findings regarding peer group influences.[50] They assert that tests for the influence of other students' attributes did not include adequate controls for the influence of a student's own attributes. If one is willing to believe that parents place their children in schools attended by children from similar backgrounds, this criticism implies that tests for peer group influences may be picking up only the effects of a pupil's own characteristics. Another way of saying this is that those parents who value education will place their children in schools offering the best educational opportunities.

Because altering service conditions uses resources, just as increasing inputs does, the true issue to be faced by policy makers is weighing the marginal benefit and the marginal cost of each means of providing a service. To continue the example of school integration and achievement, if the benefits of busing minority pupils to majority schools exceeds the marginal costs, then busing should be undertaken. Once this issue is decided, a great challenge to decision makers relates to the next question, i.e., how many resources to invest in order to overcome, in a cost-effective manner, difficult service conditions and how many in the form of factor inputs.

Let us examine some of the legal entitlement extensions of the 1970s. Under the Education of All Handicapped Children Act of 1975, handicapped persons are entitled to a "free, appropriate public education" with the federal government financially assisting the states.[51] The law requires that "individualized" instruction with parental participation be provided and that handicapped children be "main-streamed" (educated with the nonhandicapped) as much as is practicable. Outlays are required for ramps and wheelchairs and for hiring special teachers, audiologists, and therapists. Although federal and state assistance eases the burden somewhat, local urban governments are still left with substantial costs.

Another example of expanded entitlements is the Bilingual Education Act of 1967, which requires that instruction for "culturally deprived" schoolchildren be provided in a language other than English, if a sufficient number of pupils speaking that language are attending schools in the same system.[52] Its rationale is to extend the benefits of public education to those who have not yet learned English well enough to participate meaningfully in a regular English-language program. Because such a program requires specially trained teachers and results in small classes, it is costly, and moreover, it may retard the process of learning English.

Consolidating or Breaking Up School Districts There has never been any doubt that many rural school districts are too small to efficiently provide good

---

[50] Samuel Bowles and Henry M. Levin, "The Determinants of Scholastic Achievement—An Appraisal of Some Recent Evidence," *Journal of Human Resources* 3 (1968), pp. 3–24. Coleman replied to this article in the Spring 1968 issue of the same journal.

[51] U.S.C. 1401, et seq. (1975).

[52] 20 U.S.CA 880b.

education. And yet, because of great physical distances, consolidating these small districts, except sometimes on the high school level, has not been a viable solution. However, much of urban America faces the question of optimum school district size.

Let us examine this issue by turning to Jerome Rothenberg's theory of optimal government size,[53] which focuses on four criteria to evaluate optimal size: economies of scale, responsiveness of government to individual preferences, internalization of externalities, and attainment of redistributive goals. In this theory, optimal urban government size depends on the relative importance attributed to each of the four criteria, which are basically subjectively determined.

We start by examining whether consolidation leads to scale economies or diseconomies and, if so, under what conditions. We can make use of the analytical framework developed in Chapter 14. It permits us to deduce that since school districts have indivisible but highly adaptable fixed plants, the law of diminishing returns applies and produces a U-shaped short-run average cost function. Since each school building is quite flexible, i.e., within limits you can change the number of students without too great a loss, the average cost function has substantial flatness over observed data. If a district seeks to offer education of about similar quality in all its schools regardless of scale of operation, if schools for given grades are of similar size, have similar production functions, tend to be operated at about optimum capacity, can be readily added or closed, and if wages and prices of other inputs are fixed, then the district's long-run average cost function will tend to be horizontal over observed data. There are indications that most of these assumptions are met by school districts of elementary and secondary schools.

We next turn to Rothenberg's second criterion, government responsiveness to individual preferences. It would seem that small decentralized governments in general, and school districts in particular, are better able to fulfill the highly varied preferences of different individuals than a monolithic, centralized large government. Where there are many different jurisdictions, an individual is offered an extensive menu of choices, one of which is likely to be close to its optimum. This argument assumes that governmental units efficiently charge for the cost of public services provided, but the actual financing scheme makes this assumption unlikely to be met. Thus, while there are some benefits associated with this type of decentralization, there are some offsetting problems associated with the financing mechanism.

The third criterion relates to externalities. Although externalities abound in urban America, those associated with education appear to have much larger scope than many others. The use of funding from higher levels of government can internalize many of these externalities, but there is little

[53] Jerome Rothenberg, "Local Decentralization and the Theory of Optimal Government," in J. Margolis, ed., *The Analysis of Public Output* (New York: National Bureau of Economic Research, Columbia University Press, 1970), pp. 31–59.

evidence that the educational aid system is set up to achieve this result. Rather, the levels of aid are often determined by other considerations.

Finally, we come to the redistribution argument favoring school consolidation. It is true that some school districts in a metropolitan area are havens for industry, that others provide homes for the rich, and that still others are homes for poor residents. Under those conditions, consolidation permits pooling the tax base of the entire area and offering greater redistributive justice. As long as there are many small districts, local decisions can be made that permit wealthy residents and industrial and commercial activities to escape high taxes by moving to low-tax jurisdictions. This is not merely inequitable, but it might also prove inefficient because of the resulting distortions of the locational choices. But it is not clear why redistribution should be only over the confines of a large school district and not an entire state. State tax and spending programs can be tailored so as to deal effectively with redistributional aspects, unlike district consolidation. State tax and spending programs have the advantage of permitting fine tuning and ready adjustment as conditions change.

There is little reason to choose one form of production over another on the basis of these criteria since the evidence on the importance of any one is fairly inconclusive. This is complicated by the fact that many of the issues can be addressed by financial arrangements and incentives rather than direct production changes. In general, it seems that there are few reasons for very large school districts based on the production of schooling; however, there are strong distributional arguments for involvement of higher levels of government. Thus, we turn to the issues of financing for schooling.

/// POLICY ISSUES ABOUT FINANCING EDUCATION

The question of financing education is closely related to the issue of who is to be educated and at what cost to the student and his or her family. Americans long ago decided that every youngster should get an elementary and secondary education regardless of financial means. This commitment readily translates itself to a requirement for tax-supported elementary and secondary schools. At the same time, no such argument has been produced in relation to adult education, particularly in subjects that have mainly consumption values. As a matter of fact, it is not clear at all that adult education deserves to be publicly provided. Yet, in relation to retraining it is not easy to decide who should pay for it.[54] Higher education falls somewhat between the two cases.

---

[54] Maurice Peston, "The Finance of Recurrent Education: Some Theoretical Considerations," *Public Choice* 36 (1981), pp. 537–550.

Court-Induced Changes

Historically, elementary and secondary education has been provided by local school districts, which usually only have access to the property tax. However, since education is a people-related service it makes little sense to finance it with the aid of a property-related tax.[55] This arrangement is neither efficient nor equitable. Relative to the equity question, for example, the California Supreme Court in 1972 held in *Serrano v. Priest* that dependence on local property taxes with the resultant wide disparities in school revenue discriminates against the poor because it makes the quality of a child's education a function of the wealth of his parents and neighbors.[56] Moreover, the system allows affluent districts to provide a high quality education for their children while paying lower taxes, and the opposite holds for poor districts. The court concluded,

> In summary, so long as the assessed valuation within a district's boundaries is a major determinant of how much it can spend for its schools, only a district with a large tax base will be truly able to decide how much it really cares about education. The poor district cannot freely choose to tax itself into an excellence which its tax rolls cannot provide. Far from being necessary to promote local fiscal choice, the present financing system actually deprives the less wealthy districts of that option.[57]

At about the same time the New Jersey Supreme Court held that that state's education financing system was in violation of both the state and federal constitutions.

The major remedy of recent years has been to shift more of the financing responsibility to the state, which in most instances mainly relies for funds on people-related personal income and sales taxes.

The increase in state financing of elementary and secondary education was associated with changes in state aid formulas, brought about in part by such court decisions as *Serrano v. Priest*. Until the early 1970s, most states aided school districts on a per student basis. This practice was challenged because students in relatively poor districts were receiving the same aid as those in wealthy districts. In states with successful court challenges, legislatures were forced to devise aid plans that reduced the relationship between community wealth and per pupil spending. A popular reform was the guaranteed tax base plan or district power equalizing plan.

Under these plans a property-poor community's per pupil expenditure level depends only on the property tax rate of the community, rather than on the amount of revenue raised. For communities with a per pupil property tax

---

[55] Anthony M. Rufolo, "Efficient Local Taxation and Local Public Goods," *Journal of Public Economics* 12 (1979), pp. 351–376.

[56] 5 Cal. 3d 584, 487 P. 2d 1241 (1971).

[57] Ibid.

base smaller than the guaranteed tax base, the state must step in and transfer subsidies equal to the difference between the revenue raised and the revenue that would have been raised had the community's chosen tax rate been applied to a guaranteed tax base plan. As a result, the price of education for communities with a low per-pupil tax base is reduced. There are some indications that such finance plans (which lower the price of education to property-poor communities, but leave the communities free to choose between more spending on education or lower tax rates) do not tend to equalize per pupil spending levels across school districts. Moreover, they do not result in all districts spending sufficient amounts of money to provide students with strong, basic, academic programs.[58]

Other court rulings, such as the Mount Laurel ruling in New Jersey, held that communities could not systematically exclude the poor from higher income communities.[59] One consequence of greater integration of income groups within communities would be more uniform access to higher quality public schools. However, the judicial rulings so far have not had much effect on the housing mix within communities.

Much of the recent emphasis on school reform has focused on having the states take on even greater shares of the cost of education. Partly as a result of providing substantial amounts of funding and partly to address the criticism of the educational system, states have taken the lead in the regulation of education. They increasingly mandate length of school year, teaching of specific subjects, performance standards for teachers, as well as many other aspects of the education enterprise. Reasons for the states' increasing role include the following:

1. Unlike local jurisdictions, states rely on quite elastic taxes with rather rapidly growing bases. Thus, they have more resources.

2. The revenue limitation movement, with California's Proposition 13 a telling example, has further curtailed local governments' ability to make use of the property tax.

3. A consensus has emerged in favor of greater statewide equity, so that a child's education does not depend so much on accidents of geography.

Increasing funding at the college level is largely associated with a perception that the social returns to such education are much higher than the private returns. The major issue has been whether the aid should be in the form of direct subsidies or in the form of loans. The higher income of college graduates argues for relying more on loans rather than subsidies to this group.

58 U.S. Department of Education, *Digest of Education Statistics*, op. cit., p. 133.
59 *Southern County of Burlington NAACP v. Township of Mount Laurel*, 67 N.J. 151.363 A2d 713 (1985). For a discussion see "Housing Reform in New Jersey: The *Mount Laurel* Decision," Federal Reserve Bank of New York *Quarterly Review* 10 (Winter 1985–86), pp. 19–27.

Grants-in-Aid

As the states (and also up to the late 1970s the federal government) played an increasing financial role, issues surrounding the question of government grants to education arose. They obviously are part of the larger issue of fiscal intergovernmental relations, which were taken up in greater detail in a previous chapter. Here we focus on relatively narrow subvention issues as they affect education in general and elementary and secondary education in particular. Because education has public goods characteristics and resources to finance education are unequally distributed across geographic areas, transfers of funds to support education have been common.

A national school finance policy requires decisions on at least three levels. First there is the question of what level of government should provide the subsidy and what sources of funds should be used. Both the level of government and the source of funds can affect the net distribution of benefits and the efficiency incentives for the provision of education.

Second, the aggregate level of funding and subsidy must be determined. The funding level decision would ideally be determined by looking at the benefits of additional funds in both aggregate educational achievement and the distribution goals set to aid the disadvantaged.

Finally, a formula must be selected to distribute the funds among recipients. Gurwitz has suggested that formula design give expression to two sets of choices: the characteristics of those who are to receive funds under the formula and the relative weights that are assigned to those characteristics that are included.[60] Recipient characteristics of concern are the number of pupils in a district and their major relevant characteristics, as well as indicators of a district's fiscal health, the physical condition of its capital stock, and population density. The weight question can be illustrated in terms of how much money a district should receive for a pupil with a specific physical handicap and how much should be given to a district with a low fiscal capacity.

Grant formulas have two major dimensions. If the formula incorporates an element that represents the level of revenues raised by the district, its tax rate, or a similar local effort measure, a "matching grant" is involved. Thus, the higher level of government will seek to match some proportion of the funds raised locally. If the district's own revenue decisions do not affect the monies it receives, we talk about a "block grant." In a sense, matching grants lower the tax price district residents pay for education of a given quantity and quality.

A second dimension relates to the specificity of the grant. For example, most federal and much state aid for education must be assigned to specific educational programs, e.g., compensatory education or remedial programs; these are "categorical" or "specific" grants. They differ from "general grants," of which the Educational Consolidation and Improvement Act of 1981 is a good example.

---

[60] Aaron S. Gurwitz, *The Economics of Public School Finance* (Cambridge, MA: Ballinger, 1982), p. 111.

Subventions from state and federal governments to local school districts have both positive and negative aspects. The advantages are that people-related tax sources are used to finance people-related services and that the tax base is broadened over the state and nation, respectively. This latter aspect reduces the inequality in the means of financing education that exists across local school districts.

On the negative side is the fact that government units that are not raising their own funds tend to be less careful in spending them. The lesser problem, therefore, is that complex systems of accountability must be devised and effectively implemented, leading to a growth of bureaucracy and inflexibility. The greater danger is waste.

Other Financing Schemes

Are there financing schemes that are more conducive to efficient resource use without neglecting the fact that education has significant public goods characteristics? This is an issue about which Adam Smith worried more than 200 years ago. He judged Oxford a hopeless place because the teachers' "subsistence so far as it arises from their salaries, is derived from a fund altogether independent of their success" in teaching young men. In his opinion Oxford would remain hopeless so long as "endowments of schools and colleges diminished the necessity of application in teachers."[61] His solution was simple—to replace endowments by fees specifically tied to the educational results achieved. In short, teachers, principals, and school superintendents should have their salaries somehow linked to the educational results brought about by their efforts.

For elementary and secondary schools at least two policies have been advanced that would tie teacher and school administrator more closely to their educational results. One involves permitting open enrollment and financing each school according to the number of pupils it attracts.[62] Under such a policy open enrollment would permit parents to send their children to any school that would accept them. School boards would have a significant representation of parents of pupils currently enrolled in the school. Funds would be allocated to each school according to the number of pupils it attracted and schools would be permitted to choose how much salary to offer to attract any particular teacher.

One of the great challenges of such a policy would be to devise a system of capitation fees which would be mainly tied to the service conditions to be overcome by the school. Thus the largest capitation fee should go to schools with the most disadvantaged child. Clearly, if capitation fees for disadvantaged children were too low, it would show promptly when these children had

---

[61] Adam Smith, *Wealth of Nations* (Cannan edition, 1776).
[62] An example of such a proposal is *Save Our Schools* (London: Conservative Political Center, July 1986).

difficulty in finding a place in a school. Thus, their capitation fees would have to be raised.

A second scheme involves education vouchers, which usually involve giving parents the right to send their children to any school in the district willing to take them. A radical voucher proposal has been made by Doyle and Finn.[63] They would have a statewide public education voucher system wholly financed by state revenues. Under this system, all public education funds would be given to individual students, not the institutions. Students could select their school from schools throughout the entire state.

There has been active interest in making use of vouchers. In the 1970s, a number of school districts experimented with vouchers. The most extensive study over a number of years took place in Alum Rock, California, a mixed white-black-Latino district near San Francisco.[64] Students were given a voucher that they could use to go to any school in the district. On the whole, parents and teachers were reasonably well satisfied with the experiment. Parents seemed more satisfied during the second year than during the first. Teachers who participated were more satisfied at the end of the first year than at the beginning. Teachers appreciated the increased autonomy they enjoyed under the voucher system, and voucher school principals felt the same way. The fact that seven more schools joined the demonstration after the first year is additional evidence of acceptance by school staff and the community. However, teachers were concerned about the additional work load and the competitive atmosphere that they believed the demonstration engendered. One particularly positive outcome was increased diversity in instructional programs. There were twenty-two minischools in six schools the first year, and forty-five minischools in thirteen schools in the second year. Parents liked having these choices.

The experiment in Alum Rock differs from a full-fledged educational voucher plan in two major respects: only public schools participated and the demonstration guaranteed continued operation of schools and employment of teachers, regardless of market demand. Thus, the demonstration was more a system of open enrollment combined with decentralization of administration and instructional policy. It is interesting to note that when federal financing for its voucher experiment came to an end, Alum Rock did not continue the scheme but went instead to open enrollment plus financing for each school according to the number of pupils it attracts.

In addition to educational vouchers, other schemes have been used to increase parental school choice. For example, to make it easier for families to choose private over public schools, a number of states have sought to reduce the cost of sending students to private schools. Two major schemes have been

[63] Dennis P. Doyle and Chester E. Finn, Jr., "American Schools and the Future of Local Control," *Public Interest* 77 (Fall 1984), p. 92.

[64] Daniel Weiler, et al., *A Public School Voucher Demonstration: The First Year at Alum Rock—Summary and Conclusions*, R-1495-1 (Santa Monica, CA: RAND Corporation, June 1974).

used separately or jointly. Families in Minnesota are allowed to deduct educational expenses of up to $650 per elementary school child and $1,000 per secondary school child when figuring their state income tax liability. Since Minnesota makes this subsidy available to parents in both public and private schools, the scheme has been held constitutional. However, a study by Linda Darling-Hammond, et al. found that both non–public school administrators and parents viewed the income tax deduction feature as inconsequential to parents' school choices.[65] One important reason for the ineffectiveness of tuition tax deductions in Minnesota is that the subsidies are relatively small. Yet these tax deductions disproportionately benefit parents with higher incomes and educational level.

A second reason why tuition tax deductions have little effect is that they are taken a year after a family has made its cash outlay to pay full private tuition. This is one of the great differences between a tax deduction on the one hand and an educational voucher on the other, the latter providing for "upfront" cash to be applied against parents' costs. Thus, a tax deduction is an ineffective scheme to affect parental school choice and if successful it is a regressive form of subsidy.

A second class of schemes involves providing free transportation and books to students attending private schools. In Minnesota, which provides free bus transportation, this feature appears to have had a significant effect on parental choice, particularly for parents at the choice margin.[66]

Over the years many reforms have been proposed and some even implemented, and more of these efforts are likely to occur. Thus, it is useful to develop a model that can help evaluate some of the key implications of reform. Such models seek to describe the economic and political actors whose decisions interact and determine how many resources are to be allocated to education and how the allocation should take place. In these models, major actors are households, firms (including housing firms), educators, school districts, other local governments, the state government and the federal government. The allocation of resources to education by a household depends on the choices available to it in the light of expenditure levels and the educational output of the schools, whether public or private, available to the household. In turn, expenditure levels depend on the incomes of households, their tastes, the objectives of the schools and the price paid for education , whether in the form of a tax or a fee.

A further element of a response model represents the effects of education reform. A possible scenario, related to a state changing its school finance system, is as follows. The share of school revenue obtained by the average district increases, though some school districts see their share increase while that of others decreases. The increased state expenditures require that at least

---

[65] Linda Darling-Hammond, et al., *Tuition Tax Deductions and Parent School Choice: A Case Study of Minnesota* (Santa Monica, CA: RAND Corporation, 1985), p. vii.
[66] Ibid., p. x.

one of the general taxes increase. As a result, the pattern of school tax rate and expenditure levels changes across districts. Those receiving aid can lower taxes, spend more, or both, while those receiving less must raise taxes, lower expenditures, or both. One consequence is a change in the consumption patterns of households. Those households who are advantaged under the old system may choose to move elsewhere, though these changes take place slowly. Households in previously low-spending districts who sent their children to private schools may now turn to public education. And households that chose high-spending districts to obtain good education for their children may start sending them to private schools. Local taxes may also be adjusted as a result of the change in subsidies received from the state. To the extent that these changes bring about adjustments in the socioeconomic composition of students in districts, federal aid to them is affected. Should these quality changes in education lead to households voting with their feet, the demand for housing will change and with it their prices.

Clearly the issues discussed are complex. The actions of any one level of government affect the provision of education in a variety of ways. In particular, the responses by the consumers of education can take place over a variety of dimensions. Nevertheless, the importance of education for both economic growth and for equitable treatment of children in different socioeconomic conditions make it important to address these issues. The strong criticism of the education system in the United States in recent years points to serious problems in the way in which education is financed and produced, but there still is no widespread agreement on what must be done to change the outcome.

/// SUMMARY

Education is a large industry, accounting for about 4% of GNP. Much of the industry is in the public domain. It has been undergoing rapid changes, including its financing. Funding by the states has been on the increase and that from local sources on the decline. While the role of the federal government steadily increased until 1978, it has been on the decline ever since.

There is general agreement that a totally unfettered market for education, with each household buying just the amount of education it wants and can afford, will lead to an inefficient and inequitable allocation of educational services. If the financing of education is purely a private, voluntary situation, externalities are likely to be ignored and the level of provision will be inefficiently low. Further, equity concerns regarding the appropriate distribution of educational resources are unlikely to be met. Finally, problems in financing education would also lead to underinvestment. Alternatively, the more centralized the financing of education becomes, the less feasible it is to have different levels of education or different methods of producing education. If it becomes more difficult for people to achieve the level of education they prefer through the public sector, support for public education may erode substantially. Thus, many families may end up supporting low levels of public education and sending their children to private schools. Hence, a careful balance must be maintained between the private demand for education and the public sector issues that are closely associated with the provision of education.

A related issue is whether education should be provided directly by the public sector or whether the public should merely subsidize the private purchase of education. Historically, the direct public provision of education has predominated; but many of the controversies about the effectiveness of the educational system are related to the incentives within the current system. It is argued that the system tends to protect incompetent teachers and to discourage many prospective teachers from entering the education system, among other criticisms. A number of critics have called for more accountability for teachers and administrators in the public schools, but even the critics often disagree on what form the accountability should take. While some want to reform the administration of the public school system, others argue for its replacement by a subsidized private system.

Another major issue regarding the level of education to provide is the one of quality. While many studies find that the use of market inputs is of limited benefit in improving academic performance, there is nevertheless a clear difference in the quality of output achieved by different schools. What can and should be done about such differences is tied not only to the amount of education that should be provided but also to the methods of producing it. Attempts to improve the educational environment of some students almost invariably leave others worse off. This is particularly true with respect to decisions on whether or not to expel troublesome students.

Policy issues can also be divided into those that center around the provision of education and those around its financing. Into the first group fall decisions about the efficient and equitable allocation of resources to schools and decisions about the optimum district size, e.g., whether to consolidate or break up districts. The financing issues include finding efficient and equitable ways of raising funds for schools, particularly in the light of some recent rulings by the courts, and selecting the most appropriate instruments to allocate state and federal funds to school districts. Here, in addition to a variety of grants-in-aid schemes, open enrollment and voucher schemes, among others, have been explored.

The challenge of educational policy is to improve the equity and efficiency of the system without substantial increases in cost and while maintaining the option for individuals to spend amounts considerably above the public minimum for education.

Chapter 19 //////

Fighting Crime

The security of Americans depends on our national defense, for fighting threats from abroad, and on our criminal justice system, for protection from crime. Compared to the national defense budget, we spend relatively little on providing personal security for our citizens through police, prosecution, courts and correction. For example, it was estimated that public expenditures for criminal and civil justice functions in 1985 amounted to slightly less than 3% of all government spending.[1] (This percentage has been quite stable during the 1980s.) Of this amount 1.4% was for police protection, 0.8% for corrections, and 0.6% for all other justice services, i.e., courts, prosecution, and public defense.[2]

The 1985 government expenditures of $48.5 billion for police, judicial services, and corrections can be compared with a national defense and international relations budget of $289 billion and $206 billion for education. The difference in the size of the budgets appears minor when we compare the concentration of decision making and funding in the two areas. Whereas national defense is the sole responsibility of the federal government, which assumes highly centralized control, the criminal justice system has many separate components, all virtually autonomous and operating on different levels of the government. For example, of the total 1985 government spending of $48.5 billion on police, judicial services, and corrections, $27.4 billion was spent by local, $16.3 billion by state, and $6.4 billion by the federal government.[3] From Figure 19-1 we can see that between 1971 and 1985 the relative

---

[1] U.S. Department of Justice, Bureau of Justice Statistics, *Report to the Nation on Crime and Justice*, 2nd ed., NCJ-105506 (Washington, DC: Bureau of Justice Statistics, March 1988), p. 115.

[2] We have some recent data from the United Kingdom about the distribution of its crime-fighting budget. According to a 1988 report from the Home Office, the police budget was £3.5 billion, private security cost £1.6 billion, prisons spent £700 million, and the courts and legal aid for criminals cost another £700 millon. United Kingdom Home Office, *The Costs of Crime* (London: 1988).

[3] U.S. Department of Justice, op. cit., p. 115.

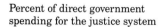

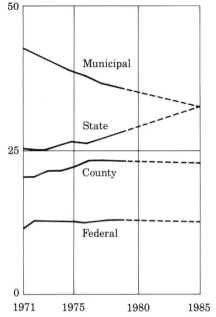

Data for 1980–84 are estimates as no
data were collected in those years.

Figure 19-1 / **Spending on Justice System by Types of Government
1971–85**

(Source: U.S. Department of Justice, Bureau of Justice Statistics, *Report to the Nation on Crime and Justice*, 2nd ed., NCJ-105506 [Washington, DC: March 1988], p. 116.)

importance of municipal spending for the justice system has significantly declined; spending by state governments increased to take up the slack, while that by county and federal governments remained stable.[4]

That the operation and funding of the justice system is carried out by governments on three levels and control is so widely dispersed is the direct result of our commitment to a federalized form of government. Accordingly, we cannot visualize federal control, except in the following exceptional circumstances: when criminal activity materially affects interstate commerce, crime occurs on a federal reservation or in the District of Columbia, crime involves large criminal organizations or conspiracies presumed to operate across state lines, the Constitution or federal law set procedural requirements for state and local law enforcement agencies, or federal programs and activities impose

[4] Ibid., p. 116.

serious financial burdens on local law enforcement agencies.[5] In short, in only relatively rare circumstances and in relatively select geographic areas does a particular crime activity warrant the establishment and exercise of federal jurisdiction.

At least in theory, states have substantial power to guide local law enforcement agencies. They exercise these powers in relation to the courts. However, in California, for example, where the appointment power is assigned to the state and virtually all the fund raising to local government, superior courts and municipal courts appear to escape careful scrutiny and control by either level of government. Fortunately, the appeals process, culminating in the authority of the state Supreme Court, assures jurisprudential review.

In the correction area there are significant intergovernmental relations. Defendants awaiting trial in state or federal courts, for example, tend to be held in local jails. There are many such prisoners, since about 60% of persons in jails have not been convicted and are awaiting trial.

Let us briefly review the meaning and nature of crime in general and as it is viewed by economists. According to Webster's dictionary a crime is an act or omission forbidden by law and punishable on conviction. For the economist, defining an action as criminal refers to the concept of social costs. A crime's social costs are not limited to the direct losses generated but include the costs of all the resources, at the value of their best alternative use, required because of the commission of that crime. They include the losses caused by criminal activity, the direct costs of fighting crime, and the indirect costs of social and education programs to discourage people from resorting to crime. The justification of expending resources on fighting crime depends on whether the criminal behavior is socially costly and whether the use of resources can reduce the incidence of such behavior.

We can regard the commission of crime as initiating a complex process of response primarily provided by government through the criminal justice system. A loose confederation of agencies at all levels of government provide the means by which we apprehend, try, and punish offenders. It is important to realize that we do not have a single criminal justice system. Instead, we have many systems, which though individually unique, resemble each other and interact frequently.

The major components of the criminal justice system are police, prosecution-defense, courts, and corrections. Police forces are mainly local, although more than fifty law enforcement agencies operate at the federal level. The federal agencies include the Federal Bureau of Investigation, the Drug Enforcement Administration, the U.S. Customs Service, the Bureau of Alcohol, Tobacco, and Firearms, and the Secret Service in the Department of the Treasury. On the local level there are more than 15,000 police agencies, including sheriffs' departments at the county level. Although each of these

---

[5] James Q. Wilson, ed., "Introduction," *Crime and Public Policy* (San Francisco, CA: Institute for Contemporary Studies, 1983), pp. 7–8.

agencies is autonomous, they tend to cooperate on specific tasks, though often only informally. The law enforcement agencies, in a similar manner, also cooperate with prosecutors, the courts, and probation agencies. Jails hold defendants before and during trials and are run and mainly funded by local governments. Prisons, where those who have been convicted serve their terms, are the responsibility of the state and federal governments.

While courts can be local, state, or federal, city and county courts are usually closely controlled by the state. The state decides how many judges should sit where, and the governor usually makes appointments to the bench.

In short, under our federalized form of government, the criminal justice system is composed of a highly complex set of independent agencies operating on all levels. Local governments hold the dominant operating and funding responsibility, though their control is often limited, and they receive some subventions from higher levels of government. Thus, fighting crime is an excellent example of expenditure and revenue decision making under federalism.

/// SOME FACTS AND TRENDS

Although police protection, judicial services, and corrections activities are carried out on all three levels of government, in terms of their expenditures, local governments are by far the most important. Municipal governments spend the largest percentage of their justice budget in providing protection, counties in court-related functions, and state governments in corrections.[6]

Criminal justice services are funded predominantly by taxes raised in the jurisdiction where the services are performed. In 1985 state and local governments also received close to $1 billion from the federal government for criminal and civil justice activities. Local governments received close to $1.4 billion from their state governments.[7] Direct justice spending varies across states in terms of state and local government funding. The state government percentages varied from a low of 27% in Nevada and Ohio to a high of 81% in Alaska.[8]

Employment figures for 1985 for police protection and corrections activities by level of government are given in Table 19-1. Thus, in 1985 almost 1.5 million persons were employed by the police and correction agencies, with police accounting for about 51%.[9] Police employment was predominantly local, i.e., on the municipal level. Correction agencies on the state level dominated employment with more than 240,000 employed by states, while

---

[6] U.S. Department of Justice, op. cit., pp. 116–117.

[7] Ibid., p. 117.

[8] Ibid., p. 117.

[9] U.S. Department of Justice, Bureau of Justice Statistics, *Sourcebook on Criminal Justice Statistics, 1987*, NCJ-111612 (Washington, DC: Bureau of Justice Statistics, 1988), p. 15.

Table 19-1 / Justice System Employment and Payroll by Type of Activity and Level of Government, United States, October 1985

Type of activity	Employment			October payroll (in thousands)
	Total	Full-time	Full-time equivalent	
Total justice system	1,437,165	1,341,865	1,368,562	$2,854,834
Federal	108,222	108,222	108,222	277,930
State	443,383	423,302	431,206	878,899
Total, local	885,560	810,341	829,134	1,698,005
County	373,058	342,614	352,606	655,120
Municipal	512,502	467,727	476,528	1,042,885
Police protection	737,741	683,754	693,245	1,515,524
Federal	61,342	61,342	61,342	157,335
State	107,606	97,110	98,656	207,784
Total, local	568,793	525,302	533,247	1,150,405
County	130,505	121,436	123,455	246,381
Municipal	438,288	403,866	409,792	904,024
Judicial (courts only)	192,504	172,104	180,590	361,380
Federal	15,455	15,455	15,455	38,358
State	61,082	57,608	60,533	151,678
Total, local	115,967	99,041	104,602	171,344
County	88,291	78,546	82,307	134,529
Municipal	27,676	20,495	22,295	36,815
Prosecution and legal services	93,742	86,727	89,624	208,832
Federal	15,791	15,791	15,791	43,904
State	23,926	22,523	23,266	53,164
Total, local	54,025	48,413	50,567	111,763
County	35,657	32,646	33,901	72,154
Municipal	18,368	15,767	16,666	39,609
Public defense	12,092	11,208	11,709	26,914
Federal	356	356	356	1,000
State	6,003	5,661	5,872	12,307
Total, local	5,733	5,191	5,481	13,607
County	54,476	4,982	5,258	12,956
Municipal	257	209	223	651
Corrections	394,677	381,988	387,209	729,699
Federal	14,448	14,448	14,448	35,025
State	240,856	236,599	239,031	446,574
Total, local	139,373	130,941	133,730	248,100
County	111,963	103,946	106,594	187,158
Municipal	27,410	26,995	27,136	60,942
Other justice activities	6,409	6,084	6,185	12,485
Federal	830	830	830	2,309
State	3,910	3,801	3,848	7,392
Total, local	1,669	1,453	1,507	2,785
County	1,166	1,058	1,091	1,941
Municipal	503	395	416	844

Subcategories may not add to total due to rounding.

(Source: U.S. Department of Justice, Bureau of Justice Statistics, *Justice Expenditure and Employment, 1985*, Bulletin NCJ-104460 [Washington, DC: U.S. Department of Justice, March 1987], p. 3, Table 4.)

counties employed 112,000 and municipalities about 27,000. Federal correction institutions employed 14,000 persons. In terms of payroll, police accounted for 53%.

The federal criminal justice budget authority and outlays for fiscal year 1986 (actual) and 1987–90 (estimated) are given in Table 19-2. Federal law enforcement outlays by such agencies as the FBI and Bureau of Alcohol, Tobacco, and Firearms accounted for more than half of the entire 1986 federal outlays.[10] Criminal investigations and border enforcement activities were by far the most important federal law enforcement outlays. The second major category was federal litigative and judicial activities, which in 1986 amounted to $2.2 billion, while federal correctional activities amounted to slightly more than half a billion dollars.

The expenditures for the four major components of the criminal justice system made by federal, state, county and municipal governments are summarized in Figure 19-2. Accordingly, 48 cents of every justice dollar is spent for police protection, 13 cents for the courts, 9 cents for prosecution-defense, and 29 cents for corrections, including probation services.[11] Figure 19-2 also shows who spends the money for each of these four major functions, with municipal governments dominating police expenditures; county governments, court and prosecution-defense expenditures; and states, correction activities.

How much does it cost to move a criminal case through the justice system? Clearly there exist great variations depending on the specific nature of the case. However, a study of three "typical" New York City robbery cases found that the cost of arresting, prosecuting, and trying defendants ranged from $851 to $32,627 in the early 1980s.[12] In the first case, the defendants pleaded guilty to a reduced charge the day after their arrest. Each defendant received a six-month sentence.

The second case cost $6,665 when the defendants pleaded guilty after being indicted but before trial. Seventy percent of the total cost was for pretrial detention; sixty-eight days after arrest, the defendants received the sentence of four to twelve years of imprisonment for the plea of guilty to robbery.

In the third case the defendant chose to go to a felony trial in which he was found guilty of robbery and sentenced to nine to eighteen years; 250 days had elapsed between arrest and sentencing. Of the total cost of $32,627, half was for pretrial detention.

To these figures must be added the cost of jail and/or imprisonment. In the late 1970s, the federal prison system reported an average annual cost per inmate of $13,000. The annual operating cost per prisoner in state prisons was found to vary from $5,800 to $23,000.[13]

Since the justice system is labor intensive, about three-quarters of state

10 Ibid., p. 13.
11 U.S. Department of Justice, *Report to the Nation on Crime and Justice*, op. cit., p. 117.
12 Ibid., p. 123.
13 Ibid., p. 123.

Table 19-2 / Federal Criminal Justice Budget Authorities and Outlays, Fiscal Year 1986 (actual) and 1987–90 (estimated) (in millions of dollars)

Type of program	1986 actual		1987 estimate		1988 estimate		1989 estimate		1990 estimate	
	Budget authority	Outlays	Budget authority	Outlays	Budget authority	Outlays	Budget authority	Outlays	Budget authority	Outlays
Federal law enforcement activities, total	$3,728	$3,632	$4,686	$4,636	$5,087	$5,150	$4,998	$4,898	$4,988	$4,871
Criminal investigations	1,522	1,538	1,794	1,759	2,006	1,984	1,973	1,954	1,969	1,956
Alcohol, tobacco, and firearms investigation	167	166	178	175	197	193	201	197	204	200
Border enforcement activities	1,375	1,291	1,992	1,986	2,056	2,154	2,022	1,957	2,003	1,916
Protection and other activities	293	290	335	329	376	369	350	343	355	348
Other enforcement	371	348	386	387	452	450	453	447	457	451
Federal litigative and judicial activities, total	2,190	2,176	2,699	2,559	2,767	2,698	2,908	2,776	2,980	2,833
Civil and criminal prosecution and representation	834	781	1,080	981	1,297	1,204	1,390	1,291	1,418	1,305
Federal judicial activities	1,063	1,090	1,314	1,275	1,471	1,458	1,519	1,485	1,563	1,528
Representation of indigents in civil cases	292	305	306	303	0	37	0	0	0	0
Federal correctional activities	595	614	868	755	971	936	964	998	988	925
Criminal justice assistance	265	181	488	344	159	387	166	232	174	129
Total	6,777	6,603	8,740	8,293	8,984	9,170	9,036	8,904	9,130	8,758

Note: These data are from the budget submitted by President Reagan to Congress in February 1987. The budget authority (actual or estimated) for each fiscal year includes appropriations for that year, as well as for future years, that have been approved by Congress. The outlays (actual or estimated) for the corresponding year are funded partially by the budget authority and partially through unspent funds allocated in previous years. "Outlays" are defined as values of checks issued, interest accrued on public debt, or other payments made, and net of refunds and reimbursements.

(Source: Executive Office of the President, Office of Management and Budget, *Budget of the United States Government, Fiscal Year 1988* [Washington, DC: USGPO, 1987], ch. 5, p. 147.)

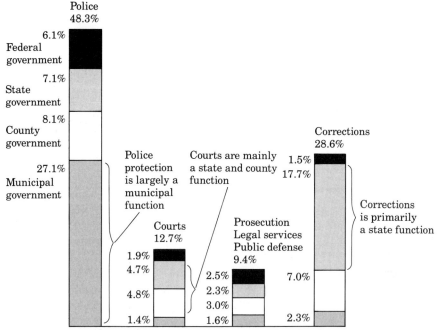

Note: An additional 1% of expenditure was for other functions.

Figure 19-2 / Justice Spending Breakdown

(Source: U.S. Department of Justice, Bureau of Justice Statistics, *Report to the Nation on Crime and Justice*, 2nd ed., NCJ-105506 [Washington, DC: March 1988], p. 117.)

and local justice dollars go for payroll. Judges have the highest salaries of criminal and civil justice employees at each level of government. Public defender salaries are generally on a par with prosecutor salaries. The salaries of state and local police officers are slightly higher than those of correctional personnel and probation and parole officers, who are usually the lowest paid employees.

What are the trends in justice expenditures, crimes, and prison population? Per capita state and local government spending for all criminal and civil justice functions in constant 1985 dollars rose steadily from 1971 to 1985, a total of 26%[14] (see Figure 19-3). Per capita expenditures for police grew 5%, courts 40%, and corrections 67%.

How has the demand for services by the criminal and civil justice system changed in recent years? We have data from the National Crime Survey, the Uniform Crime Reports, and homicide statistics from coroners' reports to the National Center for Health Statistics.[15] In 1985, 25% of all U.S. households

[14] Ibid., p. 121.
[15] Ibid., p. 14.

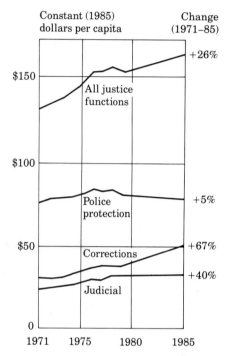

Figure 19-3 / State and Local Per Capita Spending on Justice Functions in 1985 Dollars, 1971–85

(Source: U.S. Department of Justice, Bureau of Justice Statistics, *Report to the Nation on Crime and Justice*, 2nd ed., NCJ-105506 [Washington, DC: March 1988], p. 121.)

were touched by crime. Each of these households was victimized by at least one burglary, larceny, or motor vehicle theft, or one or more of its members were victims of a rape, robbery, or assault by strangers. This was lower than the 32% touched by crime in 1975. While certain crimes per 100,000 population declined slightly between 1976 and 1985, e.g., burglaries by 4% and larceny-thefts by 1%, violent crimes increased by 19%.[16] Among them rapes increased by 38% and aggravated assaults by 30%.

Nevertheless, the absolute number of crimes committed and criminals apprehended has been increasing year after year and so has the number of convictions. As a result, the number of persons held in state and federal prisons and in local jails has been rising to a present all-time high. For example, by the end of 1983, the U.S. Bureau of Justice Statistics reported 438,830 state and federal prisoners, while on any one day an additional 210,000 prisoners were held in local jails.[17] The prison population has doubled

---

[16] Ibid., p. 14.

[17] James Austin and Barry Krisberg, "Incarceration in the United States: The Extent and Future of the Problem," *Annals of the American Academy* 478 (March 1985), pp. 16–17.

in the last ten years, while local jails were holding 30% more inmates and processing about 7 million people a year. Further increases are expected. The U.S. Government Accounting Office forecasts a national prison population of 566,170 in 1990.[18]

Governments have been increasing their spending on jails and prisons. In fiscal years 1982 and 1983, states allocated about $800 million to expand or improve prison capacity and $2.2 billion was allocated for prison construction via bond issues, while the operating budget increased to $4.4 billion.[19] But in spite of these increased financial efforts, prisons and jails are badly overcrowded. For example, the Bureau of Justice Statistics has estimated that in 1983 the nation's state prisons were operating at about 110% capacity, and that 10% of all inmates resided in prisons built before 1875.[20] Many prisons have been found unfit for use, and in the future further increases in prison funding will be required.

/// ECONOMIC MODEL OF CRIME

Earlier in this chapter we presented an overview of the components of the criminal justice system. Keeping in mind its characteristics and main components, we now offer an economic model which can help explain and guide decisions about crime.

Although there are many sociological and psychological explanations of crime, relating criminal behavior to relative deprivation, deviancy, and socially disorganized environments, we concentrate on the views of economic determinists. Though admitting that the propensity to commit a crime is possibly rooted in an individual's background and personality, they argue that the decision to engage in crime is rational and responds to incentives. Accordingly, they claim that there is an economic choice calculus with regard to criminal activity. Based on work by Gary Becker, a framework has been developed that seeks to explain how rational persons trade off expected returns from legal and illegal activities.[21] Becker's economic choice framework views crime (with the exception of crimes of passion) as an economic activity with rational participants. Persons commit criminal offenses if their expected utility exceeds the level of utility they can derive from alternative (legal) activities. They may choose to be criminals, therefore, not because their basic

[18] U.S. Government Accounting Office, *Federal District of Columbia and States Future Prison and Correctional Institution Population*, GAO/GGD-84-56 (Gartherburg, MD: Government Accounting Office, 1984).

[19] Austin and Krisberg, op. cit.

[20] U.S. Department of Justice, Bureau of Justice Statistics, *Sourcebook on Criminal Justice Statistics*, op. cit.

[21] Gary Becker, "Crime and Punishment: An Economic Approach," *Journal of Political Economy* 78 (1968), pp. 169–217.

motivation differs from that of other persons, but because their options and their evaluation of the benefits and costs differ.

We can look at the criminal justice system as designed to influence human behavior by imposing costs on criminal activities, thereby offering the individual an economic incentive to choose not to commit a criminal act; that is, a deterrent incentive. As the net rewards to crime decrease, fewer people will choose criminal activity.

Within Becker's framework, the number of crimes committed by an individual depends on the probability of conviction, the expected severity of the punishment, and the variables reflecting his or her legal income-earning potential, environment, and tastes.

This rational choice framework is based on the assumption that persons deciding whether or not to commit a crime behave as if they are responding to the relevant economic incentives. The fact that those who commit certain crimes may differ systematically in certain respects from those who do not commit them does not contradict this basic assumption that both respond to economic incentives.

Becker's model of rational choice can be extended to include other variables that affect the costs and benefits of criminal activities relative to alternative legal activities. One law enforcement variable which perhaps should be included in an extension of his rational choice framework is the probability that a person will be arrested if he or she has committed an offense. That is, irrespective of whether he or she is later convicted, the embarrassment, anxiety, fear, and temporary restrictions of activity associated with the process of being arrested in itself provides the individual with an incentive not to commit a crime.

This framework makes it possible to explore more carefully the ability of the police to make arrests that ultimately lead to conviction. Such ability is affected by a variety of constraints placed on police activity. One of the more important ones is the exclusionary rule, which bars from criminal trials evidence obtained by search or seizure made in violation of the Fourth Amendment. The rule is designed to protect the civil rights of citizens and prevent police officers from engaging in misconduct. (Suggestions have been made to deal with the second problem by providing for effective disciplinary proceedings initiated by either a judge or a citizen against any police officer engaging in misconduct. These proceedings could be combined with a citizen's ability to recover civil damages from the misbehaving officer's jurisdiction.)

Moreover, the framework makes it possible to give explicit recognition to the prosecution-defense function, which can have a major effect on the likelihood of conviction. Thus, there is the need to trade off funds for prosecution with funds for police and correction. Moreover, careful decisions must be made by prosecuting attorneys about what cases to accept for prosecution, in part with the hope of providing criminals with signals likely to have a crime-deterring effect.

There exist a number of econometric studies of the deterrence effect of the criminal justice system. We can point in particular to the econometric studies by Isaac Ehrlich,[22], R. A. Carr-Hill and N. H. Stern,[23] David L. Sjoquist,[24] Llad Phillips and Harold L. Votey,[25] J. P. Cover and P. D. Thistle,[26] S. G. Craig,[27] W. S. McManus,[28] W. K. Vicusi,[29] and V. K. Mathur.[30] Estimates of the magnitude of the deterrence effect vary; yet these studies indicate that more law enforcement activities that increase either the probability of punishment or the expected severity of punishment have been associated with a reduction in the number of offenses of somewhere between 0.3% and 1.1%.

There also is some empirical evidence on the effect of length of sentence on violent crimes. S. Van Dine and colleagues analyzed the 342 adult defendants who were charged with violent felonies and whose cases were completed in Franklin County (Columbus), Ohio, in 1973.[31] (Fifty-three percent of these defendants had no prior felony conviction, and only 18% had prior violent felony convictions.) Under existing sentencing policies, only about half of the convicted violent offenders were sentenced to serve time. By imposing a mandatory five-year term on an adult convicted of a felony, adult violent crime was reduced by 18%. If only those who were convicted of violent crimes were given the mandatory five-year term for the violent conviction and any subsequent conviction, adult violent crime would have fallen by only 6%.

In a second study, Joan Petersilia and Peter Greenwood analyzed 625 adult felons who were convicted in the Denver, Colorado, district court between 1968 and 1970.[32] (Of those defendants charged with violent crimes, only 39% had a prior adult felony conviction and 23% had no juvenile or adult record.) For this cohort, the analysis showed that the imposition of a five-year mandatory term for every conviction reduced adult violent crime by 31%. If

[22] Isaac Ehrlich, "Participation in Illegitimate Activities: A Theoretical and Empirical Investigation," *Journal of Political Economy* 81 (1973), pp. 521–565; and "On the Usefulness of Controlling Individuals: An Economic Analysis of Rehabilitation, Incapacitation, and Deterrence," *American Economic Review* 71 (1981), pp. 307–322.

[23] R. A. Carr-Hill and N. H. Stern, "An Econometric Model of the Supply and Control of Recorded Offenses in England and Wales," *Journal of Public Economics* 2 (1973), pp. 289–318.

[24] David L. Sjoquist, "Property, Crime, and Economic Behavior," *American Economic Review* 63 (1973), pp. 439–446.

[25] Llad Phillips and Harold L. Votey, "Crime Control in California," *Journal of Legal Studies* 4 (June 1975), pp. 327–350.

[26] J. P. Cover and P. D. Thistle, "Time Series, Homicide, and Deterrent Effect of Capital Punishment," *Southern Economic Journal* 54 (1988), pp. 615–622.

[27] S. G. Craig, "The Deterrent Impact of Police: An Examination of a Locally Provided Public Service," *Journal of Urban Economics* 21 (May 1987), pp. 298–311.

[28] W. S. McManus, "Estimates of the Deterrent Effect of Capital Punishment: The Importance of the Researcher's Prior Beliefs," *Journal of Political Economy* 93 (1985), pp. 417–425.

[29] W. K. Vicusi, "The Risks and Rewards of Criminal Activity: A Comprehensive Test of Criminal Deterrence," *Journal of Labor Economics* 4 (July 1986), pp. 317–340.

[30] V. K. Mathur, "Economics of Crime: An Investigation of the Deterrent Hypothesis for Urban Areas," *Review of Economics and Statistics* 60 (1978), pp. 459–466.

[31] S. Van Dine, *Restraining the Wicked* (Lexington, MA: Lexington Books, 1979).

[32] Joan Petersilia and Peter W. Greenwood, "Mandatory Prison Sentences: Their Projected Effects on Crime and Prison Populations," *Journal of Criminal Law and Criminology* 69 (1978), pp. 604–615.

the five-year mandatory term were restricted to only those convicted of violent felonies, the reduction in adult violent crime would have been 6%.

Petersilia and Greenwood estimated some of the cost implications of sentencing options. The average sentence for those convicted of a violent felony is only 1.3 years (including those who serve no time at all). If every defendant who was convicted of a violent felony was given a five-year term, the prison population would have to increase by 150% to produce a 6% reduction in adult violent crime. Incarcerating criminals for very long periods ties up prison resources that might be used more productively, particularly when society is reluctant to build new prisons. Thus, increasing prison terms for some can mean decreasing terms for others, reducing the percentage of convicted criminals sent to prison, or granting earlier parole.

Becker's framework incorporates the assumption that retribution is an important deterrent, but not all experts agree with the contention. For example, the American Bar Association's task force on crime issued a report in December 1981 that states, "There is no solid evidence to support the conclusion that sending more convicted offenders to prison for longer periods of time will deter others from committing crimes."[33]

The rational choice framework can be extended to include policy variables that aim at increasing the benefits associated with engaging in legal activities, rather than merely imposing greater costs on illegal alternatives. For example, the government may be able to lower the level of criminal activity by improving the education of individuals and thereby their income-earning possibilities in legal employment. Alternatively, reducing the level of unemployment will raise a person's chance of gaining legal employment and so increase his or her expected returns from legal, compared with illegal, alternatives.

Richard Freeman reviewed much of the existing literature on the relation between unemployment and crime. He finds that rises in unemployment or declines in labor participation rates are only in a minor way related to rises in the crime rates. Since the labor participation rate often has a closer link to crime than does unemployment, those who actually leave the labor force seem to be the most crime prone.[34]

Before we present empirical information on the crime-deterring influences of certain activities of the criminal justice system, let us recall the sequence of events that can follow the commission of a major crime, shown in Figure 19-4 as a series of branching points. The commission of a major crime can lead to the criminal's being either arrested or set free. Once arrested, he or she can be either charged or released. If charged, he or she can be either convicted or acquitted, and if convicted, he or she can be imprisoned or, in the case of murder, executed.

Brian Frost has provided some empirical estimates of what happened in

[33] As reported in the *Wall Street Journal* (December 28, 1981), p. 12.
[34] Richard B. Freeman, "Crime and Unemployment," in Wilson, op. cit., p. 96.

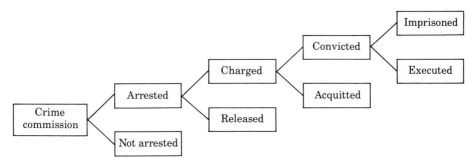

Figure 19-4 / **Flowchart Depicting Sequence of Events following Commission of a Crime**

After a crime has been committed, sequential branching points occur which, if the end of the chain is reached, lead to the imprisonment or execution of the criminal.

typical dispositions of 100 felony arrests during 1974–80.[35] Of the 65 cases that were brought to the district attorney 40 were accepted for prosecution, of which 6 were dismissed by the court. Of the remaining 34 cases, 32 led to conviction, with 20 being incarcerated and the remaining 12 put on probation.

In this framework explicit recognition is given to the probability of arrest in the commission of a crime, and clearly it is the police who have the major effect on this probability. However, it must be recognized that arrest, and with it prevention, is not the sole objective of the criminal justice system. The other objective is retribution.

The role of the police in affecting crimes can be analyzed with the aid of a police production function. It reveals the extent to which additional resources assigned to a specific police activity are likely to increase police output. This output is often measured in terms of crime prevention and retribution. If we could estimate these relationships and assign relative weights to the importance of prevention and retribution, we could progress toward devising policies beneficial to the people living in specific communities. In the abstract, the net benefits to society would be maximized if resources were allocated to police inputs to the point at which the last dollar devoted to each input yielded the same dollar benefit in the form of fewer losses from crime.

In constructing a police production function, a key issue is how to measure police output. Several alternative measures of police output have been used in the empirical literature. For example, Norman Walzer proposed using an index composed of the number of police services rendered, such as the number of complaints investigated.[36] Jeffrey Chapman and colleagues used as output

[35] Brian Frost, "Prosecution and Sentencing," in James Q. Wilson, ed., *Crime and Public Policy* (San Francisco, CA: Institute of Contemporary Studies, 1983), p. 167.

[36] Norman Walzer, "Economies of Scale and Municipal Police Services: The Illinois Experience," *Review of Economics and Statistics* 54 (1973), pp. 431–438.

measures crime prevention and the apprehension of criminals.[37] Although all these measures of police output have shortcomings, the probability of arrest or conviction is still the most useful single measure of police output, because it best conforms to the rational choice theoretical framework discussed earlier.

We can also consider a potential criminal's concern with the final stages of the criminal justice system, i.e., corrections. Here the concern is with the possibility of parole as well as the type of incarceration he or she is likely to face, if convicted. Thus, we could break out a number of correction components.

/// **MAJOR DECISION AREAS**

Economists have attempted to define society's goal of fighting crime as minimizing the social costs of crime, subject to the technical constraints of operating the criminal justice system and the behavioral relationships of society as a whole.[38]

On the assumption that it is possible to affect criminals by a variety of actions, there are trade-offs—for example, spending more for law enforcement or not spending more and having more robberies per year as a consequence. There is a certain implicit price beyond which society will not be willing to invest funds in order to reduce the number of robberies.

In a broad sense, we can argue that the interaction of the forces of the crime generation process and the criminal justice system determines the level of crime. This level, in turn, is responsible for the level of social costs that citizens must bear. We can take steps to increase the probability that the interaction between the two forces will result in an outcome that is more or less efficient. The degree of efficiency is a function of the way that society decides to use resources to combat crime and the effectiveness of these steps.

One of the most ambitious efforts to model the criminal justice system is Hellman and Naroff's model, which incorporates the impact of crime on property values and tax revenues, the impact of both revenues and crime on police expenditures, and the relationship between criminal justice expenditures and the level of crime.[39] Intergovernmental and interagency impacts within the criminal justice system are recognized. A five-equation econometric model is constructed consisting of a supply of criminal offenses function, a police production function, a police service demand function, a city revenue function, and a city property value function. The great complexity of the criminal justice system has forced the authors to make too many simplifying assumptions. This clearly reduces the usefulness of this ambitious effort.

---

[37] Jeffrey I. Chapman, et al., "Crime Prevention, the Police Production Function, and Budgeting," *Public Finance* 30 (1975), pp. 197–215.

[38] Phillips and Votey, op. cit.

[39] Daryl A. Hellman and Joel L. Naroff, *The Urban Public Sector and Urban Crime: A Simultaneous System Approach* (Washington, DC: National Institute of Justice, 1980).

We therefore concentrate on some of the more tractable policy issues, while admitting that it is easier to identify important policy issues than to subject them to careful economic analysis. The state of the art seldom permits a definitive analysis. Yet we hope to illustrate the applicability of economic concepts and frameworks developed earlier in determining the most efficient ways to allocate society's scarce resources toward fighting crime.

We have selected seven major decision areas for examination. The first concerns selecting among different crime-controlling programs. Here the term *program* is used in the program-budgeting sense of a more or less self-contained bundle of activities and expenditures designed to produce a specified output, in our case, crime prevention and reduction. The activities of a police department would be one such program that at budget-making time is traded off, for example, against funds for the jail and/or probation system.

A second policy issue is related to police departments' decisions about resource allocation. The focus is on whether additional funds for a police department are likely to give citizens greater protection against crime and, if so, what types of police inputs promise to be the most cost effective. Discussion of this issue is facilitated by a police production function which, however, places great difficulties in the path of the empirical investigator, particularly in the estimation of police output.

Another broad decision area involves efforts to effectively segment the market for police protection. We consider three segmentation possibilities: by special classes of criminals, e.g., career criminals; by type of crime, e.g., whether the particular crime is likely to be readily controllable and whether serious social harm is likely to result from it; and by geographical areas, i.e., how to distribute police resources over space.

Finally, there is the issue of taking steps to prevent the commission of crimes through means other than the police. We pay particular attention to the effectiveness of gun control on crime reduction and the allocation of resources between incarceration and parole or probation of convicts.

Selecting Among Crime-Controlling Programs

Different programs for crime control offer a choice of approach.[40] For example, crime can be reduced by greater police efforts and also by various privately financed activities, e.g., the installation of sophisticated locks and burglar alarms and the employment of private security forces. Also, funds for police can be traded off against funds for better preparation of cases by prosecutors or better parole supervision. In addition, social and educational programs for ex-convicts and potential criminals to enhance their earning capabilities can be considered as strategies for the longer term. These different

---

[40] The term *program* is used here in the program-budgeting sense. A program involves activities and expenditures aggregated in terms of a specific output package, e.g., crime control.

Input X

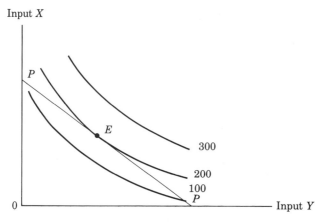

Figure 19-5 / Formalized Trade-Off between Two Crime Control Inputs

The chart shows three production isoquants representing police outputs of 100, 200, and 300 units and a price line (*PP*). The tangency at point *E* between the 200-unit isoquant and the price line indicates the combination of inputs X and Y that will result in the highest attainable police output.

approaches to controlling crime can be looked on as inputs among which society chooses in its fight against crime.

In recent years, private protection efforts have been redoubling as more and more citizens have become dissatisfied with the work of their cities' police forces in the face of spreading crime. Many people feel that their personal security is threatened more than ever before. Should citizens spend more money on police protection or on private efforts to protect themselves? This is the choice we use as an example.

Figure 19-5 presents a formalized trade-off between two classes of crime control inputs, holding the others constant. Input X can be publicly provided police protection and input Y private protection efforts, all designed to reduce criminal activities, which are designated as outputs. The question, then, is how much of each of the two inputs to select. In this instance, crime prevention may be considered the output. Efficiency requires the tangency of an isoquant and a price line, i.e., that any given quantity of output (represented by an isoquant) be attained at the least cost; or that for a given budget (represented by a price line), output be maximized (the highest possible isoquant be obtained). The tangency at E indicates that with the budget represented by the price line *PP*, 200 is the largest attainable output. With the given budget, this output is attainable only by using the combination of public and private crime-fighting inputs indicated by the coordinates of point E. In this context, trade-off can refer either to the marginal rate of substitution in buying the inputs, as represented by the slope of the price line, or to the marginal rate of substitution in using the inputs, as represented by the slope of the isoquant at any point.

The idealized equilibrium pictured in Figure 19-5 is not likely to be attained in the real world where large numbers of citizens make trade-off decisions. Private efforts to supplement those of police departments are not only diffused but also overlapping and inefficient. For example, having uncoordinated private and public police forces patrol the same street is seldom cost effective, and serious inequities can result as rich Americans spend more on personal security and cause crime to be diverted to areas that are less well protected.

The above trade-off analysis can also be applied to the different elements of the criminal justice system. We can trade off funds for the police department and for the prosecuting attorney's office or for the police and the prison system. Here is an example of such a real-life trade-off. In 1982, when the office of the Los Angeles city attorney faced major budget cuts that would have necessitated laying off thirty-nine attorneys and twenty-six support staff, the city's police chief strongly objected. He offered to give up some of the $1.6 million requested by the police department from the city council and give it to the city attorney, if necessary, "because I feel so strongly that it makes no sense for the police department to apprehend (a criminal) and then find the prosecution cannot be completed."[41]

Improving Resource Allocation of Police Departments

Local police departments as well as the FBI make major resource allocation decisions, and there is little doubt that many can stand improvement. In efforts toward this end, police output measurement and production functions play a key role. We present an empirical study that centers on two questions: Would additional funds given to a police department provide citizens greater protection against crime, and if so, which police inputs should be increased and which possibly decreased for the sake of cost-effective crime control?

Chapman and associates estimated two classes of police production functions; one selected crime prevention as output and the other chose a form of punishment.[42] They regarded a crime prevention measure in the following manner: Even if there were no police agency to catch criminals, there would be a hypothetical limit to the number of crimes committed if the marginal gain from crime (while positive) decreased. If this were true, at some point the expected legal wage would become greater than the expected illegal wage for the individual criminal. The difference between this hypothetical total potential number of crimes and the actual number of crimes committed would constitute the number of crimes prevented.

Punishment as a police output is a simpler concept. Arrests can be considered as contributing to police output because society demands that once a crime has been committed, the criminals be punished. Arrest is also a deterrent. The police agency initiates this punitive process by employing resources

---

[41] *Los Angeles Times* (January 7, 1982), p. II-1.
[42] Chapman, et al., pp. 197–215.

in apprehending criminals and bringing them to justice. Police production functions were estimated for both types of police output.

Increasing the real resources of the police agency raised both preventive and punitive outputs, particularly if resource inputs were in the form of field officers, motorcycle teams, and civilian support. A 1% increase in police employees and their associated equipment, except for nonfield officers, increased output by substantially more than 1% on the average, and often by 3% to 5%. These were indications of increasing returns to the Los Angeles Police Department as a whole between 1956 and 1970.

Let us turn finally to two studies that experimented with police-manning levels. In 1966, New York City increased its level of police manning in one of its high-crime precincts by more than 40%. An evaluation by S. J. Press, which used carefully selected control precincts to compare with what happened in the experimental precinct, found that robberies outside these precincts were reduced by 33% with the higher level of manning.[43] A second study covered the period from 1965 to 1971, during which New York City dramatically increased the number of uniformed patrol officers on its subway system in an effort to cut down on robberies. An analysis by Jan M. Chaiken and colleagues found that the number of subway robberies did indeed drop as a result of the extra police presence.[44]

Studies of this sort raise the question of whether focused police presence does not simply displace certain crimes, e.g., robberies, to another location, which indeed both the Press and Chaiken studies found to have occurred.[45]

Finally, we would like to turn to the demand for police in general and the price and income elasticity for police in particular. Jeffrey Chapman reminds us that since between 75% and 95% of police department expenditures are for labor, an analysis of the demand for police is in effect an analysis of the demand for police labor.[46] Using 1960 and 1970 data for 147 California cities with populations between 20,000 and 100,000 Chapman finds that a 1% increase in salary was associated with a 0.5% decrease in the quantity of police demanded. Thus, the demand curve was inelastic. A 1988 study of Michigan cities also finds the demand for police to be inelastic.[47]

[43] S. J. Press, *Some Effects of an Increase in Police Manpower in the 20th Precinct of New York City*, R-704-NYC (Santa Monica, CA: RAND Corporation, 1971).

[44] Jan M. Chaiken, *The Impact of Police Activity on Crime: Robberies on the New York City Subway System*, R-1424-NYC (Santa Monica, CA: RAND Corporation, 1974).

[45] Somewhat different results were obtained in a 1972 study of the Police Foundation and the Kansas City Police Department. The experiment systematically varied the level of preventive patrols across different areas of the city. In some cases the amount of preventive patrolling was doubled and in others it was eliminated. After one year, the differences in the level of patrol appeared to have had hardly any effect on crime rates or on citizens' perceptions of safety. There was no displacement of crime from the highly patrolled areas to the underpatrolled areas. L. T. Kelling, et al., *The Kansas City Preventive Patrol Experiment: A Summary Report* (Washington, DC: Police Foundation, 1974).

[46] Jeffrey I. Chapman, "The Demand for Police," *Public Finance Quarterly* 4 (1976), pp. 187–202.

[47] A. O. Gyapong and K. Gyimah-Brempong, "Factor Substitution, Price Elasticity of Factor Demand and Return to Scale in Police Production: Evidence from Michigan," *Southern Economics Journal* 54 (1988), pp. 863–878.

While median income does not appear to be an important determinant of police demand, this is not the case for property values. Per capita property values were found to be positively related to police at a very high level of significance. However, the elasticity was quite low, i.e., a 1% increase in property values was associated with a 0.2% increase in police officers demanded. Also, total per capita crimes had a significant impact on the demand for police, suggesting that decision makers hire police officers in response to increasing crime.

In summary, opinions and study results concerning the deterrence effect of police activities are far from unanimous. Charles E. Silberman offers a pessimistic view: "Looking at the available evidence, it seems clear that we need to lower our expectation of the police, at least as far as crime prevention is concerned; there is little they can do."[48]

Even if we are pessimistic about the possibility of reducing crime by feasible changes in policing, James Q. Wilson has two hopeful suggestions:

> There is reason to believe that foot patrol . . . helps promote community order and a sense of personal well being; . . . aggressive patrol, involving frequent street checks, especially of suspicious juveniles, can help reduce the rate of certain kinds of crime.[49]

Segmenting the Market for Police Services by Classes of Offenders

Should police allocate their resources by pursuing a shotgun approach or narrow targeting, and if the latter, what would be a propitious target? There are good reasons why one target should be the so-called career criminals, often referred to as recidivists. Career criminals are offenders "whose currently charged offense and criminal history are deemed sufficiently serious to justify [their] being targeted for special 'nullification' efforts by the criminal justice system."[50] Recidivists are responsible for a disproportionate amount of the serious crimes in the United States, yet they often succeed in avoiding punishment. Even after they are arrested, they often manage to delay court proceedings so that prosecution witnesses are lost, to exploit heavy court system caseloads to obtain lenient plea bargains, and to engage in "judge shopping" in order to evade stringent sentencing.

In 1974, the federal Law Enforcement Assistance Administration (LEAA) decided to investigate the proposition that crime rates can be lowered by focusing on career criminals. Its intent was to assure career criminals of certain and longer imprisonment and thereby to deter recidivism. In 1975, the

---

48 Charles E. Silberman, *Criminal Violence, Criminal Justice* (New York: Random House, 1978), p. 216.

49 James Q. Wilson, "Crime and Public Policy," *Crime and Public Policy* (San Francisco: Institute of Contemporary Studies, 1983), pp. 275–276.

50 Joan Petersilia and Marvin Lavin, *Targeting Career Criminals: A Developing Criminal Justice Strategy*, P-6173 (Santa Monica, CA: RAND Corporation, August 1978), p. 1.

LEAA established its Career Criminal Prosecution Program, enabling prosecutors to devote special attention to defendants who had been charged with targeted crimes and/or who had long criminal records. By 1978, these specialized units had prosecuted over 7,500 defendants; 83% of them were convicted and 91% of those convicted received prison sentences whose minimum terms averaged twelve years. These procedures cost about three times as much to prosecute as more routine cases,[51] so there remains the question of whether the Career Criminal Prosecution Program is cost effective. Two evaluations are available. A 1980 study by the Mitre Corporation evaluated four of the programs initially funded by the LEAA; in two of the four it found a greater likelihood of defendants being convicted of the most serious charges under the program. In none of the four was there a larger percentage of convicted defendants who were incarcerated. In one site, there was an increase in average sentence length, and in only one site was there a reduction in processing time.[52]

An evaluation of twelve programs in California found considerably more positive results,[53] a small but significant increase in conviction rates, a large increase in the number of defendants convicted of the most serious charges, increases in incarceration and imprisonment rates, and an increase in the average sentence length.[54]

To zero in on career criminals, not only the prosecution function but also the police response must be considered. The federal government has sponsored the Integrated Criminal Apprehension Program to identify and arrest career criminals. By late 1980, funding had been granted to over thirty law enforcement agencies to upgrade investigation and crime-analysis capabilities.[55]

New York City provides a good example of fruitful attention to career criminals. The New York Police Department established the Felony Augmentation Program in Manhattan in January 1980. Fifty officers were assigned to this special unit to keep watch on 500 individuals who had long criminal records and had committed at least two robberies in the borough after October 1976. Some of the targeted criminals had had as many as thirty-seven arrests.

---

[51] Peter W. Greenwood, *The Violent Offender in the Criminal Justice System*, P-6638 (Santa Monica, CA: RAND Corporation, June 1981), p. 25.

[52] E. Chelinsky and J. Dohmann, *Career Criminal Program National Evaluation Summary Report* (McLean, VA: Mitre Corporation, 1980).

[53] California Department of Justice, *Felony Arrest Disposition in California* (Sacramento, CA: Bureau of Criminal Statistics and Special Services, September 1980).

[54] Peter Greenwood explained the different evaluations: The Mitre evaluation covered the earliest programs during their first year of operation, before effective techniques were developed for the hoped-for accomplishment. Also, the initial program sites covered by the Mitre evaluation apparently were selected because of their progressive management approach. Under those circumstances there may have been little room for improvement, compared with the cases covered by the California evaluation. In California, prosecutors also have more control over the disposition of cases than they have in other states. In the Mitre evaluation the one site that consistently showed improvement in all measures, compared with the other sites, was in California, where prosecutors control plea bargaining with very little interference from the Court. Greenwood, op. cit., p. 26.

[55] Ken Auletta, "The Underclass," *The New Yorker* (November 16, 1981), p. 162.

With the aim of improving the quality of arrests, the unit called in a special investigative squad to build a solid court case, get witnesses to appear in court, and alert the district attorney to these cases in the hope that the suspects would not slip through the cracks of the criminal justice system. An all-out effort was made to prevent those who had been apprehended from receiving low bail, from being allowed to plea bargain the charge down to a misdemeanor, or to get a light jail sentence.

A number of additional suggestions have been made to assist police forces that target career criminals. For example, reduction of crimes by career criminals would be helped by routinely examining the juvenile as well as the adult arrest record of arrestees, routinely conducting urine analysis in order to identify drug users, and concentrating on young adults who are at or near the peak of their criminal activity rather than on older adults likely to be near the end of their criminal careers.[56]

Segmenting the Market for Police Services by Types of Crimes

Police resources also might usefully be concentrated on particular classes of crimes. These crimes should be classified as controllable, on the one hand, and causing serious harm, on the other.[57]

Let us first consider the issue of controllability. One type of relatively uncontrollable behavior is that in which a person perceives that the behavior offers large benefits. As long as high private costs provide insufficient deterrence, the costs associated with public sanctions probably will not provide much deterrence. For example, individuals who use heroin expose themselves to the possibility of addiction, which, where sale of heroin is illegal, means high private costs of maintaining the habit. If a rational person weighs the benefits against these high private costs and still decides to use heroin, the implied benefits of its use are great. Adding the costs of sanctions, particularly if they are low relative to the high private costs, is unlikely to change that decision. The individual who is not rationally weighing the private costs against the benefits of use is unlikely to be affected by public sanctions. Consequently, devoting police resources to controlling heroine use may not be cost effective, in spite of the great social harm of addicts engaging in street crime. The emphasis may have to be on fighting drug suppliers.

A second reason for uncontrollable behavior is high private benefits in conjunction with low private costs. Under these circumstances, individuals with a taste for such behavior will not be deterred by additional costs from sanctions. The demand for goods and services with such characteristics, e.g., marijuana, cigarettes, alcoholic beverages, gambling and betting oppor-

---

56 James Q. Wilson, op. cit., pp. 278–279.
57 Llad Phillips and Harold L. Votey, *The Economics of Crime Control* (Beverly Hills, CA: Sage Publications, 1981), p. 312.

Table 19-3 / **Controllability and Social Harm of Different Crimes**

Social Harm / Controllability	High	Moderate if conducted in public	Minimal if conducted in private	Minimal
High	Murder Burglary Rape			
Moderate if unrestricted in public		Drunkenness Marijuana use Tobacco use Nude bathing		
Minimal if conducted in private			Drunkenness Marijuana use Tobacco use Nude bathing	
Minimal				Heroin use* Gambling Prostitution Pornography

* The harm to others from heroin use may be minimal if it is decriminalized to the extent that black market activities are curtailed.

(Source: Adapted from Llad Phillips and Harold L. Votey, *The Economics of Crime Control* [Beverly Hills, CA: Sage Publications, 1981], p. 49.)

tunities, nude bathing facilities, and the services of prostitutes, tend to be inelastic with respect to price.

A litmus test of whether goods and services are of this type is the development of black markets for them once they are made illegal.[58] Rather than reducing their occurrence, criminalizing them is likely to move them underground.

We can now order some common crimes according to their behavior controllability. Street crime is highly controllable; drunkenness, marijuana use, and nude bathing are moderately so; and prostitution, pornography, drunk driving, and heroin use are the least controllable (see Table 19-3).

Turning to levels of social harm, we shall not consider such acts as killing, raping, or burglarizing, which are universally recognized as serious crimes, but concentrate on behavior that may result in private but not social harm. Accordingly, smoking cigarettes or marijuana or drinking alcohol should not be classified as crimes unless there is sufficient proof of substantial harm to others. Society should not protect individuals from their own actions, even if

[58] Ibid., pp. 45–52.

the private costs of these actions are high: smoking and drinking in private should not be illegal, regardless of the injury to the health of the individual consumer.

But if the same behavior takes place in public, it can harm others. Smoking in public, for example, offends some people and injures the health of all exposed. Some users of public facilities are offended by drunk and disorderly conduct. A family with young children may avoid strolling in a street with pornographic shops or vacationing on a beach frequented by nude bathers. If the happiness of one individual depends not only on his or her own behavior but also on that of others, then the possibility of social harm from an act arises; i.e., there are negative externalities. The social harm from these externalities can be diminished or even eliminated by regulating where these activities are permissible. Rather than criminalizing certain behavior, it is sufficient to provide smoking rooms, license taverns, allow the sale of pornographic material in select sections of town, and permit nude bathing on specified beaches. The principle should be to set aside preserves that can be avoided by those who take offense. In short, many victimless crimes are of this nature and, therefore, should be considered to have a relatively low social harm level.

If we consider both controllability and social harm and distinguish between private and public costs, a matrix of behavior can be constructed. Table 19-3 offers some guidance to the legislature as to what behaviors should or should not be criminalized and assists the police in allocating their limited resources to control behaviors that warrant police intervention.

Over half of the arrests, particularly in urban America, are for behaviors involving victimless crimes. The police in many cities devote sizable efforts to arresting prostitutes, breaking up gambling and betting rings or cockfights, and rousting drunks. Perhaps they do so because these activites are easily controlled and their success has high visibility. Police efforts to curtail these behaviors in public tend to drive the behaviors underground and are unlikely to be cost effective.

Geographic Segmentation of the Market for Police Services

Not all neighborhoods in a given jurisdiction have identical rates of crimes and their demands for police services, therefore, tend to differ. Thus, in large cities with several police divisions or precincts, each of which covers a specified area, a key decision relates to the regional distribution of police resources and, therefore, protection. In the abstract, police services can be supplied in line with one of three major distribution rules. First, service distribution based on an input equality rule requires that the resource inputs per service recipient be equalized among all service areas. Second, distribution based on an output equality rule requires that the service output per recipient be equalized among all service areas. Third is what might be called the efficiency rule, which requires that the marginal product of resource inputs be equal in all uses or, stated in another way, that the marginal cost per unit of output be

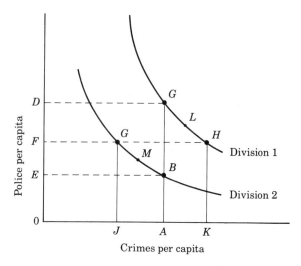

Figure 19-6 / **Police-Crime Relationship**

equal in all uses. The efficiency rule corresponds to the goal of maximum total output, using given resources.

As we stated above, because of the nature of the service, we are compelled to distribute police protection by geographic areas or divisions instead of by specific recipients such as income class or race. But in many cases, geographic location is a good proxy for the socioeconomic characteristics of its residents, and information on a geographic breakdown can be illuminating.

Assuming that the crime rate is an acceptable output measure and that we have succeeded in accurately measuring the probability of a person's becoming a victim of crime, weighted by the importance of the crime, we can apply the three distribution rules to each division. Let us hasten to point to a potential conflict between our first two distribution criteria, input equality and output equality, as illustrated in Figure 19-6.

Consider two police divisions, 1 and 2, within a city. Assume that because of social forces in division 1, e.g., the lack of employment opportunities, for any given number of police per capita, the crime rate is higher in 1 than in 2. Given the total number of police resources (police officers and equipment), an allocation of police officers that would result in an equal crime rate per capita in divisions 1 and 2 would necessitate a much higher ratio of police per capita in 1 than in 2. Such a situation is illustrated in Figure 19-6, in which each division has the same crime rate A, and division 1 has D and division 2 has E police per capita. If, instead, each division were allocated the same number of police per capita (equality in an input rather than an output sense), division 1 would have a much higher crime rate than would division 2.

Carl Shoup long ago demonstrated the conflict between the goal of output equality in terms of equal crime rates among divisions and the goal of minimizing the total number of crimes in the city.[59] This corresponds to our third distribution rule, that of efficiency. According to Figure 19-6, suppose that police resources are allocated to produce equal output per capita, so that the crime rate in each division is A; i.e., there are D police per capita in division 1 and E police per capita in division 2. Also suppose that an additional police officer in division 1 reduces the number of crimes per year by five and that an additional officer in division 2 reduces the number of crimes per year by ten. In this situation, the total number of crimes in the city would be reduced by five if one officer were removed from division 1 (increasing the number of crimes there by five) and assigned to division 2 (decreasing the number of crimes there by ten). In general, the total number of crimes in the city would be minimized only when the marginal effect of an additional police officer on the number of crimes were the same in each division. Otherwise, it would always be possible to reallocate police resources from a division in which the marginal product of police resources was lower to one in which the marginal product was higher and thereby reduce the total number of crimes in the jurisdiction. This would then lead to a departure from the criterion of equal output distribution and to a conflict between the output equality and the efficiency rules of distribution, in addition to the previously mentioned conflict between the input equality and the output equality rules.

There exists a further spatial allocation problem common to many emergency service systems, including police departments, fire departments, and ambulance services. They all require efficient allocation and dispatch of vehicles to respond to calls for services from the public. Solutions have been sought with the aid of analytical models for two problems: (1) a determination of the number of units to have on duty, by time and place, so as to develop the service's operating budget and (2) formulation of procedures for the improvement of deployment of a given number of units in existence. A number of algorithms for finding appropriate solutions have been advanced.[60]

Furthermore, analytical models have been developed for allocating crime-preventive patrol activities by police cars. With the aid of "search theory," guidelines have been provided for the frequency with which cars should patrol specific street locations consistent with prevailing crime rates. This helps estimate the total number of cars needed.

Although this discussion offers some limited general guidelines concerning the geographical distribution of police resources, some political considerations must also be mentioned. That the political clout of the inhabitants of different areas is unequal seldom goes unnoticed by the mayor and the police chief. And, of course, the maxim that the squeaking wheel gets the grease is relevant to the allocation of police resources.

[59] Carl Shoup, "Standards for Distributing a Free Governmental Service: Crime Prevention," *Public Finance* 19 (1964), pp. 386–390.

[60] Jan M. Chaiken and Richard C. Larson, *Methods for Allocating Urban Emergency Units*, $-680 (Santa Monica, CA: RAND Corporation, May 1971), pp. 1–46.

Reducing Crime by Controlling Supply of Guns, Drugs, and Alcohol

In an earlier section we raised questions about the cost-effectiveness of devoting resources to reduce the demand and use of drugs and alcohol; now we turn to control of the supply side. Let us begin by considering handgun control legislation, which has been the subject of much controversy. The effectiveness of handgun control in deterring willful homicides can be examined by reference to a police production function. Statutory gun control, in line with our general framework, would change the service conditions within which the police produce their output.

The arguments in favor of gun control assert that aggravated assaults frequently become homicides when a gun is the chosen weapon. They allege "that one of the major sources of homicide is assault, and that the use of firearms increases both the feasibility of attack and the fatality rate."[61]

The fact that weapon availability is a crucial contributing factor in homicide was demonstrated in a study by Llad Phillips.[62] To determine the relationship between handgun density and homicides, Phillips and associates developed a model that expresses the implied objective of minimizing both the losses due to crime and the costs of control.[63] Constraints are the budgets of law enforcement agencies and the behavioral relations specifying crime generation and crime control. Phillips and associates found that based on multiple regression analysis, a 10% reduction in handgun density is associated with a 27.4% reduction in the homicide offense rate.[64] They concluded that for the sake of social cost minimization, about 19.5% of California's law enforcement personnel should be assigned to homicide-related activities, although they found the current percentage to be much smaller.

These results suggest a number of potential policies. Clearly, carefully enforced laws that control the supply and possession of handguns, drugs, and alcohol would be most potent. If society is unwilling to effectively prohibit access to guns, alcohol, or drugs, our alternative policy could be to increase the cost of abusing them. If we cannot reduce the inventory of guns in private possession, we can make it riskier to carry concealed handguns. To control alcohol consumption, we could raise the price by levying high taxes on alcohol. We could also provide for severe penalties for drunk driving and thereby reduce crimes associated with alcohol. Likewise, in relation to hard drugs, our policy could be to enact laws that would make the drug very costly and hard to procure. Drug users should be encouraged to enter treatment programs by keeping the cost of the drug high and by making treatment readily available.

[61] Llad Philips, et al., "Handguns and Homicide: Minimizing Losses and the Cost of Control," *Journal of Legal Studies* 5 (1976), p. 463.

[62] Llad Phillips, "Crime Control: The Case for Deterrence," *Economics of Crime and Punishment*, vol. 65 (Washington, DC: American Enterprise Institute, 1973).

[63] Phillips, et al., "Handguns and Homicide," op. cit., pp. 463–472.

[64] Ibid., pp. 474–475.

Allocating Resources Among Incarceration, Probation, and Parole

Decisions about parole and probation of convicts may be made with retribution or crime prevention as their goal. Matters have been complicated by rapid increases in the number of prison inmates nationwide, by about 1,000 every month, with the result that every prison in the United States now houses more inmates than it was designed to hold.[65] Overcrowding has been so severe that in 1986 all but eight states were under federal court orders to bring prison populations in line with prison capacity.

There are three options for relieving prison crowding: (1) front-end options, which reduce the number of persons admitted or sentenced to prison and their sentence lengths; (2) back-end options, which increase prison releases by decreasing the amount of time served through adjustments in good-time credits or parole practices; and (3) capacity expansion, which increases the number of holding places available through new construction and renovation projects, or through redefinition of current capacity limits, for example, by double celling.

In the past, states have mainly pursued the last option, though they have recently shown an interest in early release. Thus, for example, in 1983 more than 21,000 inmates in state prisons were given early releases as fifteen states sought to cope with increasing admissions and longer sentences.[66]

Prison overcrowding also is having an effect on court decisions. For example, in interviews of state judges in thirty-one states about the impact of present overcrowding on judicial sentencing practices (carried out by ABT Associates, Inc. between October 1982 and February 1983), nearly half of the judges reported that capacity of prison facilities is a factor in the sentencing decisions of felony court judges.[67] One of the judges stated that justices in his state no longer impose prison terms for victimless crimes. Another reported that some judges in his state have set priorities in response to prison overcrowding, and that they sentence to probation offenders deemed to be least dangerous.

In short, probation and early parole have become a necessity so that prisons can accommodate new inmates. The two options have become about the only ways states presently have for reducing prisoner intake.[68] In principle, probation and parole allow the sentenced offender to remain in the community, subject to imposed conditions. In recent years, about 80% of the offenders convicted of misdemeanors and about 60% of those convicted of felonies have been given probation. As a consequence the probation popula-

---

[65] Joan Petersilia, et al., *Prison versus Probation in California: Implication for Crime and Offender Recidivism* (Santa Monica, CA: RAND Corporation, July 1986), p. 1.
[66] Austin and Krisberg, op. cit., p. 17.
[67] Peter Finn, "Judicial Responses to Present Crowding," *Judicature* 67 (February 1984), p. 318.
[68] Joan Petersilia, et al., *Prison versus Probation in California*, op. cit., p. 1.

tions have increased by about 70% in the past decade; however, probation budgets have declined by about 25%.[69]

What are the effects of incarceration versus probation? To seek an answer to this question, Petersilia et al. used a sample of 1,022 felons, all of whom had been sentenced in 1980, though half were probationers and the other half were imprisoned offenders. The probationers had on average 3.3 years of jail time while prisoners had been incarcerated for 12.5 years.[70]

To select between imprisonment and probation in terms of their crime-deterring effects, two phenomena must be investigated: first, the relationship between imprisonment and recidivism, and second, the incapacitation effect. The first issue is whether prisoners have higher or lower recidivism rates than do probationers, both across crime time, types, and in the aggregate. However, even if prisoners have higher recidivism rates, they should be expected to commit fewer crimes as long as they are incapacitated because of incarceration.

The Petersilia study found that prisoners have higher recidivism rates than probationers in the two-year follow-up period.[71] Seventy-two percent of the prisoners were rearrested compared to 63% of the probationers; 53% of the prisoners had new charges filed, though only 38% of the probationers. Finally, 47% of the prisoners were incarcerated in jail or prison, compared with 31% of the probationers. At the same time, the two groups committed about equally serious crimes.

Next we turn to the incapacitation effect, that is, imprisonment prevents offenders from committing crimes while incarcerated. The Petersilia study concluded that, on average, each prisoner committed an estimated twenty crimes and each probationer committed twenty-five crimes during the three-year period following his or her 1980 conviction.[72] On average, each probationer was arrested 2.5 times during that period and each prisoner, two times. If one assumes a constant ratio of ten crime commissions per arrest, prisoners would have committed 20% fewer crimes than the probationers during the three years.

Thus, in terms of crime prevention the Petersilia sample would conclude that under present circumstances imprisonment reduces crimes to a larger extent than does probation.

However, there are many indications that we should be able to improve the effectiveness of imprisonment and parole in preventing crime, if we had more resources and used them more efficiently. For example, there are indications that the twenty-four months after offenders are released from jail or prison constitute a watershed for recidivism, but little supervision is provided for ex-convicts and probationers. In California, for example, ex-prisoners are not even normally supervised after the first year. Insufficient funding makes it

[69] Ibid., p. 1.
[70] Ibid., p. 16.
[71] Ibid., pp. vii–viii.
[72] Ibid., p. ix.

impossible for probationers in California to be effectively supervised after probation has gone into effect.

In addition to the crime prevention aspects of imprisonment and probation, there are cost considerations. In the early 1980s probation supervision was generally assumed to cost about $1,500 per year for each probationer, whereas operational prison costs were assumed to amount to $15,000 per year for each prisoner.[73] To these direct costs the following secondary costs should be added: correction costs of initial confinement, costs of postrelease probation or parole supervision, police and court costs associated with processing postrelease arrest, and costs of any postrelease incarcerations resulting from new crimes.

When Petersilia et al. took both direct and secondary costs into consideration, they estimated that each felony probationer in their sample cost the California criminal justice system about $12,000 in the three-year period following the 1980 conviction. They found that about $6,000 went to police and court agencies to process new arrests while the offender was on probation. The cost for each prisoner over the same three-year period was about $23,000, with 70% required to cover the initial year in prison. In short, the criminal justice system spent about twice as much over the three-year period on supervising and reprocessing prisoners as it did on probationers.

/// **SUMMARY**

The fight against crime is carried out by the country's criminal justice system; although all three levels of government participate in this undertaking, the lead role is taken by local government. There exists relatively little formal cooperation between the three levels of government as local police and various federal law enforcement agencies labor to provide for personal security, prosecution places cases before the courts and judges depose of them, and convicts are put into the care of the correction system.

Economists have developed an economic model of crime, which seeks to explain how a rational person trades off expected returns from legal and illegal activities. Accordingly, crimes (other than crimes of passion) are committed if a person's expected utility from an illegal activity exceeds that from an alternative legal activity. Moreover, according to this theory the criminal justice system can reduce returns from illegal activities while a variety of educational and social programs can raise returns from legal activities.

Governments make a large variety of decisions in their efforts to combat crime. In doing so they can be helped by some economic concepts, methods of analysis, and frameworks. A few decision areas were examined in this chapter.

[73] Ibid., p. ix.

They include selection among different crime-controlling programs; a police department's resource allocation effort; decisions to effectively segment the market for police protection, e.g., by special classes of criminals, of crimes, and of neighborhoods; and selection among steps to prevent crimes by means other than law enforcement agencies, e.g., through gun control laws.

Part Four ///

Applications

Addressing the components of public finance and expenditure analysis in isolation means that some of the most interesting issues are left out. This section attempts to provide a more comprehensive analysis of some specific issues that do not fit neatly into any of the categories we have discussed so far. The first is revenue and expenditure limitations. While these efforts have gained added importance recently, there is a long history of actions intended to limit the ability of government to raise money or to spend it. Such limits are seen by some as irrational methods of trying to get something for nothing, since taxpayers frequently say that they do not want government to reduce its activities but that they do want it to spend less. Others view such limitations as a rational response to waste, inefficiency, and overspending by government. Each view has some merit, but there may also be some unintended consequences from such limits.

The inability to meet expenditures from available revenues is key to a "fiscal crisis," but it is far from the only defining characteristic. Many governments have occasional difficulties in balancing their budgets, and the federal government seems to have a chronic deficit. Yet the consequences of these deficits are far different from the experience of some government units. The last chapter seeks to determine why some governments suffer fiscal crises while others avoid them. Further, there is an interesting question of whether the experiences of the lower levels of government provide any lessons relevant to analysis of the deficits of the federal government. ///

Chapter 20 //////

Revenue and Expenditure Limitation Measures and Their Economic Effects

After decades of almost continuous increases in spending and taxation by state and local governments, a turning point came in 1978, commonly looked upon as the year when the tax revolt began. In that year federal and state-local spenders began to go their separate ways. State-local expenditures decelerated and even briefly declined while expenditures at the federal level accelerated (see Figure 20-1).

The revenue limitation movement in the United States is widely thought to have originated in California. California's Proposition 13 was passed in 1978 by an almost two-thirds majority. The taxpayers' revolt was broadly based; it has been compared to an earthquake whose aftershocks soon spread to more than half of the states.

What led to this revolt is not entirely clear. A variety of possible causes have been mentioned: unreasonably high and rapidly increasing property taxes; a large and continuously rising surplus of state funds; allegedly flabby and inefficient local government; resentment against redistribution of monies to low-income groups in general and minorities in particular; and the belief that the price at which government was providing services was too high.

There are a number of empirical investigations of what prompted voters to approve revenue limitation measures in certain states. Using data from the August 1978 California Poll, several multiple regression equations were estimated by Jack Citrin and Frank Levy, suggesting that the higher the overall property tax rate in a locality (holding constant other factors likely to influ-

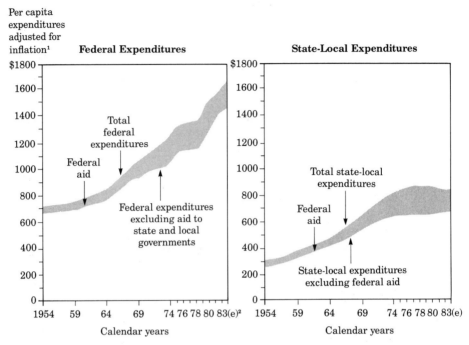

Per capita
expenditures
adjusted for
inflation[1]

Federal Expenditures

State-Local Expenditures

Total
federal
expenditures

Federal
aid

Federal expenditures
excluding aid to
state and local
governments

Total state-local
expenditures

Federal
aid

State-local expenditures
excluding federal aid

[1] Inflation adjustment by GNP Implicit Price Deflator, 1972 = 100
[2] (e) = estimated

Figure 20-1

(Source: Advisory Commission on Intergovernmental Relations, *Significant Features of Fiscal Federalism, 1982–83 Edition* [Washington, DC: January 1984], p. vii.)

ence voters), the more likely voters were to favor Proposition 13.[1] In relation to spending on welfare, the tax rate played a major role, with high tax rates boosting support for reduced welfare spending. Yet the level of actual county and city expenditures for welfare did not affect the expressed preferences for welfare spending. Neither the tax rate nor the level of educational expenditures influenced the probability of voters favoring cutbacks or increases in government spending for public education. However, as was to be expected, the presence of a child under eighteen in a household resulted in a more favorable attitude toward increased spending on education. From these specific findings Citrin and Levy concluded that California voters had been more sensitive to the tax side of the trade-off between lower taxes and reduced spending on government services.

[1] Jack Citrin and Frank Levy, "From 13 to 4 and Beyond–The Political Meaning of the Ongoing Tax Revolt in California," in George C. Kaufman and Kenneth T. Rosen, eds., *The Property Tax Revolt–The Case of Proposition 13* (Cambridge, MA: Ballinger, 1981), pp. 16–18.

A study by Paul Courant, et al., offers limited insight into the considerations that influenced voters in connection with Michigan's tax limitation measure.[2] They found that two issues dominated the Michigan revenue limitation movement: a strong desire to improve voter control of government and/or government efficiency, and the wish to reduce taxes, though apparently not taxes and spending on the local level.

To identify conditions that resulted in revenue limitation measures, a review of states with distinctly different fiscal and income characteristics is revealing. An analysis of the states of California, Massachusetts, Michigan, and Texas suggests that stringent revenue limitation measures appeared to be favored in states in which expenditures had grown very rapidly, particularly if state surpluses had accumulated.[3] California with its Proposition 13 is an extreme case, where local property taxes had been steadily increasing and a multibillion-dollar surplus had been accumulated. Property tax collections as a percentage of personal income were about one-third higher for California than the national average during 1968–77. Although property tax collections during that period in fact only increased slightly, from 6.2% of personal income in 1968 to 6.4% in 1977, many property owners perceived the property tax as becoming an ever-increasing, heavy burden. At the same time, the relatively high income elasticity of the individual income tax allowed that tax to increase from 1.5% of personal income in 1968 to 3.9% in 1980.[4] Mainly because of the high income elasticity of the individual income tax, the state of California had accumulated a surplus of about $5 billion by 1978.

In expenditure patterns, California was quite similar to the U.S. average just prior to Proposition 13. The exception was in public welfare expenditures, which claimed a somewhat higher proportion of total expenditures than in the rest of the nation over the entire ten-year period. For example, in 1977 public welfare, including Medicaid, accounted for 17.9% of all direct general expenditures in California, compared to 13.1% in the rest of the United States.

Massachusetts with its Proposition 2½ is another interesting case of relatively high taxes and high spending. In 1979 it ranked seventh in the nation in per capita state and local spending, and fifteenth in state and local spending per $1,000 of personal income. Its generous welfare programs made it third in the country in welfare spending per $1,000 of personal income. It relied heavily on the state income tax and the local property tax. Local per capita property taxes were almost twice the national average.

Michigan had suffered a ten-year squeeze on the public sector up to 1983 due to, and greatly exacerbated by, the state's deteriorating economic position.

[2] Paul B. Courant, et al., "Why Voters Support Tax Limitation Amendments: The 'Michigan Case,'" *National Tax Journal* 33 (March 1980), pp. 1–20.

[3] Peggy B. Musgrave, ed., *States Under Stress: A Report on the Finances of Massachusetts, Michigan, Texas, and California* (Berkeley: Institute of Governmental Studies, University of California, 1983).

[4] U.S. Department of Commerce, Bureau of Census, *Government Finances* in 1967–68, 1976–77, and 1978–80; and Advisory Commission on Intergovernmental Relations (ACIR), *Significant Features of Fiscal Federalism, 1980–81 Edition* and *1981–82 Edition*.

Michigan had relatively high personal income; but it had also incurred wide cyclical swings because of its heavy reliance on the manufacture of durable goods. After the 1979–80 fiscal year, a severe recession dramatically reduced the growth of the public sector even further. Without any specific expenditure limitation measures, general fund/general purpose expenditures at the state level fell by $600 million (in 1972 dollars) between 1980 and 1983, from 5.5% to 4.5% of state personal income. During this three-year period, elementary and secondary education expenditures fell from 21% to 11% of total general fund/general purpose expenditures, with police and corrections, social services, and higher education increasing their shares correspondingly.

The voters of Michigan were given a number of opportunities to enact limitation measures. Only one, the Headlee Amendment, got voter approval in November 1978, and had little direct impact. It contained the following three major provisions:

1. State revenue in any fiscal year, excluding amounts required to service general obligation bonds and federal aid, may not exceed 10% of state personal income of the previous year.

2. State aid to local jurisdictions may not fall below 41.6% of total state expenditures that such aid represented in 1979.

3. Should the assessed value of taxable property in any jurisdiction (excluding new construction) rise at a faster rate than the consumer price index, compensating reductions in tax rates must be provided.

If California is at one end of the spectrum, Texas is at the other. It is a low-tax state with a general distrust of government. Its economy has grown rapidly, and still Texas ranks thirty-ninth in the country with respect to state-local expenditures per capita and forty-first in terms of taxes as a fraction of personal income. Texas is an affluent state, with a per capita income level and growth rate above the national average, yet it ranks next to last among the states in terms of its tax effort index, i.e., at 64% of the national median. It depends for revenues on oil and gas severance taxes, a state sales tax, and a variety of excise taxes. Yet it has neither a personal nor a corporate income tax. The 1980–82 recession combined with lower energy prices had a major effect on the state's tax base.

More than forty years ago the state passed a constitutional amendment requiring expenditure appropriations not to exceed revenue estimates without new tax legislation for the coming biannum. This restriction did not pose problems during the 1970s, since tax revenues rose faster than personal income. A second limitation measure was passed in 1978. This measure required that the growth rate of state expenditures from nonearmarked revenue sources could not exceed the rate of growth of state personal income. However, expenditure growth was so low that even this more stringent measure did not provide an effective limitation. Thus, since state government had been small and lean for many years, only a very limited push for effective revenue limitation measures materialized in Texas.

/// HIGHLIGHTS OF THE REVENUE LIMITATION MOVEMENT

The tax revolt in the United States began in the late 1970s. By November 1983, twenty-nine states had enacted specific local property tax rate limits; twenty-one, property tax levy limits; twenty-one, overall property tax rates limits; six, general expenditure limits and another six, limits on assessment increases; and five states had general revenue limits. Additionally nineteen state governments had enacted state limits.[5] Massachusetts and California had voted in favor of particularly severe tax limits, and California had four such limitations.[6]

It would be a serious mistake to assume that all revenue and expenditure measures placed on state ballots were successful. Even in California, Proposition 1 was defeated while Ronald Reagan was governor. In November 1978, while Nevada and Idaho enacted a Proposition 13-type ballot measure, Michigan and Oregon rejected such proposals.

The Massachusetts measure, Proposition 2½, was partly a response to continued legislative failure to come up with viable tax reform. Enacted in November 1983 by a 59% majority, it limits the property tax levy of all communities to 2.5% of the "full and fair" market value of the properties concerned when the existing tax rates were somewhere between 6% and 12%. The total sum of the levy was to be reduced by 15% each year until it represents 2.5% of market value. Of the state's 351 cities and towns, 182 communities encompassing about 80% of the state's population were required to reduce property tax levies in the first year (fiscal year 1982) under this provision. About 40 communities were required to reduce property taxes further in fiscal year 1983, and 11 of these in fiscal year 1984. Once communities reached the 2.5% limit, their tax levies were limited to an annual growth rate of 2.5%. This growth limit also applies to all communities with rates below the 2.5% tax-rate ceiling.

In addition, the measure lowered the motor vehicle excise tax from 6.6% of valuation to 2.5%. This tax is levied at a statewide uniform rate but accrues to local treasuries. Together, these provisions reduced the total tax revenues of local governments by about 14% in fiscal year 1981. It has been estimated that

---

[5] A good description of revenue and expenditure limitation measures in force in the various states in early 1980 can be found in Frederich J. Grasburger, et al., *State and Local Tax and Expenditure Limitations: An Inventory* (Rochester, NY: Center for Governmental Research, May 1980). An in-depth analysis of California, New Jersey, Texas and Massachusetts measures can be found in Jerome G. Role, ed., *Tax and Expenditure Limitations: How to Implement and Live With Them* (Rutgers: Center for Urban Policy Research, 1982), p. 265.

[6] ACIR, *Significant Features of Fiscal Federalism, 1980–81 Edition*, M-132 (Washington, DC: December 1981), p. 12.

local governments may have lost up to $350 million in property taxes in the first year alone. The importance of this reduction can be gleaned from the fact that 60% of the city of Boston's 1981 budget of $870 million was financed by property taxes at a tax rate of 10.2% on full and fair cash value.[7]

The impact of Proposition 2½ varies dramatically across communities, primarily in response to wide variations in pre-Proposition 2½ tax rates. Typically, the larger Massachusetts communities had the higher pre-proposition tax rates; the majority rates were over 4%. Under those circumstances, many large communities needed a number of years to come down to the 2.5% tax rate limit. For example, Boston made three yearly efforts. These large property tax reductions would have required major budgetary adjustments in the absence of new state aid. The largest communities would have had to cut their budgets by up to 13% and the smallest by 5%.

The state of Massachusetts responded by increasing subventions to local government. Since Proposition 2½ made state legislators reluctant to raise state taxes the increased state aid had to be compensated for by cuts in state government spending and employment.

California's constitutional amendment known as Proposition 13 rolled back property tax assessments to their 1975 levels and restricted increases in assessments to 2% per year for as long as the property is retained by the same owner. Property taxes exceeding 1% of the property's full value are prohibited; increases in state taxes are permitted only if approved by a two-thirds majority of both houses of the state legislature; and local taxes must be approved by a two-thirds majority of a jurisdiction's voters. In the face of a multibillion-dollar state surplus, California's legislature enacted permanent bailout legislation (Assembly Bill 8). For example, in fiscal 1979–80 it provided local governments with $4.84 billion. As of July 1979, the state assumed most costs previously borne by counties for welfare programs. Part of the property taxes formerly levied by school districts were transferred to counties, cities, and special districts. As a consequence, special districts and counties now rely almost exclusively on property taxes, whereas cities, while retaining their share of the sales tax, have increased their reliance on the property tax to some degree.

The immediate effects have been startling. Whereas state and local taxes collected in California totaled $27.4 billion in fiscal 1977–78 (the last year before Proposition 13 went into effect) and would probably have climbed to $31 billion the following year in the absence of Proposition 13, collection in fiscal 1978–79 dropped to $24 billion.[8] In 1979–80, the total climbed back to $27.4 billion. However, in view of a 31% personal income increase in California during this two-year period, the relative tax burden declined from $157 per

[7] James R. Adams, "Boston's Curious Financial Crisis," *Wall Street Journal* (August 12, 1981), p. 24.

[8] Security Pacific Bank, *Monthly Summary of Business Conditions in Southern California*, 60 (March 1981), p. 4.

$1,000 of personal income in 1977–78 to $121 in 1978–79 (a 23% decline) and to $120 in 1979–80.

Expenditures by California's state and local government also changed drastically, from 10% above the national norm in fiscal 1977–78 to about the national norm in 1978–79 and slowly up to 2% above the norm in both 1981 and 1982.[9] If, for the sake of simplicity, we assign retail sales and use taxes to individuals and bank and corporation taxes to businesses, i.e., if we neglect the difficult question of tax incidence, significant tax shifts from businesses to individuals occurred. Specifically, before the passage of Proposition 13, businesses paid 39.3% of all state and local taxes, while individuals paid 60.7%. In the immediate post-Proposition 13 period, the tax share of businesses declined to 26.2%, while that of individuals increased to 73.8%.

But the effects may disappear with time. Property taxes that had amounted to 42% of the total state and local taxes in 1977 had dropped to 23% in 1980, when they began to increase slowly to 24% in 1981 and 26% in 1982.[10] A similar picture emerges when we look at property taxes as a percentage of total local tax collections. The property tax percentage declined from 85% in 1977 to 69% in 1980, when it began to increase slightly to 70% in 1981 and 71% in 1982.[11]

Property tax levies declined in California from an all-time high of $11.7 billion in 1977–78 to $5.6 billion in 1978–79. Thereafter they increased slowly to $6.2 billion in 1979–80, $7.2 billion in 1980–81, and $8 billion in 1981–82.[12] In the first year after passage of Proposition 13, counties, cities, and school districts lost more than half of their previous year's property tax levies. After four years, school districts were the slowest to recover, with 1981 –82 property tax revenues only half of those they had received in 1977–78.

In terms of expenditures, fiscal year 1984–85 saw large, even enormous increases by both the state and various local governments. The state's general fund expenditures increased from $16.5 billion in fiscal year 1978–79 to $25.4 billion in 1984–85. And the general fund expenditures of Los Angeles County, amounting in 1978–79 to $3.95 billion, increased to $6.05 billion in 1984–85.

In addition to Proposition 13-type measures, which have in common cutbacks on existing property tax rates (and sometimes assessments) and limits on future rates of revenue increases, there are also a host of measures that limit government growth. Such growth-limiting measures, rather than reflecting opposition to high and rising property taxes as Proposition 13-type measures do, express the sentiment that current levels of taxes and government should not be exceeded.

---

[9] ACIR, *Significant Features of Fiscal Federalism, 1980–81 Edition*, M-132 (Washington, DC: December 1981), p. 16.
[10] Ibid., p. 47.
[11] Ibid., p. 48.
[12] California Assembly Committee on Revenue and Taxation, *The Property Tax—Four Years After Proposition 13* (Sacramento, CA: California Legislature, October 1982), p. 7.

California's Proposition 4, a constitutional amendment approved by the voters in November 1979, limits the rate of growth of state and local appropriations to amounts spent in fiscal year 1978–79, plus an adjustment for inflation and population increase. The limit applies only to revenues that are "proceeds of taxes." Items excluded from this category include user fees and charges, benefit assessments, and federal monies. Revenues collected in excess of the appropriations limit are to be returned to the taxpayers within two years. This measure strongly resembles Nevada's appropriations limit; however, the limit is statutory.

Proposition 4 is somewhat atypical of fiscal limits. Most state limits, like Michigan's or Arizona's, are tied to changes in the level of statewide personal income. Others, like Texas' and Hawaii's, are based on the rate of growth of the state's economy. Since Proposition 4 expenditure limits apply to local as well as state government, it is likely to have a strong impact on cities and counties. Particular problems are likely in those areas with limited population growth but increasing public service demands, such as central cities with substantial employment growth.

/// EFFICIENCY EFFECTS

The large number and great variety of specific revenue limitation measures would make an encompassing or even selective effort at analysis necessarily superficial. Therefore we focus here on California's Proposition 13. Because of its severity and broad coverage, it should prove a good example for the analysis of efficiency, distributional, and debt effects.

We look upon revenue limitation measures as having the immediate purpose of bringing about significant across-the-broad reductions in local property taxes, while their longer range objective is to keep down tax increases. If successful, these reductions change the economic and institutional environment within which local governments make decisions. There are direct efficiency effects of service, expenditure, and revenue decisions. But there are also secondary efficiency effects that relate to private sector decisions made in the new local government environment. Again, effects in the private sector stem from changed local government services and expenditures on the one hand and local revenues on the other.

In line with the considerations expressed in the preceding paragraph, we examine major efficiency effects. Our general framework is presented in Figure 20-2. It can be used to prepare a balance sheet which records on one side likely positive efficiency effects and on the other, likely negative ones. We begin by examining the four boxes of Figure 20-2. Box 1 includes four major direct local government service and expenditure effects. First there is the wholesale transfer of power from local governments to a centralized state government. Second, major distortions in resource use by local governments

<table>
<tr><td>

1. *Direct Local Government Service and Expenditure Effects:*
   a. Transfer of power to centralized state government
   b. Distorted resource use by local governments
   c. Increased uncertainty
   d. Pressures for heightened efficiency

</td><td>

2. *Direct Local Revenue Effects:*
   a. Higher borrowing costs interfere with capital investment
   b. Altered revenue mix distorts some resource uses and improves others

</td></tr>
<tr><td>

3. *Indirect Effects on Private Sector:*
   a. Decreased private spending and investment and economic growth
   b. Distorted private investment and economic growth

</td><td>

4. *Indirect Effects on Private Sector:*
   a. Increased private spending and investment and economic growth (supply-side effects)
   b. Distorted private investment and economic growth
   c. Emergence of rent control with, on balance, a negative effect on rental housing quality and supply

</td></tr>
</table>

Figure 20-2 / **Revenue Limitation in the Form of Local Property Tax Reduction**

are likely to occur, resulting in underinvestment in capital improvements, repair maintenance as well as innovation. A third major effect relates to increased instability and unpredictability of local revenue.[13] A fourth consideration is an improved environment for public managers and employees to become more productive as revenues decline.

Box 2 identifies two direct local revenue effects. One effect relates to heightened borrowing costs in a revenue limitation era and the second to an altered revenue mix which in turn distorts resource use; in some cases it produces mainly negative and in others positive results.

As the private sector adjusts to the new local government service and expenditure environment, two major effects are likely, as presented in Box 3. Private spending and investment, and therefore economic growth, can be retarded as well as distorted. But perhaps even more significant are the likely indirect effects on the private sector that result from the new revenue environment, presented in Box 4. Advocates of revenue limitation measures have

---

[13] As the relative importance of property taxes has fallen, more cyclical taxes have taken their place. Moreover, since states are facing serious fiscal problems, their subventions to local governments have become less and less dependable. For example, the California bailout legislation includes a safety valve in the form of a deflator. It permits the state to cut its subsidies by almost one-half in any year when a state revenue shortfall in excess of $200 million is expected. Although so far such a drastic cut has not been made, subsidies have been reduced by almost $0.5 billion.

tended to emphasize their supply-side effect and have promised substantial increases in private spending, investment, and economic growth. A second, indirect effect involves distorted private investment and economic growth resulting from steps taken by local governments to replace property tax losses. Finally, as a far-fetched case, we would like to mention that property tax reductions that have pitted landlords against tenants have contributed to the imposition of rent control in some major California jurisdictions. The efficiency effects of rent control include a tendency to artificially reduce rental housing quality and supply.

Rather than discussing each of the elements presented in Figure 20-2, we concentrate on a few of the major efficiency effects, first those that promise to be on balance mainly positive, then those that are likely to be mainly negative.

Financial Exigencies Tend to Heighten Local Government Efficiency

As funding levels, or at least their annual growth rates, have declined, many local governments have been forced to make major changes in the manner in which they produce and deliver services. The goal is to make do with less money. In addition to eliminating some services, four major approaches toward raising productivity have been tried. Measuring the performance of the labor force is a first step, which many governments have pursued more aggressively than before. In this effort they are being aided by recent improvements in electronic and computer-based office machines. Thus, better performance measurement has enabled local governments to tie wages more closely to performance. Some have even begun to institutionalize the monitoring and evaluation of their employees through productivity bargaining and basing wage increases on agreed-upon performance standards to be met by workers.

A second set of steps relates to the performance of local government managers. Managers can raise the productivity of local government employees in two major ways: by selecting and implementing efficient production and distribution methods, and by inducing workers under their supervision to exert themselves more and thereby become more productive. Some local governments have begun to make changes in the methods by which they fulfill their missions.

But perhaps even more important has been the effort by managers to inspire their employees to exert themselves more fully. To do this, managers' performance was tied more closely to their rewards, which could be taken in various ways. Two examples are the performance appraisal system established by the city of Phoenix, Arizona, in 1978 and the system used by San Francisco, started shortly thereafter. Both include a "cafeteria" benefit plan for senior managers. The "cafeteria plan" offers a list of items a manager may choose to "buy" with his or her merit increases at no greater cost to the government. Managers can take cash over such items as health insurance with built-in income protection, family dental plan, reimbursed tuition, membership dues in professional associations, paid attendance at professional conferences or seminars, sabbatical leave, and so forth.

Some governments have begun to shift their managers horizontally in place of the conventional intradepartmental promotions. Moving managers horizontally avoids many of the shortcomings of the old vertical movement of management personnel. Managing in a given department at different levels tends to perpetuate a static, often outdated vision. Moreover, friendships tend to be formed and obligations accumulated, all of which can interfere with the tough decision making necessary for improved performance. Finally, as managers stay in their old jobs because no openings occur at higher levels, they tend to go stale and spend much of their time covering up mistakes made earlier in their administration.

Perhaps the most exciting steps have been in a third direction, which seeks to provide a more competitive environment for the delivery of local government services. Contracting out or privatization has increased by leaps and bounds. Major efficiency gains have resulted. E. S. Savas has studied refuse collection in the city of Minneapolis and 1,377 communities in 200 SMSAs.[14] He found the per household cost of trash collection in large cities to be 29% greater for municipal than for private collection.

A fourth step involves changes in the legal environment that controls local government employees. For example, a number of local governments have begun to modify their civil service provisions, placing more emphasis on merit and less on seniority in determining promotions. Furthermore, procedures have been streamlined to implement discipline. In some instances, adverse action can now be taken against public employees who perform poorly by merely requiring managers to show "substantial evidence" rather than "preponderance of evidence" to prove a case. Also, the appeals procedure (which in the past entitled employees to an evidentiary hearing, which could be followed by a rehearing and then an appeal to a court) is now being reserved only for major disciplinary action.

A further legal development is the repeal of prevailing wage laws by a number of local jurisdictions. Being forced to pay wages at least equal to those in private employment has had an inflationary wage effect, which some governments are seeking to counteract.

A caveat is in order here. Quite a few decisions made to cope with declining revenue are not governed primarily by efficiency considerations. It is often politically easier to use a meat-ax approach, in which all departments are cut back by roughly the same percentage. Since various local government services

---

[14] E. S. Savas, "An Empirical Study of Competition in Municipal Service Delivery," *Public Administration Review* 37 (November–December 1977), pp. 717–724; and "Policy Analysis for Local Government: Public Versus Private Refuse Collection," *Policy Analysis* 3 (Winter 1977), pp. 1–26.

tend to have distinctly different demand elasticities, an across-the-board cut is inefficient. Also, layoffs are rarely selective with regard to performance; many of the least productive workers are protected by seniority rules.[15]

Supply-Side Effects

Supply-side economics is commonly associated with the name of Arthur B. Laffer, who has emphasized the macroeconomic effects of tax reductions on aggregate savings, investment, and labor supply as well as on tax revenues, which in turn affect the general level of economic activity.[16] If we consider supply-side economics as the application of price theory to government fiscal measures, we must focus on how tax rate changes affect the relative prices of leisure, consumption, nonmarket production, and investment. Though perhaps less so than an income tax reduction, a substantially lower property tax rate also ultimately raises the relative price of leisure and of current compared to future consumption, and increases the value of market work compared to work in the underground economy and of taxable investment compared to tax shelter.

Supply-siders like to talk about a capital wedge, the divergence between the return to the lender and the cost to the borrower resulting from the fact that taxes are paid to government. If taxes are high, a substantial reduction can increase the amount of capital demanded and the amount of capital supplied. This occurs because of the size of the wedge. The increase in the use of capital leads to output and employment growth.

Figure 20-3 illustrates the capital wedge which comes about because taxes paid to government increase the capital cost to entrepreneurs beyond what they actually pay for capital. Only in the extreme case at E, i.e., in the absence of taxes, will the price paid for capital and the price received for it be equal. As taxes on capital income increase, the cost of capital rises and the return to those who provide capital declines, and vice versa. The tax increase, therefore, causes a decline in capital demanded as well as supplied. Consequently, the size of the wedge in Figure 20-3 increases up to Y_2, indicating a growing divergence between the cost of capital and yield to those who provide capital (D_c is the demand function for capital and S_c the supply function for capital). At Q_1 capital spending, capital cost is Y_2, whereas those who provide capital receive only Y_1. As taxes decline, we move toward E and Q_2, and a smaller wedge and greater capital spending. This analysis can be applied to a statewide property tax reduction by using the "new view"[17] of the incidence of

[15] Ronald G. Ehrenberg, "The Effect of Tax Limitation Legislation on Public Sector Labor Markets: A Comment," *National Tax Journal* 32 (June 1979), supplement, pp. 261–266.

[16] Victor A. Cantor, Douglas H. Joines, and Arthur B. Laffer, "Tax Rates, Factor Employment, and Market Production," in Laurence H. Meyer, ed., *The Supply-Side Effects of Economic Policy* (St. Louis, MO: Federal Reserve Bank of St. Louis, 1981), pp. 3–33.

[17] Peter W. Mieszkowski, "The Property Tax: An Excise Tax or a Property Tax," *Journal of Public Economics* 1 (1972), pp. 72–96.

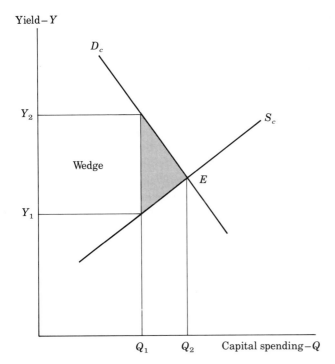

Figure 20-3

property tax, though it is most applicable to a property tax that is uniform nationwide (for more detail on the "new view" see Chapter 10). According to the "new view," the incidence of a uniform property tax is borne at least partly by all owners of capital instead of the consumers or just the owners of land. The burden cannot be passed entirely to consumers because their mobility allows them to move out of the jurisdiction to escape increased prices. The burden cannot be passed entirely to landowners because the supply of developed land is not a fixed factor.

Since the property tax is a tax on land and capital, the after-tax rate of return on capital in the state will increase if property taxes are reduced. (To the extent that labor is immobile and land is fixed, they will bear parts of the tax incidence.) Capital will shift into the jurisdictions. With the supply of capital not being perfectly elastic, this decrease in the supply of capital outside the state will result in an upward adjustment in the rate of return to all owners of capital. The capital wedge is decreased due to the increase in the after-tax demand for capital.

This decrease in the capital wedge will not be as dramatic as the decrease caused by a capital income tax reduction of equal relative magnitude. We have only a statewide, not a nationwide property tax. Still, the implications of the reduction in the capital wedge are the same: an increase in the total stock of capital, an increase in the remuneration to labor, and an increase in productivity.

There is virtually no empirical evidence of the supply-side effect, and most economists apparently expect it to be rather small, at best. Lawrence R. Klein has well summarized the principal behavioral argument of proponents of supply-side economics, i.e., "that . . . large and repetitive . . . tax rate [reductions] would . . . [enable] people . . . to retain larger and larger portions of every dollar saved, . . . this would promote savings to such an extent that investment expansion could take place without causing upward pressure on market rates of interest." Klein's evaluation, however, was, "This did not happen at all. Savings fell drastically. The rate of personal savings dipped to a low point of about 4% and interest rates soared to unprecedented levels. Productivity did pick up from its stagnant or falling values of recent years, but it remains below par . . . we have . . . the usual business-cycle recovery of productivity, not a supply-side-inspired increase."

He further argued that,

> [t]he tax cuts of 1981–82 and 1983 slowed the growth in tax revenue which, together with expenditure increases, propelled the federal budget into the biggest deficit in our peacetime history. Far from moving toward balance from the initial deficit point of $60 billion, we move towards the outlandish figure of $100 billion, followed by almost $200 billion, bringing the whole world's financial market into near-panic by the summer of 1982.[18]

We are not aware of any careful empirical analysis of the supply-side effect of Proposition 13 on the state or local level. The generally available statistics do not appear to indicate that the 1978 local property tax reductions in California of almost $7 billion have had an appreciable effect on the state's economic growth and employment. Part of the reason may be that the reduction was accompanied by an increase in federal income tax obligations of at least $2.5 billion. This resulted from the fact that property taxes are deductible from federal income taxes and that whatever user fees were levied in place of property taxes cannot be deducted.

Improved Government Resource Use by Altered Revenue Mix

Since local revenue limitation measures have rolled back property taxes, the relative importance of the latter has declined while that of sales taxes, subventions from higher levels of government, and various fees have increased. This tendency has become even more pronounced where state governments increased their subventions which are predominantly financed by income and sales tax. When property taxes vary from community to community, as they did in California prior to Proposition 13, local communities have a strong

---

[18] Lawrence R. Klein, "Supply Side: 0 Wins, 4 Losses, 1 Tie," *Los Angeles Times* (June 26, 1984), p. IV-3.

incentive to practice exclusionary zoning, which can result in inefficient resource use.[19] These tendencies are reduced once a uniform statewide property tax is imposed.

Furthermore, in the face of a reduction in the relative importance of property taxes, governments that provide people-related services tend to become more efficient. This condition holds for school districts and for county governments which in many states provide mainly health and welfare services. Municipal governments and special districts that provide flood control or street repair and street cleaning, i.e., those who mainly engage in property-related services, tend to lose some efficiency.

Transfer of Power to Centralized State Government

Even if the state does not increase the flow of funds to local governments after their property taxes have been slashed, the relative share of state funds in support of local budgets increases. However, in most states local property tax reductions have been followed by major increases in state subventions. For example, following the passage of Proposition 13, state annual aid to local governments increased by about $5 billion in real terms, and with it power and control has shifted away from local governments to the state. The result has been a general decline in home rule and local control and greater intervention by a centralized state government. Citizens, special interest business groups, and labor unions are increasingly negotiating with the state legislature and governor, rather than with local officials. The latter have fewer resources with which to respond to pleas.

The efficiency implications of increased control over local governmental services by state government are, by and large, negative. It can be demonstrated that, in the absence of economies of scale due to centralization and of spillover effects between localities, decentralized provision of a publicly provided good is more efficient than centralized provision. If communities arrive at different choices concerning how much of a publicly provided good to consume, we can assume that their decisions reflect their divergent tastes. To the extent that members of a community "vote with their feet," small communities particularly tend to be composed of members with roughly similar preferences regarding major public goods, e.g., education and police protection.[20] Centralization can take into account few of these differences among communities and would probably result in imposing a uniform quantity of good. Each community could have chosen this level under decentralization, but not all did. Hence, the uniform quantity is likely to be inefficient.

Of course, in any real-life situation inefficiencies of centralization must be

[19] Werner Z. Hirsch, "The Efficiency of Restrictive Land Use Instruments," *Land Economics* 53 (May 1977), pp. 145–156.
[20] Charles M. Tiebout, "A Pure Theory of Local Expenditures," *Journal of Political Economy* 64 (1956), pp. 416–424.

balanced against gains due to economies of scale and internalization of spillover effects. For certain services gains from centralization tend to out-weigh losses due to centralization, but this does not seem likely for the major local government services. There is no reason to expect large economies of scale to result from more centralized decision making about, for example, police and fire protection and education, since production will continue in about the same units. The issue of spillovers, however, is less clear. There are spillover effects in the sense that other communities benefit from one locality's provision, for example, of education when an individual moves to one of those other areas. However, if these effects were very significant, one would expect to see high-expenditure communities reducing the amounts they spend because they do not fully receive the benefits they provide. The final result would be a more or less uniformly low level of public expenditures across communites. In fact, this is not observed in California, for example, where before the passage of Proposition 13 there were large differences among jurisdictions in the resources they devoted to various local government services. Since neither economies of scale nor spillover effects appears to be significant in relation to most public services, centralized financing and decision making is likely to result in inefficiencies in a revenue limitation environment.

Distorted Resource Use by a Local Government

Drastic revenue limitation measures can lead to major distortions in using resources. Specifically, tight local budgets can lead to underinvestment in capital improvements, repair, maintenance, and innovation. At the same time, overinvestment is likely in state and federally funded, compared to locally funded, programs for two reasons. One reason is related to the match-ing features of most of the programs and a second to the functional disjuncture between spending and revenue raising. We discuss these issues in turn.

When budgets are slashed by revenue limitation measures, politicians are more inclined to defer new capital investment, repair and maintenance, and innovative programs than to cut operating funds for the present delivery of services. This strategy tends to minimize the political damage that elected officials fear will result from service cuts. This tendency is reinforced by the higher borrowing costs of local governments in the wake of revenue limitation measures, discussed below.

The postponement of capital investment can distort America's settlement pattern. Insufficient funds to build new physical infrastructure tends to retard suburban and exurban development and growth. While it might be argued that such a tendency is desirable in a high energy cost era, the fact remains that lack of investment funds is an arbitrary influence and possibly results in inefficient resource use. Moreover, the former automatic link between in-frastructure expense and public revenue from property taxes has been weak-ened, if not altogether broken. This has led to inefficiency.

Let us next examine the issue of underinvestment in repair, maintenance, and innovation. As local governments find themselves short of funds, another of the less painful decisions open to elected officials is to defer repair and maintenance. Yet as upkeep of buildings, roads, bridges, sewer systems, and buses is underfinanced year after year, large losses are likely to occur. These losses, in both monetary and human terms, are compounded by the fact that the eventual cost of restoring these facilities tends to be substantially higher than the savings from deferred maintenance—the well-known principle that preventive maintenance is less costly over the long run than corrective maintenance. Possible losses can result not only from public buildings and bridges collapsing, but also from accidents caused by washed-out roads and inadequate mechanical maintenance of trucks, buses, and other equipment used by the public sector.

Maintenance expenditures in each period should be increased until the increase in benefits due to slower depreciation is balanced by the increase in repair costs.[21] Such a pattern of expenditure should constitute an optimum annual policy. If, because of political considerations, these expenditures are curtailed, the optimum will not obtain. The net benefit would shift up by the amount of cost savings, but the increase in the depreciation would more than offset this gain. The result would be a net social loss.

We have some tentative empirical information on budgetary changes. Although expenditures budgeted for fiscal year 1979 by California counties increased more than 12% over actual fiscal 1978 expenses, budgets for property management (which includes custodial services and maintenance and remodeling of facilities) declined by 0.5%. Los Angeles County, for example, planned to delay building maintenance and alterations and to cancel the scheduled replacement of all nonemergency county vehicles.[22] A further example is capital spending on libraries, which as a percentage of all spending declined in Los Angeles County from 11.1% in 1978 to 0.9% in 1980.[23]

Funding on research and innovation also has been cut in California. For example, the Los Angeles city attorney reduced his staff in the Planning and Research Division by more than 50%, while all planning, research, and innovation activities of California's criminal justice system suffered.[24] Moreover, to the extent that new-book circulation reflects innovative activities, such circulation per thousand persons declined from 1978 to 1980 in Los Angeles City from 50 to 9 and in Los Angeles County from 293 to 174.[25] Warren E.

---

[21] The analysis here was inspired by work dealing with the maintenance of housing, specifically Stephen E. Margolis, *Depreciation of Capital in Housing*, unpublished Ph.D. dissertation, UCLA (1977).

[22] Legislative Analyst, State of California, *An Analysis of the Effect of Proposition 13 on Local Governments* (Sacramento, CA: October 1979); and Comptroller General of the United States, *Proposition 13: How California Government Coped with a $6 Billion Revenue Loss*, Report GGD-79-88 (Washington, DC: December 23, 1979).

[23] Mark D. Menshik, et al., *How Fiscal Restraint Affects Spending and Services in Cities*, R-2644 (Santa Monica, CA: RAND Corporation, January 1982), p. 39.

[24] Warren E. Walker, et al., *The Impact of Proposition 13 on Local Criminal Justice Agencies: Emerging Patterns*, N-1521-DOJ (Santa Monica, CA: RAND Corporation, June 1980), p. 61.

[25] Menshik, et al., op. cit., p. 85.

Walker and Jan M. Chaiken, in a study of innovation, concluded, ". . . fiscal contraction will cause the innovative process in the public sector to fall on hard times."[26] Together, these reduced levels of planning, research, and innovation effects tend to be inefficient.

Finally, let us consider the tendency to overinvest in state and federal funded programs. When local revenues decline, officials tend to protect federally and state subsidized programs at the expense of locally funded programs, which are cut more severely. The result is distorted local government resource use. In a program funded 75% by federal and state funds, for example, a cut that saves only 25% in local revenue would nevertheless have the consequence of reducing the program by a ratio of 4:1. This reduction of $4 of total program resulting from $1 of local fund reduction must be compared to a $1 loss per dollar of local funding cut.

This hypothesis is borne out in New York City where budget-cutting in 1975 and 1976 led to major cuts primarily in locally funded services not eligible for federal or state funds, e.g., police, fire, and sanitation.[27] Likewise, passage of Proposition 13 resulted in local government proposing greater retrenchment in locally supported basic services than in social-service programs that receive high federal and state funding.[28]

Further distortions and inefficiencies can result from local governments in cost cutting, in relation to locally versus nonlocally funded programs. The functional disjuncture between spending and raising revenue relative to heavily subsidized local operations weakens local incentive and determination to be cost-effective.

Impeding and Distorting Economic Growth

Under most revenue limitation measures, local government's property taxes cannot exceed a specific, relatively low rate of market value; thus, new land uses can cost governments more in services than will be covered by prospective tax receipts. Moreover, since governments have great difficulty in floating bond issues to fund infrastructure, construction permits tend to be denied, even when construction is actually efficient. Growth may be further retarded because some firms facing location decisions will not tolerate service cuts. Their decision against locating in the jurisdictions tends to redistribute the geographic demand for public services.

When construction permits are granted, onerous terms are frequently imposed on the developer. An example is a construction permit issued by the city of Santa Monica, California, after lengthy negotiations for the develop-

---

[26] Warren E. Walker and Jan M. Chaiken, *The Effects of Fiscal Contraction on Innovation in the Public Sector*, P-6610 (Santa Monica, CA: RAND Corporation, April 1981), p. 42.

[27] Temporary Commission on City Finances (TCCF), *An Historical and Comparative Analysis of Expenditures in the City of New York* (New York: TCCF, 1976).

[28] Comptroller General of the United States, op. cit.

ment of commercial property on fifteen acres.[29] After the development company had made a multimillion dollar investment in land, starting before a city-imposed construction moratorium was enacted, a development agreement was signed to break the moratorium. The conditions were severe. Under the agreement, the developer was forced to dedicate 29% of the land to open space and parks (land for which he had paid $1.9 million); to pay an arts and social services fee of 1.5% of the development's value, amounting to about half a million dollars; build a day care center of not less than 800 square feet and a community center of not less than 1,500 square feet and maintain them together with the park in perpetuity; and build thirty units of residential housing with at least forty-three bedrooms under inclusionary zoning terms.[30]

When burdens on developers in the form of construction fees, in lieu fees, exactions and inclusionary zoning provisions exceed costs placed on the community by the development, they have a chilling effect on new construction and retard economic growth. Inefficiencies result, as do distortions. Where fees and exactions are not used, the relative decline in property taxes associated with revenue limitation will tend to increase investment in real property as compared to capital. Likewise, as a result of reassessment features exemplified by Proposition 13, repair of existing facilities will be more advantageous than constructing new ones.

This reassessment feature also has an effect on oil, gas, coal, and other mineral resources exploration. For example, crude oil has substantially increased in price after the 1974 oil embargo. Yet it qualifies for a 1975 base year evaluation plus 2% per year. Thus, the property tax payments on crude oil lands are relatively small compared to what they would be if assessments were in terms of high market values. One result can be delay in exploration for crude oil.

The opposite result can occur in relation to investments in orchards and vineyards, which cost relatively little and have a low cost per unit of property investment. Although the economic productivity of orchards and vineyards increases with the passage of time, the initial low value is used as the evaluation base. Specifically, because assessed valuation is assessed upon fair market value at the time of planting, plus 2% a year compounded, compared to other investments orchards and vineyards are grossly undertaxed, which in turn can result in overinvestment.

In summary, of the various efficiency effects of revenue limitation measures, three on balance are likely to be positive. Shrinking funding levels, or at

---

[29] Development agreement between Colorado Place Associates, a California General Partnership, and the City of Santa Monica, California, December 24, 1981, p. 37.
[30] The inclusionary zoning provisions provided that (1) at least seven units will be affordable and rented to persons and families with an annual income of less than 50% of median income, (2) at least sixteen units will be affordable and rented to persons and families with an annual income from 50% to 99% of median income, and (3) the remainder shall be affordable and rented to persons and families with an annual income of less than 120% of median income. The annual rental rate for each unit can be no greater than 25% of the income of the three groups.

least growth rates, have had a salubrious, disciplining effect on public managers and their employees. As a result government officials are willing to consider methods that can substantially increase efficiency. These tendencies are mitigated by a lack of funds and by archaic civil service rules that often leave the less productive workers on the public payroll. Second, so far there is little evidence of a positive supply-side effect of the tax cuts although they occurred in a period of prosperity. If heightened investment and economic growth will make their appearance somewhat later, we expect them to be rather small. Third, the revenue mix change that has resulted from a decline in the importance of the local property tax is likely to have had, on balance, a small positive efficiency effect.

A number of other effects are strongly negative. By shifting much decision-making power from local governments to the state, great centralization of power has occurred and with it homogenization of services and service levels. The result has been a significant efficiency loss. A similar effect has probably resulted from distortions in the use of resources by local governments. The distortions have been in the form of underinvestment in capital improvements, repair and maintenance, and innovative activities on the one hand and overinvestment in state and federally funded compared to locally funded programs. Also, private sector investment and economic growth have been retarded and distorted, in part as a consequence of local governments' justifiable reluctance to issue building permits or only after attaching onerous terms. Moreover, the changed property tax provisions have distorted major investment decisions as well as decisions about the exploitation of mineral resources. Finally, it is quite likely that in California, local rent control has resulted from a clash between landlords and tenants who saw themselves denied rent reductions as property taxes were rolled back. As a consequence, there exists a tendency for the quality of rental housing to deteriorate and for overall supply to shrink.

/// DISTRIBUTIONAL EFFECTS

Rather than making as detailed an analysis of the distributional effects of Proposition 13 as we did of the efficiency effects, we focus on some major ones. First, we examine some expenditure, service and employment effects and then some revenue effects.

Any local revenue limitation measure, unless offset by increased intergovernmental transfers and/or productivity enhancement, will affect spending levels. Major spending cuts mean service cutbacks, which have major distributional implications. For example, in California county governments were forced to reduce health and welfare services, and the cuts in benefits fell almost exclusively on low-income groups. There was also a reduction in some education programs. In particular, summer school and some special programs were trimmed for a number of years, and fees paid by students attending institutions of higher learning were slightly increased. To the extent that the rich send their children to private schools and colleges, reduction in services and higher fees have fallen mainly on low-income groups. In addition, state-financed programs for disadvantaged youth education, compensatory education, special reading programs, bilingual education programs and child nutrition programs were all cut back. Library and recreational services were cut severely. At the same time, provisions in the bailout laws insured that basic police and fire services that benefit all citizens were not reduced. For these reasons, Robert D. Reischauer concluded, "California has tended to hold harmless basic services directed at the middle class or the majority of the population."[31]

Proposition 13 has also affected public employment. When local government cut back employment, it did so particularly with regard to low-paying menial jobs. In addition, wage and hiring freezes were instituted. Since they took place in a period of high inflation, wage freezes resulted in a reduction in real income, particularly burdensome for low-income groups. Hiring freezes produced a marked decline in job opportunities, especially affecting the low-income and disadvantaged segments of the population. Reducing employment opportunities in the state and local sector is particularly damaging, since its employment in recent years has grown 50% faster than that in the economy as a whole. This slowdown particularly affected women, minorities, and low-income, low-skilled persons, since these are the groups that this public sector has hired in disproportionate numbers. They likewise suffer most when layoffs occur, since those with the least seniority are the first to be dismissed.[32]

We next turn to the distributional effects on the revenue side. Because Proposition 13 has reduced local property taxes and increased reliance on state sales and income taxes, Reischauer expected Proposition 13 to

> ...have a negative impact on vertical equity but a positive impact on horizontal equity.... A reduction in property taxes and increased dependence on sales, income and other state-level taxes will therefore lead to a more uniform sharing of the costs of providing public services. But if arbitrary limitations are placed on the rate at which property assessments can rise,... new and even greater inequities might soon characterize the property tax.[33]

Proposition 13 has increased the reliance on state income and sales taxes while reducing that on the local property tax, so the tax system has become more progressive. There also has been an increased use of user fees and charges including those for swimming pools, school transportation, recrea-

[31] Robert D. Reischauer, "Intergovernmental Responsibility for Meeting the Equity Considerations of Proposition 13: The Federal Role," in Selma J. Mushkin, ed., *Proposition 13 and Its Consequences for Public Management* (Cambridge, MA: ABT Books, 1979), p. 16.
[32] Ibid., pp. 17–18.
[33] Ibid., p. 13.

tional facilities and libraries. They are likely to burden relatively more heavily the lower than the upper income groups.

The main beneficiaries from property tax reductions have been commercial, industrial, and residential properties owned by parties who did not sell their properties since 1978. Reischauer estimated in 1979 that 29.9% of the first year's $6.4 billion reduction in local property taxes would go to owners of commercial and industrial property, little of which he expected to be passed on in the form of lower prices to consumers. Another 14.7% would accrue to owners of agricultural land, few of whom in 1978 were struggling small farmers.[34]

Homeowners would receive 36.5% of the reduction, with 54.1% of it accruing to families with incomes under $20,000 and only 26.2% to homeowners with incomes under $15,000. Finally, rental property would receive 18.7% of the total tax relief. Whereas 72.9% would be relief for rental properties occupied by families with incomes under $15,000, few if any of the savings that accrued to landlords would be passed on to tenants, particularly since at that time the housing market was very tight. This disappointment has led to strong tenant pressure resulting in rent control ordinances in a number of California jurisdictions. Since homeowners tend to belong on average to higher income groups than do tenants, Proposition 13 aided the rich more than the poor. At the same time, in those communities where rent control ordinances were enacted, sitting tenants were aided while landlords and prospective tenants were hurt.

The reassessment-at-sale feature discriminates against young, first-time home buyers. For example, a condominium with an assessed value of $38,000 as of 1975 had a tax bill of about $450 in 1980. An identical unit in the same complex was purchased that year by a young couple for $150,000 and their 1980 tax bill was about $1,800.

The equity advantages that accrued to personal and corporate property owners in California as Proposition 13 slashed their property taxes is somewhat offset by increased federal income tax liability. As local property taxes were cut, these property owners had smaller itemized deductions and lower expenses to list on their federal tax return.

Some equity effects of Proposition 13 tend to be positive. A substantial reduction in local property taxes will lead to a larger state role in financing services now provided by local government. As the role of the state in financing increases, differences in the availability and quality of services across jurisdictions will decline. Likewise, local tax differences will be diminished. The augmented state aid to local governments will have positive distributional effects, because the distribution of state aid will tend to reflect relative differences in need and fiscal capacity.[35]

In summary, Proposition 13 appears to have a distinct distributive effect.

---

[34] Ibid., p. 14.
[35] Ibid., p. 19.

On balance the benefits from expenditure, service, employment, and revenue effects appear to have favored the higher income groups.[36]

/// EFFECTS ON GOVERNMENT DEBT

As was mentioned earlier, Proposition 13 had a far-reaching effect on efforts by local governments to float debt instruments and on their interest rates. Fortunately, we have some empirical research on this matter.[37] It examines changes in the issuance and mix of local debt instruments and in interest rates that occurred during the first three to four years after passage of Proposition 13.

The focus is again on California's 429 cities, mainly during the period 1977 to 1982. Rather than cover all local governments, we focus on cities for two reasons. First, not all local governments have been equally affected by Proposition 13 and its legislative followup. Second, because passage of Proposition 13 coincided with the peaking of federal aid to local governments, it is useful to concentrate on those governments that historically have been minor recipients of such aid and therefore were little affected by aid cuts.

California's 5,500 units of local government (including its 429 cities) have relied on bonds to raise funds for the construction of water systems, sanitation works, streets, sewers, flood control channels, hospitals, fire houses and equipment, ports and harbors, parks, airports, libraries, parking, and general public utilities. Most recently, notes have been used to supplement bonds. Both have important tax features which exempt them from federal and usually also from state income taxation, though they have lower interest rates than do federal or corporate bonds.

Some Hypotheses

Following are some hypotheses about how Proposition 13 affects the issuance of municipal bonds. Cities fearing difficulties in issuing new bonds under Proposition 13 will tend to float as many as possible before election day in June 1978; following the hiatus after passage, cities will not issue bonds for a few months. Thus, we expect a gap in the issuance of bonds after June 1978 and a

36 Isabel V. Sawhill, "Poverty in the U.S.: Why Is It So Persistent?" *Journal of Economic Literature* 26 (September 1988), pp. 1073–1119.

37 Werner Z. Hirsch, "Revenue Limitation Measures and Their Effects on Municipal Bonds: The Case of California Municipalities," *Public Finance and Public Debt*, Proceedings of the 40th Congress of the International Institute of Public Finance (Detroit, MI: Wayne State University Press, 1986), pp. 293–305. Earlier studies include N. E. Thomas, "Physical Limitations and Municipal Debt – The Extreme Case of Proposition 13," in G. G. Kaufman and K. T. Rosen, eds., *The Property Tax Revolt – The Case of Proposition 13* (Cambridge, MA: Ballinger, 1981), pp. 105–116; Jack H. Beebe, "California Bonds After Proposition 13," in Kaufman and Rosen, op. cit., pp. 1336–1361; and Ronald Forbes, et al., "The Effects of Proposition 13 and Tax-Supported Municipal Bonds in California," in Kaufman and Rosen, op. cit., pp. 117–133.

change in the mix of debt instruments. For example, since debt service is not exempt from limitations imposed by Proposition 13 (except debt approved by voters prior to July 1, 1978), local governments should be handicapped in using credit markets, especially in the sale of general obligation bonds. To make up for this lost opportunity, cities are likely to turn to both short-term notes and long-term bonds, which are not subject to the 1% property tax rate limitation. However, to the extent that Proposition 13 has compromised the backing of these instruments, interest rates are likely to rise, reducing the ability of cities to sell new debt instruments. Since the interest rate for low-quality bonds is likely to be particularly high, few such bonds will be sold.

Of the different types of bonds, general obligation bonds should be most difficult, if not impossible, to float. They would need a two-thirds majority of the electorate, which is seldom attainable. At the other extreme are tax or grant anticipation notes, which can be sold by a vote of the elected officials; they are much more easily floated.

We can also hypothesize about the interest cost of bonds. To the extent that the property tax ceiling has become inflexible under Proposition 13, it reduces the ability of municipalities to make service payments and thereby increases the probability of default. Investors tend to consider this debt more risky. They would therefore insist on higher interest than before. When general obligation bonds that receive voter approval prior to July 1, 1978 are actually issued, they should be little affected by Proposition 13. Their debt service is exempted from the 1% tax rate ceiling and they allow payment without additional voter-approval. Jack Beebe has reported that ". . . some analysts have suggested that such secure debt would command a premium price and thus a lower yield."[38] Since revenue bonds are issued to finance revenue-producing facilities with their fees pledged for debt service, they too should be little affected by Proposition 13. To the extent that a municipality pledges its property tax revenue as backup security, higher interest rates could be expected as Proposition 13 compromises this backup. Tax allocation bonds fund redevelopment projects and are secured and financed mainly by the tax-increment revenues generated by the specific project. Because Proposition 13 lowers assessed values and property tax rates, it has a chilling effect on tax allocation bonds. The increased default risk should result in higher net interest costs for new issues.

Effects on the Sale of Debt Instruments and Their Mix

On June 30, 1981, the total debt of all local governments in California amounted to $18.2 billion, 35% in the form of general obligation bonds, 31% in revenue bonds, and 12% in lease-purchase bonds. California cities accounted for about 40%, i.e., $5.8 billion of all general obligation, revenue, and lease

---

[38] Beebe, op. cit., p. 141.

bonds. Revenue bonds were by far the most important, accounting for nearly 65%, i.e., $3.7 billion of these major municipal bonds.

On the basis of data taken from the *Daily Bond Buyer* we find that shortly after passage of Proposition 13, issuance of new municipal bonds declined from $980 million in 1977 to $890 million in 1978 and $834 million in 1979.[39] Thereafter, except for the recession year of 1981, a recovery set in (see Table 20-1). However, when deflated to 1977 values, subsequent issuances have not matched the 1977 level. The amount issued in 1982, when deflated, was only $819 million, about 15% less than the amount issued in 1977. At the same time, a change in mix occurred.

Clearly the issuance volume and the mix of debt instruments were also affected by changes in the level of economic activity and interest rates, which in general terms affected bond markets. The decline in the issuance of debt instruments by California cities is not paralleled by changes in the issuance of such instruments in the rest of the United States. Municipal debt issuances in the United States rose from $66 billion in 1977 to $67 billion in 1978 at a time when California cities had reduced their issuances. By 1982, total municipal debt issuance in the U.S. had increased to $121 billion, i.e., by 83%, a much larger percentage than California's 33%. Another way to look at this phenomenon is to make annual comparisons of California issuances as a percentage of all municipal debt issuances. This percentage fell from 1.5% in 1977 to 1.3% in 1978 and 1.1% in 1982.

As can be seen from Table 20-1, revenue bonds have remained the single most important bond newly issued by city governments (1981 is the only exception). General obligation bonds, which apparently had lost some of their earlier importance for municipal governments, changed little after the passage of Proposition 13. Apparently there were still a number of these that had been authorized before 1978, to be floated only in subsequent years. What has increased most significantly in the post-Proposition 13 period are short-term notes of different types, e.g., tax and revenue anticipation, grant anticipation, and bond anticipation notes. They were barely used in the pre-Proposition 13 era, but in 1981 they were about as important a revenue source as all other major bonds combined; they have increased from $8 million in 1977 to $629 million in 1983. The importance of notes increased much more in California than in the U.S. in general. While the 1977–83 percentage increase in California was 7,366%, that in the U.S. was only 68%.[40]

This change in mix has a distinct effect on the net interest cost of municipalities. Since anticipation notes are short term and have reasonably reliable backing in the form of taxes, grants, or bonds, they have been sold at relatively low interest rates if compared with long-term bonds, many of which had their backing eroded because of Proposition 13. Notes in the early 1980s were

[39] National municipal debt issuance data gathered from *Moody's Municipal & Government Manual*, vol. 1 (1984), p. A6.
[40] Ibid., p. A6.

Table 20-1 / **Debt Instruments Issued by California Cities and All U.S. Municipal Governments, 1977–83**

	California Cities												United States Total	
	Revenue Bonds		General Obligation Bonds		Tax Allocation Bonds		Lease Purchase Bonds		Notes		All Debt Instruments		Municipal Notes	All Municipal Debt Instruments
Year	#	$000	#	$000	#	$000	#	$000	#	$000	#	$000	$ millions	
1977	31	591,095	39	47,500	32	251,350	13	81,015	4	8,424	119	979,324	21,349	66,409
1978	24	447,955	10	53,463	29	270,850	6	67,475	4	50,375	73	890,118	21,642	67,857
1979	25	520,065	24	67,873	14	146,010	5	99,255	1	3,300	69	836,503	20,897	63,150
1980	38	1,255,265	21	44,700	7	63,600	4	26,140	3	33,200	73	1,422,905	26,449	73,582
1981	13	144,592	10	27,240	11	135,895	4	19,260	17	304,316	55	631,303	34,443	80,577
1982	35	745,984	17	44,545	40	307,370	4	26,480	26	179,410	122	1,303,794	43,390	120,569
1983	—	—	—	—	—	—	—	—	26	628,895	—	—	35,760	116,961

(Source: *Daily Bond Buyer* [January 1, 1977–December 31, 1983]; and *Moody's Municipal and Government Manual*, vol. 1 [1984], p. A6.)

perhaps 200–250 basic points below most comparable bonds. However, replacing long-term bonds with short-term notes also includes the costs of administration and the uncertainty of what the interest rates will be at the time of refunding.

/// SUMMARY

In the late 1970s taxpayers increasingly revolted against rising taxes. More than half of the states responded by initiating revenue limitation measures and a few supplemented them with expenditure limitation measures. Whereas the former severely reined in local government expenditures, at least for a few years, expenditure limitation measures had relatively mild effects. This chapter, after briefly reviewing revenue and limitation measures in California, Massachusetts, Michigan and Texas, was mainly devoted to the analysis of California's Proposition 13, perhaps the most stringent of all measures.

But did these draconic measures to reduce state and local taxes (or at least reduce increases) succeed, and if so for how long? There appears to be general agreement that the immediate result of most revenue limitation measures was indeed a reduction in specific taxes, for example in the case of California local property taxes. However, in many instances state subsidies to local government increased and, more importantly, many expenditure reductions were short-lived.

Nevertheless there is persuasive evidence that the revenue and expenditure limitation measures of the late 1970s slowed down the expenditure increases of state and local governments. We can compare the 4.4% annual per capita expenditure increase of state and local governments (adjusted for inflation) between 1958 and 1978 with the 0.54% increase during 1978–81.[41] The change was even more pronounced in terms of public employment. Between 1957 and 1978 public employment per 1,000 population increased annually an average of 2.7%, but it decreased by 1.1% between 1978 and 1981. However, since then significant expenditure and employment increases have resumed.

Thus, while tax, revenue, and employment reductions were not one-year events, they appear to have limited staying power. Alvin Rabushka and Pauline Ryan concluded *The Tax Revolt* by stating, "In 1978, most Americans were highly enthusiastic about cutting taxes and telling government that it had to reform its spending habits. By 1981, public opinion changed. In fact,

---

[41] ACIR, *Significant Features of Fiscal Federalism, 1981–82 Edition* (Washington, DC: April 1983), p. 2.

the wheel had come full circle. . . . Almost overnight, it seemed, the tax revolt had died."[42] Reasons for the difficulty of sustaining tax revolts tend to focus on a ". . . coalition of taxing and spending interests that links together politicians, bureaucrats, public employees, and recipients of government benefits."[43]

---

[42] Alvin Rabushka and Pauline Ryan, *The Tax Revolt* (Stanford, CA: Hoover Institution, 1982), p. 201.
[43] Ibid. Most likely the reasons are more complex. Thus, it is not clear that this conclusion is valid since membership in special interest groups is substantially smaller than the general group of citizens/taxpayers. Perhaps taxpayer revolts are more expressions of frustrations rather than carefully reasoned, rational policy alternatives. Although extreme measures can be destructive and lead to great inefficiencies, a taxpayers' revolt also has salubrious effects. It warns elected and appointed officials that specific changes are in order. In such an environment, public officials often are forced to reexamine their priorities and take steps to cut costs. Such steps, because they are painful, otherwise would not have been taken.

Chapter 21 //////

Fiscal Crises

In 1975 New York City was technically in default on its debts. It was unable to pay off large amounts of short-term notes that were due and it was unable to borrow the money to continue the debts. While New York was the focus of world attention, smaller cities have more quietly faced similar crises. In 1983 a special district, the Washington Public Power Supply System, defaulted on over $2.2 billion in bonds. This was the largest default in the history of the municipal bond market.

Although local governments and special districts are more likely to reach a "crisis" stage, higher levels of government can also face serious problems. States may struggle with unexpected shortfalls or with chronic difficulty in balancing a budget. At the federal level, government runs deficits in the hundreds of billions of dollars, and it seems unable to bring expenditures and revenues into balance. Questions are raised about how long this can continue and whether the federal deficits will lead to some type of crisis of their own. Exactly what is a "fiscal crisis," how does it develop, and what can be done about it? These are the questions we address in this chapter.

Most of the attention associated with the fiscal problems of government has been focused on the lower levels of government, because this is where most of the acute problems have occurred. In addition, the higher levels of government have more tools and resources at their disposal, so they are less likely to be unable to meet their obligations. Nevertheless, all units of government have some similarities and it is worthwhile to consider whether there are lessons for the higher levels of government in the experience of the lower levels.

We start by reviewing the issues that arise in trying to determine an ideal allocation of responsibilities and funding sources in a federal system. Next we look at some of the factors suggested as possible causes of local fiscal problems. Then we consider the New York default in some detail to sort through these various possible causes. Finally, we see if there are similarities between local fiscal problems and the situations faced by higher levels of government.

/// DEFINING THE PROBLEM

It is helpful to start by considering exactly what a fiscal crisis is and how it differs from ordinary budget problems. Every government faces a budget constraint. There are always demands for more goods and services than any government could realistically expect to meet. This combination of high demand and limited resources creates a variety of conflicts. Some people want more spent on specific goods and services; others have different priorities. All want to keep their tax bills as low as possible. In addition, the workers whom the government must hire to provide these items want good salaries and comfortable working conditions, so there is also upward pressure on costs. Yet these are just standard economic problems. The budget constraint becomes the mechanism by which the various competing claims on resources are reconciled. Crises develop when the ability to reconcile the competing demands breaks down.

Normally, a government would not agree to expenditures that it could not fund. There are always unexpected ups and downs in the economy which affect both expenditures and revenues, but these items should be within the capability of the government to address. Short-term revenue losses or unexpected expenditures can be met by cutting low-priority expenditures, by raising revenues, or by borrowing. Every government faces such situations regularly; these problems cannot be considered as crises. However, they are likely to precipitate a crisis when a government reaches a state such that the normal budgetary flexibility no longer exists. If no combination of acceptable expenditure cuts, revenue increases, and borrowing exists, then the government is in a crisis situation.

It is important to understand the distinction between the event that precipitates a crisis and the true cause of the crisis. The true cause must be a long-term mismatch between revenue and expenditures. As a government uses up its tools for coping with short-term problems in trying to avoid the long-term one, it will find that eventually a short-term problem is added to the long-term one, and this creates the crisis situation. However, in most cases, the problem goes substantially beyond the short-term cause.

Possible Causes

As was discussed in Chapter 14, there are a variety of reasons why government costs might rise over time. Increasing interaction of the population due to higher density or reduced transportation costs increases the number of externalities created, and this in turn calls for more government action. The demand for government services might be very income-elastic, so it may be rising over time because the population is better off and wants more of the goods and services that government provides. The cost of government services may be rising relative to the cost of private goods and services because of rising real wages and limited opportunity for productivity improvements in government activities.

In addition to the reasons why all governments might be facing increasing costs, there are specific reasons why some governments may face problems different from others. A major reason could be that the local economy is being buffeted by economic conditions. Perhaps the local area is losing its population and tax base because of decline in some important local industry, or there is an influx of low-income residents who are demanding more services just as the ability of the government to pay starts to decline.

Local tax conditions are also likely to be an important issue. If the region depends heavily on energy production taxes, then a decline in the energy industry creates a drop in tax revenue to accompany any employment losses and increases in demand for services. Alternatively, restrictions on raising taxes may make it impossible to pay for increased expenditures even if the economy is healthy.

Some regions may also find themselves on the negative end of intergovernmental relations. Mandates from higher levels of government may force new expenditures with no increases in intergovernmental revenues; or such revenues may simply be declining, leaving the lower level of government to make up the difference.

Finally, a jurisdiction can create problems for itself, such as unwise use of debt over long periods of time or refusing to face the need to balance expenditures with revenue. Inefficient management of the public sector might also contribute by leaving costs high relative to other areas and encouraging people and resources to move elsewhere.

Given the decentralized form of government we have in the United States, it would probably be surprising to find that all government units faced the same fiscal conditions. The real issue from an intergovernmental perspective is to determine the causes of fiscal problems and the appropriate responses both from other units of government and from citizens.

Although there are no generally accepted definitions of the term *fiscal crisis*, it appears to be used often to describe a situation in which a government unit faces high and rising costs relative to its revenue base. As the demands rise and the resources shrink, there often appears to be little that officials can do to salvage the system. In particular, local governments tend to ask the state to provide more resources or to pick up some of the burdens. States ask the federal government to do the same for them; and the federal government may respond to its own problems by reducing aid to lower levels. There may be times when a government unit should look to others for help; but there are also likely to be times when such aid could be counterproductive. It is important to be able to distinguish these situations for policy purposes.

/// THE FEDERAL SYSTEM

Within a federal system, each level of government has certain responsibilities and certain powers to use in meeting those responsibilities. Recall from our discussion in Chapter 2 that the economic view of government shows essentially three reasons for government intervention in the economy. The first is to stabilize the economy at the national level. This is almost exclusively the concern of the federal government, and the analysis of the actions that it can take is left for a course in macroeconomics. The second purpose is redistribution of income. Since almost everything government does results in some people being made better off and others worse off, there is some redistribution in almost all government activity. However, redistribution is best left to the higher levels of government. Redistribution at lower levels results in people and resources changing their locations in response, and this usually results in an efficiency cost to the economy. The third area of desirable government activity is in the allocation of resources; here, there are significant activities at all levels of government.

Changing economic conditions across geographic lines create a difficult situation for governments at higher levels. Declining areas often have a concentration of problems and declining resources, but attempts to alleviate such problems may interfere with efficient economic shifts. Further, not all problems of decline are caused by external forces. To the extent that problems are caused by poor policies or other factors under government control, attempts to alleviate the problems by higher levels of government may only encourage continuation of the inappropriate policies.

When distortions are created by having local governments provide goods or services for which there are externalities, economies of scale, or significant income redistribution, higher levels of government can intervene in a variety of ways, through intergovernmental grants and through regulation of the lower levels of government. Different types of intervention would be appropriate under different circumstances.

The Ideal System

The ideal federal system would be one in which there are many different local governments with a wide variety of public services available. Each family would be charged a price for living in the community equal to the marginal (and average) cost of providing the package of goods and services they receive. All other charges by the government would come from marginal cost user charges. There would be no externalities between governments, or if there were, higher levels of government would provide grants to offset the externalities. Goods and services with large economies of scale or with significant redistributive features would be financed by higher levels of government. All subnational governments would maintain substantial reserves to deal with the uncertainties caused by changing economic conditions. Higher levels of government would provide all redistributive funding for low-income families. All the goods and services provided by any government would be provided efficiently, and each subnational government would have a balanced budget following accepted financial practices.

In the real world almost none of these conditions are met. Taxes are not clearly tied to services at the local level, and externalities are likely to be extensive. Almost all government activity involves some redistribution among residents. The simple requirement that each person have equal access to the good or service while the tax contribution is based on some other characteristic guarantees that some gain relative to others. Net gainers lobby for expansion of government activity, while net losers lobby for government spending to be cut. Those who gain have an incentive to move into the community, those who lose have an incentive to move out.

Wherever the poor end up, they place a burden on the local government. Management of local government production does not have the appropriate incentives to be efficient, so productivity improvements are likely to stay low. Few governments are prepared to make adjustments in response to negative economic changes, and many do not follow accepted financial practices when making budgets. Finally, higher levels of government are unlikely to take responsibility for all the costs of all low-income people.

The Economic Factors

Geographic differences in economic activity have been substantial through most of the history of the United States. It is not uncommon for one region to have substantially better or worse conditions than the country as a whole. Such circumstances may persist for long periods of time or they may respond to the business cycle. Other problems arise when economic forces cause an area to face long periods of economic decline or short periods of very rapid growth. These economic problems can also be seen within geographic areas as some parts of the area grow and prosper while others are faced with declining populations, employment, and tax bases coupled with increasing service demands. The latter set of characteristics appears to be relevant to a number of larger, older central cities.

Either rapid growth or rapid decline can create substantial problems for a local government. Rapid growth creates the demand for additional infrastructure, which generally requires substantial short-term expenditures. While the community growth creates the increased tax base to fund the rising expenditures, it is not always possible to raise taxes and fees to provide the appropriate funding or to borrow in recognition of the higher tax base. However, such situations are seldom described as a crisis. Some method of raising funds to accommodate the growth is usually found; even if growth is restricted, the local government can continue to function. Instead, rapid decline makes a crisis situation possible. Loss of jobs and tax base coupled with rising demand for services can easily create incentives to use any means possible to balance the budget, and this can lead to a fiscal problem. Many people feel that a local government should not have to cut its services because its wealthiest residents move away. They feel that government output should be made equally available to all no matter where they live and that it is inappropriate to reduce the net benefits going to the remaining population because they have come to expect a certain level of service for their tax payments. Changes in either taxes or services would then be capitalized into property values and could create a substantial loss for the remaining residents.

Unfortunately, it is very inefficient for government not to act in response to its changing economic conditions; failure to act could also create long-term fiscal problems. The inefficiency arises because having each unit of local government provide the same level of service takes away the opportunity for those who want higher levels of service to purchase them. In effect, the ideal system calls for the local governments to simply sell a package of goods and services. Under such a system the poor would be less able to purchase these goods and services just as they are less able to purchase most other things. This also indicates why mandating high levels of service may be inefficient. Since the poor lack many things, it is unlikely that the best way to improve their status is to provide large amounts of the goods and services supplied by government. Rather, they would probably choose to spend only a small part of any increment to income on better government services. Thus, to the extent that the public sector is attempting to redistribute income, doing it by providing high levels of government services is not effective from the perspective of the recipients.

Similar issues arise with respect to activities within a politically fragmented urban area. Urban economics and urban geography teach that the allocation of activities within an urban area follow certain patterns. To a large extent these patterns are efficient ways to allocate activities among the various locations. However, the political jurisdictions into which the area is divided are often arbitrary. Thus, the provision of goods and services by political jurisdictions is influenced by the particular set of jurisdictions that exists. In the early urbanization of the country, cities simply expanded their boundaries as their population grew. This is still possible for cities in some states, such as Texas. However, in most states the ability of the central city to expand its boundaries was significantly constrained. Rather, people moving outside the city boundaries had the option of choosing to set up separate local governments. The creation of these separate local governments led to the current pattern of a central city surrounded by a varying number of suburbs.

Since World War II, improvements in transportation have resulted in larger urban areas with more political jurisdictions within each one. Thus, we find the familiar pattern of a central city surrounded by suburbs with each jurisdiction undergoing changes associated with the changing patterns of land use and the changing composition of population in each jurisdiction.

The pattern of location that prevails in most U.S. urban areas is for the very low-income and some of the high-income residents to live near the center of the urban area with the middle-income and the rest of the high-income residents living further out. When everyone in an urban area lived in the same jurisdiction, the pattern of location was not much of a problem from the public finance perspective. However, as the number of jurisdictions increased, the effect was that the growth of the urban area also created a particular pattern of location by income. The middle-income residents and many of the high-income residents remained at the outside of the urban area as it grew. This means that many now live outside the central cities of urban areas. So we tend to find a pattern within urban areas of the low-income residents increasingly concentrated in the central city.

This concentration means that there is a tendency for the demand for services to increase or for the conditions to provide those services to deteriorate. This may happen at the same time that the tax base needed to pay for these services is remaining stagnant or declining. Some of these cities even face a declining total population. Thus, the cities find themselves providing either fewer services or raising taxes to fund the existing set of services. Further, during periods of national economic decline, the low-income residents of the urban area may be more likely to lose their jobs or fail to get new ones. Thus, during recessions the unemployment rates in cities tend to rise relative to the nation as a whole.

Intergovernmental Relations

How much money should come to a city from the state or federal governments? What criteria should be used to judge the amount and distribution of such intergovernmental aid? These questions are clearly related to issues of fiscal crisis because the actions of higher levels of government have so much impact on the finances of a city. Most people think in terms of how much the higher level governments give to the cities, but it is also important to see how this money changes the behavior patterns within a city. Also, the use of tax credits or deductions can significantly reduce the impact of local taxes on local residents or businesses.

When should a higher level of government aid a lower level of government? We have already seen that the appropriate method of financing some local services is for the state or federal government to raise the revenue and then finance a local government to actually provide the good or service. However, there are some conditions under which increased aid from higher levels of government can be detrimental to the local unit. For example, a matching grant may induce the local government to spend money on an activity that is of fairly low priority; this reduces the revenue available for use on high-priority items. This can be particularly perverse when the matching grant imposes a maintenance of effort provision on a city faced with rapid economic decline.

Most economists agree that the higher levels of government should finance activities that are largely redistributional in nature. Thus, the federal and state governments pay most of the costs of the welfare programs. However, local governments seem to get into trouble because the tax base and the service recipients are often unrelated. One can make the case that the property tax is reasonably closely related to the amount of cost that property imposes on a community for fire protection, police protection, and street cleaning. However, it is hard to argue that the property tax is related to education, health, or welfare services in any clear-cut way. This is especially a problem because such a large percentage of school expenditures are raised from the property tax and so much of the tax revenue goes to funding education.

A strong case can be made for funding education from the state level. However, this could create even more serious efficiency problems if the system does not create better incentives for efficient behavior. To accomplish this, many economists recommend that the state finance the provision of education and provide parents with vouchers to use in purchasing the education from schools. This would remove the dependence on the property tax and reduce some of the fiscal incentives for homogeneous communities. In addition, greater parental control over the choice of school should give the schools the incentive to provide their output efficiently. Some argue that schools financed in this manner would not provide good education because it would be cheaper to provide poor education. Most such concerns should be addressed by parents in looking for schools, but some of them can be met with state standards for certain subjects.

In the absence of such state funding, there are likely to be distortions created by local government finance, and to the extent that education is a merit good, local financing would lead to underprovision for low-income families. However, it is also important to keep in mind the issue of efficiency. Simply providing more money to a local government that is having problems is not going to create incentives to solve those problems. If intergovernmental aid is focused on districts that have serious problems, it may actually create an incentive for the local government to create problems so as to get aid. Even if this is not the case, the aid may remove incentives to improve inefficient management or address other problems. Thus, there is likely to be some trade-off between attempts by higher levels of government to alleviate fiscal pressure and the need to create incentives for efficiency.

/// FISCAL STRAIN

If we look at the central cities of many large urban areas, we see a number of factors that have contributed to the perception of stress on the local governments. The city is likely to have had a loss in both employment and population over time and the mix of population has changed toward more low-income and more minority residents.[1] In recent years, the level of aid from the federal government is also likely to have declined, but there may be mandates that

---

[1] Many of these issues are discussed in Paul E. Peterson, ed., *The New Urban Reality* (Washington, DC: Brookings, 1985).

require substantial additional costs.[2] In the presence of these complications, how do we address the issues raised? The concept of fiscal crisis is usually associated with a city closed down because of the business cycle or some other downturn in city finances. However, this is more likely to be a precipitating factor than a sole cause of such problems. Several studies of fiscal stress point out that many local governments with severe economic problems nevertheless maintain a balance between their revenues and expenditures while many other cities with better economic conditions are unable to do so.[3] We consider first some of the issues raised by the concentration of the poor in particular jurisdictions and then analyze the most spectacular fiscal crisis that the U.S. has yet seen, New York City's 1975 problems.

Decentralization and Older Cities

Proponents of aid to central cities often note the rising concentration of the poor in the cities while higher income residents move to the suburban communities. In the past, the city was the area where the wealthiest part of the population lived, and the high tax base allowed the provision of large amounts of services for all residents. Now the cities face growing demands amid signs of decay. Many believe that this is due to the abandonment of the central city by middle-income and high-income families intent on getting away from the crime, congestion, and other negative aspects of many cities. They argue that the city could be saved if higher levels of government provide aid.

Another view is that the shift in population is the result of strong economic forces which would make it difficult, if not impossible, to reverse the trend. These economic forces are reductions in transportation and communications costs along with growth in the urban areas themselves. According to this view, the improvements in transportation and communication have allowed the urban areas to spread out more. This has reduced the need to concentrate activities. It is relatively more efficient to have low-income people live near the city center, because they would not save much in rents by moving to a suburban location but would still face the cost of access to jobs and so on. When coupled with growth of urban areas, these forces create the observed pattern if the political boundaries remain fixed. Once the general pattern of location is set, the government tends to reinforce it by providing specific goods and services to each type of population. Thus, the low-income area is more likely to be served by mass transit and to have many of the medical and other services which the city provides to the indigent. This becomes an attraction to

---

[2] For example, the EPA recently found that a set of its proposed regulations would place severe financial burdens on some cities. See Ellen Perlman, "EPA Study Held No Surprises," *City and State* (June 6, 1988), p. 2.

[3] See, for example, Terry Nichols Clark, "Fiscal Strain: How Different Are Snowbelt and Sunbelt Cities?" in Peterson, op. cit.; and First National Bank of Boston and Touche Ross and Co., *Urban Fiscal Stress: A Comparative Analysis of 66 Cities* (New York: Touche Ross, 1979).

others requiring these services and tends to reinforce the concentration of the poor in certain areas.

It is important to know which of these explanations is closer to explaining what happened because they imply vast differences in the effectiveness of various policies that attempt to aid cities. If the decline is simply due to the rise in crime rates, the deterioration of the housing, and the fiscal problems that the cities face, then pumping money into the cities would have the desired effect. However, if the decline is due to underlying changes in transportation and communication costs, the proposed policies would have little long-term effect.[4] The evidence seems to favor the economic forces interpretation but there is still some effect from the push associated with negative conditions in the city.[5]

People versus Place Prosperity

If higher levels of government provide cities with the resources to rebuild and to subsidize the return of wealthier households, the effect is likely to be to push low-income households out. That in fact is what the urban renewal program essentially tried to do by destroying much low-income housing and replacing it with higher income units. The poor were to become a smaller portion of the total population.[6] It is not clear how this is supposed to help the low-income household, but the intended effect for the city is clear: it is an attempt to give the city a better mix of population at the expense of other political jurisdictions. The higher tax base and reduced demand for services would leave the city with fewer financial problems. If the poor only congregate in the city because it has the oldest, cheapest housing, destroying some of that housing may lead to a dispersal of the poor among the many jurisdictions in the area; however, there is little evidence that this in fact occurred.

It is important to recognize that many of the programs to aid the city have this side effect of trying to redistribute population among political jurisdictions. To the extent that this is the purpose, one can seriously question why higher levels of government should assist lower levels of government in achieving this goal. The issue is sometimes referred to as one of people versus place prosperity.[7] Is the higher level of government concerned with the well-being of the people residing in the lower level jurisdiction or is there some reason to want the place to prosper, even at the expense of its residents? It is clear that low-income families do not always see the return of the high-income families

---

[4] Wallace E. Oates, et al., "The Analysis of Public Policy in Dynamic Urban Models," *Journal of Political Economy* (January 1971), pp. 142–153.

[5] David F. Bradford and Harry H. Kelejian, "An Econometric Model of the Flight to the Suburbs," *Journal of Political Economy* (May/June 1973), pp. 566–589.

[6] William Gorham and Nathan Glazer, eds., *The Urban Predicament* (Washington, DC: The Urban Institute, 1976), p. 4.

[7] Matthew Edel, "'People' versus 'Places' in Urban Impact Analysis," in Norman Glickman, ed., *The Urban Impacts of Federal Policies* (Baltimore, MD: Johns Hopkins University Press, 1980), pp. 175–191.

as a benefit. One of the serious questions that arises when an area "gentrifies" is what happens to the previous residents. In some cities the low-income groups that have been displaced have protested the upgrading of their neighborhoods.

The relevant question is whether the actions that benefit the city also benefit its residents. For example, the easiest way to raise average income in a city would be to force out all the low-income residents and replace them with high-income residents. Both sets of residents may feel that they are worse off than before the change, but the city is better off. This may seem to be a perverse way to measure city well-being, but it is exactly what happens in many cases. For example, the recent concern with the decline in city income appears to be this kind of change. It is probably not the case that the current residents in a city in decline feel that they themselves are worse off. Rather, low-income families are more concentrated in the central city, and the replacement of a high-income family by a low-income one brings down the average income in the city.

This concentration of low-income families in the central city does indeed create problems for the city. The concentration of low-income families leads to higher costs for the city to provide the same level of service at the same time that it leads to a deterioration in the tax base. Low-income families tend to make more use of many government services, and it is often more expensive to provide certain services. For example, the cost of providing a given level of education services to a poor child is likely to be higher than it is for a middle-class child because of the differences in the home environment. Thus, expenditure per child should probably increase as the number of poor children in a jurisdiction increases. To the extent that the school district relies on local property taxes, however, the more likely outcome is that the funding for schooling will decrease as the residential composition changes.

This change creates a dilemma for city government. Should the quality of schooling be allowed to deteriorate or should taxes be raised? Either response is likely to create more incentive for high-income families to move out of the city. Thus, many mayors call for additional funds from higher levels of government. The problem is that the source of the marginal funds for schooling is not related to the cost of providing the service; therefore, the property tax is a poor choice for use in funding schooling. The preferred solution would be to change the method of funding schools, but that may not be a feasible response. Does any other policy response achieve a desired result?

Overburdened Cities?

First, one should ask if there is or is not already an excessive burden on city taxpayers. Some argue that the suburban communities exploit the central cities in a number of ways. For example, many commuters come into the city each day and use city services, but they do not pay any taxes to the city. The suburbanites do not pay their fair share of the cost of providing services to the poor. The first argument is convincing to many people. However, it ignores certain very important facts. First, the city has a large concentration of employment relative to population. The factories and skyscrapers where people work are the source of significant amounts of property tax revenue. In fact, most communities compete with each other to try to attract businesses, because they pay more in taxes than it costs the jurisdiction to provide them with services. Hence, the city has the benefit of the employment-based property tax without having to provide many of the most expensive services for the employees of that company. Thus, it would appear that the lack of tax payments from the employees does not really hurt the city. The other argument is best analyzed by trying to determine exactly how the tax base should be apportioned. If we look at tax base per capita, it is not clear that the city is any worse off than the suburbs. While many suburbs have more expensive housing than the central cities, this is often offset by much greater concentrations of nonresidential property in the cities.

The changing composition of city population does leave the city in a relatively worse financial situation, but this is not necessarily an absolutely worse financial situation than is faced by many of the suburbs. Further, additional intergovernmental aid may not end up aiding the poor residents of a city. From the city's perspective, it is just as good to change the population as it is to make existing residents better off. Thus, it is not at all clear that additional intergovernmental grants would be used to pay for services for the poor. Rather, cities are likely to continue to try to attract those who pay more in taxes than it costs to provide them with services and to repel those who cost more to provide services to than they pay in taxes.

However, much of this misses the point. If we look at the financial condition of many cities, does the concentration of the poor explain the problems? One important item to consider is that the largest fiscal problem occurred in one of the wealthiest cities in the country. While New York has many poor people, its average income is well above the average for the United States. Further, look at nearby Newark, New Jersey. Newark has a far higher concentration of poverty than does New York, and it does not have anywhere near New York's resources. Yet it did not go into default. It would probably make more sense for higher levels of government to find a more direct way of aiding cities in paying for the services to low-income residents, but targeting that aid at cities with fiscal problems may be perverse. In particular, cities that have few resources but have made a determined effort to balance their budget would be passed over in favor of aid to other cities that may have substantially more resources but did not balance their budgets.

The difference between the cities with fiscal problems and those without appears to be the attitude of the city toward balanced budgets. In New York, as in virtually all U.S. municipalities, a balanced budget is a legal requirement. However, New York used a series of gimmicks over a period of fifteen years to run deficits. Many of the cities in worse shape than New York could not do this because they could not borrow the money. In a certain sense, New York is an example of what can happen when even a wealthy entity chooses to continue to spend more than it receives on an ongoing basis. As an illustration of just what happened it is worth looking into the New York case in more detail.

/// NEW YORK'S FISCAL CRISIS

Economic Conditions

Between 1969 and 1976, New York lost over 600,000 jobs. This was indicative of a major restructuring of the city's economy. Such a massive loss of jobs certainly had a negative effect on the city's fiscal situation. However, the loss of jobs did not directly result in a loss of the equivalent tax base. The property base in the city was not greatly affected. There was a loss of revenue in terms of the city's income tax and there was an increase in the demand on the city's services because of rising unemployment. This would not have caused the city's financial problems if there had not been an ongoing problem with debt.

Debt Financing in New York

Municipal governments are usually restricted in their use of debt financing. They are only supposed to use debt to finance capital purchases, i.e., buildings or other long-lived assets, or to smooth over short-term fluctuations in their income relative to expenditures. Use of debt for capital financing allows for a general matching between the benefits an asset generates and the tax payments needed to finance it. The major alternative is pay-as-you-go financing, which requires that the capital be purchased from current revenues. This is likely to create problems when the capital expense is large relative to normal expenditures, and it may lead a jurisdiction to forgo important capital improvements because the cash is not available. On the other hand, pay-as-you-go financing is one way to make sure that no money is borrowed for inappropriate purposes.

Short-term borrowing to cover fluctuations in income is expected to be paid off within one year. This type of borrowing might be done when property taxes are due near the end of the fiscal year but expenditures occur evenly throughout the year. If it must be rolled over at each maturity, i.e., more money must be borrowed to pay for the old loan, then the debt is unlikely to be true short-term debt. Rather, it is a very risky type of long-term loan. This is the situation that New York faced in its default. A large amount of short-term debt was maturing and no one would lend the city the money to pay off the old debts.

It is interesting to note that by law the city budget for New York is required to be balanced; it met the requirements of the law for each of the fifteen years before it went into default. Yet there is widespread agreement that the city in fact ran a deficit for each of those years. To understand the difference it may be useful to consider some of the issues in defining a city budget.

Municipal Budgeting

Each budget must have information on the receipts and expenditures of the city. However, these numbers do not always mean what they appear to mean. First, many items do not show up on the city's budget at all. These off-budget items can be related to independent operating agencies of the government or they might simply be expenses handled through separate budgets of the local government. For example, a capital budget might be kept separately from the general budget. In many ways, this makes sense since capital expenditures provide benefits for many years and should be treated differently from current expenditures. However, the separate budget also allows more opportunity for gimmicks in the budgeting process.

Another thing to be aware of is the difference between municipal budgeting and standard budgeting in the corporate sector. There are many differences in how municipal budgets are kept, and some of these differences allow problems to go unnoticed by budget observers. For example, when a private firm does buy a long-lived asset it shows depreciation of the asset from year to year, which is intended to reflect using up the asset. This depreciation is treated as part of the firm's expense in each year. However, municipal governments do not show any such expenses. This is no problem if the capital budget has interest and principal expenditures that are exactly equal to the depreciation that occurs, but it is a problem when the depreciation occurs on an asset that is fully owned. In the latter case, the city is really running up a form of hidden debt since the asset will have to be replaced at some time and there will be no money set aside to replace it. Also, in the interim, the service from the deteriorating asset is likely to decline over time.

A final factor in the difference between municipal accounting and that in the private sector is that the municipal government does not have to acknowledge debts associated with pension plans for workers who have not yet retired. The standard followed in the private sector is to put aside a certain amount of money each year that a worker is employed. If this money is not set aside, the company must still treat it as an expenditure and treat the money not set aside as a form of debt. There must also be a plan to retire this debt within a certain number of years. The amount of money to be set aside is determined from actuarial calculations that take into account the age of the workers, the amount promised at retirement, and the expected earnings on the investment in the interim. A municipal government would not have to make similar payments. It is exempt from the federal laws that require an employer to make such payments.

The municipal exemption from the Employees' Retirement and Income Security Act allows it to effectively borrow from its retirement funds without letting the potential losers know. This is because any money that should be set aside and is not will have to be made up with interest at some point in the future. When existing employees seek to retire, they will draw on the balances in the fund. Beyond some point there will not be enough money to pay all the promised benefits, and the government will either have to default on its promised benefits or put additional money into paying pensions. In some of the worst cases this can result in expenditures on pensions that exceed expenditures on wages and salaries.[8] This is in comparison with a typical city, which spends only about 6% to 10% of its expenditures for labor on pensions.

Pensions tend to be larger in the municipal sector than they are in the private sector. This is attributed to a variety of causes. One cause is the bargaining power that public employees are likely to have during wage negotiations near an election. Officials would like to avoid either a tax boost or a strike. One compromise is an increase in pension benefits. If no money has to be set aside now, the increase in pension benefits will not force a tax increase. However, the workers understand the future benefits to them and are often willing to make such a trade. The cost of this promise will have to be paid only after the current politicians leave office.

There are a variety of other ways in which a city can undertake debt without appearing to have an unbalanced budget. A city's discretion in deciding what its revenue will be can border on the absurd. Turning back to New York we find that the revenue projections for the city were often whatever the mayor wanted them to be. The mayor had the right to simply state what the revenue stream from a particular source would be and then use that in the budget preparation.[9]

This point brings up the distinction between a budget balanced *ex ante* and one balanced *ex post*. The former term means that the budget as written before the beginning of the fiscal year must be balanced. The latter term means that the budget must be balanced at the end of the fiscal year. If the requirement is simply that the mayor plan to have a balanced budget then the failure to achieve it does not necessarily violate the law. In practice, it is often impossible to guarantee a budget that is balanced at the end. Hence, there is usually a provision for carrying a deficit into the next budget as long as it is treated as part of the expenditure for that budget and the new budget is balanced after paying off the old deficit. However, this situation can lead to a growing debt problem. In particular, the mayor of New York could determine anticipated revenues in any manner he chose. Thus, each year he could raise his estimate of revenues so as to cover the past deficit and perhaps increase it a bit.[10] For example, property taxes are never collected at 100% of assessment. Some taxes are defaulted each year and some are never paid. This is particularly a problem in New York where over 20,000 housing units were abandoned each year. However, there was nothing to prevent the mayor from maintaining these properties on the tax rolls and projecting the collection of the tax due as well as interest and penalties. Clearly, no one really expected this money to be paid, but it allowed the city to legally borrow short-term in anticipation that it

[8] George E. Peterson, "Finance," in Gorham and Glazer, op. cit., p. 46.
[9] Ken Auletta, *The Streets Were Paved with Gold* (New York: Random House, 1979), pp. 97–103.
[10] Ibid.

would be collected. Then at the end of the fiscal year, the budget would be balanced by claiming the outstanding taxes as uncollected revenue.

The various mayors of New York showed great skill in juggling the budget to allow for other deficits as well. One item which New York used and which others followed was the movements of expenses forward in time to make them the responsibility of the next budget. If this is done for a recurring item it creates a one-time windfall for the budget. This year's expense is postponed to next year, and next year's to the year after. Thus, no year has two years' worth of expenses, and all future budgets appear to be the same as they would have been without the gimmick. Unfortunately, they are not exactly the same. The city will face the next fiscal year with an expenditure at the beginning that would previously have come at the end, and it must either borrow money to cover the expense or reduce its interest-earning reserves. Thus, it essentially pays the interest on that amount of money for the entire year, and it must do that each year in the future. This is essentially the equivalent of having borrowed the money in the first year. The interest payments are not really different from the ones that would have been made for an explicit loan, but this loan does not show up as part of an illegal deficit.

Another tactic is to change the timing of the fiscal year. Most cities collect property taxes once per year and use that money for the whole year. They borrow in anticipation of the tax revenue before the taxes are collected, and they collect interest on balances until they are spent. However, if a city collects its property taxes in January and runs on a calendar year basis, then it will have money collecting interest for most of the year. Suppose, however, that the city were to change from the calendar year to a July-to-June fiscal year. In order to do this the city must have a transition year in which the fiscal year is either six months long or eighteen months long. In the former case, it receives its full property taxes, but it has only six months' worth of expenses. However, in the future it starts the fiscal year borrowing and has balances for only half the fiscal year. This is the same as having borrowed in the original fiscal year, and it will generate an expense for the city either in terms of lower interest earnings or higher interest payments for each year in the future.

By using a variety of other ingenious mechanisms, New York and other cities managed to run large deficits while still having legally balanced budgets. These methods included treating current expenditures as capital expenditures; changing the way in which federal intergovernmental grants were treated so as to create a one-year bulge in revenue; and ignoring maintenance and other items for streets, subways, and other parts of the city's capital stock.

Government Expenditure

Expenditures by municipal governments have been growing over time, but New York had expenditures that were high by anyone's standards. Certainly we expect a larger city to have more demands on government services because of the larger number of interactions occurring. We expect that the cost of providing these services will be higher in a large city than in a small one. We expect that the scope of services will be wider in New York than in most other municipalities because New York encompasses many of the functions of counties or other levels of government in smaller jurisdictions. Yet the conclusion appears to be that even after extrapolating to take all these factors into account, New York's cost was simply out of line with other jurisdictions. If we look at the expenditures common to most local governments, we find that New York was high even after making adjustments for its size and other unique characteristics.[11] (However, some characteristics of economic decline are likely to work against a city; see Box 21-1.)

Related to the cost of service argument is the argument that suburbanites using city services create costs for which the city is not reimbursed. We have already seen that at least some of these arguments are offset by the higher tax base created by the destinations of these suburbanites. In fact, many of the businesses are considered very desirable by local governments because they tend to generate more in tax revenue than they cost the city for direct services. However, not all of these destination organizations pay taxes. The large number of tax-exempt organizations in a city can seriously limit its revenue capabilities. The net impact depends on the costs these organizations impose on the city. In many cases, these costs are more associated with the costs imposed by employees than by the organizations themselves.

Some local governments have tried to tap this revenue source by taxing the employees rather than the businesses. Since tax-exempt organizations do not pass their tax exemption on to employees, the employees would have to pay any payroll or income taxes levied by the city. While such taxes clearly do get around the problem of taxing tax-exempt organizations, they also create other problems. In particular, the tax must be levied on all employees in the jurisdiction. Thus, there may be a loss of employment in the city. Further, the tax has little direct relation to the services provided or the cost of providing them. Finally, the use of wage and income taxes increases the cyclical sensitivity of the revenue collected. This last point is somewhat offset by the likely growth in the tax base over time, although there is little evidence that the property tax base has been growing at a slower rate than the wage base within cities. Certainly, the property base does not usually decline as rapidly as the wage or income base during a period of population loss.

The Federal Government

Senator Moynihan of New York used to publish a set of numbers each year showing how much more New Yorkers sent to Washington than they got back. Essentially, the study added up all the tax payments and then allocated

---

[11] Edward M. Gramlich, "The New York Fiscal Crisis: What Happened and What Is to Be Done?" *American Economic Review* 66 (May 1976), pp. 415–429. Reprinted in Stephen L. Mehay and Geoffrey E. Nunn, eds., *Urban Economic Issues: Readings and Analysis* (Glenview, IL: Scott, Foresman, 1984), pp. 200–210.

Box 21-1

////// Taxes and Economic Decline

When a city is faced with a decline in population or in other parts of its tax base, the short-run constraints on its actions may force it into action contrary to what economic theory would indicate is the best response. Since each city is supposed to have a balanced budget each year, tax payments can be viewed as being tied to the average cost of the city's services. If the average cost goes up, then, all else equal, the tax rate must also rise. Similarly, if the average cost goes down, the tax rate could be expected to follow it. This change in taxes can be viewed as a change in the cost of living in the city. Yet this change in cost is in exactly the opposite direction of how prices would change for a private firm faced with a similar change in demand.

A private firm lowers price when the demand for its output declines in the short run. It continues to sell as long as the price it receives is at least as great as the marginal cost of pro-

duction. In such a situation, the marginal cost is likely to be below the average cost. Hence, the private firm would lower its price. This can be seen in Figure 1. The intersection of D_1 and MC is the equilibrium for both the city and the private firm in the initial circumstances. While the short-run demand curve is not perfectly elastic, we can assume that the pricing does not take this into account because of a much more elastic long-run curve. In the event of a decline in demand from D_1 to D_2 the private firm will lower its price to P_2 and have quantity decline only to Q_2. However, the firm is not covering all its cost at this point. Average revenue is below average cost. Nevertheless, this is the most efficient point because marginal benefits equal marginal cost.

In contrast, the city will have to raise its tax price to be able to cover its average cost. Thus, it will have to charge the price P_3. At this price, even more people leave the city and

---

federal expenditures to states. Invariably, the older states of the Northeast and North Central regions would be shown as sending more money than they received back while many of the states in the South or West would receive more back than they sent. This was used as evidence of a federal bias against the older areas and as an argument for more federal assistance.

A number of problems have been identified with such studies. The first is that the numbers themselves are somewhat suspect. Tax collections, for example, are credited to the region from which the tax payment was sent. Thus if a national company has operations in all fifty states but keeps its headquarters in New York, this type of study would credit New York with having paid that amount of federal tax. Such calculations bear little resemblance to the actual

Box 21-1 *(continued)*

the quantity declines to Q_3. Hence, in this case the requirement for a balanced budget leads to an inefficient increase in taxes. It is interesting that this increase in taxes may or may not lead to an increase in revenue; it depends on the elasticity of demand. Thus, revenue will likely rise in the short run but decline in the long run.

The fixed costs of the city must be considered when looking at the effects of such a pricing policy. Many of these fixed costs reflect the usual capital investments associated with the production process; however, there are also costs associated with the accumulation of debt.

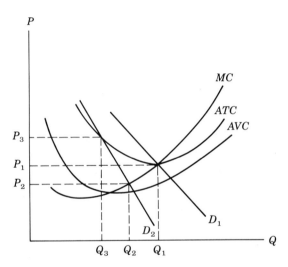

Figure 1 / Marginal Cost versus Tax Price

incidence of the tax in many cases. A similar problem arises on the expenditure side because the information often is available only for the prime contractor. However, most prime contractors for big items subcontract large portions of the contract. These subcontractors are often located in other parts of the country. Hence, it is not appropriate to allocate all the expenditure to one particular region just because the final product is assembled there.

Another problem with the expenditure numbers is that they are often made for items that are not available in all regions of the country. For example, New York would be hard pressed to provide the federal government with oil. Similarly, the harsh winters tend to make it less attractive for military bases. After all the relatively uncontrollable parts of the budget have been allocated there is comparatively little that can be accomplished with the expenditure pattern of the federal government. Although federal expenditures can certainly make a big difference for one city (e.g., the effect of NASA headquarters in Houston is thought to be quite large), the amount of money available for discretionary-type spending is fairly small. Hence, the federal government probably would not be able to direct more activity to each city requesting it. Further, some studies have found that the federal government is fairly generous to many older cities with its allocation of redistribution and service expenditures. For example, New York is found to receive the highest level of aid for virtually all the categories studied under social services. This finding is partly due to the high cost of living and doing business in New York. However, this is not likely to be a good argument to convince people that the larger, older cities require more aid.

A related problem is that the federal tax code is intended to be progressive in terms of its ultimate incidence. Thus, wealthy areas should end up paying more in taxes than poor areas, and despite its problems, New York remains one of the wealthiest cities in the country. Finally, much of the tax flow from New York to the South is associated with Social Security payments. Many New Yorkers like to retire to warmer climates. Thus, they pay their Social Security taxes while they are working in the Northeast. These taxes are treated as contributions by the state. When the money is paid out, it is credited with the state in which the recipient lives. Thus, one way to stop much of the tax code redistribution would be to prevent retirees from moving away from the place where they last worked. Clearly, this type of restriction would be unacceptable. Overall, the general conclusion is that the direct policies of the federal government have little impact on the fiscal differences between cities.

Indirect Effects

Some areas of federal activity do have significant effects on the well-being of older central cities, but these effects are usually indirect rather than direct. The indirect effects occur when the federal government does something for some other purpose and ends up having created additional incentive or opportunity for groups to flee the city. In this context, an increase in the Social Security tax to fund better pensions would create a greater drain on New York. However, other types of activities are more often cited for their impact on the older cities.

One of the biggest areas of impact is the funding of construction for new development. The federal government has subsidized such construction for a variety of reasons; however, this construction is directed more at new, growing areas. The subsidized provision of such infrastructure made the suburbs much more competitive with respect to the central city. Thus, more building is likely to occur outside the city if the federal government is paying most of the cost of new sewers and other infrastructure. This movement of activity outside the area is thus an indirect effect of the actions of the federal government. However, several analysts have concluded that the indirect effects exceed the direct effects by a large margin.[12]

The Carter administration thought that the indirect effects were so important that agencies were directed to prepare urban impact statements when making proposals. These statements were supposed to trace the impact of new laws on older urban areas. Those activities with a negative impact would be less likely to be implemented, those with a positive impact would be more likely to be implemented. A large number of such studies were done, but this procedure is no longer a part of policy and hence is seldom considered.[13]

Another type of indirect federal impact occurs when the federal government either withdraws funding for a program or imposes new conditions on the receipt of money from a program. Such situations amount to the federal government imposing new expenditures on the state and local governments. These new expenditures can be a particular hardship on older, declining cities. These cities often feel the most pressure to maintain various services, thus it is very difficult for them to close something down just because the federal government cuts funding. A project that would not have had any support if it had never been funded can develop tremendous support after a few years. It has the support of the people working to provide the good or service and it has an identifiable group of recipients. These recipients may not have known what they would get before funding became available, but they know what they will lose if it is cut off.

The imposition of conditions also can be very costly. For a community that has become accustomed to the level of funding associated with a program, the imposition of new conditions is equivalent to a mandate from the higher level of government, and this mandate must be funded from the local government's resources. For example, when the federal government wanted to ensure access to mass transit for the handicapped, it simply mandated that local governments would make such access available or have mass transit funds cut off. Since the federal government provides so much in transit funding, the cutoff would be a major loss; however, the cost of providing the access was quite large in many cases. Even with so much money at risk some cities refused to go along with the federal government completely. Nevertheless, most of the goals of the federal government were met and most local governments felt that they had paid the cost.

So we see that while the federal government is not as directly responsible for the problems of some local governments as is often claimed, some federal policies can indirectly create substantial problems, in particular, sudden changes in funding or in the "strings" attached to funding.

---

12 For example, see Roger J. Vaughan, "The Urban Impacts of Federal Policies," in Peter Morrison, et al., *Recent Contributions to the Urban Policy Debate* (Santa Monica: RAND Corporation, March 1979).
13 See Norman Glickman, *The Urban Impacts of Federal Policies* (Baltimore, MD: Johns Hopkins University Press, 1980).

"Lessons" from the New York Experience

It has been argued that the plight of New York was due to circumstances beyond its control. The economic decline of the early 1970s certainly did not help the situation. The large number of poor and homeless created a drain on city services. Some federal policies also contributed to the city's problems. Yet it is hard to look at a city as wealthy as New York and feel that somehow the rest of the country let it down. Poor people exist in all cities, and there were rural poor long before there were urban poor. Other cities managed to deal with these problems with fewer resources than New York had, and the poor existed in great numbers outside New York City. It seems that the New York problem was wanting to do everything but not wanting to pay for it. The tone was set by Mayor Wagner in 1965 when he said, "I do not propose to permit our fiscal problems to set the limits of our commitments to meet the essential needs of the people of the city."[14] Another writer stated that in 1975, New York rediscovered the budget constraint.[15] Perhaps more accurately, it was observed that "in New York, the natives proved incapable of self-government."[16]

If we look at the problem of the older central cities, it is hard to separate the self-serving claims of benevolence from the true distortions in the economic system. While services to the poor are certainly more extensive and expensive in New York than almost anywhere else in the country, there are also many city workers getting high salaries while delivering low productivity and many middle and higher income residents receiving their own pet benefits or escaping some of the taxes that should be targeted for the city's coffers.

Perhaps what New York proved was that no matter how wealthy you are, if you continue to spend more than your income you will eventually be forced to curb your expenditures. It is too simplistic to say that cities should learn to live within their budgets, but this is clearly one of the most important lessons of New York's problem. There are many ways to address a city's problems, but simply trying to spend them away is not the answer. The other major lesson is that you cannot always believe what you see in a government budget. It is not enough to mandate that a budget be balanced, because governments have used a variety of ways to get around this requirement. Improvements in accounting procedures would at least allow for earlier detection of problems.

/// HIGHER LEVELS OF GOVERNMENT

While the federal government is unlikely to go into default the way New York City did, it is unnerving to observe the parallels between the federal actions of recent years and those of New York prior to its default. There is a

---

[14] Auletta, op. cit., p. 30.
[15] Peterson, op. cit., p. 35.
[16] Quoted in Auletta, op. cit., p. 223.

chronically unbalanced budget, which leads to increased borrowing each year. This is supplemented by a substantial number of budget gimmicks, which make the deficit look smaller than it really is. For example, the federal government uses the sale of assets and the surpluses of its trust funds to help reduce its reported budget deficits, but these do nothing to bring spending in line with revenues. One impact of the rise in borrowing is a substantial increase in interest payments each year. This makes it even harder to balance the budget in the future. It also appears that there is less emphasis on building and maintaining the nation's capital stock, and problems associated with an inadequate capital stock build up slowly.

Whether one believes that the federal budget is unbalanced because of too much spending or too little taxation, the impact is to make the nation as a whole poorer over time. This may not lead to a dramatic fiscal problem, but it does constrain the government's options in many policy areas and creates substantial future liabilities which will have to be funded at some time. The rising debt and its associated problems have caused people to suggest a variety of mechanisms to bring the federal budget into balance. Before we discuss these mechanisms, it may be helpful to consider the experiences of the state governments.

State Budget Balancing

Unlike the federal government, forty-nine of the fifty states had balanced budget requirements in 1984.[17] However, as we have seen, the legal requirement for a balanced budget can sometimes be met with budgets that are not truly balanced. Further, despite the apparent uniformity in requiring balanced budgets, the stringency of these requirements varied greatly across the states. In some states the requirement was simply that the governor submit a balanced budget for consideration by the legislature; in other states there were substantial restrictions on the ability to carry a deficit into the next fiscal year.

The Advisory Commission on Intergovernmental Relations found that the states with the more stringent requirements were indeed more likely to have surpluses and less likely to carry over deficits.[18] Of course, this finding does not automatically mean that the requirements affect the state's fiscal behavior. It is almost as likely that the states that are more amenable to conservative fiscal strategy are more amenable to laws consistent with these practices. Nevertheless, this offers at least limited support to the contention that reform of the budget process would be effective in reducing the federal deficit.

---

[17] Advisory Commission on Intergovernmental Relations, *Fiscal Discipline in the Federal System: National Reform and the Experience of the States*, A-107 (Washington, DC: July 1987), p. 38.
[18] Ibid., pp. 39–46.

Federal Budget Reform

Many different proposals have been offered as methods to bring federal revenues and expenditures more in line. We have already discussed a number of them in previous chapters so we offer here a brief comment on some of the strengths and weaknesses of the various approaches. The most basic approach to budget balancing is some form of legislative or constitutional requirement that the budget be balanced. This is essentially what the Gramm-Rudman approach does legislatively and what a constitutional balanced budget amendment would attempt. While the results from the study of such restrictions at the state level are encouraging, there are enough problems with ensuring compliance that this method should be approached with caution. In particular, the use of budget gimmicks to meet the letter of the law could create new problems in the budget process.

The other major approach to budget discipline is to give the president more responsibility for expenditure or to force Congress to link revenue and expenditure more closely. For example, the president might be given the power to veto specific items in the budget rather than having to veto whole appropriation bills, or Congress might have to specify the taxes to be raised to fund additional expenditure. Although there are problems with these approaches, they have the benefit of making the deficit someone's responsibility. One clear lesson from the experience of the lower levels of government is that deficits that can be treated as if they did not exist will not go away.

/// SUMMARY

There is no general definition of a *fiscal crisis*, but it typically refers to a situation in which a government unit is unable to pay its current bills. Since most governments have some authority to borrow, a crisis situation also implies that no sources of credit were available. The term *fiscal stress* is often used to indicate a situation in which a government is unable to meet current expenditures without using unduly high tax rates, and the implication is that there will be a crisis if something is not changed. Neither of these terms can be used with precision, but there is much concern about crises in various units of government.

If we simply define a fiscal problem as a situation in which a government unit is unable to meet current expenses with current revenues and does not have access to the credit markets, we can also group the potential causes of such a situation. The first possible cause is that the government unit faces restrictions on taxes and/or expenditures which create severe pressure on the community for some action. Thus, a wealthy community could have a fiscal crisis if the community were also under a severe revenue limitation measure, as appears to be happening to a number of county governments in California.

The second type of cause is associated with unexpected economic decline. No one can predict the future perfectly, so it is not unreasonable to expect surprises in terms of the level of activity that will locate in a particular place. However, if these unexpected fluctuations are large relative to the economy, they could push the government unit into a fiscal corner.

The third possible cause is that the government unit has been assigned responsibilities that it cannot handle under a federal system. Redistribution at the local level is particularly troublesome. There is little explicit redistribution at the local level, but many federal programs are funneled through local government units. In addition, many local governments provide additional indirect redistribution by charging property taxes, which are then used to finance people-related services. The imbalance between the demand for services and the supply of revenues creates a problem for the decision maker: Should the higher income person get better services because of the higher level of taxes paid, or should there be complete equalization of services, leading to an incentive for the higher income people to leave the community?

The fourth class of causes for fiscal imbalance relate to the use of budget gimmicks by local governments to make it look as if they have a revenue-expenditure balance. Without an operative budget constraint they can go on providing the same level of services without having to raise taxes; but in reality the budget is not balanced and a hidden deficit is being created, which eventually must be addressed either through lower levels of service or higher taxes.

Cities clearly face problems because the allocation of activities among levels of government does not fit well with what we would define as an efficient system. Yet in most cases these problems are not sufficient by themselves to lead to fiscal crises. Many of the problems we observe are associated with an unwillingness to accept budget limits rather than an inability to do so.

Name Index //////

Subject Index //////